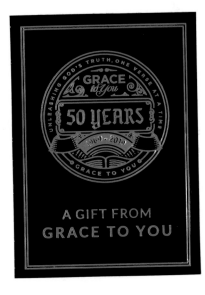

ONE
FAITHFUL
LIFE

ONE FAITHFUL LIFE

A HARMONY OF THE LIFE
AND LETTERS *of the* APOSTLE PAUL

JOHN MACARTHUR

General Editor

THOMAS NELSON
Since 1798

Published in Nashville, Tennessee, by Thomas Nelson. Thomas Nelson is a registered trademark of HarperCollins Christian Publishing, Inc.

Special thanks to Nathan Busenitz and also to the team at Thomas Nelson for their help in the completion of this project.

Thomas Nelson titles may be purchased in bulk for educational, business, fund-raising, or sales promotional use. For information, please e-mail SpecialMarkets@ThomasNelson.com.

Scripture quotations are taken from the New King James Version®. © 1982 by Thomas Nelson. Used by permission. All rights reserved.

ISBN 9780785229469 (eBook)

ISBN 9780785229261 (HC)

Library of Congress Control Number: 2019930171
ISBN 9780785229261

Printed in the United States of America

19 20 21 22 23   LSC   10 9 8 7 6 5 4 3 2 1

Contents

Paul's Life of Gospel Faithfulness*

Paul was unique among the apostles. Unlike the rest of them, he never spent time with Christ during our Lord's earthly ministry. In fact, he would not have been a good fit in the circle of the twelve disciples. They were mostly common provincial Galileans, lacking any spiritual credentials or academic clout. The best known and most influential of the Twelve included fishermen (Peter, Andrew, James, and John), a tax collector (Matthew), and a former Zealot (Simon)—a mix of working men and outcasts.

By contrast, Paul (or more precisely Saul of Tarsus, as he was known in those days) was a well-respected, well-educated, and well-read rabbi, born into a family of Pharisees and thoroughly trained in the Pharisees' ultra-orthodox traditions. He was amazingly cosmopolitan—a Roman citizen, a seasonal traveler, a distinguished legal scholar who was born in Tarsus, educated in Jerusalem at the feet of Gamaliel (Acts 22:3), and full of zeal—a Hebrew of Hebrews. "If anyone else thinks he may have confidence in the flesh," he wrote, "I more so" (Phil. 3:4). His *curriculum vitae* always outshone everyone else's. Saul of Tarsus would never lose in any contest of intellectual or academic achievements. In that regard, he stands in sharp contrast to all the other apostles.

Saul's mentor, Gamaliel, was by all accounts the most prestigious and influential rabbi in early first-century Jerusalem. Gamaliel was a grandson of the legendary Hillel the Elder—one of the most learned and quotable rabbis ever. Acts 5:34 tells us Gamaliel was "held in respect by all the people." He clearly had tremendous influence among the Sanhedrin (vv. 34–40). That council, consisting of seventy-one elite priests and scholars, was Judaism's highest ruling court of religious affairs. As a group, the Sanhedrin of Paul's

---

* This introduction is adapted from John MacArthur, *The Gospel According to Paul* (Nashville, TN: Thomas Nelson, 2017).

and Jesus' time was notoriously corrupt and often motivated by sheer political expediency. But Gamaliel stands out, even in the New Testament narrative, as a learned, peaceful, cautious, and basically honorable man. The Mishnah, a record of Hebrew oral traditions written in the early third century, refers to him as "Gamaliel the Elder" and quotes him numerous times. In all the world, there was no more highly venerated Hebrew scholar—and Saul of Tarsus was trained at his feet. So the apostle's academic credentials were impressive by any measure.

Before his famous encounter with the risen Jesus on the Damascus Road, Saul of Tarsus despised any challenge to the Pharisees' traditions. When we first meet him in Scripture, he is "a young man" (Acts 7:58) so thoroughly averse to Christ and so hostile to the faith of Jesus' followers that he presides over the stoning of the first Christian martyr, Stephen. Giving his testimony years later, Paul confessed:

> This I also did in Jerusalem, and many of the saints I shut up in prison, having received authority from the chief priests; and when they were put to death, I cast my vote against them. And I punished them often in every synagogue and compelled them to blaspheme; and being exceedingly enraged against them, I persecuted them even to foreign cities.
>
> *Acts 26:10, 11*

The fact that he had a vote in such matters suggests that he was either a member of the Sanhedrin or part of a tribunal appointed by them to judge religious dissidents. Rarely were young men appointed to such positions. But Paul was clearly a precocious scholar who stood out to his generation as a zealous activist, a ready worker, a gifted administrator, and a tough enforcer. (He was probably a skilled politician as well.)

Yet after his dramatic conversion on the road to Damascus, Paul was a completely different kind of man. He spurned every pretense of superiority. He abominated the notion that human wisdom might add anything of value to the preaching of the gospel. He emphatically opposed any suggestion that eloquence and erudition could enhance the native power of the gospel. He therefore took great pains *not* to put any stress on his own intellectual and academic achievements, lest he unwittingly undermine the simplicity of the evangelistic message. To the church at Corinth, he wrote:

> And I, brethren, when I came to you, did not come with excellence of speech or of wisdom declaring to you the testimony of God. For I determined not to know anything among you except Jesus Christ and Him crucified. I was with you in weakness, in fear, and in much trembling. And my speech and my preaching were not with persuasive words of human wisdom, but in demonstration of the Spirit and of power, that your faith should not be in the wisdom of men but in the power of God.
>
> *1 Cor. 2:1–5*

In Philippians 3:5, 6, in order to refute the claims of some false teachers, it became necessary for Paul to list some of his most impressive religious and academic achievements. "But," he quickly added, "what things were gain to me, these I have counted loss for Christ. Yet indeed I also count all things loss for the excellence of the knowledge of Christ Jesus my Lord, for whom I have suffered the loss of all things, and count them as rubbish [literally, "dung"], that I may gain Christ."

Still, Paul's towering intellect is obvious in the way he worked and in the words he wrote. He could with equal alacrity rattle off lines in Greek from ancient Mediterranean poets or quote from memory any number of passages from the Hebrew Scriptures. He spoke with bold confidence to the most elite philosophers in Athens. He also stood fearlessly in royal courts where his life was on the line. No one intimidated him. On the contrary, his driving ambition was to stand in the throne room of the Roman capitol, give his testimony in Caesar's presence, and thereby preach the gospel to the world's most powerful ruler in the hub of the largest, most far-reaching empire the world had ever seen.

Appointed for the Defense of the Gospel

Of all the apostles, Paul was the one most intent on guarding the purity, accuracy, and clarity of the evangelistic message. Christ uniquely commissioned him for that purpose—"the defense and confirmation of the gospel" (Phil. 1:7). He embraced that role as a personal assignment from on high.

He wrote, "I am appointed for the defense of the gospel" (v. 17). This was so deeply ingrained in Paul's consciousness that when he spoke of the gospel, he often referred to it as "my gospel" (Rom. 2:16; 16:25; 2 Tim. 2:8).

Of course Paul was in no way taking credit for the gospel or declaring private ownership of it. Never would it occur to him to question the divine origin of the gospel. Just as frequently, he referred to it as "the gospel of God" (Rom. 1:1; 15:16; 2 Cor. 11:7; 1 Thess. 2:2, 8, 9). More often still, he called it "the gospel of Christ" (Rom. 1:16; 15:19; 1 Cor. 9:12, 18; 2 Cor. 9:13; 10:14; Gal. 1:7; Phil. 1:27; 1 Thess. 3:2), or "the gospel of the glory of Christ" (2 Cor. 4:4). Sometimes it was "the gospel of peace" (Eph. 6:15), or "the gospel of your salvation" (Eph. 1:13).

These were not disparate gospels, but Paul's assorted titles for the one true gospel. The suggestion that there is more than one gospel would have been met with fierce opposition by the apostle Paul. He sternly instructed the Galatian churches, "But even if we, or an angel from heaven, preach any other gospel to you than what we have preached to you, let him be accursed" (Gal. 1:8). And to make his point as emphatic as possible, he repeated the curse again in the very next sentence: "As we have said before, so now I say again, if anyone preaches any other gospel to you than what you have received, let him be accursed" (v. 9).

A Survey of Paul's Epistles

Virtually every one of Paul's New Testament epistles defends and clarifies some crucial point of doctrine germane to the gospel message. The book of Romans is a carefully ordered discussion of the doctrines that constitute the very heart of gospel truth. It is laid out in a careful, logical, ordered outline. Starting with the doctrine of universal sin and human depravity, Paul moves systematically through the whole catalogue of gospel truth, dealing with justification, sanctification, eternal security, election, reprobation, the grafting of Gentiles into the people of God, and the ultimate restoration of Israel. Romans is Paul's most ordered and comprehensive exposition of gospel doctrines.

In 1 Corinthians he defends the gospel against various corruptions that were being smuggled in under either the guise of human wisdom or a cloak of carnal chaos. In 2 Corinthians he answers attacks that had come against the gospel from false teachers who evidently self-identified as "the most eminent apostles" (11:5; 12:11). These heretics seemed to understand that in order to subvert the true gospel they needed to discredit the apostle Paul, so they focused their attack on him in particular. Paul was forced therefore to answer those attacks. But he was really defending the authority and purity of the gospel, not merely his own reputation (2 Cor. 11:1–4).

Paul's epistle to the Galatians is a wall-to-wall argument against false teachers (commonly known as the Judaizers) who insisted that Gentile converts must adhere to Old Testament ceremonial law in order to be saved. In particular, they taught that Gentile men could not become Christians unless they were first circumcised. Their doctrine was an implicit denial that faith is the sole instrument of justification. That error was so subtle that even Peter and Barnabas seemed prepared to go along with it (Gal. 2:11–13). So Paul wrote the Galatian epistle to demonstrate why the Judaizers' doctrine was a fatal corruption of the Christian message—a completely "different gospel" (Gal. 1:6). That is why Galatians begins with that famous double curse against "any other gospel" (vv. 8, 9).

Ephesians is a simple rehearsal of gospel principles, with an emphasis on the essential truth that lies at the heart of the message: salvation is entirely God's work. It is not something any sinner can amplify or embellish with human merit. Much less can a fallen person achieve redemption for himself. "For by grace you have been saved through faith, and that not of yourselves; it is the gift of God, not of works, lest anyone should boast. For we are His workmanship, created in Christ Jesus for good works, which God prepared beforehand that we should walk in them." (Eph. 2:8–10)

Although the theme of Philippians is joy, and the epistle is mostly filled with practical counsel and exhortations, chapter 3 includes a sharp warning about "dogs," "evil workers," and mutilators of the flesh (v. 2). These were clearly the very same type of gospel-corrupters Paul refuted so thoroughly in his epistle to the Galatians. He goes on in Philippians 3 to give a personal testimony that ingeniously summarizes the very heart of the gospel message.

There were some in the early church who tried to corrupt the gospel with high-flown human philosophy, ascetic forms of self-denial, manmade traditions, and other standard religious contrivances. Paul's epistle to the Colossians addresses all such deliberate attempts to make the gospel seem complex or ostentatious. Of all the apostles, the profound scholar Paul was chosen by the Holy Spirit to defend the gospel's simplicity against any hint of academic elitism or philosophical gentrification.

Paul begins 1 Thessalonians with a powerful commendation for the church in Thessalonica because of the way they had eagerly embraced the gospel from the very start. He writes, "For our gospel did not come to you in word only, but also in power, and in the Holy Spirit and in much assurance" (1:5). The closing two verses of that opening chapter (vv. 9, 10) contain this crisp summary of gospel truth: "You turned to God from idols to serve the living and true God, and to wait for His Son from heaven, whom He raised from the dead, even Jesus who delivers us from the wrath to come." Paul goes on in 1 and 2 Thessalonians to instruct and encourage that church to continue their patient waiting for Christ's return while living in a way that honors the far-reaching implications of the gospel.

The epistles to Timothy and Titus are full of urgings for those two young pastors to carry on Paul's legacy by carefully safeguarding the truth of the gospel. In 1 Timothy 6:20, for example, when Paul writes, "O Timothy! Guard what was committed to your trust," it should be clear that he is talking about the gospel. He had previously described "the glorious gospel of the blessed God" as that "which was committed to my trust" (1:11). To Titus, Paul writes one of his trademark summaries of the gospel message. This is simple, profound, and amazingly comprehensive:

> For the grace of God that brings salvation has appeared to all men, teaching us that, denying ungodliness and worldly lusts, we should live soberly, righteously, and godly in the present age, looking for the blessed hope and glorious appearing of our great God and Savior Jesus Christ, who gave Himself for us, that He might redeem us from every lawless deed and purify for Himself His own special people, zealous for good works.
>
> *Titus 2:11–14*

Then he adds this exhortation: "Speak these things, exhort, and rebuke with all authority. Let no one despise you" (v. 15).

Paul's shortest epistle, the letter to Philemon, is an intensely personal, practical note written to help reconcile a runaway slave (Onesimus) with his master (Philemon). But even here, Paul manages to paint a crystal-clear picture of gospel truth while exemplifying the spirit of Christ through his own actions. He includes this plea, which perfectly epitomizes what Christ did for His people: "receive him as you would me. But if he has wronged you or owes anything, put that on my account" (Philem. vv. 17, 18). Thus Paul illustrates in a very real and practical way the principles of imputation and vicarious atonement.

Nothing But the Gospel

Gospel truth permeates everything Paul ever wrote. The gospel was at the center of his thoughts at all times. That was deliberate. He wrote, "Necessity is laid upon me; yes, woe is me if I do not preach the gospel!" (1 Cor. 9:16). "I am determined not to know anything among you expect, Jesus Christ and Him crucified" (1 Cor. 2:2). "God forbid that I should boast except in the cross of our Lord Jesus Christ, by whom the world has been crucified to me, and I to the world' (Gal. 6:14). "As much as is in me, I am ready to preach the gospel" (Rom. 1:15).

All the apostles had important roles to play in the founding and spread of the early church. John was the only one who lived to old age. The rest became martyrs, starting with James, whom Herod "killed . . . with the sword" (Acts 12:2). Some of them took the gospel to the far reaches of the known world. Early church history records, for example, that Thomas went as far as the east coast of the Indian subcontinent. Legend has it that Nathaniel (also called Bartholomew) took the gospel to Armenia and was martyred there. Although Scripture does not record the final whereabouts for each of the apostles, we know for sure that they very quickly spread the gospel far and wide throughout the known world. In Acts 17:6, the angry mob who seized Paul and Silas in Thessalonica referred to them as "these who have turned the world upside down."

No one did more than Paul to spread the gospel across the face of the Roman Empire. Luke carefully chronicled Paul's three missionary journeys in the Book of Acts. Beginning in Acts 13 through the end of that book, Paul becomes the central figure. And Luke's record of Paul's ministry is breathtaking. Paul's influence was profound wherever he set foot. He preached the gospel, planted churches, and left new believers in his wake no matter where he went—from the land of Israel, throughout Asia Minor, across Greece, through Malta, Sicily, and finally to Rome. And while doing all this, Paul wrote more New Testament epistles than any other author. In an age long before modern conveniences made travel and communication relatively easy, Paul's accomplishments were extraordinary.

More important, God used no one more than Paul to define, delimit, and defend the gospel. The other apostles clearly gained an appreciation for Paul's devotion to the gospel. Their belief that he was appointed by Christ to be an apostle "born out of due time" (1 Cor. 15:8) was rooted in the fact that he had learned from the risen Christ the very same truths that they themselves, during their Lord's earthly ministry, had been trained and commissioned to proclaim (Gal. 2:2, 6–9). Paul learned nothing about the gospel from the other disciples that he had not already heard from Christ by special revelation (Gal. 1:11, 12; 2:6).

Faithful to the End

It's no wonder Paul felt such a significant weight of responsibility to preach and defend the gospel. Wherever he went, agents of opposition to the gospel followed close behind, attacking the message he proclaimed. The powers of darkness seemed keenly aware of Paul's strategic role, and they focused their relentless attacks against the churches where his influence was especially strong. Therefore Paul was constantly engaged in "the defense and confirmation of the gospel" (Phil. 1:7). So much controversy surrounded Paul and his ministry that almost no one wanted to be identified with him. In the final epistle he wrote before giving his life for the gospel, he described how his arraignment in Rome had gone: "At my first defense no one stood with me, but all forsook me" (2 Tim. 4:16). In the opening chapter of that letter he told Timothy, "All those in Asia have turned away from me" (1:15). And his closing words included this doleful plea:

> Be diligent to come to me quickly; for Demas has forsaken me, having loved this present world, and has departed for Thessalonica—Crescens for Galatia, Titus for Dalmatia. Only Luke is with me. Get Mark and bring him with you, for he is useful to me for ministry.
>
> *2 Tim. 4:9–11*

Had Paul not been a man of such profound faith, he might have died feeling alone and abandoned. As it is, he most likely did not fully realize how far his shadow would extend over the church and how deeply his influence would be felt by generation after generation of believers. But he did not die discouraged. He knew the truth of the gospel would ultimately triumph. He understood that the gates of hell would never prevail against the church Christ was building. He remained confident that God's purposes would assuredly be fulfilled—and that God's plan was indeed already being fulfilled, even in Paul's own impending martyrdom. He wrote,

> For I am already being poured out as a drink offering, and the time of my departure is at hand. I have fought the good fight, I have finished the race, I have kept the faith. Finally, there is laid up for me the crown of righteousness, which the Lord, the righteous Judge, will give to me on that Day, and not to me only but also to all who have loved His appearing.
>
> *2 Tim. 4:6–8*

According to tradition, not long after penning those words, Paul was led by Roman soldiers to a place of execution where he would be beheaded for the sake of Christ. Even in death, the apostle was triumphant. He knew that to be absent from the body is to be present with the Lord (2 Cor. 5:8). As his sojourn on this earth ended, with the flash of a Roman sword, Paul was ushered into the presence of his Savior. There he was undoubtedly greeted with these words, "Well done, My good and faithful servant. Enter into the joy of your Master."

PART I

From Pharisee
to Pastor

ca. A.D. *30–47*

1. The Hypocrisy of the Pharisees
Matthew 23:1–22

NOTE: *As a young man, Saul of Tarsus (whose Greek name is Paul) was trained as a Pharisee. In Acts 26:4, 5, he explained, "My manner of life from my youth, which was spent from the beginning among my own nation at Jerusalem, all the Jews know. They knew me from the first, if they were willing to testify, that according to the strictest sect of our religion I lived a Pharisee." His testimony in Philippians 3:3–5 reveals his unwavering dedication to keeping their legalistic traditions. Yet, his zeal for God was devoid of true salvation. He was a prime example of a religious hypocrite. Though Saul was probably not in the crowd on the occasion recorded in Matthew 23, the rebuke Jesus issued to the Pharisees in this chapter would have described the spiritual condition of the unconverted Saul.*

Then Jesus spoke to the multitudes and to His disciples, saying: "The scribes and the Pharisees sit in ᵃMoses' seat. Therefore whatever they tell you to observe, that ᵇobserve and do, but do not do according to their works; for they say, and do not do. For they bind heavy burdens, hard to bear, and lay them on men's shoulders; but they themselves will not move them with one of their fingers. But all their works they do to be seen by men. They make their ᶜphylacteries broad and enlarge the ᵈborders of their garments. They

---

a. **Moses' seat.** The expression is equivalent to a university's "chair of philosophy." To "sit in Moses' seat" was to have the highest authority to instruct people in the law. The expression here may be translated, "[they] have seated themselves in Moses' seat"—stressing the fact that this was an imaginary authority they claimed for themselves. There was a legitimate sense in which the priests and Levites had authority to decide matters of the law (Deut. 17:9), but the scribes and Pharisees had gone beyond any legitimate authority and were adding human tradition to the Word of God (Matt. 15:3–9). For that Jesus condemned them.

b. **observe and do.** I.e., insofar as it accords with the Word of God. The Pharisees were prone to bind "heavy burdens" of extrabiblical traditions and put them on others' shoulders. Jesus explicitly condemned that sort of legalism.

c. **phylacteries.** Leather boxes containing a parchment on which is written in 4 columns Ex. 13:1–10; 11–16; Deut. 6:4–9; 11:13–21. These are worn by men during prayer—one on the middle of the forehead and one on the left arm just above the elbow. The use of phylacteries was based on an overly literal interpretation of passages like Ex. 13:9, 10; Deut. 6:8. Evidently the Pharisees would broaden the leather straps by which the phylacteries were bound to their arms and foreheads, in order to make the phylacteries more prominent.

d. **the borders of their garments.** I.e., the tassels. Jesus Himself wore them (see Matt.

3

love the best places at feasts, the best seats in the synagogues, greetings in the marketplaces, and to be called by men, 'Rabbi, Rabbi.' But you, do not be called a'Rabbi'; for One is your Teacher, the Christ, and you are all brethren. Do not call anyone on earth your father; for One is your Father, He who is in heaven. And do not be called teachers; for One is your Teacher, the Christ. But he who is greatest among you shall be your servant. And whoever exalts himself will be humbled, and he who humbles himself will be exalted.

"But woe to you, scribes and Pharisees, hypocrites! For you shut up the kingdom of heaven against men; for you neither go in yourselves, bnor do you allow those who are entering to go in. Woe to you, scribes and Pharisees, hypocrites! For you devour widows' houses, and for a pretense make long prayers. Therefore you will receive greater condemnation.

"Woe to you, scribes and Pharisees, hypocrites! For you travel land and sea to win one cproselyte, and when he is won, you make him twice as much da son of hell as yourselves.

"Woe to you, blind guides, who say, 'Whoever swears by the temple, eit is nothing; but whoever swears by the gold of the temple, he is obliged to perform it.' Fools and blind! For which is greater, the gold or the temple that sanctifies the gold? And, 'Whoever swears by the altar, it is nothing; but whoever swears by the gift that is on it, he is obliged to perform it.' Fools and blind! For which is greater, the gift or the altar that sanctifies the gift? Therefore he who swears by the altar, swears by it and by all things on it. He

---

9:20), so it was not the tassels themselves that He condemned, only the mentality that would lengthen the tassels to make it appear that one was especially spiritual.

a. **Rabbi . . . father . . . teachers.** Here Jesus condemns pride and pretense, not titles per se. Paul repeatedly speaks of "teachers" in the church, and even refers to himself as the Corinthians' "father" (1 Cor. 4:15). Obviously, this does not forbid the showing of respect, either (cf. 1 Thess. 5:11, 12; 1 Tim. 5:1). Christ is merely forbidding the use of such names as spiritual titles, or in an ostentatious sense that accords undue spiritual authority to a human being, as if he were the source of truth rather than God.

b. **nor do you allow.** The Pharisees, having shunned God's righteousness, were seeking to establish a righteousness of their own (Rom. 10:3)—and teaching others to do so as well. Their legalism and self-righteousness effectively obscured the narrow gate by which the kingdom must be entered.

c. **proselyte.** A Gentile convert to Judaism.

d. **a son of hell.** I.e., someone whose eternal destination is hell.

e. **it is nothing.** This was an arbitrary distinction the Pharisees had made, which gave them a sanctimonious justification for lying with impunity. If someone swore "by the temple" (or the altar, Matt. 23:18; or heaven, Matt. 23:22), his oath was not considered binding, but if he swore "by the gold of the temple," he could not break his word without being subject to the penalties of Jewish law. Our Lord makes it clear that swearing by those things is tantamount to swearing by God Himself.

who swears by the temple, swears by it and by Him who dwells in it. And he who swears by heaven, swears by the throne of God and by Him who sits on it.

2. CHRIST CONTINUES TO CONFRONT
Matthew 23:23–39

NOTE: *Jesus' rebuke of the Pharisees continued with these words:*

"Woe to you, scribes and Pharisees, hypocrites! For you pay ᵃtithe of mint and anise and cummin, and have neglected the weightier matters of the law: justice and mercy and faith. These you ought to have done, without leaving the others undone. Blind guides, who ᵇstrain out a gnat and swallow a camel!

"Woe to you, scribes and Pharisees, hypocrites! For ᶜyou cleanse the outside of the cup and dish, but inside they are full of extortion and self-indulgence. Blind Pharisee, first cleanse the inside of the cup and dish, that the outside of them may be clean also.

"Woe to you, scribes and Pharisees, hypocrites! For you are like ᵈwhite-washed tombs which indeed appear beautiful outwardly, but inside are full

---

a. **tithe of mint and anise and cummin.** Garden herbs, not really the kind of farm produce that the tithe was designed to cover (Lev. 27:30). But the Pharisees fastidiously weighed out a tenth of every herb, perhaps even counting individual anise seeds. Jesus' point, however, was not to condemn their observance of the law's fine points. The problem was that they "neglected the weightier matters" of justice and mercy and faith—the moral principles underlying all the laws. They were satisfied with their focus on the incidentals and externals but willfully resisted the spiritual meaning of the law. He told them they should have concentrated on those larger issues "without leaving the others undone."

b. **strain out a gnat and swallow a camel.** Some Pharisees would strain their beverages through a fine cloth to make sure they did not inadvertently swallow a gnat—the smallest of unclean animals (Lev. 11:23). The camel was the largest of all the unclean animals (Lev. 11:4).

c. **you cleanse the outside.** The Pharisees' focus on external issues lay at the heart of their error. Who would want to drink from a cup that had been washed on the outside but was still filthy inside? Yet the Pharisees lived their lives as if external appearance were more important than internal reality. That was the very essence of their hypocrisy, and Jesus rebuked them for it repeatedly.

d. **whitewashed tombs.** Tombs were regularly whitewashed to make them stand out. Accidentally touching or stepping on a grave caused ceremonial uncleanness (Num. 19:16). A freshly whitewashed tomb would be brilliantly white and clean-looking—and sometimes spectacularly ornate. But the inside was full of defilement and decay. Contrast Jesus' words here and in Luke 11:44.

of dead men's bones and all uncleanness. Even so you also outwardly appear righteous to men, but inside you are full of hypocrisy and lawlessness.

"Woe to you, scribes and Pharisees, hypocrites! Because you build the tombs of the prophets and adorn the monuments of the righteous, and say, 'If we had lived in the days of our fathers, ᵃwe would not have been partakers with them in the blood of the prophets.'

"Therefore you are witnesses against yourselves that you are sons of those who murdered the prophets. Fill up, then, the measure of your fathers' guilt. Serpents, brood of vipers! How can you escape the condemnation of hell? Therefore, indeed, I send you ᵇprophets, wise men, and scribes: some of them you will kill and crucify, and some of them you will scourge in your synagogues and persecute from city to city, that on you may come all the righteous blood shed on the earth, from the blood of righteous ᶜAbel to the blood of Zechariah, ᵈson of Berechiah, whom you murdered between the temple and the altar. Assuredly, I say to you, all these things will come upon ᵉthis generation.

"O Jerusalem, Jerusalem, the one who kills the prophets and stones those who are sent to her! How often ᶠI wanted to gather your children together, as

a. **we would not have been partakers.** A ridiculous claim to self-righteousness when they were already plotting the murder of the Messiah (cf. John 11:47–53).

b. **prophets, wise men, and scribes.** I.e., the disciples, as well as the prophets, evangelists, and pastors who followed them (cf. Eph. 4:11).

c. **Abel . . . Zechariah.** The first and last OT martyrs, respectively.

d. **son of Berechiah.** (Zech. 1:1). The OT does not record how he died. However, the death of another Zechariah, son of Jehoiada, is recorded in 2 Chr. 24:20, 21. He was stoned in the court of the temple, exactly as Jesus describes here. All the best manuscripts of Matthew contain the phrase "Zechariah, son of Berechiah" (though it does not appear in Luke 11:51). Some have suggested that the Zechariah in 2 Chr. 24 was actually a grandson of Jehoiada, and that his father's name was also Berechiah. But there is no difficulty if we simply take Jesus' words at face value and accept His infallible testimony that Zechariah the prophet was martyred between the temple and the altar, in a way very similar to how the earlier Zechariah was killed.

e. **this generation.** Historically, this was the generation that experienced the utter destruction of Jerusalem and the burning of the temple in A.D. 70. Jesus' lament over Jerusalem and His removal of the blessing of God from the temple (Matt. 23:37, 38) strongly suggest that the sacking of Jerusalem in A.D. 70 was the judgment He was speaking about.

f. **I wanted . . . but you were not willing!** God is utterly sovereign and therefore fully capable of bringing to pass whatever He desires (cf. Is. 46:10)—including the salvation of whomever He chooses (Eph. 1:4, 5). Yet, He sometimes expresses a wish for that which He does not sovereignly bring to pass (cf. Gen. 6:6; Deut. 5:29; Ps. 81:13; Is. 48:18). Such expressions in no way suggest a limitation on the sovereignty of God or imply any actual change in Him (Num. 23:19). But these statements do reveal essential aspects of the divine character: He is full of compassion, sincerely good to all, desirous of good, not evil—and therefore not delighting in the destruction of the wicked (Ezek. 18:32; 33:11). While affirming God's sovereignty, one must understand His pleas for the repentance of the reprobate as well meant appeals—and His goodness toward the wicked as a genuine mercy designed to provoke them to repentance (Rom. 2:4). The emotion displayed by Christ here (and in all similar passages, such as Luke

a hen gathers her chicks under her wings, but you were not willing! See! ᵃYour house is left to you desolate; for I say to you, you shall ᵇsee Me no more till you say, 'Blessed is He who comes in the name of the Lᴏʀᴅ!'"

3. Tʜᴇ Aꜱᴄᴇɴꜱɪᴏɴ ᴏꜰ ᴛʜᴇ Rɪꜱᴇɴ Cʜʀɪꜱᴛ

Acts 1:1–11

Nᴏᴛᴇ: *Though Jesus was arrested and crucified by the corrupt religious leaders, His death did not spell defeat. Rising victorious from the grave, He appeared to His disciples over a period of forty days. It is at this point that Luke begins his historical account in the Book of Acts, chronicling the birth and growth of the church. Luke likely wrote this book during Paul's house arrest in Rome, more than three decades after the Lord's resurrection. Because he wrote under Paul's apostolic authority, Luke's account of the early church in the book of Acts undoubtedly reflects Paul's influence and perspective.*

ᶜThe former account I made, O ᵈTheophilus, of ᵉall that Jesus began both to do and teach, until the day in which He was ᶠtaken up, after He ᵍthrough

---

19:41) is obviously a deep, sincere passion. All Christ's feelings must be in perfect harmony with the divine will (cf. John 8:29)—and therefore these lamentations should not be thought of as mere exhibitions of His humanity.

a. **Your house is left to you desolate.** A few days earlier, Christ had referred to the temple as His Father's "house" (Matt. 21:13). But the blessing and glory of God were being removed from Israel (see 1 Sam. 4:21). When Christ "departed from the temple" (Matt. 24:1), the glory of God went with Him. Ezekiel 11:23 described Ezekiel's vision of the departure of the Shekinah glory in His day. The glory left the temple and stood on the Mt. of Olives, (see Matt. 24:3; Luke 19:29) exactly the same route Christ followed here (cf. Matt. 24:3).

b. **you shall see Me no more.** Christ's public teaching ministry was over. He withdrew from national Israel until the time yet future when they will recognize Him as Messiah (Rom. 11:23–26). Then Christ quoted from Ps. 118:26.

c. **former account.** The Gospel of Luke. That account chronicled the life and teaching of Jesus, through His death, resurrection, and ascension (Luke 24:51).

d. **Theophilus.** The original recipient of this book.

e. **all that Jesus began both to do and teach.** Jesus taught the disciples by word and deed the truth necessary to carry on His work. On the cross, He finished the work of redemption, but He had only started the proclamation of its glories.

f. **taken up.** Christ's ascension to the Father (cf. Luke 24:51). Luke uses this term 3 other times (Acts 1:9, 11, 22) to describe the end of the Lord's earthly ministry (cf. John 6:62; 13:1, 3; 16:28; 17:13; 20:17).

g. **through the Holy Spirit had given commandments.** The Spirit was the source and power of Jesus' earthly ministry (cf. Matt. 4:1; 12:18; Mark 1:12; Luke 3:22; 4:1, 14, 18) and of

the Holy Spirit had given commandments to the apostles whom ᵃHe had chosen, to whom He also ᵇpresented Himself alive after His suffering by many infallible proofs, being seen by them during ᶜforty days and speaking of the things pertaining to the ᵈkingdom of God.

And ᵉbeing assembled together with them, He commanded them not to depart from Jerusalem, but to ᶠwait for the Promise of the Father, "which," He said, "you have heard from Me; for John truly baptized with water, but you shall be ᵍbaptized with the Holy Spirit ʰnot many days from now." Therefore, when they had come together, they asked Him, saying, "Lord, will You at this time ⁱrestore the kingdom to Israel?" And He said to them, "It is not for you to know times or seasons which the Father has put in His own authority. ʲBut you shall ᵏreceive power when the Holy Spirit has come upon you; and

the apostles' service (cf. Luke 24:49; John 14:16, 17; 16:7). "Commandments" are authoritative NT truths, revealed to the apostles (cf. John 14:26; 16:13–15).

a. **He had chosen.** The Lord sovereignly chose the apostles for salvation and service (cf. John 6:70; 15:16).

b. **presented Himself . . . by many infallible proofs.** Cf. John 20:30; 1 Cor. 15:5–8. To give the apostles confidence to present His message, Jesus entered a locked room (John 20:19), showed His crucifixion wounds (Luke 24:39), and ate and drank with the disciples (Luke 24:41–43).

c. **forty days.** The time period between Jesus' death and ascension during which He appeared at intervals to the apostles and others (1 Cor. 15:5–8) and provided convincing evidence of His resurrection.

d. **kingdom of God.** Cf. Acts 8:12; 14:22; 19:8; 20:25; 28:23, 31. Here this expression refers to the sphere of salvation, the gracious domain of divine rule over believers' hearts (cf. Acts 17:7; Col. 1:13, 14; Rev. 11:15; 12:10). This was the dominant theme during Christ's earthly ministry (cf. Matt. 4:23; 9:35; Mark 1:15; Luke 4:43; 9:2; John 3:3–21).

e. **being assembled together with them.** An alternative reading, "eating with them," is preferred (see Acts 10:41; cf. Luke 24:42, 43). The fact that Jesus ate provides additional proof of His bodily resurrection.

f. **wait for the Promise of the Father.** Jesus repeatedly promised that God would send them His Spirit (Luke 11:13; 24:49; John 7:39; 14:16, 26; 15:26; 16:7).

g. **baptized with the Holy Spirit.** The apostles had to wait until the Day of Pentecost, but since then all believers are baptized with the Holy Spirit at salvation (cf. Rom. 8:9; 1 Cor. 6:19, 20; 12:13; Titus 3:5, 6).

h. **not many days from now.** God's promise was fulfilled just 10 days later.

i. **restore the kingdom to Israel.** The apostles still believed the earthly form of the kingdom of Messiah would soon be re-established (cf. Luke 19:11; 24:21). They also knew that Ezek. 36 and Joel 2 connected the coming of the kingdom with the outpouring of the Spirit whom Jesus had promised.

j. **times or seasons.** These two words refer to features, eras, and events that will be part of His earthly kingdom reign, which will begin at the second coming (Matt. 25:21–34). The exact time of His return, however, remains unrevealed (Mark 13:32; cf. Deut. 29:29). This verse shows that the apostles' expectation of a literal, earthly kingdom mirrored what Christ taught and what the OT predicted. Otherwise, He would have corrected them about such a crucial aspect of His teaching.

k. **receive power.** The apostles had already experienced the Holy Spirit's saving, guiding, teaching, and miracle-working power. Soon they would receive His indwelling presence and a new dimension of power for witness (see Acts 2:4; 1 Cor. 6:19, 20; Eph. 3:16, 20).

you shall be ªwitnesses to Me in Jerusalem, and in all ᵇJudea and Samaria, and to the end of the earth."

Now when He had spoken these things, while they watched, He was ᶜtaken up, and ᵈa cloud received Him out of their sight. And while they looked steadfastly toward heaven as He went up, behold, ᵉtwo men stood by them in white apparel, who also said, ᶠ"Men of Galilee, why do you stand gazing up into heaven? This same Jesus, who was taken up from you into heaven, will so come ᵍin like manner as you saw Him go into heaven."

4. The Disciples Wait in the Upper Room
Acts 1:12–26

Then they returned to Jerusalem from the ʰmount called Olivet, which is near Jerusalem, a ⁱSabbath day's journey. And when they had entered, they went up into the ʲupper room where they were staying: Peter, James, John,

a. **witnesses.** People who tell the truth about Jesus Christ (cf. John 14:26; 1 Pet. 3:15). The Gr. word means "one who dies for his faith" because that was commonly the price of witnessing.

b. **Judea.** The region in which Jerusalem was located. The apostles' mission of spreading the gospel was the major reason the Holy Spirit empowered them. This event dramatically altered world history, and the gospel message eventually reached all parts of the earth.

c. **taken up.** God the Father took Jesus, in His resurrection body, from this world to His rightful place at the Father's right hand (Luke 24:51; cf. 2:33; John 17:1–6).

d. **a cloud.** A visible reminder that God's glory was present as the apostles watched the ascension. For some of them, this was not the first time they had witnessed divine glory (Mark 9:26); neither will it be the last time clouds accompany Jesus (Mark 13:26; 14:62; Rev. 1:7).

e. **two men . . . in white apparel.** Two angels in the form of men (cf. Gen. 18:2; Josh. 5:13–15; Mark 16:5).

f. **Men of Galilee.** All the apostles were from Galilee except for Judas, who had killed himself by this time.

g. **in like manner.** Christ one day will return to earth (to the Mt. of Olives), in the same way He ascended (with clouds), to set up His kingdom (cf. Dan. 7:13; Zech. 14:4; Matt. 24:30; 26:64; Rev. 1:7; 14:14).

h. **mount called Olivet.** Located across the Kidron Valley, E of Jerusalem, this large hill rising about 200 ft. higher in elevation than the city, was the site from which Jesus ascended into heaven (Luke 24:50, 51).

i. **Sabbath day's journey.** One-half of a mi. (about 2,000 cubits), the farthest distance a faithful Jew could travel on the Sabbath to accommodate the prohibition of Ex. 16:29. This measurement was derived from tradition based on Israel's encampments in the wilderness. The tents farthest out on the camp's perimeter were 2,000 cubits from the center tabernacle—the longest distance anyone had to walk to reach the tabernacle on the Sabbath (Josh. 3:4; cf. Num. 35:5).

j. **upper room.** Where the Last Supper may have been celebrated (Mark 14:15) and where Jesus had appeared to the apostles after His resurrection.

and Andrew; Philip and Thomas; [a]Bartholomew and Matthew; [b]James the son of Alphaeus and Simon the Zealot; and [c]Judas the son of James. These all [d]continued with one accord in prayer and supplication, [e]with the women and [f]Mary the mother of Jesus, and with His [g]brothers.

And [h]in those days [i]Peter stood up in the midst of the disciples (altogether the number of names was about a hundred and twenty), and said, [j]"Men and brethren, [k]this Scripture had to be fulfilled, which the [l]Holy Spirit spoke before by the mouth of David concerning Judas, who became a guide to those who arrested Jesus; for he was numbered with us and [m]obtained a part in this ministry."

(Now this man [n]purchased a field with the wages of iniquity; and falling headlong, he burst open in the middle and all his entrails gushed out. And

---

a. **Bartholomew.** See Matt. 10:3. This disciple is also called Nathanael (John 1:45–49; 21:2).

b. **James the son of Alphaeus.** See Matt. 10:2. The same person as James the younger, also called "the Less" to distinguish him from James, the brother of John (Mark 15:40).

c. **Judas the son of James.** The preferred rendering is "the brother of." See Matt. 10:3. He was also known as Thaddaeus (Mark 3:18).

d. **continued . . . in prayer.** The pattern of praying in the name of Jesus started at this time (cf. John 14:13, 14).

e. **with the women.** Doubtless they included Mary Magdalene, Mary the wife of Clopas, the sisters Mary and Martha, and Salome. Some of the apostles' wives also may have been present (cf. 1 Cor. 9:5).

f. **Mary the mother of Jesus.** See Luke 1:27, 28. Mary's name does not appear again in the NT.

g. **brothers.** Jesus' half-brothers, named in Mark 6:3 as James, Joses, Judas, and Simon. James was the leader of the Jerusalem church (Acts 12:17; 15:13–22) and author of the epistle that bears his name. Judas (Jude) wrote the epistle of Jude. At this time they were new believers in Jesus as God, Savior, and Lord, whereas only 8 months earlier John had mentioned their unbelief (John 7:5). Their conversions are not recorded in the NT, but James may have been saved following a post-resurrection appearance by Jesus (1 Cor. 15:7).

h. **in those days.** Some unspecified time during the believers' 10 days of prayer and fellowship between the ascension and Pentecost.

i. **Peter.** See Matt. 10:2. The acknowledged leader of the apostles took charge.

j. **Men and brethren.** The 120 believers who were gathered (Acts 1:15).

k. **this Scripture had to be fulfilled.** The two OT passages Peter quotes in Acts 1:20 are Pss. 69:25; 109:8. When God gives prophecies, they will come to pass (cf. Ps. 115:3; Is. 46:10; 55:11).

l. **Holy Spirit . . . by the mouth of David.** Scripture contains no clearer description of divine inspiration. God spoke through David's mouth, actually referring to his writing (see 2 Pet. 1:21).

m. **obtained a part in this ministry.** Judas Iscariot was a member of the 12, but was never truly saved which is why he was called "the son of perdition" (John 17:12). See Matt. 26:24; John 6:64, 70, 71; cf. 2:23; Luke 22:22.

n. **this man purchased a field.** Because the field was bought with the money the Jewish leaders paid Judas to betray Jesus, which he returned to them (Matt. 27:3–10), Luke refers to Judas as if he was the buyer (cf. Zech. 11:12, 13). **wages of iniquity.** The 30 pieces of silver paid to Judas. **falling headlong.** Apparently the tree on which Judas chose to hang himself (Matt. 27:5) overlooked a cliff. Likely, the rope or branch broke (or the knot slipped) and his body was shattered on the rocks below.

it became known to all those dwelling in Jerusalem; so that field is called in their own language, ᵃAkel Dama, that is, Field of Blood.)

"For ᵇit is written in the Book of Psalms:

> 'Let his dwelling place be desolate,
> And let no one live in it';

and,

> 'Let another take his office.'

"Therefore, of these men who have accompanied us all the time that the Lord Jesus ᶜwent in and out among us, beginning from the ᵈbaptism of John to that day when He was taken up from us, one of these must become a witness with us of His resurrection."

And they proposed two: Joseph called ᵉBarsabas, who was surnamed Justus, and Matthias. And they prayed and said, "You, O Lord, who know the hearts of all, show which of these two You have chosen to take part in this ministry and apostleship from which Judas by transgression fell, that he might go to ᶠhis own place." And they ᵍcast their lots, and the lot fell on Matthias. And he was numbered with the eleven apostles.

---

a. **Akel Dama . . . Field of Blood.** This is the Aram. name of the field bought by the Jewish leaders. Traditionally, the field is located S of Jerusalem in the Valley of Hinnom, where that valley crosses the Kidron Valley. The soil there was good for making pottery, thus Matthew identifies it as "the potter's field" (Matt. 27:7, 10).

b. **it is written.** Peter used the most compelling proof, Scripture, to reassure the believers that Judas' defection and the choice of his replacement were both in God's purpose (cf. Ps. 55:12–15).

c. **went in and out among us.** The first requirement for Judas' successor was that he had participated in Jesus' earthly ministry.

d. **baptism of John.** Jesus' baptism by John the Baptist (Matt. 3:13–17; Mark 1:9–11; Luke 3:21–23). a witness with us of His resurrection. A second requirement for Judas' successor was that he had to have seen the resurrected Christ. The resurrection was central to apostolic preaching (cf. Acts 2:24, 32; 3:15; 5:30; 10:40; 13:30–37).

e. **Barsabas . . . Justus.** Barsabas means "son of the Sabbath." Justus ("the righteous") was Joseph's Lat. name. Many Jews in the Roman Empire had equivalent Gentile names. Matthias. The name means "gift of God." The ancient historian Eusebius claims Matthias was among the 70 of Luke 10:1.

f. **his own place.** Judas chose his own fate of hell by rejecting Christ. It is not unfair to say that Judas and all others who go to hell belong there (cf. John 6:70).

g. **cast their lots.** A common OT method of determining God's will (cf. Lev. 16:8–10; Josh. 7:14; Prov. 18:18; see Prov. 16:33). This is the last biblical mention of lots—the coming of the Spirit made them unnecessary.

5. THE CHURCH IS BORN

Acts 2:1–13

When the ªDay of Pentecost had fully come, they were all with one accord in one place. And suddenly there came ᵇa sound from heaven, as of a rushing mighty wind, and it filled the whole house where they were sitting. Then there appeared to them divided ᶜtongues, as of fire, and one sat upon each of them. And they were ᵈall ᵉfilled with the Holy Spirit and began to speak ᶠwith other tongues, as the Spirit gave them utterance.

And there were dwelling in Jerusalem ᵍJews, devout men, from every nation under heaven. And when ʰthis sound occurred, the multitude came together, and were confused, because everyone heard them ⁱspeak in his own language. Then they were all amazed and marveled, saying to one another, "Look, are not all these who speak ʲGalileans? And how is it that we hear,

a. **Day of Pentecost.** "Pentecost" means "fiftieth" and refers to the Feast of Weeks (Ex. 34:22, 23) or Harvest (Lev. 23:16), which was celebrated 50 days after Passover in May/June (Lev. 23:15–22). It was one of 3 annual feasts for which the nation was to come to Jerusalem (see Ex. 23:14–19). At Pentecost, an offering of firstfruits was made (Lev. 23:20). The Holy Spirit came on this day as the firstfruits of the believer's inheritance (cf. 2 Cor. 5:5; Eph. 1:11, 14). Those gathered into the church then were also the firstfruits of the full harvest of all believers to come after.

b. **a sound . . . as . . . mighty wind.** Luke's simile described God's action of sending the Holy Spirit. Wind is frequently used in Scripture as a picture of the Spirit (cf. Ezek. 37:9, 10; John 3:8).

c. **tongues, as of fire.** Just as the sound, like wind, was symbolic, these were not literal flames of fire but supernatural indicators, like fire, that God had sent the Holy Spirit upon each believer. In Scripture, fire often denoted the divine presence (cf. Ex. 3:2–6). God's use of a fire-like appearance here parallels what He did with the dove when Jesus was baptized (Matt. 3:11; Luke 3:16).

d. **all.** The apostles and the 120. Cf. Joel 2:28–32.

e. **filled with the Holy Spirit.** In contrast to the baptism with the Spirit, which is the one-time act by which God places believers into His body (see 1 Cor. 12:13), the filling is a repeated reality of Spirit-controlled behavior that God commands believers to maintain (see Eph. 5:18). Peter and many others in Acts 2 were filled with the Spirit again (e.g., Acts 4:8, 31; 6:5; 7:55) and so spoke boldly the Word of God. The fullness of the Spirit affects all areas of life, not just speaking boldly (cf. Eph. 5:19–33).

f. **with other tongues.** Known languages (1 Cor. 14:1–25), not ecstatic utterances. These languages given by the Spirit were a sign of judgment to unbelieving Israel (see 1 Cor. 14:21, 22). They also showed that from then on God's people would come from all nations, and marked the transition from Israel to the church. Tongues speaking occurs only twice more in Acts (10:46; 19:6).

g. **Jews, devout men.** Hebrew males who made the pilgrimage to Jerusalem. They were expected to celebrate Pentecost (see v. 1) in Jerusalem, as part of observing the Jewish religious calendar. See Ex. 23:14–19.

h. **this sound.** The noise like gusty wind, not the sound of the various languages.

i. **speak in his own language.** As the believers were speaking, each pilgrim in the crowd recognized the language or dialect from his own country.

j. **Galileans.** Inhabitants of the mostly rural area of northern Israel around the Sea

each in our own ᵃlanguage in which we were born? ᵇParthians and ᶜMedes and ᵈElamites, those dwelling in ᵉMesopotamia, ᶠJudea and ᵍCappadocia, Pontus and Asia, Phrygia and Pamphylia, ʰEgypt and the parts of ⁱLibya adjoining Cyrene, visitors from ʲRome, both ᵏJews and proselytes, ˡCretans and ᵐArabs—we hear them speaking in our own tongues the ⁿwonderful works of God." So they were all amazed and perplexed, saying to one another, "Whatever could this mean?"

Others mocking said, "They are full of ᵒnew wine."

6. Peter Preaches the Gospel in Jerusalem
Acts 2:14–36

But Peter, standing up ᵖwith the eleven, raised his voice and said to them, "Men of Judea and all who dwell in Jerusalem, let this be known to you, and

---

of Galilee. Galilean Jews spoke with a distinct regional accent and were considered to be unsophisticated and uneducated by the southern Judean Jews. When Galileans were seen to be speaking so many different languages, the Judean Jews were astonished.

a. **language.** The listing of specific countries and ethnic groups proves again that these utterances were known human languages.

b. **Parthians.** They lived in what is modern Iran.

c. **Medes.** In Daniel's time, they ruled with the Persians, but had settled in Parthia.

d. **Elamites.** They were from the southwestern part of the Parthian Empire.

e. **Mesopotamia.** This means "between the rivers" (the Tigris and Euphrates). Many Jews still lived there, descendants of those who were in captivity and who never returned to Palestine (cf. 2 Chr. 36:22, 23).

f. **Judea.** All the region once controlled by David and Solomon, including Syria.

g. **Cappadocia, Pontus and Asia, Phrygia and Pamphylia.** All were districts in Asia Minor, in what is now Turkey.

h. **Egypt.** Many Jews lived there, especially in the city of Alexandria. The nation then covered the same general area as modern Egypt.

i. **Libya adjoining Cyrene.** These districts were W of Egypt, along the North African coast.

j. **Rome.** The capital of the Empire had a sizeable Jewish population, dating from the second century B.C.

k. **proselytes.** Gentile converts to Judaism. Jews in Rome were especially active in seeking such converts.

l. **Cretans.** Residents of the island of Crete, off the southern coast of Greece.

m. **Arabs.** Jews who lived S of Damascus, among the Nabatean Arabs (cf. Gal. 1:17).

n. **wonderful works of God.** The Christians were quoting from the OT what God had done for His people (cf. Ex. 15:11; Pss. 40:5; 77:11; 96:3; 107:21). Such praises were often heard in Jerusalem during festival times.

o. **new wine.** A drink that could have made one drunk.

p. **with the eleven.** This number of the apostles included the newly-appointed Matthias, who replaced Judas Iscariot (see Acts 1:23, 24).

heed my words. For these are not drunk, as you suppose, since it is only [a]the third hour of the day. But this is what was spoken by [b]the prophet Joel:

'And it shall come to pass in the [c]last days, says God,

That I will pour out of My Spirit on [d]all flesh;

Your sons and your daughters shall [e]prophesy,

Your young men shall see [f]visions,

Your old men shall dream dreams.

And on My menservants and on My maidservants

I will pour out My Spirit in those days;

And they shall prophesy. I will show [g]wonders in heaven above

And signs in the earth beneath:

[h]Blood and fire and vapor of smoke.

The [i]sun shall be turned into darkness,

And the moon into blood,

---

a. **the third hour.** Calculated in Jewish fashion from sunrise, this was 9:00 a.m.

b. **the prophet Joel.** Joel's prophecy will not be completely fulfilled until the millennial kingdom and the final judgment. But Peter, by using it, shows that Pentecost was a pre-fulfillment, a taste of what will happen in the millennial kingdom when the Spirit is poured out on all flesh (cf. Acts 10:45).

c. **last days.** This phrase refers to the present era of redemptive history from the first coming of Christ (Heb. 1:2; 1 Pet. 1:20; 1 John 2:18) to His return.

d. **all flesh.** This indicates all people will receive the Holy Spirit, because everyone who enters the millennial kingdom will be redeemed (cf. Matt. 24:29—25:46; Rev. 20:4–6).

e. **prophesy.** The proclamation of God's truth will be pervasive in the millennial kingdom.

f. **visions . . . dreams.** Dreams (Gen. 20:3; Dan. 7:1) and visions (Gen. 15:1; Rev. 9:17) were some of God's most memorable means of revelation since they were pictorial in nature. While they were not limited to believers (e.g., Abimelech, Gen. 20:3 and Pharaoh, Gen. 41:1–8), they were primarily reserved for prophets and apostles (cf. Num. 12:6). While frequent in the OT, they were rare in the NT. In Acts, all of God's visions were given to either Peter (chaps. 10, 11) or Paul (chaps. 9, 18; cf. 2 Cor. 12:1). Most frequently they were used to reveal apocalyptic imagery (cf. Ezek., Dan., Zech., Rev.). They were not considered normal in biblical times, nor should they be so now. The time will come, however, when God will use visions and dreams during the Tribulation period as predicted by Joel 2:28–32.

g. **wonders . . . signs.** Cf. Acts 4:30; 5:12; 14:3; 15:12. "Wonders" is the amazement people experience when witnessing supernatural works (miracles). "Signs" point to the power of God behind miracles—marvels have no value unless they point to God and His truth. Such works were often done by the Holy Spirit through the apostles (Acts 5:12–16) and their associates (Acts 6:8) to authenticate them as the messengers of God's truth. Cf. 2 Cor. 12:12.

h. **Blood . . . fire . . . vapor of smoke.** These phenomena are all connected with events surrounding Christ's second coming and signal the establishment of the earthly kingdom: blood (Rev. 6:8; 8:7, 9; 9:15; 14:20; 16:3); fire (Rev. 8:5, 7, 8, 10); and smoke (Rev. 9:2, 3, 17, 18; 18:9, 18).

i. **sun . . . darkness . . . moon into blood.** Cf. Matt. 24:29, 30; see Rev. 6:12.

Before the coming of the great and awesome [a]day of the LORD.
And it shall come to pass
That [b]whoever calls on the name of the Lord
Shall be saved.'

"Men of Israel, hear these words: [c]Jesus of Nazareth, a Man [d]attested by God to you by miracles, wonders, and signs which God did through Him in your midst, as you yourselves also know—Him, being delivered [e]by the determined purpose and foreknowledge of God, you have taken by [f]lawless hands, have crucified, and put to death; whom God raised up, having loosed the pains of death, because it was [g]not possible that He should be held by it. For [h]David says concerning Him:

'I foresaw the Lord always before my face,
For He is at my right hand, that I may not be shaken.
Therefore my heart rejoiced, and my tongue was glad;
Moreover my flesh also will rest in hope.
For You will not leave my soul in [i]Hades,
Nor will You allow Your Holy One to see corruption.

---

a. **day of the LORD.** See 1 Thess. 5:2. This Day of the Lord will come with the return of Jesus Christ (cf. 2 Thess. 2:2; Rev. 19:11–15).

b. **whoever calls.** Up to that hour of judgment and wrath, any who turn to Christ as Lord and Savior will be saved (see Rom. 10:10–13).

c. **Jesus of Nazareth.** The humble name that often identified the Lord during His earthly ministry (Matt. 21:11; Mark 10:47; Luke 24:19; John 18:5).

d. **attested . . . by miracles, wonders, and signs.** By a variety of supernatural means and works, God validated Jesus as the Messiah (cf. Matt. 11:1–6; Luke 7:20–23; John 3:2; 5:17–20; 8:28; Phil. 2:9; see 1:3; 2:19).

e. **by the determined purpose and foreknowledge of God.** From eternity past (2 Tim. 1:9; Rev. 13:8) God predetermined that Jesus would die an atoning death as part of the His pre-ordained plan (Acts 4:27, 28; 13:27–29).

f. **lawless hands, have crucified.** An indictment against "men of Israel" (v. 22), those unbelieving Jews who instigated Jesus' death, which was carried out by the Romans. That the crucifixion was predetermined by God does not absolve the guilt of those who caused it.

g. **not possible.** Because of His divine power (John 11:25; Heb. 2:14) and God's promise and purpose (Luke 24:46; John 2:18–22; 1 Cor. 15:16–26), death could not keep Jesus in the grave.

h. **David says.** The Lord was speaking of His resurrection prophetically through David (see Ps. 16:8–11).

i. **Hades.** Cf. Acts 2:31; see Luke 16:23. The NT equivalent of the OT grave or "sheol." Though sometimes it identifies hell (Matt. 11:23), here it refers to the general place of the dead.

You have made known to me the ways of life;
You will make me full of joy in Your presence.'

"Men and brethren, let me speak freely to you of the patriarch David, that he is both dead and buried, and ᵃhis tomb is with us to this day. Therefore, ᵇbeing a prophet, and knowing that God had sworn with an oath to him that of the fruit of his body, according to the flesh, He would raise up the Christ to sit on his throne, he, foreseeing this, ᶜspoke concerning the resurrection of the Christ, that His soul was not left in Hades, nor did His flesh see corruption. This Jesus ᵈGod has raised up, of which ᵉwe are all witnesses. Therefore being exalted to the right hand of God, and having received from the Father the ᶠpromise of the Holy Spirit, He poured out this which you now see and hear.

"For David did not ascend into the heavens, but he says himself:

ᵍ'The Lᴏʀᴅ said to my Lord,
"Sit at My right hand,
Till I make Your enemies Your footstool."'

ʰ"Therefore let all the house of Israel know assuredly that God has made this Jesus, whom you crucified, both Lord and Christ."

---

a. **his tomb is with us.** A reminder to the Jews that David's body had never been raised, so he could not be the fulfillment of the prophecy of Ps. 16.

b. **being a prophet.** Peter quoted Ps. 132:11. As God's spokesman, David knew that God would keep His oath (2 Sam. 7:11–16) and Christ would come.

c. **spoke.** Peter is referring to David's words in Ps. 16:10. Peter exposits the meaning of Ps. 16 as referring not to David, but to Jesus Christ. He would be raised to reign (cf. Pss. 2:1–9; 89:3; 138:1–8).

d. **God has raised up.** Cf. Acts 2:24; 10:40; 17:31; 1 Cor. 6:14; Eph. 1:20. That He did so attests to His approval of Christ's work on the cross.

e. **we are all witnesses.** The early preachers preached the resurrection (Acts 3:15, 26; 4:10; 5:30; 10:40; 13:30, 33, 34, 37; 17:31).

f. **promise of the Holy Spirit.** After Jesus was risen and ascended, God's promise to send the Holy Spirit was fulfilled (cf. John 7:39; Gal. 3:14) and manifest that day.

g. **The Lᴏʀᴅ said to my Lord.** Peter quoted another psalm (Ps. 110:1) concerning the exaltation of Messiah by ascension to the right hand of God, and reminds the reader that it was not fulfilled by David, but by Jesus Christ. Peter had been an eyewitness to that ascension (Acts 1:9–11).

h. **Therefore.** Peter summarizes his sermon with a powerful statement of certainty: The OT prophecies of resurrection and exaltation provide evidence that overwhelmingly points to the crucified Jesus as the Messiah. **both Lord and Christ.** Jesus is God as well as anointed Messiah (cf. Rom. 1:4; 10:9; 1 Cor. 12:3; Phil. 2:9, 11).

7. THE EARLY CHURCH

Acts 2:37–47

Now when they heard this, they were ᵃcut to the heart, and said to Peter and the rest of the apostles, "Men and brethren, what shall we do?"

Then Peter said to them, ᵇ"Repent, and let every one of you ᶜbe baptized ᵈin the name of Jesus Christ ᵉfor the remission of sins; and you shall receive the gift of the Holy Spirit. For the promise is to you and to your children, and to ᶠall who are afar off, ᵍas many as the Lord our God will call."

And with many other words he testified and exhorted them, saying, "Be saved from this perverse generation." Then those who gladly received his word were baptized; and that day about ʰthree thousand souls were added to

---

a. **cut to the heart.** The Gr. word for "cut" means "pierce" or "stab," and thus denotes something sudden and unexpected. In grief, remorse, and intense spiritual conviction, Peter's listeners were stunned by his indictment that they had killed their Messiah.

b. **Repent.** This refers to a change of mind and purpose that turns an individual from sin to God (1 Thess. 1:9). Such change involves more than fearing the consequences of God's judgment. Genuine repentance knows that the evil of sin must be forsaken and the person and work of Christ totally and singularly embraced. Peter exhorted his hearers to repent, otherwise they would not experience true conversion (see Matt. 3:2; cf. Acts 3:19; 5:31; 8:22; 11:18; 17:30; 20:21; 26:20; Matt. 4:17).

c. **be baptized.** This Gr. word lit. means "be dipped or immersed" in water. Peter was obeying Christ's command from Matt. 28:19 and urging the people who repented and turned to the Lord Christ for salvation to identify, through the waters of baptism, with His death, burial, and resurrection (cf. Acts 19:5; Rom. 6:3, 4; 1 Cor. 12:13; Gal. 3:27; see Matt. 3:2). This is the first time the apostles publicly enjoined people to obey that ceremony. Prior to this, many Jews had experienced the baptism of John the Baptist, (see Matt. 3:1–3) and were also familiar with the baptism of Gentile converts to Judaism (proselytes).

d. **in the name of Jesus Christ.** For the new believer, it was a crucial but costly identification to accept.

e. **for the remission of sins.** This might better be translated "because of the remission of sins." Baptism does not produce forgiveness and cleansing from sin. See 1 Pet. 3:20, 21. The reality of forgiveness precedes the rite of baptism (v. 41). Genuine repentance brings from God the forgiveness (remission) of sins (cf. Eph. 1:7), and because of that the new believer was to be baptized. Baptism, however, was to be the ever-present act of obedience, so that it became synonymous with salvation. Thus to say one was baptized for forgiveness was the same as saying one was saved. See "one baptism" in Eph. 4:5. Every believer enjoys the complete remission of sins (Matt. 26:28; Luke 24:47; Eph. 1:7; Col. 2:13; 1 John 2:12).

f. **all who are afar off.** Gentiles, who would also share in the blessings of salvation (cf. Eph. 2:11–13).

g. **as many as the Lord our God will call.** Salvation is ultimately from the Lord. See Rom. 3:24.

h. **three thousand.** Peter's use of a specific number suggests records were kept of conversions and baptisms. Archaeological work on the S side of the temple mount has uncovered numerous Jewish mikvahs, large baptistry-like facilities where Jewish worshipers would immerse themselves in ritual purification before entering the temple. More than enough existed to facilitate the large number of baptisms in a short amount of time.

them. And they continued steadfastly in the ªapostles' doctrine and ᵇfellowship, in the ᶜbreaking of bread, and in ᵈprayers. Then fear came upon every soul, and many ᵉwonders and signs were done through the apostles. Now all who believed were together, and had ᶠall things in common, and ᵍsold their possessions and goods, and divided them among all, as anyone had need.

So continuing ʰdaily with one accord in the temple, and ⁱbreaking bread from house to house, they ate their food with ʲgladness and simplicity of heart, praising God and having favor with all the people. And the ᵏLord added to the church daily those who were being saved.

8. THE MINISTRY OF PETER AND JOHN

Acts 3:1–10

Now Peter and John went up together to the temple at the ˡhour of prayer, the ninth hour. And a certain man lame from his mother's womb was carried,

---

a. **apostles' doctrine.** The foundational content for the believer's spiritual growth and maturity was the Scripture, God's revealed truth, which the apostles received (see John 14:26; 15:26, 27; 16:13) and taught faithfully. See 2 Pet. 1:19–21; 3:1, 2, 16.

b. **fellowship.** Lit. "partnership," or "sharing." Because Christians become partners with Jesus Christ and all other believers (1 John 1:3), it is their spiritual duty to stimulate one another to righteousness and obedience (cf. Rom. 12:10; 13:8; 15:5; Gal. 5:13; Eph. 4:2, 25; 5:21; Col. 3:9; 1 Thess. 4:9; Heb. 3:13; 10:24, 25; 1 Pet. 4:9, 10).

c. **breaking of bread.** A reference to the Lord's Table, or Communion, which is mandatory for all Christians to observe (cf. 1 Cor. 11:24–29).

d. **prayers.** Of individual believers and the church corporately (see Acts 1:14, 24; 4:24–31; cf. John 14:13, 14).

e. **wonders and signs.** See Acts 2:19. In the NT, the ability to perform miracles was limited to the apostles and their close colleagues (e.g., Philip in 8:13; cf. 2 Cor. 12:12; Heb. 2:3, 4). These produced awe and respect for divine power.

f. **all things in common.** See Acts 4:32. This phrase conveys not that the early Christians lived in a commune or pooled and redistributed everything equally, but that they held their own possessions lightly, ready to use them at any moment for someone else, as needs arose.

g. **sold their possessions.** This indicates that they had not pooled their resources (Acts 2:44) but sold their own possessions to provide money for those of the church in need (cf. Acts 2:46; 4:34–37; 2 Cor. 8:13, 14).

h. **daily . . . in the temple.** Believers went to the temple to praise God (Acts 2:47), observe the daily hours of prayer (cf. Acts 3:1), and witness to the gospel (Acts 2:47; 5:42).

i. **breaking bread from house to house.** This has reference to the daily means that believers shared with one another.

j. **gladness and simplicity of heart.** The Jerusalem church was joyful because its single focus was on Jesus Christ. See 2 Cor. 11:3; Phil. 3:13, 14.

k. **the Lord added.** Cf. Acts 2:39; 5:14. See Matt. 16:18. Salvation is God's sovereign work.

l. **hour of prayer, the ninth hour.** 3:00 p.m. The Jews had 3 daily times of prayer (Ps. 55:17); the other two were 9:00 a.m. (third hour) and 12:00 noon (sixth hour).

whom they laid daily at the ªgate of the temple which is called Beautiful, to ask alms from those who entered the temple; who, seeing Peter and John about to go ᵇinto the temple, asked for alms. And fixing his eyes on him, with John, Peter said, "Look at us." So he gave them his attention, expecting to receive something from them. Then Peter said, "Silver and gold I do not have, but what I do have I give you: In the name of Jesus Christ of Nazareth, rise up and walk." And he took him by the right hand and lifted him up, and immediately his feet and ankle bones received strength. So he, leaping up, stood and walked and entered the temple with them—walking, leaping, and praising God. And all the people saw him walking and praising God. Then they knew that it was he who sat begging alms at the Beautiful Gate of the temple; and they were filled with wonder and amazement at what had happened to him.

9. Peter's Second Sermon

Acts 3:11–26

Now as the lame man who was healed held on to Peter and John, all the people ran together to them in the ᶜporch which is called Solomon's, greatly amazed. So when Peter saw it, he responded to the people: "Men of Israel, why do you marvel at this? Or why look so intently at us, as though by our own power or godliness we had made this man walk? ᵈThe God of Abraham, Isaac, and Jacob, the God of our fathers, glorified ᵉHis Servant Jesus, whom you delivered

---

a. **gate of the temple . . . called Beautiful.** A large and ornate gate inside the temple mount on the eastern side, separating the Court of the Gentiles from the Court of the Women.

b. **into the temple.** Beggars considered the temple the best site to operate because the daily throngs came to impress God with their pious good works, including offerings at the temple treasury.

c. **3:11 porch . . . Solomon's.** A portico surrounding the temple's Court of the Gentiles. This was also where Jesus had taught about the Good Shepherd (John 10:23). Cf. Is. 35:6.

d. **The God of Abraham, Isaac, and Jacob.** A description of God familiar to Peter's Jewish audience (cf. Ex. 3:6, 15; 1 Kin. 18:36; 1 Chr. 29:18; 2 Chr. 30:6; Matt. 22:32). He used this formula, which stressed God's covenant faithfulness, to demonstrate that he declared the same God and Messiah whom the prophets had proclaimed.

e. **His Servant Jesus.** Peter depicted Jesus as God's personal representative. This is an unusual NT title for Jesus, used only 4 other places (Acts 3:26; 4:27, 30; Matt. 12:18), but a more familiar OT name for Messiah (Is. 42:1–4, 19; 49:5–7; 52:13—53:12; cf. Matt. 20:28; John 6:38; 8:28; 13:1–7).

up and denied in the presence of ªPilate, when he was determined to let Him go. But you denied ᵇthe Holy One and the Just, and asked for a ᶜmurderer to be granted to you, and ᵈkilled the ᵉPrince of life, whom God raised from the dead, of which we are witnesses. And His name, through faith in His name, has made this man strong, whom you see and know. Yes, the faith which comes through Him has given him this perfect soundness in the presence of you all.

"Yet now, brethren, I know that you did it in ignorance, as did also your rulers. But those things which God ᶠforetold by the mouth of all His prophets, that the Christ would suffer, He has thus fulfilled. ᵍRepent therefore and be converted, that ʰyour sins may be blotted out, so that ⁱtimes of refreshing may come from the presence of the Lord, and that He may send Jesus Christ, who was preached to you before, whom heaven must receive until the times of restoration of all things, which God has spoken by the mouth of all His holy prophets since the world began. For ʲMoses truly said to the fathers, 'The Lord your God will raise up for you a Prophet like me from your brethren. Him you shall hear in all things, whatever He says to you. And it shall be

---

a. **Pilate . . . determined to let Him go.** Pontius Pilate, the Roman governor at Jesus' trial, came from a national tradition that strongly supported justice (cf. Acts 16:37, 38; 22:25–29; 25:16). He knew Jesus' crucifixion would be unjust and therefore declared Him innocent 6 times (Luke 23:4, 14, 15, 22; John 18:38; 19:4, 6) and repeatedly sought to release Him (Luke 23:13–22; John 19:12, 13).

b. **the Holy One.** Cf. Ps. 10:10; Luke 4:34; John 6:69.

c. **murderer.** Barabbas (Matt. 27:16–21; Mark 15:11; Luke 23:18; John 18:40).

d. **killed . . . God raised . . . we are witnesses.** Peter's confident and forceful declaration (cf. 1 Cor. 15:3–7) was a clear defense of and provided further evidence for Christ's resurrection. Peter's claim was undeniable; the Jews never showed any evidence, such as Jesus' corpse, to disprove it.

e. **Prince of life.** The Gr. word for "prince" means originator, pioneer, or beginner of something. Both Heb. 2:10 and 12:2 translate it "author." It describes Jesus as the Divine Originator of life (cf. Ps. 36:9; Heb. 2:10; 12:2; 1 John 5:11, 20).

f. **foretold by the mouth of all His prophets.** Cf. Gen. 3:15; Ps. 22; Is. 53; Zech. 12:10.

g. **Repent . . . be converted.** See 2:38; Matt. 3:2. "Converted" is a frequent NT word that relates to sinners turning to God (Acts 9:35; 14:15; 26:18, 20; Luke 1:16, 17; 2 Cor. 3:16; 1 Pet. 2:25).

h. **your sins . . . blotted out.** Cf. Ps. 51:9; Is. 43:25; 44:22. "Blotted out" compares forgiveness to the complete wiping away of ink from the surface of a document (Col. 2:14).

i. **times of refreshing . . . times of restoration of all things.** "Times" means epoch, era, or season. Two descriptions are given to the coming era of the millennial kingdom. This is clear because they bracket the reference to Jesus Christ being sent from God to bring those times. Peter points to Christ's earthly reign (see Acts 1:7; cf. Rom. 11:26). The period will be marked by all kinds of blessings and renewal (cf. Is. 11:6–10; 35:1–10; Ezek. 34:26; 44:3; Joel 2:26; Matt. 19:28; Rev. 19:1–10).

j. **Moses truly said.** Quoted from Deut. 18:15, 19. Moses was revered by the Jews as their first and greatest prophet, and the Jews viewed the prophet "like him" to refer to the Messiah.

that every soul who will not hear that Prophet shall be utterly destroyed from among the people.' Yes, and all the ᵃprophets, from Samuel and those who follow, as many as have spoken, have also foretold these days. You are sons of the prophets, and of the covenant which God made with our fathers, saying to Abraham, 'And ᵇin your seed all the families of the earth shall be blessed.' To you first, God, having raised up His Servant Jesus, sent Him to bless you, in turning away every one of you from your iniquities."

10. Peter Tried by the Sanhedrin
Acts 4:1–22

Now as they spoke to the people, the ᶜpriests, the ᵈcaptain of the temple, and the Sadducees came upon them, being greatly disturbed that they taught the people and ᵉpreached in Jesus the resurrection from the dead. And they laid hands on them, and put them in custody until the next day, for it was ᶠalready evening. However, many of those who heard the word believed; and the number of the men came to be about ᵍfive thousand.

---

a. **prophets, from Samuel.** Samuel was called a prophet in the OT (1 Sam. 3:20). Although he did not directly prophesy about Christ, he did anoint David as king and speak of his kingdom (1 Sam. 13:14; 15:28; 16:13; 28:17), and the promises David received were and will be fulfilled in Christ (cf. 2 Sam. 7:10–16).

b. **in your seed.** Quoted from Gen. 22:18; 26:4. Jesus Christ was the ultimate fulfillment of the Abrahamic Covenant and its blessings (Gal. 3:16), which are still available to the Jews.

c. **priests.** The office of priest in the OT began with Aaron and his sons (Lev. 8). They became the human intermediaries between holy God and sinful humanity. They were characterized by 3 qualities: 1) they were chosen and set apart for priestly service by God; 2) they were to be holy in character; and 3) they were the only ones allowed to come near to God on behalf of the people with the High-Priest being the chief go-between on the Day of Atonement (Lev. 16). Cf. Num. 16:5.

d. **captain of the temple.** Chief of the temple police force (composed of Levites) and second-ranking official to the High-Priest. The Romans had delegated the temple-policing responsibility to the Jews.

e. **preached in Jesus the resurrection.** This part of the apostles' message was the most objectionable to the Jewish leaders. They had executed Christ as a blasphemer and now Peter and John were proclaiming His resurrection.

f. **already evening.** The Jews detained Peter and John overnight in jail because Jewish law did not permit trials at night. It had been too late to convene the Sanhedrin that afternoon, so the apostles would face a hearing the next day before that council.

g. **five thousand.** The cumulative total of men in the Jerusalem church by this time, not the number of those converted after Peter's latest message.

And it came to pass, on the next day, that their [a]rulers, elders, and scribes, as well as [b]Annas the high priest, Caiaphas, [c]John, and Alexander, and as many as were of the family of the high priest, were gathered together at Jerusalem. And when they had set them in the midst, they asked, "By what power or by what name have you done this?"

Then Peter, [d]filled with the Holy Spirit, said to them, "Rulers of the people and elders of Israel: If we this day are judged for a good deed done to a helpless man, by what means he has been made well, let it be known to you all, and to all the people of Israel, that by the name of Jesus Christ of Nazareth, whom you crucified, whom God raised from the dead, by Him this man stands here before you whole. This is the 'stone which was [e]rejected by you builders, which has become the chief cornerstone.' Nor is there salvation in any other, for there is [f]no other name under heaven given among men by which we must be saved."

Now when they saw the boldness of Peter and John, and perceived that they were [g]uneducated and untrained men, they marveled. And they realized that they had been with Jesus. And seeing the man who had been healed standing with them, they could say nothing against it. But when they had commanded them to go aside out of the [h]council, they [i]conferred among themselves, saying, "What shall we do to these men? For, indeed, that a notable miracle has been done through them is evident to all who dwell in

---

a. **rulers, elders, and scribes.** These positions made up the Jewish ruling body, the Sanhedrin.

b. **Annas . . . Caiaphas.** See John 18:13. Even though Annas (A.D. 6–15) had been replaced and Caiaphas was now High-Priest (A.D. 18–36), he retained his title and wielded great influence.

c. **John . . . Alexander.** Their identities are uncertain. "John" could be an alternate reading for "Jonathan," who was one of Annas' sons and replaced Caiaphas as High-Priest in A.D. 36.

d. **filled with the Holy Spirit.** See Acts 2:4. Because Peter was under the control of the Spirit, he was able to face persecution and preach the gospel with power (cf. Luke 12:11, 12).

e. **rejected . . . the chief cornerstone.** Quoted from Ps. 118:22; cf. Eph. 2:19–22; 1 Pet. 2:4–8.

f. **no other name.** This refers to the exclusivism of salvation by faith in Jesus Christ. There are only two religious paths: the broad way of works salvation leading to eternal death, and the narrow way of faith in Jesus, leading to eternal life (Matt. 7:13, 14; cf. John 10:7, 8; 14:6). Sadly, the Sanhedrin and its followers were on the first path.

g. **uneducated and untrained men.** Peter and John were not educated in the rabbinical schools and had no formal training in OT theology.

h. **council.** The Sanhedrin, the Jews' national ruling body and supreme court. It had 71 members, including the High-Priest.

i. **conferred.** It would be risky to punish the two apostles when they had broken no laws and had performed a miracle that captured the entire city's attention. But the Sanhedrin believed it had to stop the preaching of the incriminating truth that its members had executed the Messiah.

Jerusalem, and we cannot deny it. But so that it spreads no further among the people, let us severely threaten them, that from now on they speak to no man in this name."

So they called them and commanded them not to speak at all nor teach in the name of Jesus. But Peter and John answered and said to them, "Whether it is right in the sight of God [a]to listen to you more than to God, you judge. For we cannot but speak the things which we have seen and heard." So when they had further threatened them, they let them go, finding no way of punishing them, because of the people, since they all glorified God for what had been done. For the man was over forty years old on whom this miracle of healing had been performed.

11. The Resolve of the Early Church
Acts 4:23–37

And [b]being let go, they went to their own companions and reported all that the chief priests and elders had said to them. So when they heard that, they raised their voice to God with one accord and said: [c]"Lord, You are God, who made heaven and earth and the sea, and all that is in them, who [d]by the mouth of Your servant David have said:

> 'Why did the nations rage,
> And the people plot vain things?
> The kings of the earth took their stand,
> And the rulers were gathered together
> Against the LORD and against His Christ.'

---

a. **to listen to you more than to God.** Christians should obey governmental authority (Rom. 13:1–7; 1 Pet. 2:13–17), but when government decrees are clearly contrary to God's Word, God must be obeyed (cf. Ex. 1:15–17; Dan. 6:4–10).

b. **being let go.** Peter and John's experience did not frighten or discourage the other disciples, but exhilarated them. They took confidence in God's sovereign control of all events, even their sufferings. Furthermore, they were comforted that the opposition whom they were facing was foreseen in the OT.

c. **Lord.** The Gr. word is an uncommon NT title for God that means "absolute master" (Luke 2:29; 2 Tim. 2:21; 2 Pet. 2:1; Jude 4; Rev. 6:10), which represented the disciples' recognition of God's sovereignty.

d. **by the mouth of Your servant David.** See Acts 1:16. In the events of recent days, the disciples saw a fulfillment of Ps. 2:1, 2 which they quoted.

"For truly against Your holy Servant Jesus, whom You anointed, both Herod and Pontius Pilate, with the Gentiles and the people of Israel, were gathered together to do whatever Your hand and Your purpose determined before to be done. Now, Lord, look on their threats, and grant to Your servants that with all boldness they may speak Your word, by stretching out [a]Your hand to heal, and that signs and wonders may be done through the name of Your holy Servant Jesus."

And when they had prayed, the place where they were assembled together [b]was shaken; and they were all filled with the Holy Spirit, and they spoke the word of God with boldness.

Now the multitude of those who believed were of one heart and one soul; neither did anyone say that any of the things he possessed was his own, but they had [c]all things in common. And with great power the apostles gave witness to the resurrection of the Lord Jesus. And [d]great grace was upon them all. Nor was there anyone among them who lacked; for all who were possessors of lands or houses sold them, and brought the proceeds of the things that were sold, and laid them at the apostles' feet; and they distributed to each as anyone had need.

And [e]Joses, who was also named Barnabas by the apostles (which is translated Son of Encouragement), a Levite of the country of [f]Cyprus, [g]having land, sold it, and brought the money and laid it at the apostles' feet.

---

a. **Your hand and Your purpose.** God has written all of history according to His eternal plan. The crucifixion of Jesus was no exception (see Acts 2:23; cf. Rom. 8:29, 30; 1 Cor. 2:7; Eph. 1:5–11).

b. **was shaken.** As on Pentecost, a physical phenomenon indicated the presence of the Holy Spirit (see Acts 2:2, 3).

c. **all things in common.** See Acts 2:44–46. Believers understood that all they had belonged to God, and therefore when a brother or sister had a need those who could meet it were obligated to do so (cf. James 2:15, 16; 1 John 3:17). The method was to give the money to the apostles who would distribute it.

d. **great grace.** This means "favor" and carries a twofold meaning here: 1) favor from the people outside the church. Because of the believers' love and unity, the common people were impressed (cf. 2:47); and 2) favor from God who was granting blessing.

e. **Joses . . . Barnabas . . . a Levite.** Luke introduces Barnabas as a role model from among those who donated property proceeds. Barnabas was a member of the priestly tribe of the Levites and a native of the island of Cyprus. He becomes an associate of Paul and a prominent figure later in the book (cf. Acts 9:26, 27; 11:22–24, 30; chaps. 13–15).

f. **Cyprus.** The third largest island in the Mediterranean after Sicily and Sardinia, located some 60 mi. W off the Syrian coast (see Acts 13:4).

g. **having land, sold it.** The OT prohibited Levites from owning property in Israel (Num. 18:20, 24; Deut. 10:9), but that law was apparently no longer in force. It is also possible that the land was in Cyprus.

12. THE PURITY OF THE EARLY CHURCH

Acts 5:1–21a

But a certain man named [a]Ananias, with Sapphira his wife, sold a possession. And [b]he kept back part of the proceeds, his wife also being aware of it, and brought a certain part and laid it at the apostles' feet. But Peter said, "Ananias, why has [c]Satan filled your heart to [d]lie to the Holy Spirit and keep back part of the price of the land for yourself? While it remained, was it not your own? And after it was sold, was it not in your own control? Why have you conceived this thing in your heart? You have not lied to men but to God."

Then Ananias, hearing these words, fell down and breathed his last. So [e]great fear came upon all those who heard these things. And the young men arose and wrapped him up, carried him out, and [f]buried him.

Now it was about three hours later when his wife came in, not knowing what had happened. And Peter answered her, "Tell me whether you sold the land for so much?"

She said, "Yes, for so much."

Then Peter said to her, "How is it that you have agreed together to [g]test the Spirit of the Lord? Look, the feet of those who have buried your husband

---

a. **Ananias . . . Sapphira.** These are two classic examples of hypocrisy among Christians who faked their spirituality to impress others (cf. Matt. 6:1–6, 16–18; 15:7; 23:13–36). They were "in the congregation of those who believed" (Acts 4:32) and were involved with the Holy Spirit, but remained hypocrites.

b. **he kept back part of the proceeds.** This was not a sin in and of itself. However, they had promised, perhaps publicly, that they were giving the full amount received to the Lord. Their outward sin was lying about how much they were giving to the church, but the deeper, more devastating sin was their spiritual hypocrisy based on selfishness.

c. **Satan filled your heart.** Ananias and Sapphira were satanically inspired in contrast to Barnabas' Spirit-filled gesture (Acts 4:37).

d. **lie to the Holy Spirit.** Ananias must have promised the Lord he would give the whole amount. He lied to the ever-present Holy Spirit in him (1 Cor. 6:19, 20) and in the church (Eph. 2:21, 22).

e. **great fear.** They were afraid about the seriousness of hypocrisy and sin in the church. The people learned that death can be the consequence of sin (see 1 Cor. 11:30–32; 1 John 5:16). That fear extended beyond those present to all who heard about the divine judgment. Cf. 1 Pet. 3:10; 4:17.

f. **buried.** The Jews did not embalm, but customarily buried the dead the same day, especially someone who died by divine judgment (see Deut. 21:22, 23).

g. **test the Spirit of the Lord.** Sapphira had gone too far in presuming upon God's forbearance. The folly of such blatant human presumption had to be shown as a sin, hence the ultimate divine chastening that followed.

are at the door, and they will carry you out." Then immediately she fell down at his feet and breathed her last. And the young men came in and found her dead, and carrying her out, buried her by her husband. So great fear came upon all the ªchurch and upon all who heard these things.

And through the hands of the apostles many signs and wonders were done among the people. And they were all with one accord in Solomon's Porch. Yet ᵇnone of the rest dared join them, but the people esteemed them highly. And ᶜbelievers were increasingly added to the Lord, multitudes of both men and women, so that they brought the sick out into the streets and laid them on beds and couches, that at least the ᵈshadow of Peter passing by might fall on some of them. Also a multitude gathered from the surrounding cities to Jerusalem, bringing sick people and those who were tormented by ᵉunclean spirits, and they were all healed.

Then the ᶠhigh priest rose up, and all those who were with him (which is the sect of the Sadducees), and they were filled with indignation, and laid their hands on the apostles and put them in the ᵍcommon prison. But at night ʰan angel of the Lord opened the prison doors and brought them out, and said, "Go, stand in the temple and speak to the people all ⁱthe words of this life."

And when they heard that, they entered the temple early in the morning and taught.

---

a. **church.** This is the first use of "church" in Acts, although it is the most common word used to describe the assembly of those who had believed (cf. Acts 4:32).

b. **none . . . dared join them.** These unbelievers had respect for the followers of Jesus, but feared the deadly potential of joining the church.

c. **believers . . . both men and women.** While the unbelievers stayed away due to fear of the consequence of sin, there were multitudes who heard the gospel witness, gladly believed, and joined the church.

d. **shadow of Peter.** The people truly believed he had divine healing power and that it might even extend to them through his shadow (cf. Acts 3:1–10). But Scripture does not say Peter's shadow ever healed anyone; in fact, the healing power of God through him seemed to go far beyond his shadow (Acts 5:16, "multitude . . . all were healed"). This outpouring of healing was an answer to the prayer in Acts 4:29, 30.

e. **unclean spirits.** Cf. Matt. 10:1; 12:43–45; Mark 1:23–27; 5:1–13; 6:7; 9:25; Luke 4:36; 8:29; 9:42. They are demons, fallen angels (Rev. 12:3) who are so designated because of their vile wickedness. They frequently live inside unbelievers, particularly those who vent their wicked nature.

f. See Acts 4:6. Here the title could refer to Annas or Caiaphas.

g. **common prison.** The public jail.

h. **an angel of the Lord.** This person should not be confused with "the Angel of the Lord" in the OT (see Ex. 3:2).

i. **the words of this life.** The gospel (cf. Phil. 2:16; 1 John 1:1–4). Jesus Christ came into this world to provide abundant and eternal life to spiritually dead people (cf. John 1:4; 11:25; 1 John 5:20).

13. THE APOSTLES ARE TRIED BY THE SANHEDRIN
Acts 5:21b–42

But the high priest and those with him came and called the council together, with all the elders of the children of Israel, and sent to the prison to have them brought.

But when the officers came and did not find them in the prison, they returned and reported, saying, "Indeed we found the prison shut securely, and the guards standing outside before the doors; but when we opened them, we found no one inside!" Now when the high priest, the captain of the temple, and the chief priests heard these things, they wondered what the outcome would be. So one came and told them, saying, "Look, the men whom you put in prison are standing in the temple and teaching the people!"

Then the captain went with the officers and brought them without violence, for they feared the people, lest they should be stoned. And when they had brought them, they set them before the council. And the high priest asked them, saying, "Did we not strictly command you not to teach in this name? And look, you have filled Jerusalem with your ᵃdoctrine, and intend to bring ᵇthis Man's blood on us!"

But Peter and the other apostles answered and said: "We ought to obey God rather than men. The God of our fathers raised up Jesus whom you murdered by ᶜhanging on a tree. ᵈHim God has exalted to His right hand to be Prince and Savior, to give ᵉrepentance to Israel and forgiveness of sins. And we are His witnesses to these things, and ᶠso also is the Holy Spirit whom God has given to those who obey Him."

When they heard this, they were furious and plotted to kill them. Then one in the council stood up, a Pharisee named ᵍGamaliel, a teacher of the law held

---

a. **doctrine.** The gospel of Jesus Christ (see Acts 2:14–40; 4:12, 13).

b. **this Man's blood on us.** The Sanhedrin had apparently forgotten the brash statement its supporters had made before Pilate that the responsibility for Jesus' death should be on them and their children (Matt. 27:25).

c. **hanging on a tree.** Cf. Deut. 21:23; Gal. 3:13.

d. **Him God has exalted to His right hand.** See Acts 1:9; Mark 6:19; Phil. 2:9–11.

e. **repentance to Israel.** Salvation for the Jews. Salvation demands repentance (cf. 2:38; 3:19; 17:30; 20:21; 26:20). For the nature of repentance, see 2 Cor. 7:9–12.

f. **so also is the Holy Spirit.** Every believer receives the Spirit the moment one is saved by obeying the gospel (see Acts 2:4; cf. Rom. 8:9; 1 Cor. 6:19, 20).

g. **Gamaliel.** Like his grandfather, the prominent rabbi Hillel, Gamaliel the most noted

in respect by all the people, and commanded them to put the apostles outside for a little while. And he said to them: "Men of Israel, take heed to yourselves what you intend to do regarding these men. For some time ago [a]Theudas rose up, claiming to be somebody. A number of men, about four hundred, joined him. He was slain, and all who obeyed him were scattered and came to nothing. After this man, [b]Judas of Galilee rose up in the [c]days of the census, and drew away many people after him. He also perished, and all who obeyed him were dispersed. And now I say to you, keep away from these men and let them alone; for if this plan or this work is of men, it will come to nothing; but if it is of God, you cannot overthrow it—lest you even be found to fight against God."

And they [d]agreed with him, and when they had called for the apostles and [e]beaten them, they commanded that they should not speak in the name of Jesus, and let them go. So they departed from the presence of the council, rejoicing that they were counted worthy to suffer shame for His name. And daily in the temple, and in every house, they did not cease teaching and preaching Jesus as the Christ.

14. THE MINISTRY OF STEPHEN

Acts 6:1–15

Now in those days, when the number of the disciples was [f]multiplying, there arose a complaint against the [g]Hebrews by the Hellenists, because their

---

rabbi of his time, led the liberal faction of the Pharisees. His most famous student was the Apostle Paul (Acts 22:3).

a. **Theudas.** An otherwise unknown individual who led a revolt in Judea in the early years of the first century, not to be confused with a later Theudas cited in Josephus as a revolutionary.

b. **Judas of Galilee rose up.** The founder of the Zealots who led another revolt in Palestine early in the first century. Zealots, a party of Jews who were fanatical nationalists, believed that radical action was required to overthrow the Roman power in Palestine. They even sought to take up arms against Rome.

c. **days of the census.** One ordered by Quirinius, governor of Syria, in A.D. 6–7 (cf. Luke 2:2).

d. **agreed.** Members of the Sanhedrin heeded Gamaliel's words concerning the apostles. But, based on his knowledge of Scripture, Gamaliel should have been more decisive and less pragmatic about accepting Jesus as the risen Messiah.

e. **beaten them.** The apostles were unjustly flogged, probably with 39 lashes, the standard number given to avoid exceeding the OT legal limit of 40 (cf. Deut. 25:3).

f. **multiplying.** The figure could have reached over 20,000 men and women.

g. **Hebrews . . . Hellenists.** "Hebrews" were the native Jewish population of Palestine; "Hellenists" were Jews from the Diaspora. The Hellenists' absorption of aspects of Gr. culture made them suspect to the Palestinian Jews.

[a]widows were neglected in the daily distribution. Then the twelve summoned the multitude of the disciples and said, "It is not desirable that we should leave the word of God and [b]serve tables. Therefore, brethren, seek out from among you [c]seven men of good reputation, full of the Holy Spirit and wisdom, whom we may appoint over this business; but we will give ourselves continually to [d]prayer and to the ministry of the word."

And the saying pleased the whole multitude. And [e]they chose Stephen, a man full of faith and the Holy Spirit, and Philip, Prochorus, Nicanor, Timon, Parmenas, and Nicolas, a proselyte from Antioch, whom they set before the apostles; and when they had [f]prayed, they laid hands on them.

Then the word of God spread, and the [g]number of the disciples multiplied greatly in Jerusalem, and a [h]great many of the priests were obedient to the faith.

And Stephen, full of faith and power, did great wonders and signs among the people. Then there arose some from what is called the [i]Synagogue of

---

a. **widows were neglected.** The Hellenists believed their widows were not receiving an adequate share of the food the church provided for their care (cf. 1 Tim. 5:3–16).

b. **serve tables** The word translated "tables" can refer to tables used in monetary matters (cf. Matt. 21:12; Mark 11:15; John 2:15), as well as those used for serving meals. To be involved either in financial matters or in serving meals would take the 12 away from their first priority.

c. **seven men.** These were not deacons in terms of the later church office (1 Tim. 3:8–13), although they performed some of the same duties. Stephen and Philip (the only ones of the 7 mentioned elsewhere in Scripture) clearly were evangelists, not deacons. Acts later mentions elders (Acts 14:23; 20:17), but not deacons. It seems, therefore, that a permanent order of deacons was not established at that time.

d. **prayer . . . ministry of the word.** Prayer and the ministry of the Word define the highest priorities of church leaders.

e. **they chose Stephen . . . Nicolas.** For Stephen's ministry, see Acts 6:9—7:60. His martyrdom became the catalyst for the spread of the gospel beyond Palestine (Acts 8:1–4; 11:19). Philip also played a key role in the spread of the gospel (cf. Acts 8:4–24, 26–40). Nothing certain is known of the other 5. According to some early traditions, Prochorus became the Apostle John's amanuensis when he wrote his gospel and Nicholas was a Gentile convert to Judaism from Antioch. The 7 men chosen by the church all had Gr. names, implying they were all Hellenists. The church, in a display of love and unity, may have chosen them to rectify the apparent imbalance involving the Hellenistic widows.

f. **prayed . . . laid hands on them.** This expression was used of Jesus when He healed (Mark 6:5; Luke 4:40; 13:13; cf. Acts 28:8) and sometimes indicated being taken prisoner (5:18; Mark 14:46). In the OT, offerers of sacrifices laid their hands on the animal as an expression of identification (Lev. 8:14, 18, 22; Heb. 6:2). But in the symbolic sense, it signified the affirmation, support, and identification with someone and his ministry. See 1 Tim. 4:14; 5:22; 2 Tim. 1:6; cf. Num. 27:23.

g. **number.** One of Luke's periodic statements summarizing the growth of the church and the spread of the gospel (cf. Acts 2:41, 47; 4:4; 5:14; 9:31; 12:24; 13:49; 16:5; 19:20).

h. **great many of the priests.** The conversion of large numbers of priests may account for the vicious opposition that arose against Stephen.

i. **Synagogue.** These were meeting places which began in the intertestamental period

the [a]Freedmen ([b]Cyrenians, [c]Alexandrians, and those from [d]Cilicia and Asia), [e]disputing with Stephen. And they were not able to resist the wisdom and the Spirit by which he spoke. Then they secretly induced men to say, "We have heard him speak [f]blasphemous words against Moses and God." And they stirred up the people, the elders, and the scribes; and they came upon him, seized him, and brought him to the council. They also set up false witnesses who said, "This man does not cease to speak blasphemous words against this holy place and the law; for we have heard him say that this [g]Jesus of Nazareth will destroy this place and change the customs which Moses delivered to us." And all who sat in the council, looking steadfastly at him, saw his [h]face as the face of an angel.

15. Stephen's Powerful Sermon

Acts 7:1–29

Note: *In light of Acts 7:58, Saul was undoubtedly in the audience to hear Stephen deliver this remarkable message focusing on the reality that Jesus is the Messiah whom the religious leaders had rejected.*

---

where the dispersed Jews (usually Hellenists), who did not have temple access, could meet in their community to worship and read the OT. See Mark 1:21. It seems that this verse describes 3 synagogues: the Synagogue of the Freedmen, a second composed of Cyrenians and Alexandrians, and a third composed of those from Cilicia and Asia. Cultural and linguistic differences among the 3 groups make it unlikely they all attended the same synagogue.

a. **Freedmen.** Descendants of Jewish slaves captured by Pompeii (63 b.c.) and taken to Rome. They were later freed and formed a Jewish community there.

b. **Cyrenians.** Men from Cyrene, a city in North Africa. Simon, the man conscripted to carry Jesus' cross, was a native of Cyrene (Luke 23:26).

c. **Alexandrians.** Alexandria, another major North African city, was located near the mouth of the Nile River. The powerful preacher Apollos was from Alexandria (see Acts 18:24).

d. **Cilicia and Asia.** Roman provinces in Asia Minor (modern Turkey). Since Paul's hometown (Tarsus) was located in Cilicia, he probably attended this synagogue.

e. **disputing with Stephen.** The word translated "disputing" signifies a formal debate. They no doubt focused on such themes as the death and resurrection of Jesus, and the OT evidence that He was the Messiah.

f. **blasphemous words against Moses and God.** Unable to prevail over Stephen in open debate, his enemies resorted to deceit and conspiracy. As with Jesus (Matt. 26:59–61), they secretly recruited false witnesses to spread lies about Stephen. The charges were serious, since blasphemy was punishable by death (Lev. 24:16).

g. **Jesus of Nazareth will destroy this place.** Another lie, since Jesus' words (John 2:19) referred to His own body (John 2:21).

h. **face of an angel.** Pure, calm, unruffled composure, reflecting the presence of God (cf. Ex. 34:29–35).

Then the [a]high priest said, [b]"Are these things so?"

And [c]he said, "Brethren and fathers, listen: [d]The God of glory appeared to our father [e]Abraham when he was in Mesopotamia, before he dwelt in Haran, and said to him, 'Get out of your country and from your relatives, and come to a land that I will show you.' Then he came out of the [f]land of the Chaldeans and dwelt in Haran. And from there, [g]when his father was dead, He moved him to this land in which you now dwell. And God gave him no inheritance in it, not even enough to set his foot on. But even when Abraham had no child, He promised to give it to him for a possession, and to his descendants after him. But God spoke in this way: that his descendants would dwell in a foreign land, and that they would bring them into bondage and oppress them [h]four hundred years. 'And the nation to whom they will be in bondage I will judge,' said God, 'and after that they shall come out and serve Me in this place.' Then He gave him the [i]covenant of circumcision; and so Abraham begot Isaac and circumcised him on the eighth day; and Isaac begot Jacob, and Jacob begot the [j]twelve patriarchs.

"And the patriarchs, becoming envious, sold Joseph into Egypt. But God was with him and delivered him out of all his troubles, and gave him favor

a. **high priest.** See Acts 4:6. Probably Caiaphas (see John 18:13), who remained in office until A.D. 36.

b. **Are these things so?** In modern legal terminology, "How do you plead?"

c. **he said.** Stephen's response does not seem to answer the High-Priest's question. Instead, he gave a masterful, detailed defense of the Christian faith from the OT and concluded by condemning the Jewish leaders for rejecting Jesus.

d. **The God of glory.** A title used only here and in Ps. 29:3. God's glory is the sum of His attributes (see Ex. 33:18, 19).

e. **Abraham . . . Mesopotamia, before he dwelt in Haran.** Genesis 12:1–4 refers to the repeat of this call after Abraham had settled in Haran (ca. 500 mi. NW of Ur). Evidently, God had originally called Abraham while he was living in Ur (cf. Gen. 15:7; Neh. 9:7), then repeated that call at Haran (see Gen. 11:31—12:3).

f. **land of the Chaldeans.** Where Abraham's original home city of Ur was located (Gen. 11:28, 31; 15:7; Neh. 9:7).

g. **when his father was dead.** At first glance, Gen. 11:26, 32 and 12:4 seem to indicate that Terah lived for 60 years after Abraham's departure from Haran. Terah was 70 when his first son was born (Gen. 11:26); Abraham was 75 when he left Haran (Gen. 12:4; Terah would have been 145); and Terah lived to be 205 (Gen. 11:32). The best solution to this apparent difficulty is that Abraham was not Terah's firstborn son, but was mentioned first (Gen. 11:26) because he was most prominent. Abraham, then, would have been born when Terah was 130.

h. **four hundred years.** This is taken directly from Gen. 15:13, 14 where God Himself rounded off the exact length of Israel's sojourn in Egypt (430 years, Ex. 12:40).

i. **covenant of circumcision.** Circumcision was the sign of the Abrahamic Covenant (see Gen. 17:11).

j. **twelve patriarchs.** The 12 sons of Jacob, who became the heads of the 12 tribes of Israel (Gen. 35:22–26).

and wisdom in the presence of Pharaoh, king of Egypt; and he made him governor over Egypt and all his house. Now a famine and great trouble came over all the land of Egypt and Canaan, and our fathers found no sustenance. But when Jacob heard that there was grain in Egypt, he sent out our fathers first. And the ᵃsecond time Joseph was made known to his brothers, and Joseph's family became known to the Pharaoh. Then Joseph sent and called his father ᵇJacob and all his relatives to him, seventy-five people. So Jacob went down to Egypt; and he died, he and our fathers. And ᶜthey were carried back to Shechem and laid in ᵈthe tomb that Abraham bought for a sum of money from the sons of Hamor, the father of Shechem.

"But when the time of the promise drew near which God had sworn to Abraham, the people grew and multiplied in Egypt till another ᵉking arose who did not know Joseph. This man dealt treacherously with our people, and oppressed our forefathers, making them ᶠexpose their babies, so that they might not live. At this time ᵍMoses was born, and was well pleasing to God; and he was brought up in his father's house for three months. But when he was set out, Pharaoh's daughter took him away and brought him up as her own son. And Moses was learned in all the wisdom of the Egyptians, and was mighty in words and deeds.

"Now when he was ʰforty years old, it came into his heart to visit his breth-

---

a. **second time.** Joseph revealed himself to his brothers on their second trip to Egypt to buy grain (Gen. 43:1–3; 45:1–3).

b. **Jacob and all his relatives . . . seventy-five people.** Genesis 46:26, 27; Ex. 1:5; Deut. 10:22 give the figure as 70. However the LXX (the Gr. translation of the OT, which as a Hellenist Stephen would have used) in Gen. 46:27 reads "seventy-five." The additional 5 people were Joseph's descendants born in Egypt.

c. **they were . . . laid in the tomb.** "They" refers to Joseph (Josh. 24:32) and his brothers, but not Jacob, who was buried in Abraham's tomb at Machpelah (Gen. 50:13).

d. **the tomb that Abraham bought . . . of Shechem.** Joshua 24:32 states that Jacob bought this tomb, although Abraham had earlier built an altar at Shechem (Gen. 12:6, 7), and probably purchased the land on which he built it. Abraham did not settle there, however, and the land apparently reverted to the people of Hamor. Jacob then repurchased it from Shechem (Gen. 33:18–20), much like Isaac repurchased the well at Beersheba (Gen. 26:28–31) that Abraham had originally bought (Gen. 21:27–30). It is clear that Joseph was buried at Shechem as he requested (Gen. 50:25; Ex. 13:19; Josh. 24:32). The OT does not record where Joseph's brothers were buried, but Stephen reveals it was in Shechem.

e. **king . . . did not know Joseph.** See Ex. 1:8.

f. **expose their babies.** Only the male babies (Ex. 1:15–22).

g. **Moses . . . was set out.** In God's providence, however, he was rescued by Pharaoh's daughter. See Ex. 2:5–10.

h. **he was forty years old.** Moses' life may be divided into three 40 year periods. The first 40 years encompassed his birth and life in Pharaoh's court; the second his exile in Midian

ren, the children of Israel. And seeing one of them suffer wrong, he defended and avenged him who was oppressed, and struck down the Egyptian. For he supposed that his brethren would have understood that God would deliver them by his hand, but they did not understand. And the next day he appeared to two of them as they were fighting, and tried to reconcile them, saying, 'Men, you are brethren; why do you wrong one another?' But he who did his neighbor wrong pushed him away, saying, 'Who made you a ruler and a judge over us? Do you want to kill me as you did the Egyptian yesterday?' Then, at this saying, Moses ªfled and became a dweller in the land of Midian, where he had two sons.

16. STEPHEN'S POWERFUL SERMON— CONTINUED

Acts 7:30–53

"And when forty years had passed, an ᵇAngel of the Lord appeared to him in a flame of fire in a bush, in the wilderness of Mount Sinai. When Moses saw it, he marveled at the sight; and as he drew near to observe, the voice of the Lord came to him, saying, 'I am the God of your fathers—the God of Abraham, the God of Isaac, and the God of Jacob.' And Moses trembled and dared not look. 'Then the Lord said to him, "Take your sandals off your feet, for the place where you stand is holy ground. I have surely seen the oppression of My people who are in Egypt; I have heard their groaning and have come down to deliver them. And now come, I will send you to Egypt."'

ᶜ "This Moses whom they rejected, saying, ᵈ'Who made you a ruler and a judge?' is the one God sent to be a ruler and a deliverer by the hand of the Angel who appeared to him in the bush. He brought them out, after he had

---

(Acts 7:29, 30); and the third revolved around the events of the Exodus and the years of Israel's wilderness wandering (Acts 7:36).

a. **fled . . . Midian.** Because he feared Pharaoh would learn of his killing of the Egyptian (Acts 7:28) and view him as the leader of a Jewish rebellion.

b. **Angel.** The Angel of the Lord (v. 30). See Ex. 3:2.

c. **This Moses . . . sent to be a ruler and a deliverer.** Thus began Israel's long history of rejecting her God-sent deliverers (cf. Matt. 21:33–46; 23:37).

d. **Who made you.** Quoted from Ex. 2:14.

shown [a]wonders and signs in the land of Egypt, and in the Red Sea, and in the wilderness forty years.

"This is that Moses who said to the children of Israel, 'The Lord your God will raise up for you a [b]Prophet like me from your brethren. Him you shall hear.'

"This is he who was in [c]the congregation in the wilderness with [d]the Angel who spoke to him on Mount Sinai, and with our fathers, the one who received the [e]living oracles to give to us, whom our fathers [f]would not obey, but rejected. And in their hearts they turned back to Egypt, saying to Aaron, [g]'Make us gods to go before us; as for this Moses who brought us out of the land of Egypt, we do not know what has become of him.' And they made [h]a calf in those days, offered sacrifices to the idol, and rejoiced in the works of their own hands. Then [i]God turned and gave them up to worship [j]the host of heaven, as it is written in the book of the Prophets:

> 'Did you offer Me slaughtered animals and sacrifices during
> forty years in the wilderness, O house of Israel?
> You also took up the tabernacle of Moloch,
> And the star of your god Remphan,
> Images which you made to worship;
> And I will carry you away beyond [k]Babylon.'

a. **wonders and signs.** The 10 plagues in Egypt, and the miracles during the wilderness wandering (e.g., the parting of the Red Sea, Ex. 14:1–31; the miraculous provision of water at Rephidim, Ex. 17:1–7; and the destruction of Korah, Dathan, and Abiram, Num. 16:1–40).

b. **Prophet like me.** Quoted from Deut. 18:15, this refers to the Messiah (cf. John 1:21, 25; 6:14; 7:40).

c. **the congregation in the wilderness.** Israel (cf. Ex. 12:3, 6, 19, 47; 16:1, 2, 9, 10; 17:1; 35:1; Lev. 4:13; 16:5; Num. 1:2; 8:9; 13:26; 14:2; Josh. 18:1).

d. **the Angel . . . on Mount Sinai.** Most likely this is the Angel of the Lord (Acts 7:30, 35) who was assisted by a multitude of angels (cf. Deut. 33:3; Gal. 3:19; Heb. 2:2).

e. **living oracles.** The law given to Moses by God through the Angel of the Lord and a whole host of angels (cf. Heb. 4:12; 1 Pet. 1:23).

f. **would not obey.** Israel rejected Moses' leadership and longed to return to slavery in Egypt (cf. Num. 11:5).

g. **Make us gods.** A man-made representation of the true God (Ex. 32:1–5) which was forbidden (Ex. 20:4). Quoted from Ex. 32:1, 23.

h. **a calf.** See Ex. 32:4.

i. **God . . . gave them up.** Quoted from Amos 5:25–27. Judicially abandoning the people to their sin and idolatry (cf. Hos. 4:17; see Rom. 1:24, 26, 28).

j. **the host of heaven.** Israel's idolatrous worship of the sun, moon, and stars began in the wilderness and lasted through the Babylonian captivity (cf. Deut. 4:19; 17:3; 2 Kin. 17:16; 21:3–5; 23:4; 2 Chr. 33:3, 5; Jer. 8:2; 19:13; Zeph. 1:5).

k. **Babylon.** Amos wrote Damascus (Amos 5:27), while Stephen said Babylon. Amos was prophesying the captivity of the northern kingdom in Assyria, a deportation beyond

"Our fathers had the ᵃtabernacle of witness in the wilderness, as He appointed, instructing Moses to make it according to the pattern that he had seen, which our fathers, having received it in turn, also brought with Joshua into the land possessed by the Gentiles, whom God drove out before the face of our fathers until the days of David, who found favor before God and asked to find a dwelling for the God of Jacob. But Solomon built Him a house.

"However, the ᵇMost High does not dwell in temples made with hands, as ᶜthe prophet says:

> 'Heaven is My throne,
> And earth is My footstool.
> What house will you build for Me? says the Lord,
> Or what is the place of My rest?
> Has My hand not made all these things?'

"You ᵈstiff-necked and ᵉuncircumcised in heart and ears! You always ᶠresist the Holy Spirit; as your fathers did, so do you. Which of the prophets did your fathers not persecute? And they killed those who foretold the coming of the Just One, of whom you now have become the betrayers and murderers, who have received the ᵍlaw by the direction of angels and have not kept it."

Damascus. Later the southern kingdom was taken captive to Babylon. Stephen, inspired to do so, extended the prophecy to embrace the judgment on the whole nation summarizing their idolatrous history and its results.

a. **tabernacle of witness.** The predecessor of the temple (Ex. 25:8, 9, 40).

b. **Most High.** A common OT title for God (cf. Gen. 14:18–20, 22; Num. 24:16; Deut. 32:8; 2 Sam. 22:14; Pss. 7:17; 9:2; 18:13; 21:7; 73:11; 87:5; 91:1; 107:11; Is. 14:14; Lam. 3:35, 38; Dan. 4:17, 24, 25, 32, 34; 7:25).

c. **the prophet says.** Quoted from Is. 66:1, 2. Stephen's point is that God is greater than the temple, and thus the Jewish leaders were guilty of blaspheming by confining God to it.

d. **stiff-necked.** Obstinate, like their fathers (Ex. 32:9; 33:5). The climax of Stephen's sermon indicted the Jewish leaders for rejecting God in the same way that their ancestors had rejected Him in the OT.

e. **uncircumcised in heart and ears!** Thus as unclean before God as the uncircumcised Gentiles (see Deut. 10:16; Jer. 4:4; Rom. 2:28, 29).

f. **resist the Holy Spirit.** By rejecting the Spirit's messengers and their message. Cf. Jesus' sermon in Matt. 23:13–39.

g. **law by the direction of angels.** See Deut. 33:2; Gal. 3:19; Heb. 2:2. Scripture does not delineate their precise role in the giving of the law, but clearly states the fact of their presence.

17. THE MARTYRDOM OF STEPHEN

Acts 7:54—8:3

When they heard these things they were cut to the heart, and they [a]gnashed at him with their teeth. But he, being full of the Holy Spirit, gazed into heaven and saw [b]the glory of God, and Jesus standing at the right hand of God, and said, "Look! I see the heavens opened and the Son of Man [c]standing at the right hand of God!"

Then they cried out with a loud voice, stopped their ears, and ran at him with one accord; and they cast him out of the city and stoned him. And the witnesses [d]laid down their clothes at the feet of a young man named Saul. And they [e]stoned Stephen as he was calling on God and saying, "Lord Jesus, receive my spirit." Then he knelt down and cried out with a loud voice, "Lord, [f]do not charge them with this sin." And when he had said this, [g]he fell asleep.

Now Saul was [h]consenting to his death.

At that time a great persecution arose against the church which was at Jerusalem; and they were all [i]scattered throughout the regions of Judea and Samaria, [j]except the apostles. And [k]devout men carried Stephen to his burial, and made great lamentation over him.

---

a. **gnashed . . . with their teeth.** In anger and frustration (cf. Pss. 35:16; 37:12; Matt. 8:11, 12; 13:41, 42, 50; 22:13; 24:51; 25:30; Luke 13:28).

b. **the glory of God.** Isaiah (Is. 6:1–3), Ezekiel (Ezek. 1:26–28), Paul (2 Cor. 12:2–4), and John (Rev. 1:10) also received visions of God's glory in heaven.

c. **standing at the right hand of God.** Jesus is frequently so depicted (Acts 2:34; cf. Matt. 22:44; 26:64; Luke 22:69; Eph. 1:20; Col. 3:1; Heb. 1:3; 8:1; 10:11, 12; 12:2).

d. **laid down their clothes . . . Saul.** Paul's first appearance in Scripture. That he was near enough to the action to be holding the clothes of Stephen's killers reflects his deep involvement in the sordid affair (see Acts 8:1).

e. **stoned.** This was the punishment prescribed in the law for blasphemy (Lev. 24:16); however, this was not a formal execution but an act of mob violence.

f. **do not charge them with this sin.** As had Jesus before him (Luke 23:34), Stephen prayed for God to forgive his killers.

g. **he fell asleep.** A common NT euphemism for the death of believers (cf. John 11:11–14; 1 Cor. 11:30; 15:20, 51; 1 Thess. 4:14; 5:10).

h. **consenting.** Paul's murderous hatred of all believers was manifested here in his attitude toward Stephen (1 Tim. 1:13–15).

i. **scattered.** Led by a Jew named Saul of Tarsus, the persecution scattered the Jerusalem fellowship and led to the first missionary outreach of the church. Not all members of the Jerusalem church were forced to flee; the Hellenists, because Stephen was likely one, bore the brunt of the persecution (cf. Acts 11:19, 20).

j. **except the apostles.** They remained because of their devotion to Christ, to care for those at Jerusalem, and to continue evangelizing the region (cf. Acts 9:26, 27).

k. **devout men.** Probably pious Jews (cf. Luke 2:25) who publicly protested Stephen's death.

As for Saul, [a]he made havoc of the church, entering every house, and dragging off men and women, committing them to prison.

18. PHILIP PREACHES THE GOSPEL IN SAMARIA
Acts 8:4–25

Therefore those who were scattered [b]went everywhere preaching the word. Then [c]Philip went down to the [d]city of Samaria and preached Christ to them. And the multitudes with one accord heeded the things spoken by Philip, hearing and seeing the miracles which he did. For unclean spirits, crying with a loud voice, came out of many who were possessed; and many who were paralyzed and lame were healed. And there was great joy in that city.

But there was a certain man called Simon, who previously practiced [e]sorcery in the city and astonished the people of Samaria, claiming that he was someone great, to whom they all gave heed, from the least to the greatest, saying, "This man is [f]the great power of God." And they heeded him because he had astonished them with his sorceries for a long time. But when they believed Philip as he preached the things concerning the kingdom of God and the name of Jesus Christ, both men and women were baptized. Then [g]Simon

---

a. **he made havoc of the church.** "Made havoc" was used in extrabiblical writings to refer to the destruction of a city or mangling by a wild animal.

b. **went everywhere.** This Gr. word is used frequently in Acts for missionary efforts (Acts 8:40; 9:32; 13:6; 14:24; 15:3, 41; 16:6; 18:23; 19:1, 21; 20:2).

c. **Philip.** Cf. Acts 6:5. The first missionary named in Scripture and the first to be given the title "evangelist" (Acts 21:8).

d. **the city of Samaria.** The ancient capital of the northern kingdom of Israel, which eventually fell to the Assyrians (722 B.C.) after over 200 years of idolatry and rebellion against God. After resettling many of the people in other lands, the Assyrians located Gentiles from other areas into the region, resulting in a mix of Jews and Gentiles who became known as Samaritans (see John 4:9, 20).

e. **sorcery.** Magic which originally referred to the practices of the Medo-Persians: a mixture of science and superstition, including astrology, divination, and the occult (see Deut. 18:9–12; Rev. 9:21).

f. **the great power of God.** Simon claimed to be united to God. The early church Fathers claimed he was one of the founders of Gnosticism, which asserted there were a series of divine emanations reaching up to God. They were called "Powers," and the people believed he was at the top of the ladder.

g. **Simon . . . believed.** His belief was motivated by purely selfish reasons and could never be considered genuine. Cf. John 2:23, 24. He saw it as an external act useful to gain the power he believed Philip possessed. By following Philip, he also was able to maintain contact with his former audience.

himself also believed; and when he was baptized he continued with Philip, and was amazed, seeing the miracles and signs which were done.

Now when the apostles who were at Jerusalem heard that Samaria had received the word of God, they sent Peter and John to them, who, when they had come down, prayed for them that they might receive the Holy Spirit. For ᵃas yet He had fallen upon none of them. They had only been baptized in the name of the Lord Jesus. Then they ᵇlaid hands on them, and they ᶜreceived the Holy Spirit.

And when Simon saw that through the laying on of the apostles' hands the Holy Spirit was given, he offered them money, saying, "Give me this power also, that anyone on whom I lay hands may receive the Holy Spirit."

But Peter said to him, "Your money perish with you, because you thought that the gift of God could be purchased with money! You have neither part nor portion in this matter, for your heart is not right in the sight of God. Repent therefore of this your wickedness, and pray God if perhaps the thought of your heart may be forgiven you. For I see that you are poisoned by bitterness and bound by iniquity."

Then ᵈSimon answered and said, "Pray to the Lord for me, that none of the things which you have spoken may come upon me."

So when they had testified and preached the word of the Lord, they returned to Jerusalem, preaching the gospel in many villages of the Samaritans.

---

a. **as yet . . . upon none of them.** This verse does not support the false notion that Christians receive the Holy Spirit subsequent to salvation. This was a transitional period in which confirmation by the apostles was necessary to verify the inclusion of a new group of people into the church. Because of the animosity that existed between Jews and Samaritans, it was essential for the Samaritans to receive the Spirit, in the presence of the leaders of the Jerusalem church, for the purpose of maintaining a unified church. The delay also revealed the Samaritans' need to come under apostolic authority. The same transitional event occurred when the Gentiles were added to the church (Acts 13:44–46; cf. 15:6–12; 19:6).

b. **laid hands on them.** This signified apostolic affirmation and solidarity. See Acts 6:6.

c. **received the Holy Spirit.** That this actually occurred likely demonstrated that believers also spoke in tongues here, just as those who received the Spirit did on the Day of Pentecost (see Acts 2:4), as the Gentiles did when they received the Spirit (Acts 10:46), and as those followers of John did (Acts 19:6). As Samaritans, Gentiles, and believers from the Old Covenant were added to the church, the unity of the church was established. No longer could one nation (Israel) be God's witness people, but the church made up of Jews, Gentiles, half-breed Samaritans, and OT saints who became NT believers (19:1–7). To demonstrate the unity, it was imperative that there be some replication in each instance of what had occurred at Pentecost with the believing Jews, such as the presence of the apostles and the coming of the Spirit manifestly indicated through speaking in the languages of Pentecost (Acts 2:5–12).

d. **Simon answered.** Although he was certainly fearful, he was unwilling to repent and seek forgiveness, wanting only to escape the consequences of his sin.

19. PHILIP PREACHES THE GOSPEL TO AN ETHIOPIAN PROSELYTE

Acts 8:26—40

Now an angel of the Lord spoke to Philip, saying, "Arise and go toward the south along the road which goes down from Jerusalem to ᵃGaza." This is desert. So he arose and went. And behold, a man of ᵇEthiopia, a ᶜeunuch of great authority under ᵈCandace the queen of the Ethiopians, who had charge of all her treasury, and had come to Jerusalem to worship, was returning. And sitting in his chariot, he was ᵉreading Isaiah the prophet. Then the Spirit said to Philip, "Go near and overtake this chariot."

So Philip ran to him, and heard him reading the prophet Isaiah, and said, "Do you understand what you are reading?"

And he said, "How can I, unless someone guides me?" And he asked Philip to come up and sit with him. ᶠThe place in the Scripture which he read was this:

> "He was led as a sheep to the slaughter;
> And as a lamb before its shearer is silent,
> So He opened not His mouth.
> In His humiliation His justice was taken away,
> And who will declare His generation?
> For His life is taken from the earth."

---

a. **Gaza.** One of 5 chief cities of the Philistines. The original city was destroyed in the first century B.C. and a new city was built near the coast.

b. **Ethiopia.** In those days, a large kingdom located S of Egypt.

c. **eunuch.** This can refer to one who had been emasculated or generally, to a government official. It is likely he was both since Luke refers to him as a eunuch and as one who held a position of authority in the queen's court—that of treasurer, much like a Minister of Finance or Secretary of the Treasury. As a physical eunuch, he would have been denied access to the temple (Deut. 23:1) and the opportunity to become a full proselyte to Judaism.

d. **Candace.** Probably not a name, but an official title (like Pharaoh or Caesar) given to the queen mothers in that land.

e. **reading Isaiah.** He knew the importance of seeking God through the Scripture (Luke 24:25–27; John 5:39, 46; Rom. 10:12–15).

f. **The place . . . he read.** Isaiah 53:7, 8.

So the eunuch answered Philip and said, "I ask you, of ᵃwhom does the prophet say this, of himself or of some other man?" Then Philip opened his mouth, and beginning at this Scripture, preached Jesus to him. Now as they went down the road, they came to some water. And the eunuch said, "See, here is water. What hinders me from being baptized?"

Then Philip said, "If you believe with all your heart, you may."

And he answered and said, "I believe that Jesus Christ is the Son of God."

So he commanded the chariot to stand still. And both Philip and the eunuch went down into the water, and he baptized him. Now when they came up out of the water, the Spirit of the Lord ᵇcaught Philip away, so that the eunuch saw him no more; and he went on his way rejoicing. But Philip was found at ᶜAzotus. And passing through, he preached in all the cities till he came to Caesarea.

20. SAUL'S REMARKABLE CONVERSION

Acts 9:1—9

Then ᵈSaul, still breathing ᵉthreats and murder against the disciples of the Lord, went to the high priest and asked letters from him to the synagogues of ᶠDamascus, so that if he found any ᵍwho were of the Way, whether men or women, he might bring them bound to Jerusalem.

---

a. **whom does the prophet say . . . ?** His confusion was understandable. Even the Jewish religious experts were divided on the meaning of this passage. Some believed the slaughtered sheep represented Israel, others thought Isaiah was referring to himself, and others thought the Messiah was Isaiah's subject.

b. **caught Philip away.** Elijah (1 Kin. 18:12; 2 Kin. 2:16) and Ezekiel (Ezek. 3:12, 14; 8:3) were also snatched away in a miraculous fashion. This was a powerful confirmation to the caravan that Philip was God's representative.

c. **Azotus.** The first-century name for the ancient Philistine city of Ashdod, located 20 mi. N of Gaza. **Caesarea.** Where Philip and his family probably lived (Acts 21:9; see 9:30).

d. **Saul.** The Apostle Paul was originally named Saul, after the first king of Israel. He was born a Jew, studied in Jerusalem under Gamaliel (Acts 22:3), and became a Pharisee (Acts 23:6). He was also a Roman citizen, a right he inherited from his father (Acts 22:8). Acts 9:1–19 record the external facts of his conversion (see also Acts 22:1–22; 26:9–20). Philippians 3:1–14 records the internal spiritual conversion.

e. **threats and murder.** See 1 Tim. 1:12, 13; 1 Cor. 15:9.

f. **Damascus.** An ancient city, the capital of Syria, located 60 mi. inland from the Mediterranean and ca. 160 mi. NE of Jerusalem. Apparently, it had a large population of Jews, including Hellenist believers who fled Jerusalem to avoid persecution (Acts 8:2).

g. **who were of the Way.** This description of Christianity, derived from Jesus' description of Himself (John 14:6), appears several times in Acts (19:9, 23; 22:4; 24:14, 22). This is an

As he journeyed he came near Damascus, and ªsuddenly ᵇa light shone around him from heaven. Then he fell to the ground, and heard a voice saying to him, "Saul, Saul, ᶜwhy are you persecuting Me?"

And he said, "Who are You, Lord?"

Then the Lord said, "I am Jesus, whom you are persecuting. It is hard for you to kick against the ᵈgoads."

So he, trembling and astonished, said, "Lord, what do You want me to do?"

Then the Lord said to him, "Arise and go into the city, and you will be told what you must do."

And the men who journeyed with him stood speechless, hearing a voice but seeing no one. Then Saul arose from the ground, and when his eyes were opened he saw no one. But they led him by the hand and brought him into Damascus. And he was three days without sight, and neither ate nor drank.

21. Paul's Later Testimony before the Jewish Leaders

Acts 22:1–16

Note: *Paul gave this account of his conversion shortly after his arrest in Jerusalem, nearly 25 years after his experience on the road to Damascus.*

"Brethren and fathers, hear my defense before you now." And when they heard that he spoke to them in the ᵉHebrew language, they kept all the more silent.

---

appropriate title because Christianity is the way of God (18:26), the way into the Holy Place (Heb. 10:19, 20), and the way of truth (John 14:6; 2 Pet. 2:2).

a. **suddenly.** This was the first of 6 visions to be seen by Paul in Acts (cf. 16:9, 10; 18:9, 10; 22:17, 18; 23:11; 27:23, 24).

b. **a light . . . from heaven.** The appearance of Jesus Christ in glory (cf. Acts 22:6; 26:13), visible only to Saul (26:9).

c. **why are you persecuting Me?** An inseparable union exists between Christ and His followers. Saul's persecution represented a direct attack on Christ. Cf. Matt. 18:5, 6.

d. **goads.** Sticks for prodding cattle (cf. Acts 26:14).

e. **Hebrew language.** Aramaic, the language commonly spoken in Palestine (cf. 2 Kin. 18:26; Is. 36:11). See Acts 21:37.

Then he said: [a]"I am indeed a Jew, born in Tarsus of [b]Cilicia, but [c]brought up in this city at the feet of [d]Gamaliel, taught according to the strictness of our [e]fathers' law, and was zealous toward God as you all are today. [f]I persecuted this Way to the death, binding and delivering into prisons both men and women, as also the high priest bears me witness, and all the [g]council of the elders, from whom I also received letters to the brethren, and went to Damascus to bring in chains even those who were there to Jerusalem to be punished.

"Now it happened, as I journeyed and came near Damascus at [h]about noon, suddenly a great light from heaven shone around me. And I fell to the ground and heard a voice saying to me, 'Saul, Saul, why are you persecuting Me?' So I answered, 'Who are You, Lord?' And He said to me, 'I am Jesus of Nazareth, whom you are persecuting.'

"And those who were with me indeed saw the light and were afraid, but they [i]did not hear the voice of Him who spoke to me. So I said, 'What shall I do, Lord?' And the Lord said to me, 'Arise and go into Damascus, and there you will be told all things which are appointed for you to do.' And since I could not see for the [j]glory of that light, being led by the hand of those who were with me, I came into Damascus.

"Then a certain [k]Ananias, a devout man according to the law, having a

---

a. **I am indeed a Jew.** A response to the false charges raised by the Asian Jews (see Acts 21:21).

b. **Cilicia.** See Acts 6:9. Tarsus was the chief city of Cilicia.

c. **brought up in this city.** Paul was born among the Hellenistic Jews of the Diaspora, but had been brought up in Jerusalem.

d. **Gamaliel.** See Acts 5:34. That Paul had studied under the most celebrated rabbi of that day was further evidence that the charges against him were absurd.

e. **fathers' law.** As a student of Gamaliel, Paul received extensive training both in the OT law, and in the rabbinic traditions. Also, though he did not mention it to the crowd, he also had been a Pharisee. In light of all that, the charge that Paul opposed the law (see Acts 21:21) was ridiculous.

f. **I persecuted this Way.** See Acts 9:2. As the leading persecutor of the Christian church after Stephen's martyrdom (cf. Gal. 1:13), Paul's zeal for his Jewish heritage far outstripped that of his hearers.

g. **council of the elders.** The Sanhedrin (see Acts 4:15; cf. Matt. 26:59).

h. **about noon.** Paul's reference to the time of day emphasizes how bright the light from heaven really was. It outshone the sun at its peak.

i. **did not hear the voice.** This is no contradiction with Acts 9:7. Since Jesus spoke only to Paul, only he understood the Lord's words. His companions heard the sound, but could not make out the words (cf. John 12:29).

j. **glory of that light.** Paul's companions saw the light, but only he saw the Lord Jesus Christ (Acts 9:7, 17, 27; 26:16; 1 Cor. 9:1; 15:8).

k. **Ananias.** See Acts 9:10. His testimony as a respected member of Damascus' Jewish

---

good testimony with all the Jews who dwelt there, came to me; and he stood and said to me, 'Brother Saul, receive your sight.' And at that same hour I looked up at him. Then he said, 'The God of our fathers has chosen you that you should know His will, and see ªthe Just One, and hear the voice of His mouth. For you will be ᵇHis witness to all men of what you have seen and heard. And now why are you waiting? Arise and be baptized, and ᶜwash away your sins, calling on the name of the Lord.'"

22. Paul's Later Testimony before Agrippa
Acts 26:1–20

Note: *Paul gave this account of his conversion when standing trial before King Herod Agrippa II.*

So Paul stretched out his hand and answered for himself: "I think myself happy, King Agrippa, because today I shall answer for myself before you concerning all the things of which I am accused by the Jews, especially because you are ᵈexpert in all customs and questions which have to do with the Jews. Therefore I beg you to hear me patiently.

"My manner of life from my youth, which was spent from the beginning among my own nation at Jerusalem, all the Jews know. They knew me from the first, if they were willing to testify, that according to the strictest sect of our religion I lived a Pharisee. And now I stand and am judged for ᵉthe hope

---

community would carry weight with Paul's hostile audience.

a. **the Just One.** A title given to the Messiah (cf. Acts 3:14; 7:52; Is. 53:11).

b. **His witness.** Paul never wavered in his claim to have seen the risen, glorified Christ on the Damascus road.

c. **wash away your sins.** Grammatically this phrase, "calling on the name of the Lord," precedes "arise and be baptized." Salvation comes from calling on the name of the Lord (Rom. 10:9, 10, 13), not from being baptized (see Acts 2:38).

d. **expert in all customs and questions . . . with the Jews.** See Acts 25:26. Paul's main purpose was not to defend himself but to convert Agrippa and the others.

e. **the hope of the promise.** The coming of the Messiah and His kingdom (cf. Acts 1:6; 3:22–24; 13:23–33; Gen. 3:15; Is. 7:14; 9:6; Dan. 7:14; Mic. 5:2; Titus 2:13; 1 Pet. 1:11, 12). Paul found it inconceivable that he should be condemned for believing in the resurrection—the great hope of the Jewish people (see Acts 24:15).

of the promise made by God to our fathers. To this promise our [a]twelve tribes, earnestly serving God night and day, hope to attain. For this hope's sake, King Agrippa, I am accused by the Jews. Why should it be thought incredible by you that God raises the dead?

"Indeed, I myself thought I must do many things contrary to the name of Jesus of Nazareth. This I also did in Jerusalem, and many of the saints I shut up in prison, having received authority from the chief priests; and when they were put to death, [b]I cast my vote against them. And I punished them often in every synagogue and [c]compelled them to blaspheme; and being exceedingly enraged against them, I persecuted them even to foreign cities.

"While thus occupied, as I journeyed to Damascus with authority and commission from the chief priests, at midday, O king, along the road I saw a light from heaven, brighter than the sun, shining around me and those who journeyed with me. And when we all had fallen to the ground, I heard a voice speaking to me and saying in the Hebrew language, 'Saul, Saul, why are you persecuting Me? It is hard for you to kick against the goads.' So I said, 'Who are You, Lord?' And He said, 'I am Jesus, whom you are persecuting. But rise and stand on your feet; for I have appeared to you for this purpose, to make you a minister and a witness both of the things which you have seen and of the [d]things which I will yet reveal to you. I will deliver you from the Jewish people, as well as from the [e]Gentiles, to whom I now send you, [f]to open their eyes, in order to turn them [g]from darkness to light, and from the power of

---

a. **twelve tribes.** A common NT designation for Israel (cf. Matt. 19:28; James 1:1; Rev. 21:12). The 10 northern tribes were not lost. Representatives from each intermingled with the two southern tribes before and after the Exile—a process that had begun during the reigns of Hezekiah (2 Chr. 30:1–11) and Josiah (2 Chr. 34:1–9).

b. **I cast my vote.** Lit. "I threw my pebble"—a reference to the ancient custom of recording votes by means of colored pebbles. This verse may also indicate that Paul had once been a member of the Sanhedrin.

c. **compelled them to blaspheme.** To renounce their faith in Jesus Christ.

d. **things which I will yet reveal to you.** See Acts 18:9, 10; 22:17–21; 23:11; 2 Cor. 12:1–7; Gal. 1:11, 12.

e. **Gentiles to whom I now send you.** Paul's commissioning as the apostle to the Gentiles (Rom. 11:13; 1 Tim. 2:7).

f. **to open their eyes.** Unbelievers are blinded to spiritual truth by Satan (2 Cor. 4:4; 6:14; cf. Matt. 15:14).

g. **from darkness to light.** Since unbelievers are in the darkness of their spiritual blindness, the Bible often uses light to picture salvation (v. 23; 13:47; Matt. 4:16; John 1:4, 5, 7–9; 3:19–21; 8:12; 9:5; 12:36; 2 Cor. 4:4; 6:14; Eph. 5:8, 14; Col. 1:12, 13; 1 Thess. 5:5; 1 Pet. 2:9; 1 John 1:7; 2:8–10).

Satan to God, that they may receive ªforgiveness of sins and ᵇan inheritance among those who are ᶜsanctified by faith in Me.'

"Therefore, King Agrippa, I was not disobedient to the heavenly vision, but declared first to those in Damascus and in Jerusalem, and throughout all the region of Judea, and then to the Gentiles, that they should repent, turn to God, and do ᵈworks befitting repentance."

23. SAUL'S BAPTISM AND EARLY MINISTRY
Acts 9:10–22

Now there was a certain disciple at Damascus named ᵉAnanias; and to him the Lord said in a vision, "Ananias."

And he said, "Here I am, Lord."

So the Lord said to him, "Arise and go to the ᶠstreet called Straight, and inquire at the house of Judas for one called Saul of ᵍTarsus, for behold, he is praying. And in a vision he has seen a man named Ananias coming in and putting his hand on him, so that he might receive his sight."

Then Ananias answered, "Lord, I have heard from many about this man, how much harm he has done to Your saints in Jerusalem. And here he has authority from the chief priests to bind all who call on Your name."

---

a. **forgiveness of sins.** This is the most significant result of salvation (see 2:38; cf. 3:19; 5:31; 10:43; 13:38; Matt. 1:21; 26:28; Luke 1:77; 24:47; 1 Cor. 15:3; Gal. 1:4; Col. 1:14; Heb. 8:12; 9:28; 10:12; 1 Pet. 2:24; 3:18; 1 John 2:1, 2; 3:5; 4:10; Rev. 1:5).

b. **an inheritance.** The blessings believers will enjoy throughout eternity in heaven (cf. 20:32; Eph. 1:11, 14, 18; Col. 1:12; 3:24; Heb. 9:15).

c. **sanctified by faith.** The Bible plainly and repeatedly teaches that salvation comes solely through faith apart from human works (13:39; 15:9; 16:31; John 3:14–17; 6:69; Rom. 3:21–28; 4:5; 5:1; 9:30; 10:9–11; Gal. 2:16; 3:11, 24; Eph. 2:8, 9; Phil. 3:9).

d. **works befitting repentance.** Genuine repentance is inseparably linked to a changed lifestyle (see 2:38; Matt. 3:8; James 2:18).

e. **Ananias.** One of the leaders of the Damascus church, and therefore, one of Saul's targets (cf. Acts 22:12).

f. **street called Straight.** This street, which runs through Damascus from the E gate to the W, still exists and is called Darb el-Mustaqim.

g. **Tarsus.** The birthplace of Paul and a key city in the Roman province of Cilicia, located on the banks of the Cydnus River near the border of Asia Minor and Syria. It served as both a commercial and educational center. The wharves on the Cydnus were crowded with commerce, while its university ranked with those of Athens and Alexandria as the finest in the Roman world.

But the Lord said to him, "Go, for he is a ªchosen vessel of Mine to bear My name ᵇbefore Gentiles, kings, and the children of Israel. For I will show him how many things he must suffer for My name's sake."

And Ananias went his way and entered the house; and laying his hands on him he said, "Brother Saul, the Lord Jesus, who appeared to you on the road as you came, has sent me that you may receive your sight and ᶜbe filled with the Holy Spirit." Immediately there fell from his eyes something like scales, and he received his sight at once; and he arose and was baptized.

So when he had received food, he was strengthened. Then Saul spent some days with the disciples at Damascus.

Immediately he preached the Christ in the synagogues, that He is the Son of God.

Then all who heard were amazed, and said, "Is this not he who destroyed those who called on this name in Jerusalem, and has come here for that purpose, so that he might bring them bound to the chief priests?"

But Saul increased all the more in strength, and confounded the Jews who dwelt in Damascus, proving that this Jesus is the Christ.

24. Time in Arabia and Escape from Damascus
Acts 9:23–25; Gal. 1:11–18a; 2 Cor. 11:32–33

Note: *In the book of Galatians, Paul gives more detail about the events that transpired in the years following his conversion. These include a three-year*

---

a. **chosen vessel.** Lit. "a vessel of election." There was perfect continuity between Paul's salvation and his service; God chose him to convey His grace to all men (Gal. 1:1; cf. 1 Tim. 2:7; 2 Tim. 1:11). Paul used this same word 4 times (Rom. 9:21, 23; 2 Cor. 4:7; 2 Tim. 2:21).

b. **before Gentiles, kings, and the children of Israel.** Paul began his ministry preaching to Jews (Acts 13:14; 14:1; 17:1, 10; 18:4; 19:8), but his primary calling was to Gentiles (Rom. 11:13; 15:16). God also called him to minister to kings such as Agrippa (Acts 25:23—26:32) and likely Caesar (cf. Acts 25:10–12; 2 Tim. 4:16, 17).

c. **be filled with the Holy Spirit.** See Acts 2:4. The Spirit had already been active in Paul's life: convicting him of sin (John 16:9), convincing him of the Lordship of Christ (1 Cor. 12:3), transforming him (Titus 3:5), and indwelling him permanently (1 Cor. 12:13). He was then filled with the Spirit and empowered for service (cf. 2:4, 14; 4:8, 31; 6:5; see also note on Eph. 5:16). Saul received the Spirit without any apostles present because he was a Jew (the inclusion of Jews in the church had already been established at Pentecost) and because he was an apostle in his own right because Christ personally chose him and commissioned him for service (Rom. 1:1).

period in Arabia and an initial trip to Jerusalem in which Paul met with Peter and James.

^{GAL} But I ^amake known to you, brethren, that the ^bgospel which was preached by me is not according to man. For I ^cneither received it from man, nor was I taught it, but it came ^dthrough the revelation of Jesus Christ. For you have heard of my former conduct in ^eJudaism, how I ^fpersecuted the church of God beyond measure and tried to destroy it. And I ^gadvanced in Judaism beyond many of my contemporaries in my own nation, being more ^hexceedingly zealous for the ⁱtraditions of my fathers.

But when it pleased God, who ^jseparated me from my mother's womb and ^kcalled me through His grace, to ^lreveal His Son in me, that I might

---

a. **make known to you.** The strong Gr. verb Paul used here often introduced an important and emphatic statement (1 Cor. 12:3; 2 Cor. 8:1).

b. **the gospel . . . not according to man.** The gospel Paul preached was not human in origin or it would have been like all other human religion, permeated with works righteousness born of man's pride and Satan's deception (Rom. 1:16).

c. **neither received it from man, nor was I taught it.** In contrast to the Judaizers, who received their religious instruction from rabbinic tradition. Most Jews did not study the actual Scriptures; instead they used human interpretations of Scripture as their religious authority and guide. Many of their traditions not only were not taught in Scripture but also contradicted it (Mark 7:13).

d. **through the revelation.** This refers to the unveiling of something previously kept secret—in this case, Jesus Christ. While he knew about Christ, Paul subsequently met Him personally on the road to Damascus and received the truth of the gospel from Him (Acts 9:1–16).

e. **Judaism.** The Jewish religious system of works righteousness, based not primarily on the OT text, but on rabbinic interpretations and traditions. In fact, Paul will argue that a proper understanding of the OT can lead only to Christ and His gospel of grace through faith (Gal. 3:6–29).

f. **persecuted.** The tense of this Gr. verb emphasizes Paul's persistent and continual effort to hurt and ultimately exterminate Christians. See Acts 8:1–3; 9:1; 1 Cor. 15:9; 1 Tim. 1:12–14.

g. **advanced . . . beyond.** The Gr. word for "advanced" means "to chop ahead," much like one would blaze a trail through a forest. Paul blazed his path in Judaism (see Phil. 3:5, 6), and because he saw Jewish Christians as obstacles to its advancement, he worked to cut them down.

h. **exceedingly zealous.** Paul demonstrated this by the extent to which he pursued and persecuted Christians (see Acts 8:1–3; 26:11).

i. **traditions of my fathers.** The oral teachings about OT law commonly known as the "Halakah." This collection of interpretations of the law eventually carried the same authority as, or even greater than, the law (Torah) itself. Its regulations were so hopelessly complex and burdensome that even the most astute rabbinical scholars could not master it by either interpretation or conduct.

j. **separated me from my mother's womb.** Paul is not talking about being born, separated physically from his mother, but being separated or set apart to God for service from the time of his birth. The phrase refers to God's election of Paul without regard for his personal merit or effort (see Is. 49:1; Jer. 1:5; Luke 1:13–17; Rom. 9:10–23).

k. **called me through His grace.** This refers to God's effectual call (see Rom. 1:7; 8:30). On the Damascus Road God actually brought Saul, whom He had already chosen, to salvation.

l. **reveal His Son in me.** Not only was Christ revealed to Paul on the Damascus Road, but in him as God gave him the life, light, and faith to believe in Him.

^apreach Him among the Gentiles, I did not immediately ^bconfer with flesh and blood, nor did I go up to ^cJerusalem to those who were apostles before me; but I went to Arabia, and returned again to Damascus.

Then after three years, ^{ACTS} after many days were past, the Jews plotted to kill [Saul]. But their plot became known to Saul. And they watched the gates day and night, to kill him. Then the disciples took him by night and let him down through the wall in a large basket.

^{2 COR} In Damascus the governor, under Aretas the king, was guarding the city of the Damascenes with a garrison, desiring to arrest me; but I was let down in a basket through a window in the wall, and escaped from his hands.

25. SAUL VISITS JERUSALEM
Acts 9:26–31; 22:17–20; Gal. 1:18, 19, 21–23

^{GAL} I went up to Jerusalem to see Peter, and remained with him fifteen days. But I saw none of the other apostles except ^dJames, the Lord's brother.

^{ACTS 9} And when Saul had come to Jerusalem, he tried to join the disciples; but they were all afraid of him, and did not believe that he was a disciple. But Barnabas took him and brought him to the apostles [namely, Peter and James]. And he declared to them how he had seen the Lord on the road, and that He had spoken to him, and how he had preached boldly at Damascus in the name of Jesus. So he was with them at Jerusalem, coming in and going out. And he spoke boldly in the name of the Lord Jesus and disputed against the ^eHellenists, but they attempted to kill him.

---

a. **preach Him among the Gentiles.** Paul's specific call to proclaim the gospel to non-Jews (see Acts 9:15; 26:15–18; cf. Rom. 1:13–16; 11:13; 15:18).

b. **confer with flesh and blood.** Paul did not look to Ananias or other Christians at Damascus for clarification of or addition to the revelation he received from Christ (Acts 9:19, 20).

c. **Jerusalem . . . Arabia . . . Damascus.** Rather than immediately travel to Jerusalem to be instructed by the apostles, Paul instead went to Nabatean Arabia, a wilderness desert that stretched E of Damascus down to the Sinai peninsula. After being prepared for ministry by the Lord, he returned to minister in nearby Damascus.

d. **James, the Lord's brother.** Cf. Acts 2:9, 12; 15:13.

e. **Hellenists.** The same group Stephen debated (cf. Acts 6:1).

ACTS 22 "Now it happened, ᵃwhen I returned to Jerusalem and was praying in the temple, that I was in a ᵇtrance and saw Him saying to me, 'Make haste and get out of Jerusalem quickly, for they will not receive your testimony concerning Me.' So I said, 'Lord, they know that in every synagogue I imprisoned and beat those who believe on You. And when the blood of Your martyr Stephen was shed, I also was standing by consenting to his death, and guarding the clothes of those who were killing him.' Then He said to me, 'Depart, for I will send you far from here to the Gentiles.'"

ACTS 9 When the brethren found out, they brought him [Paul] down to ᶜCaesarea and ᵈsent him out to Tarsus.

GAL Afterward I went into the regions of ᵉSyria and Cilicia. And I was ᶠunknown by face to the churches of Judea which were in Christ. But they were hearing only, "He who formerly persecuted us now preaches the faith which he once tried to destroy." And ᵍthey glorified God in me.

ACTS 9 Then ʰthe churches throughout all Judea, Galilee, and Samaria had peace and were edified. And walking in the fear of the Lord and in the comfort of the Holy Spirit, they were multiplied.

---

a. **when I returned to Jerusalem.** After a brief ministry in Damascus (Acts 9:20–25) and 3 years in Nabatean Arabia (Gal. 1:17, 18).

b. **trance.** Paul was carried beyond his senses into the supernatural realm to receive revelation from Jesus Christ. The experience was unique to the apostles, since only Peter (Acts 10:10; 11:5) and John (Rev. 1:10) had similar revelations. This was the fourth of 6 visions received by Paul in Acts (cf. 9:3–6; 16:9, 10; 18:9, 10; 23:11; 27:23, 24).

c. **Caesarea.** Cf. Acts 8:40. An important port city on the Mediterranean located 30 mi. N of Joppa. As the capital of the Roman province of Judea and the home of the Roman procurator, it served as the headquarters of a large Roman garrison.

d. **sent him out to Tarsus.** Paul disappeared from prominent ministry for several years, although he possibly founded some churches around Syria and Cilicia (Acts 15:23; Gal. 1:21).

e. **Syria and Cilicia.** Cf. Acts 9:30; 15:23. This area included his home town of Tarsus. He was preaching in that region for several years. When word of revival in that area reached Jerusalem, they sent Barnabas (see Acts 11:20–26). Paul stayed on in that region as a pastor in the church at Antioch. With Barnabas, they went from there on the first missionary journey (Acts 13:1–3), and afterward returned to Antioch (Acts 13:1–3) from where they were sent to the Jerusalem Council (Acts 14:26—15:4).

f. **unknown by face to the churches of Judea.** Excepting the church in Jerusalem, Paul had not visited the churches throughout Judea.

g. **they glorified God in me.** Proof that the gospel Paul preached was the same one the other apostles had taught the Judean believers.

h. **the churches . . . had peace and were edified.** Paul's conversion and political changes contributed to the rest. A stricter Roman governor and the expansion of Herod Agrippa's authority restricted the persecution.

26. Peter Performs Miraculous Signs
Acts 9:32–43

Now it came to pass, as Peter went through all parts of the country, that he also came down to the saints who dwelt in ªLydda. There he found a certain man named ᵇAeneas, who had been bedridden eight years and was paralyzed. And Peter said to him, "Aeneas, Jesus the Christ heals you. Arise and make your bed." Then he arose immediately. So all who dwelt at Lydda and ᶜSharon saw him and turned to the Lord.

At ᵈJoppa there was a certain disciple named ᵉTabitha, which is translated Dorcas. This woman was full of good works and charitable deeds which she did. But it happened in those days that she became sick and died. When they had washed her, they laid her in an ᶠupper room. And since Lydda was ᵍnear Joppa, and the disciples had heard that Peter was there, they sent two men to him, imploring him not to delay in coming to them. Then Peter arose and went with them. When he had come, they brought him to the upper room. And all the widows stood by him weeping, showing the ʰtunics and garments which Dorcas had made while she was with them. But Peter put them all out, and knelt down and prayed. And turning to the body he said, "Tabitha, arise." And she opened her eyes, and when she saw Peter she sat up. Then he gave her his hand and lifted her up; and when he had called the saints and widows, he presented her alive. And it became known throughout all Joppa, and many believed on the Lord. So it was that he stayed many days in Joppa with ⁱSimon, a tanner.

---

a. **Lydda.** Lod in the OT. Located about 10 mi. SE of Joppa, it was a hub servicing roads from Egypt to Syria and from Joppa to Jerusalem.

b. **Aeneas.** Use of "certain man" to describe him means he was an unbeliever. His paralysis was incurable by the limited medical knowledge of that day.

c. **Sharon.** The plain surrounding Lydda and Joppa and extending N to Caesarea.

d. **Joppa.** A seacoast town today known as Jaffa, S of Tel Aviv.

e. **Tabitha.** She was more commonly known by her Gr. name, "Dorcas." Both names mean "gazelle."

f. **upper room.** This arrangement was similar to that of the upstairs room in Acts 1:13; 2:1. While it was customary to bury a body immediately, the believers in Joppa had another plan.

g. **near Joppa.** 10 mi. SE.

h. **tunics . . . garments.** Close fitting undergarments and long outer robes.

i. **Simon, a tanner.** Cf. Acts 10:5, 6. Peter breaks down a cultural barrier by staying with a tanner, an occupation despised by Jewish society because the tanner dealt with the skins of dead animals. The local synagogue probably shunned Simon.

27. THE VISION OF THE UNCLEAN ANIMALS
Acts 10:1–23

There was a certain man in Caesarea called Cornelius, a ^acenturion of what was called the ^bItalian Regiment, a devout man and one who ^cfeared God with all his household, who gave alms generously to the people, and prayed to God always. ^dAbout the ninth hour of the day he saw clearly in a vision an angel of God coming in and saying to him, "Cornelius!"

And when he observed him, he was afraid, and said, "What is it, lord?"

So he said to him, "Your prayers and your alms have come up for a ^ememorial before God. Now send men to Joppa, and send for Simon whose surname is Peter. He is lodging with Simon, a tanner, whose house is by the sea. He will tell you what you must do." And when the angel who spoke to him had departed, Cornelius called two of his household servants and a devout soldier from among those who waited on him continually. So when he had explained all these things to them, he sent them to Joppa.

The next day, as they went on their journey and drew near the city, Peter went up on the ^fhousetop to pray, about the ^gsixth hour. Then he became very hungry and wanted to eat; but while they made ready, he fell into a trance and saw heaven opened and an object like a great sheet bound at the four corners, descending to him and let down to the earth. In it were ^hall kinds of four-footed animals of the earth, wild beasts, creeping things, and birds of the air. And a voice came to him, "Rise, Peter; ⁱkill and eat."

---

a. **centurion.** One of 60 officers in a Roman legion, each of whom commanded 100 men (see Matt. 8:5).

b. **Italian Regiment.** Or "Italian Cohort." Ten cohorts of 600 men each made up a legion.

c. **feared God.** A technical term used by Jews to refer to Gentiles who had abandoned their pagan religion in favor of worshiping Jehovah God. Such a person, while following the ethics of the OT, had not become a full proselyte to Judaism through circumcision. Cornelius was to receive the saving knowledge of God in Christ (see Rom. 1:20).

d. **About the ninth hour.** 3:00 p.m.

e. **memorial.** A remembrance. Cornelius' prayers, devotion, faith, and goodness were like a fragrant offering rising up to God.

f. **housetop to pray.** All kinds of worship occurred on the flat roofs of Jewish homes (2 Kin. 23:12; Jer. 19:13; 32:29).

g. **sixth hour.** 12:00 noon.

h. **all kinds of four-footed animals.** Both clean and unclean animals. To keep the Israelites separate from their idolatrous neighbors, God set specific dietary restrictions regarding the consumption of such animals (cf. Lev. 11:25, 26).

i. **kill and eat.** With the coming of the New Covenant and the calling of the church, God ended the dietary restrictions (cf. Mark 7:19).

But Peter said, "Not so, Lord! For I have never eaten anything ªcommon or unclean."

And a voice spoke to him again the second time, "What ᵇGod has cleansed you must not call common." This was done three times. And the object was taken up into heaven again.

Now while Peter wondered within himself what this vision which he had seen meant, behold, the men who had been sent from Cornelius had made inquiry for Simon's house, and stood before the gate. And they called and asked whether Simon, whose surname was Peter, was lodging there.

While Peter thought about the vision, the Spirit said to him, "Behold, three men are seeking you. Arise therefore, go down and go with them, doubting nothing; for I have sent them." Then Peter went down to the men who had been sent to him from Cornelius, and said, "Yes, I am he whom you seek. For what reason have you come?"

And they said, "Cornelius the centurion, a just man, one who fears God and has a good reputation among all the nation of the Jews, was divinely instructed by a holy angel to summon you to his house, and to hear words from you." Then he ᶜinvited them in and lodged them.

On the next day Peter went away with them, and ᵈsome brethren from Joppa accompanied him.

28. Peter Preaches the Gospel to the Gentiles

Acts 10:24–48

And the following day they entered Caesarea. Now Cornelius was waiting for them, and had called together his relatives and close friends. As Peter was

---

a. **common or unclean.** Unholy or defiled.

b. **God has cleansed.** More than just abolishing the OT dietary restrictions, God made unity possible in the church of both Jews, symbolized by the clean animals, and Gentiles, symbolized by the unclean animals, through the comprehensive sacrificial death of Christ (see Eph. 2:14).

c. **invited them in.** Self-respecting Jews did not invite any Gentiles into their home, especially soldiers of the hated Roman army.

d. **some brethren.** Six Jewish believers (Acts 11:12), identified as "those of the circumcision" in Acts 10:45.

coming in, Cornelius met him and fell down at his feet and worshiped him. But Peter lifted him up, saying, "Stand up; [a]I myself am also a man." And as he talked with him, he went in and found many who had come together. Then he said to them, "You know how [b]unlawful it is for a Jewish man to keep company with or go to one of another nation. But God has shown me that I should not call any man common or unclean. Therefore I came without objection as soon as I was sent for. I ask, then, for what reason have you sent for me?"

So Cornelius said, "Four days ago I was fasting until this hour; and at the ninth hour I prayed in my house, and behold, a man stood before me in bright clothing, and said, 'Cornelius, your prayer has been heard, and your alms are remembered in the sight of God. Send therefore to Joppa and call Simon here, whose surname is Peter. He is lodging in the house of Simon, a tanner, by the sea. When he comes, he will speak to you.' So I sent to you immediately, and you have done well to come. Now therefore, we are all present before God, to hear all the things commanded you by God."

Then Peter opened his mouth and said: "In truth I perceive that [c]God shows no partiality. But in every nation whoever fears Him and works righteousness is [d]accepted by Him. The word which God sent to the children of Israel, [e]preaching peace through Jesus Christ—He is Lord of all—that word you know, which was proclaimed throughout all Judea, and began from Galilee after [f]the baptism which John preached: [g]how God anointed Jesus of Nazareth with the Holy Spirit and with power, who went about doing good and healing all who were oppressed by the devil, for God was with Him. And we are witnesses of all things which He did both in the land of the Jews and in Jerusalem, whom they killed by hanging on a tree. Him God raised up on the third day, and showed Him openly, not to

---

a. **I myself am also a man.** Cf. Acts 14:11–15; Rev. 22:8, 9. Only the triune God deserves our worship.

b. **unlawful.** Lit. "breaking a taboo." Peter followed the Jewish standards and traditions his whole life. His comments reveal his acceptance of a new standard in which Jews no longer were to consider Gentiles profane.

c. **God shows no partiality.** Taught in both the OT (Deut. 10:17; 2 Chr. 19:7; Job 34:19) and NT (Rom. 2:11; 3:29, 30; James 2:1). The reality of this truth was taking on new dimensions for Peter.

d. **accepted.** This Gr. word means "marked by a favorable manifestation of the divine pleasure."

e. **preaching peace.** Christ, by paying the price of sin through His sacrificial death, established peace between man and God (see Rom. 5:1–11).

f. **the baptism which John preached.** Cf. Acts 1:22; 13:24; 18:25; 19:34; see Matt. 3:2–12.

g. **how God anointed Jesus.** Cf. Acts 4:27. The beginning of Jesus' earthly ministry (cf. Matt. 3:13–17; Luke 3:21, 22).

all the people, but ᵃto witnesses chosen before by God, even to us who ate and drank with Him after He arose from the dead. And He commanded us to preach to the people, and to testify that it is He who was ordained by God to be Judge of the living and the dead. To Him all the prophets witness that, through His name, whoever ᵇbelieves in Him will receive remission of sins."

While Peter was still speaking these words, ᶜthe Holy Spirit fell upon all those who heard the word. and those of ᵈthe circumcision who believed were astonished, as many as came with Peter, because the gift of the Holy Spirit had been poured out on the Gentiles also. For they heard them speak with ᵉtongues and magnify God.

Then Peter answered, "Can anyone forbid water, that these should not be baptized who have received the Holy Spirit just as we have?" And he commanded them to be baptized in the name of the Lord. Then they asked him to stay a few days.

29. THE JERUSALEM CHURCH LEARNS OF GENTILE CONVERSIONS
Acts 11:1–18

Now the apostles and brethren who were in Judea heard that the Gentiles had also received the word of God. And when Peter came up to Jerusalem, those of the circumcision contended with him, saying, "You went in to uncircumcised men and ᶠate with them!"

But Peter explained it to them in order from the beginning, saying: "I was in the city of Joppa praying; and in a trance I saw a vision, an object descending like a great sheet, let down from heaven by four corners; and it came to me. When I observed it intently and considered, I saw four-footed animals of the earth, wild beasts, creeping things, and birds of the air. And I

---

a. **to witnesses chosen.** Jesus became visible after His resurrection only to believers (cf. 1 Cor. 15:5–8).

b. **believes in Him.** The means of salvation—faith in Christ alone (see Rom. 1:16; cf. John 3:14–17; 6:69; Rom. 10:11; Gal. 3:22; Eph. 2:8, 9).

c. **the Holy Spirit fell.** Cf. Acts 2:4; 8:17.

d. **the circumcision.** Cf. Acts 11:2. Jewish Christians.

e. **tongues.** See Acts 2:4; 8:17.

f. **ate with them!** The Jewish believers were outraged over such a blatant breach of Jewish custom. It was difficult for them to conceive that Jesus could be equally Lord of Gentile believers.

heard a voice saying to me, 'Rise, Peter; kill and eat.' But I said, 'Not so, Lord! For nothing common or unclean has at any time entered my mouth.' But the voice answered me again from heaven, 'What God has cleansed you must not call common.' Now this was done three times, and all were drawn up again into heaven. At that very moment, three men stood before the house where I was, having been sent to me from Caesarea. Then the Spirit told me to go with them, doubting nothing. Moreover these six brethren accompanied me, and we entered the man's house. And he told us how he had seen an angel standing in his house, who said to him, 'Send men to Joppa, and call for Simon whose surname is Peter, who will tell you words by which you and all ªyour household will be saved.' And as I began to speak, the Holy Spirit fell upon them, as upon us ᵇat the beginning. Then I remembered the word of the Lord, how He said, 'John indeed baptized with water, but you shall be ᶜbaptized with the Holy Spirit.' If therefore God gave them the same gift as He gave us when we believed on the Lord Jesus Christ, who was I that I could withstand God?"

When they heard these things they became silent; and they glorified God, saying, "Then ᵈGod has also granted to the Gentiles repentance to life."

30. BARNABAS AND SAUL PASTOR A GENTILE CHURCH IN ANTIOCH

Acts 11:19—30

Now those who were scattered after the persecution that arose over Stephen traveled as far as ᵉPhoenicia, ᶠCyprus, and ᵍAntioch, preaching the word to no

---

a. **your household.** All who were under Cornelius' authority and care, who could comprehend the gospel and believe (cf. Acts 16:15, 31). This does not include infants.

b. **at the beginning.** God attested to the reality of Gentile salvation with the same phenomenon that occurred at Pentecost.

c. **baptized with the Holy Spirit.** See Acts 1:5.

d. **God has also granted to the Gentiles repentance to life.** One of the most shocking admissions in Jewish history, but an event that the OT had prophesied (Is. 42:1, 6; 49:6; see Acts 2:38).

e. **Phoenicia.** The coastal region directly N of Judea, containing the trading ports of Tyre and Sidon.

f. **Cyprus.** See Acts 4:36.

g. **Antioch.** Located some 200 mi. N of Sidon, Antioch was a major pagan metropolis, the third largest in the Roman Empire, behind Rome and Alexandria.

one but the Jews only. But some of them were [a]men from Cyprus and Cyrene, who, when they had come to Antioch, spoke to the [b]Hellenists, preaching the Lord Jesus. And the [c]hand of the Lord was with them, and a great number believed and turned to the Lord.

Then news of these things came to the ears of the church in Jerusalem, and they sent out [d]Barnabas to go as far as Antioch. When he came and had seen the grace of God, he was glad, and encouraged them all that with purpose of heart they should continue with the Lord. For he was a good man, full of the Holy Spirit and of faith. And a great many people were added to the Lord.

Then Barnabas departed for Tarsus [e]to seek Saul. And when he had found him, he brought him to Antioch. So it was that for a whole year they assembled with the church and taught a great many people. And the disciples were first called [f]Christians in Antioch.

And in these days [g]prophets came from Jerusalem to Antioch. Then one of them, named [h]Agabus, stood up and showed by the Spirit that there was going to be a [i]great famine throughout [j]all the world, which also happened in the days of [k]Claudius Caesar. Then the disciples, each according to his ability, determined to send relief to the brethren dwelling in Judea. This they also did, and sent it to [l]the elders by the hands of Barnabas and Saul.

---

a. **men from Cyprus and Cyrene.** See Acts 6:9; 13:4.

b. **Hellenists.** Cf. Acts 6:1; 9:29. The preferred reading is "Greeks," or Greek-speaking non-Jews (see Acts 6:1).

c. **hand of the Lord.** This refers to God's power expressed in judgment (cf. Ex. 9:33; Deut. 2:15; Josh. 4:24; 1 Sam. 5:6; 7:13) and in blessing (Ezra 7:9; 8:18; Neh. 2:8, 18). Here, it refers to blessing.

d. **Barnabas.** See Acts 4:36. Since he was a Cypriot Jew, he came from a similar background to the founders of the Antioch church.

e. **to seek Saul.** This was to be no easy task. Several years had elapsed since Saul fled Jerusalem (Acts 9:30). Apparently, he had been disinherited and forced to leave his home due to his new allegiance to Christianity (Phil. 3:8).

f. **Christians.** A term of derision meaning "of the party of Christ." Cf. Acts 26:28; 1 Pet. 4:16.

g. **prophets.** Preachers of the NT (cf. 1 Cor. 14:32; Eph. 2:20; see 13:1; 21:9; Eph. 4:11).

h. **Agabus.** One of the Jerusalem prophets who years later played an important part in Paul's ministry (Acts 21:10, 11).

i. **a great famine.** Several ancient writers (Tacitus [Annals XI.43], Josephus [Antiquities 20.2.5], and Suetonius [Claudius 18]) affirm the occurrence of great famines in Israel ca. A.D. 45–46.

j. **all the world.** The famine reached beyond the region of Palestine.

k. **Claudius Caesar.** Emperor of Rome (A.D. 41–54).

l. **the elders.** This is the first mention of the men who were pastor-overseers of the churches (Acts 15:4, 6, 22, 23; 16:4; 21:18); i.e., a plurality of godly men responsible to lead the church (see 1 Tim. 3:1–7; Titus 1:5–9). They soon began to occupy the leading role in the churches, transitioning from the apostles and prophets, who were foundational (cf. Eph. 2:20; 4:11).

31. PETER ESCAPES FROM PRISON

Acts 12:1–17

Now about that time Herod the king stretched out his hand to harass some from the church. Then he killed [a]James the brother of John [b]with the sword. And because he saw that it pleased the Jews, he proceeded further to seize Peter also. Now it was [c]during the Days of Unleavened Bread. So when he had arrested him, he put him in prison, and delivered him to [d]four squads of soldiers to keep him, intending to bring him before the people after Passover.

Peter was therefore kept in prison, but constant prayer was offered to God for him by the church. And when Herod was about to bring him out, that night Peter was sleeping, bound with two chains between two soldiers; and the guards before the door were keeping the prison. Now behold, an angel of the Lord stood by him, and a light shone in the prison; and he struck Peter on the side and raised him up, saying, "Arise quickly!" And his chains fell off his hands. Then the angel said to him, "Gird yourself and tie on your sandals"; and so he did. And he said to him, "Put on your garment and follow me." So he went out and followed him, and did not know that what was done by the angel was real, but thought he was seeing a vision. When they were past the first and the second guard posts, they came to the iron gate that leads to the city, which opened to them of its own accord; and they went out and went down one street, and immediately the angel departed from him.

And when Peter had come to himself, he said, "Now I know for certain that the Lord has sent His angel, and has delivered me from the hand of Herod and from all the expectation of the Jewish people."

So, when he had considered this, he came to the house of Mary, the mother of [e]John whose surname was Mark, where many were gathered together

---

a. **James.** The first of the apostles to be martyred (see Matt. 10:2).

b. **with the sword.** The manner of his execution indicates James was accused of leading people to follow false gods (cf. Deut. 13:12–15).

c. **during the Days of Unleavened Bread.** The weekly feast following Passover (see Ex. 23:14–19; Matt. 26:17).

d. **four squads.** Each squad contained four soldiers and rotated the watch on Peter. At all times two guards were chained to him in his cell, while the other two stood guard outside the cell door.

e. **John . . . Mark.** Cousin of Barnabas (Col. 4:10), acquaintance of Peter in his youth (1 Pet. 5:13), he accompanied Barnabas and Paul to Antioch (Acts 12:25) and later to Cyprus

praying. And as Peter knocked at the door of the gate, a girl named Rhoda came to answer. When she recognized Peter's voice, because of her gladness she did not open the gate, but ran in and announced that Peter stood before the gate. But they said to her, "You are beside yourself!" Yet she kept insisting that it was so. So they said, "It is ªhis angel."

Now Peter continued knocking; and when they opened the door and saw him, they were astonished. But motioning to them with his hand to keep silent, he declared to them how the Lord had brought him out of the prison. And he said, "Go, tell these things to ᵇJames and to the brethren." And ᶜhe departed and went to another place.

32. King Herod's Dramatic Death
Acts 12:18–24

Then, as soon as it was day, there was no small stir among the soldiers about what had become of Peter. But when Herod had searched for him and not found him, he examined the guards and commanded that they should be ᵈput to death.

And he went down from Judea to Caesarea, and stayed there.

Now Herod had been very angry with the people of ᵉTyre and Sidon; but they came to him with one accord, and having made ᶠBlastus the king's

---

(Acts 13:4, 5). He deserted them at Perga (Acts 13:13) and Paul refused to take him on his second missionary journey because of that desertion (Acts 15:36–41). He accompanied Barnabas to Cyprus (Acts 15:39). He disappeared until he was seen with Paul at Rome as an accepted companion and co-worker (Col. 4:10; Philem. 24). During Paul's second imprisonment at Rome, Paul sought John Mark's presence as useful to him (2 Tim. 4:11). He wrote the second gospel that bears his name, being enriched in his task by the aid of Peter (1 Pet. 5:13).

    a. **his angel.** According to Jewish superstition, each person had his own guardian angel who could assume that person's form.

    b. **James.** The Lord's brother, now head of the Jerusalem church (see Acts 15:13).

    c. **he departed.** Except for a brief appearance in chap. 15, Peter fades from the scene as the rest of Acts revolves around Paul and his mini.stry.

    d. **put to death.** According to Justinian's Code (ix. 4:4), a guard who allowed a prisoner to escape would suffer the same fatal penalty that awaited the prisoner.

    e. **Tyre and Sidon.** Two port cities N of Caesarea, in a region call Phoenicia. Mutual interdependence existed between these cities and Galilee, although Tyre and Sidon were more dependent on Galilee (see Mark 3:8).

    f. **Blastus.** The king's treasurer acted as an intermediary between Herod and the representatives of Tyre and Sidon.

personal aide their friend, they asked for peace, because their country was supplied with food by the king's country.

ᵃSo on a set day Herod, arrayed in royal apparel, sat on his throne and gave an oration to them. And the people kept shouting, "The voice of a god and not of a man!" Then immediately an angel of the Lord struck him, because he ᵇdid not give glory to God. And he was ᶜeaten by worms and died.

But the word of God grew and multiplied.

---

a. **So on a set day.** A feast in honor of Herod's patron, the Roman emperor Claudius.

b. **did not give glory to God.** The crime for which Herod was executed by God (A.D. 44), who will eventually condemn and execute all who are guilty of this crime (Rom. 1:18–23).

c. **eaten by worms.** According to Josephus, Herod endured terrible pain for 5 days before he died.

PART II

———◆———

Paul's First Missionary Journey & the Jerusalem Council

A.D. 47–50

33. Paul and Barnabas Depart from Antioch

Acts 12:25—13:12

And Barnabas and Saul returned from Jerusalem when they [a]had fulfilled their ministry, and they also took with them John whose surname was Mark. Now in the church that was at Antioch there were certain [b]prophets and teachers: Barnabas, [c]Simeon who was called Niger, [d]Lucius of Cyrene, Manaen [e]who had been brought up with [f]Herod the tetrarch, and Saul. As they [g]ministered to the Lord and [h]fasted, the Holy Spirit said, "Now separate to Me Barnabas and Saul for the work to which I have called them." Then, having fasted and prayed, and laid hands on them, they sent them away.

So, being sent out by the Holy Spirit, they went down to [i]Seleucia, and from there they sailed to [j]Cyprus. And when they [k]arrived in Salamis, they

---

a. **had fulfilled their ministry.** After Herod's death, they delivered the famine relief to the Jerusalem church (Acts 11:30). Chapter 13 marks a turning point in Acts. The first 12 chapters focus on Peter; the remaining chapters revolve around Paul. With Peter, the emphasis is the Jewish church in Jerusalem and Judea; with Paul, the focus is the spread of the Gentile church throughout the Roman world, which began at the church in Antioch.

b. **prophets.** These had a significant role in the apostolic church (see 1 Cor. 12:28; Eph. 2:20). They were preachers of God's Word and were responsible in the early years of the church to instruct local congregations. On some occasions, they received new revelation that was of a practical nature (cf. Acts 11:28; 21:10), a function that ended with the cessation of the temporary sign gifts. Their office was also replaced by pastor-teachers and evangelists (see Eph. 4:11).

c. **Simeon . . . called Niger.** "Niger" means "black." He may have been a dark-skinned man, an African, or both. No direct evidence exists to equate him with Simon of Cyrene (Mark 15:21).

d. **Lucius of Cyrene.** Not the Lucius of Rom. 16:21, or Luke, the physician and author of Acts.

e. **who had been brought up with.** Can be translated "foster-brother." Manean was reared in Herod the Great's household.

f. **Herod the tetrarch.** Herod Antipas, the Herod of the gospels (see Matt. 14:1).

g. **ministered.** This is from a Gr. word which in Scripture describes priestly service. Serving in leadership in the church is an act of worship to God, and consists of offering spiritual sacrifices to Him, including prayer, oversight of the flock, plus preaching and teaching the Word.

h. **fasted.** This is often connected with vigilant, passionate prayer (cf. Neh. 1:4; Ps. 35:13; Dan. 9:3; Matt. 17:21; Luke 2:37), and includes either a loss of desire for food or the purposeful setting aside of eating to concentrate on spiritual issues (see Matt. 6:16, 17).

i. **Seleucia.** This city served as the port for Antioch, some 16 mi. away at the mouth of the Orontes River.

j. **Cyprus.** See Acts 4:36. Saul and Barnabas chose to begin their missionary outreach there because it was Barnabas' home, which was only a two-day journey from Antioch, and had a large Jewish population.

k. **arrived in Salamis.** The chief port and commercial center of Cyprus.

preached the word of God in the ᵃsynagogues of the Jews. They also had John as their assistant.

Now when they had gone through the island to ᵇPaphos, they found ᶜa certain sorcerer, a false prophet, a Jew whose name was Bar-Jesus, who was with ᵈthe proconsul, Sergius Paulus, an intelligent man. This man called for Barnabas and Saul and sought to hear the word of God. But ᵉElymas the sorcerer (for so his name is translated) withstood them, seeking to turn the proconsul away from the faith. Then ᶠSaul, who also is called Paul, filled with the Holy Spirit, looked intently at him and said, "O full of all deceit and all fraud, you son of the devil, you enemy of all righteousness, will you not cease perverting the straight ways of the Lord? And now, indeed, the hand of the Lord is upon you, and you shall be blind, not seeing the sun for a time."

And immediately a dark mist fell on him, and he went around seeking someone to lead him by the hand. Then the proconsul believed, when he saw what had been done, being astonished at the teaching of the Lord.

34. PAUL PREACHES IN ANTIOCH OF PISIDIA
Acts 13:13–41

Now when Paul and his party set sail from Paphos, they ᵍcame to Perga in Pamphylia; and ʰJohn, departing from them, returned to Jerusalem. But when

---

a. **synagogues.** See Acts 6:9. Paul established the custom of preaching to the Jews first whenever he entered a new city (cf. Acts 13:14, 42; 14:1; 17:1, 10, 17; 18:4, 19, 26; 19:8) because he had an open door, as a Jew, to speak and introduce the gospel. Also, if he preached to Gentiles first, the Jews would never have listened to him.

b. **Paphos.** The capital of Cyprus and thus the seat of the Roman government. It also was a great center for the worship of Aphrodite (Venus), and thus a hotbed for all kinds of immorality.

c. **a certain sorcerer . . . a Jew.** "Sorcerer" is better translated "magician." Originally it carried no evil connotation, but later was used to describe all kinds of practitioners and dabblers in the occult. This particular magician put his knowledge to evil use (see Acts 8:9).

d. **the proconsul.** A Roman official who served as provincial governor (cf. Acts 18:12).

e. **Elymas.** The Gr. name of Bar-Jesus, a transliteration of the Arab. word for magician.

f. **Saul . . . called Paul.** Paul's Hebrew and Roman names.

g. **came to Perga in Pamphylia.** Perga was a major city in the Roman province of Pamphylia, in Asia Minor—some 200 mi. N across the Mediterranean from Cyprus.

h. **John, departing from them.** Whatever reason John Mark gave for leaving, Paul didn't accept it (Acts 15:38). While his desertion did not hamper the mission, it did later create

they departed from Perga, they came to [a]Antioch in Pisidia, and went into the synagogue on the Sabbath day and sat down. And after the [b]reading of the Law and the Prophets, the [c]rulers of the synagogue sent to them, saying, "Men and brethren, if you have any word of exhortation for the people, say on."

Then Paul stood up, and motioning with his hand said, "Men of Israel, and you who fear God, listen: The God of this people Israel chose our fathers, and exalted the people when they dwelt as strangers in the land of Egypt, and with an uplifted arm He brought them out of it. Now for a time of about forty years He put up with their ways in the wilderness. And when He had destroyed [d]seven nations in the land of Canaan, He distributed their land to them [e]by allotment.

"After that He gave them judges for [f]about four hundred and fifty years, until [g]Samuel the prophet. And afterward they asked for a king; so God gave them Saul the son of Kish, a man of the tribe of Benjamin, for forty years. And when He had removed him, He raised up for them David as king, to whom also He gave testimony and said, 'I have found David the son of Jesse, [h]a man after My own heart, who will do all My will.' From this man's seed, [i]according to the promise, God raised up for Israel a Savior—Jesus—after John had first preached, before His coming, the [j]baptism of repentance to

---

dissension between Paul and Barnabas (Acts 15:36–40). This was finally resolved (cf. Col. 4:10; 2 Tim. 4:11).

a. **Antioch in Pisidia.** Not to be confused with Antioch in Syria, the location of the first Gentile church. This Antioch was located in the mountains of Asia Minor (modern Turkey).

b. **reading of the Law and the Prophets.** The reading of the Scriptures. This occupied the third part in the liturgy of the synagogue, after the recitation of the shema (Deut. 6:4) and further prayers, but before the teaching, which was usually based on what had been read from the Scriptures.

c. **rulers of the synagogue.** Those who had general oversight of the synagogue (see 6:9), including designating who would read from the Scriptures.

d. **seven nations.** Cf. Deut. 7:1.

e. **by allotment.** A better reading would be, "as an inheritance."

f. **about four hundred and fifty years.** Four hundred years of captivity in Egypt, 40 years wandering in the wilderness, and about 10 years from the crossing of the Jordan to the division of the Land (Josh. 14:1–5).

g. **Samuel the prophet.** The last judge who anointed the first king, Saul.

h. **a man after My own heart.** See 1 Sam. 13:14. Some would question the reality of this designation for David since he proved to be such a sinner at times (cf. 1 Sam. 11:1–4; 12:9; 21:10—22:1). No man after God's own heart is perfect; yet he will recognize sin and repent of it, as did David (cf. Pss. 32, 38, 51). Paul quoted from 1 Sam. 13:14 and Ps. 89:20.

i. **according to the promise.** OT prophecy points to Messiah as a descendant of David (cf. 2 Sam. 7:12–16; Ps. 132:11; Is. 11:10; Jer. 23:5). Jesus is the fulfillment of the OT prophecies of the coming Messiah (Matt. 1:1, 20, 21; Rom. 1:3; 2 Tim. 2:8).

j. **baptism of repentance.** Cf. Acts 1:22; 10:37.

all the people of Israel. And as John was finishing his course, he said, 'Who do you think I am? I am not He. But behold, there comes One after me, the sandals of whose feet I am not worthy to loose.'

"Men and brethren, sons of the family of Abraham, and those among you who fear God, to you the word of this salvation has been sent. For those who dwell in Jerusalem, and their ªrulers, because they did not know Him, nor even the voices of the Prophets which are read every Sabbath, have fulfilled them in condemning Him. And though they found no cause for death in Him, they asked Pilate that He should be put to death. Now when they had fulfilled all that was written concerning Him, they took Him down from the ᵇtree and laid Him in a tomb. But God raised Him from the dead. He was seen for many days by those who came up with Him from Galilee to Jerusalem, who are His ᶜwitnesses to the people. And we declare to you glad tidings—that promise which was made to the fathers. God has fulfilled this for us their children, in that He has raised up Jesus. As it is also written in the ᵈsecond Psalm:

'You are My Son,
Today I have begotten You.'

"And that He raised Him from the dead, no more to return to corruption, He has spoken thus:

'I will give you the sure mercies of David.'
Therefore He also says in another Psalm:
'You will not allow Your Holy One to see corruption.'

"For David, after he had served his own generation by the will of God, fell asleep, was buried with his fathers, and saw corruption; but He whom

---

a. **rulers.** The supposed experts in the OT, including the scribes, Pharisees, Sadducees, and priests.

b. **tree . . . tomb . . . God raised.** The OT predicted the crucifixion of Christ on a cross (Ps. 22; Num. 34), at the time when this particular form of execution was not used. His burial in a "tomb" was also prophesied (Is. 53:9), yet victims of crucifixions were commonly tossed into mass graves. The climax of Paul's message was the resurrection of Christ, the ultimate proof that Jesus is the Messiah, and the fulfillment of 3 specific prophecies.

c. **witnesses.** More than 500 (cf. 1 Cor. 15:5–8).

d. **second Psalm.** Quoted from Ps. 2:7.

God raised up saw no corruption. Therefore let it be known to you, brethren, that through this Man is preached to you the forgiveness of sins; and by Him everyone who believes is ^ajustified from all things from which ^byou could not be justified by the law of Moses. Beware therefore, lest what has been ^cspoken in the prophets come upon you:

> 'Behold, you despisers,
> Marvel and perish!
> For I work a work in your days,
> A work which you will by no means believe,
> Though one were to declare it to you.'"

35. Paul's Audience Responds with Hostility

Acts 13:42–52

So when the Jews went out of the synagogue, the Gentiles begged that these words might be preached to them the next Sabbath. Now when the congregation had broken up, many of the Jews and ^ddevout proselytes followed Paul and Barnabas, who, speaking to them, persuaded them to ^econtinue in the grace of God.

On the next Sabbath almost the whole city came together to hear the word of God. But when the Jews saw the multitudes, they were filled with

---

a. **justified from.** This is better translated "freed from."

b. **you could not be justified by the law of Moses.** Keeping the law of Moses did not free anyone from their sins (cf. Rom. 3:28; 1 Cor. 1:30; Gal. 2:16; 3:11; Phil. 3:9). But the atoning death of Jesus completely satisfied the demands of God's law, making forgiveness of all sins available to all who believe (Gal. 3:16; Col. 2:13, 14). Only the forgiveness Christ offers can free people from their sins (Rom. 3:20, 22).

c. **spoken in the prophets.** This is a quotation from Hab. 1:5.

d. **devout proselytes.** Full converts to Judaism who had been circumcised.

e. **continue in the grace of God.** Those who are truly saved persevere and validate the reality of their salvation by continuing in the grace of God (cf. John 8:31; 15:1–6; Col. 1:21–23; 1 John 2:19). With such encouragement, Paul and Barnabas hoped to prevent those who were intellectually convinced of the truths of the gospel, yet had stopped short of saving faith, from reverting to legalism rather than embracing Christ completely.

envy; and contradicting and blaspheming, they opposed the things spoken by Paul. Then Paul and Barnabas grew bold and said, "It was necessary that the word of God should be spoken ªto you first; but since you reject it, and judge yourselves unworthy of everlasting life, behold, ᵇwe turn to the Gentiles. For so the Lord has commanded us:

'I have set you as a light to the Gentiles,
That you should be for salvation to the ends of the earth.'"

Now when the Gentiles heard this, they were glad and glorified the word of the Lord. And as many as had been ᶜappointed to eternal life believed.

And the word of the Lord was being spread throughout all the region. But the Jews stirred up the devout and prominent women and the chief men of the city, raised up persecution against Paul and Barnabas, and expelled them from their region. But they ᵈshook off the dust from their feet against them, and came to Iconium. And the disciples were ᵉfilled with joy and with the Holy Spirit.

36. Paul's Ministry in Iconium

Acts 14:1–7

Now it happened in ᶠIconium that they went together to the synagogue of the Jews, and so spoke that a great multitude both of the Jews and of the Greeks

---

a. **to you first.** God offered the plan of salvation to the Jews first (Matt. 10:5, 6; 15:24; Luke 24:47; Rom. 1:16). Although the thrust of Paul's ministry was to Gentiles, he had a desire to see Jews saved (Rom. 9:1–5; 10:1), preaching to them first in many cities.

b. **we turn to the Gentiles.** Because the Jews rejected the gospel. But God never planned salvation as an exclusive possession of the Jews (Is. 42:1, 6; 49:6).

c. **appointed to eternal life.** One of Scripture's clearest statements on the sovereignty of God in salvation. God chooses man for salvation, not the opposite (John 6:65; Eph. 1:4; Col. 3:12; 2 Thess. 2:13). Faith itself is a gift from God (Eph. 2:8, 9).

d. **shook off the dust from their feet.** The Jews' antagonism toward Gentiles extended to their unwillingness to even bring Gentile dust into Israel. The symbolism of Paul and Barnabas' act is clear that they considered the Jews at Antioch no better than heathen. There could have been no stronger condemnation.

e. **filled . . . with the Holy Spirit.** See Acts 2:4; Eph. 5:18.

f. **Iconium.** A cultural melting pot of native Phrygians, Greeks, Jews, and Roman colonists, located 80 mi. SE of Pisidian Antioch.

believed. But the unbelieving Jews stirred up the Gentiles and poisoned their minds against the brethren. Therefore they stayed there a long time, speaking boldly in the Lord, who was bearing witness to the word of His grace, ᵃgranting signs and wonders to be done by their hands.

But the multitude of the city was divided: part sided with the Jews, and part with the ᵇapostles. And when a violent attempt was made by both the Gentiles and Jews, with their rulers, to abuse and ᶜstone them, they became aware of it and fled to ᵈLystra and Derbe, cities of Lycaonia, and to the surrounding region. And they were preaching the gospel there.

37. PAUL STONED IN LYSTRA

Acts 14:8—20

And in Lystra a certain man without strength in his feet was sitting, a cripple from his mother's womb, who had never walked. This man heard Paul speaking. Paul, observing him intently and seeing that he had faith to be healed, said with a loud voice, "Stand up straight on your feet!" And he leaped and walked. Now ᵉwhen the people saw what Paul had done, they raised their

---

a. **granting signs and wonders.** See Acts 2:19. Acts of such divine power confirmed that Paul and Barnabas spoke for God.

b. **apostles.** See Rom. 1:1; Eph. 4:11. Barnabas was not an apostle in the same sense as Paul and the 12 since he was not an eyewitness of the resurrected Christ nor had he been called by Him. It is best to translate "apostles" here as "messengers" (cf. 2 Cor. 8:23; Phil. 2:25). The verb means "to send." The 12 and Paul were "apostles of Christ," (2 Cor. 11:13; 1 Thess. 2:6), while Barnabas and others were "apostles of the churches" (2 Cor. 8:23).

c. **stone them.** This proves that their Jewish opponents were the instigators, since stoning was a Jewish form of execution, usually for blasphemy.

d. **Lystra and Derbe, cities of Lycaonia.** Lycaonia was a district in the Roman province of Galatia. Lystra was about 18 mi. from Iconium, and was the home of Lois, Eunice, and Timothy (Acts 16:1; 2 Tim. 1:5). Luke mentions no synagogue in connection with Lystra, and since Paul began his ministry there by preaching to a crowd, it likely had a small Jewish population. Derbe was about 40 mi. SE of Lystra.

e. **when the people saw.** The strange reaction by the people of Lystra to the healing had its roots in local folklore. According to tradition, the gods Zeus and Hermes visited Lystra incognito, asking for food and lodging. All turned them away except for a peasant named Philemon and his wife, Baucis. The gods took vengeance by drowning everyone in a flood. But they turned the lowly cottage of Philemon and Baucis into a temple, where they were to serve as priest and priestess. Not wanting to repeat their ancestors' mistake, the people of Lystra believed Barnabas to be Zeus and Paul to be Hermes.

voices, saying in the [a]Lycaonian language, "The gods have come down to us in the likeness of men!" And Barnabas they called Zeus, and Paul, Hermes, because he was the chief speaker. Then the [b]priest of Zeus, whose temple was in front of their city, brought oxen and garlands to the gates, intending to sacrifice with the multitudes.

But when the apostles Barnabas and Paul heard this, they [c]tore their clothes and ran in among the multitude, crying out and saying, "Men, why are you doing these things? We also are men with the same nature as you, and [d]preach to you that you should turn from these [e]useless things to the living God, who made the heaven, the earth, the sea, and all things that are in them, who in bygone generations [f]allowed all nations to walk in their own ways. Nevertheless He [g]did not leave Himself without witness, in that He did good, gave us rain from heaven and fruitful seasons, filling our hearts with food and gladness." And with these sayings they could scarcely restrain the multitudes from sacrificing to them.

Then Jews from Antioch and Iconium came there; and having persuaded the multitudes, [h]they stoned Paul and dragged him out of the city, supposing him to be dead. However, when the disciples gathered around him, he rose up and went into the city. And the next day he departed with Barnabas to Derbe.

---

a. **Lycaonian language.** Paul and Barnabas were unable to understand the intentions of the people.

b. **priest of Zeus.** It was his job to lead the people in worship of the two men they believed to be gods.

c. **tore their clothes.** A Jewish expression of horror and revulsion at blasphemy (see Matt. 26:65).

d. **preach to you.** Because the crowd at Lystra was pagan and had no knowledge of the OT, Paul adjusted his message to fit the audience. Instead of proclaiming the God of Abraham, Isaac, and Jacob, he appealed to the universal and rational knowledge of the One who created the world (cf. Acts 17:22–26; Jon. 1:9).

e. **useless things.** An appropriate description of idolatry and all false religions.

f. **allowed all nations.** The path that they all have walked is described in Rom. 1:18–32.

g. **did not leave Himself without witness.** God's providence and His creative power testify to man's reason of His existence (Rom. 1:18–20), as does man's own conscience, which contains His moral law (Rom. 2:13–15).

h. **they stoned Paul . . . supposing him to be dead.** Paul did not die from the stoning as some claim, who link it to his third-heaven experience in 2 Cor. 12. "Supposing" usually means "to suppose something that is not true." The main NT use of this word argues that the crowd's supposition was incorrect and that Paul was not dead. Another argument in favor of this position is that if Paul was resurrected, why didn't Luke mention it? Also, the dates of Paul's third-heaven experience and the time of the stoning do not reconcile.

38. Paul and Barnabas Strengthen the Churches
Acts 14:21–28

And when they had preached the gospel to that city and made many disciples, they returned to Lystra, Iconium, and Antioch, strengthening the souls of the disciples, exhorting them to continue in the faith, and saying, "We must through many tribulations enter the kingdom of God." So when they had appointed elders in every church, and prayed with fasting, they commended them to the Lord in whom they had believed. And after they had passed through ªPisidia, they came to ᵇPamphylia. Now when they had preached the word in Perga, they went down to Attalia. ᶜFrom there they sailed to Antioch, where they had been commended to the grace of God for the work which they had completed.

Now when they had come and gathered the church together, they reported all that God had done with them, and that He had opened the door of faith to the Gentiles. So they stayed there ᵈa long time with the disciples.

39. False Teachers Threaten the Gospel
Acts 15:1–5

And ᵉcertain men came down from Judea and taught the brethren, ᶠ"Unless you are circumcised according to the custom of Moses, you cannot be saved."

---

a. **Pisidia.** A mountainous and rugged region that offered no opportunities for evangelism.

b. **Pamphylia.** See Acts 13:13.

c. **From there.** Thus ended Paul's first missionary journey.

d. **a long time.** About one year.

e. **certain men.** Judaizers—false teachers who were self-appointed guardians of legalism, teaching a doctrine of salvation by works. Throughout its history, the church's leaders have met to settle doctrinal issues. Historians point to 7 ecumenical councils in the church's early history, especially the Councils of Nicea (A.D. 325) and Chalcedon (A.D. 451). Yet the most important council was the first one—the Jerusalem Council—because it established the answer to the most vital doctrinal question of all: "What must a person do to be saved?" The apostles and elders defied efforts to impose legalism and ritualism as necessary prerequisites for salvation. They forever affirmed that salvation is totally by grace through faith in Christ alone.

f. **Unless you are circumcised . . . you cannot be saved.** The heresy propagated by the Judaizers. See Gen. 17:10–12.

Therefore, when Paul and Barnabas had no small dissension and dispute with them, they determined that Paul and Barnabas and certain others of them should go up to Jerusalem, to the apostles and elders, about this question.

So, being sent on their way by the church, they passed through Phoenicia and Samaria, describing the conversion of the Gentiles; and they caused great joy to all the brethren. And when they had come to Jerusalem, they were received by the church and the apostles and the ªelders; and ᵇthey reported all things that God had done with them. But some of the sect of the Pharisees who believed rose up, saying, "It is necessary to circumcise them, and to command them to keep the law of Moses."

40. Paul Meets Privately with Peter, John, and James

Gal. 2:1–10

Note: *In Acts 15, Luke describes the public events of the Jerusalem Council. In Galatians 2, Paul gives a personal account of the private meetings he had with Peter, John, and James leading up to the public council.*

Then after ᶜfourteen years I went up again to Jerusalem with ᵈBarnabas, and also took ᵉTitus with me. And I went up ᶠby revelation, and communicated to

---

a. **elders.** Leaders of the Jerusalem church (see Acts 11:30).

b. **they reported all things.** Paul and Barnabas and others went into great detail to report the many works God was accomplishing through their efforts. No doubt they provided sufficient evidence to verify the genuineness of the Gentiles' salvation (cf. Acts 10:44–48; 11:17, 18).

c. **fourteen years . . . again to Jerusalem.** This was the period from the time of his first visit to Jerusalem (Gal. 1:18) to the one Paul refers to here, which probably was for the Jerusalem Council (Acts 15:1–22) called to resolve the issue of Gentile salvation. Linguistically, the word "again" need not refer to the next visit; it can just as easily mean "once again" without respect to how many visits took place in between. And in fact, Paul did visit Jerusalem during that 14-year period to deliver famine relief to the church there (Acts 11:27–30; 12:24, 25), but he does not refer to that visit here since it had no bearing on his apostolic authority.

d. **Barnabas.** See Acts 4:36. Paul's first ally who vouched for him before the apostles at Jerusalem (Acts 9:27), and became his traveling companion on his first missionary journey (Acts 13:2, 3).

e. **Titus.** A spiritual child of Paul and a co-worker (Titus 1:4, 5). As an uncircumcised Gentile, Titus was fitting proof of the effectiveness of Paul's ministry.

f. **by revelation.** This revelation from God was the voice of the Holy Spirit (see Acts 13:2–4). He refers to the divine commissioning of his visit in order to refute any suggestion by the Judaizers that they had sent Paul to Jerusalem to have the apostles correct his doctrine.

them that gospel which I preach among the Gentiles, but privately to ᵃthose who were of reputation, lest by any means I ᵇmight run, or had run, in vain. Yet not even Titus who was with me, being a Greek, was ᶜcompelled to be circumcised. And this occurred because of ᵈfalse brethren secretly brought in (who came in by stealth ᵉto spy out our ᶠliberty which we have in Christ Jesus, that they might bring us into ᵍbondage), to whom ʰwe did not yield submission even for an hour, that the ⁱtruth of the gospel might continue with you.

But from ʲthose who seemed to be something—whatever they were, it makes no difference to me; God shows ᵏpersonal favoritism to no man—for those who seemed to be something added nothing to me. But ˡon the contrary,

a. **those who were of reputation.** The 3 main leaders of the Jerusalem church: Peter, James (the Lord's brother, Gal. 1:19), and John (cf. Gal. 2:9). This phrase was typically used of authorities and implied a position of honor. Paul refers to them in a similar way two other times (Gal. 2:6, 9), suggesting a hint of sarcasm directed toward the Judaizers, who claimed they had apostolic approval for their doctrine and Paul did not. They had likely made a habit of exalting these 3 leaders at the expense of Paul.

b. **might run . . . in vain.** Paul hoped the Jerusalem leaders would support his ministry to the Gentiles and not soften their opposition to legalism. He did not want to see his ministry efforts wasted because of conflict with the other apostles.

c. **compelled to be circumcised.** At the core of the Judaizers' works system was the Mosaic prescription of circumcision (see Gen. 17:9–14; Rom. 4:9–12). They were teaching that there could be no salvation without circumcision (Acts 15:1, 5, 24). Paul and the apostles denied that and it was settled at the Jerusalem Council (Acts 15:1–22). See Gal. 5:2–12; 6:15; Rom. 4:10–12; 1 Cor. 7:19. As a true believer, Titus was living proof that circumcision and the Mosaic regulations were not prerequisites or necessary components of salvation. The apostles' refusal to require Titus' circumcision verified the church's rejection of the Judaizers' doctrine (cf. Timothy, Acts 16:1–3).

d. **false brethren.** The Judaizers, who pretended to be true Christians. Yet, their doctrine, because it claimed allegiance to Christ, was opposed to traditional Judaism, and because it demanded circumcision and obedience to the Mosaic law as prerequisites for salvation, was opposed to Christianity.

e. **to spy out.** This Gr. word pictures spies or traitors entering by stealth into an enemy's camp. The Judaizers were Satan's undercover agents sent into the midst of the church to sabotage the true gospel.

f. **liberty.** Christians are free from the law as a means of salvation, from its external ceremonial regulations as a way of living, and from its curse for disobedience to the law—a curse that Christ bore for all believers (Gal. 3:13). This freedom is not, however, a license to sin (Rom. 6:18; Gal. 5:13; 1 Pet. 2:16).

g. **bondage.** Conveys the idea of absolute slavery to an impossible system of works righteousness.

h. **we did not yield.** Paul and Titus never budged from their position of salvation by grace alone through faith alone.

i. **truth of the gospel.** The true gospel as opposed to the different (Gal. 1:6–8) and false one propagated by the Judaizers (see Rom. 1:1).

j. **those who seemed to be something.** Another reference to Peter, James, and John.

k. **personal favoritism.** The unique privileges of the 12 did not make their apostleship more legitimate or authoritative than Paul's—Christ commissioned them all (cf. Rom. 2:11). Paul never saw himself as apostolically inferior (see 2 Cor. 12:11, 12).

l. **on the contrary.** The Judaizers claimed Paul was preaching a deviant gospel, but the apostles confirmed that he proclaimed the true gospel. It was the same gospel Peter proclaimed, but to a different audience.

when they saw that the gospel ᵃfor the uncircumcised had been committed to me, as the gospel for the ᵇcircumcised was to Peter (for ᶜHe who worked effectively in Peter for the apostleship to the circumcised also worked effectively in me toward the Gentiles), and when ᵈJames, Cephas, and John, who seemed to be ᵉpillars, perceived the ᶠgrace that had been given to me, they gave me and Barnabas ᵍthe right hand of fellowship, that we ʰshould go to the Gentiles and they to the circumcised. They desired only that we should ⁱremember the poor, the very thing which I also was eager to do.

41. THE JERUSALEM COUNCIL: PETER SPEAKS
Acts 15:6–12

Now the apostles and elders came together to consider this matter. And when there had been much dispute, ʲPeter rose up and said to them: "Men and

---

a. **for the uncircumcised.** Better translated "to the uncircumcised." Paul preached the gospel primarily to the Gentiles (also to Jews in Gentile lands, as his pattern was to go to the synagogue first; cf. Acts 13:5).

b. **circumcised . . . Peter.** Peter's ministry was primarily to the Jews.

c. **He who worked effectively in Peter . . . in me.** The Holy Spirit, who has but one gospel, empowered both Peter and Paul in their ministries.

d. **James, Cephas, and John.** This James was Jesus' half-brother (Gal. 1:19), who had risen to a prominent role in the Jerusalem church. Cephas (Peter) and John (the brother of James the apostle, martyred in Acts 1Gal. 2:2), were two of Christ's closest companions and became the main apostles in the Jerusalem church (see Acts 2–12).

e. **pillars.** Emphasizing the role of James, Peter, and John in establishing and supporting the church.

f. **grace . . . given to me.** The only conclusion these leaders could make was that God's grace was responsible for the powerful preaching of the gospel and the building of the church through Paul's efforts.

g. **the right hand of fellowship.** In the Near East, this represented a solemn vow of friendship and a mark of partnership. This act signified the apostles' recognition of Paul as a teacher of the true gospel and a partner in ministry.

h. **should go to the Gentiles.** Further confirmation of Paul's divine call to ministry and a blow to the Judaizers, since the apostles directed him to continue in his already flourishing ministry to the Gentiles.

i. **remember the poor.** A practical reminder for Paul and the growing ranks of Gentile Christians. The number of Christians in Jerusalem grew rapidly at first (cf. Acts 2:41–45; 6:1) and many who were visiting the city for the feast of Pentecost (Acts 2:1, 5) remained and never returned to their homes. While the believers initially shared their resources (Acts 2:45; 4:32–37), many had little money. For years the Jerusalem church was economically pressed. See Acts 11:29, 30.

j. **Peter rose up.** Peter gave the first of 3 speeches at the Council that amount to one of the strongest defenses of salvation by grace through faith alone contained in Scripture.

brethren, you know that a good while ago God chose among us, that by my mouth the Gentiles should hear the word of the gospel and believe. So God, who knows the heart, acknowledged them by ªgiving them the Holy Spirit, just as He did to us, and made no distinction between us and them, purifying their hearts by faith. Now therefore, why do you test God by putting ᵇa yoke on the neck of the disciples which neither our fathers nor we were able to bear? But we believe that ᶜthrough the grace of the Lord Jesus Christ we shall be saved in the same manner as they."

Then all the multitude kept silent and listened to ᵈBarnabas and Paul declaring how many miracles and wonders God had worked through them among the Gentiles.

42. THE JERUSALEM COUNCIL: JAMES SPEAKS
Acts 15:13—29

And after they had become silent, ᵉJames answered, saying, "Men and brethren, listen to me: Simon has declared how God at the first visited the Gentiles to take out of them a people for His name. And with this the words of the prophets agree, just as ᶠit is written:

Peter began his defense by reviewing how God saved Gentiles in the early days of the church without a requirement of circumcision, law keeping, or ritual—referring to the salvation of Cornelius and his household (Acts 10:44–48; 11:17, 18). If God did not require any additional qualifications for salvation, neither should the legalists.

    a. **giving them the Holy Spirit.** The Judaizers could have argued that Cornelius and the others could not have been saved because they did not meet the legalistic requirements. To thwart that potential argument, Peter reiterates that God gave them the Holy Spirit, thus proving the genuineness of their salvation (see Acts 2:4).

    b. **a yoke.** A description of the law and the legalism of the scribes and Pharisees (Matt. 23:4; cf. Luke 11:46). The legalists expected the Gentiles to carry a load they themselves were unwilling to bear.

    c. **through the grace of the Lord Jesus Christ.** A resounding affirmation of salvation by grace through faith alone (see Rom. 3:24, 25).

    d. **Barnabas and Paul.** They delivered the second speech in which they recounted the work of God on their just completed first missionary journey among Gentiles.

    e. **James answered.** He delivers the third speech in defense of salvation by faith alone by relating how God's future plans for Gentile salvation agree with His current work.

    f. **it is written.** James quotes Amos' prophecy (Amos 9:11, 12) of the millennial kingdom to prove that Gentile salvation was not contrary to God's plan for Israel. In fact, in the kingdom God's messengers will announce salvation to the Gentiles (Zech. 8:20–23).

'After this I will return
And will rebuild the tabernacle of David, which has fallen down;
I will rebuild its ruins,
And I will set it up;
So that the rest of mankind may seek the LORD,
Even all the ᵃGentiles who are called by My name,
Says the LORD who does all these things.'

"Known to God from eternity are all His works. Therefore I judge that ᵇwe should not trouble those from among the Gentiles who are turning to God, but that we write to them to abstain from ᶜthings polluted by idols, from ᵈsexual immorality, from ᵉthings strangled, and from blood. For Moses has had throughout many generations those who preach him in every city, being read in the synagogues every Sabbath."

Then it pleased the apostles and elders, with the whole church, to send chosen men of their own company to Antioch with Paul and Barnabas, namely, ᶠJudas who was also named Barsabas, and ᵍSilas, leading men among the brethren.

They wrote this letter by them:

---

a. **Gentiles . . . called by My name.** James' point is that Amos makes no mention of Gentiles becoming Jewish proselytes. If Gentiles can be saved without becoming Jews in the kingdom, there is no need for Gentiles to become proselytes in the present age.

b. **we should not trouble.** The Gr. word for "trouble" means "to throw something in the path of someone to annoy them." The decision of the Jerusalem Council, after considering all the evidence, was that keeping the law and observing rituals were not requirements for salvation. The Judaizers were to cease troubling and annoying the Gentiles. James and the other leaders did not want the Gentiles to revel in their freedom in Christ, which could cause the Jewish believers to follow that same liberty and violate their consciences. So James proposed that the Gentiles abstain from 4 pagan, idolatrous practices that were violations of the law of Moses so as not to offend Jews.

c. **things polluted by idols.** Food offered to pagan gods and then sold in temple butcher shops. Because idolatry was so repulsive to Jews and forbidden by God (cf. Ex. 20:3; 34:17; Deut. 5:7), they would avoid anything to do with idols, including meat offered to idols (cf. 1 Cor. 8:1–13).

d. **sexual immorality.** Sexual sins in general, but particularly the orgies associated with the worship of pagan gods. The Gentiles were to avoid being offensive to Jewish sensibilities in their marriages and any relationship with the opposite sex.

e. **things strangled, and from blood.** Dietary restrictions (Gen. 9:4; Lev. 3:17; 7:26; 17:12–14; 19:26; Deut. 12:16, 23; 15:23; 1 Sam. 14:34; Ezek. 33:25).

f. **Judas.** Nothing more is known about him except that he was a prophet (Acts 15:32).

g. **Silas.** Also known as Silvanus, he accompanied Paul on his second missionary journey (Acts 15:40; 16:19, 25, 29; 17:4, 10, 14, 15; 18:5) and later was Peter's amanuensis (scribe) for his first epistle (1 Pet. 5:12).

The apostles, the elders, and the brethren,

To the brethren who are of the Gentiles ªin Antioch, Syria, and Cilicia:

Greetings.

Since we have heard that some who went out from us have ᵇtroubled you with words, unsettling your souls, saying, "You must be circumcised and keep the law" —to whom we gave no such commandment—it seemed good to us, being assembled with one accord, to send chosen men to you with our beloved Barnabas and Paul, men who have ᶜrisked their lives for the name of our Lord Jesus Christ. We have therefore sent Judas and Silas, who will also report the same things by word of mouth. For it seemed good to the Holy Spirit, and to us, to lay upon you no greater burden than these necessary things: that you abstain from things offered to idols, from blood, from things strangled, and from sexual immorality. If you keep yourselves from these, you will do well.

Farewell.

43. Paul and Barnabas Return to Antioch
Acts 15:30–35

So when they were sent off, they came to Antioch; and when they had gathered the multitude together, they delivered the letter. When they had read it, they rejoiced over its encouragement. Now Judas and Silas, themselves being prophets also, exhorted and strengthened the brethren with many words. And after they had stayed there for a time, they were sent back with greetings from the brethren to the apostles.

---

a. **in Antioch, Syria, and Cilicia.** Antioch was the capital of Syria and Cilicia, which was administered as a single Roman district. The churches in Cilicia were probably founded by Paul when he went there after fleeing Jerusalem (Acts 9:30).

b. **troubled . . . unsettling.** "Troubled" is a different Gr. word from the one in Acts 15:19, meaning "to deeply upset," "to deeply disturb," "to perplex," or "to create fear." The Gr. word for "unsettling" was used in extrabiblical writings to speak of someone going bankrupt. Together these words aptly describe the chaos caused by the Judaizers.

c. **risked their lives.** On the first missionary journey they faced persecution (Acts 13:50) and Paul was nearly killed (Acts 14:19, 20).

However, it seemed good to Silas to remain there. Paul and Barnabas also remained in Antioch, teaching and preaching the word of the Lord, with many others also.

44. PAUL WRITES A LETTER TO THE CHURCHES OF GALATIA

Introduction to Galatians:

Galatians derives its title (*pros Galatas*) from the region in Asia Minor (modern Turkey) where the churches addressed were located. It is the only one of Paul's epistles specifically addressed to churches in more than one city (Gal. 1:2; cf. 3:1; 1 Cor. 16:1).

Author and Date

There is no reason to question the internal claims that the apostle Paul wrote Galatians (Gal. 1:1; 5:2). Paul was born in Tarsus, a city in the province of Cilicia, not far from Galatia. Under the famous rabbi, Gamaliel, Paul received a thorough training in the OT Scriptures and in the rabbinic traditions at Jerusalem (Acts 22:3). A member of the ultra-orthodox sect of the Pharisees (Acts 23:6), he was one of first-century Judaism's rising stars (Gal. 1:14; cf. Phil. 3:5, 6).

The course of Paul's life took a sudden and startling turn when, on his way to Damascus from Jerusalem to persecute Christians, he was confronted by the risen, glorified Christ (see Acts 9). That dramatic encounter turned Paul from Christianity's chief persecutor to its greatest missionary. His 3 missionary journeys and trip to Rome turned Christianity from a faith that included only a small group of Palestinian Jewish believers into an Empire-wide phenomenon. Galatians is one of 13 inspired letters he addressed to Gentile congregations or his fellow workers.

In chap. 2, Paul described his visit to the Jerusalem Council of Acts 15, so he must have written Galatians after that event. Since most scholars date the Jerusalem Council about A.D. 49, the most likely date for Galatians is shortly thereafter.

Background and Setting

In Paul's day, the word Galatia had two distinct meanings. In a strict ethnic sense, Galatia was the region of central Asia Minor inhabited by the Galatians. They were a Celtic people who had migrated to that region from Gaul (modern France) in the third century B.C. The Romans conquered the Galatians in 189 B.C. but allowed them to have some measure of independence until 25 B.C. when Galatia became a Roman province, incorporating some regions not inhabited by ethnic Galatians (e.g., parts of Lycaonia, Phrygia, and Pisidia). In a political sense, Galatia came to describe the entire Roman province, not merely the region inhabited by the ethnic Galatians.

Paul founded churches in the southern Galatian cities of Antioch, Iconium, Lystra, and Derbe (Acts 13:14—14:23). These cities, although within the Roman province of Galatia, were not in the ethnic Galatian region. There is no record of Paul's founding churches in that northern, less populated region.

Those two uses of the word Galatia make it more difficult to determine who the original recipients of the epistle were. Some interpret Galatia in its strict racial sense and argue that Paul addressed this epistle to churches in the northern Galatian region, inhabited by the ethnic descendants of the Gauls. Although the apostle apparently crossed the border into the fringes of ethnic Galatia on at least two occasions (Acts 16:6; 18:23), Acts does not record that he founded any churches or engaged in any evangelistic ministry there.

Because neither Acts nor Galatians mentions any cities or people from northern (ethnic) Galatia, it is reasonable to believe that Paul addressed this epistle to churches located in the southern part of the Roman province, but outside of the ethnic Galatian region. Acts records the apostle's founding of such churches at Pisidian Antioch (13:14–50), Iconium (13:51—14:7; cf. 16:2), Lystra (14:8–19; cf. 16:2), and Derbe (14:20, 21; cf. 16:1). In addition, the churches Paul addressed had apparently been established before the Jerusalem Council (Gal 2:5), and the churches of southern Galatia fit that criterion, having been founded during Paul's first missionary journey before the Council met. Paul did not visit northern (ethnic) Galatia until after the Jerusalem Council (Acts 16:6).

Paul wrote Galatians to counter judaizing false teachers who were undermining the central NT doctrine of justification by faith (see Rom. 3:24). Ignoring the express decree of the Jerusalem Council (Acts 15:23–29), they spread their dangerous teaching that Gentiles must first become Jewish proselytes and submit to all the Mosaic law before they could become Christians (see Gal. 1:7; 4:17, 21; 5:2–12; 6:12, 13). Shocked by the Galatians' openness to that damning heresy (cf. Gal. 1:6), Paul wrote this letter to defend justification by faith, and warn these churches of the dire consequences of abandoning that essential doctrine. Galatians is the only epistle Paul wrote that does not contain a commendation for its readers—that obvious omission reflects how urgently he felt about confronting the defection and defending the essential doctrine of justification.

Historical and Theological Themes

Galatians provides valuable historical information about Paul's background (chaps. 1, 2), including his three-year stay in Nabatean Arabia (1:17, 18), which Acts does not mention; his fifteen-day visit with Peter after his stay in Arabia (1:18, 19); his trip to the Jerusalem Council (2:1–10); and his confrontation of Peter (2:11–21).

As already noted, the central theme of Galatians (like that of Romans) is justification by faith. Paul defends that doctrine (which is the heart of the gospel) both in its theological (chaps. 3, 4) and practical (chaps. 5, 6) ramifications. He also defends his position as an apostle (chaps. 1, 2) since, as in Corinth, false teachers had attempted to gain a hearing for their heretical teaching by undermining Paul's credibility. The main theological themes of Galatians are strikingly similar to those of Romans, e.g., the inability of the law to justify (Gal. 2:16; cf. Rom. 3:20); the believer's deadness to the law (Gal. 2:19; cf. Rom. 7:4); the believer's crucifixion with Christ (Gal. 2:20; cf. Rom. 6:6); Abraham's justification by faith (3:6; cf. Rom. 4:3); that believers are Abraham's spiritual children (Gal. 3:7; cf. Rom. 4:10, 11) and therefore blessed (3:9; cf. Rom. 4:23, 24); that the law brings not salvation but God's wrath (Gal. 3:10; cf. Rom. 4:15); that the just shall live by faith (Gal. 3:11; cf. Rom. 1:17); the universality of sin (3:22; cf. Rom. 11:32); that believers are spiritually baptized into Christ (Gal. 3:27; cf. Rom. 6:3); believers' adoption as God's spiritual children (Gal. 4:5–7; cf. Rom. 8:14–17); that love fulfills the law (Gal. 5:14; cf. Rom. 13:8–10); the importance of walking in the Spirit (Gal. 5:16; cf. Rom. 8:4); the warfare of the flesh against the Spirit (Gal. 5:17; cf. Rom. 7:23, 25); and the importance of believers bearing one anothers' burdens (Gal. 6:2; cf. Rom. 15:1).

Interpretive Challenges

First, Paul described a visit to Jerusalem and a subsequent meeting with Peter, James, and John (Gal. 2:1–10). There is a question to be resolved in that text, as to whether that was his visit to the Jerusalem Council (Acts 15), or his earlier visit bringing famine relief to the Jerusalem church (Acts 11:27–30). Second, those who teach baptismal regeneration (the false doctrine that baptism is necessary for salvation) support their view from Gal. 3:27. Third, others have used this epistle to support their attacks on the biblical roles of men and women, claiming that the spiritual equality taught in Gal. 3:28 is incompatible with the traditional concept of authority and submission. Fourth, those who reject the doctrine of eternal security argue that the phrase "you have fallen from grace" (Gal. 5:4) describes believers who lost their salvation. Fifth, there is disagreement whether Paul's statement "see with what large letters I have written to you with my own hand!" refers to the entire letter, or merely the concluding verses. Finally, many claim that Paul erased the line between Israel and the church when he identified the church as the "Israel of God" (Gal. 6:16). Those challenges will be addressed in the notes on the appropriate passages.

45. FALSE TEACHING REBUKED

Gal. 1:1–9

Paul, [a]an apostle ([b]not from men nor through man, but through Jesus Christ and God the Father who [c]raised Him from the dead), and all the brethren who are with me,

---

a. **an apostle.** In general terms, it means "one who is sent with a commission." The apostles of Jesus Christ—the 12 and Paul—were special ambassadors or messengers chosen and trained by Christ to lay the foundation of the early church and be the channels of God's completed revelation (see Rom. 1:1; cf. Acts 1:2; 2:42; Eph. 2:20).

b. **not from men . . . but through Jesus Christ.** To defend his apostleship against the false teachers' attack, Paul emphasized that Christ Himself appointed him as an apostle before he met the other apostles (cf. Gal. 1:17, 18; Acts 9:3–9).

c. **raised Him from the dead.** See Rom. 1:4. Paul included this important fact to show that the risen and ascended Christ Himself appointed him (see Acts 9:1–9, 15), thus Paul was a qualified witness of His resurrection (cf. Acts 1:22).

To the ^achurches of Galatia:

^bGrace to you and peace from God the Father and our Lord Jesus Christ, who gave Himself ^cfor our sins, that He might deliver us from this ^dpresent evil age, according to ^ethe will of our God and Father, to whom be glory forever and ever. Amen.

I marvel that you are ^fturning away ^gso soon from Him who ^hcalled you in the ⁱgrace of Christ, to a ^jdifferent gospel, which is not another; but there are some who ^ktrouble you and want to ^lpervert ^mthe gospel of Christ. But even if ⁿwe, or an angel from heaven, preach any other gospel to you than what we

---

a. **churches of Galatia.** The churches Paul founded at Antioch of Pisidia, Iconium, Lystra, and Derbe during his first missionary journey (Acts 13:14—14:23).

b. **Grace to you and peace.** See Rom. 1:1. Even Paul's typical greeting attacked the Judaizers' legalistic system. If salvation is by works as they claimed, it is not of "grace" and cannot result in "peace," since no one can be sure he has enough good works to be eternally secure.

c. **for our sins.** No one can avoid sin by human effort or law-keeping (Rom. 3:20); therefore it must be forgiven, which Christ accomplished through His atoning death on the cross (Gal. 3:13; see 2 Cor. 5:19–21; 1 Pet. 2:24).

d. **present evil age.** The Gr. word for "age" does not refer to a period of time but an order or system, and in particular to the current world system ruled by Satan (see Rom. 12:2; 1 John 2:15, 16; 5:19).

e. **the will of our God.** The sacrifice of Christ for salvation was the will of God designed and fulfilled for His glory. Cf. Matt. 26:42; John 6:38–40; Acts 2:22, 23; Rom. 8:3, 31, 32; Eph. 1:7, 11; Heb. 10:4–10.

f. **turning away.** This is better translated "deserting." The Gr. word was used of military desertion, which was punishable by death. The form of this Gr. verb indicates that the Galatian believers were voluntarily deserting grace to pursue the legalism taught by the false teachers (see Gal. 5:4).

g. **so soon.** This Gr. word can mean either "easily" or "quickly" and sometimes both. No doubt both senses characterized the Galatians' response to the false teachers' heretical doctrines.

h. **called you.** This could be translated, "who called you once and for all" (cf. 2 Thess. 2:13, 14; 2 Tim. 1:8, 9; 1 Pet. 1:15), and refers to God's effectual call to salvation (see Rom. 1:7).

i. **grace of Christ.** God's free and sovereign act of mercy in granting salvation through the death and resurrection of Christ, totally apart from any human work or merit (see Rom. 3:24).

j. **different gospel.** Cf. 2 Cor. 11:4. The Judaizers' perversion of the true gospel. They added the requirements, ceremonies, and standards of the Old Covenant as necessary prerequisites to salvation. See Gal. 3:3; 4:9; 5:7; Phil. 3:2.

k. **trouble.** The Gr. word could be translated "disturb" and means "to shake back and forth," meaning to agitate or stir up. Here, it refers to the deep emotional disturbance the Galatian believers experienced.

l. **pervert.** To turn something into its opposite. By adding law to the gospel of Christ, the false teachers were effectively destroying grace, turning the message of God's undeserved favor toward sinners into a message of earned and merited favor.

m. **the gospel of Christ.** The good news of salvation by grace alone through faith alone in Christ alone (see Rom. 1:1; 1 Cor. 15:1–4).

n. **we, or an angel from heaven.** Paul's point is hypothetical, calling on the most unlikely examples for false teaching—himself and holy angels. The Galatians should receive

have preached to you, let him be ªaccursed. ᵇAs we have said before, so now I say again, if ᶜanyone preaches any other gospel to you than what you have received, let him be accursed.

46. PAUL'S TESTIMONY

Gal. 1:10–24

For do I now persuade men, or God? Or do I seek to please men? For if I ᵈstill pleased men, I would not be a ᵉbondservant of Christ.

But I ᶠmake known to you, brethren, that ᵍthe gospel which was preached by me is not according to man. For I ʰneither received it from man, nor was I taught it, but it came ⁱthrough the revelation of Jesus Christ.

---

no messenger, regardless of how impeccable his credentials, if his doctrine of salvation differs in the slightest degree from God's truth revealed through Christ and the apostles.

a. **accursed.** The translation of the familiar Gr. word *anathema*, which refers to devoting someone to destruction in eternal hell (cf. Rom. 9:3; 1 Cor. 12:3; 16:22). Throughout history God has devoted certain objects, individuals, and groups of people to destruction (Josh. 6:17, 18; 7:1, 25, 26). The NT offers many examples of one such group: false teachers (Matt. 24:24; John 8:44; 1 Tim. 1:20; Titus 1:16). Here the Judaizers are identified as members of this infamous company.

b. **As we have said before.** This refers to what Paul taught during an earlier visit to these churches, not to a previous comment in this epistle.

c. **anyone.** Paul turns from the hypothetical case of the previous verse (the apostle or heavenly angels preaching a false gospel) to the real situation faced by the Galatians. The Judaizers were doing just that, and were to be devoted to destruction because of their damning heresy.

d. **still pleased men.** Paul's previous motivation when he used to persecute Christians on behalf of his fellow Jews. Because the false teachers sought to undermine Paul's spiritual credentials, he set out to defend his apostleship, explaining once again that he was appointed by God and not by men.

e. **bondservant of Christ.** See Rom. 1:1. Paul had become a willing slave of Christ, which cost him a great deal of suffering from others (Gal. 6:17). Such personal sacrifice is exactly opposite the goal of pleasing men (Gal. 6:12).

f. **make known to you.** The strong Gr. verb Paul used here often introduced an important and emphatic statement (1 Cor. 12:3; 2 Cor. 8:1).

g. **the gospel . . . not according to man.** The gospel Paul preached was not human in origin or it would have been like all other human religion, permeated with works righteousness born of man's pride and Satan's deception (Rom. 1:16).

h. **neither received it from man, nor was I taught it.** In contrast to the Judaizers, who received their religious instruction from rabbinic tradition. Most Jews did not study the actual Scriptures; instead they used human interpretations of Scripture as their religious authority and guide. Many of their traditions not only were not taught in Scripture but also contradicted it (Mark 7:13).

i. **through the revelation.** This refers to the unveiling of something previously kept secret—in this case, Jesus Christ. While he knew about Christ, Paul subsequently met Him personally on the road to Damascus and received the truth of the gospel from Him (Acts 9:1–16).

83

For you have heard of my former conduct in [a]Judaism, how I [b]persecuted the church of God beyond measure and tried to destroy it. And I [c]advanced in Judaism beyond many of my contemporaries in my own nation, being more [d]exceedingly zealous for the [e]traditions of my fathers.

But when it pleased God, who [f]separated me from my mother's womb and [g]called me through His grace, to [h]reveal His Son in me, that I might [i]preach Him among the Gentiles, I did not immediately [j]confer with flesh and blood, nor did I go up to [k]Jerusalem to those who were apostles before me; but I went to Arabia, and returned again to Damascus.

Then after [l]three years I went [m]up to Jerusalem to see [n]Peter, and remained

---

a. **Judaism.** The Jewish religious system of works righteousness, based not primarily on the OT text, but on rabbinic interpretations and traditions. In fact, Paul will argue that a proper understanding of the OT can lead only to Christ and His gospel of grace through faith (Gal. 3:6–29).

b. **persecuted.** The tense of this Gr. verb emphasizes Paul's persistent and continual effort to hurt and ultimately exterminate Christians. See Acts 8:1–3; 9:1; 1 Cor. 15:9; 1 Tim. 1:12–14.

c. **advanced . . . beyond.** The Gr. word for "advanced" means "to chop ahead," much like one would blaze a trail through a forest. Paul blazed his path in Judaism (cf. Phil. 3:5, 6), and because he saw Jewish Christians as obstacles to its advancement, he worked to cut them down.

d. **exceedingly zealous.** Paul demonstrated this by the extent to which he pursued and persecuted Christians (cf. Acts 8:1–3; 26:11).

e. **traditions of my fathers.** The oral teachings about OT law commonly known as the "Halakah." This collection of interpretations of the law eventually carried the same authority as, or even greater than, the law (Torah) itself. Its regulations were so hopelessly complex and burdensome that even the most astute rabbinical scholars could not master it by either interpretation or conduct.

f. **separated me from my mother's womb.** Paul is not talking about being born, separated physically from his mother, but being separated or set apart to God for service from the time of his birth. The phrase refers to God's election of Paul without regard for his personal merit or effort (cf. Is. 49:1; Jer. 1:5; Luke 1:13–17; Rom. 9:10–23).

g. **called me through His grace.** This refers to God's effectual call (see Rom. 1:7; 8:30). On the Damascus Road God actually brought Saul, whom He had already chosen, to salvation.

h. **reveal His Son in me.** Not only was Christ revealed to Paul on the Damascus Road, but in him as God gave him the life, light, and faith to believe in Him.

i. **preach Him among the Gentiles.** Paul's specific call to proclaim the gospel to non-Jews (see Acts 9:15; 26:15–18; cf. Rom. 1:13–16; 11:13; 15:18).

j. **confer with flesh and blood.** Paul did not look to Ananias or other Christians at Damascus for clarification of or addition to the revelation he received from Christ (Acts 9:19, 20).

k. **Jerusalem . . . Arabia . . . Damascus.** Rather than immediately travel to Jerusalem to be instructed by the apostles, Paul instead went to Nabatean Arabia, a wilderness desert that stretched E of Damascus down to the Sinai peninsula. After being prepared for ministry by the Lord, he returned to minister in nearby Damascus.

l. **three years.** The approximate time from Paul's conversion to his first journey to Jerusalem. During those years he made a visit to Damascus and resided in Arabia, under the instruction of the Lord. This visit is discussed in Acts 9:26–30 (see Acts 9:23).

m. **up to Jerusalem.** Travelers in Israel always speak of going up to Jerusalem because of its higher elevation (see Acts 18:22).

n. **Peter.** See Matt. 10:2. The apostle who was the personal companion of the Lord and the most powerful spokesman in the early years of the Jerusalem church (Acts 1–12).

with him fifteen days. But I saw none of the other apostles except ªJames, the Lord's brother. (Now concerning the things which I write to you, indeed, before God, I do not ᵇlie.)

Afterward I went into the regions of ᶜSyria and Cilicia. And I was unknown by face to the churches of Judea which were in Christ. But they were hearing only, "He who formerly persecuted us now preaches the faith which he once tried to destroy." And they ᵈglorified God in me.

47. VISIT TO JERUSALEM

Gal. 2:1–10

Then after ᵉfourteen years I went up again to Jerusalem with ᶠBarnabas, and also took ᵍTitus with me. And I went up ʰby revelation, and communicated to them that gospel which I preach among the Gentiles, but privately to ⁱthose

---

a. **James, the Lord's brother.** Cf. Gal. 2:9, 12; see Acts 15:13.

b. **lie.** The directness of this statement indicates that Paul had been accused by the Jewish legalists of being a liar, who was shameless or deluded.

c. **Syria and Cilicia.** See Acts 15:23; cf. Acts 9:30. This area included his home town of Tarsus. He was preaching in that region for several years. When word of revival in that area reached·Jerusalem, they sent Barnabas (see Acts 11:20–26). Paul stayed on in that region as a pastor in the church at Antioch. With Barnabas, they went from there on the first missionary journey (Acts 13:1–3), and afterward returned to Antioch (Acts 13:1–3) from where they were sent to the Jerusalem Council (Acts 14:26—15:4).

d. **they glorified God in me.** Proof that the gospel Paul preached was the same one the other apostles had taught the Judean believers.

e. **fourteen years . . . again to Jerusalem.** This was the period from the time of his first visit to Jerusalem (Gal. 1:18) to the one Paul refers to here, which probably was for the Jerusalem Council (Acts 15:1–22) called to resolve the issue of Gentile salvation. Linguistically, the word "again" need not refer to the next visit; it can just as easily mean "once again" without respect to how many visits took place in between. And in fact, Paul did visit Jerusalem during that 14-year period to deliver famine relief to the church there (Acts 11:27–30; 12:24, 25), but he does not refer to that visit here since it had no bearing on his apostolic authority.

f. **Barnabas.** See Acts 4:36. Paul's first ally who vouched for him before the apostles at Jerusalem (Acts 9:27), and became his traveling companion on his first missionary journey (Acts 13:2, 3).

g. **Titus.** A spiritual child of Paul and a co-worker (Titus 1:4, 5). As an uncircumcised Gentile, Titus was fitting proof of the effectiveness of Paul's ministry.

h. **by revelation.** This revelation from God was the voice of the Holy Spirit (see Acts 13:2–4). He refers to the divine commissioning of his visit in order to refute any suggestion by the Judaizers that they had sent Paul to Jerusalem to have the apostles correct his doctrine.

i. **those who were of reputation.** The 3 main leaders of the Jerusalem church: Peter, James (the Lord's brother, Gal. 1:19), and John (cf. Gal. 2:9). This phrase was typically used of authorities and implied a position of honor. Paul refers to them in a similar way two other

who were of reputation, lest by any means I [a]might run, or had run, in vain. Yet not even Titus who was with me, being a Greek, was [b]compelled to be circumcised. And this occurred because of [c]false brethren secretly brought in (who came in by stealth to spy out our [d]liberty which we have in Christ Jesus, that they might bring us into [e]bondage), to whom [f]we did not yield submission even for an hour, that the [g]truth of the gospel might continue with you.

But from [h]those who seemed to be something—whatever they were, it makes no difference to me; God shows [i]personal favoritism to no man—for those who seemed to be something added nothing to me. But [j]on the contrary, when they saw that the gospel [k]for the uncircumcised had been committed to me, as the gospel

---

times (Gal. 2:6, 9), suggesting a hint of sarcasm directed toward the Judaizers, who claimed they had apostolic approval for their doctrine and Paul did not. They had likely made a habit of exalting these 3 leaders at the expense of Paul.

a. **might run . . . in vain.** Paul hoped the Jerusalem leaders would support his ministry to the Gentiles and not soften their opposition to legalism. He did not want to see his ministry efforts wasted because of conflict with the other apostles.

b. **compelled to be circumcised.** At the core of the Judaizers' works system was the Mosaic prescription of circumcision (see Gen. 17:9–14; Rom. 4:9–12). They were teaching that there could be no salvation without circumcision (Acts 15:1, 5, 24). Paul and the apostles denied that and it was settled at the Jerusalem Council (Acts 15:1–22). See 5:2–12; 6:15; Rom. 4:10–12; 1 Cor. 7:19. As a true believer, Titus was living proof that circumcision and the Mosaic regulations were not prerequisites or necessary components of salvation. The apostles' refusal to require Titus' circumcision verified the church's rejection of the Judaizers' doctrine (cf. Timothy, Acts 16:1–3).

c. **false brethren.** The Judaizers, who pretended to be true Christians. Yet, their doctrine, because it claimed allegiance to Christ, was opposed to traditional Judaism, and because it demanded circumcision and obedience to the Mosaic law as prerequisites for salvation, was opposed to Christianity. **to spy out.** This Gr. word pictures spies or traitors entering by stealth into an enemy's camp. The Judaizers were Satan's undercover agents sent into the midst of the church to sabotage the true gospel.

d. **liberty.** Christians are free from the law as a means of salvation, from its external ceremonial regulations as a way of living, and from its curse for disobedience to the law—a curse that Christ bore for all believers (Gal. 3:13). This freedom is not, however, a license to sin (Rom. 6:18; Gal. 5:13; 1 Pet. 2:16).

e. **bondage.** Conveys the idea of absolute slavery to an impossible system of works righteousness.

f. **we did not yield.** Paul and Titus never budged from their position of salvation by grace alone through faith alone.

g. **truth of the gospel.** The true gospel as opposed to the different (Gal. 1:6–8) and false one propagated by the Judaizers (see Rom. 1:1).

h. **those who seemed to be something.** Another reference to Peter, James, and John.

i. **personal favoritism.** The unique privileges of the 12 did not make their apostleship more legitimate or authoritative than Paul's—Christ commissioned them all (cf. Rom. 2:11). Paul never saw himself as apostolically inferior (see 2 Cor. 12:11, 12).

j. **on the contrary.** The Judaizers claimed Paul was preaching a deviant gospel, but the apostles confirmed that he proclaimed the true gospel. It was the same gospel Peter proclaimed, but to a different audience.

k. **for the uncircumcised.** Better translated "to the uncircumcised." Paul preached the gospel primarily to the Gentiles (also to Jews in Gentile lands, as his pattern was to go to the synagogue first; cf. Acts 13:5).

for the ^acircumcised was to Peter (for ^bHe who worked effectively in Peter for the apostleship to the circumcised also worked effectively in me toward the Gentiles), and when ^cJames, Cephas, and John, who seemed to be ^dpillars, perceived the ^egrace that had been given to me, they gave me and Barnabas ^fthe right hand of fellowship, that ^gwe should go to the Gentiles and they to the circumcised. They desired only that we should ^hremember the poor, the very thing which I also was eager to do.

48. PAUL CONFRONTS PETER

Gal. 2:11–21

Now when Peter had come to ⁱAntioch, I withstood him to his face, because he was ^jto be blamed; for before ^kcertain men came from James, he would eat with the Gentiles; but when they came, he ^lwithdrew and separated himself,

---

a. **circumcised . . . Peter.** Peter's ministry was primarily to the Jews.

b. **He who worked effectively in Peter . . . in me.** The Holy Spirit, who has but one gospel, empowered both Peter and Paul in their ministries.

c. **James, Cephas, and John.** This James was Jesus' half-brother (Gal. 1:19), who had risen to a prominent role in the Jerusalem church. Cephas (Peter) and John (the brother of James the apostle, martyred in Acts 12:2), were two of Christ's closest companions and became the main apostles in the Jerusalem church (see Acts 2–12).

d. **pillars.** Emphasizing the role of James, Peter, and John in establishing and supporting the church.

e. **grace . . . given to me.** The only conclusion these leaders could make was that God's grace was responsible for the powerful preaching of the gospel and the building of the church through Paul's efforts.

f. **the right hand of fellowship.** In the Near East, this represented a solemn vow of friendship and a mark of partnership. This act signified the apostles' recognition of Paul as a teacher of the true gospel and a partner in ministry.

g. **we should go to the Gentiles.** Further confirmation of Paul's divine call to ministry and a blow to the Judaizers, since the apostles directed him to continue in his already flourishing ministry to the Gentiles.

h. **remember the poor.** A practical reminder for Paul and the growing ranks of Gentile Christians. The number of Christians in Jerusalem grew rapidly at first (cf. Acts 2:41–45; 6:1) and many who were visiting the city for the feast of Pentecost (Acts 2:1, 5) remained and never returned to their homes. While the believers initially shared their resources (Acts 2:45; 4:32–37), many had little money. For years the Jerusalem church was economically pressed. See Acts 11:29, 30.

i. **Antioch.** See Acts 11:19. The location of the first Gentile church.

j. **to be blamed.** Better translated, "stood condemned." Peter was guilty of sin by aligning himself with men he knew to be in error and because of the harm and confusion he caused his Gentile brethren.

k. **certain men . . . from James.** Peter, knowing the decision the Jerusalem Council had made (Acts 15:7–29), had been in Antioch for some time, eating with Gentiles. When Judaizers came, pretending to be sent by James, they lied, giving false claims of support from the apostles. Peter had already given up all Mosaic ceremony (Acts 10:9–22) and James had at times held only to some of it (Acts 21:18–26).

l. **withdrew.** The Gr. term refers to strategic military withdrawal. The verb's form may

[a]fearing those who were of the circumcision. And the [b]rest of the Jews also played the [c]hypocrite with him, so that even Barnabas was carried away with their hypocrisy.

But when I saw that they were not [d]straightforward about the truth of the gospel, I said to [e]Peter before them all, "If you, being a Jew, live in the [f]manner of Gentiles and not as the Jews, why do you [g]compel Gentiles to live as Jews? We who are Jews by nature, and not [h]sinners of the Gentiles, knowing that a man is not justified by the [i]works of the law but by faith in Jesus Christ, even we have believed in Christ Jesus, that we might be [j]justified by faith in Christ and not by the [k]works of the law; for by the works of the law no flesh shall be justified.

"But if, while we seek to be justified by Christ, [l]we ourselves also are found

imply that Peter's withdrawal was gradual and deceptive. To eat with the Judaizers and decline invitations to eat with the Gentiles, which he had previously done, meant that Peter was affirming the very dietary restrictions he knew God had abolished (Acts 10:15) and thus striking a blow at the gospel of grace.

a. **fearing those . . . of the circumcision.** The true motivation behind Peter's defection. He was afraid of losing popularity with the legalistic, Judaizing segment of people in the church, even though they were self-righteous hypocrites promoting a heretical doctrine.

b. **the rest of the Jews.** The Jewish believers in Antioch.

c. **hypocrite.** This Gr. word refers to an actor who wore a mask to depict a mood or certain character. In the spiritual sense, it refers to someone who masks his true character by pretending to be something he is not (cf. Matt. 6:1–6). They were committed to the gospel of grace, but pretended to accept Jewish legalism.

d. **straightforward.** Lit. to walk "straight" or "uprightly." By withdrawing from the Gentile Christians, Peter and the other Jewish believers were not walking in line with God's Word.

e. **Peter.** Paul's rebuke of Peter serves as one of the most dynamic statements in the NT on the absolute and unwavering necessity of the doctrine of justification by grace through faith (see Rom. 3:24). Peter's apparent repentance acknowledged Paul's apostolic authority and his own submission to the truth (cf. 2 Pet. 3:15, 16).

f. **manner of Gentiles.** Before his gradual withdrawal, Peter regularly had fellowship and ate with the Gentiles, thus modeling the ideal of Christian love and liberty between Jew and Gentile.

g. **compel Gentiles to live as Jews.** By his Judaizing mandate, he was declaring theirs was the right way.

h. **sinners of the Gentiles.** This is used in the legal sense since Gentiles were sinners by nature because they had no revealed divine written law to guide them toward salvation or living righteously.

i. **works . . . faith.** Three times in this verse Paul declares that salvation is only through faith in Christ and not by law. The first is general, "a man is not justified"; the second is personal, "we might be justified"; and the third is universal, "no flesh shall be justified."

j. **justified.** This basic forensic Gr. word describes a judge declaring an accused person not guilty and therefore innocent before the law. Throughout Scripture it refers to God's declaring a sinner not guilty and fully righteous before Him by imputing to him the divine righteousness of Christ and imputing the man's sin to his sinless Savior for punishment, (see Rom. 3:24; Phil. 3:8, 9).

k. **works of the law.** Keeping the law is a totally unacceptable means of salvation because the root of sinfulness is in the fallenness of man's heart, not his actions. The law served as a mirror to reveal sin, not a cure for it (see Gal. 3:22–24; Rom. 7:7–13; 1 Tim. 1:8–11).

l. **we . . . are found sinners.** If the Judaizers' doctrine was correct, then Paul, Peter, Barnabas, and the other Jewish believers fell back into the category of sinners because they had been eating and fellowshiping with Gentiles, who according to the Judaizers were unclean.

sinners, is Christ therefore a [a]minister of sin? Certainly not! For if I build again those [b]things which I destroyed, I make myself a transgressor. For I through the law [c]died to the law that I might live to God. [d]I have been crucified with Christ; it is no longer I who live, but [e]Christ lives in me; and the life which I now live in the flesh I live by faith in the Son of God, who loved me and [f]gave Himself for me. I do not set aside the grace of God; for if righteousness comes through the law, then [g]Christ died in vain."

49. JUSTIFICATION AND ABRAHAM

Gal. 3:1–9

O [h]foolish Galatians! [i]Who has [j]bewitched you that you should not obey the truth, before whose eyes Jesus Christ was [k]clearly portrayed among you as

---

a. **minister of sin.** If the Judaizers were right, then Christ was wrong and had been teaching people to sin because He taught that food could not contaminate a person (Mark 7:19; cf. Acts 10:13–15). He also declared that all who belong to Him are one with Him and therefore each other (John 17:21–23). Paul's airtight logic condemned Peter, because by his actions he had in effect made it appear as if Christ was lying. This thought is utterly objectionable and causes Paul to use the strongest Gr. negative ("certainly not"; cf. Gal. 3:21; Rom. 6:1, 2; 7:13).

b. **things which I destroyed.** The false system of salvation through legalism (see Gal. 1:13), done away with by the preaching of salvation by grace alone through faith alone.

c. **died to the law.** When a person is convicted of a capital crime and executed, the law has no further claim on him. So it is with the Christian who has died in Christ (who paid the penalty for his sins in full) and rises to new life in Him—justice has been satisfied and he is forever free from any further penalty.

d. **I have been crucified with Christ.** See Rom. 6:2–6. When a person trusts in Christ for salvation, he spiritually participates with the Lord in His crucifixion and His victory over sin and death.

e. **Christ lives in me.** The believer's old self is dead (see Eph. 4:22), having been crucified with Christ (Rom. 6:3, 5). The believer's new man has the privilege of the indwelling Christ empowering him and living through him (see Rom. 8:9, 10).

f. **gave Himself for me.** The manifestation of Christ's love for the believer through His sacrificial death on the cross (John 10:17, 18; Rom. 5:6–8; Eph. 5:25–30).

g. **Christ died in vain.** This can be better translated, "Christ died needlessly." Those who insist they can earn salvation by their own efforts undermine the foundation of Christianity and render unnecessary the death of Christ.

h. **foolish.** This refers not to lack of intelligence, but to lack of obedience (cf. Luke 24:25; 1 Tim. 6:9; Titus 3:3). Paul expressed his shock, surprise, and outrage at the Galatians' defection.

i. **Who . . . ?** The Judaizers, the Jewish false teachers were plaguing the Galatian churches.

j. **bewitched.** Charmed or misled by flattery and false promises. The term suggests an appeal to the emotions by the Judaizers.

k. **clearly portrayed.** The Gr. word describes the posting of official notices in public places. Paul's preaching had publicly displayed the true gospel of Jesus Christ before the Galatians.

ᵃcrucified? This only I want to learn from you: ᵇDid you receive the Spirit by the works of the law, or by the hearing of faith? ᶜAre you so foolish? Having ᵈbegun in the Spirit, are you now being made perfect by the flesh? Have you ᵉsuffered so ᶠmany things in vain—ᵍif indeed it was in vain?

Therefore He who supplies the Spirit to you and works miracles among you, does He do it by the works of the law, or by the hearing of faith?—just as ʰAbraham "believed God, and it was accounted to him for righteousness." Therefore know that only those who are of faith are ⁱsons of Abraham. And the ʲScripture, foreseeing that God would justify the Gentiles by faith, ᵏpreached the gospel to Abraham beforehand, saying, "In you all the nations shall be blessed." So then ˡthose who are of faith are blessed with believing Abraham.

---

a. **crucified.** The crucifixion of Christ was a one time historical fact with continuing results into eternity. Christ's sacrificial death provides eternal payment for believers' sins (cf. Heb. 7:25), and does not need to be supplemented by any human works.

b. **Did you receive the Spirit . . . ?** The answer to Paul's rhetorical question is obvious. The Galatians had received the Spirit when they were saved (Rom. 8:9; 1 Cor. 12:13; 1 John 3:24; 4:13), not through keeping the law, but through saving faith granted when hearing the gospel (cf. Rom. 10:17). The hearing of faith is actually hearing with faith. Paul appealed to the Galatians' own salvation to refute the Judaizers' false teaching that keeping the law is necessary for salvation.

c. **Are you so foolish?** Incredulous at how easily the Galatians had been duped, Paul asked a second rhetorical question, again rebuking them for their foolishness.

d. **begun in the Spirit . . . by the flesh.** The notion that sinful, weak (Matt. 26:41; Rom. 6:19), fallen human nature could improve on the saving work of the Holy Spirit was ludicrous to Paul.

e. **suffered.** The Gr. word has the basic meaning of "experienced," and does not necessarily imply pain or hardship. Paul used it to describe the Galatians' personal experience of salvation in Jesus Christ.

f. **many things.** This refers to all the blessings of salvation from God, Christ, and the Holy Spirit (cf. Eph. 1:3).

g. **if indeed it was in vain.** See Luke 8:13; Acts 8:13, 21; 1 Cor. 15:2; 2 Cor. 6:1; 13:5, 6.

h. **Abraham.** As he does in Romans (see Rom. 4:3), Paul uses Abraham as proof that there has never been any other way of salvation than by grace through faith. Even the OT teaches justification by faith.

i. **sons of Abraham.** Quoted from Gen. 15:6. Believing Jews and Gentiles are the true spiritual children of Abraham because they follow his examples of faith (cf. Gal. 3:29; Rom. 4:11, 16).

j. **Scripture, foreseeing.** Personifying the Scriptures was a common Jewish figure of speech (cf. Gal. 4:30; John 7:38, 42; 19:37; Rom. 9:17; 10:11; 11:2; 1 Tim. 5:18). Because Scripture is God's Word, when it speaks, God speaks.

k. **preached the gospel to Abraham.** The "good news" to Abraham was the news of salvation for all the nations (quoted from Gen. 12:3; 18:18). See Gen. 22:18; John 8:56; Acts 26:22, 23. Salvation has always, in every age, been by faith.

l. **those who are of faith . . . Abraham.** Whether Jew or Gentile. The OT predicted that Gentiles would receive the blessings of justification by faith, as did Abraham. Those blessings are poured out on all because of Christ (cf. John 1:16; Rom. 8:32; Eph. 1:3; 2:6, 7; Col. 2:10; 1 Pet. 3:9; 2 Pet. 1:3, 4).

50. JUSTIFICATION AND THE LAW

Gal. 3:10–24

For [a]as many as are of the works of the law are [b]under the curse; for it is written, "Cursed is everyone who does not continue in [c]all things which are written in the book of the law, to do them." But that no one is [d]justified by the law in the sight of God is evident, for [e]"the just shall live by faith." Yet [f]the law is not of faith, but "the man who does them shall live by them."

[g]Christ has redeemed us from the curse of the law, [h]having become a curse for us (for [i]it is written, "Cursed is everyone who hangs on a tree"), that the [j]blessing of Abraham might come upon the Gentiles in Christ Jesus, that we might receive the [k]promise of the Spirit through faith.

[l] Brethren, I speak in the [m]manner of men: Though it is only a man's covenant, yet if it is confirmed, no one annuls or adds to it. Now to Abraham

---

a. **as many as are of the works of the law.** Those attempting to earn salvation by keeping the law.

b. **under the curse.** Quoted from Deut. 27:26 to show that failure to perfectly keep the law brings divine judgment and condemnation. One violation of the law deserves the curse of God. Cf. Deut. 27, 28.

c. **all things.** See James 2:10. No one can keep all the commands of the law—not even strict Pharisees like Saul of Tarsus (Rom. 7:7–12).

d. **justified.** Made righteous before God. See Rom. 3:24.

e. **the just shall live by faith.** See Rom. 1:17. Paul's earlier OT quote (cf. Deut. 27:26) showed that justification does not come from keeping the law; this quote from Hab. 2:4 shows that justification is by faith alone (cf. Heb. 10:38).

f. **the law is not of faith.** Justification by faith and justification by keeping the law are mutually exclusive, as Paul's OT quote from Lev. 18:5 proves.

g. **Christ has redeemed us from the curse of the law.** The Gr. word translated "redeemed" was often used to speak of buying a slave's or debtor's freedom. Christ's death, because it was a death of substitution for sin, satisfied God's justice and exhausted His wrath toward His elect, so that Christ actually purchased believers from slavery to sin and from the sentence of eternal death (4:5; Titus 2:14; 1 Pet. 1:18; cf. Rom. 3:24; 1 Cor. 1:30; Eph. 1:7; Col. 1:14; Heb. 9:12).

h. **having become a curse for us.** By bearing God's wrath for believers' sins on the cross (see 2 Cor. 5:21; cf. Heb. 9:28; 1 Pet. 2:24; 3:18), Christ took upon Himself the curse pronounced on those who violated the law (see v. 10).

i. **it is written.** The common NT way (61 times) of introducing OT quotes, (see Rom. 3:10). Deut. 21:23 is quoted.

j. **the blessing of Abraham.** Faith in God's promise of salvation.

k. **promise of the Spirit.** From God the Father. Cf. Is. 32:15; 44:3; 59:19–21; Ezek. 36:26, 27; 37:14; 39:29; Joel 2:28, 29; Luke 11:13; 24:49; John 7:37–39; 14:16, 26.

l. **Brethren.** This term of endearment reveals Paul's compassionate love for the Galatians—which they may have begun to question in light of his stern rebuke.

m. **manner of man . . . man's covenant.** Even human covenants, once confirmed, are considered irrevocable and unchangeable, how much more a covenant made by an unchanging God (Mal. 3:6; James 1:17).

and his [a]Seed were the [b]promises made. He does not say, "And to seeds," as of many, but as of one, "And to your Seed," who is Christ. And this I say, that the law, which was [c]four hundred and thirty years later, cannot annul [d]the covenant that was [e]confirmed before by God in Christ, that it should make the promise of no effect. For if the [f]inheritance is of the law, it is no longer of promise; but God gave it to Abraham by promise.

What purpose then does the law serve? It [g]was added because of transgressions, till the Seed should come to whom the promise was made; and it was appointed [h]through angels by the hand of a mediator. Now a [i]mediator does not mediate for one only, but God is one.

Is the law then against the promises of God? [j]Certainly not! For if there

---

a. **Seed.** The quote is from Gen. 12:7. The singular form of the Heb. word, like its Eng. and Gr. counterparts, can be used in a collective sense. Paul's point is that in some OT passages (e.g., Gen. 3:15; 22:18), "seed" refers to the greatest of Abraham's descendants, Jesus Christ.

b. **promises.** Those associated with the Abrahamic Covenant (Gen. 12:3, 7; 13:15, 16; 15:5, 18; 17:8; 22:16–18; 26:3, 4; 28:13, 14). Because they were made both to Abraham and his descendants, they did not become void when Abraham died, or when the law came.

c. **four hundred and thirty years.** From Israel's sojourn in Egypt (cf. Ex. 12:40) to the giving of the law at Sinai (ca. 1445 B.C.) The law actually came 645 years after the initial promise to Abraham (ca. 2090 B.C.; cf. Gen. 12:4; 21:5; 25:26; 47:9), but the promise was repeated to Isaac (Gen. 26:24) and later to Jacob (ca. 1928 B.C.; Gen. 28:15). The last known reaffirmation of the Abrahamic Covenant to Jacob occurred in Gen. 46:2–4 (ca. 1875 B.C.) just before he went to Egypt—430 years before the Mosaic law was given.

d. **the covenant.** The Abrahamic Covenant.

e. **confirmed before by God.** The term means "ratified." Once God ratified the covenant officially (see Gen. 15:9–21), it had lasting authority so that nothing and no one could annul it. The Abrahamic Covenant was unilateral (God made the promise to Himself), eternal (it provided for everlasting blessing), irrevocable (it will never cease), unconditional (in that it depended on God, not man), but its complete fulfillment awaits the salvation of Israel and the millennial kingdom of Jesus Christ.

f. **inheritance.** Paul again emphasized that there is no middle ground between law (works) and promise (grace); the two principles are mutually exclusive ways of salvation (cf. Rom 4:14). An "inheritance" by definition is something granted, not worked for, as proven in the case of Abraham.

g. **was added because of transgressions.** Paul's persuasive argument that the promise is superior to the law raises an obvious question: What was the purpose of the law? Paul's answer is that the law reveals man's utter sinfulness, inability to save himself, and desperate need of a Savior—it was never intended to be the way of salvation (cf. Rom. 7:1–13).

h. **through angels.** The Bible teaches that angels were involved in the giving of the law (cf. Acts 7:53; Heb. 2:2), but does not explain the precise role they played.

i. **mediator.** Paul's point is apparently that a "mediator" is required when more than one party is involved, but God alone ratified the covenant with Abraham (see Gen. 15:7–21).

j. **Certainly not!** Paul uses the strongest Gr. negative (see Gal. 2:17) to disdain the idea that the law and the promise are at opposite purposes. Since God gave them both and does not work against Himself, law and promise work in harmony; the law reveals man's sinfulness and need for the salvation freely offered in the promise. If the law could have provided righteousness and eternal life, there would be no gracious promise.

had been a law given which could have given life, truly righteousness would have been by the law. But the Scripture has ªconfined all under sin, that the promise by faith in Jesus Christ might be given to those who believe. But ᵇbefore faith came, we were ᶜkept under guard by the law, kept for ᵈthe faith which would afterward be revealed. Therefore the law was our ᵉtutor to bring us to Christ, that we might be justified by faith.

51. THE SONSHIP OF BELIEVERS
Gal. 3:25—4:7

But after faith has come, we are no longer under a tutor. For you are all ᶠsons of God through faith in Christ Jesus. For as many of you as were ᵍbaptized into Christ have ʰput on Christ. There is neither Jew nor Greek, there is

---

a. **confined all under sin.** The Gr. verb translated "confined" means "to enclose on all sides." Paul portrays all mankind as hopelessly trapped in sin, like a school of fish caught in a net. That all people are sinners is the express teaching of Scripture (see Rom. 3:19; cf. 1 Kin. 8:46; Ps. 143:2; Prov. 20:9; Eccl. 7:20; Is. 53:6; Rom. 3:9–19, 23; 11:32).

b. **before faith came.** From the viewpoints of both the history of redemption and through all times in the area of individual salvation (cf. Gal. 3:19, 24, 25; 4:1–4), only saving faith unlocks the door of the prison where the law keeps men bound.

c. **kept under guard by the law.** Paul personifies the law as a jailer of guilty, condemned sinners, on death row awaiting God's judgment (Rom. 6:23).

d. **the faith which would afterward be revealed.** Again Paul was looking at the coming of Christ, historically and at each believer's salvation, individually. Faith in Christ alone releases people from bondage to law, whether the Mosaic law, or the law written on the hearts of Gentiles (Rom. 2:14–16).

e. **tutor.** The Gr. word denotes a slave whose duty it was to take care of a child until adulthood. The "tutor" escorted the children to and from school and watched over their behavior at home. Tutors were often strict disciplinarians, causing those under their care to yearn for the day when they would be free from their tutor's custody. The law was our tutor which, by showing us our sins, was escorting us to Christ.

f. **sons of God.** While God is the Father of all people in a general sense because He created them (Acts 17:24–28), only those who have put their faith in Jesus Christ are God's true spiritual children. Unbelievers are the children of Satan (Matt. 13:38; John 8:38, 41, 44; Acts 13:10; 1 John 3:10; cf. Eph. 2:3; 1 John 5:19). Believers, through faith in Jesus Christ, have come of age as God's children. Thus, they are not under the tutelage of the law (Rom. 6:14), although they are still obligated to obey God's holy and unchanging righteous standards which are now given authority in the New Covenant (Gal. 6:2; Rom. 8:4; 1 Cor. 9:21).

g. **baptized into Christ.** This is not water baptism, which cannot save (see Acts 2:38; 22:16). Paul used the word "baptized" in a metaphorical manner to speak of being "immersed," or "placed into" Christ (cf. 2:20) by the spiritual miracle of union with Him in His death and resurrection. See Rom. 6:3–5; cf. 1 Cor. 6:17.

h. **put on Christ.** The result of the believer's spiritual union with Christ. Paul was emphasizing the fact that we have been united with Christ through salvation. Positionally before God,

neither slave nor free, there is neither male nor female; for ᵃyou are all one in Christ Jesus. And if you are Christ's, then you are ᵇAbraham's seed, and ᶜheirs according to the promise.

Now I say that the heir, as long as he is a ᵈchild, does not differ at all from a slave, though he is master of all, but is under ᵉguardians and stewards until the time appointed by the father. Even so we, ᶠwhen we were children, were in bondage under ᵍthe elements of the world. But when ʰthe fullness of the time had come, ⁱGod

---

we have put on Christ, His death, resurrection, and righteousness (see Phil. 3:8–10). Practically, we need to "put on Christ" before men, in our conduct (Rom. 13:14).

a. **you are all one in Christ Jesus.** All those who are one with Jesus Christ are one with each other. This verse does not deny that God has designed for racial, social, and sexual distinctions among Christians, but it affirms that those do not imply spiritual inequality before God. Nor is this spiritual equality incompatible with the God-ordained roles of headship and submission in the church, society, and at home. Jesus Christ, though fully equal with the Father, assumed a submissive role during His incarnation (Phil. 2:5–8).

b. **Abraham's seed.** Not all physical children of Abraham are the "Israel of God" (cf. Gal. 6:16), that is, true spiritual children of Abraham (Rom. 9:6–8). Gentile believers who are not physical children of Abraham are, however, his spiritual children in the sense that they followed the pattern of his faith (see Rom. 4:11).

c. **heirs according to the promise.** All believers are heirs of the spiritual blessing that accompanied the Abrahamic Covenant—justification by faith (Gen. 15:6; cf. Rom. 4:3–11).

d. **child.** The Gr. word refers to a child too young to talk; a minor, spiritually and intellectually immature and not ready for the privileges and responsibilities of adulthood. Paul expands on the analogy of a child's coming of age (cf. Gal. 3:24–26), contrasting believers' lives before salvation (as children and servants), with their lives after salvation (as adults and sons). Both Paul's Jewish and Gentile readers readily understood this imagery, since the Jews, Greeks, and Romans all had a ceremony to mark a child's coming of age.

e. **guardians and stewards.** "Guardians" were slaves entrusted with the care of underage boys, while "stewards" managed their property for them until they came of age. Along with the tutor (Gal. 3:24), they had almost complete charge of the child—so that, for all practical purposes, a child under their care did not differ from a slave.

f. **when we were children . . . in bondage.** Before our "coming of age" when we came to saving faith in Jesus Christ.

g. **the elements of the world.** "Elements" is from a Gr. word meaning "row," or "rank," and was used to speak of basic, foundational things like the letters of the alphabet. In light of its use in v. 9, it is best to see it here as a reference to the basic elements and rituals of human religion (see Col. 2:8). Paul describes both Jewish and Gentile religions as elemental because they are merely human, never rising to the level of the divine. Both Jewish religion and Gentile religion centered on man-made systems of works. They were filled with laws and ceremonies to be performed so as to achieve divine acceptance. All such rudimentary elements are immature, like behaviors of children under bondage to a guardian.

h. **the fullness of the time.** In God's timetable, when the exact religious, cultural, and political conditions demanded by His perfect plan were in place, Jesus came into the world.

i. **God sent forth His Son.** As a father set the time for the ceremony of his son becoming of age and being released from the guardians, stewards, and tutors, so God sent His Son at the precise moment to bring all who believe out from under bondage to the law—a truth Jesus repeatedly affirmed (John 5:30, 36, 37; 6:39, 44, 57; 8:16, 18, 42; 12:49; 17:21, 25; 20:21). That the Father sent Jesus into the world teaches His pre-existence as the eternal second member of the Trinity. See Phil. 2:6, 7; Heb. 1:3–5; cf. Rom. 8:3, 4.

sent forth His Son, [a]born of a woman, born [b]under the law, to redeem [c]those who were under the law, that we might receive [d]the adoption as sons.

And because you are sons, God has sent forth the [e]Spirit of His Son into your hearts, crying out, [f]"Abba, Father!" Therefore you are no longer a slave but a son, and if a son, then an heir of God through Christ.

52. THE FUTILITY OF RITUALISM
Gal. 4:8–20

But then, indeed, [g]when you did not know God, you served those which [h]by nature are not gods. [i]But now after you have known God, or rather are [j]known

---

a. **born of a woman.** This emphasizes Jesus' full humanity, not merely His virgin birth (Is. 7:14; Matt. 1:20–25). Jesus had to be fully God for His sacrifice to be of the infinite worth needed to atone for sin. But, He also had to be fully man so He could take upon Himself the penalty of sin as the substitute for man. See Luke 1:32, 35; John 1:1, 14, 18.

b. **under the law.** Like all men, Jesus was obligated to obey God's law. Unlike anyone else, however, He perfectly obeyed that law (John 8:46; 2 Cor. 5:21; Heb. 4:15; 7:26; 1 Pet. 2:22; 1 John 3:5). His sinlessness made Him the unblemished sacrifice for sins, who "fulfilled all righteousness," i.e., perfectly obeyed God in everything. That perfect righteousness is what is imputed to those who believe in Him.

c. **those . . . under the law.** Guilty sinners who are under the law's demands and its curses (see Gal. 3:10, 13) and in need of a savior (see Gal. 3:23).

d. **the adoption as sons.** "Adoption" is the act of bringing someone who is the offspring of another into one's own family. Since unregenerate people are by nature children of the devil (see Gal. 3:26), the only way they can become God's children is by spiritual adoption (Rom. 8:15, 23; Eph. 1:5).

e. **Spirit of His Son.** It is the Holy Spirit's work to confirm to believers their adoption as God's children (see Rom. 8:15). Assurance of salvation is a gracious work of the Holy Spirit and does not come from any human source.

f. **Abba.** An Aram. term of endearment, used by young children to speak to their fathers; the equivalent of the word "Daddy" (see Rom. 8:15).

g. **when you did not know God.** Before coming to saving faith in Christ, no unsaved person knows God. See Eph. 4:17–19; 2 Cor. 4:3–6.

h. **by nature are not gods.** The Greco-Roman pantheon of nonexistent deities the Galatians had imagined they worshiped before their conversion (cf. Rom. 1:23; 1 Cor. 8:4; 10:19, 20; 12:2; 1 Thess. 1:9).

i. **But now after.** While salvation is the free gift of God (Rom. 5:15, 16, 18; 6:23; Eph. 2:8), it brings with it serious responsibility (cf. Luke 12:48). God requires believers to live a holy life because they are children of a holy God and desire to love and worship Him (Matt. 5:48; 1 Pet. 1:15–18). That obligation was to the unchanging moral and spiritual principles that forever reflect the nature of God; however, it did not include the rituals and ceremonies unique to Israel under Mosaic law as the Judaizers falsely claimed.

j. **known by God.** We can know God only because He first knew us, just as we choose Him only because He first chose us (John 6:44; 15:16), and we love Him only because He first loved us (1 John 4:19).

by God, how is it that you turn again to the weak and beggarly elements, to which you desire again to be in bondage? You observe ᵃdays and months and seasons and years. I am afraid for you, lest I have ᵇlabored for you in vain.

Brethren, I urge you to ᶜbecome like me, for I became like you. ᵈYou have not injured me at all. You know that because of ᵉphysical infirmity I preached the gospel to you at the first. And my trial which was in my flesh you did not despise or reject, but ᶠyou received me as an angel of God, even as Christ Jesus. What then was the ᵍblessing you enjoyed? For I bear you witness that, if possible, you would have ʰplucked out your own eyes and given them to me. Have I therefore become ⁱyour enemy because I tell you the truth?

They ʲzealously court you, but for no good; yes, they want to exclude you,

---

a. **days . . . years.** The rituals, ceremonies, and festivals of the Jewish religious calendar which God had given, but were never required for the church. Paul warns the Galatians, as he did the Colossians (see Rom. 14:1–6; Col. 2:16, 17), against legalistically observing them as if they were required by God or could earn favor with Him.

b. **labored . . . in vain.** Paul feared that his effort in establishing and building the Galatian churches might prove to be futile if they fell back into legalism (cf. Gal. 3:4; 1 Thess. 3:5).

c. **become like me, for I became like you.** Paul had been a proud, self-righteous Pharisee, trusting in his own righteousness to save him (cf. Phil. 3:4–6). But when he came to Christ, he abandoned all efforts to save himself, trusting wholly in God's grace (Phil. 3:7–9). He urged the Galatians to follow his example and avoid the legalism of the Judaizers.

d. **You have not injured me.** Though the Jews persecuted him when he first went to Galatia, the Galatian believers had not harmed Paul, but had enthusiastically received him when he preached the gospel to them (cf. Acts 13:42–50; 14:19). How, he asked, could they reject him now?

e. **physical infirmity.** Some think the illness Paul refers to was malaria, possibly contracted in the coastal lowlands of Pamphylia. That could explain why Paul and Barnabas apparently did not preach at Perga, a city in Pamphylia (cf. Acts 13:13, 14). The cooler and healthier weather in Galatia and especially at Pisidian Antioch (3,600 ft. above sea level), where Paul went when he left Perga, would have brought some relief to the fever caused by malaria. Although malaria is a serious, debilitating disease, its attacks are not continuous; Paul could have ministered between bouts with fever.

f. **you received me.** The Galatians welcomed Paul in spite of his illness, which in no way was a barrier to his credibility or acceptance.

g. **blessing you enjoyed.** "Blessing" can also be translated "happiness," or "satisfaction." Paul points out that the Galatians had been happy and content with his gospel preaching (cf. Acts 13:48) and wonders why they had turned against him.

h. **plucked out your own eyes.** This may be a figure of speech (cf. Matt. 5:29; 18:9), or an indication that Paul's bodily illness (see Gal. 4:13) had somehow affected his eyes (cf. Gal. 6:11). In either case, it reflects the great love the Galatians had initially expressed for the apostle.

i. **your enemy.** The Galatians had become so confused that, in spite of their previous affection for Paul, some had come to regard him as their enemy. The apostle reminds them that he had not harmed them, but merely told them the truth—a truth that had once brought them great joy.

j. **zealously.** With a serious concern, or warm interest (the same word is used in Gal. 1:14 to describe Paul's former zeal for Judaism). The Judaizers appeared to have a genuine interest in the Galatians, but their true motive was to exclude the Galatians from God's gracious salvation and win recognition for themselves.

that you may be zealous for them. But it is good to be zealous in a good thing always, and [a]not only when I am present with you. [b]My little children, for whom I labor in birth again [c]until Christ is formed in you, I would like to be present with you now and to change my tone; for I have [d]doubts about you.

53. THE ILLUSTRATION FROM SCRIPTURE
Gal. 4:21–31

Tell me, you who desire to be under the law, do you not hear the law? For [e]it is written that Abraham had [f]two sons: the one by a bondwoman, the other by a freewoman. But he who was of the bondwoman was born [g]according to the flesh, and he of the freewoman [h]through promise, which things are [i]symbolic. For these are the [j]two covenants: the one from Mount Sinai which gives birth

---

a. **not only when I am present.** Paul encouraged the Galatians to have the same zeal for the true gospel of grace that they had had when he was with them.

b. **My little children.** Paul's only use of this affectionate phrase, which John uses frequently (1 John 2:1, 18, 28; 3:7, 18; 4:4; 5:21).

c. **until Christ is formed in you.** In contrast to the evil motives of the Judaizers (see Gal. 3:1), Paul sought to bring the Galatians to Christlikeness. This is the goal of salvation (see Rom. 8:29).

d. **doubts.** The verb means "to be at wits end."

e. **it is written.** Paul, continuing to contrast grace and law, faith and works, employs an OT story as an analogy or illustration of what he has been teaching.

f. **two sons.** Ishmael, son of Sarah's Egyptian maid Hagar (Gen. 16:1–16), and Isaac, Sarah's son (Gen 21:1–7).

g. **according to the flesh.** Ishmael's birth was motivated by Abraham and Sarah's lack of faith in God's promise and fulfilled by sinful human means.

h. **through promise.** God miraculously enabled Abraham and Sarah to have Isaac when Sarah was well past childbearing age and had been barren her entire life.

i. **symbolic.** The Gr. word was used of a story that conveyed a meaning beyond the literal sense of the words. In this passage, Paul uses historical people and places from the OT to illustrate spiritual truth. This is not an allegory, nor are there any allegories in Scripture. An allegory is a fictional story where real truth is the secret, mysterious, hidden meaning. The story of Abraham, Sarah, Hagar, Ishmael, and Isaac is actual history and has no secret or hidden meaning. Paul uses it only as an illustration to support his contrast between law and grace.

j. **two covenants.** Paul uses the two mothers, their two sons, and two locations as a further illustration of two covenants. Hagar, Ishmael, and Mt. Sinai (earthly Jerusalem) represent the covenant of law; Sarah, Isaac and the heavenly Jerusalem the covenant of promise. However, Paul cannot be contrasting these two covenants as different ways of salvation, one way for OT saints, another for NT saints—a premise he has already denied (Gal. 2:16; 3:10–14, 21, 22). The purpose of the Mosaic Covenant was only to show all who were under its demands and condemnation their desperate need for salvation by grace alone (Gal. 3:24)—it was never intended to portray the way of salvation. Paul's point is that those, like the Judaizers, who attempt to earn righteousness by keeping the law receive only bondage and condemnation

to bondage, which is ªHagar—for this Hagar is ᵇMount Sinai in Arabia, and ᶜcorresponds to Jerusalem which now is, and is in bondage with her children—but the ᵈJerusalem above is free, which is ᵉthe mother of us all. For ᶠit is written:

> "Rejoice, O barren,
> You who do not bear!
> Break forth and shout,
> You who are not in labor!
> For the desolate has many more children
> Than she who has a husband."

Now we, brethren, as Isaac was, are ᵍchildren of promise. But, as he who was born according to the flesh then ʰpersecuted him who was born according to the Spirit, ⁱeven so it is now. Nevertheless what does the Scripture say? ʲ"Cast out the bondwoman and her son, for the son of the bondwoman shall not be heir with the son of the freewoman." So then, brethren, we are not children of the bondwoman but of the free.

(Gal. 3:10, 23). While those who partake of salvation by grace—the only way of salvation since Adam's sin—are freed from the law's bondage and condemnation.

a. **Hagar.** Since she was Sarah's slave (Gen. 16:1), Hagar is a fitting illustration of those under bondage to the law (cf. Gal. 3:23; 4:5, 21). She was actually associated with Mt. Sinai through her son Ishmael, whose descendants settled in that region.

b. **Mount Sinai.** An appropriate symbol for the old covenant, since it was at Mt. Sinai that Moses received the law (Ex. 19).

c. **corresponds to Jerusalem.** The law was given at Sinai and received its highest expression in the temple worship at Jerusalem. The Jewish people were still in bondage to the law.

d. **Jerusalem above is free.** Heaven (Heb. 12:18, 22). Those who are citizens of heaven (Phil. 3:20) are free from the Mosaic law, works, bondage, and trying endlessly and futilely to please God by the flesh.

e. **the mother.** Believers are children of the heavenly Jerusalem, the "mother-city" of heaven. In contrast to the slavery of Hagar's children, believers in Christ are free (Gal. 5:1; cf. Is. 61:1; Luke 4:18; John 8:36; Rom. 6:18, 22; 8:2; 2 Cor. 3:17).

f. **it is written.** Paul applies the passage from Is. 54:1 to the Jerusalem above.

g. **children of promise.** Just as Isaac inherited the promises made to Abraham (Gen. 26:1–3), so also are believers the recipients of God's redemptive promises (1 Cor. 3:21–23; Eph. 1:3), because they are spiritual heirs of Abraham (see Gal. 3:29).

h. **persecuted him who was born according to the Spirit.** Isaac, whom Ishmael mocked at the feast celebrating Isaac's weaning (see Gen. 21:8, 9).

i. **even so it is now.** Ishmael's descendants (Arabs) have always persecuted Isaac's (Jews). So unbelievers have always persecuted believers (cf. Matt. 5:11; 10:22–25; Mark 10:30; John 15:19, 20; 16:2, 33; 17:14; Acts 14:22; 2 Tim. 3:12; Heb. 11:32–37; 1 Pet. 2:20, 21; 3:14; 4:12–14).

j. **Cast out the bondwoman.** Quoted from Gen. 21:10 to illustrate that those who are attempting to be justified on the basis of keeping the law will be cast out of God's presence forever (Matt. 8:12; 22:12, 13; 25:30; Luke 13:28; 2 Thess. 1:9).

54. Freedom from Legalistic Ritual
Gal. 5:1–12

[a]Stand fast therefore in the liberty by which Christ has made us [b]free, and do not be [c]entangled again with a [d]yoke of bondage. Indeed I, Paul, say to you that if you become [e]circumcised, [f]Christ will profit you nothing. And I testify again to every man who becomes circumcised that he is a [g]debtor to keep the whole law. You have become [h]estranged from Christ, you who attempt to be justified by law; you have fallen from grace. For we through the Spirit eagerly wait for [i]the hope of righteousness by faith. For in Christ Jesus neither circumcision nor uncircumcision avails anything, but faith working through love.[j]

---

a. **Stand fast.** Stay where you are, Paul asserts, because of the benefit of being free from law and the flesh as a way of salvation and the fullness of blessing by grace.

b. **free.** Deliverance from the curse that the law pronounces on the sinner who has been striving unsuccessfully to achieve his own righteousness (Gal. 3:13, 22–26; 4:1–7), but who has now embraced Christ and the salvation granted to him by grace (see Gal. 2:4; 4:26; cf. Rom. 7:3; 8:2).

c. **entangled again.** Better translated "to be burdened by," "to be oppressed by," or "to be subject to," because of its connection with a yoke.

d. **yoke of bondage.** "Yoke" refers to the apparatus used to control a domesticated animal. The Jews referred to the "yoke of the law" as a good thing, the essence of true religion. Paul argued that for those who pursued it as a way of salvation, the law was a yoke of slavery. See Matt. 11:29, 30.

e. **circumcised.** Paul had no objection to circumcision itself (cf. Acts 16:1–3; Phil. 3:5). But he objected to the notion that it had some spiritual benefit or merit with God and was a prerequisite or necessary component of salvation. Circumcision had meaning in Israel when it was a physical symbol of a cleansed heart (cf. Deut. 30:6; Jer. 4:4; 9:24–26) and served as a reminder of God's covenant of salvation promise (Gen. 17:9, 10).

f. **Christ . . . profit you nothing.** The atoning sacrifice of Christ cannot benefit anyone who trusts in law and ceremony for salvation.

g. **a debtor to keep the whole law.** God's standard is perfect righteousness, thus a failure to keep only one part of the law falls short of the standard.

h. **estranged from Christ . . . fallen from grace.** The Gr. word for "estranged" means "to be separated," or "to be severed." The word for "fallen" means "to lose one's grasp on something." Paul's clear meaning is that any attempt to be justified by the law is to reject salvation by grace alone through faith alone. Those once exposed to the gracious truth of the gospel, who then turn their backs on Christ (Heb. 6:4–6) and seek to be justified by the law are separated from Christ and lose all prospects of God's gracious salvation. Their desertion of Christ and the gospel only proves that their faith was never genuine (cf. Luke 8:13, 14; 1 John 2:19).

i. **the hope of righteousness by faith.** Christians already possess the imputed righteousness of Christ, but they still await the completed and perfected righteousness that is yet to come at glorification (Rom. 8:18, 21).

j. **faith working through love.** Saving faith proves its genuine character by works of love. The one who lives by faith is internally motivated by love for God and Christ (cf. Matt. 22:37–40), which supernaturally issues forth in reverent worship, genuine obedience, and self-sacrificing love for others.

^aYou ran well. Who hindered you from ^bobeying the truth? ^cThis persuasion does not come from Him who calls you. ^dA little leaven leavens the whole lump. I have ^econfidence in you, in the Lord, that you will have no other mind; but he who troubles you shall bear his ^fjudgment, whoever he is.

And I, brethren, if I ^gstill preach circumcision, why do I still suffer persecution? Then the ^hoffense of the cross has ceased. I could wish that those who trouble you would even ⁱcut themselves off!

55. Freedom in the Spirit

Gal. 5:13–26

For you, brethren, have been called to liberty; only do not use liberty as an ^jopportunity for the flesh, but through love ^kserve one another.

a. **You ran well.** Cf. Gal. 3:3. Paul compares the Galatians' life of faith with a race, a figure he used frequently (2:2; Rom. 9:16; 1 Cor. 9:24). They had a good beginning—they had received the gospel message by faith and had begun to live their Christian lives by faith as well.

b. **obeying the truth.** See 1 Peter 1:22. A reference to believers' true way of living, including both their response to the true gospel in salvation (cf. Acts 6:7; Rom. 2:8; 6:17; 2 Thess. 1:8), and their consequent response to obey the Word of God in sanctification. Paul wrote more about salvation and sanctification being a matter of obedience in Rom. 1:5; 6:16, 17; 16:26. The legalistic influence of the Judaizers prevented the unsaved from responding in faith to the gospel of grace and true believers from living by faith.

c. **This persuasion.** Salvation by works. God does not promote legalism. Any doctrine that claims His gracious work is insufficient to save is false (see Gal. 1:6, 7).

d. **leaven.** A common axiomatic saying (cf. 1 Cor. 5:6) regarding the influence of yeast in dough. Leaven is often used in Scripture to denote sin (Matt. 16:6, 12) because of its permeating power.

e. **confidence in you.** Paul expresses encouraging assurance that the Lord will be faithful to keep His own from falling into the gross heresy. See John 6:39, 40; 10:28, 29; Rom. 8:31–39; Phil. 1:6, 7. They will persevere and be preserved (Jude 24).

f. **judgment.** All false teachers will incur strict and devastating eternal condemnation. See 2 Pet. 2:2, 3, 9.

g. **still preach circumcision.** Apparently the Judaizers had falsely claimed that Paul agreed with their teaching. But he makes the point that if he was preaching circumcision as necessary for salvation, why were the Judaizers persecuting him instead of supporting him?

h. **offense of the cross.** The Gr. word for "offense" can mean "trap," "snare," or "stumbling block." Any offer of salvation that strips man of the opportunity to earn it by his own merit breeds opposition (cf. Rom. 9:33).

i. **cut themselves off.** Better translated "mutilate themselves." The Gr. word was often used of castration, such as in the cult of Cybele, whose priests were self-made eunuchs. Paul's ironic point is that since the Judaizers were so insistent on circumcision as a means of pleasing God, they should go to the extreme of religious devotion and mutilate themselves.

j. **opportunity for the flesh.** The Gr. word for "opportunity" was often used to refer to a central base of military operations (cf. Rom. 7:8). In the context, "flesh" refers to the sinful inclinations of fallen man (see Rom. 7:5). The freedom Christians have is not a base from which they can sin freely and without consequence.

k. **serve one another.** Christian freedom is not for selfish fulfillment, but for serving others. Cf. Rom. 14:1–15.

For ᵃall the law is fulfilled in one word, even in this: "You shall love your neighbor as yourself." But if you ᵇbite and devour one another, beware lest you be consumed by one another!

I say then: ᶜWalk in the Spirit, and you shall not fulfill the lust of ᵈthe flesh. For the flesh lusts against the Spirit, and the Spirit against the flesh; and these are ᵉcontrary to one another, so that you do not do the things that you wish. But if you are ᶠled by the Spirit, you are not under the law.

Now the ᵍworks of the flesh are ʰevident, which are: adultery, ⁱfornication, uncleanness, ʲlewdness, idolatry, ᵏsorcery, hatred, ˡcontentions, jealousies, outbursts of wrath, selfish ambitions, dissensions, heresies, envy, murders,

---

a. **all the law.** The ethics of the former OT law are the same as those of the NT gospel as indicated in the quote from Lev. 19:18 (see Rom. 7:12; 8:4; cf. James 2:8–10). When a Christian genuinely loves others, he fulfills all the moral requirements of the former Mosaic law concerning them (Matt. 22:36–40; cf. Deut. 6:5; Rom. 13:8–10). This is the ruling principle of Christian freedom (Gal. 5:6, 13).

b. **bite and devour one another.** The imagery is of wild animals savagely attacking and killing each other—a graphic picture of what happens in the spiritual realm when believers do not love and serve each other.

c. **Walk in the Spirit.** All believers have the presence of the indwelling Holy Spirit (cf. Rom. 8:9; 1 Cor. 6:19, 20) as the personal power for living to please God. The form of the Gr. verb translated "walk" indicates continuous action, or a habitual lifestyle. Walking also implies progress; as a believer submits to the Spirit's control—that is, responds in obedience to the simple commands of Scripture—he grows in his spiritual life (see Rom. 8:13; Eph. 5:18; Col. 3:16).

d. **the flesh.** This is not simply the physical body, but includes the mind, will, and emotions which are all subject to sin. It refers in general to our unredeemed humanness. See Rom. 7:5; 8:23; cf. v. 13.

e. **contrary to one another.** The flesh opposes the work of the Spirit and leads the believer toward sinful behavior he would not otherwise be compelled to do (see Rom. 7:14–25).

f. **led by the Spirit . . . not under the law.** Take your choice; these are mutually exclusive. Either you live by the power of the Holy Spirit which results in righteous behavior and spiritual attitudes (Gal. 5:22–26) or by the law which can only produce unrighteous behavior and attitudes (vv. 19–21). Cf. 1 Cor. 15:56.

g. **works of the flesh.** These sins characterize all unredeemed mankind living under the impotent commands of the law which produces only iniquity, though not every person manifests all these sins nor exhibits them to the same degree. Paul's list, which is not exhaustive, encompasses 3 areas of human life: sex, religion, and human relationships. For other such lists, see Rom. 1:24–32; 1 Cor. 6:9, 10.

h. **evident.** The flesh manifests itself in obvious and certain ways.

i. **fornication.** The Gr. word is *porneia*, from which the Eng. word "pornography" comes. It refers to all illicit sexual activity, including (but not limited to) adultery, premarital sex, homosexuality, bestiality, incest, and prostitution.

j. **lewdness.** The word originally referred to any excessive behavior or lack of restraint, but eventually became associated with sexual excess and indulgence.

k. **sorcery.** The Gr. word *pharmakeia*, from which the Eng. word "pharmacy" comes, originally referred to medicines in general, but eventually only to mood- and mind-altering drugs, as well as the occult, witchcraft, and magic. Many pagan religious practices required the use of these drugs to aid in the communication with deities.

l. **contentions . . . heresies.** Many of these sins manifested in the area of human relationships have to do with some form of anger: "Hatred" results in "contentions" (strife). "Jealousies"

^adrunkenness, revelries, and the like; of which I tell you beforehand, just as I also told you in time past, that those who ^bpractice such things ^cwill not inherit the kingdom of God.

But the ^dfruit of the Spirit is ^elove, ^fjoy, ^gpeace, ^hlongsuffering, ⁱkindness, ^jgoodness, ^kfaithfulness, ^lgentleness, ^mself-control. Against such there is ⁿno law. And those who are Christ's have ^ocrucified the flesh with its passions and

---

(hateful resentment) result in "outbursts of wrath" (sudden, unrestrained expressions of hostility). The next 4 represent animosity between individuals and groups.

a. **drunkenness, revelries.** Probably a specific reference to the orgies that characterized pagan, idolatrous worship. Generally, it refers to all rowdy, boisterous, and crude behavior.

b. **practice.** Here is the key word in Paul's warning. The sense of this Gr. verb describes continual, habitual action. Although believers undoubtedly can commit these sins, those people whose basic character is summed up in the uninterrupted and unrepentant practice of them cannot belong to God (see 1 Cor. 6:11; 1 John 3:4–10).

c. **will not inherit the kingdom of God.** See Matt. 5:3. The unregenerate are barred from entering the spiritual kingdom of redeemed people over whom Christ now rules, and they will be excluded from His millennial kingdom and the eternal state of blessing that follows it.

d. **fruit of the Spirit.** Godly attitudes that characterize the lives of only those who belong to God by faith in Christ and possess the Spirit of God. The Spirit produces fruit which consists of 9 characteristics or attitudes that are inextricably linked with each and are commanded of believers throughout the NT.

e. **love.** One of several Gr. words for love, *agape*, is the love of choice, referring not to an emotional affection, physical attraction, or a familial bond, but to respect, devotion, and affection that leads to willing, self-sacrificial service (John 15:13; Rom. 5:8; 1 John 3:16, 17).

f. **joy.** A happiness based on unchanging divine promises and eternal spiritual realities. It is the sense of well being experienced by one who knows all is well between himself and the Lord (1 Pet. 1:8). Joy is not the result of favorable circumstances, and even occurs when those circumstances are the most painful and severe (John 16:20–22). Joy is a gift from God, and as such, believers are not to manufacture it but to delight in the blessing they already possess (Rom. 14:17; Phil. 4:4).

g. **peace.** The inner calm that results from confidence in one's saving relationship with Christ. The verb form denotes binding together and is reflected in the expression "having it all together." Like joy, peace is not related to one's circumstances (John 14:27; Rom. 8:28; Phil. 4:6, 7, 9).

h. **longsuffering.** Patience which refers to the ability to endure injuries inflicted by others and the willingness to accept irritating or painful situations (Eph. 4:2; Col. 3:12; 1 Tim. 1:15, 16).

i. **kindness.** Tender concern for others, reflected in a desire to treat others gently, just as the Lord treats all believers (Matt. 11:28, 29; 19:13, 14; 2 Tim. 2:24).

j. **goodness.** Moral and spiritual excellence manifested in active kindness (Rom. 5:7). Believers are commanded to exemplify goodness (Gal. 6:10; 2 Thess. 1:11).

k. **faithfulness.** Loyalty and trustworthiness (Lam. 3:22; Phil. 2:7–9; 1 Thess. 5:24; Rev. 2:10).

l. **gentleness.** Better translated "meekness." It is a humble and gentle attitude that is patiently submissive in every offense, while having no desire for revenge or retribution. In the NT, it is used to describe 3 attitudes: submission to the will of God (Col. 3:12), teachability (James 1:21), and consideration of others (Eph. 4:2).

m. **self-control.** This refers to restraining passions and appetites (1 Cor. 9:25; 2 Pet. 1:5, 6).

n. **no law.** When a Christian walks by the Spirit and manifests His fruit, he needs no external law to produce the attitudes and behavior that please God (cf. Rom. 8:4).

o. **have crucified the flesh.** One of 4 uses of "crucified" that does not refer to Christ's crucifixion (Rom. 2:20; 6:6, 14). Here Paul states that the flesh has been executed, yet the spiritual battle still rages in the believer (see Rom. 7:14–25). Paul's use looks back to the cross of Christ, where the death of the flesh and its power to reign over believers was actually accomplished (Rom. 6:1–11). Christians must wait until their glorification before they are finally

desires. If we live in the Spirit, let us also walk in the Spirit. Let us not become conceited, provoking one another, envying one another.

56. Freedom from Spiritual Bondage
Gal. 6:1–10

Brethren, if a man is overtaken in any trespass, ᵃyou who are spiritual ᵇrestore such a one in a ᶜspirit of gentleness, ᵈconsidering yourself lest you also be tempted. ᵉBear one another's burdens, and so fulfill ᶠthe law of Christ. For if anyone thinks himself to be something, when he is nothing, he deceives himself. But let each one ᵍexamine his own work, and then he will ʰhave rejoicing in himself alone, and not in another. For each one shall ⁱbear his own load.

Let him who is taught the word share in ʲall good things with him who teaches.

---

rid of their unredeemed humanness (Rom. 8:23), yet by walking in the Spirit they can please God in this world.

a. **you . . . spiritual.** Those believers who are walking in the Spirit (see Gal. 5:16), filled with the Spirit (see Eph. 5:18–20; Col. 3:16), and evidencing the fruit of the Spirit (see Gal. 5:22, 23).

b. **restore.** Sometimes used metaphorically of settling disputes or arguments, it lit. means "to mend" or "repair," and was used of setting a broken bone or repairing a dislocated limb (Heb. 12:12, 13; see Rom. 15:1; 1 Thess. 5:14). The basic process of restoration is outlined in Matt. 18:15–20.

c. **spirit of gentleness.** See Gal. 5:23 (cf. 2 Cor. 2:7; 2 Thess. 3:15).

d. **considering.** Also "looking to, observing." The Gr. form strongly emphasizes a continual, diligent attentiveness.

e. **Bear one another's burdens.** "Burdens" are extra heavy loads, which here represent difficulties or problems people have trouble dealing with. "Bear" connotes carrying something with endurance.

f. **the law of Christ.** The law of love which fulfills the entire law (see Gal. 5:14; John 13:34; Rom. 13:8, 10).

g. **examine.** Lit. "to approve something after testing it." Believers first must be sure their lives are right with God before giving spiritual help to others (cf. Matt. 7:3–5).

h. **have rejoicing in himself.** If a believer rejoices or boasts, it should be only boasting in the Lord for what God has done in him (cf. 2 Cor. 10:12–18), not for what he supposedly has accomplished compared to other believers (see 1 Cor. 1:31).

i. **bear his own load.** This is not a contradiction to Gal. 6:2. "Load" has no connotation of difficulty; it refers to life's routine obligations and each believer's ministry calling (cf. Matt. 11:30; 1 Cor. 3:12–15; 2 Cor. 5:10). God requires faithfulness in meeting those responsibilities.

j. **all good things.** Although this expression could refer to material compensation, the context suggests that Paul is referring to the spiritually and morally excellent things learned from the Word, in which they fellowship together. Paul uses this same term to describe the gospel (Rom. 10:15; cf. Heb. 9:11).

Do not be deceived, God is not mocked; for [a]whatever a man sows, that he will also reap. For he who [b]sows to his flesh will of the flesh reap [c]corruption, but he who [d]sows to the Spirit will of the Spirit reap [e]everlasting life. And let us not grow weary while doing good, for in due season we shall reap if we do not lose heart. Therefore, as we have [f]opportunity, let us do good to all, [g]especially to those who are of the household of faith.

57. Paul Concludes Galatians

Gal. 6:11–18

See [h]with what large letters [i]I have written to you with my own hand! As many as desire to make a [j]good showing in the flesh, these would compel you to

---

a. **whatever a man sows . . . reap.** This agricultural principle, applied metaphorically to the moral and spiritual realm, is universally true (cf. Job 4:8; Prov. 1:31–33; Hos. 8:7; 10:12). This law is a form of God's wrath. See Rom. 1:18.

b. **sows to his flesh.** See Gal. 5:16–19; Rom. 7:18; 8:23. Here it means pandering to the flesh's evil desires.

c. **corruption.** From the Gr. word for degeneration, as in decaying food. Sin always corrupts and, when left unchecked, always makes a person progressively worse in character (cf. Rom. 6:23).

d. **sows to the Spirit.** To walk by the Holy Spirit (see Gal. 5:16–18; Eph. 5:18; cf. John 8:31; 15:7; Rom. 12:1, 2; Col. 2:6; 3:2).

e. **everlasting life.** This expression describes not only a life that endures forever but, primarily, the highest quality of living that one can experience (cf. Ps. 51:12; John 10:10; Eph. 1:3, 18).

f. **opportunity.** This Gr. word refers to a distinct, fixed time period, rather than occasional moments. Paul's point is that the believer's entire life provides the unique privilege by which he can serve others in Christ's name.

g. **especially . . . the household of faith.** Our love for fellow Christians is the primary test of our love for God (see John 13:35; Rom. 12:10–13; 1 John 4:20, 21).

h. **with what large letters.** This can be interpreted in two ways: 1) Paul's poor eyesight forced him to use large letters (cf. Gal. 4:13, 15); or 2) instead of the normal cursive style of writing used by professional scribes, he used the large, block letters (frequently employed in public notices) to emphasize the letter's content rather than its form. It was a visible picture that contrasted his concern with the content of the gospel for the Judaizers' only concern: appearances. The expression served as a transition to his concluding remarks. This closing section of the letter is Paul's final rhetorical attack against the Judaizers' doctrine (see Gal. 1:7–9) and motives. It is also a positive statement of his own godly motives in preaching the true gospel.

i. **I have written . . . my own hand.** As a good translation of the Gr. verb, this indicates that Paul wrote the entire letter by his own hand, not merely penning a brief statement at the end of dictation to a secretary as he did other times (cf. 1 Cor. 16:21; Col. 4:18; 2 Thess. 3:17). Paul wrote this letter himself to make sure the Galatians knew he—not some forger—was writing it, and to personalize the document, given the importance and severity of its contents.

j. **good showing.** The Judaizers were motivated by religious pride and wanted to impress others with their external piety (cf. Matt. 6:1–7).

be circumcised, only that they may [a]not suffer persecution for the cross of Christ. For not even those who are circumcised keep the law, but they desire to have you [b]circumcised that they may [c]boast in your flesh. But God forbid that I should [d]boast except in the cross of our Lord Jesus Christ, by whom the world has been [e]crucified to me, and I to [f]the world. For in Christ Jesus neither circumcision nor uncircumcision avails anything, but [g]a new creation.

And as many as walk according to this rule, [h]peace and mercy be upon them, and upon the [i]Israel of God.

From now on let no one trouble me, for I bear in my body the [j]marks of the Lord Jesus. Brethren, the [k]grace of our Lord Jesus Christ be with your spirit. Amen.

---

a. **may not suffer persecution.** The Judaizers were more concerned about their personal safety than correct doctrine. By adhering more to the Mosaic law than to the gospel of Jesus, they hoped to avoid social and financial ostracism from other Jews and maintain their protected status as Jews within the Roman Empire.

b. **circumcised.** Specifically, in this case, the Judaizers (see Gal. 2:7, 8; cf. Acts 10:45; 11:2).

c. **boast in your flesh.** They zealously worked to win Gentile converts to the law so they could brag about their effective proselytizing (cf. Matt. 23:15).

d. **boast except in the cross.** The Gr. word for "boast" is a basic expression of praise, unlike the Eng. word, which necessarily includes the aspect of pride. Paul glories and rejoices in the sacrifice of Jesus Christ (cf. Rom. 8:1–3; 1 Cor. 2:2; 1 Pet. 2:24).

e. **crucified to me, and I to the world.** The world is spiritually dead to believers, and they are dead to the world (see 2:20; Rom. 6:2–10; 1 John 5:4, 5; cf. Phil. 3:20, 21).

f. **the world.** The evil, Satanic system (see 1 John 2:15, 16; 5:19).

g. **a new creation.** The new birth (see John 3:3; 2 Cor. 5:17).

h. **peace and mercy.** The results of salvation: "Peace" is the believer's new relationship to God (Rom. 5:1; 8:6; Col. 3:15), and "mercy" is the forgiveness of all his sins and the setting aside of God's judgment (Ps. 25:6; Dan. 9:18; Matt. 5:7; Luke 1:50; Rom. 12:1; Eph. 2:4; Titus 3:5).

i. **Israel of God.** All Jewish believers in Christ, i.e., those who are both physical and spiritual descendants of Abraham (see Gal. 3:7, 18; cf. Rom. 2:28, 29; 9:6, 7).

j. **marks.** The physical results of persecution (scars, wounds, etc.) that identified Paul as one who had suffered for the Lord (cf. Acts 14:19; 16:22; 2 Cor. 11:25; see 2 Cor. 1:5; 4:10; Col. 1:24).

k. **grace.** Even Paul's final benediction implicitly extols the superiority of the gospel of grace over any man-made system of works righteousness.

PART III

PAUL'S SECOND MISSIONARY JOURNEY

ca. A.D. 50–53

58. Paul and Silas Visit the Churches of Galatia

Acts 15:36—16:5

Then after some days Paul said to Barnabas, "Let us now go back and visit our brethren in every city where we have preached the word of the Lord, and ^asee how they are doing." Now Barnabas was determined to take with them ^bJohn called Mark. But Paul insisted that they should not take with them the one who had departed from them in Pamphylia, and had not gone with them to the work. Then the ^ccontention became so sharp that they parted from one another. And so Barnabas took Mark and sailed to Cyprus; but Paul chose ^dSilas and departed, being commended by the brethren to the grace of God. And he went through ^eSyria and Cilicia, strengthening the churches.

Then he came to Derbe and Lystra. And behold, a certain disciple was there, named ^fTimothy, the son of a certain Jewish woman who believed, but ^ghis father was Greek. He was well spoken of by the brethren who were at Lystra and Iconium. Paul wanted to have him go on with him. And he took him and ^hcircumcised him because of the Jews who were in that region,

---

a. **see how they are doing.** In addition to proclaiming the gospel, Paul also recognized his responsibility to mature the new believers in their faith (Matt. 28:19, 20; Eph. 4:12, 13; Phil. 1:8; Col. 1:28; 1 Thess. 2:17). So he planned his second missionary journey to retrace his first one.

b. **John called Mark.** See Acts 12:12; 13:13.

c. **contention . . . parted.** This was not an amicable parting—they were in sharp disagreement regarding John Mark. The weight of the evidence favors Paul's decision, especially since he was an apostle of Jesus Christ. That alone should have caused Barnabas to submit to his authority. But they eventually did reconcile (1 Cor. 9:6).

d. **Silas.** He was perfectly suited to be Paul's companion, since he was a prophet and could proclaim and teach the Word. Being a Jew gave him access to the synagogues (see Acts 6:9). Because he was a Roman citizen (Acts 16:37), he enjoyed the same benefits and protection as Paul. His status as a respected leader in the Jerusalem fellowship helped to reinforce Paul's teaching that Gentile salvation was by grace alone through faith alone.

e. **Syria and Cilicia.** Paul visited congregations he had most likely founded before his connection with the Antioch church (Gal. 1:21). The circumcision question had been raised there also.

f. **a certain disciple . . . Timothy.** A young man (late teens or early 20s) of high regard, a "true child in the faith" (1 Tim. 1:2; cf. 2 Tim. 1:2), who eventually became Paul's right-hand man (1 Cor. 4:17; 1 Thess. 3:2; Phil. 2:19). In essence, he became John Mark's replacement. After being commissioned by the elders of the local church (1 Tim. 4:14; 2 Tim. 1:6), he joined Paul and Silas.

g. **his father was Greek.** The grammar likely suggests his father was dead. By being both Jew and Gentile, Timothy had access to both cultures—an indispensable asset for missionary service.

h. **circumcised him.** This was done to aid his acceptance by the Jews and provide full access to the synagogues (see Acts 6:9) he would be visiting with Paul and Silas. If Timothy had

for they all knew that his father was Greek. And as they went through the cities, they delivered to them ᵃthe decrees to keep, which were determined by the apostles and elders at Jerusalem. So the churches were strengthened in the faith, and increased in number daily.

59. PAUL TRAVELS TO MACEDONIA

Acts 16:6—19

Now when they had gone through Phrygia and the region of Galatia, they were forbidden by the ᵇHoly Spirit to preach the word in Asia. After they had come to ᶜMysia, they tried to go into ᵈBithynia, but ᵉthe Spirit did not permit them. So passing by Mysia, they came down to Troas. And a ᶠvision appeared to Paul in the night. A man of ᵍMacedonia stood and pleaded with him, saying, "Come over to Macedonia and help us." Now after he had seen the vision, immediately ʰwe sought to go to Macedonia, concluding that the Lord had called us to preach the gospel to them.

Therefore, sailing from Troas, we ran a straight course to ⁱSamothrace, and the next day came to ʲNeapolis, and from there to ᵏPhilippi, which is the

not been circumcised, the Jews could have assumed he had renounced his Jewish heritage and had chosen to live as a Gentile.

a. **the decrees.** The determinations of the Jerusalem Council (see Acts 15:23–29).

b. **Holy Spirit . . . Asia.** Paul was not allowed to fulfill his intention to minister in Asia Minor (modern Turkey) and to such cities as Ephesus, Smyrna, Philadelphia, Laodicea, Colosse, Sardis, Pergamos, and Thyatira.

c. **Mysia . . . Troas.** The NW part of the province of Asia Minor.

d. **Bithynia.** A separate Roman province NE of Mysia.

e. **the Spirit did not permit them.** Once the Holy Spirit had providentially stopped their travel N, they had nowhere else to go but Troas, a seaport on the Aegean Sea.

f. **vision.** This was the second of 6 visions received by the apostle (cf. Acts 9:3–6; 18:9, 10; 22:17, 18; 23:11; 27:23, 24).

g. **Macedonia.** The region located across the Aegean Sea on the mainland of Greece. The cities of Philippi and Thessalonica were located there. Most significantly, going there was to take the gospel from Asia into Europe.

h. **we.** A change from the third person pronoun to the second person indicates that Luke joined up with Paul, Silas, and Timothy.

i. **Samothrace.** An island in the Aegean Sea about halfway between Asia Minor and the Greek mainland. They stayed there overnight to avoid the hazards associated with sailing in the dark.

j. **Neapolis.** The port city for Philippi.

k. **Philippi.** Located 10 mi. inland from Neapolis, Philippi was named for Philip II of Macedon (the father of Alexander the Great).

foremost city of that part of Macedonia, a ªcolony. And we were staying in that city for some days. And on the Sabbath day we went out of the city ᵇto the riverside, where prayer was customarily made; and we sat down and spoke to the ᶜwomen who met there. Now a certain woman named ᵈLydia heard us. She was a ᵉseller of purple from the city of Thyatira, ᶠwho worshiped God. ᵍThe Lord opened her heart to heed the things spoken by Paul. And when she and her household were baptized, she begged us, saying, "If you have judged me to be faithful to the Lord, come to my house and stay." So she persuaded us.

Now it happened, as we went to prayer, that a certain slave girl possessed with ʰa spirit of divination met us, who brought her masters much profit by fortune-telling. This girl followed Paul and us, and cried out, saying, "These men are the servants of ⁱthe Most High God, who proclaim to us the way of salvation." And this she did for many days.

But Paul, greatly annoyed, turned and said to the spirit, ʲ"I command you in the name of Jesus Christ to come out of her." And he came out that very hour. But when her masters saw that their hope of profit was gone, they seized Paul and Silas and dragged them into the marketplace to the authorities.

---

a. **colony.** Philippi became a Roman colony in 31 B.C., so it carried the right of freedom (it was self-governing and independent of the provincial government), the right of exemption from tax, and the right of holding land in full ownership.

b. **to the riverside.** Evidently, the Jewish community did not have the minimum of 10 Jewish men who were heads of households required to form a synagogue. In such cases, a place of prayer under the open sky and near a river or sea was adopted as a meeting place. Most likely this spot was located where the road leading out of the city crossed the Gangites River.

c. **women who met there.** In further evidence of the small number of Jewish men, it was women who met to pray, read from the OT law, and discuss what they read.

d. **Lydia . . . from the city of Thyatira.** Her home city was located in the Roman province of Lydia, thus the name "Lydia" was probably associated with her place of origin.

e. **seller of purple.** "Purple" fabrics. Because purple dye was extremely expensive, purple garments were usually worn by royalty and the wealthy. As a result, Lydia's business turned a nice profit, which enabled her to have a house large enough to accommodate the missionary team (Acts 16:15) and the new church at Philippi (Acts 16:40).

f. **who worshiped God.** Like Cornelius, she believed in the God of Israel but had not become a full proselyte (cf. Acts 10:2).

g. **The Lord opened her heart.** This is another proof of the sovereignty of God in salvation (see Acts 13:48).

h. **a spirit of divination.** Lit. "a python spirit." That expression comes from Gr. mythology; Python was a snake that guarded the oracle at Delphi. Essentially, this girl was a medium in contact with demons who could supposedly predict the future. See Deut. 18:9–12.

i. **the Most High God.** El Elyon, the Absolutely Sovereign God, is an OT title (used about 50 times) for the God of Israel (see Gen. 14:18–22; Ps. 78:35; Dan. 5:18).

j. **I command you in the name of Jesus Christ.** The demon left the girl in obedience to Paul's command and his apostolic authority. The ability to cast out demons was a special ability of Christ's apostles (Mark 3:15; 2 Cor. 12:12).

60. THE PHILIPPIAN JAILER

Acts 16:20–40

And they brought them to the magistrates, and said, "These men, being ªJews, exceedingly trouble our city; and they ᵇteach customs which are not lawful for us, being Romans, to receive or observe." Then the multitude rose up together against them; and the ᶜmagistrates tore off their clothes and commanded them to be ᵈbeaten with rods. And when they had laid many stripes on them, they threw them into prison, commanding the jailer to keep them securely. Having received such a charge, he put them into the ᵉinner prison and fastened their feet in the stocks.

But at midnight Paul and Silas were praying and singing hymns to God, and the prisoners were listening to them. Suddenly there was a great earthquake, so that the foundations of the prison were shaken; and immediately all the doors were opened and everyone's chains were loosed. And the keeper of the prison, awaking from sleep and seeing the ᶠprison doors open, supposing the prisoners had fled, drew his sword and was about to kill himself. But Paul called with a loud voice, saying, "Do yourself no harm, for we are all here."

Then he called for a light, ran in, and fell down trembling before Paul and Silas. And he brought them out and said, "Sirs, what must I do to be saved?"

So they said, ᵍ"Believe on the Lord Jesus Christ, and you will be saved,

---

a. **Jews . . . trouble our city.** Anti-Semitism was alive even then. The Emperor Claudius issued an order around that time expelling the Jews from Rome (Acts 18:2). This may explain why they apprehended only Paul and Silas, since Luke was a Gentile and Timothy half-Gentile.

b. **teach customs . . . not lawful for us . . . Romans.** It was technically true that Roman citizens were not to engage in any foreign religion that had not been sanctioned by the state. But it was a false charge that they were creating chaos.

c. **magistrates.** Every Roman colony had two of these men serving as judges. In this case, they did not uphold Roman justice: They did not investigate the charges, conduct a proper hearing, or give Paul and Silas the chance to defend themselves.

d. **beaten.** This was an illegal punishment since they had not been convicted of any crime. The officers under the command of the magistrates administered the beating with rods tied together in a bundle. Paul received the same punishment on two other occasions (2 Cor. 11:25).

e. **inner prison . . . in the stocks.** The most secure part of the prison. The jailer took further precautions by putting their feet "in the stocks." This particular security measure was designed to produce painful cramping so the prisoner's legs were spread as far apart as possible.

f. **prison doors open . . . about to kill himself.** Instead of waiting to face humiliation and a painful execution. A Roman soldier, who let a prisoner escape, paid for his negligence with his life (Acts 12:19; 27:42).

g. **Believe on the Lord Jesus Christ.** One must believe He is who He claimed to be (John 20:31) and believe in what He did (1 Cor. 15:3, 4; see Rom. 1:16).

[a]you and your household." Then they spoke the word of the Lord to him and to all who were in his house. And he took them the same hour of the night and washed their stripes. And immediately he and all his family were baptized. Now when he had brought them into his house, he set food before them; and he rejoiced, having believed in God with all his household.

And when it was day, the magistrates sent the officers, saying, "Let those men go."

So the keeper of the prison reported these words to Paul, saying, "The magistrates have sent to let you go. Now therefore depart, and go in peace."

But Paul said to them, "They have beaten us openly, uncondemned Romans, and have thrown us into prison. And now do they put us out secretly? No indeed! Let them come themselves and get us out."

And the officers told these words to the magistrates, and they were afraid when they heard that they were [b]Romans. Then they came and pleaded with them and brought them out, and asked them to depart from the city. So they went out of the prison and entered the house of Lydia; and when they had seen the brethren, they encouraged them and departed.

61. PAUL PREACHES IN THESSALONICA
Acts 17:1–15

Now when they had passed through [c]Amphipolis and Apollonia, they came to Thessalonica, where there was a [d]synagogue of the Jews. Then Paul, [e]as his custom was, went in to them, and for [f]three Sabbaths reasoned with them from

---

a. **you and your household.** All of his family, servants, and guests who could comprehend the gospel and believe heard the gospel and believed (see Acts 11:14). This does not include infants.

b. **Romans.** To inflict corporal punishment on a Roman citizen was a serious crime, and made more so since Paul and Barnabas did not receive a trial. As a result, the magistrates faced the possibility of being removed from office, and having Philippi's privileges as a Roman colony revoked.

c. **Amphipolis and Apollonia . . . Thessalonica.** SW from Philippi along the Egnatian Way. "Amphipolis" was about 30 mi. from Philippi, and "Apollonia" another 30 mi. beyond. The narrative indicates that the travelers stopped only for the night in those cities. Forty mi. beyond "Apollonia" was "Thessalonica," the capital city of Macedonia with a population of 200,000. It was a major port city and an important commercial center.

d. **synagogue.** See Acts 13:5. Luke refers to a synagogue only in Thessalonica, which may explain why Paul and his companions did not stay in the other two cities.

e. **as his custom was.** Paul began his ministry in each town with the Jews (see Acts 13:5).

f. **three Sabbaths.** The length of his initial public ministry. The actual amount of time spent in Thessalonica would have been longer, extending perhaps to 4–6 months.

the Scriptures, explaining and demonstrating that the Christ had to suffer and rise again from the dead, and saying, "This Jesus whom I preach to you is the Christ." And some of them were persuaded; and a great multitude of the devout Greeks, and not a few of the leading women, joined Paul and Silas.

But the Jews who were not persuaded, becoming envious, took some of the evil men from the marketplace, and gathering a mob, set all the city in an uproar and attacked ᵃthe house of Jason, and sought to bring them out to the people. But when they did not find them, they dragged Jason and some brethren to the rulers of the city, crying out, "These who have turned the world upside down have come here too. Jason has harbored them, and these are all acting ᵇcontrary to the decrees of Caesar, saying there is another king—Jesus." And they troubled the crowd and the rulers of the city when they heard these things. So when they had ᶜtaken security from Jason and the rest, they let them go.

Then the brethren immediately sent Paul and Silas away by night to ᵈBerea. When they arrived, they went into the synagogue of the Jews. These were more fair-minded than those in Thessalonica, in that they received the word with all readiness, and searched the Scriptures daily to find out whether these things were so. Therefore many of them believed, and also not a few of the Greeks, prominent women as well as men. But when the Jews from Thessalonica learned that the word of God was preached by Paul at Berea, they came there also and stirred up the crowds. Then immediately the brethren sent Paul away, to go to the sea; but both Silas and Timothy remained there. So those who conducted Paul brought him to ᵉAthens; and receiving a command for Silas and Timothy to come to him with all speed, they departed.

---

a. **the house of Jason.** The mob assumed Paul, Silas, and Timothy were staying there. Nothing is known of Jason except that he was probably Jewish, since Jason was a name adopted by many of the dispersed Jews.

b. **contrary to the decrees of Caesar.** One of the most serious crimes in the Roman Empire was to acknowledge allegiance to any king but Caesar (cf. John 19:15).

c. **taken security.** A pledge or bond, which would be forfeited by Jason should Paul and his companions cause more trouble. As a result, they had no choice but to leave Thessalonica.

d. **Berea.** An important town that was not on a main route.

e. **Athens.** The cultural center of Greece. At its zenith, Athens was home to the most renowned philosophers in history, including Socrates, Plato, and Aristotle, who was arguably the most influential philosopher of all. Two other significant philosophers taught there: Epicurus, founder of Epicureanism, and Zeno, founder of Stoicism—two of the dominant philosophies in that day.

62. PAUL PREACHES IN ATHENS

Acts 17:16–34

Now while Paul waited for them at Athens, his spirit was provoked within him when he saw that the city was ªgiven over to idols. Therefore he reasoned in the synagogue with the Jews and with the Gentile worshipers, and in the marketplace daily with those who happened to be there. Then certain ᵇEpicurean and Stoic philosophers encountered him. And some said, "What does this ᶜbabbler want to say?"

Others said, "He seems to be a proclaimer of foreign gods," because he preached to them Jesus and the resurrection.

And they took him and brought him to ᵈthe Areopagus, saying, "May we know what this new doctrine is of which you speak? For you are bringing some strange things to our ears. Therefore we want to know what these things mean." For all the Athenians and the foreigners who were there spent their time in nothing else but either to tell or to hear some new thing.

Then Paul stood in the midst of the Areopagus and said, "Men of Athens, I perceive that in all things you are very ᵉreligious; for as I was passing through and considering the objects of your worship, I even found an altar with this inscription:

ᶠTO THE UNKNOWN GOD.

---

a. **given over to idols.** Athens was also the religious center of Greece—virtually every deity known to man could be worshiped there. Paul viewed Athens as a city of lost humanity, all doomed to a Christless eternity because of rampant pagan idolatry.

b. **Epicurean and Stoic philosophers.** Epicurean philosophy taught that the chief end of man was the avoidance of pain. Epicureans were materialists—they did not deny the existence of God, but they believed He did not become involved with the affairs of men. When a person died, they believed his body and soul disintegrated. Stoic philosophy taught self-mastery—that the goal in life was to reach a place of indifference to pleasure or pain.

c. **babbler.** Lit. "seed picker." Some of the philosophers viewed Paul as an amateur philosopher—one who had no ideas of his own but only picked among prevailing philosophies and constructed one with no depth.

d. **The Areopagus.** A court named for the hill on which it once met. Paul was not being formally tried; only being asked to defend his teaching.

e. **religious.** Lit. "in fear of Gods."

f. **TO THE UNKNOWN GOD.** The Athenians were supernaturalists—they believed in supernatural powers that intervened in the course of natural laws. They at least acknowledged the existence of someone beyond their ability to understand who had made all things. Paul thus had the opportunity to introduce them to the Creator-God who could be known (Deut. 4:35; 1 Kin. 8:43; 1 Chr. 28:9; Ps. 9:10; Jer. 9:24; 24:7; 31:34; John 17:3). When evangelizing

Therefore, the One whom you worship without knowing, Him I proclaim to you: [a]"God, who made the world and everything in it, since He is Lord of heaven and earth, does not dwell in temples made with hands. Nor is He worshiped with men's hands, as though He needed anything, since He gives to all life, breath, and all things. And He has made from [b]one blood every nation of men to dwell on all the face of the earth, and has [c]determined their preappointed times and [d]the boundaries of their dwellings, so that they should [e]seek the Lord, in the hope that they might grope for Him and find Him, though He is not far from each one of us; for [f]in Him we live and move and have our being, as also some of your own poets have said, 'For we are also His offspring.' Therefore, since we are [g]the offspring of God, we ought not to think that the Divine Nature is like gold or silver or stone, something shaped by art and man's devising. Truly, these [h]times of ignorance God overlooked, but now commands all men everywhere to repent, because He has appointed a day on which He will judge the world in righteousness by the [i]Man whom He has ordained. He has given assurance of this to all by raising Him from the dead."

And when they heard of the [j]resurrection of the dead, some mocked, while

---

pagans, Paul started from creation, the general revelation of God (cf. Acts 14:15–17). When evangelizing Jews, he started from the OT (Acts 17:10–13).

a. **God, who made the world.** This teaching flatly contradicted both the Epicureans, who believed matter was eternal and therefore had no creator, and the Stoics, who as pantheists believed God was part of everything and could not have created Himself. Paul's teaching finds its support throughout Scripture (Gen. 1:1; Ps. 146:5, 6; Is. 40:28; 45:18; Jer. 10:12; 32:17; Jon. 1:9; Zech. 12:1; Eph. 3:9; Col. 1:16; Rev. 4:11; 10:6).

b. **one blood.** All men are equal in God's sight since all came from one man, Adam. This teaching was a blow to the national pride of the Greeks, who believed all non-Greeks were barbarians (see Rom. 1:14).

c. **determined their preappointed times.** God sovereignly controls the rise and fall of nations and empires (cf. Dan. 2:36–45; Luke 21:24).

d. **the boundaries of their dwellings.** God is responsible for establishing nations as to their racial identity and their specific geographical locations (Deut. 32:8) and determining the extent of their conquests (cf. Is. 10:12–15).

e. **seek the Lord.** God's objective for man in revealing Himself as the creator, ruler, and controller of the world. Men have no excuse for not knowing about God because He has revealed Himself in man's conscience and in the physical world (see Rom. 1:19, 20; 2:15).

f. **in Him we live and move and have our being.** A quote from the Cretan poet Epimendes.

g. **the offspring of God.** A quote from Aratus, who came from Paul's home region of Cilicia. **not . . . like gold or silver.** If man is the offspring of God, as the Greek poet suggested, it is foolish to think that God could be nothing more than a man-made idol. Such reasoning points out the absurdity of idolatry (cf. Is. 44:9–20).

h. **times of ignorance God overlooked.** See Rom. 3:25.

i. **Man whom He has ordained.** Jesus Christ (John 5:22–27).

j. **resurrection of the dead.** Gr. philosophy did not believe in bodily resurrection.

others said, "We will hear you again on this matter." So Paul departed from among them. However, some men joined him and believed, among them Dionysius the ªAreopagite, a woman named Damaris, and others with them.

63. PAUL MINISTERS IN CORINTH
Acts 18:1–18a

After these things Paul departed from Athens and went to ᵇCorinth. And he found a certain Jew named ᶜAquila, born in Pontus, who had recently come from Italy with his wife Priscilla (because Claudius had ᵈcommanded all the Jews to depart from Rome); and he came to them. So, because he was of the same trade, he stayed with them and worked; for by occupation they were ᵉtentmakers. And he reasoned in the synagogue every Sabbath, and persuaded both Jews and Greeks.

When ᶠSilas and Timothy had come from Macedonia, Paul was compelled by the Spirit, and testified to the Jews that Jesus is the Christ. But when they opposed him and blasphemed, he shook his garments and said to them, ᵍ"Your blood be upon your own heads; I am clean. From now on I will go to the Gentiles." And

a. **the Areopagite.** A member of the Areopagus court.

b. **Corinth.** The leading political and commercial center in Greece. It was located at a strategic point on the isthmus of Corinth, which connected the Peloponnesian peninsula with the rest of Greece. Virtually all traffic between northern and southern Greece had to pass through the city. Because Corinth was a trade center and host to all sorts of travelers, it had an unsettled population that was extremely debauched. It also housed the temple of Aphrodite, the goddess of love. One thousand temple priestesses, who were ritual prostitutes, came each evening into the city to practice their trade.

c. **Aquila . . . Priscilla.** This husband and wife team were to become Paul's close friends who even risked their lives for him (Rom. 16:3, 4). The remaining 5 times they are mentioned in Scripture, Priscilla is listed first, which could imply she had a higher social rank than Aquila or that she was the more prominent of the two in the church. They probably were Christians when Paul met them, having come from Rome where a church already existed (Rom. 1:7, 8).

d. **commanded all the Jews to depart from Rome.** The decree that forced Priscilla and Aquila to leave Rome ca. A.D. 49.

e. **tentmakers.** This could also refer to leatherworkers.

f. **Silas and Timothy had come from Macedonia.** As Paul desired, Silas and Timothy joined him in Athens (17:15). From there he sent Timothy back to Thessalonica (1 Thess. 3:1–6). Paul evidently sent Silas somewhere in Macedonia, possibly Philippi (cf. Phil. 4:15; 2 Cor. 11:9), since he returned to Corinth from that province.

g. **Your blood be upon your own heads.** Paul held his opponents completely responsible for blaspheming Christ and rejecting his message (cf. Josh. 2:19; 2 Sam. 1:16; 1 Kin. 2:37; Ezek. 18:13; 33:4; Matt. 27:25).

he departed from there and entered the ᵃhouse of a certain man named Justus, one who worshiped God, whose house was next door to the synagogue. Then ᵇCrispus, the ruler of the synagogue, believed on the Lord with all his household. And many of the Corinthians, hearing, believed and were baptized.

Now the Lord spoke to Paul in the night by a ᶜvision, "Do not be afraid, but speak, and do not keep silent; for I am with you, and no one will attack you to hurt you; for ᵈI have many people in this city." And he continued there ᵉa year and six months, teaching the word of God among them.

ᶠWhen Gallio was proconsul of Achaia, the Jews with one accord rose up against Paul and brought him to the ᵍjudgment seat, saying, "This fellow persuades men to worship God ʰcontrary to the law."

And when Paul was about to open his mouth, ⁱGallio said to the Jews, "If it were a matter of wrongdoing or wicked crimes, O Jews, there would be reason why I should bear with you. But if it is a question of words and names and your own law, look to it yourselves; for I do not want to be a judge of such matters." And he drove them from the judgment seat. Then all the Greeks took ʲSosthenes, the ruler of the synagogue, and beat him before the judgment seat. But Gallio took no notice of these things. So Paul still remained a good while.

---

a. **house of . . . Justus.** A Gentile who showed interest in the God of Israel and was associated with the synagogue next door. His name indicates he was a Roman, and since Romans usually had 3 names, his may have been Gaius Titius Justus, meaning he was the same Gaius mentioned in Rom. 16:23 and 1 Cor. 1:14

b. **Crispus, the ruler of the synagogue.** The conversion of this respected leader must have sent shock waves throughout the Jewish community (see Acts 6:9).

c. **vision.** This was the third of 6 visions given to Paul (cf. Acts 9:3–6; 16:9, 10; 22:17, 18; 23:11; 27:23, 24).

d. **I have many people in this city.** God had appointed a number of people in Corinth for salvation, who had not yet heard the gospel (cf. Acts 13:48; Rom. 10:13–15). The effect of Paul's preaching would be to bring the elect to faith (Titus 1:1).

e. **a year and six months.** Paul's longest stay in any city, except Ephesus (Acts 20:31) and Rome (Acts 28:30).

f. **When Gallio was proconsul of Achaia.** From July, A.D. 51 to June, A.D. 52.

g. **judgment seat.** A large, raised stone platform in the marketplace, situated in front of the residence of the proconsul, where he would try public cases.

h. **contrary to the law.** While Judaism was not an official religion, it was officially tolerated in the Roman world, and Christianity was viewed as a sect of Judaism. The Jews in Corinth claimed that Paul's teaching was external to Judaism, and therefore should be banned. Had Gallio ruled in the Jews' favor, Christianity could have been outlawed throughout the Empire.

i. **Gallio said.** Gallio was no fool and saw through the Jews' plan. He refused to get caught up in what he viewed as an internal squabble within Judaism. In essence, he rendered what would be called a summary judgment—he officially ruled that no crime had been committed, that the dispute was over semantics, and threw the case out.

j. **Sosthenes . . . beat him.** The Greeks had reasons for being hostile to Sosthenes; they were venting general hostility toward Jews on him, or they may have been angry with

64. Paul Writes His First Letter to the Thessalonians
Introduction to 1 Thessalonians

In the Greek NT, 1 Thessalonians is listed literally as "To the Thessalonians." This represents the Apostle Paul's first canonical correspondence to the church in the city of Thessalonica (cf. 1 Thess. 1:1).

Author and Date

The Apostle Paul identified himself twice as the author of this letter (1 Thess. 1:1; 2:18). Silvanus (Silas) and Timothy (1 Thess. 3:2, 6), Paul's traveling companions on the second missionary journey when the church was founded (Acts 17:1–9), were also mentioned in Paul's greeting (1 Thess. 1:1). Though Paul was the single inspired author, most of the first person plural pronouns (we, us, our) refer to all 3. However, during Timothy's visit back to Thessalonica, they refer only to Paul and Silvanus (1 Thess. 3:1, 2, 6). Paul commonly used such editorial plurals because the letters came with the full support of his companions.

Paul's authorship has not been questioned until recently by radical critics. Their attempts to undermine Pauline authorship has failed in light of the combined weight of evidence favoring Paul such as: 1) the direct assertions of Paul's authorship (1 Thess. 1:1; 2:18); 2) the letter's perfect correlation with Paul's travels in Acts 16–18; 3) the multitude of intimate details regarding Paul; and 4) the confirmation by multiple, early historical verifications starting with Marcion's canon in A.D. 140.

The first of Paul's two letters written from Corinth to the church at Thessalonica is dated ca. A.D. 51. This date has been archeologically verified by an inscription in the temple of Apollos at Delphi (near Corinth) which dates Gallio's service as proconsul in Achaia to A.D. 51–52 (Acts 18:12–17). Since Paul's letter to the churches of Galatia was probably written ca. A.D. 49–50, this was his second piece of canonical correspondence.

---

his unsuccessful attempt, as leader of the Jews, at prosecuting the case against Paul. Since he was the ruler of the synagogue, he would have presented the case to Gallio. Later, he converted to Christ (1 Cor. 1:1).

Background and Setting

Thessalonica (modern Salonica) lies near the ancient site of Therma on the Thermaic Gulf at the northern reaches of the Aegean Sea. This city became the capital of Macedonia (ca. 168 B.C.) and enjoyed the status of a "free city" which was ruled by its own citizenry (Acts 17:6) under the Roman Empire. Because it was located on the main east-west highway, Via Egnatia, Thessalonica served as the hub of political and commercial activity in Macedonia, and became known as "the mother of all Macedonia." The population in Paul's day reached 200,000 people.

Paul had originally traveled 100 mi. from Philippi via Amphipolis and Apollonia to Thessalonica on his second missionary journey (A.D. 50; Acts 16:1—18:22). As his custom was upon arrival, he sought out the synagogue in which to teach the local Jews the gospel (Acts 17:1, 2). On that occasion, he dialogued with them from the OT concerning Christ's death and resurrection in order to prove that Jesus of Nazareth was truly the promised Messiah (Acts 17:2, 3). Some Jews believed and soon after, Hellenistic proselytes and some wealthy women of the community also were converted (Acts 17:4). Mentioned among these new believers were Jason (Acts 17:5), Gaius (Acts 19:29), Aristarchus (Acts 20:4), and Segundus (Acts 20:4).

Because of their effective ministry, the Jews had Paul's team evicted from the city (Acts 17:5–9), so they went south to evangelize Berea (Acts 17:10). There Paul had a similar experience to Thessalonica with conversions followed by hostility, so the believers sent Paul away. He headed for Athens, while Silvanus and Timothy remained in Berea (Acts 17:11–14). They rejoined Paul in Athens (cf. Acts 17:15, 16 with 1 Thess. 3:1), from which Timothy was later dispatched back to Thessalonica (1 Thess. 3:2). Apparently, Silas afterwards traveled from Athens to Philippi while Paul journeyed on alone to Corinth (Acts 18:1). It was after Timothy and Silvanus rejoined Paul in Corinth (Acts 18:5), that he wrote 1 Thessalonians in response to Timothy's good report of the church.

Paul undoubtedly had multiple reasons for writing, all coming out of his supreme concern for the flock from which he had been separated. Some of Paul's purposes clearly included: 1) encouraging the church (1 Thess. 1:2–10); 2) answering false allegations (2:1–12); 3) comforting the persecuted flock (2:13–16); 4) expressing his joy in their faith (2:17—3:13); 5) reminding them of the importance of moral purity (4:1–8); 6) condemning the sluggard lifestyle (4:9–12); 7) correcting a wrong understanding of prophetic events (4:13—5:11); 8) defusing tensions within the flock (5:12–15); and 9) exhorting the flock in the basics of Christian living (5:16–22).

Historical and Theological Themes

Both letters to Thessalonica have been referred to as "the eschatological epistles." However, in light of their more extensive focus upon the church, they would better be categorized as the church epistles. Five major themes are woven together in 1 Thessalonians: 1) an apologetic theme with the historical correlation between Acts and 1 Thessalonians; 2) an ecclesiastical theme with the portrayal of a healthy, growing church; 3) a pastoral theme with the example of shepherding activities and attitudes; 4) an eschatological theme with the focus on future events as the church's hope; and 5) a missionary theme with the emphasis on gospel proclamation and church planting.

Interpretive Challenges

Primarily the challenges for understanding this epistle involve the sections that are eschatological in nature: 1) the coming wrath (1 Thess. 1:10; 5:9); 2) Christ's return (2:19; 3:13; 4:15; 5:23); 3) the rapture of the church (4:13–18); and 4) the meaning and time of the Day of the Lord (5:1–11). These issues will be addressed in the notes on the appropriate passages.

65. THANKSGIVING FOR THE CHURCH
1 Thess. 1:1—10

ªPaul, ᵇSilvanus, and ᶜTimothy,

---

a. **1:1 Paul.** Biographical details for the former Saul of Tarsus (Acts 9:11) can be found in Acts 9:1–30; 11:19—28:31; see Rom. 1:1. For autobiographical material, see 2 Cor. 11:16—12:10; Gal. 1:11—2:21; Phil. 3:4–6; and 1 Tim. 1:12–17.

b. **Silvanus.** A companion of Paul on the second missionary journey (Acts 15–18), later a writer for Peter (1 Pet. 5:12), also called Silas.

c. **Timothy.** Paul's most notable disciple (Phil. 2:17–23) who traveled on the second and third missionary journeys and stayed near Paul during his first Roman imprisonment (Phil. 1:1; Col. 1:1; Philem. 1). Later he served in Ephesus (1 Tim. 1:3) and spent some time in prison (Heb. 13:23). Paul's first letter to Timothy, while he was ministering in the church at Ephesus, instructed him regarding life in the church (cf. 1 Tim. 3:15). In his second letter, Paul called

To the church of the Thessalonians in [a]God the Father and the Lord Jesus Christ:

Grace to you and peace from God our Father and the Lord Jesus Christ.

We give thanks to God always for you all, making mention of you in [b]our prayers, remembering without ceasing your [c]work of faith, labor of love, and patience of hope in our Lord Jesus Christ in the sight of our God and Father, knowing, beloved brethren, [d]your election by God. For [e]our gospel did not come to you in [f]word only, but also in power, and in the Holy Spirit and in much assurance, as you know [g]what kind of men we were among you for your sake.

And you became [h]followers of us and of the Lord, having received the word in much affliction, with [i]joy of the Holy Spirit, so that you became [j]examples to all in Macedonia and Achaia who believe. For from you the word

Timothy to be strong (2 Tim. 2:1) and faithfully preach as he faced death and was about to turn his ministry over to Timothy (2 Tim. 4:1–8).

a. **God the Father and the Lord Jesus Christ.** Since Paul's initial converts were Jewish, he made it unmistakably clear that this "church" was not a Jewish assembly, but rather one which gathered in the name of Jesus, the Son of God (Acts 17:2, 3), who is both Lord God and Messiah. This emphasis on the equality between God and the Lord Jesus is a part of the introduction in all Paul's epistles (cf. 1 John 2:23).

b. **our prayers.** Paul and his companions prayed frequently for the entire flock and 3 of those prayers are offered in this letter (1 Thess. 1:2, 3; 3:11–13; 5:23, 24).

c. **work of faith.** The threefold combination of faith, hope, and love is a Pauline favorite (1 Thess. 5:8; 1 Cor. 13:13; Col. 1:4, 5). Paul refers here to the fulfillment of ministry duties which resulted from these three spiritual attitudes.

d. **your election by God.** The church is commonly called "the elect" (cf. Rom. 8:33; Col. 3:12; 2 Tim. 2:10; Titus 1:1). In salvation, the initiating will is God's not man's (cf. John 1:13; Acts 13:46–48; Rom. 9:15, 16; 1 Cor. 1:30; Col. 1:13; 2 Thess. 2:13; 1 Pet. 1:1, 2; see Eph. 1:4, 5). Man's will participates in response to God's promptings as Paul makes clear when he says the Thessalonians received the Word (v. 6) and they turned to God from idols (v. 9). These two responses describe faith and repentance, which God repeatedly calls sinners to do throughout Scripture (e.g., Acts 20:21).

e. **our gospel.** Paul called his message "our gospel," because it was for him and all sinners to believe and especially for him to preach. He knew it did not originate with him, but was divinely authored; thus he also called it "the gospel of God" (1 Thess. 2:2, 9; cf. Rom. 1:1). Because the person who made forgiveness possible is the Lord Jesus, he also referred to it as "the gospel of Christ" (1 Thess. 3:2).

f. **word only.** It had to come in word (cf. Rom. 10:13–17), and not word only, but in Holy Spirit power (cf. 2 Cor. 2:4, 5) and in confidence (cf. Is. 55:11).

g. **what kind of men.** The quality of the message was confirmed by the character of the lives of the preachers. Paul's exemplary life served as an open book for all men to read, establishing the credibility of the power and grace of God essential to making the message of redemption believable to sinners (see 2 Cor. 1:12).

h. **followers.** The Thessalonians had become third generation mimics of Christ. Christ is the first; Paul is the second; and the Thessalonians are the third (1 Cor. 4:16; 11:1).

i. **joy of the Holy Spirit.** Cf. Rom. 14:17. Joy in the midst of suffering evidenced the reality of their salvation, which included the indwelling Holy Spirit (1 Cor. 3:16; 6:19).

j. **examples.** The Gr. word was used to describe a seal that marked wax or a stamp that minted coins. Paul commended the Thessalonians for being model believers leaving their mark on others.

of the Lord has ªsounded forth, not only in ᵇMacedonia and Achaia, but also in every place. Your faith toward God has gone out, so that ᶜwe do not need to say anything. For they themselves declare concerning us what manner of entry we had to you, and how you ᵈturned to God from idols ᵉto serve the living and true God, and ᶠto wait for His Son from heaven, whom He raised from the dead, even Jesus who ᵍdelivers us from the wrath to come.

66. REMINDERS FOR THE CHURCH
1 Thess. 2:1–16

For you yourselves know, brethren, that our coming to you was ʰnot in vain. But even after we had suffered before and were ⁱspitefully treated at Philippi,

---

a. **sounded forth.** The idea is to reverberate. Wherever the Thessalonians went, the gospel given by the word of the Lord was heard. It resulted in a local outreach to Thessalonica, a national outreach to Macedonia and Achaia, and an international outreach to regions beyond.

b. **Macedonia and Achaia.** The two Roman provinces which compromised Greece, Macedonia being to the N and Achaia to the S.

c. **we do not need to say anything.** Though it may appear that this church developed such a testimony in only 3 Sabbaths of preaching (cf. Acts 17:2) spanning as little as 15 days, it is better to understand that Paul preached 3 Sabbaths in the synagogue before he had to relocate elsewhere in the city. In all likelihood, Paul spent months not weeks, which accounts for: 1) the two collections he received from Philippi (Phil. 4:16); 2) the time he worked night and day (2:9; 2 Thess. 3:8); and 3) the depth of pastoral care evidenced in the letter (1 Thess. 2:7, 8, 11).

d. **turned.** This word describes what the Bible elsewhere calls repentance (Matt. 3:1, 2; 4:17; Acts 2:38; 3:19; 5:31; 20:21). Salvation involves a person's turning from sin and trusting in false gods to Christ. Cf. 2 Cor. 7:8–11.

e. **to serve the living and true God.** Those converted to Christ abandoned the worship of dead idols to become willing slaves to the living God.

f. **to wait.** This is a recurring theme in the Thessalonian letters (1 Thess. 3:13; 4:15–17; 5:8, 23; 2 Thess. 3:6–13; cf. Acts 1:11; 2 Tim. 4:8; Titus 2:11–13). These passages indicate the imminency of the deliverance; it was something Paul felt could happen in their lifetime.

g. **delivers us from the wrath to come.** This can mean to evacuate out of a current distress (Rom. 7:24; Col. 1:13) or to exempt from entering into a distress (John 12:27; 2 Cor. 1:10). The wrath can refer either to God's temporal wrath to come on the earth (Rev. 6:16, 17; 19:15) or to God's eternal wrath (John 3:36; Rom. 5:9, 10). First Thessalonians 5:9 develops the same idea. The emphasis in both passages on Christ's work of salvation from sin favors this being understood as the deliverance from the eternal wrath of God in hell because of salvation.

h. **not in vain.** Paul's ministry among the Thessalonians was so fruitful that not only were people saved and a vibrant, reproducing church planted, but the church also grew and flourished even after Paul left (cf. 1 Thess. 1:5–8).

i. **spitefully treated at Philippi.** Paul and Silas had been brutalized in Philippi before coming to Thessalonica (cf. Acts 16:19–24, 37). They suffered physically when beaten (Acts 16:22, 23) and incarcerated (Acts 16:24). They were arrogantly mistreated with false accusations (Acts 16:20, 21) and illegally punished in spite of their Roman citizenship (Acts 16:37).

as you know, we were bold in our God to speak to you the gospel of God in [a]much conflict. For our exhortation did not come from [b]error or uncleanness, nor was it in deceit.

But as we have been [c]approved by God to be entrusted with the gospel, even so we speak, not as pleasing men, but God who tests our hearts. For neither at any time did we use [d]flattering words, as you know, nor a cloak for covetousness—God is witness. Nor did we seek glory from men, either from you or from others, when we might have made demands as [e]apostles of Christ. But we were [f]gentle among you, just as a nursing mother cherishes her own children. So, affectionately longing for you, we were well pleased to impart to you not only the gospel of God, but also our own lives, because you had become dear to us. For you remember, brethren, our labor and toil; for [g]laboring night and day, that we might not be a burden to any of you, we preached to you [h]the gospel of God.

---

a. **much conflict.** Like their treatment in Philippi, Paul's team was falsely accused of civil treason in Thessalonica (Acts 17:7) and suffered physical intimidation (Acts 17:5, 6).

b. **error or uncleanness . . . deceit.** Paul used 3 distinctly different words to affirm the truthfulness of his ministry, each expressing a contrast with what was characteristic of false teachers. He first asserted that "his message" was true and not erroneously false. His "manner of life" was pure, not sexually wicked. His "method of ministry" was authentic, not deceptive (see 2 Cor. 4:2).

c. **approved by God.** It could be that some false teachers came into the church to discredit Paul's ministry. This would account for his emphasis in 1 Thess. 2:1–12 on his divine appointment, approval, integrity, and devotion to them. Cf. Acts 9:15; 16:9, 10

d. **flattering words.** Paul used 3 disclaimers to affirm the purity of his motives for ministry: 1) he denied being a smooth talking preacher who tried to make favorable impressions in order to gain influence for selfish advantage; 2) he did not pretend to be poor and work night and day (cf. v. 9) as a pretense to get rich in the ministry at their expense; and 3) he didn't use his honored position as an apostle to seek personal glory, only God's glory (cf. 1 Cor. 10:31).

e. **apostles of Christ.** This plural is designed to include Paul with the 12 for the sake of emphasizing his unique authority. Silvanus and Timothy were "apostles (messengers) of the church" (cf. Rom. 16:7; Phil. 2:15).

f. **gentle . . . as a nursing mother.** Paul may have had in mind Moses' portrayal of himself as a nursing mother to Israel (cf. Num. 11:12). He used the same tender picture with the Corinthians (cf. 2 Cor. 12:14, 15) and the Galatians (cf. Gal. 4:19). Paul's affection for the Thessalonians was like that felt by a mother willing to sacrifice her life for her child as was Christ who was willing to give up His own life for those who would be born again into the family of God (cf. Matt. 20:28)

g. **laboring night and day.** Paul explained this in 2 Thess. 3:7–9. He did not ask for any money from the Thessalonians but rather lived on what he earned and what the Philippians sent (Phil. 4:16), so that his motives could not be questioned, unlike the false teachers who always sought money (cf. 1 Pet. 5:2).

h. **the gospel of God.** Cf. Rom. 1:1. The good news from God which Paul preached included these truths: 1) the authority and truthfulness of Scripture (1 Thess. 2:13); 2) the deity of Christ (Rom. 10:9); 3) the sinfulness of mankind (Rom. 3:23); 4) Christ's death and

[a]You are witnesses, and God also, how devoutly and justly and blamelessly we behaved ourselves among you who believe; as you know how we [b]exhorted, and comforted, and charged every one of you, as a father does his own children, that you would walk worthy of God who calls you into [c]His own kingdom and glory.

For this reason we also thank God without ceasing, because when you received the word of God which you heard from us, you welcomed it not as the word of men, but as it is in truth, the [d]word of God, which also [e]effectively works in you who believe. For you, brethren, became [f]imitators of the churches of God which are in Judea in Christ Jesus. For you also suffered the same things from your own countrymen, just as they did from the Judeans, [g]who killed both the Lord Jesus and their own prophets, and have persecuted us; and they do not please God and are [h]contrary to all men, forbidding us to speak to the Gentiles that they may be saved, so as always to fill up the measure of their sins; but [i]wrath has come upon them to the uttermost.

---

resurrection (1 Cor. 15:4, 5); and 5) salvation by God's grace through man's faith (Eph. 2:8, 9). Paul's summary of the gospel is in 1 Cor. 15:1–5.

a. **you are witnesses.** Under OT law it took two or more witnesses to verify truth (Num. 35:30; Deut. 17:6; 19:15; 2 Cor. 13:1). Here Paul called on both the Thessalonians and God as witnesses to affirm his holy conduct in the ministry. Cf. 2 Cor. 1:12.

b. **exhorted . . . comforted . . . charged.** Paul used these 3 words to describe his fatherly relationship with the Thessalonians since they were his children in the faith. They emphasized the personal touch of a loving father (cf. 1 Cor. 4:14, 15).

c. **His own kingdom and glory.** This speaks of the sphere of eternal salvation (cf. Col. 1:13, 14) culminating in the splendor of heaven.

d. **the word of God.** Paul's message from God is equated with the OT (Mark 7:13). It was the message taught by the apostles (Acts 4:31; 6:2). Peter preached it to the Gentiles (Acts 11:1). It was the word Paul preached on his first missionary journey (Acts 13:5, 7, 44, 48, 49), his second (Acts 16:32; 17:13; 18:11), and his third (Acts 19:10). Cf. Col. 1:25.

e. **effectively works.** The work of God's Word includes: saving (Rom. 10:17; 1 Pet. 1:23); teaching and training (2 Tim. 3:16, 17); guiding (Ps. 119:105); counseling (Ps. 119:24); reviving (Ps. 119:154); restoring (Ps. 19:7); warning and rewarding (Ps. 19:11); nourishing (1 Pet. 2:2); judging (Heb. 4:12); sanctifying (John 17:17); freeing (John 8:31, 32); enriching (Col. 3:16); protecting (Ps. 119:11); strengthening (Ps. 119:28); making wise (Ps. 119:17–100); rejoicing the heart (Ps. 19:8); and prospering (Josh. 1:8, 9). All this is summarized in Ps. 19:7–9.

f. **imitators.** Not only were the Thessalonians imitators of Paul and the Lord (cf. 1:6), but also of the churches in Judea in the sense that they both were persecuted for Christ's sake (cf. Acts 4:1–4; 5:26; 8:1). They drank Christ's cup of sufafering (Matt. 26:39) and walked in the way of the OT prophets (Matt. 21:33–46; Luke 13:34).

g. **who killed . . . the Lord Jesus.** There is no question that the Jews were responsible for the death of their Messiah, though the Romans carried out the execution. It was the Jews who brought the case against Him and demanded His death (cf. Luke 23:1–24, 34–38), just as they had killed the prophets (cf. Matt. 22:37; Mark 5:1–8; Acts 7:51, 52).

h. **contrary to all men.** Just as it is God's will that all men be saved (1 Tim. 2:4; 2 Pet. 3:9), so it was the will of the Jews that no one find salvation in Christ. Paul at one time had embraced this blasphemy of trying to prevent gospel preaching (cf. 1 Tim. 1:12–17).

i. **wrath has come upon them.** God's wrath (cf. 1 Thess. 1:10; 5:9) on the Jews who

67. CONCERNS FOR THE CHURCH

1 Thess. 2:17—3:13

But we, brethren, [a]having been taken away from you for a short time in presence, not in heart, endeavored more eagerly to see your face with great desire. Therefore we wanted to come to you—even I, Paul, time and again—but [b]Satan hindered us. For what is our hope, or joy, or [c]crown of rejoicing? Is it not even you in the presence of our Lord Jesus Christ [d]at His coming? For you are our glory and joy.

Therefore, when we could [e]no longer endure it, we thought it good to be left [f]in Athens alone, and sent Timothy, our brother and minister of God,

---

"pile up their sins to the maximum limit" (cf. Matt. 23:32; Rom. 2:5), thus filling up the cup of wrath, can be understood: 1) historically of the Babylonian exile (Ezek. 8–11); 2) prophetically of Jerusalem's destruction in A.D. 70; 3) eschatologically of Christ's second coming in judgment (Rev. 19); or 4) soteriologically in the sense that God's promised eternal wrath for unbelievers is so certain that it is spoken of as having come already as does the Apostle John (cf. John 3:18, 36). This context relates to the fourth option.

a. **having been taken away.** Paul had been forcedly separated from his spiritual children (cf. Acts 17:5–9). His motherly (1 Thess. 2:7) and fatherly instincts (v. 11) had been dealt a severe blow. Lit. the Thessalonians had been orphaned by Paul's forced departure.

b. **Satan hindered us.** Satan, which means "adversary," continually attempted to tear down the church that Christ promised to build (cf. Matt. 16:18). He was said to be present at the churches of Jerusalem (Acts 5:1–10), Smyrna (Rev. 2:9, 10), Pergamum (Rev. 2:13), Thyatira (Rev. 2:24), Philadelphia (Rev. 3:9), Ephesus (1 Tim. 3:6, 7), and Corinth (2 Cor. 2:1–11). He thwarted Paul in the sense that a military foe would hinder the advance of his enemy. This could very possibly refer to the pledge that Jason made (Acts 17:9), if that pledge was a promise that Paul would not return to Thessalonica.

c. **crown of rejoicing.** The Bible speaks of eternal life like a wreath awarded for an athletic victory. It is spoken of in terms of: 1) the imperishable wreath that celebrates salvation's victory over corruption (1 Cor. 9:25); 2) the righteous wreath that celebrates salvation's victory over unrighteousness (2 Tim. 4:8); 3) the unfading wreath of glory that celebrates salvation's victory over defilement (1 Pet. 5:4); 4) the wreath of life that celebrates salvation's victory over death (James 1:12, Rev. 2:10); and here 5) the wreath of exultation which celebrates salvation's victory over Satan and mankind's persecution of believers.

d. **at His coming.** "Coming" or parousia, lit. means "to be present." It can be understood as: 1) actual presence (Phil. 2:2); 2) moment of arrival (1 Cor. 16:17); or 3) expected coming (2 Cor. 7:6). In regard to Christ and the future, it can refer to: 1) Christ's coming at the Rapture (4:15), or 2) Christ's second coming prior to His 1,000 year millennial reign (Matt. 24:37; Rev. 19:11—20:6). Paul referred directly to Christ's coming 4 times in 1 Thess. (see also 3:13; 4:15; 5:23) and once indirectly (1:10). Context indicates Paul most likely refers here to Christ's coming for the rapture of the church.

e. **no longer endure it.** The agony of separation between spiritual parent Paul and his children in Thessalonica became unbearably painful.

f. **in Athens alone.** Paul and Silas stayed behind while Timothy returned. This would not be the last time that Timothy went to a church in Paul's place (cf. 1 Cor. 4:17; 16:10; Phil. 2:19–24; 1 Tim. 1:3).

and our fellow laborer in the gospel of Christ, to ^aestablish you and encourage you concerning your faith, that no one should be shaken by these afflictions; for you yourselves know that we are ^bappointed to this. For, in fact, we told you before when we were with you that we would ^csuffer tribulation, just as it happened, and you know. For this reason, when I could no longer endure it, I sent to know your faith, lest by some means ^dthe tempter had tempted you, and our labor might be in vain.

But now that Timothy has come to us from you, and brought us good news of ^eyour faith and love, and that you always have good remembrance of us, greatly desiring to see us, as we also to see you—therefore, brethren, in all our affliction and distress we were comforted concerning you by your faith. For now we live, if you ^fstand fast in the Lord.

For what thanks can we render to God for you, for all the ^gjoy with which we rejoice for your sake before our God, night and day ^hpraying exceedingly that we may see your face and perfect what is ⁱlacking in your faith?

---

a. **establish . . . encourage . . . your faith.** This was a common ministry concern and practice of Paul (cf. Acts 14:22; 15:32; 18:23). Paul's concern did not focus on health, wealth, self-esteem, or ease of life, but rather the spiritual quality of life. Their faith was of supreme importance in Paul's mind as evidenced by 5 mentions in 1 Thess. 3:1–10 (see also vv. 5, 6, 7, 10). Faith includes the foundation of the body of doctrine (cf. Jude 3) and their believing response to God in living out that truth (cf. Heb. 11:6).

b. **appointed.** God had promised Paul future sufferings when He commended him to ministry through Ananias (Acts 9:16). Paul reminded the Thessalonians of this divine appointment so that they would not think that: 1) God's plan was not working out as evidenced by Paul's troubles, or 2) Paul's afflictions demonstrated God's displeasure with him. To think that way would upset the church's confidence in Paul and fulfill Satan's deceptive purposes. Cf. 2 Cor. 4:8–15; 6:1–10; 11:23–27; 12:7–10.

c. **suffer tribulation.** Paul had told them to expect him to suffer as he had already suffered before his Thessalonian experience (1 Thess. 2:14–16; Acts 13, 14). During (Acts 17:1–9) and following (Acts 17:10—18:11) his time at Thessalonica, Paul also knew tribulation.

d. **the tempter.** Satan had already been characterized as a hinderer (1 Thess. 2:18) and now as a tempter in the sense of trying/testing for the purpose of causing failure (cf. Matt. 4:3; 1 Cor. 7:5; James 1:12–18). Paul was not ignorant of Satan's schemes (2 Cor. 2:11; 11:23) nor vulnerable to his methods (Eph. 6:11), so Paul took action to counterattack Satan's expected maneuver and to assure that all his efforts were not useless (cf. 1 Thess. 2:1).

e. **your faith and love.** Timothy returned to report the Thessalonians' trust in God, their response to one another, and to Paul's ministry. This news convinced Paul that Satan's plans to disrupt God's work had not been successful and settled Paul's anxiety.

f. **stand fast.** Pictured here is an army that refuses to retreat even though it is being assaulted by the enemy. This is a frequent Pauline injunction (1 Cor. 16:13; Gal. 5:1; Eph. 6:11, 13, 14; Phil. 1:27; 4:1; 2 Thess. 2:15).

g. **joy.** Paul, like John (3 John 4), found the highest sense of ministry joy in knowing that his children in the faith were growing and walking in the truth. It led him to the worship of God in thanksgiving and rejoicing.

h. **praying.** As to frequency, Paul prayed night and day just as he worked night and day (1 Thess. 2:9). As to fervency, Paul prayed superabundantly (cf. Eph. 3:20).

i. **lacking.** Paul was not criticizing the church but rather acknowledging that they had

Now may our God and Father Himself, and our Lord Jesus Christ, ᵃdirect our way to you. And may the Lord make you increase and abound in ᵇlove to one another and to all, just as we do to you, so that He may establish your hearts ᶜblameless in holiness before our God and Father at the coming of our Lord Jesus Christ with all ᵈHis saints.

68. MORAL PURITY AND DISCIPLINED LIVING
1 Thess. 4:1–12

Finally then, brethren, we urge and exhort ᵉin the Lord Jesus that you should abound more and more, just as you received from us how you ought to walk and to please God; for you know what commandments we gave you through the Lord Jesus.

For this is ᶠthe will of God, your sanctification: that you should abstain

---

not yet reached their full potential, for which he prayed and labored. The themes of 1 Thess. 4, 5 deal with areas of this lack.

a. **direct our way.** Paul knew that Satan had hindered his return (1 Thess. 2:18). Even though Timothy had visited and returned with a good report, Paul still felt the urgency to see his spiritual children again. Paul followed the biblical admonition of the Psalms (Ps. 37:1–5) and Proverbs (Prov. 3:5, 6) to entrust difficult situations to God.

b. **love to one another.** With over 30 positive and negative "one anothers" in the NT, love appears by far most frequently (cf. 1 Thess. 4:9; Rom. 12:10; 13:8; 2 Thess. 1:3; 1 Pet. 1:22; 1 John 3:11, 23; 4:7, 11; 2 John 5). It is the overarching term that includes all of the other "one anothers." Its focus is on believers in the church. **to all.** In light of the fact that God loved the world and sent His son to die for human sin (John 3:16), believers who were loved when they were unlovely (Rom. 5:8) are to love unbelievers (see Matt. 5:43, 44). Other NT commands concerning all men include pursuing peace (Rom. 12:18), doing good (Gal. 6:10), being patient (Phil. 4:5), praying (1 Tim. 2:1), showing consideration (Titus 3:2), and honoring (1 Pet. 2:17).

c. **blameless in holiness.** Paul prayed that there would be no grounds of accusation because of unholiness. Cf. 1 Cor. 1:8; 2 Cor. 11:2; Eph. 5:25–27; 1 Pet. 3:16, 17; Jude 24.

d. **His saints.** Since this exact term is not used elsewhere in the NT of angels (see Jude 14), but is commonly used for believers, it is best to understand the coming of the Lord to rapture all His church (see 1 Thess. 4:13–18) and take them to heaven to enjoy His presence (see John 14:1–3).

e. **in the Lord Jesus.** To give added weight to his words, Paul appealed here to the fact that he wrote with the authority of Christ Himself (see 1 Thess. 4:2, 15; 5:27; 2 Thess. 3:6, 12; cf. 2:4, 15; 2 Cor. 5:9; Eph. 5:10, 17; Col. 1:10; Heb. 11:6; 13:15, 16; 1 John 3:22). This is done by obedience to the Word of God (cf. 1 Thess. 4:3).

f. **the will of God.** All of God's Word contains God's will—both affirmations and prohibitions. Specifically, God's will includes salvation (1 Tim. 2:4), self-sacrifice (Rom. 12:1, 2), Spirit filling (Eph. 5:18), submission (1 Pet. 2:13–15), suffering (1 Pet. 3:17), satisfaction (5:18), settledness (Heb. 10:36), and particularly here—sanctification, which literally refers to a state of being set apart from sin to holiness. In this context, it means being set apart from sexual

from sexual immorality; that each of you should know how to ªpossess his own vessel in sanctification and honor, not in passion of lust, like ᵇthe Gentiles who do not know God; that no one should take advantage of and ᶜdefraud his brother in this matter, because the Lord is the ᵈavenger of all such, as we also forewarned you and testified. For God did not ᵉcall us to uncleanness, but in holiness. Therefore he who rejects this does not reject man, but God, who has also ᶠgiven us His Holy Spirit.

But concerning brotherly love you have no need that I should write to you, for you yourselves are ᵍtaught by God to love one another; and indeed you do so toward all the brethren who are in all Macedonia. But we urge you, brethren, that you increase more and more; that you also aspire to lead ʰa quiet life, to mind your own business, and to ⁱwork with your own hands, as we commanded you, that you may walk properly toward ʲthose who are outside, and that you may lack nothing.

---

impurity in particular, holding oneself away from immorality by following the instruction in 1 Thess. 4:4–8.

   a. **possess his own vessel.** Two interpretations of "vessel" are usually offered. The term can mean: 1) the wife (cf. Ruth 4:10 LXX; 1 Pet. 3:7) which one acquires, or 2) the body (2 Cor. 4:7; 2 Tim. 2:21) which one possesses. The latter is most likely since: 1) vessel in 1 Pet. 3:7 is used only in a comparative sense ("weaker vessel") referring to vessel in terms of general humanity not femaleness; 2) being married does not guarantee sexual purity; 3) Paul would be contradicting what he taught in 1 Cor. 7 about the superlative state of singleness (cf. 7:8, 9); and 4) if taken in the sense of "acquiring a wife," Paul would be talking to men only and ignoring how women were to stay pure. Therefore, "possess his own body" is the preferred translation/interpretation.

   b. **the Gentiles.** Used here in a spiritual sense referring to non-Christians, and indicated by the defining statement, "who do not know God."

   c. **defraud his brother.** The context, which remains unchanged throughout vv. 1–8, demands that this refer to all the destructive social and spiritual implications of illegitimate sexual activity. See Matt. 18:6–10.

   d. **avenger.** This means it is God who ultimately works out just recompense for such sins (cf. Col. 3:4–7; Heb. 13:4).

   e. **call us.** Whenever the epistles refer to the "call" of God, it is always a reference to His effectual, saving call, never to a general plea. It is linked to justification (cf. Rom. 8:30).

   f. **given us His Holy Spirit.** God's Spirit is a free gift to all who believe in the Lord Jesus Christ for salvation. Cf. Acts 2:38; Rom. 8:9; 1 Cor. 3:16; 12:13; 2 Cor. 6:16.

   g. **taught by God to love.** Through God's Word (Ps. 119:97–102) and by God Himself, they were loving believers (cf. Rom. 5:5; 1 John 2:7–11; 3:14; 4:7, 8, 12).

   h. **a quiet life.** This refers to one who does not present social problems (see 1 Tim. 2:2) or generate conflict among those people in his life, but whose soul rests easy even in the midst of difficulty (cf. 1 Pet. 3:4). Paul later deals with those who did not "mind their own business" at Thessalonica (cf. 2 Thess. 3:6–15).

   i. **work with your own hands.** Greek culture looked down on manual labor but Paul exalts it (see Eph. 4:28).

   j. **those . . . outside.** Non-Christians are in view here (cf. 1 Cor. 5:2; Col. 4:5; 1 Tim. 3:7).

69. Death and the Rapture

1 Thess. 4:13–18

But I do not want you to be ᵃignorant, brethren, concerning ᵇthose who have fallen asleep, lest you sorrow as others who have no hope. For if we believe that Jesus died and rose again, even so ᶜGod will bring with Him those who sleep in Jesus.

For this we say to you by ᵈthe word of the Lord, that ᵉwe who are alive

---

a. ignorant. Even though Paul's ministry in Thessalonica was brief, it is clear the people had come to believe in and hope for the reality of their Savior's return (cf. 1 Thess. 1:3, 9, 10; 2:19; 5:1, 2; 2 Thess. 2:1, 5). They were living in expectation of that coming, eagerly awaiting Christ. First Thess. 4:13 (cf. 2 Thess. 2:1–3) indicates they were even agitated about some things that were happening to them that might affect their participation in it. They knew Christ's return was the climactic event in redemptive history and didn't want to miss it. The major question they had was "What happens to the Christians who die before He comes? Do they miss His return?" Clearly, they had an imminent view of Christ's return and Paul had left the impression it could happen in their lifetime. Their confusion came as they were being persecuted, an experience they thought they were to be delivered from by the Lord's return (cf. 1 Thess. 3:3, 4).

b. those who have fallen asleep. Sleep is the familiar NT euphemism for death which describes the appearance of the deceased (see 1 Cor. 11:30). It describes the dead body, not the soul (cf. 2 Cor. 5:1–9; Phil. 1:23). Sleep is used of Jarius' daughter (Matt. 9:24) whom Jesus raised from the dead and Stephen who was stoned to death (Acts 7:60; cf. John 11:11; 1 Cor. 7:39; 15:6, 18, 51; 2 Pet. 3:4). Those who sleep are identified in v. 16 as "the dead in Christ." The people, in ignorance, had come to the conclusion that those who die miss the Lord's return and they were grieved over their absence at such a glorious event. Thus the departure of a loved one brought great anguish to the soul. But there is no reason for Christians to sorrow when a brother dies as if some great loss to that person has come.

c. God will bring with Him. As Jesus died and rose, so also will those who die believing in Him rise again so they can be taken to heaven with the Lord (see John 14:1–3; 1 Cor. 15:51–58). These texts describe the rapture of the church, which takes place when Jesus comes to collect His redeemed and take them back to heaven. Those who have died before that time (called "those who sleep") will be gathered and taken back to heaven with the Lord.

d. the word of the Lord. Was Paul referring to some saying of Jesus found in the gospels? No. There are none exact or even close. The only explicit reference to the Rapture in the gospel is John 14:1–3. Some suggest that Jesus had said the words while on earth, their substance being recorded later in such places as Matt. 24:30, 31 and John 6:39, 40; 11:25, 26. Similarities between this passage in 1 Thess. and the gospel accounts include a trumpet (Matt. 24:31), a resurrection (John 1:26), and a gathering of the elect (Matt. 24:31). Yet dissimilarities between it and the canonical sayings of Christ far outweigh the resemblances. Some of the differences between Matt. 24:30, 31 and vv. 15–17 are as follows: 1) in Matt. the Son of Man is coming on the clouds (but see Mark 13:26; Luke 21:27), in 1 Thess. ascending believers are in them; 2) in the former the angels gather, in the latter Christ does personally; 3) in the former nothing is said about resurrection, while in the latter this is the main theme; and 4) Matthew records nothing about the order of ascent, which is the principal lesson in Thessalonians. On the other hand, did he mean a statement of Jesus that was spoken but not recorded in the gospels (Acts 20:35)? No. There is reason to conclude this since Paul affirmed that he taught the Rapture as a heretofore hidden truth (1 Cor. 15:51), i.e., "mystery." Apparently, the Thessalonians were informed fully about the Day of the Lord judgment (cf. 5:1, 2), but not the preceding event—the rapture of the church. Until Paul revealed it as the revelation from God to him, it had been a secret, with the only prior mention being Jesus' teaching in John 14:1–3. This was new revelation of what had previously been an unrevealed mystery.

e. we who are alive and remain. This refers to Christians alive at the time of the Rapture,

and remain until the coming of the Lord will by no means precede those who are asleep. For [a]the Lord Himself will descend from heaven with a shout, with the voice of an [b]archangel, and with the [c]trumpet of God. And the dead in Christ will rise first. Then we who are alive and remain shall be [d]caught up together with them in the clouds to meet the Lord in the air. And thus we shall always be with the Lord. Therefore [e]comfort one another with these words.

---

those who live on this earth to see the coming of the Lord for His own. Since Paul didn't know God's timing, he lived and spoke as if it could happen in his lifetime. As with all early Christians, he believed the event was near (cf. Rom. 13:11; 1 Cor. 6:14; 10:11; 16:22; Phil. 3:20, 21; 1 Tim. 6:14; Titus 2:13). Those alive at the Rapture will follow those dead who rise first (1 Thess. 4:16).

    a. **the Lord Himself will descend.** This fulfills the pledge of John 14:1–3 (cf. Acts 1:11). Until then, He remains in heaven (cf. 1 Thess. 1:10; Heb. 1:1–3).

    b. **archangel.** Very little is known about the organization or rank of angels (cf. Col. 1:17). While only Michael is named as an archangel (Jude 9), there seems to be more than one in the angelic ranks (Dan. 10:13). Perhaps it is Michael, the archangel, whose voice is heard as he is identified with Israel's resurrection in Dan. 12:1–3. At that moment (cf. 1 Cor. 15:52, "twinkling of an eye"), the dead rise first. They will not miss the Rapture, but be the first participants.

    c. **trumpet of God.** Cf. 1 Cor. 15:52. This trumpet is not the judgment trumpets of Rev. 8–11, but is illustrated by the trumpet of Ex. 19:16–19, which called the people out of the camp to meet God. It will be a trumpet of deliverance (cf. Zeph. 1:16; Zech. 9:14).

    d. **caught up.** After the dead come forth, their spirits, already with the Lord (2 Cor. 5:8; Phil. 1:23), now being joined to resurrected new bodies (see 1 Cor. 15:35–50), the living Christians will be raptured, lit. snatched away (cf. John 10:28; Acts 8:39). This passage, along with John 14:1–3 and 1 Cor. 15:51, 52, form the biblical basis for "the Rapture" of the church. The time of the Rapture cannot be conclusively determined from this passage alone. However, when other texts such as Rev. 3:10 and John 14:3 are consulted and compared to the texts about Christ's coming in judgment (Matt. 13:34–50; 24:29–44; Rev. 19:11–21) at the end of a 7 year tribulation, it has to be noted that there is a clear difference between the character of the "Rapture" in that there is no mention of any judgment, while the other texts feature judgment. So then, it is best to understand that the Rapture occurs at a time different from the coming of Christ in judgment. Thus, the Rapture has been described as pretribulational (before the wrath of God unfolded in the judgments of Rev. 6–19). This event includes complete transformation (cf. 1 Cor. 15:51, 52; Phil 3:20, 21) and union with the Lord Jesus Christ that never ends.

    e. **comfort one another.** The primary purpose of this passage is not to teach a scheme of prophecy, but rather to provide encouragement to those Christians whose loved ones have died. The comfort here is based on the following: 1) the dead will be resurrected and will participate in the Lord's coming for His own; 2) when Christ comes the living will be reunited forever with their loved ones; and 3) they all will be with the Lord eternally.

70. HOLY LIVING AND THE DAY OF THE LORD
1 Thess. 5:1–11

[a]But concerning the [b]times and the seasons, brethren, you have no need that I should write to you. For you yourselves know perfectly that the [c]day of the Lord so comes as a [d]thief in the night. For when they say, [e]"Peace and safety!" then sudden destruction comes upon them, as [f]labor pains upon a pregnant woman. And they shall not escape. [g]But you, brethren, are

---

a. **But.** Paul used familiar Gr. words here to indicate a change of topics within the same general subject of prophecy (cf. 1 Thess. 4:9, 13; 1 Cor. 7:1, 25; 8:1; 12:1; 16:1). The expression here points to the idea that within the broader context of the end time coming of the Lord Jesus, the subject is changing from a discussion of the blessings of the rapture of believers to the judgment of unbelievers.

b. **times and the seasons.** These two terms mean the measurement of time and the character of the times respectively (cf. Dan. 2:21; Acts 1:7). Many of them expected the Lord to come in their lifetime and were confused and grieved when their fellow believers died before His coming (see 4:13–18). They were concerned about the delay. Apparently, the Thessalonians knew all that God intended believers to know about coming judgment, and Paul had taught them what they hadn't known about the Rapture (4:13–18), so Paul exhorted them to live godly lives in light of coming judgment on the world, rather than to be distracted by probing into issues of prophetic timing. They could not know the timing of God's final judgment, but they knew well that it was coming unexpectedly (1 Thess. 5:2).

c. **day of the Lord.** There are 19 indisputable uses of "the Day of the Lord" in the OT and 4 in the NT (cf. Acts 2:20; 2 Thess. 2:2; 2 Pet. 3:10). The OT prophets used "Day of the Lord" to describe near historical judgments (see Is. 13:6–22; Ezek. 30:2–19; Joel 1:15; 3:14; Amos 5:18–20; Zeph. 1:14–18) or far eschatological divine judgments (see Joel 2:30–32; Zech. 14:1; Mal. 4:1, 5). Six times it is referred to as the "day of doom" and 4 times "day of vengeance." The NT calls it a day of "wrath," day of "visitation," and the "Great Day of God Almighty" (Rev. 16:4). These are terrifying judgments from God (cf. Joel 2:30, 31; 2 Thess. 1:7–10) for the overwhelming sinfulness of the world. The future "Day of the Lord" which unleashes God's wrath, falls into two parts: 1) the end of the 7 year tribulation period (cf. Rev. 19:11–21), and 2) the end of the Millennium. These two are actually 1,000 years apart and Peter refers to the end of the 1,000 year period in connection with the final "Day of the Lord" (cf. 2 Pet. 3:10; Rev. 20:7–15). Here, Paul refers to that aspect of the "Day of the Lord," which concludes the tribulation period.

d. **a thief in the night.** This phrase is never used to refer to the rapture of the church. It is used of Christ's coming in judgment on the Day of the Lord at the end of the 7 year tribulation which is distinct from the rapture of the church (see 1 Thess. 4:15) and it is used of the judgment which concludes the Millennium (2 Pet. 3:10). As a thief comes unexpectedly and without warning, so will the Day of the Lord come in both its final phases.

e. **"Peace and safety!"** Just as false prophets of old fraudulently forecast a bright future, in spite of the imminence of God's judgment (Jer. 6:14; 8:11; 14:13, 14; Lam. 2:14; Ezek. 13:10, 16; Mic. 3:5), so they will again in future days just before the final Day of the Lord destruction.

f. **labor pains.** The Lord used this same illustration in the Olivet Discourse (see Matt. 24:8). It portrays the inevitability, suddenness, inescapable nature, and painfulness of the Day of the Lord.

g. **But you, brethren.** Paul dramatically shifts from the third person plural pronoun (3 times in v. 3) to the second person plural. Because the church is raptured before the judgment

[a]not in darkness, so that this Day should overtake you as a thief. You are all sons of light and [b]sons of the day. We are not of the night nor of darkness. Therefore [c]let us not sleep, as others do, but let us watch and be sober. For those who sleep, sleep at night, and those who get drunk are drunk at night. But let us who are of the day be sober, putting on the [d]breastplate of faith and love, and as a helmet the hope of salvation. For God did not appoint us to [e]wrath, but to obtain salvation through our Lord Jesus Christ, who died for us, that whether [f]we wake or sleep, we should live together with Him.

Therefore comfort each other and edify one another, just as you also are doing.

---

of the Day of the Lord, believers will not be present on earth to experience its terrors and destruction.

a. **not in darkness.** Believers have no part in the Day of the Lord, because they have been delivered from the domain of darkness and transferred to the kingdom of light (Col. 1:13). Jesus taught that to believe in Him would remove a person from spiritual darkness (John 8:12; 12:46). The contrast between believers and the lost is emphatic and Paul draws it out all the way through 1 Thess. 5:7. Believers will not experience the wrath of God because they are different in nature. Unbelievers are in darkness (cf. v. 2, "in the night"), engulfed in mental, moral, and spiritual darkness because of sin and unbelief (cf. John 1:5; 3:19; 8:12; 2 Cor. 4:6; Eph. 4:17, 18; 5:8, 11). All these people are children of Satan (cf. John 8:44) who is called "the power of darkness" (Luke 22:53). The Day of the Lord will "overtake" them suddenly and with deadly results.

b. **sons of light.** This is a Heb. expression that characterizes believers as children of God, their heavenly Father, who is light and in whom is no darkness at all (1 John 1:5–7). Cf. Luke 16:8; John 8:12; 12:36. Believers live in a completely different sphere of life than those who will be in the Day of the Lord.

c. **let us not sleep.** Because believers have been delivered from the domain of darkness, they are taken out of the night of sin and ignorance and put into the light of God. Because Christians are in the light, they should not sleep in spiritual indifference and comfort, but be alert to the spiritual issues around them. They are not to live like the sleeping, darkened people who will be jolted out of their coma by the Day of the Lord, but to live alert, balanced, godly lives under control of the truth.

d. **breastplate.** Paul pictured the Christian life in military terms as being a life of soberness (alertness) and proper equipping. The "breastplate" covers the vital organs of the body. "Faith" is an essential protection against temptations, because it is trust in God's promise, plan, and truth. It is unwavering belief in God's Word that protects us from temptation's arrows. Looking at it negatively, it is unbelief that characterizes all sin. When believers sin, they have believed Satan's lie. Love for God is essential, as perfect love for Him yields perfect obedience to Him. Elsewhere the warrior's breastplate has been used to represent righteousness (Is. 59:17; Eph. 6:14). Faith elsewhere is represented by a soldier's shield (Eph. 6:16). The "helmet" is always associated with salvation in its future aspects (cf. Is. 59:17; Eph. 6:17). Our future salvation is guaranteed, nothing can take it away (Rom. 13:11). Paul again combined faith, love, and hope (cf. 1 Thess. 1:3).

e. **wrath.** This is the same wrath referred to in 1 Thess. 1:9. In this context (note especially the contrast), it appears obvious that this wrath refers to God's eternal wrath, not His temporal wrath during the tribulation period (cf. Rom. 5:9).

f. **wake or asleep.** This analogy goes back to 1 Thess. 4:13–15 and refers to being physically alive or dead with the promise that, in either case, we will one day live together (cf. 4:17; John 14:1–3) forever with the Savior who died as the substitute for our sins. Cf. Rom. 4:9; Gal. 1:4; 2 Cor. 5:15, 21.

71. CHRISTIAN LIVING AND FINAL BENEDICTION

1 Thess. 5:12–28

And we urge you, brethren, to [a] recognize those who labor among you, and are over you in the Lord and admonish you, and to [b]esteem them very highly in love for their work's sake. Be at peace among yourselves.

Now [c]we exhort you, brethren, warn those who are unruly, comfort the fainthearted, uphold the weak, be patient with all. See that no one renders evil for evil to anyone, but always pursue what is good both for yourselves and for all.

[d]Rejoice always, [e]pray without ceasing, in everything [f]give thanks; for this is the will of God in Christ Jesus for you.

Do not [g] quench the Spirit. Do not despise [h]prophecies. [i]Test all things; hold fast what is good. Abstain from every form of evil.

---

a. **recognize.** This does not mean simple face recognition, but that the people are to lit. know their pastors well enough to have an intimate appreciation for them and to respect them because of their value. The work of pastors is summarized in a threefold description which includes: 1) laboring, working to the point of exhaustion; 2) overseeing, lit. standing before the flock to lead them in the way of righteousness; and 3) admonishing, instructing in the truths of God's Word. Cf. Heb. 13:7, 17.

b. **esteem.** In addition to knowing pastors, congregations are to think rightly and lovingly of their pastors, not because of their charm or personality, but because of the fact that they work for the Chief Shepherd as His special servants (cf. 1 Pet. 5:2–4). They are also to submit to their leadership so that "peace" prevails in the church.

c. **we exhort you.** Paul has discussed how the pastors are to serve the people and how the people are to respond to the pastors. In these verses, he presents how the people are to treat each other in the fellowship of the church. The "unruly," those out of line, must be warned and taught to get back in line. The "fainthearted," those in fear and doubt, must be encouraged and made bold. The "weak," those without spiritual and moral strength, must be held up firmly. Patience, forgiveness and acts of goodness must prevail between all the people.

d. **Rejoice.** Joy is appropriate at all times. Cf. Phil. 2:17, 18; 3:1; 4:4.

e. **pray.** This does not mean pray repetitiously or continuously without a break (cf. Matt. 6:7, 8), but rather pray persistently (cf. Luke 11:1–13; 18:1–8) and regularly (cf. Eph. 6:18; Phil. 4:6; Col. 4:2, 12).

f. **give thanks.** Thanklessness is a trait of unbelievers (cf. Rom. 1:21; 2 Tim. 3:1–5). "This is the will of God" includes 1 Thess. 5:16, 17.

g. **quench.** The fire of God's Spirit is not to be doused with sin. Believers are also instructed to not grieve the Holy Spirit (Eph. 4:30), but to be controlled by the Holy Spirit (Eph. 5:18) and to walk by the Holy Spirit (Gal. 5:16).

h. **prophecies.** This word can refer to a spoken revelation from God (cf. Acts 11:27, 28; 1 Tim. 1:18; 4:14), but most often refers to the written word of Scripture (cf. Matt. 13:14; 2 Pet. 1:19–21; Rev. 1:3; 22:7, 10, 18, 19). These "prophecies" are authoritative messages from God through a well recognized spokesman for God that, because of their divine origin, are not to be treated lightly. When God's Word is preached or read, it is to be received with great seriousness.

i. **Test all things.** This call for careful examination and discernment is in response to

Now may the ᵃGod of peace Himself sanctify you completely; and may your ᵇwhole spirit, soul, and body be preserved blameless ᶜat the coming of our Lord Jesus Christ. He who ᵈcalls you is faithful, who also will do it.

Brethren, pray for us.

Greet all the brethren with a ᵉholy kiss.

I charge you by the Lord that this epistle ᶠbe read to all the holy brethren.

The grace of our Lord Jesus Christ be with you. Amen.

72. PAUL WRITES HIS SECOND LETTER TO THE THESSALONIANS

Introduction to 2 Thessalonians

In the Greek NT, 2 Thessalonians is listed as "To the Thessalonians." This represents the Apostle Paul's second canonical correspondence to the fellowship of believers in the city of Thessalonica (cf. 1:1).

the command of v. 20. One is never to downgrade the proclamation of God's Word, but to examine the preached word carefully (cf. Acts 17:10, 11). What is found to be "good" is to be wholeheartedly embraced. What is "evil" or unbiblical is to be shunned.

a. **God . . . sanctify you.** Having concluded all the exhortations beginning in 1 Thess. 4:1, and especially from vv. 16–22, Paul's ending benediction acknowledged the source for obeying and fulfilling them all. It is not within human power to be sanctified in all these ways (cf. Zech. 4:6; 1 Cor. 2:4, 5; Eph. 3:20, 21; Col. 1:29). Only God (cf. Rom. 15:33; 16:20; Phil. 4:9; Heb. 13:20 for references to God as "peace") "Himself" can separate us from sin to holiness "completely."

b. **whole spirit, soul, and body.** This comprehensive reference makes the term "completely" more emphatic. By using spirit and soul, Paul was not indicating that the immaterial part of man could be divided into two substances (cf. Heb. 4:12). The two words are used interchangeably throughout Scripture (cf. Heb. 6:19; 10:39; 1 Pet. 2:11; 2 Pet. 2:8). There can be no division of these realities, but rather they are used as other texts use multiple terms for emphasis (cf. Deut. 6:5; Matt. 22:37; Mark 12:30; Luke 10:27). Nor was Paul a believer in a 3-part human composition (cf. Rom. 8:10; 1 Cor. 3:11; 5:3–5; 7:34; 2 Cor. 7:1; Gal. 6:18; Col. 2:5; 2 Tim. 4:22), but rather two parts: material and immaterial.

c. **at the coming.** This fourth mention of Christ's parousia refers to the rapture of the church as it has previously at 1 Thess. 2:19; 3:13; 4:15.

d. **calls you.** This, as every time the divine call is mentioned in the NT, refers to God's effectual call of His chosen ones to salvation (cf. 1 Thess. 2:12; 4:7; Rom. 1:6, 7; 8:28; 1 Cor. 1:9; Eph. 4:1, 4; 2 Tim. 1:9; 1 Pet. 2:9; 5:10; 2 Pet. 1:10). The God who calls will also bring those whom He calls to glory and none will be lost (cf. John 6:37–44; 10:28, 29; Rom. 8:28–39; Phil. 1:6; Jude 24).

e. **holy kiss.** This gesture of affection is commanded 5 times in the NT (Rom. 16:16; 1 Cor. 16:20; 2 Cor. 13:12; 1 Pet. 5:14) and refers to the cultural hug and kiss greeting of the first century which for Christians was to be done righteously in recognition that believers are brothers and sisters in the family of God.

f. **be read.** Public reading was the foundation of spiritual accountability (cf. Gal. 4:16; 2 Thess. 3:14).

Author and Date

Paul, as in 1 Thessalonians, identified himself twice as the author of this letter (1:1; 3:17). Silvanus (Silas) and Timothy, Paul's co-laborers in founding the church, were present with him when he wrote. Evidence, both within this letter and with regard to vocabulary, style, and doctrinal content, strongly supports Paul as the only possible author. The time of this writing was surely a few months after the first epistle, while Paul was still in Corinth with Silas and Timothy (1:1; Acts 18:5) in late A.D. 51 or early A.D. 52 (see Introduction to 1 Thessalonians: Author and Date).

Background and Setting

For the history of Thessalonica, see Introduction to 1 Thessalonians: Background and Setting. Some have suggested that Paul penned this letter from Ephesus (Acts 18:18–21), but his 18 month stay in Corinth provided ample time both for the Thessalonian epistles to be authored (Acts 18:11).

Apparently, Paul had stayed appraised of the happenings in Thessalonica through correspondence and/or couriers. Perhaps the bearer of the first letter brought Paul back an update on the condition of the church, which had matured and expanded (1:3); but pressure and persecution had also increased. The seeds of false doctrine concerning the Lord had been sown, and the people were behaving disorderly. So Paul wrote to his beloved flock who were: 1) discouraged by persecution and needed incentive to persevere; 2) deceived by false teachers who confused them about the Lord's return; and 3) disobedient to divine commands, particularly by refusing to work. Paul wrote to address those 3 issues by offering: 1) comfort for the persecuted believers (1:3–12); 2) correction for the falsely taught and frightened believers (2:1–15); and 3) confrontation for the disobedient and undisciplined believers (3:6–15).

Historical and Theological Themes

Although chaps. 1, 2 contain much prophetic material because the main issue was a serious misunderstanding generated by false teachers about the coming Day of the Lord (Paul reveals that the Day had not come and would not until certain other events occur), it is still best to call this "a pastoral letter." The emphasis is on how to maintain a healthy church with an effective testimony in proper response to sound eschatology and obedience to the truth.

Eschatology dominates the theological issues. One of the clearest statements on personal eschatology for unbelievers is found in 1:9. Church discipline is the major focus of 3:6–15, which needs to be considered along with Matt. 18:15–20; 1 Cor. 5:1–13; Gal. 6:1–5, and 1 Tim. 5:19, 20 for understanding the complete Biblical teaching on this theme.

Interpretive Challenges

Eternal reward and retribution are discussed in 1:5–12 in such general terms that it is difficult to precisely identify some of the details with regard to exact timing. Matters concerning the Day of the Lord (2:2), the restrainer (2:6, 7), and the lawless one (2:3, 4, 8–10) provide challenging prophetic material to interpret. These issues are addressed in the notes.

73. PAUL'S COMFORT FOR AFFLICTION
2 Thess. 1:1–12

Paul, Silvanus, and Timothy,

To the church of the Thessalonians in God our Father and the Lord Jesus Christ: Grace to you and peace from God our Father and the Lord Jesus Christ.

We are ªbound to thank God always for you, brethren, as it is fitting, because your faith grows exceedingly, and the love of every one of you all abounds toward each other, so that we ourselves boast of you among the churches of God for your ᵇpatience and faith in all your persecutions and tribulations that you endure, which is manifest evidence of the righteous judgment of God, that you may be counted worthy of the kingdom of God,

---

a. **bound to thank.** There is a spiritual obligation to thank God in prayer when He accomplishes great things in the lives of His saints. That was the case with the obedient Thessalonians, who had demonstrated growth in faith and love since the first letter. This was in direct answer to Paul's prayers (cf. 1 Thess. 1:3; 3:12).

b. **patience and faith.** Nowhere was their growth in faith and love (2 Thess. 1:3) more evident than in the way they patiently and faithfully endured hostilities and suffering from the enemies of Christ. Although there was no need to speak, since the Thessalonians' lives spoke clearly enough (1 Thess. 1:8), Paul's joy before the Lord over their perseverance bubbled up.

for which you also ᵃsuffer; since it is a righteous thing with ᵇGod to repay with tribulation those who trouble you, and to give you who are troubled ᶜrest with us ᵈwhen the Lord Jesus is revealed from heaven with His mighty angels, ᵉin flaming fire ᶠtaking vengeance on those who ᵍdo not know God, and on those who do not obey the gospel of our Lord Jesus Christ. These shall be punished with ʰeverlasting destruction from the presence of the Lord and from

---

a. **suffer.** Having a right attitude toward suffering is essential, and that required attitude is concern for the kingdom of God. They were not self-centered, but concentrated on God's kingdom. Their focus was not on personal comfort, fulfillment, and happiness, but on the glory of God and the fulfillment of His purposes. They were not moaning about the injustice of their persecutions. Rather, they were patiently enduring the sufferings they did not deserve (v. 4). This very attitude was "manifest evidence" or positive proof that God's wise process of purging, purifying, and perfecting through suffering was working to make His beloved people worthy of the kingdom (cf. 2:12) by being perfected (cf. James 1:2–4; 1 Pet. 5:10). For believers, afflictions are to be expected (cf. 1 Thess. 3:3) as they live and develop Christian character in a satanic world. Suffering is not to be thought of as evidence that God has forsaken them, but evidence that He is with them, perfecting them (cf. Matt. 5:10; Rom 8:18; 2 Cor. 12:10). So the Thessalonians demonstrated that their salvation, determined by faith alone in the Lord Jesus Christ, was genuine because they, like Christ, were willing to suffer on account of God and His kingdom. They suffered unjustly as objects of man's wrath against Christ and His kingdom (Acts 5:41; Phil. 3:10; Col. 1:24). "Kingdom of God" is used here in its spiritual sense of salvation (see Matt. 3:2).

b. **God to repay.** Just as the righteous judgment of God works to perfect believers (v. 5), so it works to "repay" the wicked (cf. 2 Thess. 1:8). Vindication and retribution are to be exercised by God, not man, in matters of spiritual persecution (cf. Deut. 32:35; Prov. 25:21, 22; Rom. 12:19–21; 1 Thess. 5:15; Rev. 19:2). When God repays and how God repays are to be determined by Him.

c. **rest with us.** Paul was a fellow-sufferer for the just cause of Christ. He, like the Thessalonians, hoped for that ultimate rest and reward for their suffering for the kingdom that was to come when Christ returned to judge the ungodly. The Lord Jesus promised this twofold coming for rest and retribution (cf. Matt. 13:40–43; 24:39–41; 25:31–33; Luke 21:27, 28, 34–36; John 5:24–29).

d. **when the Lord Jesus is revealed.** This undoubtedly refers to Christ being unveiled in His coming as Judge. The first aspect of this revealing occurs at the end of the 7 year tribulation period (cf. Matt. 13:24–30, 36–43; 24:29–51; 25:31–46; Rev. 19:11–15). The final and universal revelation of Christ as Judge occurs at the Great White Throne judgment following Christ's millennial reign on the earth (Rev. 20:11–15). Angels always accompany Christ in His coming for judgment (cf. Matt 13:41, 49; 24:30, 31; 25:31; Rev. 14:14, 15).

e. **in flaming fire.** Fire is a symbol of judgment (cf. Ex. 3:2; 19:16–20; Deut. 5:4; Ps. 104:4; Is. 66:15, 16; Matt. 3:11, 12; Rev. 19:12).

f. **taking vengeance.** Lit. these words mean "to give full punishment" (cf. Deut. 32:35; Is. 59:17; 66:15; Ezek. 25:14; Rom. 12:19).

g. **do not know God.** Cf. 1 Thess. 4:5. This speaks to the lack of a personal relationship with God through Jesus Christ (cf. John 17:3; Gal. 4:8; Eph. 2:12; 4:17, 18; Titus 1:16). Retribution is not dealt out because of persecuting Christians, but rather because they did not obey God's command to believe (cf. Acts 17:30, 31; Rom. 1:5; 10:16; 15:18; 16:19) and call upon the name of the Lord to be saved from their sin (Rom. 10:9–13; 1 Cor. 16:22; Heb. 10:26–31). Salvation is never obtained by works but always by placing one's faith alone in the Lord Jesus Christ (Eph. 2:8–10).

h. **everlasting destruction.** See Matt. 25:46. Paul explained the duration and extent of what is elsewhere in Scripture called "hell." First, it is forever, thus it is not a reversible experience. Second, destruction means ruin and does not involve annihilation, but rather a new state of conscious being which is significantly worse than the first (cf. Rev. 20:14, 15). This is described as the absence of God's presence and glory (cf. Matt. 8:12; 22:13; 25:30; Luke 16:24–26).

the glory of His power, ᵃwhen He comes, in that Day, to be glorified in His saints and to be admired among all those who believe, because our testimony among you was believed.

Therefore ᵇwe also pray always for you ᶜthat our God would count you worthy of this calling, and fulfill all the good pleasure of His goodness and the work of faith with power, that the name of our Lord Jesus Christ may be glorified in you, and you in Him, according to the grace of our God and the Lord Jesus Christ.

74. PAUL'S CORRECTION FOR PROPHETIC ERROR

2 Thess. 2:1–17

Now, brethren, ᵈconcerning the coming of our Lord Jesus Christ and our gathering together to Him, we ask you, not to be ᵉsoon shaken in mind or

---

a. **when He comes.** When the Day of the Lord arrives bringing retribution and ruin for unbelievers. As Christ's great glory is displayed the result will be rest and relief for believers and the privilege of sharing His glory (cf. Phil. 3:21; 1 John 3:2). This is the "glorious manifestation" of believers of which Paul spoke (Rom. 8:18, 19). At the time, all believers will adore and worship Him, including those in the Thessalonian church who believed Paul's testimony of the gospel.

b. **we also pray.** Paul's prayer life is exemplified 4 times in this letter (cf. 2 Thess. 1:12; 2:16, 17; 3:1–5, 16). Here he prayed as he did in v. 5, that they might behave in ways consistent with their identity as Christians (cf. 1 Thess. 2:19; Eph. 4:1; Col. 1:10), living up to their "calling to salvation" (cf. Rom 8:30; 11:29; Gal. 4:13–15; 1 Cor. 1:26; Col. 1:3–5; 1 Thess. 2:12) with lives marked by goodness and powerful works of faith.

c. **that.** The worthy walk of 2 Thess. 1:11 allows God to be glorified in us, the light of all purposes (cf. 2 Thess. 2:14; 1 Cor. 10:31; 1 Pet. 4:11).

d. **coming of our Lord Jesus Christ.** This is the fifth mention of Christ's coming in the Thessalonian letters (cf. 1 Thess. 2:19; 3:13; 4:15; 5:23; see 1 Thess. 2:19). The aspect of His particular coming in view here is identified by the next phrase "our gathering together," which conveys the idea of all believers meeting together with the Lord Jesus, obviously referring to the rapture of the church described in 1 Thess. 4:13–18 and John 14:1–3. Cf. Heb. 10:25 for the only other use of this phrase in the NT. This was the event the Thessalonians were anticipating (cf. 1 Thess. 1:10; 3:13; 5:9).

e. **soon shaken.** This term has been used of an earthquake (Acts 16:26) and a ship at anchor slipping its mooring in the midst of a heavy wind. Along with the word "troubled," it describes the state of agitation and alarm that had gripped the church. They were greatly distressed because they had expected the Rapture, the gathering together to the Lord, to take place before the Day of the Lord. They had expected to be taken to glory and heavenly rest, not left to persecution and divine wrath. Paul must have taught them that they would miss the Day of the Lord (1 Thess. 5:2–5; cf. Rev. 3:10), but they had become confused by the persecution they were experiencing, thinking they may have been in the Day of the Lord.

troubled, either by spirit or by word or by letter, as if from us, as though
[a]the day of Christ had come. Let no one deceive you by any means; for that
Day will not come unless [b]the falling away comes first, and the man of sin is
revealed, the son of perdition, who opposes and exalts himself above all that is
called God or that is worshiped, so that he sits as God in the temple of God,
showing himself that he is God.

This error had been reinforced by some messages to them claiming that they were indeed in
the Day of the Lord. Paul noted the source of these as "spirit," "word," and "letter." A "spirit"
would most likely refer to a false prophet claiming divine revelation as in 1 John 4:1–3. A
"word" would refer to a sermon or speech given, while a "letter" indicated a written report.
The powerful but harmful effect of this false information was gained by claiming it was from
the Apostle Paul ("as if from us"). Whoever was telling them they were in the Day of the Lord
claimed that it came from Paul who heard it, preached it, and wrote it. Thus their lie was
given supposed apostolic sanction. The result was shock, fear, and alarm. Obviously, they
had expected the Rapture before the Day of the Lord. For if they had expected it after, they
would have rejoiced because Christ's coming was to be soon. Apostolic authenticity in this
letter which corrects the error was important and accounts for Paul's care to close the letter
in his distinctive handwriting (2 Thess. 3:17; cf. Gal. 6:11).

a. **the day of Christ.** The better text sources indicate "the Lord" rather than "Christ,"
The idea that the Day of the Lord had already come conflicted with what Paul had previously
taught them about the Rapture. This error, which so upset the Thessalonians, is what Paul
corrected in vv. 3–12, where he showed that the day hadn't come and couldn't until certain
realities were in place, most especially "the man of sin" (2 Thess. 1:3).

b. **the falling away.** The Day of the Lord cannot occur until a deliberate abandonment
of a formerly professed position, allegiance, or commitment occurs, (the term was used to
refer to military, political, or religious rebellion). Some have suggested, on questionable
linguistic evidence, that this refers to "departure" in the sense of the Rapture. Context, however,
points to a religious defection, which is further described in v. 4. The language indicates a
specific event, not general apostasy which exists now and always will. Rather, Paul has in mind
the apostasy. This is an event which is clearly and specifically identifiable and unique, the
consummate act of rebellion, an event of final magnitude. The key to identifying the event is
to identify the main person, which Paul does, calling him the "man of sin." Some texts have
"man of lawlessness," but there is no real difference in meaning since sin equals lawlessness
(1 John 3:4). This is the one who is called "the prince who is to come" (Dan. 9:26) and "the
little horn" (Dan. 7:8), whom John calls "the beast" (Rev. 13:2–10, 18) and most know as the
Antichrist. The context and language clearly identify a real person in future times who actually
does the things prophesied of him in Scripture. He is also called "the son of perdition" or
destruction, a term used of Judas Iscariot (John 17:12). "The falling away" is the abomination
of desolation that takes place at the midpoint of the Tribulation, spoken of in Dan. 9:27; 11:31
and Matt. 24:15. This man is not Satan, although Satan is the force behind him (v. 9) and he
has motives like the desires of the devil (cf. Is. 14:13, 14). Paul is referring to the very act of
ultimate apostasy which reveals the final Antichrist and sets the course for the events that
usher in the Day of the Lord. Apparently, he will be seen as supportive of religion so that God
and Christ will not appear as his enemies until the apostasy. He exalts himself and opposes
God by moving into the temple, the place for worship of God, declaring himself to be God
and demanding the worship of the world. In this act of Satanic self-deification, he commits
the great apostasy in defiance of God. For the first 3½ years of the Tribulation, he maintains
relations with Israel, but halts those (cf. Dan. 9:27); and for the last 3½ years, there is great
tribulation under his reign (cf. Dan. 7:25; 11:36–39; Matt. 24:15–21; Rev. 13:1–8) culminating
with the Day of the Lord.

Do you not remember that when I was still with you [a]I told you these things? And now you know what is [b]restraining, that he may be revealed in his own time. For [c]the mystery of lawlessness is already at work; only He who now restrains will do so until He is [d]taken out of the way. [e]And then the lawless one will be revealed, whom [f]the Lord will consume with the breath of His mouth and destroy with the brightness of [g]His coming. The coming of [h]the lawless one is according to the working of Satan, with all power, signs, and lying wonders, and with all unrighteous deception among those who perish,

a. **I told you.** The imperfect tense is used indicating repeated action in past time. Apparently, Paul on numerous occasions had taught them the details of God's future plans. Here, he reminded them of the issues which proved the false teachers wrong about the Day of the Lord. Paul had before told them that the revealing of the Antichrist preceded the Day of the Lord; since he has not yet been revealed they could not possibly be in that Day.

b. **restraining.** While the Thessalonians already had been taught and thus knew what was restraining the coming of the Antichrist, Paul does not say specifically in this letter; thus many suggestions have been made to identify the restraining force of 2 Thess. 2:6, 7. These include: 1) human government; 2) preaching of the gospel; 3) the binding of Satan; 4) the providence of God; 5) the Jewish state; 6) the church; 7) the Holy Spirit; and 8) Michael. Whatever now restrains the Antichrist of vv. 3, 4, 8–10 from being revealed in the fullness of his apostasy and evil, must be more than human or even angelic power. The power that holds back Satan from bringing the final apostasy and unveiling of his Satan-possessed false Christ must be divinely supernatural. It must be God's power in operation that holds back Satan, so that the man of sin, the son of destruction, won't be able to come until God permits it by removing the restraining power. The reason for the restraint was so that Antichrist would be revealed at God's appointed time and no sooner, just as was Christ (cf. Gal. 4:4), because God controls Satan.

c. **the mystery of lawlessness.** This is the spirit of lawlessness already prevalent in society (cf. 1 John 3:4; 5:17), but still a mystery in that it is not fully revealed as it will be in the one who so blatantly opposes God that he blasphemously assumes the place of God on earth which God has reserved for Jesus Christ. The spirit of such a man is already in operation (cf. 1 John 2:18; 4:3), but the man who fully embodies that spirit has not come. For more on mystery, see Matt. 13:11; 1 Cor. 2:7; Eph. 3:4, 5.

d. **taken out of the way.** This refers not to spatial removal (therefore it could not be the rapture of the church) but rather "a stepping aside." The idea is "out of the way," not gone (cf. Col. 2:14 where our sins are taken out of the way as a barrier to God). This restraint will be in place until the Antichrist is revealed, at the midpoint of the Tribulation, leaving him 42 months to reign (Dan. 7:25; Rev. 13:5).

e. **And then the . . . revealed.** At the divinely decreed moment in the middle of the Tribulation when God removes the divine restraint, Satan, who has been promoting the spirit of lawlessness (v. 7), is finally allowed to fulfill his desire to imitate God by indwelling a man who will perform his will as Jesus did God's. This also fits God's plan for the consummation of evil and the judgment of the Day of the Lord.

f. **the Lord will consume.** Death occurs at God's hand (cf. Dan 7:26; Rev. 17:11) and this man and his partner, the false prophet, will be cast alive into the lake of fire which burns with brimstone, where he will be eternally separated from God. (Rev. 19:20; 20:10).

g. **His coming.** The aspect of His coming in view here is not the rapture of the church, but the Lord's coming in judgment on that day when He conquers the forces of Satan and sets up his millennial kingdom (Rev. 19:11–21).

h. **the lawless one.** He will do mighty acts pointing to himself as supernaturally empowered. His whole operation will be deceptive, luring the world to worship him and be damned. The career of the coming lawless one is more fully described in Rev. 13:1–18.

because they did not receive the love of the truth, that they might be saved. And for this reason God will send them strong delusion, that they should believe the lie, that they all may be condemned who did not believe the truth but had pleasure in unrighteousness.

But we are bound to give thanks to God always for you, brethren beloved by the Lord, because God from the beginning chose you for salvation through sanctification by the Spirit and belief in the truth, to which He called you by our gospel, for the obtaining of the glory of our Lord Jesus Christ. Therefore, brethren, stand fast and hold the traditions which you were taught, whether by word or our epistle.

Now may our Lord Jesus Christ Himself, and our God and Father, who has loved us and given us everlasting consolation and good hope by grace, comfort your hearts and establish you in every good word and work.

75. Paul's Concern for the Church
2 Thess. 3:1–18

Finally, brethren, [a]pray for us, that the word of the Lord may run swiftly and be glorified, just as it is with you, and that we may be delivered from [b]unreasonable and wicked men; for not all have faith.

But [c]the Lord is faithful, who will establish you and guard you from the evil one. And we have confidence in the Lord concerning you, both that you do and will do the things we command you.

Now may the Lord direct your hearts into the love of God and into the patience of Christ.

---

a. **pray for us.** Paul frequently enlisted prayer support from the churches for his ministry (cf. Rom. 15:30–32; Eph. 6:18, 19; Col. 4:2, 3; 1 Thess. 5:25; Philem. 22). In particular, he asked them to pray that the word of God would continue to spread rapidly as it had been already (cf. Acts 6:7; 12:24; 13:44–49), and be received with the honor it deserved.

b. **unreasonable and wicked men.** These were Paul's enemies at Corinth, where he ministered when he wrote (cf. Acts 18:9–17), who were perverse and aggressively unrighteous in their opposition of him and the gospel.

c. **the Lord is faithful.** Cf. Lam. 3:23. God is faithful in regard to creation (Ps. 119:90), His promises (Deut. 7:9; 2 Cor. 1:18; Heb. 10:23), salvation (1 Thess. 5:24), temptation (1 Cor. 10:13), suffering (1 Pet. 4:19), and here faithful to strengthen and protect from Satan (cf. John 17:15; Eph. 6:16; 1 Thess. 3:5).

But [a]we command you, brethren, in the name of our Lord Jesus Christ, that you withdraw from every brother who walks disorderly and not according to [b]the tradition which he received from us. For you yourselves know how you ought to [c]follow us, for we were not disorderly among you; nor did we eat anyone's bread free of charge, but [d]worked with labor and toil night and day, that we might not be a burden to any of you, not because we do not have authority, but to make ourselves an example of how you should follow us.

For even when we were with you, we commanded you this: If anyone will not work, neither shall he eat. For [e]we hear that there are some who walk among you in a disorderly manner, not working at all, but are busybodies. Now those who are such we command and exhort through our Lord Jesus Christ that they work in quietness and eat their own bread.

But as for you, brethren, [f]do not grow weary in doing good. And if anyone does not obey our word in this epistle, note that person and [g]do not keep company with him, that he may be ashamed. Yet do not count him as an [h]enemy, but admonish him as a brother.

Now may [i]the Lord of peace Himself give you peace always in every way. The Lord be with you all.

---

a. **we command you.** Paul's directions were not mere suggestions but rather they carried the weight and authority of a judge's court order which the apostle delivered and enforced (cf. 2 Thess. 3:4, 6, 10, 12). Here, he required separation so that obedient Christians were not to fellowship with habitually disobedient believers. This is further explained at v. 14.

b. **the tradition.** There were false traditions (Mark 7:2–13; Col. 2:8) and true (cf. 2 Thess. 2:15). Paul's traditions were the inspired teachings he had given.

c. **follow us.** Paul called for them to imitate him (cf. 1 Thess. 1:6) because he imitated Christ's example (cf. 1 Cor. 4:16; 11:1; Eph. 5:1).

d. **worked.** The specific issue related to working diligently to earn one's living. Though Paul had the "authority" as an apostle to receive support, he chose rather to earn his own living to set an example (cf. 1 Cor. 9:3–14; Gal. 5:4, 6; 1 Tim. 5:17, 18).

e. **we hear.** Word had come that, in spite of Paul teaching them to work and writing to them about it (1 Thess. 4:11), some were still not willing to work (cf. 1 Tim. 5:13). These were commanded to settle down and begin an ordered life of work.

f. **do not grow weary.** The hard working believers were tired of having to support the lazy, and were ready to stop all help to those in need, giving up all charity. Paul reminded them that the truly needy still required help and that the Thessalonians must not be negligent toward them.

g. **do not keep company.** This means to "mix it up" in the sense of social interaction. Blatantly disobedient Christians were to be disfellowshipped (2 Thess. 3:6) to produce shame and, hopefully, repentance if they refused to obey the Word of God. See Matt. 18:15–17; 1 Cor. 5:9–13; Gal. 6:1 for additional details on how to deal with those engaged in unrepentant and repeated sin.

h. **enemy . . . brother.** The purpose of this disfellowship discipline is not final rejection. While an unrepentant pattern of sin is to be dealt with decisively, it is to be continually kept in mind that the one with whom one deals is a brother in the Lord, so all further warnings to him about his sin are done with a brotherly attitude. For instruction on the manner of church discipline, see Matt. 18:15–20.

i. **the Lord of peace.** Paul knew this characteristic of God would be most meaningful

The salutation of Paul with my own hand, which is [a]a sign in every epistle; so I write.

The grace of our Lord Jesus Christ be with you all. Amen.

76. Paul Returns to Antioch
Acts 18:18b–22

Then he [Paul] took leave of the brethren [in Corinth] and sailed for Syria, and [b]Priscilla and Aquila were with him. [c]He had his hair cut off at [d]Cenchrea, for he had taken a vow. And he came to [e]Ephesus, and [f]left them there; but he himself entered the synagogue and reasoned with the Jews. When they asked him to stay a longer time with them, he did not consent, but took leave of them, saying, "I must by all means keep this coming feast in Jerusalem; but I will return again to you, God willing." And he sailed from Ephesus.

And when he had landed at Caesarea, and [g]gone up and greeted the church, he went down to Antioch.

to reflect upon in light of the intense spiritual battle that raged all around the Thessalonians (cf. 2 Thess. 1:2; 1 Thess. 1:1; 5:23). Cf. Paul's other benedictions to this church in 1 Thess. 3:11–13; 5:23; 2 Thess. 2:16, 17; 3:5.

a. **a sign.** Paul often wrote through a secretary (cf. Rom. 16:22). When that was the case, as most likely with this letter, Paul added an identifying signature (cf. 1 Cor. 16:21; Col. 4:18) so that readers could be sure he was truly the author.

b. **Priscilla and Aquila.** That they could accompany Paul means there was sufficient leadership in Corinth, with men such as Gaius, Sosthenes, Stephanas, and Crispus.

c. **He had his hair cut off . . . he had taken a vow.** To show God his gratitude for helping him through a difficult time in Corinth, he took a Nazirite vow—a special pledge of separation and devotion to God (cf. Num. 6:2–5, 13–21). The vow generally lasted a specific period of time, although Samson (Judg. 13:5), Samuel (1 Sam. 1:11), and John the Baptist (Luke 1:15) were Nazirites for life. In Paul's day, if someone made the vow while away from Jerusalem, at the termination of his vow he would shave his head, as Paul did, and afterwards present the shorn hair at the temple within 30 days.

d. **Cenchrea.** The eastern port of Corinth.

e. **Ephesus.** The most important city in Asia Minor.

f. **left them there.** Priscilla and Aquila remained in Ephesus to establish their business. Apparently they lived in Ephesus for several years—a church met in their home (1 Cor. 16:19)—before they returned to Rome (Rom. 16:3–5).

g. **gone up . . . went down to Antioch.** Although Luke does not mention it in detail, his description of the geography indicates Paul went to Jerusalem to greet the church. Because Jerusalem was elevated over the surrounding region, travelers had to go "up" to get there and "down" to any other place. Paul also had to return to Jerusalem so he could fulfill his vow. This ended the second missionary journey.

77. MINISTRY WITH APOLLOS IN EPHESUS

Acts 18:23—19:7

After he [Paul] had spent ᵃsome time there [in Antioch], he departed and went over the region of ᵇGalatia and Phrygia in order, strengthening all the disciples.

Now a certain Jew named ᶜApollos, born at ᵈAlexandria, an eloquent man and ᵉmighty in the Scriptures, came to Ephesus. This man had been instructed in ᶠthe way of the Lord; and being fervent in spirit, he spoke and taught accurately the things of the Lord, though he knew only the ᵍbaptism of John. So he began to speak boldly in the synagogue. When Aquila and Priscilla heard him, they took him aside and explained to him ʰthe way of God more accurately. And when he desired to cross to ⁱAchaia, ʲthe brethren wrote, exhorting the disciples to receive him; and when he arrived, he greatly

---

a. **some time there.** Possibly from the summer of A.D. 52 to the spring of A.D. 53.

b. **Galatia and Phrygia.** See Acts 16:6. Paul's return to those regions marked the beginning of his third missionary journey.

c. **Apollos.** An OT saint and follower of John the Baptist (Acts 18:25). After further instruction by Aquila and Priscilla (v. 26), he became a powerful Christian preacher. His ministry profoundly influenced the Corinthians (cf. 1 Cor. 1:12).

d. **Alexandria.** An important city in Egypt located near the mouth of the Nile. In the first century, it had a large Jewish population. Thus Apollos, though born outside of Israel, was reared in a Jewish cultural setting.

e. **mighty in the Scriptures.** Used only here, this phrase refers to Apollos' knowledge of the OT Scriptures. That knowledge, combined with his eloquence, allowed him to crush his Jewish opponents in debate (Acts 18:28).

f. **the way of the Lord.** This did not include the Christian faith. The OT uses the phrase to describe the spiritual and moral standards God required His people to observe (Gen. 18:19; Judg. 2:22; 1 Sam. 12:23; 2 Sam. 22:22; 2 Kin. 21:22; 2 Chr. 17:6; Pss. 18:21; 25:8, 9; 138:5; Prov. 10:29; Jer. 5:4, 5; Ezek. 18:25, 29; 33:17, 20; Hos. 14:9).

g. **baptism of John.** Despite his knowledge of the OT, Apollos did not fully understand Christian truth. John's baptism was to prepare Israel for the Messiah's arrival (cf. Luke 1:16, 17; see 2:38; Matt. 3:6). Apollos accepted that message, even acknowledging that Jesus of Nazareth was Israel's Messiah. He did not, however, understand such basic Christian truths as the significance of Christ's death and resurrection, the ministry of the Holy Spirit, and the church as God's new witness people. He was a redeemed OT believer.

h. **the way of God more accurately.** Aquila and Priscilla completed Apollos' training in divine truth by instructing him in the fullness of the Christian faith.

i. **Achaia.** Apollos planned to cross from Asia Minor (modern Turkey) to Corinth on the Greek mainland (Acts 19:1).

j. **the brethren wrote.** Such letters of commendation were common in the early church (cf. Rom 16:1, 2; 1 Cor. 16:10; 2 Cor. 3:1, 2; Col. 4:10). The Ephesian Christians wrote to inform their Corinthian brethren that Apollos was now a fully informed Christian.

helped those who had believed through grace; for he vigorously refuted the Jews publicly, showing from the Scriptures that Jesus is ᵃthe Christ.

And it happened, while Apollos was at Corinth, that Paul, having passed through ᵇthe upper regions, came to Ephesus. And finding ᶜsome disciples he said to them, ᵈ"Did you receive the Holy Spirit when you believed?"

So they said to him, "We have not so much as heard whether there is a Holy Spirit."

And he said to them, "Into what then were you baptized?"

So they said, "Into John's baptism."

Then Paul said, "John indeed baptized with a ᵉbaptism of repentance, saying to the people that they should believe on Him who would come after him, that is, on Christ Jesus."

When they heard this, they were ᶠbaptized in the name of the Lord Jesus. And when ᵍPaul had laid hands on them, the Holy Spirit came upon them, and they ʰspoke with tongues and prophesied. Now the men were about twelve in all.

---

a. **the Christ.** The Messiah of Israel.

b. **the upper regions.** The area of Asia Minor N of Ephesus, where Luke left Paul before the interlude describing Apollos' ministry (Acts 18:23). By going through that area, Paul took the direct route to Ephesus, not the more common trade route.

c. **some disciples.** They were of John the Baptist (Acts 19:3); hence OT seekers. That they did not yet fully understand the Christian faith is evident from their reply to Paul's question (v. 2). The word "disciple" means "learner," or "follower," and does not always refer to Christians (cf. Matt. 9:14; 11:2; Mark 2:18; Luke 5:33; 7:18, 19; 11:1; John 1:35; 6:66). Followers of John the Baptist, like this group, existed into the second century.

d. **"Did you receive the Holy Spirit when you believed?"** The question reflects Paul's uncertainty about their spiritual status. Since all Christians receive the Holy Spirit at the moment of salvation (see Rom. 8:9; 1 Cor. 12:13), their answer revealed they were not yet fully Christians. They had not yet received Christian baptism (having been baptized only "into John's baptism") which further evidenced that they were not Christians (see Acts 2:38).

e. **baptism of repentance . . . believe on . . . Christ Jesus.** These disciples did not realize Jesus of Nazareth was the One to whom John's baptism pointed. Paul gave them instruction not on how to receive the Spirit, but about Jesus Christ.

f. **baptized in the name of the Lord Jesus.** They believed Paul's presentation of the gospel and came to saving faith in the Lord Jesus Christ (cf. Acts 2:41). Although required of all Christians, baptism does not save (see Acts 2:38).

g. **Paul . . . laid hands on them.** This signified their inclusion into the church (see Acts 8:17). Apostles were also present when the church was born (Acts 2), and when the Samaritans (Acts 8) and Gentiles (Acts 10) were included. In each case, God's purpose was to emphasize the unity of the church.

h. **spoke with tongues and prophesied.** This served as proof that they were part of the church (see Acts 8:17). They also needed tangible evidence that the Holy Spirit now indwelt them, since they had not heard that He had come.

78. TEACHING THE DISCIPLES IN EPHESUS
Acts 19:8—22

And he went into the synagogue and spoke boldly for [a]three months, reasoning and persuading concerning the things of the kingdom of God. But when some were [b]hardened and did not believe, but spoke evil of the Way before the multitude, he departed from them and withdrew the disciples, reasoning daily in [c]the school of Tyrannus. And this continued for [d]two years, so that [e]all who dwelt in Asia heard the word of the Lord Jesus, both Jews and Greeks.

Now God worked [f]unusual miracles by the hands of Paul, so that even [g]handkerchiefs or aprons were brought from his body to the sick, and the diseases left them and the evil spirits went out of them. Then some of the [h]itinerant Jewish exorcists took it upon themselves to call the name of the Lord Jesus over those who had evil spirits, saying, "We exorcise you by the Jesus whom Paul preaches." Also there were seven sons of [i]Sceva, a Jewish chief priest, who did so.

---

a. **three months.** Paul's longest stay in any synagogue, with the possible exception of the one at Corinth.

b. **hardened.** The Gr. word always refers to defiance against God (Rom. 9:18; Heb. 3:8, 13, 15; 4:7). Truth rejected leads to a hardened heart, causing the life-giving message of salvation to become "the aroma of death leading to death" (2 Cor. 2:16).

c. **the school of Tyrannus.** Tyrannus was either the owner of the lecture hall, or a philosopher who taught there. If the latter, his name, which means "our tyrant," may have been a nickname given him by his students. Paul used the hall during the afternoon break (from about 11:00 a.m. to 4:00 p.m.), when it would otherwise be unoccupied.

d. **two years.** The length of time Paul taught in the school of Tyrannus, not the total length of his ministry at Ephesus (cf. Acts 20:31).

e. **all . . . in Asia heard.** Though Paul probably never left Ephesus, his converts (cf. 2 Tim. 2:2) spread the gospel throughout the province of Asia Minor (modern Turkey). This two-year period saw the founding of the churches at Colosse and Hierapolis, and possibly some of the 7 churches mentioned in Rev. 2, 3, beyond the one at Ephesus.

f. **unusual miracles.** These confirmed that Paul was God's messenger, since there was no completed NT to use to determine the truth of his message (cf. 2 Cor. 12:12; Heb. 2:3, 4).

g. **handkerchiefs . . . aprons.** The headbands and outer clothing Paul wore while making tents. The belief that mystical power could be so transmitted was widespread in the ancient world, e.g., believing that Peter's shadow could heal (cf. Acts 5:15; Matt. 9:21).

h. **itinerant Jewish exorcists.** Simon Magus (Acts 8:9–25) and Bar-Jesus (Acts 13:6–12) were other possible examples of such charlatans (cf. Matt. 12:27). In contrast to the absolute authority exercised by Jesus and the apostles over demons, those exorcists sought to expel the demons by attempting to call on a more potent spirit being—in this case the Lord Jesus.

i. **Sceva, a Jewish chief priest.** Since there is no record of a Jewish High-Priest by that name, he probably assumed that title falsely to impress people.

And the evil spirit answered and said, [a]"Jesus I know, and Paul I know; but who are you?"

Then the man in whom the evil spirit was leaped on them, overpowered them, and prevailed against them, so that they fled out of that house naked and wounded. This became known both to all Jews and Greeks dwelling in Ephesus; and fear fell on them all, and the name of the Lord Jesus was magnified. And many who had believed came confessing and telling their deeds. Also, many of those who had practiced magic brought their [b]books together and burned them in the sight of all. And they counted up the value of them, and it totaled [c]fifty thousand pieces of silver. So the word of the Lord grew mightily and prevailed.

When these things were accomplished, Paul [d]purposed in the Spirit, when he had passed through [e]Macedonia and Achaia, to go to Jerusalem, saying, "After I have been there, [f]I must also see Rome." So he sent into Macedonia two of those who ministered to him, Timothy and Erastus, but he himself stayed in Asia for a time.

79. PAUL WRITES A LETTER TO THE CORINTHIAN CHURCH
Introduction to 1 Corinthians

The letter is named for the city of Corinth, where the church to whom it was written was located. With the exception of personal epistles addressed

---

a. **Jesus . . . Paul I know.** Recognizing that the exorcists had no authority over him (unlike Jesus and Paul), the demon rejected their attempt to expel him from his victim. This confirms that the power to cast out demons belonged to Jesus and the apostles and no one else. Even the demons give testimony to that.

b. **books.** Of secret magical spells. Burning them proved the genuineness of the magicians' repentance (see 2:38); having destroyed these books, they could not easily resume their practices.

c. **fifty thousand pieces of silver.** Fifty thousand days' wages for a common laborer—an astonishing sum of money given to indicate how widespread the practice of magic was in Ephesus.

d. **purposed in the Spirit.** Probably his own spirit, not the Holy Spirit (contra. the NKJV translation).

e. **Macedonia and Achaia.** See Acts 16:9; 18:12. Located on the Greek mainland, these provinces were in the opposite direction from Jerusalem. Paul, however, took this roundabout route to collect an offering for the needy in the Jerusalem church (Rom. 15:25–27; 1 Cor. 16:1–4; 2 Cor. 8, 9).

f. **I must also see Rome.** Paul had not visited the Imperial capital, but because of the strategic importance of the church there, he could stay away no longer. In addition, Paul intended to use Rome as a jumping off point for ministry in the strategic region of Spain (Rom. 15:22–24). This simple declaration marked a turning point in Acts; from this point on, Rome became Paul's goal. He would ultimately arrive there as a Roman prisoner (Acts 28:16).

to Timothy, Titus, and Philemon, all Paul's letters bear the name of the city where the church addressed existed.

Author and Date

As indicated in the first verse, the epistle was written by the Apostle Paul, whose authorship cannot be seriously questioned. Pauline authorship has been universally accepted by the church since the first century, when 1 Corinthians was penned. Internally, the apostle claimed to have written the epistle (1 Cor. 1:1, 13; 3:4–6; 4:15; 16:21). Externally, this correspondence has been acknowledged as genuine since A.D. 95 by Clement of Rome, who was writing to the Corinthian church. Other early Christian leaders who authenticated Paul as author include Ignatius (ca. A.D. 110), Polycarp (ca. A.D. 135), and Tertullian (ca. A.D. 200).

This epistle was most likely written in the first half of A.D. 55 from Ephesus (1 Cor. 16:8, 9, 19) while Paul was on his third missionary journey. The apostle intended to remain on at Ephesus to complete his 3 year stay (Acts 20:31) until Pentecost (May/June) A.D. 55 (16:8). Then he hoped to winter (A.D. 55–56) at Corinth (16:6; Acts 20:2). His departure for Corinth was anticipated even as he wrote (4:19; 11:34; 16:8).

Background and Setting

The city of Corinth was located in southern Greece, in what was the Roman province of Achaia, ca. 45 mi. W from Athens. This lower part, the Peloponnesus, is connected to the rest of Greece by a 4-mile-wide isthmus, which is bounded on the E by the Saronic Gulf and on the W by the Gulf of Corinth. Corinth is near the middle of the isthmus and is prominently situated on a high plateau. For many centuries, all N-S land traffic in that area had to pass through or near this ancient city. Since travel by sea around the Peloponnesus involved a 250 mile voyage that was dangerous and obviously time consuming, most captains carried their ships on skids or rollers across the isthmus directly past Corinth. Corinth understandably prospered as a major trade city, not only for most of Greece but for much of the Mediterranean area, including North Africa, Italy, and Asia Minor. A canal across the isthmus was begun by the emperor Nero during the first century A.D., but was not completed until near the end of the nineteenth century.

The Isthmian games, one of the two most famous athletic events of that day (the other being the Olympian games), was hosted by Corinth, causing more people-traffic. Even by the pagan standards of its own culture, Corinth became so morally corrupt that its very name became synonymous with debauchery and moral depravity. To "corinthianize" came to represent gross immorality and drunken debauchery. In 1 Cor. 6:9, 10, Paul lists some of the specific sins for which the city was noted and which formerly had characterized many believers in the church there. Tragically, some of the worst sins were still found among some church members. One of those sins, incest, was condemned even by most pagan Gentiles (5:1).

Like most ancient Greek cities, Corinth had an acropolis (lit. "a high city"), which rose 2,000 feet and was used both for defense and for worship. The most prominent edifice on the acropolis was a temple to Aphrodite, the Greek goddess of love. Some 1, 000 priestesses, who were "religious" prostitutes, lived and worked there and came down into the city in the evening to offer their services to male citizens and foreign visitors.

The church in Corinth was founded by Paul on his second missionary journey (Acts 18:1ff). As usual, his ministry began in the synagogue, where he was assisted by two Jewish believers, Priscilla and Aquila, with whom he lived for a while and who were fellow tradesmen. Soon after, Silas and Timothy joined them and Paul began preaching even more intensely in the synagogue. When most of the Jews resisted the gospel, he left the synagogue, but not before Crispus, the leader of the synagogue, his family, and many other Corinthians were converted (Acts 18:5–8).

After ministering in Corinth for over a year and a half (Acts 18:11), Paul was brought before a Roman tribunal by some of the Jewish leaders. Because the charges were strictly religious and not civil, the proconsul, Gallio, dismissed the case. Shortly thereafter, Paul took Priscilla and Aquila with him to Ephesus. From there he returned to Israel (vv. 18–22).

Unable to fully break with the culture from which it came, the church at Corinth was exceptionally factional, showing its carnality and immaturity. After the gifted Apollos had ministered in the church for some time, a group of his admirers established a clique and had little to do with the rest of the church. Another group developed that was loyal to Paul, another claimed special allegiance to Peter (Cephas), and still another to Christ alone (see 1 Cor. 1:10–13; 3:1–9).

The most serious problem of the Corinthian church was worldliness, an unwillingness to divorce the culture around them. Most of the believers could not consistently separate themselves from their old, selfish, immoral, and pagan ways. It became necessary for Paul to write to correct this, as well as to command the faithful Christians not only to break fellowship with the disobedient and unrepentant members, but to put those members out of the church (5:9–13).

Before he wrote this inspired letter, Paul had written the church other correspondence (see 5:9), which was also corrective in nature. Because a copy of that letter has never been discovered, it has been referred to as "the lost epistle." There was another non-canonical letter after 1 Corinthians, usually called "the severe letter" (2 Cor. 2:4).

Historical and Theological Themes

Although the major thrust of this epistle is corrective of behavior rather than of doctrine, Paul gives seminal teaching on many doctrines that directly relate to the matters of sin and righteousness. In one way or another, wrong living always stems from wrong belief. Sexual sins for example, including divorce, are inevitably related to disobeying God's plan for marriage and the family (7:1–40). Proper worship is determined by such things as recognition of God's holy character (3:17), the spiritual identity of the church (12:12–27) and pure partaking of the Lord's Supper (11:17–34). It is not possible for the church to be edified faithfully and effectively unless believers understand and exercise their spiritual gifts (12:1—14:40). The importance of the doctrine of the resurrection, of course, cannot be overestimated because if there is no resurrection of the dead, then Christ is not risen. And if Christ is not risen, then preaching is empty and so is faith (15:13, 14).

In addition to those themes, Paul deals briefly with God's judgment of believers, the right understanding of which will produce right motives for godly living (see 3:13–15). The right understanding of idols and of false gods, in general, was to help the immature Corinthians think maturely about such things as eating meat that had been sacrificed to idols (8:1—11:1). The right understanding and expression of genuine, godly love was mandatory to right use of the gifts and even to right knowledge about all the things of God (13:1–13).

So Paul deals with the cross, divine wisdom and human wisdom, the work of the Spirit in illumination, carnality, eternal rewards, the transformation of salvation, sanctification, the nature of Christ, union with Him, the divine role for women, marriage and divorce, Spirit baptism, indwelling and gifting, the unity of the church in one body, the theology of love, and the doctrine of resurrection. All these establish foundational truth for godly behavior.

Interpretive Challenges

By far the most controversial issue for interpretation is that of the sign gifts discussed in chaps. 12–14, particularly the gifts of miracles and tongues-speaking. Many believe that all the gifts are permanent, so that the gift of speaking in tongues will cease (13:8) only at the time the gifts of prophecy and of knowledge cease, namely, when that which is perfect has come (v. 10). Those who maintain that tongues and miracles are still valid spiritual gifts in the church today believe they should be exercised with the same power they were in NT times by the apostles. Others believe the miraculous sign gifts have ceased. This controversy will be resolved in the appropriate notes on chaps. 12–14.

The issue of divorce is a troubling one for many. Chapter 7 addresses the subject, but calls for careful interpretation to yield consistent biblical doctrine on the matter.

Advocates of universalism, the idea that all men will eventually be saved, use 15:22 in support of that view, claiming that, just as every human being died spiritually because of Adam's sin, they will all be saved through Christ's righteousness. The note on that verse will confront the challenge of such universalists.

From that same chapter, the obscure phrase "baptized for the dead" (v. 29) is used to defend the notion that a dead person can be saved by being baptized vicariously through a living Christian. There have been over 40 suggested explanations for this baptism. As the notes will point out, regardless of how that particular verse is interpreted, the falsehood of dead people having the opportunity to be saved is proven by many other texts that are indisputably clear.

A much less serious issue concerns the meaning of 6:4, which pertains to Christians taking other Christians to court before unbelievers. The resolution of that problem lies primarily in being obedient to a verse which is unambiguous.

80. The Calling and Benefits of Sainthood

1 Cor. 1:1–9

Paul, called to be an ᵃapostle of Jesus Christ through the will of God, and ᵇSosthenes our brother,

To the church of God which is at Corinth, to those who are sanctified in Christ Jesus, called to be ᶜsaints, with all who in every place call on the name of Jesus Christ our Lord, both theirs and ours:

ᵈGrace to you and peace from God our Father and the Lord Jesus Christ.

I thank my God always concerning you for the ᵉgrace of God which was given to you by Christ Jesus, that you were ᶠenriched in everything by Him in all ᵍutterance and ʰall knowledge, even as the ⁱtestimony of Christ was confirmed in you, ʲ so that you come short in no gift, eagerly waiting for ᵏthe

---

a. **apostle.** Lit. "a sent one." Paul establishes his authority as an emissary of the Lord Jesus by God's appointment (1 Cor. 9:1; 15:8; cf. Acts 9:3–6, 17; 22:11–15), made especially necessary because so much of the message of this epistle is corrective (1 Cor. 2:1–7). See Rom. 1:1; Eph. 4:11. Since he was delegated by God to speak and write, resisting him was resisting God.

b. **Sosthenes.** Probably Paul's secretary, a former leader of the Corinthian synagogue who had become a brother in Christ. On one occasion, he was beaten for bringing Paul before the civil court at Corinth (Acts 18:12–17).

c. **saints.** Not referring to a specially pious or revered person canonized by an ecclesiastical body, but a reference to everyone who by salvation has been sanctified, that is, set apart from sin in Christ Jesus (cf. Gal. 1:6; Eph. 4:1, 4; Col. 3:15–17; 1 Tim. 6:12; Heb. 10:10, 14; 1 Pet. 2:9, 21; 3:9; 2 Pet. 1:3; Jude 1).

d. **Grace to you and peace.** A greeting Paul used in all his letters. The basic meaning of "grace" is favor; "peace" is a result of God's saving grace (John 14:27; Phil. 4:7).

e. **grace of God . . . given.** This looks at the past, i.e., their salvation, when God justified them by undeserved and unrepayable love and mercy, forgiving their sin through the work of His Son.

f. **enriched in everything by Him.** In the present, the believer has everything the Lord has to give and therefore everything he needs (see 1 Cor. 3:21; Eph. 1:3; Col. 2:10; 2 Pet. 1:3). The two particular blessings spoken of here are related to presenting the truth of God's Word.

g. **utterance.** In regard to speaking for God (cf. Acts 4:29, 31; Eph. 6:19; 2 Tim. 2:15; 1 Pet. 3:15), believers are able to speak when God wants them to because of His enablement. Prayer reaches out for that ability (cf. Acts 4:29, 31; Eph. 6:19), and diligence in study of God's Word aids it (2 Tim. 2:15; 1 Pet. 3:15).

h. **all knowledge.** God provides believers with all the knowledge they need in order to speak effectively for Him (cf. 1 Cor. 2:9; Matt. 11:15; 2 Cor. 4:6; Col. 1:9, 10).

i. **testimony of Christ . . . confirmed in you.** This is a reference to the moment of salvation when the gospel was heard and believed and settled in the heart. At that moment, the enabling of 1 Cor. 1:4 took place, because one became a recipient of the grace of God.

j. **come short in no gift.** "Gift" in Gr. is specifically "a gift of grace." While the blessings of speech and knowledge were primarily for evangelizing the lost, the spiritual gifts (1 Cor. 12–14) edify the church. Because these gifts are given to each believer (1 Cor. 12:11, 12) without regard for maturity or spirituality, the Corinthians, though sinful, had them in full.

k. **the revelation.** Paul looks to the blessing of future grace. At the Lord's second coming,

revelation of our Lord Jesus Christ, who will also confirm you to the end, that you may be blameless in ªthe day of our Lord Jesus Christ. ᵇGod is faithful, ᶜby whom you were called into the fellowship of His Son, Jesus Christ our Lord.

81. THE SIN OF DIVISIVENESS

1 Cor. 1:10–17

Now I plead with you, brethren, by the name of our Lord Jesus Christ, that you all ᵈspeak the same thing, and that there be no divisions among you, but that you be perfectly ᵉjoined together in the ᶠsame mind and in the same judgment. For it has been declared to me concerning you, my brethren, by those of ᵍChloe's household, that there are contentions among you. Now I say

His full glory, honor, and majesty will be revealed in blazing splendor (Rev. 4:11; 5:12; 17:14), at which time all true believers will be fixed solidly forever as holy and without sin in full resurrected glory and purity to live in heaven with God forever. See Eph. 5:25–27; 2 Cor. 11:2.

a. **the day of our Lord Jesus Christ.** Cf. 1 Cor. 5:5; 2 Cor. 1:14. This refers to the coming of the Lord for His church, the rapture (John 14:1–3; 1 Thess. 4:13–18; Rev. 3:10). This is to be distinguished from the Day of the Lord (1 Thess. 5:2, 4; 2 Thess. 2:2), a term referring to judgment on the ungodly.

b. **God is faithful.** Because of God's sovereign and unchangeable promise, believers are assured of this grace—past, present, and future—and will remain saved, assured of future glory at Christ's appearing (Eph. 5:26, 27).

c. **by whom you were called.** This call, as always in the epistles of the NT, refers to an effectual call that saves (see Rom. 8:30). God who calls to salvation and heaven will be faithful to give the grace needed to fulfill that call.

d. **speak the same thing.** Paul is emphasizing the unity of doctrine in the local assembly of believers, not the spiritual unity of His universal church. Doctrinal unity, clearly and completely based on Scripture, must be the foundation of all church life (cf. John 17:11, 21–23; Acts 2:46, 47). Both weak commitment to doctrine and commitment to disunity of doctrine will severely weaken a church and destroy the true unity. In its place, there can be only shallow sentimentalism or superficial harmony.

e. **joined together.** The basic idea is that of putting back together something that was broken or separated so it is no longer divided. The term is used in both the NT and in classical Gr. to speak of mending such things as nets, broken bones or utensils, torn garments, and dislocated joints. Cf. Rom. 16:17; Phil. 1:27.

f. **same mind . . . same judgment.** Cf. Phil 3:15, 16. The demand is for unity internally in their individual minds and externally in decisions made among themselves—unified in truth by beliefs, convictions, standards, and in behavior by applied principles of living (Acts 4:32; Eph. 4:3). The only source of such unity is God's Word which establishes the standard of truth on which true unity rests.

g. **Chloe's household.** Probably a prominent person in the Corinthian church who had written or come to visit Paul in Ephesus to tell him of the factions in the church. It is not known whether Chloe was a man or a woman.

this, that each of you says, "I am of Paul," or "I am of ᵃApollos," or "I am of ᵇCephas," or "I am of Christ." ᶜIs Christ divided? Was Paul crucified for you? Or were you baptized in the name of Paul?

I thank God that I baptized none of you except ᵈCrispus and ᵉGaius, lest anyone should say that I had baptized in my own name. Yes, I also baptized the household of Stephanas. Besides, I do not know whether I baptized any other. For Christ ᶠdid not send me to baptize, but to preach the gospel, not with wisdom of words, lest the cross of Christ should be made of no effect.

82. THE WISDOM OF GOD

1 Cor. 1:18–31

For the ᵍ message of the cross is ʰfoolishness to those who are ⁱperishing, but to us who are being saved it is the power of God. For ʲit is written:

---

a. **Apollos.** See 1 Cor. 16:12; Acts 18:24–28.

b. **Cephas.** The Apostle Peter.

c. **Is Christ divided?** No human leader, not even an apostle, should be given the loyalty that belongs only to the Lord. Such elevation of leaders leads only to contention, disputes, and a divided church. Christ is not divided and neither is His body, the church. Paul depreciates his worth in comparison to the Lord Jesus. For passages on unity, see 1 Cor. 12:12, 13; Rom. 12:5; Eph. 4:4–6.

d. **Crispus.** The leader of the synagogue in Corinth who was converted under Paul's preaching (Acts 18:8). His conversion led to that of many others.

e. **Gaius.** Since Romans was written from Corinth, this man was probably the host referred to in Rom. 16:23.

f. **did not send me to baptize.** This verse does not mean that people should not be baptized (cf. Acts 2:38), but that God did not send Paul to start a private cult of people personally baptized by him. See Acts 26:16–18. He was called to preach the gospel and bring people to oneness in Christ, not baptize a faction around himself.

g. **message of the cross.** God's total revelation, i.e., the gospel in all its fullness, which centers in the incarnation and crucifixion of Christ (1 Cor. 2:2); the entire divine plan and provision for the redemption of sinners, which is the theme of all Scripture, is in view.

h. **foolishness.** Translates the word from which "moron" is derived.

i. **perishing . . . being saved.** Every person is either in the process of salvation (though not completed until the redemption of the body; see Rom. 8:23; 13:11) or the process of destruction. One's response to the cross of Christ determines which. To the Christ-rejectors who are in the process of being destroyed (cf. Eph. 2:1, 2) the gospel is nonsense. To those who are believers it is powerful wisdom.

j. **it is written.** Quoted from Is. 29:14 to emphasize that man's wisdom will be destroyed. Isaiah's prophecy will have its ultimate fulfillment in the last days when Christ sets up His kingdom (cf. Rev. 17:14) and all of human wisdom dies.

"I will destroy the wisdom of the wise,

And bring to nothing the understanding of the prudent."

[a]Where is the wise? Where is the [b]scribe? Where is the [c]disputer of this age? Has not God made foolish the wisdom of this world? For since, [d]in the wisdom of God, the world through wisdom did not know God, it pleased God through the foolishness of the message preached to save those [e]who believe. For Jews request [f]a sign, and Greeks seek after [g]wisdom; but we preach [h]Christ crucified, to the Jews a stumbling block and to the Greeks foolishness, [i]but to those who are called, both Jews and Greeks, Christ the power of God and the wisdom of God. Because the foolishness of God is [j]wiser than men, and the weakness of God is stronger than men.

---

a. **Where is the wise?** Paul paraphrased Is. 19:12, where the prophet was referring to the wise men of Egypt who promised, but never produced wisdom. Human wisdom always proves to be unreliable and impermanent (cf. 1 Cor. 1:17; Prov. 14:12; Is. 29:14; Jer. 8:9; Rom. 1:18–23).

b. **scribe.** Probably Paul has in mind the Assyrians, who sent scribes along with their soldiers to record the booty taken in battle. God saw to it they had nothing to record (Is. 33:18).

c. **disputer.** This was a Gr. word with no OT counterpart, identifying those who were adept at arguing philosophy.

d. **in the wisdom of God.** God wisely established that men could not come to know Him by human wisdom. That would exalt man, so God designed to save helpless sinners through the preaching of a message that was so simple the "worldly wise" deemed it nonsense. Cf. Rom 1:18–23.

e. **who believe.** From the human side, salvation requires and comes only through faith. Cf. John 1:12; Rom. 10:8–17.

f. **a sign.** Unbelieving Jews still wanted supernatural signs (Matt. 12:38–44), yet they refused to accept the most glorious of all the supernatural sign-works of God, namely providing salvation through a virgin-born, crucified, and risen Messiah. In fact, the sign was a stumbling block to them (cf. Rom. 9:31–33).

g. **wisdom.** Gentiles wanted proof by means of human reason, through ideas they could set forth, discuss, and debate. Like the Athenian philosophers, they were not sincere, with no interest in divine truth, but merely wanting to argue intellectual novelty (Acts 17:21).

h. **Christ crucified.** The only true sign and the only true wisdom. This alone was the message Paul would preach (1 Cor. 2:2) because it alone had the power to save all who believed.

i. **called.** To all the "called," the message of the cross, which seems so pointless and irrelevant to man's proud, natural mind, actually exhibits God's greatest power and greatest wisdom.

j. **wiser than man** God disdained human wisdom, not only by disallowing it as a means to knowing Him, but also by choosing to save the lowly. He does not call to salvation many whom the world would call wise, mighty, and noble (cf. Matt. 11:25; 18:3, 4). God's wisdom is revealed to the foolish, weak, and common, i.e., those considered nothing by the elite, who trust in Jesus Christ as Savior and Lord. God clearly received all the credit and the glory for causing such lowly ones to know Him and the eternal truths of His heavenly kingdom. No saved sinner can boast that he has achieved salvation by his intellect (1 Cor. 1:29).

For you see ᵃyour calling, brethren, that not many wise according to the flesh, not many mighty, not many noble, are called. But God has chosen the foolish things of the world to put to shame the wise, and God has chosen the weak things of the world to put to shame the things which are mighty; and the base things of the world and the things which are despised God has chosen, and the things which are not, to bring to nothing the things that are, that no flesh should glory in His presence. But of Him you are in Christ Jesus, who became for us wisdom from God—and righteousness and sanctification and redemption—that, as it is written, ᵇ"He who glories, let him glory in the LORD."

83. THE SOURCE OF SPIRITUAL WISDOM
1 Cor. 2:1–16

And I, brethren, when I came to you, did not come with excellence of speech or of wisdom declaring to you the testimony of God. For I determined not to know anything among you except Jesus Christ and Him ᶜcrucified. I was with you in ᵈweakness, in fear, and in much trembling. And my speech and my preaching were not with persuasive words of human wisdom, but in demonstration of the Spirit and of power, that your faith should not be in the wisdom of men but in the power of God.

---

a. **your calling.** The redeemed not only are given salvation by God's wisdom rather than by their own, but are also graciously given ("by His doing") a measure of His divine wisdom, as well as imputed righteousness (Rom. 4:5; 2 Cor. 5:21), sanctification from sin (Eph. 2:10), and redemption by God (Eph 1:14; 1 Pet. 1:18, 19) in order that, above all else, the Lord will be glorified (cf. Gal. 6:4).

b. **He who glories.** Quoted from Jer. 9:24.

c. **crucified.** Though Paul expounded the whole counsel of God to the church (Acts 20:27) and taught the Corinthians the Word of God (Acts 18:11), the focus of his preaching and teaching to unbelievers was Jesus Christ, who paid the penalty for sin on the cross (Acts 20:20; 2 Cor. 4:2; 2 Tim. 4:1, 2). Until someone understands and believes the gospel, there is nothing more to say to them. The preaching of the cross (1 Cor. 1:18) was so dominant in the early church that believers were accused of worshiping a dead man.

d. **weakness . . . fear . . . trembling.** Paul came to Corinth after being beaten and imprisoned in Philippi, run out of Thessalonica and Berea, and scoffed at in Athens (Acts 16:22–24; 17:10, 13, 14, 32), so he may have been physically weak. But in that weakness, he was most powerful (see 1 Cor. 2:4, 5; 2 Cor. 12:9, 10) There were no theatrics or techniques to manipulate people's response. His fear and shaking was because of the seriousness of his mission.

However, we speak wisdom among those who are ᵃmature, yet not the wisdom of this age, nor of the ᵇrulers of ᶜthis age, who are coming to nothing. But we speak the wisdom of God in a ᵈmystery, the hidden wisdom which God ordained before the ages ᵉfor our glory, which none of the rulers of this age knew; for ᶠhad they known, they would not have crucified the Lord of glory.

But as ᵍit is written:

> "Eye has not seen, nor ear heard,
> Nor have entered into the heart of man
> The things which God has prepared for those who love Him."

ʰBut God ⁱhas revealed them ʲto us through His Spirit. For the Spirit searches all things, yes, the deep things of God. For what man knows the things of a man except the spirit of the man which is in him? Even so no one knows the things of God except the Spirit of God. Now ᵏwe have received, not

---

a. **mature.** Paul uses this word to refer to genuine believers who have been saved by Christ, as in Heb. 6:1; 10:14.

b. **rulers.** Those in authority. See 1 Cor. 1:19, 20.

c. **this age.** All periods of human history until the Lord returns.

d. **mystery.** This term does not refer to something puzzling, but to truth known to God before time, that He has kept secret until the appropriate time for Him to reveal it. See Matt. 13:11; Eph. 3:4, 5.

e. **for our glory.** The truth God established before time and revealed in the NT wisdom of the gospel is the truth that God will save and glorify sinners. See Eph. 3:8–12.

f. **had they known.** The crucifixion is proof that the rulers/Jewish religious leaders lacked wisdom. Cf. 1 Tim. 1:12, 13.

g. **it is written.** These words from Is. 64:4, often incorrectly thought to refer to the wonders of heaven, refer rather to the wisdom God has prepared for believers. God's truth is not discoverable by eye or ear (objective, empirical evidence), nor is it discovered by the mind (subjective, rational conclusions).

h. **But God.** The wisdom that saves, which man's wisdom can't know, is revealed to us by God. He makes it known by revelation, inspiration, and illumination. Revelation (1 Cor. 2:10, 11) and inspiration (vv. 12, 13) were given to those who wrote the Bible; illumination (vv. 14–16) is given to all believers who seek to know and understand that divinely written truth. In each case, the Holy Spirit is the divine agent doing the work (cf. 2 Pet. 1:21).

i. **has revealed them.** By the Holy Spirit, God disclosed His saving truth (cf. Matt. 11:25; 13:10–13). The Spirit alone was qualified because He knows all that God knows, Himself being God.

j. **to us.** As with the "we's" in 1 Cor. 2:6, 7 and vv. 12, 13, Paul is, first of all, speaking of himself (as in John 14:26; 15:26, 27), and, in a sense, of believers who have been given the Word as recorded by the apostles and their associates who wrote the NT.

k. **we have received.** The "we" and "us" refer to the apostles and other writers of the Word of God. The means was inspiration (see 2 Tim. 3:16; 2 Pet. 1:20, 21), by which God freely gave the gift of His Word. It was this process of inspiration that turned the spiritual thoughts into spiritual words to give life (cf. Matt. 4:4).

the spirit of the world, but the Spirit who is from God, that we might know the things that have been freely given to us by God.

These things we also speak, not in words which man's wisdom teaches but which the Holy Spirit teaches, comparing spiritual things with spiritual. But the ªnatural man does not receive the things of the Spirit of God, for they are foolishness to him; nor can he know them, because they are ᵇspiritually discerned. But he who is spiritual judges all things, yet he himself is rightly ᶜjudged by no one. For "who has known the mind of the LORD that he may instruct Him?" But we have the ᵈmind of Christ.

84. BUILDING ON THE FOUNDATION

1 Cor. 3:1–15

And I, brethren, could not speak to you as to spiritual people but as to ᵉcarnal, as to ᶠbabes in Christ. I fed you with ᵍmilk and not with ʰsolid food; for until now you were not able to receive it, and even now you are still not able; for

---

a. **natural man.** This refers to the unconverted, who lack supernatural life and wisdom.

b. **spiritually discerned.** Through illumination of the Word, the Holy Spirit provides His saints the capacity to discern divine truth (see Ps. 119:18), which the spiritually dead are unable to comprehend (cf. John 5:37–39; see 1 John 2:20, 27). The doctrine of illumination does not mean we know everything (cf. Deut. 29:29), that we do not need teachers (cf. Eph. 4:11, 12), or that understanding does not require hard work (cf. 2 Tim. 2:15).

c. **judged by no one.** Obviously, unbelievers are able to recognize Christians' faults and shortcomings; but they are not able to evaluate their true nature as spiritual people who have been transformed into children of God (cf. 1 John 3:2).

d. **mind of Christ.** Quoted from Is. 40:13. The same word is translated "understanding" in 14:14, 15, 19. Believers are allowed, by the Word and the Spirit, to know the thoughts of their Lord. Cf. Luke 24:45.

e. **carnal.** Although Corinthian believers were no longer "natural," they were not "spiritual" (fully controlled by the Holy Spirit). In fact, they were "carnal" (controlled by the fallen flesh). Though all believers have the Holy Spirit (cf. Rom. 8:9) they still battle the fallen flesh (see Rom. 7:14–25; 8:23).

f. **babes in Christ.** The carnality of those believers was indicative of their immaturity. They had no excuse for not being mature, since Paul implied that he should have been able to write to them as mature, in light of all he had taught them. See Heb. 5:12–14; 1 Pet. 2:1, 2.

g. **milk.** Not a reference to certain doctrines, but to the more easily digestible truths of doctrine that were given to new believers.

h. **solid food.** The deeper features of the doctrines of Scripture. The difference is not in kind of truth, but degree of depth. Spiritual immaturity makes one unable to receive the richest truths.

you are still carnal. For where there are ᵃenvy, strife, and divisions among you, are you not carnal and behaving like ᵇmere men? For when one says, "I am of ᶜPaul," and another, "I am of Apollos," are you not carnal?

ᵈWho then is Paul, and who is Apollos, but ministers through whom you believed, as ᵉthe Lord gave to each one? I planted, Apollos watered, but God gave the increase. So then neither he who plants is anything, nor he who waters, but God who gives the increase. Now he who plants and he who waters ᶠare one, and each one will receive his own reward according to his own labor.

For ᵍwe are God's fellow workers; you are God's field, you are ʰGod's building. According to the grace of God which was given to me, as a wise ⁱmaster builder I have laid the foundation, and another builds on it. But let each one take heed how he builds on it. For ʲno other foundation can anyone lay than that which is laid, which is Jesus Christ. Now ᵏif anyone builds on this foundation with ˡgold, silver, precious stones, ᵐwood, hay, straw, each

---

a. **envy, strife.** Carnality produces the attitude of envy, a severe form of selfishness, which produces the action of strife and the subsequent divisions.

b. **mere men.** Apart from the will of the Spirit, hence carnal, not spiritual.

c. **Paul . . . Apollos.** Factionalism was the divisive product of carnality. Cf. 1 Cor. 1:11–13.

d. **Who then is Paul . . . Apollos.** A humble, but accurate assessment of the roles that ministers play.

e. **the Lord gave . . . God gave . . . God who gives.** It is the Lord alone who can give the faith to the spiritually ignorant and dead. Salvation is God's work of grace to whom He chooses to give it (see Rom. 9:15–19; Eph. 2:8, 9).

f. **are one.** All the human instruments God uses to produce salvation life are equally considered and rewarded for their willingness to be used by God. But all the glory goes to Him, who alone saves. Because of that, the silly favoritism of 1 Cor. 1:12; 3:4 is condemned. See Matt. 20:1–16.

g. **we.** Paul, Apollos, Peter, and all ministers are equal workers in the field, but the spiritual life from that field is entirely by God's grace and power.

h. **God's building.** Paul shifts the imagery from agricultural to construction (1 Cor. 3:10–17).

i. **master builder . . . foundation.** The Gr. word is the root for architect, but contained the idea of builder as well as designer. Paul's specialty was designing and building spiritual foundations (cf. Rom. 15:20). He was used by God to establish the groundwork for churches in Asia Minor, Macedonia, and Greece. Others (e.g., Timothy, Apollos) built the churches up from his foundations. That God used him in that way was all of grace (cf. 1 Cor. 3:7; 15:20; Rom. 15:18; Eph. 3:7, 8; Col. 1:29).

j. **no other foundation.** Paul did not design the foundation, he only laid it down by preaching Christ. Cf. 1 Pet. 2:6–8.

k. **if anyone builds.** This is, first of all, in reference to the evangelists and pastors, and then to all believers who are called to build the church through faithful ministry.

l. **gold, silver, precious stones.** His quality materials represent dedicated, spiritual service to build the church.

m. **wood, hay, straw.** Inferior materials implying shallow activity with no eternal value. They do not refer to activities that are evil.

one's work will become clear; for [a]the Day will declare it, because it will be [b]revealed by fire; and the fire will test each one's work, of what sort it is. If anyone's work which he has built on it [c]endures, he will receive a [d]reward. If anyone's work is burned, he will suffer loss; but he himself will be [e]saved, yet so as [f]through fire.

85. THE TEMPLE OF GOD

1 Cor. 3:16−23

Do you not know that you are the temple of God and that the Spirit of God dwells in you? If anyone defiles the temple of God, God will destroy him. For the temple of God is holy, which temple you are.

Let no one [g]deceive himself. If anyone among you seems to be wise in this age, let him become a fool that he may become wise. For the wisdom of this world is foolishness with God. For [h]it is written, "He catches the wise in their own craftiness"; and again, "The LORD knows the thoughts of the wise, that they are futile." Therefore let no one [i]boast in men. For [j]all things are

---

a. **the Day.** Refers to the time of the Judgment Seat of Christ (see 2 Cor. 5:10).

b. **revealed by fire.** The fire of God's discerning judgment (cf. Job 23; 10; Zech. 13:9; 1 Pet. 1:17, 18; Rev. 3:18). Second Corinthians 5:10 indicates that the wood, hay, and straw are "worthless" things that don't stand the test of judgment fire (cf. Col. 2:18).

c. **endures.** All that which has been accomplished in His power and for His glory will survive (cf. Matt. 25:21, 23; 2 Cor. 5:9; Phil. 3:13, 14; 1 Thess. 2:19, 20; 2 Tim. 4:7, 8; James 1:12; 1 Pet. 5:4; Rev. 22:12).

d. **reward.** Cf. Rev. 22:12. This is not a judgment for sin. Christ has paid that price (Rom. 8:1), so that no believer will ever be judged for sin. This is only to determine eternal reward (cf. 1 Cor. 4:5, "each one's praise").

e. **be saved.** No matter how much is worthless, no believer will forfeit salvation.

f. **through fire.** Here is a severe warning to any who would try to interfere with or destroy the building of the church on the foundation of Christ. See Matt. 18:6, 7.

g. **deceive himself.** See 1 Cor. 1:18–25. Those who defile the church and think they can succeed in destroying it by their human wisdom, would be far better to reject that wisdom and accept the foolishness of Christ's cross.

h. **it is written.** With quotations from Job 5:13 and Ps. 94:11, Paul reinforces his point from 1 Cor. 1:18–25 by reminding them that human wisdom which cannot save, also cannot either build a church or prevent its growth.

i. **boast in men.** Paul, Apollos, and all others receive no credit for the building of the church.

j. **all things are yours.** All believers share equally in God's most important and valuable provisions and glories; human boasting, therefore, is ludicrous as well as sinful.

yours: whether Paul or Apollos or Cephas, or ªthe world or ᵇlife or death, or
ᶜthings present or ᵈthings to come—ᵉall are yours. And you are ᶠChrist's, and
Christ is God's.

86. THE NEED FOR SERVANTHOOD

1 Cor. 4:1–13

Let a man ᵍso consider us, as ʰservants of Christ and ⁱstewards of the ʲmysteries
of God. Moreover it is required in stewards that one be found ᵏfaithful. But
with me it is a very small thing that I should be judged by you or by a ˡhuman
court. In fact, I do not even judge myself. For I know of ᵐnothing against

---

a. **the world.** Although the universe is now in Satan's grip, it is still the God-given and
God-made possession of Christians (2 Cor. 4:15; 1 John 5:19). In the millennial kingdom and
throughout eternity, however, believers will possess both the recreated and eternal earth in
an infinitely more complete and rich way (Matt. 5:5; Rev. 21).

b. **life or death.** Spiritual, eternal life (cf. John 14:23; cf. 2 Pet. 1:3, 4) or spiritual, eternal
death (1 Cor. 15:54–57; Phil. 1:21–24).

c. **things present.** Everything the believer has or experiences in this life (cf. Rom. 8:37–39).

d. **things to come.** All the blessings of heaven. Cf. 1 Pet. 1:3, 4.

e. **all are yours.** In Christ, all good and holy things are for believers' blessing and for
God's glory. Cf. Eph. 1:3; 2 Pet. 1:3.

f. **Christ's . . . God's.** Knowing that believers belong to Christ and therefore to each
other is the greatest incentive for unity in the church (1 Cor. 6:17; cf. John 9:9, 10, 21–23;
Phil. 2:1–4).

g. **so consider us.** Paul wanted everyone to view him and his fellow ministers only as the
humble messengers God ordained them to be (cf. 1 Cor. 3:9, 22).

h. **servants.** Paul expresses his humility by using a word lit. meaning "under rowers,"
referring to the lowest, most menial, and most despised galley slaves, who rowed on the
bottom tier of a ship (1 Cor. 9:16; see Luke 1:2; Acts 20:19).

i. **stewards.** Paul defines his responsibilities as an apostle by using a word originally
referring to a person entrusted with and responsible for his master's entire household: e.g.,
buildings, fields, finances, food, other servants, and sometimes even children of the owner.
Cf. 1 Pet. 4:10.

j. **mysteries of God.** "Mystery" is used in the NT to refer to divine revelation previously
hidden. See 2:7; Matt. 13:11; Eph. 3:4, 5. Here the word is used in its broadest sense as God's
full revealed truth in the NT (Acts 20:20, 21, 27; 2 Tim. 2:15; 3:16). It was all that truth which
Paul had to oversee and dispense as God's servant and steward.

k. **faithful.** The most essential quality of a servant or steward is obedient loyalty to his
master (1 Cor. 4:17; 7:25; cf. Matt. 24:45–51; Col. 1:7; 4:7).

l. **human court.** Paul is not being arrogant or saying that he is above fellow ministers,
other Christians, or even certain unbelievers. He is saying that a human verdict on his life is
not the one that matters, even if it was his own.

m. **nothing against myself.** Paul was not aware of any unconfessed or habitual sin in his
own life, but his limited understanding assumed that his was not the final verdict (see 2 Cor. 1:12).

myself, yet I am ªnot justified by this; but He who judges me is ᵇthe Lord. Therefore judge nothing before the time, until the Lord comes, who will both bring to light the ᶜhidden things of darkness and reveal the counsels of the hearts. Then each one's praise will come from God.

Now ᵈthese things, brethren, I have figuratively transferred to myself and Apollos for ᵉyour sakes, that you may learn in us not to think beyond ᶠwhat is written, that none of you may be ᵍpuffed up on behalf of one against the other. For who makes you differ from another? And what do you have that you did not receive? ʰNow if you did indeed receive it, why do you boast as if you had not received it?

You are already ⁱfull! You are already rich! You have reigned as kings without us—and indeed I could wish you did ʲreign, that we also might reign with you! For I think that God has displayed us, the apostles, ᵏlast, as men condemned to death; for we have been made a spectacle to the world,

---

a. **not justified by this.** Paul's own sincere evaluation of his life did not acquit him of all failures to be faithful.

b. **the Lord.** He is the ultimate and only qualified Judge of any man's obedience and faithfulness (2 Tim. 2:15). See 2 Cor. 5:9, 10.

c. **hidden things of darkness . . . counsels of the hearts.** These refer to the inner motives, thoughts, and attitudes which only God can know. Since final rewards will be based, not just on outward service, but on inward devotion (cf. 10:31), only God can give the praise each deserves. See 1 Cor. 3:12–14.

d. **these things.** Paul is referring to the analogies he used to depict those who minister for the Lord, including himself and Apollos: farmers (1 Cor. 3:6–9), builders (1 Cor. 3:10–15), and servant-stewards (1 Cor. 4:1–5).

e. **your sakes.** Paul's humility, expressed in light of God's judgment on the greatest apostles and preachers, was useful to teach believers not to exalt any of them (cf. Gen. 18:27; 32:10; Ex. 3:11; Judg. 6:15; Matt. 3:14; Luke 5:8; John 1:26, 27; Acts 20:19; 2 Cor. 3:5; Eph. 3:8).

f. **what is written.** God's faithful servants are to be treated with respect only within the bounds of what is scriptural (1 Thess. 5:12; 1 Tim. 5:17; Heb. 13:7, 17).

g. **puffed up.** Pride and arrogance were great problems in the Corinthian church (see 1 Cor. 4:18, 19; 5:2; 8:1; 13:4; 2 Cor. 12:20).

h. **boast.** Pride is deception, since everything a person possesses is from God's providential hand (cf. 1 Chr. 29:11–16; Job 1:21; James 1:17).

i. **full . . . rich . . . reigned.** In a severe rebuke, Paul heaps on false praise, sarcastically suggesting that those Corinthians who were self-satisfied had already achieved spiritual greatness. They were similar to the Laodiceans (see Rev. 3:17). Cf. Phil 3:12; 2 Tim. 4:8; James 1:12; 1 Pet. 5:4.

j. **reign.** Yet, Paul genuinely wished it really were the coronation time of the Millennium, so that they all might share in the glory of the Lord.

k. **last.** The imagery is of condemned prisoners brought into a Roman arena to fight and die; the last ones brought out for slaughter were the grand finale. In His sovereign wisdom and for His ultimate glory, God chose to display the apostles figuratively before men and angels during the present age as just such worthless and condemned spectacles (cf. Matt. 19:28). Like doomed gladiators, they were ridiculed, spit on, imprisoned, and beaten; yet, God glorified His name through them as He used them to build His kingdom.

both to angels and to men. We are ᵃfools for Christ's sake, but you are wise in Christ! We are weak, but you are strong! You are distinguished, but we are dishonored! To the present hour we both hunger and thirst, and ᵇwe are poorly clothed, and beaten, and homeless. And we labor, working with ᶜour own hands. Being reviled, we bless; being persecuted, we endure; being defamed, we entreat. We have been made as the ᵈfilth of the world, the offscouring of all things until now.

87. THE ADMONITION OF A FATHER
1 Cor. 4:14–21

ᵉI do not write these things to shame you, but as my beloved children I ᶠwarn you. For though you might have ᵍten thousand instructors in Christ, yet you do not have many fathers; for in Christ Jesus I have begotten you through the gospel. Therefore I urge you, ʰimitate me. For this reason I have sent ⁱTimothy

---

a. **fools . . . wise.** Again using sarcasm, this time on himself as if mimicking the attitude of the proud Corinthians toward him, Paul rebukes them (cf. Acts 17:18).

b. **we are poorly clothed.** The apostles and early preachers lived at the lowest levels of society. While the Corinthians believers thought they were kings (1 Cor. 4:8), the apostle knew he was a suffering slave (cf. 2 Cor. 1:8, 9; 4:8–12; 6:4–10; 11:23–28).

c. **our own hands.** The apostles did manual labor which Greeks, including some in the church at Corinth, considered beneath their dignity and suitable only for slaves. But Paul was not resentful about any necessary labor needed to support gospel preaching (cf. Acts 18:3; 20:34; 2 Cor. 11:23–28; 1 Thess. 2:9; 2 Thess. 3:8; 2 Tim. 3:12).

d. **filth . . . offscouring.** The scum and dregs scraped from a dirty dish or garbage pot, figuratively used of the lowest, most degraded criminals who were often sacrificed in pagan ceremonies. Not in God's sight, but in the world's, Paul and his fellow preachers were so designated. What a rebuke of the proud, carnal Corinthians who saw themselves at the top, while the humble apostle considered himself at the bottom.

e. **beloved children.** Despite their carnal, even sometimes hateful immaturity, Paul always looked on the Corinthian believers with affection (cf. 2 Cor. 12:14, 15; Gal. 4:19; Phil. 1:23–27; 3 John 4).

f. **warn.** Lit. "put in mind," with the purpose of admonishing and reproving, presupposing that something is wrong and should be corrected (cf. Matt. 18:15–20; Acts 20:31; 1 Thess. 2:7–12; 5:14).

g. **ten thousand instructors.** The terms actually say "countless tutors," referring by hyperbole to an unlimited number of moral guardians used with children. Only Paul was their spiritual father; hence, no one cared like him.

h. **imitate me.** See 1 Cor. 11:1. A bold, but justified exhortation. Spiritual leaders must set an example of Christlikeness to follow (cf. 1 Tim. 4:12; Heb. 13:7)

i. **Timothy.** He had been so faithfully discipled by Paul that he could be sent in the great apostle's place with confidence that he would perfectly represent him. Cf. 2 Tim. 2:2; 3:10–14.

to you, who is my beloved and faithful son in the Lord, who will remind you of my ways in Christ, as [a]I teach everywhere in every church.

Now some are [b]puffed up, as though I were not coming to you. But I will come to you shortly, if the Lord wills, and I will know, not the word of those who are puffed up, but the power. For the kingdom of God is not in [c]word but in power. What do you want? Shall I come to you with a [d]rod, or in love and a spirit of gentleness?

88. IMMORALITY CONFRONTED

1 Cor. 5:1–12

It is actually reported that there is [e]sexual immorality among you, and such sexual immorality as is not even named among the Gentiles—that a man has [f]his father's wife! And you are [g]puffed up, and have not rather mourned, that he who has done this deed might be [h]taken away from among you. For I indeed, as absent in body but present in spirit, have [i]already judged (as though I were present) him who has so done this deed. In the [j]name of our Lord Jesus

---

a. **I teach.** Referring to doctrine, not advice. By his own instruction and example, Timothy would reinforce the eternal truths Paul had taught him.

b. **puffed up.** They were arrogant, thinking they would never have to face Paul again. But, if God allowed, he was planning to see them soon. He would not let their proud sinning go unchallenged, for their own sake as well as the gospel's (cf. Heb. 12:6). The reality of how much real spiritual power they had would become clear in that confrontation.

c. **word . . . power.** Spiritual character is measured not by the impressiveness of words, but in the power of the life (cf. Matt. 7:21–23).

d. **rod.** Spiritual leaders need to use the rod of correction if people persist in sin. The pattern for that correction is illustrated and explained in 1 Cor. 5:1–13; cf. Matt. 18:15–18.

e. **sexual immorality.** This sin was so vile that even the church's pagan neighbors were doubtless scandalized by it. The Corinthians had rationalized or minimized this sin which was common knowledge, even though Paul had written them before about it (v. 9). The Gr. for "immorality" is the root of the Eng. word "pornography."

f. **his father's wife.** The man's stepmother, with whom having sexual relations bore the same sinful stigma as if between him and his natural mother. Incest was punishable by death in the OT (Lev. 18:7, 8, 29; cf. Deut. 22:30) and was both uncommon ("not even named") and illegal under Roman law.

g. **puffed up.** So arrogant and carnal as to excuse even that extreme wickedness.

h. **taken away.** Excommunicated as in v. 7 (see Matt 18:15–17; Eph. 5:3, 11; 2 Thess. 3:6).

i. **already judged.** Paul had passed judgment on the sinner, and the church also needed to.

j. **name of our Lord.** Consistent with His holy person and will.

Christ, when you are ᵃgathered together, along with my spirit, with the ᵇpower of our Lord Jesus Christ, ᶜdeliver such a one to Satan for the ᵈdestruction of the flesh, that his ᵉspirit may be saved in the ᶠday of the Lord Jesus.

Your ᵍglorying is not good. Do you not know that a little ʰleaven leavens the ⁱwhole lump? Therefore purge out the old leaven, that you may be a new lump, since you truly are unleavened. For indeed ʲChrist, our Passover, was sacrificed for us.ᵏTherefore let us keep the feast, not with old leaven, nor with the leaven of malice and wickedness, but with the unleavened bread of sincerity and truth.

I wrote to you in ˡmy epistle not to keep company with sexually immoral people. Yet I certainly did not mean with the sexually immoral ᵐpeople of

---

a. **gathered together.** This action is to be done when the church meets publicly (see Matt. 18:15–18).

b. **power.** Authority is in view. Action against unrepentant sinning in the church carries the weight of the Lord's authority.

c. **deliver . . . to Satan.** "Deliver" is a strong term, used of judicial sentencing. This is equal to excommunicating the professed believer. It amounts to putting that person out of the blessing of Christian worship and fellowship by thrusting him into Satan's realm, the world system. See 1 Tim. 1:20.

d. **destruction of the flesh.** This refers to divine chastening for sin that can result in illness and even death. See 1 Cor. 11:29–32; cf. Acts 5:1–11.

e. **spirit . . . saved.** The unrepentant person may suffer greatly under God's judgment, but will not be an evil influence in the church; and he will more likely be saved under that judgment than if tolerated and accepted in the church.

f. **day of the Lord Jesus.** This is the time when the Lord returns with His rewards for His people. See 1 Cor. 1:8.

g. **glorying.** Better, "boasting." It was not good because their proud sense of satisfaction blinded them to their duty in regard to blatant sin that devastated the church.

h. **leaven.** See Mark 8:15. In Scripture, it is used to represent influence, in most cases evil influence, although in Matt. 13:33 it refers to the good influence of the kingdom of heaven (cf. Ex. 13:3, 7).

i. **whole lump.** When tolerated, sin will permeate and corrupt the whole local church.

j. **Christ, our Passover.** Just as unleavened bread symbolized being freed from Egypt by the Passover (Ex. 12:15–17), so the church is to be unleavened, since it has been separated from the dominion of sin and death by the perfect Passover Lamb, the Lord Jesus Christ. The church is, therefore, to remove everything sinful in order to be separate from the old life, including the influence of sinful church members.

k. **keep the feast.** In contrast to the OT Passover feast celebrated annually, believers constantly celebrate the "feast" of the new Passover—Jesus Christ. As the Jews who celebrate Passover do so with unleavened bread, so believers celebrate their continual Passover with unleavened lives.

l. **my epistle.** A previous letter that Paul had written the church at Corinth instructed them to disassociate with the immoral (cf. 1 Cor. 5:11; 2 Thess. 3:6–15).

m. **people of this world.** Evidently, the church had misinterpreted the advice in that letter and had stopped having contact with the unsaved in the world, while continuing to tolerate the sin of those in the church, which was even more dangerous to the fellowship. See John 17:15, 18. God intends us to be in the world as witnesses (cf. Matt. 5:13–16; Acts 1:8; Phil. 2:15).

this world, or with the covetous, or extortioners, or idolaters, since then you would need to go out of the world. But now I have written to you not to keep company with anyone [a]named a brother, who is sexually immoral, or covetous, or an idolater, or a reviler, or a drunkard, or an extortioner—[b]not even to eat with such a person.

For what have I to do with judging those also who are outside? Do you not judge those who are inside? But those who are [c]outside God judges. Therefore [d]"put away from yourselves the evil person."

89. LAWSUITS AND STRIFE FORBIDDEN
1 Cor. 6:1—11

[e]Dare any of you, having [f]a matter against another, go to law before the [g]unrighteous, and not [h]before the saints? Do you not know that the saints will [i]judge the world? And if the world will be judged by you, are you unworthy to judge the smallest matters? Do you not know that we shall [j]judge angels? How much more, things that pertain to this life? If then you have judgments

---

a. **named a brother.** Paul clarifies his intention in the earlier letter. He expected them to disassociate with all who said they were brothers, but had a consistent pattern of sin.

b. **not even to eat.** The meal was a sign of acceptance and fellowship in those days. See 2 Thess. 3:6, 14.

c. **outside.** Paul never intended himself or the church to be judges of unbelievers outside the church, but to judge those inside (cf. 1 Pet. 4:17). Those on the outside are for God to judge and believers to evangelize. Those who sin on the inside, the church is to put out.

d. Quoted from Deut. 17:7.

e. **Dare.** Suing another believer in a secular law court is a daring act of disobedience because of its implications related to all sin—the displeasure of God.

f. **a matter against another.** The phrase in Gr. was commonly used of a lawsuit ("go to law").

g. **unrighteous.** This does not refer to their moral character, but to their unsaved spiritual condition.

h. **before the saints.** Believers are to settle all issues between themselves within the church.

i. **judge the world.** Because Christians will assist Christ to judge the world in the millennial kingdom (Rev. 2:26, 27; 3:21; cf. Dan. 7:22), they are more than qualified with the truth, the Spirit, the gifts, and the resources they presently have in Him to settle small matters that come up among themselves in this present life.

j. **judge angels.** The Gr. word can mean "rule or govern." Since the Lord Himself will judge fallen angels (2 Pet. 2:4; Jude 6), it is likely this means we will have some rule in eternity over holy angels. Since angels are "ministering spirits" to serve the saints (Heb. 1:14), it seems reasonable that they will serve us in glory.

concerning things pertaining to this life, do you appoint those who are [a]least esteemed by the church to judge? I say this to your [b]shame. Is it so, that there is not a wise man among you, not even one, who will be able to judge between his brethren? But brother goes to law against brother, and that before unbelievers!

Now therefore, it is already an utter failure for you that you go to law against one another. [c]Why do you not rather accept wrong? Why do you not rather let yourselves be [d]cheated? No, [e]you yourselves do wrong and cheat, and you do these things to your brethren! Do you not know that the unrighteous will [f]not inherit the kingdom of God? Do not be deceived. Neither fornicators, nor [g]idolaters, nor [h]adulterers, nor [i]homosexuals, nor sodomites, nor [j]thieves, nor covetous, nor drunkards, nor [k]revilers, nor [l]extortioners will inherit the

---

a. **least esteemed.** This is a difficult verse to translate, as suggested by the widely varying Eng. renderings. But the basic meaning is clear: when Christians have earthly quarrels and disputes among themselves, it is inconceivable that they would turn to those least qualified (unbelievers) to resolve the matter. The most legally untrained believers, who know the Word of God and are obedient to the Spirit, are far more competent to settle disagreements between believers than the most experienced unbeliever, void of God's truth and Spirit.

b. **shame.** Such conduct as suing a fellow believer is not only a sinful shame (1 Cor. 6:5), but a complete failure to act obediently and righteously. Christians who take fellow Christians to court suffer moral defeat and spiritual loss even before the case is heard, and they become subject to divine chastening (cf. Heb. 12:3ff).

c. **Why . . . not . . . accept wrong?** The implied answer is because of the shameful sin (1 Cor. 6:5) and the moral defeat (v. 8) that result from selfishness, a willingness to discredit God, His wisdom, power, and sovereign purpose, and to harm the church and the testimony of Christ's gospel.

d. **cheated.** Christians have no right to insist on legal recourse in a public court. It is far better to trust God's sovereign purposes in trouble and lose financially, than to be disobedient and suffer spiritually (see Matt. 5:39, 40; 18:21–35).

e. **you yourselves do wrong and cheat.** He is referring to those who sue their brothers in Christ being as guilty of the same misconduct they are suing to rectify.

f. **not inherit the kingdom.** The kingdom is the spiritual sphere of salvation where God rules as king over all who belong to Him by faith (see Matt. 5:3, 10). All believers are in that spiritual kingdom, yet are waiting to enter into the full inheritance of it in the age to come. People who are characterized by these iniquities are not saved. See 1 John 3:9, 10. While believers can and do commit these sins, they do not characterize them as an unbroken life pattern. When they do, it demonstrates that the person is not in God's kingdom. True believers who do sin, resent that sin and seek to gain the victory over it (cf. Rom. 7:14–25).

g. **idolaters.** Those who worship any false god or follow any false religious system.

h. **adulterers.** Married persons who indulge in sexual acts outside their marriage.

i. **homosexuals . . . sodomites.** These terms refer to those who exchange and corrupt normal male-female sexual roles and relations. Transvestism, sex changes, and other gender perversions are included (cf. Gen. 1:27; Deut. 22:5). Sodomites are so-called because the sin of male-male sex dominated the city of Sodom (Gen. 18:20; 19:4, 5). This sinful perversion is condemned always, in any form, by Scripture (cf. Lev. 18:22; 20:13; Rom. 1:26, 27; 1 Tim. 1:10).

j. **thieves . . . covetous.** Both are guilty of the same basic sin of greed. Those who are covetous desire what belongs to others; thieves actually take it.

k. **revilers.** People who try to destroy others with words.

l. **extortioners.** Swindlers and embezzlers who steal indirectly, taking unfair advantage of others for their own financial gain.

kingdom of God. ^aAnd such were ^bsome of you. But you were ^cwashed, but you were ^dsanctified, but you were ^ejustified in the name of the Lord Jesus and ^fby the Spirit of our God.

90. SEXUAL SIN CONDEMNED

1 Cor. 6:12–20

^gAll things are lawful for me, but all things are not helpful. All things are lawful for me, but I will not be brought under the ^hpower of any. ⁱFoods for

---

a. **fornicators.** All who indulge in sexual immorality, but particularly unmarried persons.

b. **some of you.** Though not all Christians have been guilty of all those particular sins, every Christian is equally an ex-sinner, since Christ came to save sinners (cf. Matt. 9:13; Rom. 5:20). Some who used to have those patterns of sinful life were falling into those old sins again, and needed reminding that if they went all the way back to live as they used to, they were not going to inherit eternal salvation, because it would indicate that they never were saved (cf. 2 Cor. 5:17).

c. **washed.** Refers to new life, through spiritual cleansing and regeneration (cf. John 3:3–8; 2 Cor. 5:17; Eph. 2:10; Titus 3:5).

d. **sanctified.** This results in new behavior, which a transformed life always produces. Sin's total domination is broken and replaced by a new pattern of obedience and holiness. Though not perfection, this is a new direction (see Rom. 6:17, 18, 22).

e. **justified.** This refers to a new standing before God, in which the Christian is clothed in Christ's righteousness. In His death, the believer's sins were put to His account and He suffered for them, so that His righteousness might be put to an account, so that we might be blessed for it (Rom. 3:26; 4:22–25; 2 Cor. 5:21; Phil. 3:8, 9; 1 Pet. 3:18).

f. **by the Spirit.** The Holy Spirit is the agent of salvation's transformation (cf. John 3:3–5).

g. **All things are lawful . . . not helpful.** That may have been a Corinthian slogan. It was true that no matter what sins a believer commits, God forgives (Eph. 1:7), but not everything they did was profitable or beneficial. The price of abusing freedom and grace was very high. Sin always produces loss. As one who is washed, sanctified, and justified eternally by God's grace, the believer is set free (cf. Rom. 8:21, 33; Gal. 5:1, 13). The Corinthians had done with that freedom just what Paul had warned the Galatians not to do: "Do not use your liberty as an opportunity for the flesh" (Gal. 5:13). So in this section, Paul exposed the error in the Corinthian Christians' rationalization that they were free to sin, because it was covered by God's grace.

h. **power.** Sin has power. The word means "mastered" (cf. Rom. 6:14), and no sin is more enslaving than sexual sin. While it can never be the unbroken pattern of a true believer's life, it can be the recurring habit that saps joy, peace, usefulness and brings divine chastening and even church discipline (cf. 1 Cor. 5:1ff). See 1 Thess. 4:3–5. Sexual sin controls, so the believer must never allow sin to have that control, but must master it in the Lord's strength (see 1 Cor. 9:27). Paul categorically rejects the ungodly notion that freedom in Christ gives license to sin (cf. Rom. 7:6; 8:13, 21).

i. **Foods . . . stomach.** Perhaps this was a popular proverb to celebrate the idea that sex is purely biological, like eating. The influence of philosophical dualism may have contributed to this idea since it made only the body evil; therefore, what one did physically was not preventable and thus inconsequential. Because the relationship between these two is purely biological and temporal, the Corinthians, like many of their pagan friends, probably used that analogy to justify sexual immorality.

the stomach and the stomach for foods, but God will destroy both it and them. Now [a]the body is not for sexual immorality but for the Lord, and the Lord for the body. And God both raised up the Lord and will also raise us up by His power.

Do you not know that your bodies are [b]members of Christ? Shall I then take the members of Christ and make them members of a harlot? [c]Certainly not! Or do you not know that he who is joined to a harlot is one body with her? For "the two," He says, "shall become [d]one flesh." But he who is joined to the Lord is [e]one spirit with Him.

Flee sexual immorality. [f]Every sin that a man does is outside the body, but he who commits sexual immorality sins against his own body. Or do you not know that your body is the temple of the Holy Spirit who is in you, whom you have from God, and you are [g]not your own? For you were bought at [h]a price; therefore [i]glorify God in your body and in your spirit, which are God's.

---

a. **the body . . . the Lord.** Paul rejects the convenient justifying analogy. Bodies and food are temporal relations that will perish. Cf. Acts 2:32; Eph. 1:19. Bodies of believers and the Lord have an eternal relationship that will never perish. He is referring to the believer's body to be changed, raised, glorified, and made heavenly. See 1 Cor. 15:35–54; cf. Phil. 3:20, 21.

b. **members.** The believer's body is not only for the Lord here and now (v. 14) but is of the Lord, a part of His body, the church (Eph. 1:22, 23). The Christian's body is a spiritual temple in which the Spirit of Christ lives (1 Cor. 12:3; John 7:38, 39; 20:22; Acts 1:8; Rom. 8:9; 2 Cor. 6:16); therefore, when a believer commits a sexual sin, it involves Christ with a harlot. All sexual sin is harlotry.

c. **Certainly not!** These words translate the strongest Gr. negative—"May it never be so."

d. **one flesh.** Paul supports his point in the previous verse by appealing to the truth of Gen. 2:24 that defines the sexual union between a man and a woman as "one flesh." When a person is joined to a harlot, it is a one flesh experience; therefore Christ spiritually is joined to that harlot.

e. **one spirit with Him.** Further strengthening the point, Paul affirms that all sex outside of marriage is sin; but illicit relationships by believers are especially reprehensible because they profane Jesus Christ with whom believers are one (John 14:18–23; 15:4, 7; 17:20–23; Rom. 12:5). This argument should make such sin unthinkable.

f. **Every sin . . . is outside.** There is a sense in which sexual sin destroys a person like no other, because it is so intimate and entangling, corrupting on the deepest human level. But Paul is probably alluding to venereal disease, prevalent and devastating in his day and today. No sin has greater potential to destroy the body, something a believer should avoid because of the reality given in 1 Cor. 6:19, 20.

g. **not your own.** A Christian's body belongs to the Lord, is a member of Christ, and is the Holy Spirit's temple. See Rom. 12:1, 2. Every act of fornication, adultery, or any other sin is committed by the believer in the sanctuary, the Holy of Holies, where God dwells. In the OT, the High-Priest only went in there once a year, and only after extensive cleansing, lest he be killed (Lev. 16).

h. **a price.** The precious blood of Christ (see 1 Pet. 1:18, 19).

i. **glorify God.** The Christian's supreme purpose (1 Cor. 10:31).

91. Marriage and Singleness

1 Cor. 7:1–16

Now concerning [a]the things of which you wrote to me:

[b]It is good for a man not to [c]touch a woman. Nevertheless, because of [d]sexual immorality, let each man have his own wife, and let each woman have her own husband. Let the husband [e]render to his wife the affection due her, and likewise also the wife to her husband. The wife does not have [f]authority over her own body, but the husband does. And likewise the husband does not have authority over his own body, but the wife does. Do not [g]deprive one another except with consent for a time, that you may give yourselves to fasting and prayer; and [h]come together again [i]so that Satan does not tempt you because of your lack of self-control. But I say this as a [j]concession, not as

---

a. **the things of which you wrote to me.** This section (1 Cor. 7–11) comprises Paul's answers to practical questions about which the Corinthians had written him (1 Cor. 7:1) in a letter probably delivered by Stephanas, Fortunatus, and Achaicus (1 Cor. 16:17). The first of those questions had to do with marriage, an area of trouble due to the moral corruption of the culture which tolerated fornication, adultery, homosexuality, polygamy, and concubinage.

b. **it is good.** Some had the notion that because of all the sexual sin and marital confusion, it would be better to be single, even more spiritual to be celibate. This could lead some falsely pious people to advocate divorce in order to be single. These verses elevate singleness, as long as it is celibate, but they in no way teach that marriage is either wrong or inferior.

c. **touch a woman.** This is a Jewish euphemism for sexual intercourse (see, e.g., Gen. 20:6; Ruth 2:9; Prov. 6:29). Paul is saying that it is good not to have sex, that is, to be single and celibate. It is not, however, the only good or even better than marriage (cf. Gen. 1:28; 2:18).

d. **sexual immorality.** There is a great danger of sexual sin when single (cf. Matt. 19:12). Marriage is God's only provision for sexual fulfillment. Marriage should not be reduced simply to that, however. Paul has a much higher view and articulates it in Eph. 5:22, 23. He is, here, stressing the issue of sexual sin for people who are single.

e. **render . . . affection due.** Married believers are not to sexually deprive their spouses. While celibacy is right for the single, it is wrong for the married. The practice of deprivation may have been most common when a believer had an unsaved spouse.

f. **authority.** By the marriage covenant, each partner is given the right over the spouse's body for the satisfaction of the other.

g. **deprive.** Lit. "stop depriving each other!" This command may indicate that this kind of deprivation was going on among believers, perhaps reacting to the gross sexual sins of their past and wanting to leave all that behind. Husbands and wives may abstain temporarily from sexual activity, but only when they mutually agree to do so for intercession, as a part of their fasting.

h. **come together again.** Sexual intercourse is to be soon renewed after the spiritual interruption.

i. **so that Satan does not tempt.** Cf. 1 Thess. 3:5. After the agreed-upon "time" of abstinence, sexual desires intensify and a spouse becomes more vulnerable to sinful desire. See Matt. 4:1–11; 2 Cor. 2:11.

j. **concession.** A better translation of the Gr. would be "awareness" or "to have a

a commandment. For I wish that all men were even ᵃas I myself. But each one has his own ᵇgift from God, one in this manner and another in that.

But I say to the ᶜunmarried and to the widows: It is good for them if they remain even ᵈas I am; but if they cannot exercise self-control, ᵉlet them marry. For it is better to marry than to burn with passion.

Now to the married I command, yet ᶠnot I but the Lord: A wife is not to ᵍdepart from her husband. But even if she does depart, let her ʰremain unmarried or be reconciled to her husband. And a husband is not to divorce his wife.

But to the rest ⁱI, not the Lord, say: If any brother has a wife who does not believe, and she is willing to live with him, let him not divorce her. And a woman who has a husband who does not believe, if he is willing to live with her, let her not divorce him. For the unbelieving husband is ʲsanctified by the wife,

---

mutual opinion." Paul was very aware of the God-ordained advantages of both singleness and marriage, and was not commanding marriage because of the temptation of singleness. Spirituality is not connected at all to marital status, though marriage is God's good gift (see 1 Pet. 3:7, "the grace of life").

a. **as I myself.** As a single person, Paul recognized the special freedom and independence he had to serve Christ (see 1 Cor. 7:32–34). But he did not expect all believers to be single, nor all who were single to stay that way, nor all who were married to act celibate as if they were single.

b. **gift from God.** Both singleness and marriage are God's gracious gifts.

c. **unmarried . . . widows.** "Unmarried" is a term used 4 times in the NT, and only in 1 Corinthians (cf. vv. 11, 32, 34). This verse makes it clear that the unmarried and widows are distinct. Verse 11 identifies the divorced as the "unmarried" to be distinguished from "widows" (1 Cor. 7:39, 40; single by death) and virgins (1 Cor. 7:25, 28; never married). Each use of "unmarried," then, refers to those formerly married, presently single, but not widowed. They are the divorced. It is likely these people who were formerly married wanted to know if they, as Christians, could or should remarry.

d. **as I am.** Paul was possibly a widower, and could here affirm his former marriage by identifying with the unmarried and widows. His first suggestion is that they stay single because of its freedoms in serving the Lord (1 Cor. 7:25–27, 32–34). See Anna in Luke 2:36–38.

e. **let them marry.** The Gr. tense indicates a command, since a person can't live a happy life and serve the Lord effectively if dominated by unfulfilled sexual passion—especially in that Corinthian society.

f. **not I but the Lord.** What Paul writes to these believers was already made clear by Jesus during His earthly ministry (Matt. 5:31, 32; 19:5–8; cf. Gen. 2:24; Mal. 2:16).

g. **depart.** This word is used as a synonym for divorce, as indicated by the parallel use of the word "divorce," in v. 11. Apparently, some Christians felt they should divorce their unsaved spouses, to live celibately or marry a believer.

h. **remain unmarried.** If a Christian divorces another Christian except for adultery (see Matt. 5:31, 32; 19:8, 9), neither partner is free to marry another person. They should reconcile, or at least remain unmarried.

i. **I . . . say.** Not a denial of inspiration or an indication that Paul is giving human opinion, but simply a way of saying that Jesus had not spoken on this and God had not previously given revelation on the matter, as Paul was then writing.

j. **sanctified.** This does not refer to salvation; otherwise the spouse would not be spoken of as unbelieving. The sanctification is matrimonial and familial, not personal or spiritual, and means that the unsaved partner is set apart for temporal blessing because the other belongs

and the unbelieving wife is sanctified by the husband; otherwise your ᵃchildren would be unclean, but now they are holy. But if the unbeliever departs, ᵇlet him depart; a brother or a sister is ᶜnot under bondage in such cases. But God has called us to peace. For how do you know, O wife, whether you will save your husband? Or how do you know, O husband, whether you will save your wife?

92. LIVE ACCORDING TO YOUR CALLING
1 Cor. 7:17–24

But ᵈas God has distributed to each one, as the Lord has ᵉcalled each one, so let him walk. And so I ordain in all the churches. Was anyone called while ᶠcircumcised? Let him not become uncircumcised. Was anyone called

---

to God. One Christian in a marriage brings grace that spills over on the spouse—even possibly leading them to salvation.

a. **children . . . are holy.** The Christian need not separate from an unbeliever because of fear that the unbelieving spouse may defile the children. God promises the opposite. They would be unclean if both parents were unsaved, but the presence of one believing parent exposes the children to blessing and brings them protection. The presence of even one Christian parent will protect children from undue spiritual harm and they will receive many blessings, and often that includes salvation.

b. **let him depart.** A term referring to divorce. When an unbelieving spouse cannot tolerate the partner's faith and wants a divorce, it is best to let that happen in order to preserve peace in the family (cf. Rom. 12:18). Some may have been reluctant to let go of their unsaved spouse, who wanted out and was creating discord in the home—thinking they could evangelize the spouse by hanging on for the purpose of seeing that one converted. Paul says there are no such assurances and it is better to divorce and be at peace, if the unsaved partner wants to end the marriage that way. The bond of marriage is broken only by death (Rom. 7:2), adultery (Matt. 19:9), or an unbeliever's leaving.

c. **not under bondage.** When the bond is broken in any of those ways, a Christian is free to marry another believer. Throughout Scripture, whenever legitimate divorce occurs, remarriage is assumed. When divorce is permitted, so is remarriage. By implication, the permission for a widow to remarry (1 Cor. 7:39, 40; Rom. 7:3) because the "bond" is broken, extends to this case where there is no more "bondage."

d. **as God has distributed.** Discontent was prevalent among these new believers in the Corinthian church. As noted up to this point (1 Cor. 7:1–16), some wanted to change their marital status, some were slaves who wanted to be free, and some used their freedom in Christ to rationalize sinning. In a general response to that, this passage plainly repeats the basic principle that Christians should willingly accept the marital condition and social situations into which God has placed them and be content to serve Him there until He leads them elsewhere.

e. **called.** As always in the epistles, this term refers to God's effectual call that saves (see Rom. 8:30).

f. **circumcised . . . uncircumcised.** With Judaizers demanding all Gentile believers in Christ to be circumcised (Gal. 5:1–6), and with some Christian Jews wanting to disassociate with Judaism and thus having a surgery to become circumcised (as addressed in rabbinic

while uncircumcised? Let him not be circumcised. Circumcision is nothing and uncircumcision is nothing, but keeping the commandments of God is what matters. Let each one remain in the same calling in which he was called. Were you called ªwhile a slave? ᵇDo not be concerned about it; but if you can be made free, rather use it. For he who is called in the Lord while a slave is the ᶜLord's freedman. Likewise he who is called while free is ᵈChrist's slave. You were bought at a ᵉprice; do not become ᶠslaves of men. Brethren, let each one remain with God in that state in which he was called.

93. INSTRUCTIONS TO THE UNMARRIED
1 Cor. 7:25–40

Now ᵍconcerning virgins: ʰI have no commandment from the Lord; yet I give judgment as one whom the Lord in His mercy has made trustworthy.

---

literature), Paul needed to clarify the issue by saying that neither was necessary. Figuratively, the idea is that when a Jew became a Christian, he was not to give up his racial and cultural identity in order to appear like a Gentile. Likewise, a Gentile was not to become culturally like a Jew (v. 19). Culture, social order, external ceremony have no bearing on spiritual life. What matters is faith and obedience.

a. **while a slave.** Paul was not approving all slavery, but is teaching that a person who is a slave is still able to obey and honor Christ (Eph. 6:5–8; Col. 3:23; 1 Tim. 6:1, 2).

b. **Do not be concerned about.** In modern society, this seems an insensitive command to those who wrongly assume that freedom is some God-given right, rather than a preferable option.

c. **the Lord's freedman.** In the ways that truly count, no man is freer than a Christian. No bondage is as terrible as that of sin, from which Christ frees the believer.

d. **Christ's slave.** Those who are not slaves, but free in the social sense, are in the spiritual sense made slaves of Christ in salvation (Rom. 6:22).

e. **price.** The blood of Christ (1 Cor. 6:20; 1 Pet. 1:19).

f. **slaves of men.** This refers to sinful slavery, i.e., becoming slaves to the ways of men, the ways of the world, and of the flesh. This is the slavery about which to be concerned.

g. **concerning virgins.** Having already established that both marriage and singleness are good and right before the Lord (1 Cor. 7:1–9), and for the person who has the gift of singleness (v. 7), that state has many practical advantages, Paul continued to answer the questions about which the Corinthians had written him (see v. 1). Paul gives 6 reasons for never marrying, in relationship to the downside of marriage, but remaining single (virgins): 1) pressure from the system (vv. 25–27); 2) problems of the flesh (v. 28); 3) passing of the world (vv. 29–31); 4) preoccupations of marriage (vv. 32–35); 5) promises from fathers (vv. 36–38); and 6) permanency of marriage (vv. 39, 40).

h. **I have no commandment.** The conviction given here is not a command, but is thoroughly dependable and sound advice to remain a virgin, which is counsel included by the inspiration of the Spirit from a trustworthy man.

I suppose therefore that this is good because of the [a]present distress—that it is good for a man to [b]remain as he is: Are you bound to a wife? Do not seek to be [c]loosed. Are you loosed from a wife? Do not seek a wife. But even if you do [d]marry, you have not sinned; and if a virgin marries, she has not sinned. Nevertheless such will have [e]trouble in the flesh, but I would spare you.

But this I say, brethren, the [f]time is short, so that from now on even those who have wives should be [g]as though they had none, those who weep as though they did not weep, those who rejoice as though they did not rejoice, those who buy as though they did not possess, and those who [h]use this world as not misusing it. For the [i]form of this world is passing away.

But I want you to [j]be without care. He who is unmarried cares for the [k]things of the Lord—how he may please the Lord. But he who is married cares about the things of the world—[l]how he may please his wife. There is a

---

a. **present distress.** An unspecified, current calamity. Perhaps Paul anticipated the imminent Roman persecutions which began within 10 years after this epistle was written.

b. **remain as he is.** Persecution is difficult enough for a single person to endure, but problems and pain are multiplied for those who are married, especially if they have children. The benefits of singleness notwithstanding, married people must remain married.

c. **loosed.** Divorce is in view.

d. **marry, you have not sinned.** Marriage is a fully legitimate and godly option for both the divorced (on biblical grounds) and virgins.

e. **trouble in the flesh.** "Trouble" means lit. "pressed together, or under pressure." Marriage can involve conflicts, demands, difficulties, and adjustments that singleness does not, because it presses two fallen people into intimate life that leads to inevitable "trouble." The troubles of singleness may be exceeded by the conflicts of marriage.

f. **time is short.** Human life is brief (cf. James 4:14; 1 Pet. 1:24).

g. **as though they had none.** This does not teach that marriage is no longer binding or treated with seriousness (cf. Eph. 5:22–33; Col. 3:18, 19), nor should there be any physical deprivation (1 Cor. 7:3–5); but Paul is teaching that marriage should not at all reduce one's devotion to the Lord and service to Him (cf. Col. 3:2). He means to keep the eternal priority. The mature Christian does not get so swept up in the emotion of this life, so as to lose motivation, hope, and purpose.

h. **use . . . not misusing.** This refers to the normal commercial materialism and pleasures that govern in the world. Believers are not to be swept up in earthly enterprises so that heavenly matters become secondary.

i. **form.** This refers to a manner of life, a fashion, or way of doing things.

j. **be without care.** A single person is free from concern about the earthly needs of a spouse and therefore potentially better able to set himself apart exclusively for the Lord's work.

k. **things of the world.** These are earthly matters connected to the passing system.

l. **how he may please his wife . . . husband.** Here is a basic and expected principle for a good marriage—each seeking to please the other. The first part of this verse is preferably

difference between a wife and a virgin. The unmarried woman cares about the things of the Lord, that she may be holy both in body and in spirit. But she who is married cares about the things of the world—how she may please her husband. And this I say for your own profit, not that I may put a leash on you, but for what is proper, and that you may serve the Lord without distraction.

But if any man thinks he is behaving improperly toward ᵃhis virgin, if she is ᵇpast the flower of youth, and thus ᶜit must be, let him do what he wishes. He does not sin; let them marry. Nevertheless he who stands steadfast in his heart, having ᵈno necessity, but has power over his own will, and has so determined in his heart that he will keep his virgin, does well. So then he who gives her in marriage does well, but he who does not give her in marriage does better.

A wife is ᵉbound by law as long as her husband lives; but if her husband dies, she is at liberty to be married to whom she wishes, ᶠonly in the Lord. But she is happier if she remains as she is, according to my judgment—and I think ᵍI also have the Spirit of God.

---

rendered in some manuscripts, "and his interests are divided. And the woman who is unmarried and the virgin. . . ." This is important because it distinguishes clearly between the "unmarried" and "virgins," who, therefore, can't be the same. "Virgins" are single people never married, while "unmarried" must be single by divorce. Widows is the term for those made single by death. Marriage does not prevent great devotion to the Lord, but it brings more potential matters to interfere with it. Singleness has fewer hindrances, though not guaranteed greater spiritual virtue.

a. **his virgin.** That is, a man's daughter. Apparently in Corinth some of the fathers intending devotion to the Lord, had dedicated their young daughters to the Lord as permanent virgins.

b. **past the flower of youth.** Fully matured as a woman capable of child-bearing.

c. **it must be.** When daughters became of marriageable age and insisted on being married, their fathers were free to break the vow and let them marry.

d. **no necessity.** This means the father who has kept his daughter a virgin and is not under constraint by the daughter to change his mind, does well to fulfill his desire for her to be singularly devoted to the Lord (1 Cor. 7:34). As with those who remain single (1 Cor. 7:28), the choice was not between right and wrong.

e. **bound by law.** God's law designed marriage for life (cf. Gen 2:24; Mal. 2:16; Rom. 7:1–3). It is so permanent that the disciples thought it may be better not to marry (see Matt. 19:10).

f. **only in the Lord.** That is, free to marry a believer only. This is true for all believers who marry or remarry (see 2 Cor. 6:14–16).

g. **I also have the Spirit.** Perhaps with a touch of sarcasm, Paul affirmed that this sound advice was given by the Holy Spirit.

94. FOOD OFFERED TO IDOLS

1 Cor. 8:1–13

Now [a]concerning [b]things offered to idols: We know that [c]we all have knowledge. Knowledge puffs up, but [d]love edifies. And if anyone thinks that he knows anything, he knows nothing yet as he ought to know. But if anyone loves God, this one is [e]known by Him.

Therefore concerning the eating of things offered to idols, we know that an idol is [f]nothing in the world, and that there is no other God but one. For even if there are [g]so-called gods, whether in heaven or on earth (as there are many gods and many lords), yet for us there is [h]one God, the Father, of whom are all things, and we for Him; and one Lord Jesus Christ, through whom are all things, and through whom we live.

However, there is not in everyone that knowledge; for some, with consciousness of the idol, until now eat it as a thing offered to an idol; and their [i]conscience, being weak, is defiled. But food does not [j]commend

---

a. **concerning.** Paul addresses liberty in the church (see Rom. 14).

b. **things offered to idols.** The Greeks and Romans were polytheistic (worshiping many gods) and polydemonistic (believing in many evil spirits). They believed that evil spirits would try to invade human beings by attaching themselves to food before it was eaten, and that the spirits could be removed only by the food's being sacrificed to a god. The sacrifice was meant not only to gain favor with the god, but also to cleanse the meat from demonic contamination. Such decontaminated meat was offered to the gods as a sacrifice. That which was not burned on the altar was served at wicked pagan feasts. What was left was sold in the market. After conversion, believers resented eating such food bought out of idol markets, because it reminded sensitive Gentile believers of their previous pagan lives and the demonic worship.

c. **we all have knowledge.** Paul and mature believers knew better than to be bothered by such food offered once to idols and then sold in the marketplace. They knew the deities didn't exist and that evil spirits did not contaminate the food. See 1 Tim. 4:3.

d. **love edifies.** Knowledge mingled with love prevents a believer from exercising freedoms that offend weaker believers and, rather, builds the others up in truth and wisdom (cf. 1 Cor. 13:1–4).

e. **anyone loves God.** Love is the proof of knowing God. Cf. 1 John 4:19—5:1.

f. **nothing.** Paul states his agreement with the well taught believers who knew idols were nothing, so food offered to idols was not defiled.

g. **so-called gods.** Some were outright fakes and some were manifestations of demons, but none were truly gods (Ps. 115:4–7; Acts 19:26).

h. **one God, the Father . . . one Lord Jesus Christ.** A powerful and clear affirmation of the essential equality of God the Father and God the Son (cf. Eph. 4:4–6).

i. **conscience . . . is defiled.** The consciences of some newer converts were still accusing them strongly with regard to allowing them to eat idol food without feeling spiritually corrupted and guilty. They still imagined that idols were real and evil. A defiled conscience is one that has been violated, bringing fear, shame, and guilt. See Rom. 14:20–23.

j. **commend us to God.** The idea is of bringing us nearer to God or making us approved by Him. Food is spiritually neutral.

us to God; for neither if we eat are we the better, nor if we do not eat are we the worse.

But beware lest somehow this liberty of yours become a ᵃstumbling block to those who are weak. For if anyone sees you who have knowledge eating in an idol's temple, will not the conscience of him who is weak be emboldened to eat those things offered to idols? And because of your knowledge shall the weak brother ᵇperish, ᶜfor whom Christ died? But when you thus sin against the brethren, and wound their weak conscience, ᵈyou sin against Christ. Therefore, if food makes my brother stumble, I will never again eat meat, lest I make my brother stumble.

95. CHRISTIAN LIBERTY: THE FREEDOM OF SELF-DENIAL

1 Cor. 9:1–18

ᵉAm I not an apostle? Am I not free? Have I not seen Jesus Christ our Lord? Are you not my work in the Lord? If I am not an apostle to others, yet doubtless I am to you. For you are the ᶠseal of my apostleship in the Lord.

My defense to those who ᵍexamine me is this: Do we have no ʰright to eat

---

a. **stumbling block.** Some believers would be caused to fall back into old sins by getting involved with foods offered to idols.

b. **perish.** This is better translated "ruined," with the idea of "come to sin." See Matt. 18:14.

c. **for whom Christ died.** Christ died for all who believe, actually bearing the penalty for their sin and fully satisfying the wrath of God.

d. **you sin against Christ.** A strong warning that causing a brother or sister in Christ to stumble is more than simply an offense against that person; it is a serious offense against the Lord Himself (see Matt. 18:6–14).

e. **Am I not an apostle?** In 1 Cor. 8, Paul set out the limits of Christian liberty. In this chapter he sets forth how he followed them in his own life. In 1 Cor. 9:1–18, he discusses his right to be financially supported by those to whom he ministers. In vv. 19–27, he explains how he would give up all rights to win people to Christ. All of these questions are rhetorical, the "yes" answer to each being assumed.

f. **seal of my apostleship.** The existence of the church in Corinth was evidence of Paul's apostolic authenticity.

g. **examine.** Using this Gr. legal term for a preliminary investigation required before a decision was reached in a case, Paul sets out to defend his rights.

h. **right to eat and drink.** Cf. Gal. 6:6; 1 Tim. 5:17, 18. He was entitled to be married (v. 5) and to receive financial support from those to whom he ministered.

and drink? Do we have no right to take along a believing wife, as do also the other apostles, the brothers of the Lord, and ^aCephas? Or is it only Barnabas and I who have no right to refrain from ^bworking? Who ever goes to war at his own expense? Who plants a vineyard and does not eat of its fruit? Or who tends a flock and does not drink of the milk of the flock?

Do I say these things as a mere man? Or does not the ^claw say the same also? For it is written in the law of Moses, "You shall not muzzle an ox while it treads out the grain." Is it oxen God is concerned about? Or does He say it altogether ^dfor our sakes? For our sakes, no doubt, this is written, that he who plows should plow in hope, and he who threshes in hope should be partaker of his hope. If we have sown spiritual things for you, is it a great thing if we reap your ^ematerial things? If ^fothers are partakers of this right over you, are we not even more?

Nevertheless we have not used this right, but ^gendure all things lest we hinder the gospel of Christ. Do you not know that those who minister the holy things eat of the things of the temple, and those who serve at the altar ^hpartake of the offerings of the altar? Even so the Lord has commanded that those who preach the gospel should ⁱlive from the gospel.

But I have used ^jnone of these things, ^knor have I written these things that it should be done so to me; for it would be ^lbetter for me to die than that

---

a. **Cephas.** Peter, who was married (cf. Mark 1:29–31).

b. **working.** With sarcasm, Paul, a tentmaker (Acts 18:3), let the Corinthians know that he and Barnabas had as much right as others to receive full financial support from their work. Except for help from a few churches (e.g., Phil. 4:15, 16), they paid their own expenses not because of obligation or necessity, but voluntarily.

c. **law.** The Scripture, as quoted from Deut. 25:4.

d. **for our sakes.** As in agriculture, men should earn their living from their labor.

e. **material things.** Financial support. See 1 Tim. 5:17. Cf. 2 Cor. 8:1–5.

f. **others are partakers.** Apparently, the church had financially supported other ministers.

g. **endure.** False teachers sought money. Paul wanted to be certain he was not classed with them, so he endured not accepting support, so as not to offend. Cf. Acts 20:34; 2 Thess. 3:8.

h. **partake of the offerings.** OT priests were supported by the tithes of crops and animals, as well as of financial gifts (Num. 18:8–24; cf. Gen. 14:18–21).

i. **live from the gospel.** This refers to earning a living by preaching the good news.

j. **none of these things.** The 6 reasons given in 1 Cor. 9:1–14 that indicate his right to financial support.

k. **nor have I written.** He was not underhandedly hoping that, despite his protest, the Corinthians would feel obligated to pay him (2 Cor. 11:8, 9; cf. 1 Thess. 2:9; 2 Thess. 3:8; 1 Pet. 5:2).

l. **better . . . to die.** He preferred death to having anyone think he ministered with a financial motive. See Acts 20:33–35; 1 Pet. 5:2.

anyone should [a]make my boasting void. For if I preach the gospel, I have [b]nothing to boast of, for [c]necessity is laid upon me; yes, [d]woe is me if I do not preach the gospel! For if I do this willingly, I have a reward; but if [e]against my will, I have been entrusted with a stewardship. What is [f]my reward then? That when I preach the gospel, I may present the gospel of Christ without charge, that I may not abuse my authority in the gospel.

96. Seeking to Serve and Striving to Win

1 Cor. 9:19–27

For though I am free from all men, I have made myself a [g]servant to all, that I might win the more; and to the Jews I [h]became as a Jew, that I might win Jews; to those who are under the law, as under the law, that I might win those who are under the law; to [i]those who are without law, as without law

---

a. **make my boasting void.** The term "boast" refers to that in which one glories or to the basis of one's glorying, and carries the idea of rejoicing. It is a statement of sincere joy, not pride (cf. 1 Cor. 1:31; Rom 15:17). He was genuinely overjoyed for the privilege of serving the Lord and did not want material support to rob him of it in any way.

b. **nothing to boast of.** That is to say, his boast (cf. 1 Cor. 9:15) was not personal. He was not proud as if it were his gospel; nor was he proud about the way he preached it, as if it were his ability.

c. **necessity.** Paul did not preach from personal pride, but from divine compulsion. He had no other choice, because God had sovereignly set him apart for service (see Acts 9:3–6, 15; 26:13–19; Gal. 1:15; Col. 1:25; cf. Jer. 1:5; 20:9; Luke 1:13–17).

d. **woe.** God's severest chastening is reserved for unfaithful ministers (Heb. 13:17; James 3:1).

e. **against my will.** This does not indicate that Paul was unwilling to obey but that his will had no part in the call itself. Since it was God's sovereign choice and call, he received not a "reward," but a "stewardship" (a valuable responsibility or duty to be carefully managed).

f. **my reward.** Not money, but the privilege of preaching the gospel without support, was Paul's reward, so that he set aside his liberty ("right").

g. **a servant.** By choice, he set aside his right to be supported, and thus "enslaved" himself to self-support, in order to remove a potential offense and win more people to Jesus Christ (cf. Prov. 11:30).

h. **became as a Jew.** Within the limits of God's Word and his Christian conscience, he would be as culturally and socially Jewish as necessary when witnessing to Jews (cf. Rom. 9:3; 10:1; 11:14). He was not bound to ceremonies and traditions of Judaism. All legal restraints had been removed, but there was the constraint of love (cf. Rom. 9:3; 10:1; 11:14). For examples of this identification with customs of the Jews, see Acts 16:3; 18:18; 21:20–26.

i. **those . . . without law.** Gentiles. Paul was not suggesting the violating of God's moral

(not being without law toward God, but under law toward Christ), that I might win those who are without law; to the ᵃweak I became as weak, that I might win the weak. I have become ᵇall things to all men, that I might by all means save some. Now this I do for the gospel's sake, that I may be partaker of it with you.

Do you not know that those who run in a ᶜrace all run, but one receives the prize? Run in such a way that you may obtain it. And everyone who competes for the prize is ᵈtemperate in all things. Now they do it to obtain a perishable ᵉcrown, but we for an imperishable crown. Therefore I run thus: ᶠnot with uncertainty. Thus I fight: not as one who ᵍbeats the air. ʰBut I discipline my body and bring it into subjection, lest, when I have preached to others, I myself should become ⁱdisqualified.

---

law, but, as he explained, not being lawless toward God, but abiding by the law of Jesus Christ (cf. James 1:25; 2:8, 12).

a. **weak.** He stooped to make the gospel clear at the lower level of comprehension, which Paul no doubt had done often while dealing with the Corinthians themselves (cf. 1 Cor. 2:1–5).

b. **all things . . . all means.** Within the bounds of God's Word, he would not offend the Jew, Gentile, or those weak in understanding. Not changing Scripture or compromising the truth, he would condescend in ways that could lead to salvation. Liberty cannot be limited without self-control, since the flesh resists limits as its freedom. Here, Paul speaks of his personal self-control.

c. **race.** The Greeks enjoyed two great athletic events, the Olympic games and the Isthmian games, and because the Isthmian events were held in Corinth, believers there were quite familiar with this analogy of running to win.

d. **temperate.** Self-control is crucial to victory.

e. **crown.** A wreath of greenery given to the winner of the race. Cf. 2 Tim. 4:8; 1 Pet. 1:4.

f. **not with uncertainty.** Four times he has mentioned his goal of winning people to salvation.

g. **beats the air.** Paul changes the metaphor to boxing to illustrate the point that he was no shadow boxer, just waving his arms without effect (cf. 1 Tim. 1:18).

h. **discipline.** From a term lit. meaning to hit under the eye. He knocked out the bodily impulses to keep them from preventing him from his mission of winning souls to Christ.

i. **disqualified.** Another metaphor from the athletic games. A contestant who failed to meet basic training requirements could not participate at all, much less have an opportunity to win. Paul may be especially referring to such fleshly sins that disqualify a man from preaching and leading the church, particularly being blameless and above reproach in the sexual area, since such sin is a disqualification (see Ps. 101:6; Prov. 6:33; 1 Tim. 3:2; Titus 1:6).

97. LESSONS FROM THE OLD TESTAMENT

1 Cor. 10:1–13

[a]Moreover, brethren, I do not want you to be unaware that [b]all our fathers were [c]under the cloud, all passed [d]through the sea, all were [e]baptized into Moses in the cloud and in the sea, all ate the same [f]spiritual food, and all drank the same spiritual drink. For they drank of [g]that spiritual Rock that followed them, and that Rock was Christ. But with most of them God was [h]not well pleased, for their bodies were scattered in the wilderness.

Now these things became [i]our examples, to the intent that we should not lust after evil things as they also lusted. And do not become [j]idolaters as were some of them. As it is written, "The people sat down to eat and drink,

---

a. **Moreover . . . unaware.** This transition leads from the lack of self-discipline and subsequent disqualification spoken of in 1 Cor. 9:27 to an illustration of it in ancient Israel.

b. **all our fathers.** Paul is referring to ancient Israel, of whom he was a descendant. Ancient Israel's 40-year journey between Egypt and Canaan (Ex. 13:21; 14:16; 16:15; 17:6) is a sobering illustration of the misuse of freedom and the dangers of overconfidence. The Israelites misused their new-found freedom, fell into idolatry, immorality, and rebelliousness, disqualifying themselves from receiving the Lord's blessing. In particular, he asked his readers to remember what had happened to Israel in the wilderness, because of freedom without self-control.

c. **under the cloud.** Guided by God's presence as a cloud by day and column of fire at night (see Ex. 13:21).

d. **through the sea.** The Red Sea, which opened for Israel to pass through and closed to drown the Egyptian army (see Ex. 14:26–31).

e. **baptized.** Israel was immersed, not in the sea, but "into Moses," indicating their oneness, or solidarity, with him as their leader.

f. **spiritual food . . . drink.** Actual food provided by the spiritual power of God. See Ex. 16:15; 17:6.

g. **that spiritual Rock.** The Jews had a legend that the actual rock Moses struck followed them throughout their wilderness wanderings, providing water for them. Paul says they have a Rock providing all they need, but it is Christ. Rock (petra) refers to a massive cliff, not simply a large stone or boulder, signifying the pre-incarnate Messiah (Christ), who protected and sustained His people. Cf. Matt. 16:18.

h. **not well pleased.** This is an understatement. Because of Israel's extreme disobedience, God allowed only two of the men who had originally left Egypt (Joshua and Caleb) to enter the Promised Land; all the others died in the wilderness, including Moses and Aaron who were disqualified from entering the Land (Num. 20:8–12, 24).

i. **our examples.** They died in the wilderness because of their failure of self-discipline and consequent indulgence of every desire (see 1 Cor. 9:27). Four major sins characterized them: idolatry (1 Cor. 10:7); sexual immorality (v. 8); testing God (v. 9); and complaining (v. 10).

j. **idolaters.** The Israelites were barely out of Egypt when they fell into idol worship. Exodus 32 records the story (v. 6 is quoted here). Some 3,000 were executed for instigating an immoral orgy at Sinai (Ex. 32:28). See Ex. 20:3; Ezek. 14:3; 1 John 5:21; Rev. 22:9.

and rose up to ᵃplay." Nor let us commit sexual immorality, as some of them did, and in one day ᵇtwenty-three thousand fell; nor let us ᶜtempt Christ, as some of them also tempted, and were destroyed by ᵈserpents; nor complain, as some of them also complained, and were destroyed by the ᵉdestroyer. Now all these things happened to them as examples, and they were written for our admonition, upon whom ᶠthe ends of the ages have come.

Therefore let him who thinks he stands ᵍtake heed lest he fall. No ʰtemptation has overtaken you except such as is ⁱcommon to man; but God is faithful, who will not allow you to be tempted beyond what you are able, but with the temptation will also make the way of escape, that you may be able to bear it.

98. CHRISTIAN LIBERTY AND THE GLORY OF GOD

1 Cor. 10:14—11:1

Therefore, my beloved, flee from idolatry. I speak as to wise men; judge for yourselves what I say. The ʲ cup of blessing which we bless, is it not the

---

a. **play.** A euphemism for the gross sexual relations which followed the excessive feasting.

b. **twenty-three thousand.** Having just quoted from Ex. 32 in v. 7, this very likely also refers to the incident in Ex. 32, not to the incident at Shittim in Num. 25 (contra. marginal ref.). Apparently 3,000 were killed by the Levites (Ex. 32:28) and 20,000 died in the plague (Ex. 32:35).

c. **tempt Christ.** Numbers 21 records this story of the people questioning the goodness and plan of the One carrying them through the wilderness, the Protector and Provider, the spiritual Rock, Christ pre-incarnate (see v. 4).

d. **serpents.** See Num. 21:6; cf. 11:30.

e. **destroyer.** This incident is recorded in Num. 16:3–41. The same angel had slain the firstborn of the Egyptians (Ex. 12:23), the 70,000 men because of David's census (2 Sam. 24:15, 16), and the entire Assyrian army that was besieging Jerusalem (2 Chr. 32:21).

f. **the ends of the ages.** The time of Messiah; the last days of redemptive history before the messianic kingdom. See Heb. 9:26; 1 John 2:18.

g. **take heed.** Cf. Prov. 16:18. The Bible is filled with examples of overconfidence (see Esth. 3–5; Is. 37:36–38; Luke 22:33, 34, 54–62; Rev. 3:1–3, 17).

h. **temptation.** See James 1:13–15; cf. Matt. 6:13.

i. **common to man.** One Gr. word meaning "that which is human."

j. **cup of blessing.** The proper name given to the third cup during the Passover Feast. At the last Passover with the disciples, Jesus used the third cup as the symbol of His blood shed for sin. That cup became the one used to institute the Lord's Supper. He set the cup apart as a token of salvation blessing before passing it to the 12 (see Luke 22:17, 20).

[a]communion of [b]the blood of Christ? [c]The bread which we break, is it not the communion of the body of Christ? For we, though many, [d]are one bread and one body; for we all partake of that one bread.

[e]Observe Israel after the flesh: Are not those who eat of the sacrifices partakers of the altar? What am I saying then? That [f]an idol is anything, or what is offered to idols is anything? Rather, that the things which the Gentiles sacrifice they sacrifice to demons and not to God, and I do not want you to have fellowship with demons. You cannot drink the cup of the Lord and the cup of demons; you cannot partake of the Lord's table and of the table of demons. Or do we provoke the Lord to [g]jealousy? Are we stronger than He?

[h]All things are lawful for me, but not all things are helpful; all things are lawful for me, but not all things [i]edify. Let no one seek his own, but each one the other's well-being.

[j]Eat whatever is sold in the meat market, asking no questions for conscience' sake; for "the earth is the LORD's, and all its fullness."

---

a. **communion.** Means "to have in common, to participate and have partnership with." The same Gr. word is used in 1:9; 2 Cor. 8:4; Phil. 2:1; 3:10. Commemorating the Lord's Supper was a regular and cherished practice in the early church, by which believers remembered their Savior's death and celebrated their common salvation and eternal life which reflected their perfect spiritual oneness.

b. **the blood of Christ.** A vivid phrase used to represent Christ's sacrificial death and full atoning work. See Rom. 5:9. See Acts 20:28; Rom. 3:25; Eph. 1:7; 2:13; Col. 1:20; 1 Pet. 1:19; 1 John 1:7; Rev. 1:5; 5:9.

c. **The bread.** This symbolized our Lord's body as the cup symbolized His blood. Both point to His death as a sacrifice for the salvation of men.

d. **are one bread.** This refers to the bread of communion as the symbol of Christ's body given for all who believe. Since we all partake of that body, we are one.

e. **Observe Israel.** In the OT sacrifices, the offering was in behalf of all who ate (see Lev. 7:15–18). By such action, the people were identifying with the offering and affirming their devotion to God to whom it was offered. Paul was, by this, implying how any sacrifice made to an idol (see 1 Cor. 10:7, 14) was identifying with and participating with that idol. It is completely inconsistent for believers to participate in any such worship (v. 21).

f. **an idol.** Idols and the things sacrificed to them have no spiritual nature or power in themselves (cf. 1 Cor. 8:4, 8), but they do represent the demonic. If pagan worshipers believe an idol was a god, demons act out the part of the imagined god (cf. 2 Thess. 2:9–11). There is not a true god in the idol, but there is a satanic spiritual force (cf. Deut. 32:17; Ps. 106:37).

g. **jealousy.** God tolerates no competition and will not allow idolatry to go unpunished. (Deut. 32:21; Jer. 25:6, 9; Rev. 21:8; cf. 11:30).

h. **All things.** In this section, Paul gives 4 principles for Christian liberty: 1) edification over gratification (1 Cor. 10:23); 2) others over self (v. 24); 3) liberty over legalism (vv. 25–27); and 4) condescension over condemnation (vv. 28–30).

i. **edify.** To build up in Christian doctrine (cf. 1 Cor. 8:1; 14:3, 4, 26; Acts 20:32; 2 Cor. 12:19; Eph. 4:12; 2 Tim. 3:16, 17).

j. **Eat whatever.** Quoting Ps. 24:1, Paul declares that believers, though not participating in idol ceremonies (see vv. 18–20), should not hesitate to buy meat once used in such ceremonies and eat it without guilt (see 1 Tim. 4:4, 5).

If any of those who do not believe invites you to dinner, and you desire to go, eat whatever is set before you, asking no question for conscience' sake. But if anyone says to you, "This was offered to idols," [a]do not eat it for the sake of the one who told you, and for conscience' sake; for "the earth is the LORD's, and all its fullness." "Conscience," I say, not your own, but that of the other. For why is [b]my liberty judged by another man's conscience? But if I partake with thanks, why am I evil spoken of for the food over which I give thanks?

Therefore, whether you eat or drink, or whatever you do, do all to the [c]glory of God. Give no offense, either to the Jews or to the Greeks or to the church of God, just as I also please all men in all things, not seeking my own profit, but the profit of many, that they may be saved. Imitate me, just as I also imitate Christ.

99. MEN'S AND WOMEN'S ROLES
1 Cor. 11:2—16

Now I praise you, brethren, that you remember me in all things and keep the [d] traditions just as I delivered them to you. But I want you to know that the head of every man is [e]Christ, the head of woman is [f]man, and the head of

---

a. **do not eat.** Even if you are the guest of an unbeliever and don't want to offend him, it is better to offend the unbeliever and not eat for the sake of the weaker Christian who would be offended to eat, since love to other believers is the strongest witness we have (John 13:34, 35).

b. **my liberty judged by another.** Offending a weaker brother with one's freedom will cause the offended person to condemn us.

c. **glory.** Christian liberty, as well as the most common behavior, is to be conducted to the honor of God. Cf. Ezek. 36:23.

d. **traditions.** In the strict sense used here, a synonym for God's Word (cf. 2 Thess. 2:15). The NT sometimes uses the word in a negative way, referring to man-made ideas or practices, especially those that conflict with Scripture (cf. Matt. 15:2–6; Gal. 1:14; Col. 2:8).

e. **Christ.** Christ is the head of the church as its Savior and Lord (cf. Eph. 1:22, 23; 4:15; Col. 1:18). He is also the Lord over every unbeliever (cf. Matt. 28:18; Heb. 2:8). Someday all will acknowledge His authority (cf. Phil. 2:10, 11).

f. **man.** Men have authority over women in the basic order of creation (cf. 1 Cor. 11:8, 9; cf. Is. 3:12; Eph. 5:22–33). See 1 Tim. 2:11–15. There is no distinction between men and women as far as personal worth, intellect, or spirituality are concerned (cf. Gal. 3:28). All believers, male and female, are equal in the Lord and complementary in the Lord's work. Their roles are different in function and relationships, not in spirituality or importance (cf. Gal. 3:28). That women function uniquely in God's order, however, submitting to men's authority, Paul affirms by several points: 1) the pattern in the Godhead (1 Cor. 11:3); 2) the divine design of male and female (v. 7); 3) the order of creation (v. 8); 4) the purpose of woman in regard to man (v. 9); 5) the concern of the angels (v. 10); and 6) and the characteristics of natural physiology (vv. 13–15).

Christ is ᵃGod. Every man praying or prophesying, having his head ᵇcovered, dishonors his head. But every ᶜwoman who prays or prophesies with her head ᵈuncovered ᵉdishonors her head, for that is one and the same as if her head were shaved. For if a woman is not covered, let her also be shorn. But if it is ᶠshameful for a woman to be shorn or shaved, let her be covered. For a man indeed ought not to cover his head, since he is the ᵍimage and glory of God; but ʰwoman is the glory of man. For man is not from woman, but woman from man. Nor was man created for the woman, but woman for the man. For this reason the woman ought to have a symbol of authority on her head, because of the ⁱangels. Nevertheless, neither is man independent of woman,

a. **God.** Christ has never been in any way inferior in essence to the Father (John 10:30; 17:21–24), but in His incarnation He willingly submitted Himself to the Father's will in humble obedience (1 Cor. 3:23; 15:24–28; cf. John 4:34; 5:30; 6:38).

b. **covered, dishonors.** Lit. "having down from head," is probably a reference to men wearing a head covering, which seems to have been a local custom. Jews began wearing head coverings during the fourth century A.D., although some may already have been wearing them in NT times. Apparently, Corinthian men were doing the same, and Paul informs them that it is a disgrace. Paul is not stating a universal law from God, but acknowledging a local custom, which did reflect divine principle. In that society, a man's uncovered head was a sign of his authority over women, who were to have their heads covered. For a man to cover his head was to suggest a reversal of proper roles.

c. **woman who prays or prophesies.** Paul makes clear directives that women are not to lead or speak in the services of the church (cf. 1 Cor. 14:34; 1 Tim. 2:12), but they may pray and proclaim the truth to unbelievers, as well as teaching children and other women (cf. 1 Tim. 5:16; Titus 2:3, 4). See Acts 21:9. Wherever and whenever women do pray and proclaim the Word appropriately, they must do so maintaining a proper distinction from men.

d. **uncovered.** In the culture of Corinth, a woman's covered head while ministering or worshiping was a symbol to signify a subordinate relationship to her husband. The apostle is not laying down an absolute law for women to wear veils or coverings in all churches for all time, but is declaring that the symbols of the divinely-established male and female roles are to be genuinely honored in every culture. As in the case of meat offered to idols (1 Cor. 8, 9), there is nothing spiritual about wearing or not wearing a covering. But manifesting rebellion against God's order was wrong.

e. **dishonors her head.** "Head" may refer to her own self being disgraced by refusing to conform to recognized symbols of submission, or to her husband, who is disgraced by her behavior.

f. **shameful . . . to be shorn.** In that day only a prostitute or a feminist would shave her head. If a Christian woman rejected the covering that symbolized her submission in that culture, she might as well have shaved her head—the shame was similar.

g. **image and glory of God.** Though men and women were both created in God's image (Gen. 1:27), it is man who bears the glory of God uniquely by his role. Like God, he is given a sphere of sovereignty as the earthly sovereign over God's created order. See Gen. 3:16, 17.

h. **woman is the glory of man.** As man carries authority delegated to him by God, so woman carries authority delegated to her by God through her husband. Man came from God; woman came from man (cf. Gen. 2:9–23; 1 Tim. 2:11–13).

i. **angels.** Women are to be submissive by wearing the symbol of authority so as not to offend these most holy and submissive creatures who watch the church (cf. Matt. 18:10; Eph. 3:9, 10), who were present (Job 38:4, 7) at creation, when God designed the order of authority for men and women.

nor woman independent of man, in the Lord. For as woman came from man, even so man also comes through woman; but all things are from God.

Judge among yourselves. [a]Is it proper for a woman to pray to God with her head uncovered? Does not even [b]nature itself teach you that if a man has long hair, it is a dishonor to him? But if a woman has long hair, it is a glory to her; for her hair is given to her for a covering. But if anyone seems to be contentious, we have [c]no such custom, nor do the churches of God.

100. Observing the Lord's Supper
1 Cor. 11:17–34

Now in giving these instructions I do not praise you, since you [d]come together not for the better but for the [e]worse. For first of all, when you come together as a church, I hear that there are [f]divisions among you, and in part I believe it. For there must also be factions among you, that those who are [g]approved may be recognized among you. Therefore when you come together in one place, [h]it is not to eat the Lord's Supper. For in eating, each one takes his own supper ahead of others; and one is hungry and another is drunk. What! Do you not have houses to

---

a. **Is it proper.** Aside from apostolic command, Paul asked, in effect, "Isn't it self-evident that women should not be uncovered?"

b. **nature.** The term can convey the idea of basic human awareness, i.e., the innate sense of what is normal and right. The male hormone, testosterone, speeds up the loss of hair in men. Estrogen causes women's hair to grow longer and for longer time. Women are rarely bald, no matter how old. This physiology is reflected in most cultures in the custom of longer hair on women. God has given her hair as a covering to show tenderness, softness, and beauty.

c. **no such custom.** Neither the Lord, the apostles, nor the churches would allow female rebellion. Women were to maintain their distinctively feminine hairdos; and when custom dictated, they should wear a covering.

d. **come together.** The early church love feasts (cf. Jude 12) usually closed with observance of the Lord's Supper. The worldly, carnal church at Corinth had turned those sacred meals into gluttonous, drunken revelries (1 Cor. 11:17; cf. 2 Pet. 2:13). Beyond that, wealthy believers brought ample food and drink for themselves but refused to share, letting their poorer brethren go away hungry (1 Cor. 11:21).

e. **worse.** A comparative Gr. word which refers to moral evil.

f. **divisions.** The church was torn by dissension (see 1 Cor. 1:10–17; 3:1–3).

g. **approved . . . recognized.** Factions revealed who passed the test of spiritual genuineness and purity (cf. 1 Thess. 2:4).

h. **it is not to eat the Lord's Supper.** The love feast and communion celebration had become so perverted that it was a sinful, selfish mockery. They could not legitimately say it was devoted to the Lord, since it was not honoring to Him.

eat and drink in? Or do you despise the church of God and shame those who have nothing? What shall I say to you? Shall I praise you in this? I do not praise you.

For I ªreceived from the Lord that which I also delivered to you: that the Lord Jesus on the same night in which He was betrayed took bread; and when He had given thanks, He broke it and said, "Take, eat; this is My body which is broken for you; do this ᵇin remembrance of Me." In the same manner He also took the cup after supper, saying, "This cup is the ᶜnew covenant in My blood. This do, as often as you drink it, in remembrance of Me."

For as often as you eat this bread and drink this cup, you ᵈproclaim the Lord's death till He comes.

Therefore whoever eats this bread or drinks this cup of the Lord ᵉin an unworthy manner will be ᶠguilty of the body and blood of the Lord. But let a man examine himself, and so let him eat of the bread and drink of the cup. For he who eats and drinks in an unworthy manner eats and drinks ᵍjudgment to himself, ʰnot discerning the Lord's body. For this reason many are weak and sick among you, and many ⁱsleep. For if we would judge ourselves, we would not be judged. But when we are judged, we are chastened by the Lord, that we may ʲnot be condemned with the world.

---

a. **received . . . delivered.** While the information was not new to the Corinthians, because Paul had previously "delivered" it, it is an important reminder. This description of Christ's final supper with his disciples is one of the most beautiful in all of Scripture, yet it was given in the midst of a strong rebuke of carnal selfishness. If this letter was written before any of the gospels (see Matt. 26:26–30; Mark 14:22–26; Luke 22:17–20; John 13:2), as most conservative scholars believe, then Paul's instruction was the first biblical record of the institution of the Lord's Supper—given directly from the Lord and not through his reading of any other apostles (cf. Gal. 1:10–12).

b. **in remembrance of Me.** Jesus transformed the third cup of the Passover into the cup of remembrance of His offering (see 1 Cor. 10:16).

c. **new covenant in My blood.** The Old Covenant was practiced repeatedly by the blood of animals offered by men; but the New Covenant has been ratified once and for all by the death of Christ (cf. Heb. 9:28).

d. **proclaim the Lord's death.** The gospel is presented through the service of communion as the elements are explained. They point to His physical incarnation, sacrificial death, resurrection, and coming kingdom.

e. **in an unworthy manner.** I.e., ritualistically, indifferently, with an unrepentant heart, a spirit of bitterness, or any other ungodly attitude.

f. **guilty.** To come to the Lord's Table clinging to one's sin does not only dishonor the ceremony, but it also dishonors His body and blood, treating lightly the gracious sacrifice of Christ for us. It is necessary to set all sin before the Lord (v. 28), then partake, so as not to mock the sacrifice for sin, by holding on to it.

g. **judgment.** I.e., chastisement.

h. **not discerning the Lord's body.** When believers do not properly judge the holiness of the celebration of Communion, they treat with indifference the Lord Himself—His life, suffering, and death (cf. Acts 7:52; Heb. 6:6; 10:29).

i. **sleep.** I.e., are dead. See 1 Cor. 15:18. The offense was so serious that God put the worst offenders to death, an extreme but effective form of church purification (cf. Luke 13:1–5; Acts 5:1–11; 1 John 5:16).

j. **not be condemned.** Believers are kept from being consigned to hell, not only by divine

Therefore, my brethren, when you come together to eat, wait for one another. But if anyone is hungry, let him eat at home, lest you come together for judgment. And the rest I will set in order when I come.

101. Spiritual Gifts in the Body of Christ
1 Cor. 12:1–31

[a]Now concerning [b]spiritual gifts, brethren, I do not want you to be ignorant: You know that you were [c]Gentiles, [d]carried away to these dumb idols, however you were led. Therefore I make known to you that no one speaking by the Spirit of God calls Jesus [e]accursed, and no one can say that [f]Jesus is Lord except by the Holy Spirit.

---

decree, but by divine intervention. The Lord chastens to drive His people back to righteous behavior and even sends death to some in the church (1 Cor. 11:30) to remove them before they could be condemned (cf. Jude 24).

a. **Now concerning.** This section (1 Cor. 12–14) focuses on spiritual gifts in the church, dealing with a vital, but controversial subject. The false religion situation in Corinth caused counterfeit spiritual manifestations that had to be confronted. The church was being informed on this subject by Paul and its behavior would be regulated by the truth and the Spirit.

b. **spiritual gifts.** The word "gifts" is not in the original but is implied by the context (cf. 1 Cor. 12:4, 9, 28, 30, 31; 14:1). The Gr. lit. means "pertaining to the Spirit," referring to that which has spiritual qualities or characteristics or is under some form of spiritual control. Spiritual gifts are divine enablements for ministry that the Holy Spirit gives in some measure to all believers and that are to be completely under His control and used for the building of the church to Christ's glory (see Rom. 12:4–8). These had to be distinguished from the mystical experiences called "ecstasy" (supernatural, sensuous communion with a deity) and "enthusiasm" (divination, dreams, revelations, visions) that were found in the pagan religions of Corinth.

c. **Gentiles.** That is, non-Christian pagans (1 Thess. 4:5; 1 Pet. 2:12).

d. **carried away.** Incredibly, some church members were mimicking certain dramatic and bizarre practices of the mystery religions in which they had been formerly involved. The practice of ecstasy, considered to be the highest expression of religious experience, involved supposed supernatural interaction with a deity, induced through frenzied hypnotic chants and ceremonies. The practice frequently included drunkenness (cf. Eph. 5:18) and sexual orgies, to which the devotees willfully yielded themselves to be led into gross sin.

e. **accursed.** This is the most severe kind of condemnation. Some of the Corinthians were fleshly and given over to ecstasies that were controlled by demons. In that condition, they actually claimed to be prophesying or teaching in the Spirit while demonically blaspheming the name of the Lord whom they were supposed to be worshiping. They had been judging the use of gifts on the basis of experience and not content. Satan always assaults the person of Christ. It is possible that the curser of Christ was a Gentile claiming to be a Christian, but holding to a philosophy that all matter was evil, including the human Jesus (i.e., pre-gnosticism). They might have said that the Christ spirit left the human Jesus before His death, and therefore Jesus died a cursed death as a mere man.

f. **Jesus is Lord.** Cf. Acts 2:36; Rom. 10:9, 10; Eph. 1:20, 21; Phil. 2:9–11. The validity

There are diversities of ᵃgifts, but the same Spirit. There are ᵇdifferences of ministries, but the same Lord. And there are diversities of activities, but it is the same God who works all in all. But the ᶜmanifestation of the Spirit is given to each one for the profit of all: for to one is given the ᵈword of wisdom through the Spirit, to another the ᵉword of knowledge through the same Spirit, ᶠto another faith by the same Spirit, to another gifts of ᵍhealings by the same

---

of any speaking exercise is determined by the truthfulness of it. If the speaker affirms the lordship of Jesus, it is the truth from the Holy Spirit. What a person believes and says about Jesus Christ is the test of whether he speaks from the Holy Spirit. He always leads people to Christ's lordship (cf. 1 Cor. 2:8–14; John 15:26; 1 John 5:6–8).

a. **gifts.** These categories of giftedness are not natural talents, skills, or abilities, such as are possessed by believers and unbelievers alike. They are sovereignly and supernaturally bestowed by the Holy Spirit on all believers (1 Cor. 12:7, 11), enabling them to spiritually edify each other effectively and thus honor the Lord. The varieties of gifts fall into two general types, speaking and serving (see vv. 8–10; cf. Rom. 12:6–8; 1 Pet. 4:10, 11). The speaking, or verbal, gifts (prophecy, knowledge, wisdom, teaching, and exhortation) and the serving, nonverbal gifts (leadership, helps, giving, mercy, faith, and discernment) are all permanent gifts that will operate throughout the church age. Their purpose is to edify the church and glorify God. The list here and in Rom. 12:3–8 is best seen as representative of categories of giftedness which the Holy Spirit draws from to give each believer whatever kind or combination of kinds He chooses. Some believers may be gifted categorically similar to others but are personally unique as the Spirit suits each grace gift to the individual. Miracles, healing, languages, and the interpretation of languages were temporary sign gifts limited to the apostolic age and have, therefore, ceased. Their purpose was to authenticate the apostles and their message as the true Word of God, until God's written Word was completed and became self-authenticating.

b. **differences of ministries . . . diversities of activities.** The Lord gives believers unique ministry arenas in which to fulfill their giftedness, and provides varieties of power to energize and accomplish them (cf. Rom. 12:6).

c. **manifestation of the Spirit.** No matter what the gift, ministry, or effect, all spiritual gifts are from the Holy Spirit. They make Him known, understood, and evident in the church and in the world, by spiritually profiting all who receive their ministry.

d. **word of wisdom.** "Word" indicates a speaking gift (cf. 1 Pet. 4:11). In the NT, "wisdom" is most often used of the ability to understand God's Word and His will, and to skillfully apply that understanding to life (cf. Matt. 11:19; 13:54; Mark 6:2; Luke 7:35; Acts 6:10; James 1:5; 3:13, 17; 2 Pet. 3:15).

e. **word of knowledge.** This gift may have been revelatory in the first century, but it is today the ability to understand and speak God's truth, with insight into the mysteries of His Word, that cannot be known apart from God's revelation (Rom. 16:25; Eph. 3:3; Col. 1:26; 2:2; 4:3; cf. 13:2). Knowledge majors on grasping the meaning of the truth; wisdom emphasizes the practical conviction and conduct that applies it.

f. **faith.** Distinct from saving faith or persevering faith, both of which all believers possess, this gift is exercised in persistent prayer and endurance in intercession, along with a strong trust in God in the midst of difficult circumstances (cf. Matt. 17:20).

g. **healings.** A temporary sign gift used by Christ (Matt. 8:16, 17), the apostles (Matt. 10:1), the seventy (Luke 10:1), and a few associates of the apostles, such as Philip (Acts 8:5–7). This ability was identified as a gift belonging to the apostles (cf. 2 Cor. 12:12). Although Christians today do not have the gift of healings, God certainly still hears and answers the faithful prayers of His children (see James 5:13–16). Some people feel that healing should be common and expected in every era, but this is not the case. Physical healings are very rare throughout the OT record. Only a few are recorded. There was never a time before the coming of Christ when healings were common. Only in His lifetime and that of His apostles was there

Spirit, to another the working of [a]miracles, to another [b]prophecy, to another [c]discerning of spirits, to another different kinds of [d]tongues, to another the

---

a veritable explosion of healing. This was due to the unique need to accredit the Messiah and to authenticate the first miracles of the gospel. Jesus and His apostles temporarily banished disease from Palestine, but that was the most monumental era of redemptive history and called for such authentication. To normalize healing would be to normalize the arrival of the Savior. This gift belonged to the sign gifts for that era only. The gift of healings were never used solely for bringing people physical health. Paul was sick but never healed himself or asked another human to heal him. His friend Epaphroditus was near death (Phil. 2:27), and Paul did not heal him. God intervened. When Timothy was sick, Paul did not heal him, but told him to take some wine (1 Tim. 5:23). Paul left Trophimus "sick at Miletus" (2 Tim. 4:20). Healings were not the everyday norm in Paul's ministry, but did occur when he entered a new region, e.g., Malta, where the gospel and its preacher needed authentication (see Acts 28:8, 9). That healing was the first mention of healing since the lame man was healed in Lystra (Acts 14:9) in connection with the arrival of Paul and the gospel there. Prior to that, the nearest healing was by Peter in Acts 9:34, and the resurrection of Tabitha in 9:41, so that people would believe the gospel Peter preached (9:42).

a. **miracles.** This temporary sign gift was for the working of divine acts contrary to nature, so that there was no explanation for the action except that it was by the power of God. This, too, was to authenticate Christ and the apostolic preachers of the gospel. John 2:11 notes that Jesus did His first miracle at Cana to "manifest His glory," not enhance the party (cf. John's purpose for recording the miracles of Jesus in this gospel, 20:30, 31). Acts 2:22 affirms that Jesus did miracles to "attest" that God was working through Him, so that people would believe in Him as Lord and Savior. Jesus performed miracles and healed only for the 3 years of His ministry, not at all in the 30 years before. His miracles began when His ministry began. Though Jesus did miracles related to nature (made wine, created food, walked on water with Peter, ascended), no apostle ever is reported to have done a miracle in the natural realm. What miracle did the apostles do? The answer is in the word "miracles," meaning "power," and is frequently connected to casting out demons (Luke 4:36; 6:18; 9:42). It is precisely that power that the Lord gave the disciples (Luke 9:1; 10:17–19; cf. Acts 6:8; 8:7; 13:6–12).

b. **prophecy.** The meaning is simply that of "speaking forth," or "proclaiming publicly" to which the connotation of prediction was added sometime in the Middle Ages. Since the completion of Scripture, prophecy has not been a means of new revelation, but is limited to proclaiming what has already been revealed in the written Word. Even the biblical prophets were preachers, proclaimers of God's truth both by revelation and reiteration. Old Testament prophets like Isaiah, Jeremiah, and Ezekiel spent lifetimes proclaiming God's Word. Only a comparatively small amount of what they preached is recorded in the Bible as God's direct revelation. They must have continually repeated and re-emphasized those truths, as preachers today repeat, explain, and re-emphasize the Word of God in Scripture. The best definition for this gift is given in 1 Cor. 14:3. The importance of this gift is given in 1 Cor. 14:1, 39. Its supremacy to other gifts, especially tongues, is the theme of chap. 14. See 1 Thess. 5:20; Rev. 19:10.

c. **discerning of spirits.** Satan is the great deceiver (John 8:44) and his demons counterfeit God's message and work. Christians with the gift of discernment have the God-given ability to recognize lying spirits and to identify deceptive and erroneous doctrine (cf. Acts 17:11; 1 John 4:1). Paul illustrated the use of this gift in Acts 16:16–18, as Peter had exercised it in Acts 5:3. When it was not being exercised in the Corinthian church, grave distortion of the truth occurred (see v. 3; 14:29). Though its operation has changed since apostolic times, because of the completion of Scripture, it is still essential to have people in the church who are discerning. They are the guardians, the watchmen who protect the church from demonic lies, false doctrines, perverted cults, and fleshly elements. As it requires diligent study of the Word to exercise gifts of knowledge, wisdom, preaching, and teaching, so it does with discernment. See 1 Thess. 5:20–22; Acts 17:11.

d. **tongues . . . interpretation.** These temporary sign gifts, using the normal words for

interpretation of tongues. But ªone and the same Spirit works all these things, distributing to each one individually as He wills.

For as the ᵇbody is one and has many members, but all the members of that one body, being many, are one body, so also is Christ. For by one Spirit we were all ᶜbaptized into one body—whether Jews or Greeks, whether slaves or free—and have all been made to ᵈdrink into one Spirit. For in fact the body is not one member but many.

ᵉIf the foot should say, "Because I am not a hand, I am not of the body," is it therefore not of the body? And if the ear should say, "Because I am not an eye, I am not of the body," is it therefore not of the body? If the whole body were an eye, where would be the hearing? If the whole were hearing, where would be the smelling? But now God has set the members, each one

---

speaking a foreign language and translating it, like the others (miracles, healings) were for the authentication of the truth and those who preached it. This true gift was clearly identified in Acts 2:5–12 as languages, which validated the gospel as divine. They were, however, because of their counterfeit in the culture, disproportionately exalted and seriously abused in Corinth. Here, Paul identified them, but throughout chap. 14 he discussed them in detail. See 1 Cor. 14:1–29.

a. **one and the same Spirit.** While stressing the diversity of gifts (1 Cor. 12:4–11), Paul also stressed the singular source in the Spirit (cf. v1 Cor. 12:4, 5, 6, 8, 9). This is the fifth mention, in this chapter, of the source of gifts being the Holy Spirit. It emphasizes that gifts are not something to seek, but to be received from the Spirit "as He wills." It is He alone who "works" or energizes all gifts as He chooses.

b. **body . . . members.** Paul used the human body as an analogy (cf. 1 Cor. 10:17) for the unity of the church in Christ.

c. **baptized.** The church, the spiritual body of Christ, is formed as believers are immersed by Christ with the Holy Spirit. Christ is the baptizer (see Matt. 3:11) who immerses each believer with the Spirit into unity with all other believers. Paul is not writing of water baptism. That outward sign depicts the believer's union with Christ in His death and resurrection (see Rom. 6:3–5). Similarly, all believers are also immersed into the body of Christ by means of the Holy Spirit. Paul's point is to emphasize the unity of believers. There cannot be any believer who has not been Spirit-baptized, nor can there be more than one Spirit baptism or the whole point of unity in the body of Christ is convoluted. Believers have all been Spirit-baptized and thus are all in one body. See Eph. 4:4–6. This is not an experience to seek, but a reality to acknowledge. See also Acts 8:17; 10:44, 45; 11:15–17.

d. **drink into one Spirit.** At salvation, all believers not only become full members of Christ's body, the church, but the Holy Spirit is placed within each of them (Rom. 8:9; cf. 6:19; Col. 2:10; 2 Pet. 1:3, 4). There is no need (or divine provision) for any such thing as a second blessing, a triumphalistic experience of a deeper life, or a formula for instantly increased spirituality (cf. John 3:34). Christ's salvation provision is perfect and He calls only for obedience and trust in what has already been given (Heb. 10:14).

e. **If the foot should say.** By his illustration of how every part of a human body is essential to the function of that body, Paul showed that unity is an indispensable need of the church; but divinely-provided diversity within that unity is also necessary. His words additionally implied that some selfish members were discontent with their gifts, wanting the gifts they had not been given. With that attitude, they in effect questioned God's wisdom and implied He had made a mistake in assignments (cf. Rom. 9:20, 21). In seeking showy abilities and power, they also became vulnerable to carnal, demonically counterfeited gifts.

of them, in the body just as He pleased. And if they were all one member, where would the body be?

But now indeed there are many members, yet one body. And the eye cannot say to the hand, "I have ªno need of you"; nor again the head to the feet, "I have no need of you." No, much rather, those members of the body which seem to be weaker are necessary. And those members of the body which we think to be less honorable, on these we bestow greater honor; and our ᵇunpresentable parts have greater modesty, but our presentable parts have no need. But God composed the body, having given greater honor to that part which lacks it, that there should be no schism in the body, but that the members should have the same care for one another. And if one member suffers, all the members suffer with it; or if one member is honored, all the members rejoice with it.

ᶜNow you are the body of Christ, and members individually. And God has appointed these in the church: first ᵈapostles, second prophets, third ᵉteachers,

---

a. **no need.** While some in Corinth were bemoaning the fact that they did not have the showy gifts (see vv. 14–20), those who did were belittling those with the more quiet and less prominent gifts. The "eye" and the "head," which are highly visible and the focus of all who engage each other, represent the people with public gifts. They so overestimated their own importance that they disdained those whom they perceived as less gifted and less significant. They were apparently indifferent ("I have no need") and self-sufficient.

b. **unpresentable parts.** Paul's answer to the pride of the more visibly gifted was to engage his analogy again and remind them that the more fragile and less lovely, in fact, ugly parts of the body which are not publicly "presentable" (1 Cor. 12:24) are given the greater respect for their necessity. He spoke of the internal organs. God has designed visible, public gifts to have a crucial place, but equally designed and more vital to life are the hidden gifts, thus maintaining the perspective of unity—all are essential to the working of the body of Christ. This is a call to mutual love and concern in the fellowship of believers (cf. Phil. 2:1–4) which maintains the unity that honors the Lord. There is one body in which all function, yet never do they lose their personal identity and the essential necessity of ministry as God has designed them to do it.

c. **God has appointed.** Again emphasizing the sovereignty of God (cf. 1 Cor. 12:7, 11, 18), Paul illustrates the individuality and unity of the body by a repeat of the representative categories of ministries, callings, and giftedness.

d. **apostles . . . prophets.** See Eph. 4:11. Their purpose was: 1) to lay the foundation of the church (Eph. 2:20); 2) to receive and declare the revelation of God's Word (Acts 11:28; 21:10, 11; Eph. 3:5); and 3) to give confirmation of that Word through signs, wonders, and miracles (2 Cor. 12:12; cf. Acts 8:6, 7; Heb. 2:3, 4). "Apostles" refers, primarily, to those 12 chosen by our Lord plus Paul and Matthias (Acts 1:26). See Rom. 1:1. In a secondary sense, others served as messengers of the church: Barnabas (Acts 14:14) Silas and Timothy (1 Thess. 2:6) and others (Rom. 16:7; 2 Cor. 8:23; Phil. 2:25). Apostles of Christ were the source of the church's doctrine (Acts 2:42); apostles of the church (2 Cor. 8:23) were its early leaders. "Prophets" were especially gifted men in the local churches, who preached God's Word (Acts 11:21–28; 13:1). Any message preached by a prophet had to be judged by the word of the apostles (see 1 Cor. 14:36, 37).

e. **teachers.** Could be the same as pastor-teachers (see Eph. 4:11), but probably should be broadened to include all who are gifted for teaching in the church, whether they have the office of pastor or not.

after that miracles, then gifts of healings, ªhelps, administrations, varieties of tongues. ᵇAre all apostles? Are all prophets? Are all teachers? Are all workers of miracles? Do all have gifts of healings? Do all speak with tongues? Do all interpret? But ᶜearnestly desire the best gifts. And yet I show you a more excellent way.

102. THE SUPERIORITY OF LOVE

1 Cor. 13:1–13

Though I speak with the ᵈtongues of men and of ᵉangels, but ᶠhave not ᵍlove, I have become sounding brass or a clanging cymbal. And though I have the

a. **helps, administration.** These less public gifts are mingled with the more public manifestations of the Spirit to show their vital necessity. "Helps" is an ability for service; in fact, the gift of ministry ("service") in Rom. 12:7 is in the same category. "Administration" is leadership. The word comes from the Gr., meaning "to pilot a ship" (Acts 27:11) and speaks of one who can lead ministries of the church efficiently and effectively.

b. **Are all apostles?** Each of these rhetorical queries expects a "no" answer. The body of Christ is diverse and God sovereignly designs it that way.

c. **earnestly desire.** In context, this could not mean that believers should desire the more prominent gifts, when the whole chapter has just been confronting the fact that they have sinfully been doing just that. Desiring a gift for selfish reasons is wrong, since they are sovereignly given by God as He wills (1 Cor. 12:7, 11, 18, 28). Therefore, this must be rendered not as an imperative (command), but, as the verb form allows, as an indicative (statement of fact), "You are desiring the showy gifts, wrongly." The real imperative is to stop doing that and learn the "more excellent way," the way of love, which Paul will explain 1 Cor. 13.

d. **tongues of men.** Cf. 1 Cor. 12:10, 28; 14:4–33. That this gift was actual languages is established in Acts 2:4–12, affirmed in this text by Paul's calling it "of men"—clearly a reference to human language. This was the gift which the Corinthians prized so highly, abused so greatly, and counterfeited so disastrously. God gave the ability to speak in a language not known to the speaker, as a sign with limited function (see 1 Cor. 14:1–33).

e. **angels.** The apostle was writing in general hypothetical terms. There is no biblical teaching of any special angelic language that people could learn to speak.

f. **have not.** Spiritual gifts were present in Corinth (1 Cor. 1:7); right doctrine was even in place (1 Cor. 11:2); but love was absent. This led to the quarrels and exhibitions of selfishness and pride that plagued the church—notably in the area of spiritual gifts (see 1 Cor. 12:14–31). Instead of selfishly and jealously desiring showy gifts which they don't have, believers should pursue the greatest thing of all—love for each other. This chapter is considered by many the greatest literary passage ever penned by Paul. It is central to his earnestly dealing with spiritual gifts (1 Cor. 12–14), because after discussing the endowment of gifts (chap. 12) and before presenting the function of gifts (chap. 14), he addresses the attitude necessary in all ministry in the church (chap. 13).

g. **love.** Self-giving love that is more concerned with giving than receiving (John 3:16; cf. 14:1; Matt. 5:44, 45; John 13:1, 34, 35; 15:9; Rom. 5:10; Eph. 2:4–7; Phil. 2:2; Col. 3:14; Heb. 10:24). The word was not admired and thus seldom used in ancient Gr. literature, but it is common in the NT. Without love, no matter how linguistically gifted one is to speak his own language, other languages, or even (hypothetically) the speech of angels, his speech is noise only. In NT times, rites honoring the pagan deities Cybele, Bacchus, and Dionysius included ecstatic noises accompanied by gongs, cymbals, and trumpets. Unless the speech of the Corinthians was done in love, it was no better than the gibberish of pagan ritual.

^agift of prophecy, and ^bunderstand all mysteries and all knowledge, and though I have ^call faith, so that I could remove mountains, but have not love, I am nothing. And though I bestow all my goods to feed the poor, and though I give my body to be ^dburned, but have not love, it profits me nothing.

^eLove suffers long and is kind; love does not envy; love does not parade itself, is not puffed up; does not behave rudely, does not seek its own, is not provoked, thinks no evil; does not rejoice in iniquity, but rejoices in the truth; bears all things, believes all things, hopes all things, endures all things.

^fLove never fails. But whether there are prophecies, they will fail; whether

---

a. **the gift of prophecy.** See 1 Cor. 12:10. In 1 Cor. 14:1–5, Paul speaks of this gift as the most essential one because it brings God's truth to people. Even this gift must be ministered in love (cf. Eph. 4:15).

b. **understand all mysteries and all knowledge.** This encompasses gifts of wisdom, knowledge, and discernment (see 1 Cor. 12:8, 10), which are to be exercised in love (see Phil. 1:9).

c. **all faith.** See Matt. 17:20. This refers to the gift of faith (enduring, believing prayer; see 1 Cor. 12:9), which is useless without selfless love for the church.

d. **burned.** The practice of burning Christians at the stake did not begin until some years later, but it was clearly understood to be an extremely horrible death. Neither volunteering for giving up all your possessions or being burned would produce any spiritual benefit if not done out of love for the body of Christ.

e. **Love.** In the previous comments (1 Cor. 13:1–3), the focus is on the emptiness produced when love is absent from ministry. In these verses, the fullness of love is described, in each case by what love does. Love is action, not abstraction. Positively, love is patient with people and gracious to them with generosity. Negatively, love never envies, or brags, or is arrogant, since that is the opposite of selfless service to others. Never rude or overbearing, love never wants its own way, is not irritated or angered in personal offense, and finds no pleasure in someone else's sin, even the sin of an enemy. On the positive side again, love is devoted to truth in everything. With regard to "all things" within God's righteous and gracious will, love protects, believes, hopes, and endures what others reject.

f. **never fails.** This refers to love's lastingness or permanence as a divine quality. Love outlasts all failures (cf. 1 Pet. 4:8; 1 John 4:16). Paul strengthens his point on the permanence of love by comparing it to the spiritual gifts which the Corinthians so highly prized: prophecy, knowledge, and languages, all of which will have an end. There may be a distinction made on how prophecy and knowledge come to an end, and how the gift of languages does. This is indicated by the Gr. verb forms used. In the case of prophecy and knowledge, they are both said to "be abolished" (in both cases the verb indicates that something will put an end to these two functions. Verses 9, 10 indicate that what will abolish knowledge and prophecy is "that which is perfect." When that occurs, those gifts will be rendered inoperative. The "perfect" is not the completion of Scripture, since there is still the operation of those two gifts and will be in the future kingdom (cf. Joel 2:28; Acts 2:17; Rev. 11:3). The Scriptures do not allow us to see "face to face" or have perfect knowledge as God does (1 Cor. 13:12). The "perfect" is not the rapture of the church or the second coming of Christ, since the kingdom to follow these events will have an abundance of preachers and teachers (cf. Is. 29:18; 32:3, 4; Joel 2:28; Rev. 11:3). The perfect must be the eternal state, when we in glory see God face to face (Rev. 22:4) and have full knowledge in the eternal new heavens and new earth. Just as a child grows to full understanding, believers will come to perfect knowledge and no such gifts will be necessary.

On the other hand, Paul uses a different word for the end of the gift of languages, thus indicating it will "cease" by itself, as it did at the end of the apostolic age. It will not end by the coming of the "perfect," for it will already have ceased. The uniqueness of the gift of languages and its interpretations was, as all sign gifts, to authenticate the message and messages of the gospel before the NT was completed (Heb. 2:3, 4). "Tongues" was also limited

there are tongues, they will cease; whether there is knowledge, it will vanish away. For we know in part and we prophesy in part. But when that which is perfect has come, then that which is in part will be done away.

When I was a child, I spoke as a child, I understood as a child, I thought as a child; but when I became a man, I put away childish things. For now we see in a mirror, dimly, but then face to face. Now I know in part, but then I shall know just as I also am known.

And now abide faith, hope, love, these three; but the [a]greatest of these is love.

103. Gifts of Prophecy and Tongues
1 Cor. 14:1—19

[b]Pursue love, and [c]desire spiritual gifts, but [d]especially that you may prophesy. For he who speaks in a tongue [e]does not speak to men but to God,

---

by being a judicial sign from the God of Israel's judgment (see 1 Cor. 14:21; cf. Is. 28:11, 12). "Tongues" were also not a sign to believers, but unbelievers (see 1 Cor. 14:22), specifically those unbelieving Jews. Tongues also ceased because there was no need to verify the true messages from God once the Scripture was given. It became the standard by which all are to be deemed true. "Tongues" was a means of edification in a way far inferior to preaching and teaching (see 1 Cor. 14:5, 12, 13, 27, 28). In fact, 1 Cor. 14 was designed to show the Corinthians, so preoccupied with tongues, that it was an inferior means of communication (vv. 1–12), an inferior means of praise (vv. 13–19), and an inferior means of evangelism (vv. 20–25). Prophecy was and is, far superior (vv. 1, 3–6, 24, 29, 31, 39). That tongues have ceased should be clear from their absence from any other books in the NT, except Acts. Tongues ceased to be an issue of record or practice in the early church, as the Scripture was being written. That tongues has ceased should be clear also from its absence through church history since the first century, appearing only sporadically and then only in questionable groups.

a. **greatest of these.** The objects of faith and hope will be fulfilled and perfectly realized in heaven, but love, the God-like virtue, is everlasting (cf. 1 John 4:8). Heaven will be the place for the expression of nothing but perfect love toward God and each other.

b. **Pursue love.** A command for every believer. Because lovelessness was a root spiritual problem in the Corinthian church, the godly love just described should have been sought after by them with particular determination and diligence.

c. **desire spiritual gifts.** Love does not preclude the use of these enablements. Since Paul has addressed not desiring showy gifts (1 Cor. 12:31) and not elevating one over the other (1 Cor. 12:14–25), some might think it best to set them all aside for unity's sake. Spiritual gifts, on the other hand, are sovereignly bestowed by God on each believer and necessary for the building of the church (1 Cor. 12:1–10). Desire for them, in this context, is in reference to their use collectively and faithfully in His service—not a personal yearning to have an admired gift that one did not possess. As a congregation, the Corinthians should be wanting the full expression of all the gifts to be exercised. "You" is plural, emphasizing the corporate desire of the church.

d. **especially . . . prophesy.** This spiritual gift was desirable in the life of the church to serve in a way that tongues cannot, namely, by edifying the entire church.

e. **does not speak to men but to God.** This is better translated, "to a god." The Gr.

for [a]no one understands him; however, in the spirit he speaks mysteries. But he who [b]prophesies speaks edification and exhortation and comfort to men. [c]He who speaks in a tongue edifies himself, but he who prophesies edifies the church. I wish you [d]all spoke with tongues, but even more that you prophesied; for he who prophesies is greater than he who speaks with tongues, unless indeed he interprets, that the church may receive edification.

But now, brethren, [e]if I come to you speaking with tongues, what shall I profit you unless I speak to you either by revelation, by knowledge, by prophesying, or by teaching? Even things without life, whether [f]flute or harp, when they make a sound, unless they make a distinction in the sounds, how will

---

text has no definite article (see similar translation in Acts 17:23, "an unknown god"). Their gibberish was worship of pagan deities. The Bible records no incident of any believer ever speaking to God in any other than normal human language.

a. **no one understands him; . . . in the spirit he speaks mysteries.** The carnal Corinthians using the counterfeit ecstatic speech of paganism were not interested in being understood, but in making a dramatic display. The spirit by which they spoke was not the Holy Spirit, but their own human spirit or some demon; and the mysteries they declared were the type associated with the pagan mystery religions, which was espoused to be the depths that only the initiated few were privileged to know and understand. Those mysteries were totally unlike the ones mentioned in Scripture (e.g., Matt. 13:11; Eph. 3:9), which are divine revelations of truths previously hidden (see 1 Cor. 12:7; Eph. 3:3–6).

b. **prophesies.** In dramatic contrast to the bedlam of counterfeit tongues was the gift of genuine prophesy or preaching of the truth (see 1 Cor. 12:10). It produced the building up in truth, the encouragement to obedience, and the comfort in trouble that God desired for His church. Spiritual gifts are always for the benefit of others, never self.

c. **a tongue.** Again, Paul uses the singular to refer to the pagan counterfeit gibberish and sarcastically marks its selfishness as some kind of self-edification. This illicit building up of self comes from pride-induced emotion which only produces more pride.

d. **all spoke with tongues . . . that you prophesied.** Here the plural, "tongues," appears as Paul was referring to the real gift of languages. Obviously this was not Paul's true desire, even for the true gift, since the very idea was impossible and contrary to God's sovereign distribution of gifts (1 Cor. 12:11, 30). He was simply suggesting hypothetically that, if they insisted on clamoring after gifts they did not possess, they at least should seek the one that was more enduring and more valuable for the church. The only purpose tongues renders to the church is when it is interpreted (the normal Gr. word for translation). Wherever God gave the gift of languages, He also gave the gift for translation, so that the sign would also be edifying. Never was the gift to be used without such translation (v. 28), so that the church would always be edified.

e. **if I come to you . . . what shall I profit?** Even an apostle who spoke in tongues did not spiritually benefit a congregation unless, through interpretation, his utterance was clarified so that the revelation and knowledge could be understandably preached and taught. Any private use of this gift is excluded for several reasons: 1) it is a sign to unbelievers (1 Cor. 14:22); 2) it must have a translator to have any meaning, even to the speaker (1 Cor. 14:2); and 3) it must edify the church (v. 6).

f. **flute or harp.** Here, Paul illustrates his previous point about the uselessness of even the true gift apart from translation for the church to understand. If even inanimate musical instruments are expected to make sensible sounds, how much more should human speech make sense, especially when it deals with the things of God? See v. 23.

it be known what is piped or played? For if the trumpet makes an uncertain sound, who will prepare for battle? So likewise you, ᵃunless you utter by the tongue words easy to understand, how will it be known what is spoken? For you will be speaking into the air. There are, it may be, so many kinds of languages in the world, and none of them is without significance. Therefore, if I do not know the meaning of the language, I shall be a foreigner to him who speaks, and he who speaks will be a foreigner to me. Even so you, since you are zealous for spiritual gifts, let it be for the ᵇedification of the church that you seek to excel.

Therefore let him who speaks in a tongue pray that he may interpret. For if I pray in a tongue, my spirit prays, but my understanding is unfruitful. What is the conclusion then? I will pray with the spirit, and I will also pray with the understanding. I will sing with the spirit, and I will also sing with the understanding. Otherwise, if you bless with the spirit, how will he who occupies the place of the ᶜuninformed say "Amen" at your giving of thanks, since he does not understand what you say? For you indeed give thanks well, but the other is not edified.

I thank my God ᵈI speak with tongues more than you all; yet in the church I would rather speak five words with my understanding, that I may ᵉteach others also, than ten thousand words in a tongue.

---

a. **unless you utter.** Paul simply points up the obvious: the purpose of every language is to communicate, not to impress and certainly not to confuse, as the Corinthians had been doing with their counterfeits. That was clearly the point in the first instance of tongues: Each heard the apostles speak in his own language (Acts 2:6, cf. v. 8). This section makes an undeniable case for the fact that the true gift of tongues was never some unintelligible gibberish, but was human language that was to be translated.

b. **edification.** Again Paul returned to the issue of edification, central to all gifts (1 Cor. 12:7).

c. **uninformed.** From the Gr. word meaning ignorant or unlearned.

d. **I speak with tongues more than you all.** Paul emphasized that by writing all of this, he was not condemning genuine tongues (plural); nor, as some may have thought to accuse him, was he envious of a gift he did not possess. At that point, he stopped speaking hypothetically about counterfeit tongue-speaking. He actually had more occasions to use the true gift than all of them (though we have no record of a specific instance). He knew the true gift and had used it properly. It is interesting, however, that the NT makes no mention of Paul's actually exercising that gift. Nor does Paul in his own writings make mention of a specific use of it by any Christian.

e. **teach others.** This is the general principle that summarizes what he has been saying, i.e., teaching others is the important matter and that requires understanding.

104. Gifts of Prophecy and Tongues—Continued

1 Cor. 14:20–40

Brethren, ^ado not be children in understanding; however, ^bin malice be babes, but in understanding be mature.

In the law ^cit is written:

> "With men of other tongues and other lips
> I will speak to this people;
> And yet, for all that, they will not hear Me,"
>
> says the Lord.

---

a. **do not be children in understanding.** This very important passage deals with the primary purpose of the gift of languages. Paul has clearly indicated that such speaking was not something for all believers to do, since it was dispensed sovereignly like all other gifts (1 Cor. 12:11); nor was it connected to the baptism with the Holy Spirit which all believers receive (1 Cor. 12:13); nor was it some superior sign of spirituality, but rather an inferior gift (v. 5). Because of all that, and the corruption of the real gift by the Corinthians, the apostle gives the principles for its proper and limited operation as a sign.

b. **in malice be babes, but in understanding be mature.** Most of the Corinthian believers were the opposite of what Paul here admonished. They were extremely experienced in evil, but greatly lacking in wisdom. Yet mature understanding was especially essential for proper comprehension and use of the gift of tongues, because the conspicuous and fascinating nature of that gift made it so attractive to the flesh. He was asking his readers to put aside emotion and experience, along with the desires of the flesh and pride, to think carefully about the purpose of tongues.

c. **it is written.** In a freely rendered quotation from Is. 28:11, 12, Paul explains that centuries earlier the Lord had predicted that one day He would use men of other tongues, that is, foreigners speaking unknown languages, as a sign to unbelieving Israel, who "will not hear Me." These "other tongues" are what they knew as the gift of languages, given solely as a sign to unbelieving Israel. That sign was threefold: cursing, blessing, and authority. To emphasize the cursing, Paul quoted Isaiah's words of warning to Judah of the judgment from Assyria (see Is. 28:11, 12). The leaders thought his words were too simple and rejected him. The time would come, the prophet said, when they would hear Assyrian, a language they could not understand, indicating judgment. Jeremiah spoke similarly of the Babylonians who were also to come and destroy Judah (cf. Jer. 5:15). When the apostles spoke at Pentecost in all those foreign languages (Acts 2:3–12), the Jews should have known that the judgment prophesied and historically fulfilled first by the Assyrians and then by the Babylonian captivity was about to fall on them again for their rejection of Christ, including the destruction of Jerusalem (A.D. 70) as it had happened in 586 B.C. under Babylonian power.

One Faithful Life

[a]Therefore tongues are for a sign, not to those who believe but to unbelievers; but [b]prophesying is not for unbelievers but for those who believe. [c]Therefore if the whole church comes together in one place, and all speak with tongues, and there come in those who are uninformed or unbelievers, will they not say that you are [d]out of your mind? [e]But if all prophesy, and an unbeliever or an uninformed person comes in, he is convinced by all, he is convicted by all. And thus the secrets of his heart are revealed; and so, falling down on his face, he will worship God and report that God is truly among you.

How is it then, brethren? Whenever you come together, [f]each of you has [g]a psalm, has [h]a teaching, has a tongue, has a [i]revelation, has [j]an interpretation. Let all things be done [k]for edification. If anyone speaks in a tongue,

a. **Therefore tongues are for a sign, not to those who believe but to unbelievers.** Explaining further, he says explicitly that all tongues are for the sake of unbelievers. In other words, that gift has no purpose in the church when everyone present is a believer. And once the sign served its purpose to pronounce judgment or cursing on Israel, and the judgment fell, the purpose ceased along with the sign gift. The blessing of that sign was that God would build a new nation of Jews and Gentiles to be his people (Gal. 3:28), to make Israel jealous and someday repent (see Rom. 11:11, 12, 25–27). The sign was thus repeated when Gentiles were included in the church (Acts 10:44–46). The sign also gave authority to those who preached both the judgment and blessing (2 Cor. 12:12), including Paul (1 Cor. 14:18).

b. **prophesying is . . . for those who believe.** In the completely opposite way, the gift of prophesying benefits only believers, who are able, by their new natures and the indwelling Holy Spirit, to understand spiritual truth (cf. 1 Cor. 2:14; 1 John 2:20, 27).

c. **Therefore if . . . all speak with tongues.** As Paul explains in more detail later (1 Cor. 14:27, 28), even for unbelievers, even when the gift of tongues was exercised in its proper time in history, when it was dominant and uncontrolled in the church, bedlam ensued and the gospel was disgraced and discredited.

d. **out of your mind.** The Gr. word means to be in an uncontrolled frenzy. When the real gift was used in Acts 2, there was no madness, and everyone understood in his own language (1 Cor. 14:11). In Corinth, there was charismatic chaos.

e. **But if all prophesy.** This means to publicly proclaim the Word of God (see 1 Cor. 2:10). "All" does not mean all at once (see 1 Cor. 14:31), but rather means that hypothetically if the cacophony of all the Corinthians could be replaced by all of them preaching the Word, the effect on unbelievers would be amazingly powerful, the gospel would be honored, and souls would be converted to worshiping God.

f. **each of you has.** It seems that chaos and lack of order was rampant in that assembly. It is interesting that no elders or pastors are mentioned, and the prophets were not even exercising control (see 1 Cor. 14:29, 32, 37). Everyone was participating with whatever expression they desired "whenever" they desired.

g. **a psalm.** The reading or singing of an OT psalm.

h. **a teaching.** This probably refers to a doctrine or subject of special interest.

i. **revelation.** Some supposed word from God, whether spurious or genuine.

j. **an interpretation.** This refers to that of a tongue's message.

k. **for edification.** This was Paul's way of calling a halt to the chaos. Edification is the goal, (1 Cor. 14:3–5, 12, 17, 26, 31) and the Corinthian chaos could not realize it (cf. 1 Thess. 5:11; Rom. 15:2, 3).

let there be two or at the most three, each in turn, and let one interpret. But if there is no interpreter, let him keep silent in church, and let him speak to himself and to God. [a]Let two or three prophets speak, and let the others judge. But if anything is revealed to another who sits by, let the first keep silent. For you can all prophesy one by one, that all may learn and all may be encouraged. And the spirits of the prophets are [b]subject to the prophets. For God is not the author of [c]confusion but of peace, [d]as in all the churches of the saints.

Let your [e]women keep silent in the churches, for they are not permitted to speak; but they are to be submissive, as the law also says. And if they want to learn something, let them ask their own husbands at home; for it is shameful for women to speak in church.

Or did the word of God come originally from you? Or was it you only that it reached? If anyone thinks himself to be a prophet or spiritual, let him

---

a. **Let two or three prophets.** These verses provide regulations for the exercise of the gift: 1) only two or three persons in a service; 2) only speaking in turn, one at a time; and 3) only with an interpreter. Without those conditions, one was to meditate and pray silently. Since Paul's pastoral epistles (1, 2 Tim.; Titus) do not mention prophets, it seems evident that this unique office had ceased to function in the church even before the end of the apostolic age. When Paul wrote the Corinthians, however, prophets were still central to the work of that church (cf. Acts 13:1). Here he gave 4 regulations for their preaching: 1) only two or three were to speak; 2) the other prophets were to judge what was said; 3) if while one was speaking, God gave a revelation, the speaker was to defer to the one hearing from God; and 4) each prophet was to speak in turn. See Eph. 2:20; 4:11.

b. **subject to the prophets.** Not only were the prophets to judge others with discernment, but they were also to have control over themselves. God does not desire out-of-spirit or out-of-mind experiences. Those who received and proclaimed the truth were to have clear minds. There was nothing bizarre, ecstatic, trance-like, or wild about receiving and preaching God's Word, as with demonic experiences.

c. **confusion.** Here is the key to the whole chapter. The church at worship before God should reflect His character and nature because He is a God of peace and harmony, order and clarity, not strife and confusion (cf. Rom. 15:33; 2 Thess. 3:16; Heb. 13:20).

d. **as in all the churches.** This phrase does not belong in 1 Cor. 14:33, but at the beginning of v. 34, as a logical introduction to a universal principle for churches.

e. **women keep silent in the churches.** The principle of women not speaking in church services is universal; this applies to all the churches, not just locally, geographically, or culturally. The context in this verse concerns prophecy, but includes the general theme of the chapter, i.e., tongues. Rather than leading, they are to be submissive as God's Word makes clear (see 1 Cor. 11:3–15; Gen. 3:16; 1 Tim. 2:11–15). It is not coincidental that many modern churches that have tongues-speaking and claim gifts of healings and miracles also permit women to lead worship, preach, and teach. Women may be gifted teachers, but they are not permitted by God "to speak" in churches. In fact, for them to do so is "shameful," meaning "disgraceful." Apparently, certain women were out of order in disruptively asking questions publicly in the chaotic services.

acknowledge that the things which I write to you are the ªcommandments of the Lord. But if anyone is ᵇignorant, let him be ignorant.

Therefore, brethren, desire earnestly to prophesy, and ᶜdo not forbid to speak with tongues. Let all things be done decently and in order.

105. The Historical Reality of the Resurrection

1 Cor. 15:1–34

Moreover, brethren, ᵈI declare to you the gospel which I ᵉpreached to you, which also you received and in which you stand, by which also you are saved, if you hold fast that word which I preached to you—ᶠunless you believed in vain.

---

a. **Commandments of the Lord.** Paul knew that the Corinthians would react to all these firm regulations that would end the free-for-all in their services. The prophets, tongues-speakers, and women may all have been resistant to words, so he anticipated that resistance by sarcastically challenging those who put themselves above his word, and thus, above Scripture by either ignoring it or interpreting it to fit their predisposed ideas. If anyone was genuinely a prophet or had the true spiritual gift of tongues, he or she would submit to the principles God had revealed through the apostle.

b. **ignorant.** That is, anyone who does not recognize the authority of Paul's teaching should himself not be recognized as a legitimate servant gifted by God.

c. **do not forbid . . . tongues.** Legitimate languages were limited in purpose and in duration, but as long as it was still active in the early church, it was not to be hindered. But prophecy was the most desirable gift to be exercised because of its ability to edify, exhort, and comfort with the truth.

d. **I declare to you.** This chapter (1 Cor. 15) is the most extensive treatment of resurrection in the Bible. Both the resurrection of Jesus Christ as recorded in the gospels and the resurrection of believers as promised in the gospels are here explained. To begin his teachings about the resurrection of believers, Paul reviewed the evidences for Jesus' resurrection: 1) the church (vv. 1, 2); 2) the Scriptures (vv. 3, 4); 3) the eyewitnesses (vv. 5–7); 4) the apostle himself (vv. 8–10); and 5) the common message (v. 11).

born out of due time. Paul was saved too late to be one of the 12 apostles. Christ had ascended before he was converted. But through a miraculous appearance (Acts 9:1–8; cf. 18:9, 10; 23:11; 2 Cor. 12:1–7), Christ revealed Himself to Paul and, according to divine purpose, Paul was made an apostle. See 1:1. He was "last of all" the apostles, and felt himself to be the "least" (1 Cor. 15:9, 10; 1 Tim. 1:12–17).

e. **preached . . . received . . . stand.** This was not a new message. They had heard of the resurrection, believed in it, and had been saved by it.

f. **unless you believed in vain.** By this qualifying statement, Paul recognized and called to their attention that some may have had a shallow, non-saving faith (see Matt. 7:13, 14, 22–27; 13:24–30, 34–43, 47–50; 25:1–30). Some believed only as the demons believed

For I delivered to you first of all that which I also received: that Christ died for our sins ªaccording to the Scriptures, and that He was buried, and that He rose again the third day according to the Scriptures, and that ᵇHe was seen by Cephas, then by the twelve. After that He was seen by over five hundred brethren at once, of whom the greater part remain to the present, but some have fallen asleep. After that He was seen by James, then by all the apostles. Then last of all He was seen by me also, as by one born out of due time.

For I am the least of the apostles, who am not worthy to be called an apostle, because I persecuted the church of God. But by the grace of God I am what I am, and His grace toward me was not in vain; but ᶜI labored more abundantly than they all, yet not I, but the grace of God which was with me. Therefore, whether it was I or they, so we preach and so you believed.

Now if Christ is preached that He has been raised from the dead, how do ᵈsome among you say that there is ᵉno resurrection of the dead? But if there

---

(James 2:19), i.e., they were convinced the gospel was true, but had no love for God, Christ, and righteousness. True believers "hold fast" to the gospel (cf. John 8:31; 2 Cor. 13:5; 1 John 2:24; 2 John 9).

a. **according to the Scriptures.** The OT spoke of the suffering and resurrection of Christ (see Luke 24:25–27; Acts 2:25–31; 26:22, 23). Jesus, Peter, and Paul quoted or referred to such OT passages regarding the work of Christ as Pss. 16:8–11; 22; Is. 53.

b. **He was seen.** The testimony of eyewitnesses, recorded in the NT, was added to support the reality of the resurrection. These included: 1) John and Peter together (John 20:19, 20), but probably also separately before (Luke 24:34); 2) the 12 (John 20:19, 20; Luke 24:36; Acts 1:22); 3) the 500, only referred to here (see 2 Pet. 3:15, 16), had all seen the risen Christ (cf. Matt. 28:9; Mark 16:9, 12, 14; Luke 24:31–39; John 21:1–23); 4) James, either one of the two so-named apostles (son of Zebedee or son of Alphaeus; cf. Mark 3:17, 18) or even James the half-brother of the Lord, the author of the epistle by that name and the key leader in the Jerusalem church (Acts 15:13–21); and 5) the apostles (John 20:19–29). Such unspecified appearances occurred over a 40 day period (Acts 1:3) to all the apostles.

c. **labored more . . . they all.** In terms of years and extent of ministry, he exceeded all those named (vv. 5–7). John outlived him but did not have the extensive ministry of Paul.

d. **some among you say.** The Corinthian Christians believed in Christ's resurrection, or else they could not have been Christians (cf. John 6:44; 11:25; Acts 4:12; 2 Cor. 4:14; 1 Thess. 4:16). But some had particular difficulty accepting and understanding the resurrection of believers. Some of this confusion was a result of their experiences with pagan philosophies and religions. A basic tenet of much of ancient Gr. philosophy was dualism, which taught that everything physical was intrinsically evil; so the idea of a resurrected body was repulsive and disgusting (Acts 17:32). In addition, perhaps some Jews in the Corinthian church formerly may have been influenced by the Sadducees, who did not believe in the resurrection even though it is taught in the OT (Job 19:26; Pss. 16:8–11; 17:15; Dan. 12:2). On the other hand, NT teaching in the words of our Lord Himself was extensive on the resurrection (John 5:28, 29; 6:44; 11:25; 14:19) and it was the theme of the apostolic preaching (Acts 4:1, 2). In spite of that clarity, the church at Corinth was in doubt about the resurrection.

e. **no resurrection.** In these verses, Paul gives 6 disastrous consequences if there were no resurrection: 1) preaching Christ would be senseless (1 Cor. 15:14); 2) faith in Christ would be useless (v. 14); 3) all the witnesses and preachers of the resurrection would be liars (v. 15); 4)

is no resurrection of the dead, then Christ is not risen. And if Christ is not risen, then our preaching is empty and your faith is also empty. Yes, and we are found false witnesses of God, because we have testified of God that He raised up Christ, whom He did not raise up—if in fact the dead do not rise. For if the dead do not rise, then Christ is not risen. And if Christ is not risen, your faith is futile; you are still in your sins! Then also those who have [a]fallen asleep in Christ have perished. If in this life only we have hope in Christ, we are of all men the [b]most pitiable.

But now Christ is risen from the dead, and has become the [c]firstfruits of those who have fallen asleep. For since by [d]man came death, by Man also came the resurrection of the dead. For as in Adam [e]all die, even so in Christ all shall be made alive. But each one [f]in his own order: Christ the firstfruits, afterward those who are Christ's at His coming. [g]Then comes the end, when

---

no one would be redeemed from sin (v. 17); 5) all former believers would have perished (v. 18); and 6) Christians would be the most pitiable people on earth (v. 19).

a. **fallen asleep.** A common euphemism for death (cf. 1 Cor. 15:6, 20; 11:30; Matt. 27:52; Acts 7:60; 2 Pet. 3:4). This is not soul sleep, in which the body dies and the soul, or spirit, supposedly rests in unconsciousness.

b. **most pitiable.** This is because of the sacrifices made in this life in light of the hope of life to come. If there is no life to come, we would be better "to eat, drink and be merry" before we die.

c. **firstfruits.** This speaks of the first installment of harvest to eternal life, in which Christ's resurrection will precipitate and guarantee that all of the saints who have died will be resurrected also. See John 14:19.

d. **man . . . Man.** Adam, who through his sin brought death on the whole human race, was human. So was Christ, who by His resurrection brought life to the race. See Rom. 5:12–19.

e. **all . . . all.** The two "alls" are alike only in the sense that they both apply to descendants. The second "all" applies only to believers (see Gal. 3:26, 29; 4:7; Eph. 3:6; cf. Acts 20:32; Titus 3:7) and does not imply universalism (the salvation of everyone without faith). Countless other passages clearly teach the eternal punishment of the unbelieving (e.g., Matt. 5:29; 10:28; 25:41, 46; Luke 16:23; 2 Thess. 1:9; Rev. 20:15).

f. **in his own order.** Christ was first, as the firstfruits of the resurrection harvest. Because of His resurrection, "those who are Christ's" will be raised and enter the eternal heavenly state in 3 stages at Christ's coming (cf. Matt. 24:36, 42, 44, 50; 25:13): 1) those who have come to saving faith from Pentecost to the Rapture will be joined by living saints at the Rapture to meet the Lord in the air and ascend to heaven (1 Thess. 4:16, 17); 2) those who come to faith during the Tribulation, with the OT saints as well, will be raised up to reign with Him during the Millennium (Rev. 20:4; cf. Dan. 12:2; cf. Is. 26:19, 20); and 3) those who die during the millennial kingdom may well be instantly transformed at death into their eternal bodies and spirits. The only people left to be raised will be the ungodly and that will occur at the end of the Millennium at the Great White Throne Judgment of God (see Rev. 20:11–15; cf. John 5:28, 29), which will be followed by eternal hell (Rev. 21:8).

g. **Then comes the end.** This third aspect of the resurrection involves the restoration of the earth to the rule of Christ, the rightful King. "End" can refer not only to what is over, but to what is complete and fulfilled.

ᵃHe delivers the kingdom to God the Father, when He puts an ᵇend to all rule and all authority and power. For He must reign till He has put ᶜall enemies under His feet. The ᵈlast enemy that will be destroyed is death. For "He has put all things under His feet." But when He says "all things are put under Him," ᵉit is evident that He who put all things under Him is excepted. Now when all things are made subject to Him, then the Son Himself will also be subject to Him who put all things under Him, that God may be ᶠall in all.

Otherwise, what will they do who are ᵍbaptized for the dead, if the dead do not rise at all? Why then are they baptized for the dead? And why do we stand in jeopardy every hour? I affirm, by the boasting in you which I have in Christ Jesus our Lord, ʰI die daily. If, in the manner of men, I have fought

---

a. **He delivers the kingdom to God.** In the culmination of the world's history, after Christ has taken over the restored world for His Father and reigned for 1,000 years, all things will be returned to the way they were designed by God to be in the sinless glory of the new heavens and new earth (see Rev. 21, 22).

b. **end to all rule.** Christ will permanently conquer every enemy of God and take back the earth that He created and that is rightfully His. During the Millennium, under Christ's rule, rebelliousness will still exist and Christ will have to "rule them with a rod of iron" (Rev. 19:15). At the end of that 1,000 years, Satan will be unleashed briefly to lead a final insurrection against God (Rev. 20:7–9). But with all who follow his hatred of God and Christ, he will be banished to hell with his fallen angels to suffer forever in the lake of fire (Rev. 20:10–15).

c. **all enemies under His feet.** This figure comes from the common practice of kings always sitting enthroned above their subjects, so that when the subjects bowed or kneeled, they were lower than the sovereign's feet. With enemies, the monarch might put his foot on the neck of a conquered ruler, symbolizing that enemy's total subjugation. In the millennial kingdom, Christ's foes will be in subjection to Him.

d. **last enemy . . . death.** Christ has broken the power of Satan, who held the power of death (Heb. 2:14), at the cross. But Satan will not be permanently divested of his weapon of death until the end of the Millennium (see Rev. 20:1–10). At that point, having fulfilled completely the prophecy of Ps. 8:6, Christ then will deliver the kingdom to His Father, and the eternal glory of Rev. 21, 22 will begin.

e. **it is evident.** Lest anyone misunderstand what should be "evident," Paul does not mean by "all things being put under Christ," that God the Father is so included. It is actually the Father who gave Christ His authority (Matt. 28:18; John 5:26, 27) and whom the Son perfectly serves.

f. **all in all.** Christ will continue to rule because His reign is eternal (Rev. 11:15), but He will reign in His former, full, and glorious place within the Trinity, subject to God in the way eternally designed for Him in full Trinitarian glory.

g. **baptized for the dead.** This difficult verse has numerous possible interpretations. Other Scripture passages, however, clarify certain things which it does not mean. It does not teach, for example, that a dead person can be saved by another person's being baptized on his behalf, because baptism never has a part in a person's salvation (Eph. 2:8; cf. Rom. 3:28; 4:3; 6:3, 4). A reasonable view seems to be that "they . . . who are baptized" refers to living believers who give outward testimony to their faith in baptism by water because they were first drawn to Christ by the exemplary lives, faithful influence, and witness of believers who had subsequently died. Paul's point is that if there is no resurrection and no life after death, then why are people coming to Christ to follow the hope of those who have died?

h. **I die daily.** Paul continually risked his life in self-sacrificing ministry. Why would he risk death daily, even hourly, if there were no life after death, no reward, and no eternal joy for all his pain? Cf. 1 Pet. 1:3, 4.

with ᵃbeasts at Ephesus, what advantage is it to me? If the dead do not rise, "Let us ᵇeat and drink, for tomorrow we die!"

Do not be deceived: ᶜ"Evil company corrupts good habits." Awake to righteousness, and do not sin; for some do not have the knowledge of God. I speak this to your shame.

106. The Future Reality of the Resurrection Body

1 Cor. 15:35–58

But ᵈsomeone will say, "How are the dead raised up? And ᵉwith what body do they come?" Foolish one, what you sow is not made alive ᶠunless it dies. And what you sow, you do not sow that body that shall be, but mere grain— perhaps wheat or some other grain. But God gives it a body as He pleases, and to each seed its own body.

All flesh is ᵍnot the same flesh, but there is one kind of flesh of men, another flesh of animals, another of fish, and another of birds.

---

a. **beasts at Ephesus.** Perhaps literal wild animals, or, metaphorically, the fierce crowd of Ephesians incited against him by Demetrius (Acts 19:23–34). In either case, these were life-threatening dangers (cf. 2 Cor. 11:23–28).

b. **eat . . . drink . . . die.** A direct quote from Is. 22:13 reflecting the hopelessness of the backslidden Israelites. Cf. Heb. 11:33, 34, 38 for a litany of sufferers who were willing to die because they looked forward to resurrection (v. 35).

c. **Evil company.** The Gr. term behind this word can also refer to a spoken message. By word or example, evil friends are a corrupting influence. Hope in the resurrection is sanctifying; it leads to godly living, not corruption. Some in the church did not know God and were a corrupting influence, but not for those who hoped for life in God's presence (see 1 John 3:2, 3).

d. **someone will say.** They had the truth but shamefully did not believe and follow it (cf. 2 Cor. 13:5); thus, these questions did not reflect a genuine interest in the resurrection but were mocking taunts, by those who denied the resurrection, perhaps under the influence of gnostic-oriented philosophy. But supposing it were true, they queried as to how it could ever happen. Cf. Acts 26:8.

e. **with what body do they come?** To the questions posed in 1 Cor. 15:35, Paul here gives 4 responses: 1) an illustration from nature (vv. 36–38); 2) a description of resurrection bodies (vv. 39–42a); 3) contrasts of earthly and resurrection bodies (vv. 42b–44); and 4) a reminder of the prototype resurrection of Jesus Christ (vv. 45–49).

f. **unless it dies.** When a seed is planted in the ground it dies; decomposing, it ceases to exist in its seed form, but life comes from inside that dead seed (see John 12:24). Just as God gives a new body to that plant that rises from the dead seed, so He can give a resurrection body to a man who dies.

g. **not the same.** As there are vastly different bodies and forms in God's created universe which are suited for all kinds of existence, so God can design a body perfect for resurrection life.

There are also celestial bodies and terrestrial bodies; but the glory of the celestial is one, and the glory of the terrestrial is another. There is one glory of the sun, another glory of the moon, and another glory of the stars; for one star differs from another star in glory.

So also is ªthe resurrection of the dead. The body is sown in corruption, it is raised in incorruption. It is sown in dishonor, it is raised in glory. It is sown in weakness, it is raised in power. It is sown a natural body, it is raised a spiritual body. There is a natural body, and there is a spiritual body. And so it is written, "The first man Adam became a living being." The last Adam became a life-giving spirit.

However, the spiritual is not first, but the natural, and afterward the spiritual. The first man was of the earth, made of dust; the second Man is the Lord from heaven. As was the man of dust, so also are those who are made of dust; and as is ᵇthe heavenly Man, so also are those who are heavenly. And as we have borne the image of the man of dust, we shall also bear the image of the heavenly Man.

Now this I say, brethren, that flesh and blood ᶜcannot inherit the kingdom of God; nor does corruption inherit incorruption. Behold, I tell you a ᵈmystery: We shall not all sleep, but we shall all be changed—in a moment, in the ᵉtwinkling of an eye, at the last trumpet. For the ᶠtrumpet will sound,

---

a. **the resurrection of the dead.** Focusing directly on the resurrection body, Paul gives 4 sets of contrasts to show how the new body will differ from the present ones (cf. 1 Cor. 15:54; Phil. 3:20, 21): 1) no more sickness and death ("corruption"); 2) no more shame because of sin ("dishonor"); 3) no more frailty in temptation ("weakness"); and 4) no more limits to the time/space sphere ("natural").

b. **the heavenly Man.** Here Paul answers the question (1 Cor. 15:35) more specifically by showing that the resurrection body of Jesus Christ is the prototype. He begins with a quotation from Gen. 2:7 with the addition of two words, "first" and "Adam." Adam was created with a natural body, not perfect, but good in every way (Gen. 3:1). The "last Adam" is Jesus Christ (Rom. 5:19, 21). He is saying that through the first Adam we received our natural bodies, but through the last Adam we will receive our spiritual bodies in resurrection. Adam's body was the prototype of the natural, Christ's body of the resurrection. We will bear the image of His body fit for heaven (Acts 1:11; Phil. 3:20, 21; 1 John 3:1–3) as we have borne the image of Adam's on earth.

c. **cannot inherit.** People cannot live in God's eternal heavenly glory the way they are. See Rom. 8:23. We have to be changed (1 Cor. 15:51).

d. **mystery.** This term refers to truth hidden in the past and revealed in the NT. See 1 Cor. 2:7 and Eph. 3:4, 5. In this case, the rapture of the church was never revealed in the OT. It was first mentioned in John 14:1–3, when it is specifically explained and is detailed in 1 Thess. 4:13–18.

e. **twinkling of an eye.** This was Paul's way of showing how brief the "moment" will be. The Gr. word for "twinkling" refers to any rapid movement. Since the eye can move more rapidly than any other part of our visible bodies, it seems to well illustrate the sudden transformation of raptured believers.

f. **trumpet will sound.** To herald the end of the church era, when all believers will be removed from the earth at the rapture (1 Thess. 4:16).

and the [a]dead will be raised incorruptible, and we shall be changed. For this corruptible must put on incorruption, and this mortal must put on immortality. So when this corruptible has put on incorruption, and this mortal has put on immortality, then shall be brought to pass the saying [b]that is written: "Death is swallowed up in victory."

> "O Death, where is your sting?
> O Hades, where is your victory?"

The sting of death is sin, and the strength of sin is the law. But thanks be to God, who gives us the victory through our Lord Jesus Christ.

Therefore, my beloved brethren, be steadfast, immovable, always [c]abounding in the work of the Lord, knowing that your labor is not in vain in the Lord.

107. Concluding Charge to the Church
1 Cor. 16:1–23

Now concerning the [d]collection for the saints, as I have given orders to the churches of Galatia, so you must do also: On the [d]first day of the week let each one of you lay something aside, storing up [e]as he may prosper, that there

---

a. **dead . . . raised.** According to 1 Thess. 4:16, they are first and the living saints follow (1 Thess. 4:17).

b. **that is written.** Paul enhanced his joy at the reality of resurrection by quoting from Is. 25:8 and Hos. 13:14. The latter quote taunts death as if it were a bee whose sting was removed. That sting was the sin that was exposed by the law of God (see Rom. 3:23; 4:15; 6:23; Gal. 3:10–13), but conquered by Christ in His death (see Rom. 5:17; 2 Cor. 5:21).

c. **abounding in the work.** The hope of resurrection makes all the efforts and sacrifices in the Lord's work worth it. No work done in His name is wasted in light of eternal glory and reward.

d. **collection.** An offering for destitute believers in the overpopulated, famine stricken city of Jerusalem (v. 3; see Acts 11:28). Paul had previously solicited funds from the churches of Galatia, Macedonia, and Achaia (Rom. 15:26; cf. Luke 10:25–37; 2 Cor. 8:1–5; 9:12–15; Gal. 6:10; 1 John 3:17).

d. **first day of the week.** This evidences that the early church met on Sunday (Acts 20:7). The point is that giving must occur regularly, not just when one feels generous, particularly led to do so, or instructed to do so for some special purpose (cf. Luke 6:38; cf. 2 Cor. 9:6, 7).

e. **as he may prosper.** No required amount or percentage for giving to the Lord's work is specified in the NT. All giving to the Lord is to be free will giving and completely discretionary (see Luke 6:38; 2 Cor. 9:6–8). This is not to be confused with the OT required giving of 3 tithes (see Lev. 27:30; Num. 18:21–26; Deut. 14:28, 29; Mal. 3:8–10) which totaled about 23 percent annually to fund the national government of Israel, take care of public festivals, and provide

be no collections when I come. And when I come, whomever you approve by your letters I will send to bear your gift to Jerusalem. But if it is fitting that I go also, they will go with me.

Now I will come to you when I pass through Macedonia (for I am passing through Macedonia). And it may be that I will remain, or even spend the winter with you, that you may send me on my journey, wherever I go. For I do not wish to see you now on the way; but I hope to stay a while with you, if the Lord permits.

But I will ᵃtarry in Ephesus until Pentecost. For a great and effective door has opened to me, and there are ᵇmany adversaries.

And if ᶜTimothy comes, see that he may be with you ᵈwithout fear; for he does the work of the Lord, as I also do. Therefore let no one despise him. But send him on his journey in peace, that he may come to me; for I am waiting for him with the brethren.

Now concerning our brother ᵉApollos, I strongly urged him to come to you with the brethren, but he was quite unwilling to come at this time; however, he will come when he has a convenient time.

Watch, stand fast in ᶠthe faith, be brave, be strong. Let all that you do be done with love.

I urge you, brethren—you know the household of Stephanas, that it is the ᵍfirstfruits of Achaia, and that they have devoted themselves to the ministry

---

welfare. Modern parallels to the OT tithe are found in the taxation system of countries (Rom. 13:6). OT giving to God was not regulated as to amount (see Ex. 25:1, 2; 35:21; 36:6; Prov. 3:9, 10; 11:24).

a. **tarry in Ephesus.** At the end of a 3 year stay in Ephesus, Paul wrote his letter and probably gave it to Timothy to deliver (1 Cor. 16:10). Paul originally planned to follow Timothy a short while after (1 Cor. 4:19), visiting Corinth on the way to and from Macedonia (2 Cor. 1:15, 16). He had to change his plan and visit only after a longer stay in Ephesus (1 Cor. 16:8), then on to Corinth after Macedonia, to stay for a while (vv. 6, 7).

b. **many adversaries.** Perhaps no NT church had such fierce opposition as the one in Ephesus (see 2 Cor. 1:8–10 where he described his experience in Ephesus; cf. Acts 19:1–21). In spite of that opposition, the door for the gospel was open wide (cf. 2 Cor. 2:12, 13 where Paul also had an open door, but no heart to remain and preach) and Paul stayed. At the end of the experience of opposition described in 2 Cor. 1:8–10, he wrote 1 Corinthians.

c. **Timothy.** Paul had sent him with Erastus to Macedonia (Acts 19:22) and then he was to travel to Corinth, perhaps to carry this epistle (1 Cor. 4:17).

d. **without fear.** I.e., of intimidation or frustration by believers in Corinth.

e. **Apollos.** See Acts 18:24. Paul felt Apollos should accompany the other brothers, Timothy and Erastus, to Corinth. Apollos refused, staying in Ephesus longer. Paul respected his convictions.

f. **the faith.** The Christian faith, i.e., sound doctrine, as in Phil. 1:27; 1 Tim. 6:12; Jude 3.

g. **firstfruits.** The members of the household of Stephanas were among the first converts in Corinth, which is located in Achaia, the southern province of Greece. Stephanas was one of the Corinthian believers Paul baptized personally (1 Cor. 1:16), and was visiting with Paul in

of the saints—that you also submit to such, and to everyone who works and labors with us.

I am glad about the coming of ªStephanas, Fortunatus, and Achaicus, for what was lacking on your part they supplied. For they refreshed my spirit and yours. Therefore acknowledge such men.

The churches of Asia greet you. ᵇAquila and Priscilla greet you heartily in the Lord, with the church that is ᶜin their house. All the brethren greet you.

Greet one another with a holy ᵈkiss.

The salutation with ᵉmy own hand—Paul's.

If anyone does not love the Lord Jesus Christ, let him be ᶠaccursed. ᵍO Lord, come!

The grace of our Lord Jesus Christ be with you. My love be with you all in Christ Jesus. Amen.

108. The Riot in Ephesus

Acts 19:23—20:1

And about that time there arose a great commotion about the Way. For a certain man named ʰDemetrius, a silversmith, who made ᶦsilver shrines of

---

Ephesus at the time this epistle was written. With Fortunatus and Achaicus (1 Cor. 16:17), he probably delivered the earlier letter from Corinth mentioned in 7:1.

a. **Stephanas, Fortunatus, and Achaicus.** Paul was glad about the arrival of his 3 friends in Ephesus who went there to be with him (cf. Prov. 25:25). The Corinthians were to give those men respect for their service to the Lord (cf. 1 Thess. 5:12, 13).

b. **Aquila and Priscilla.** See Acts 18:2. They had become good friends with Paul, since he stayed in their house during his first ministry in Corinth (Acts 18:1–3). He may have stayed with them the entire year and a half (cf. Acts 18:18, 19, 24–26).

c. **in their house.** The early church used homes of believers for worship and many other activities (see, e.g., Acts 2:46; 5:42; 10:23, 27–48; 20:7, 8; 28:23).

d. **kiss.** A pure expression of Christian love between men with men and women with women, with no sexual overtones (cf. Rom. 16:16; 2 Cor. 13:12; 1 Thess. 5:26; 1 Pet. 5:14).

e. **my own hand.** Paul dictated the main part of the letter to a scribe (Rom. 16:22), but finished and signed it himself.

f. **accursed.** I.e., devoted to destruction.

g. **O Lord, come!** In this context, Paul perhaps appeals for the Lord to take away the nominal, false Christians who threatened the spiritual well-being of the church. This was also an expression of eagerness for the Lord's return (cf. Rev. 22:20). The Aram. words are transliterated "Maranatha."

h. **Demetrius, a silversmith.** Probably not the individual commended by John (3 John 12), since the name was a common one.

i. **silver shrines.** These were of the goddess Diana (Artemis). These shrines were used as household idols, and in the worship at the temple of Diana.

ᵃDiana, ᵇbrought no small profit to the craftsmen. He called them together with the workers of similar occupation, and said: "Men, you know that we have our prosperity by this trade. ᶜMoreover you see and hear that not only at Ephesus, but throughout almost all Asia, this Paul has persuaded and turned away many people, saying that they are not gods which are made with hands. So not only is this trade of ours in danger of falling into disrepute, but also the temple of the great goddess Diana may be despised and her magnificence destroyed, whom all Asia and the world worship."

Now when they heard this, they were full of wrath and cried out, saying, "Great is Diana of the Ephesians!" So the whole city was filled with confusion, and rushed into the theater with one accord, having seized ᵈGaius and Aristarchus, Macedonians, Paul's travel companions. And when Paul wanted to go in to the people, the disciples would not allow him. Then some of the ᵉofficials of Asia, who were his friends, sent to him pleading that he would not venture into the theater. Some therefore cried one thing and some another, for the ᶠassembly was confused, and most of them did not know why they had come together. And they drew ᵍAlexander out of the multitude, the Jews putting him forward. And Alexander motioned with his hand, and wanted to

---

a. **Diana.** She was also known as "Artemis." Worship of her, centered at the great temple of Diana at Ephesus (one of the Seven Wonders of the Ancient World), was widespread throughout the Roman Empire. It is likely that the riot described in this passage took place during the annual spring festival held in her honor at Ephesus.

b. **brought no small profit.** This statement suggests Demetrius may have been the head of the silversmiths' guild—which would explain his taking the lead in opposing the Christian preachers.

c. **our prosperity.** Demetrius cleverly played upon his hearers' fears of financial ruin, religious zeal, and concern for their city's prestige. The Christian preachers, he argued, threatened the continued prosperity of Ephesus. His audience's violent reaction shows they took the threat seriously (Acts 19:28).

d. **Gaius and Aristarchus.** These men are described as Macedonians, though 20:4 lists Gaius' hometown as Derbe, a city in Galatia. Possibly the Gaius of 20:4 was a different person.

e. **officials of Asia.** Known by the title "Asiarchs," these members of the aristocracy were dedicated to promoting Roman interests. Though only one Asiarch ruled at a time, they bore the title for life. That such powerful, influential men were Paul's friends shows that they did not regard him or his message as criminal. Hence, there was no legitimate cause for the riot.

f. **assembly.** The frenzied mob gathered in the theater. Though Paul courageously sought to address them, the Asiarchs (along with the Ephesian Christians, Acts 19:30) begged him to stay away (v. 31). They feared both for the apostle's safety, and that his presence would exacerbate the already explosive situation.

g. **Alexander.** Probably not the false teacher later active at Ephesus (1 Tim. 1:20), or the individual who opposed Paul at Rome (2 Tim. 4:14), since the name was common. He was either a Christian Jew or a spokesman for Ephesus' Jewish community. Either way, the Jews' motive for putting him forward was the same—to disassociate themselves from the Christians and avoid a massacre of the Jews.

^amake his defense to the people. But when they found out that he was ^ba Jew, all with one voice cried out for about two hours, "Great is Diana of the Ephesians!"

And when the ^ccity clerk had quieted the crowd, he said: "Men of Ephesus, what man is there who does not know that the city of the Ephesians is temple guardian of the great goddess Diana, and of the ^dimage which fell down from Zeus? Therefore, since these things cannot be denied, you ^eought to be quiet and do nothing rashly. For you have brought these men here who are neither robbers of temples nor blasphemers of your goddess. Therefore, if Demetrius and his fellow craftsmen have a case against anyone, the courts are open and there are proconsuls. Let them bring charges against one another. But if you have any other inquiry to make, it shall be determined in the lawful assembly. For we are in danger of being called in question for today's uproar, there being no reason which we may give to account for this disorderly gathering." And when he had said these things, he dismissed the assembly.

After the uproar had ceased, Paul called the disciples to himself, embraced them, and ^fdeparted to go to Macedonia.

109. PAUL WRITES A SECOND LETTER TO THE CORINTHIAN CHURCH
Introduction to 2 Corinthians

This is the second NT epistle the Apostle Paul wrote to the Christians in the city of Corinth (see Introduction to 1 Corinthians).

---

a. **make his defense.** Either of the Christians, or the Jews, depending on which group he represented.

b. **a Jew.** Whatever the Jews intended by putting Alexander forward backfired; the crowd shouted him down, and in a mindless display of religious frenzy, chanted the name of their goddess for two hours.

c. **city clerk.** In modern terms, he was Ephesus' mayor. He was the liaison between the town council and the Roman authorities—who would hold him personally responsible for the riot.

d. **image which fell . . . Zeus.** This probably refers to a meteorite, since meteorites were incorporated with the worship of Diana.

e. **ought to be quiet.** The city clerk correctly blamed the crowd for the riot, noting that they should have followed proper judicial procedure and gone to the courts and proconsuls if they had any complaints, so as not to incur serious consequences from Rome.

f. **departed.** Paul left on his trip to Jerusalem via Greece (cf. Acts 19:21).

Author and Date

That the Apostle Paul wrote 2 Corinthians is uncontested; the lack of any motive for a forger to write this highly personal, biographical epistle has led even the most critical scholars to affirm Paul as its author.

Several considerations establish a feasible date for the writing of this letter. Extrabiblical sources indicate that July, A.D. 51 is the most likely date for the beginning of Gallio's proconsulship (cf. Acts 18:12). Paul's trial before him at Corinth (Acts 18:12–17) probably took place shortly after Gallio assumed office. Leaving Corinth (probably in A.D. 52), Paul sailed for Palestine (Acts 18:18), thus concluding his second missionary journey. Returning to Ephesus on his third missionary journey (probably in A.D. 52), Paul ministered there for about 2 1/2 years (Acts 19:8, 10). The apostle wrote 1 Corinthians from Ephesus toward the close of that period (1 Cor. 16:8), most likely in A.D. 55. Since Paul planned to stay in Ephesus until the following spring (cf. the reference to Pentecost in 1 Cor. 16:8), and 2 Corinthians was written after he left Ephesus (see Background and Setting), the most likely date for 2 Corinthians is late A.D. 55 or very early A.D. 56.

Background and Setting

Paul's association with the important commercial city of Corinth (see Introduction to 1 Corinthians) began on his second missionary journey (Acts 18:1–18), when he spent 18 months (Acts 18:11) ministering there. After leaving Corinth, Paul heard of immorality in the Corinthian church and wrote a letter (since lost) to confront that sin, referred to in 1 Cor. 5:9. During his ministry in Ephesus, he received further reports of trouble in the Corinthian church in the form of divisions among them (1 Cor. 1:11). In addition, the Corinthians wrote Paul a letter (1 Cor. 7:1) asking for clarification of some issues. Paul responded by writing the letter known as 1 Corinthians. Planning to remain at Ephesus a little longer (1 Cor. 16:8, 9), Paul sent Timothy to Corinth (1 Cor. 4:17; 16:10, 11). Disturbing news reached the apostle (possibly from Timothy) of further difficulties at Corinth, including the arrival of self-styled false apostles (2 Cor. 11:4, 13)

To create the platform to teach their false gospel, they began by assaulting the character of Paul. They had to convince the people to turn from Paul to them if they were to succeed in preaching demon doctrine. Temporarily abandoning the work at Ephesus, Paul went immediately to Corinth. The visit (known as the "painful visit," 2 Cor. 2:1) was not a successful one from Paul's perspective; someone in the Corinthian church (possibly one of the false apostles) even openly insulted him (2:5–8, 10; 7:12). Saddened by the Corinthians' lack of loyalty to defend him, seeking to spare them further reproof (cf. 1:23), and perhaps hoping time would bring them to their senses, Paul returned to Ephesus. From Ephesus, Paul wrote what is known as the "severe letter" (2:4) and sent it with Titus to Corinth (7:5–16). Leaving Ephesus after the riot sparked by Demetrius (Acts 19:23—20:1), Paul went to Troas to meet Titus (2:12, 13). But Paul was so anxious for news of how the Corinthians had responded to the "severe letter" that he could not minister there though the Lord had opened the door (2:12; cf. 7:5). So he left for Macedonia to look for Titus (2:13). To Paul's immense relief and joy, Titus met him with the news that the majority of the Corinthians had repented of their rebellion against Paul (7:7). Wise enough to know that some rebellious attitudes still smoldered under the surface, and could erupt again, Paul wrote (possibly from Philippi, cf. 11:9 with Phil. 4:15; also, some early manuscripts list Philippi as the place of writing) the Corinthians the letter called 2 Corinthians. In this letter, though the apostle expressed his relief and joy at their repentance (7:8–16), his main concern was to defend his apostleship (chaps. 1–7), exhort the Corinthians to resume preparations for the collection for the poor at Jerusalem (chaps. 8, 9), and confront the false apostles head on (chaps. 10–13). He then went to Corinth, as he had written (12:14; 13:1, 2). The Corinthians' participation in the Jerusalem offering (Rom. 15:26) implies that Paul's third visit to that church was successful.

Historical and Theological Themes

Second Corinthians complements the historical record of Paul's dealings with the Corinthian church recorded in Acts and 1 Corinthians. It also contains important biographical data on Paul throughout.

Although an intensely personal letter, written by the apostle in the heat of battle against those attacking his credibility, 2 Corinthians contains several important theological themes. It portrays God the Father as a merciful comforter (1:3; 7:6), the Creator (4:6), the One who raised Jesus from the dead (4:14; cf. 13:4), and who will raise believers as well (1:9). Jesus Christ is the One who suffered (1:5), who fulfilled God's promises (1:20), who was the proclaimed Lord (4:5), who manifested God's glory (4:6), and the One who in His incarnation became poor for believers (8:9; cf. Phil. 2:5–8). The letter portrays the Holy Spirit as God (3:17, 18) and the guarantee of believers' salvation (1:22; 5:5). Satan is identified as the "god of this age" (4:4; cf. 1 John 5:19), a deceiver (11:14), and the leader of human and angelic deceivers (11:15). The end times include both the believer's glorification (4:16—5:8) and his judgment (5:10). The glorious truth of God's sovereignty in salvation is the theme of 5:14–21, while 7:9, 10 sets forth man's response to God's offer of salvation-genuine repentance. Second Corinthians also presents the clearest, most concise summary of the substitutionary atonement of Christ to be found anywhere in Scripture (5:21; cf. Is. 53) and defines the mission of the church to proclaim reconciliation (5:18–20). Finally, the nature of the New Covenant receives its fullest exposition outside the book of Hebrews (3:6–16).

Interpretive Challenges

The main challenge confronting the interpreter is the relationship of chaps. 10–13 to chaps. 1–9. The identity of Paul's opponents at Corinth has produced various interpretations, as has the identity of the brother who accompanied Titus to Corinth (8:18, 22). Whether the offender mentioned in 2:5–8 is the incestuous man of 1 Cor. 5 is also uncertain. It is difficult to explain Paul's vision (12:1–5) and to identify specifically his "thorn in the flesh," the "messenger of Satan [sent] to buffet [him]" (12:7). These and other interpretive problems will be dealt with in the notes on the appropriate passages.

110. PAUL'S GREETING

2 Cor. 1:1—11

Paul, an ªapostle of Jesus Christ ᵇby the will of God, and ᶜTimothy our brother,

---

a. **apostle.** This refers to Paul's official position as a messenger sent by Christ (see Rom. 1:1).

b. **by the will of God.** Paul's mission was not a self-appointed one, or based on his own achievements. Rather, his credentials were by divine appointment and his letter reflected not his own message but the words of Christ (Acts 26:15–18).

c. **Timothy our brother.** Paul's cherished son in the faith and a dominant person in Paul's life and ministry (see 1 Tim. 1:2). Paul first met Timothy in Derbe and Lystra on his second missionary journey (Acts 16:1–4). Timothy was with him during the founding of the church in

To the church of God which is at Corinth, with all the saints who are in all Achaia:

[a]Grace to you and peace from God our Father and the Lord Jesus Christ.

Blessed be the [b]God and Father of our Lord Jesus Christ, the [c]Father of mercies and [d]God of all comfort, who comforts us in all our [e]tribulation, that [f]we may be able to comfort those who are in any trouble, with the comfort with which we ourselves are comforted by God. For as the [g]sufferings of Christ abound in us, so our consolation also abounds through Christ. Now if we are afflicted, it is for your consolation and [h]salvation, which is effective for

---

Corinth (Acts 18:1–5), which, along with Paul's mention of Timothy in 1 Corinthians (2 Cor. 4:17; 16:10, 11), indicated the Corinthians knew Timothy. Perhaps Paul mentioned him here to remind them Timothy was indeed a brother and to smooth over any hard feelings left from his recent visit (see 1 Cor. 16:10).

a. **Grace . . . peace.** Part of Paul's normal salutation in his letters (see Rom. 1:7). "Grace" is God's unmerited favor, and "peace" one of its benefits.

b. **God and Father of our Lord Jesus Christ.** Paul praised the true God who revealed Himself in His Son, who is of the same essence with the Father (see John 1:14, 18; 17:3–5; cf. John 5:17; 14:9–11; Eph. 1:3; Heb. 1:2, 3; 2 John 3). He is the anointed one (Christ) and sovereign (Lord) Redeemer (Jesus). Although the Son enjoyed this lofty position, He was willing to become a servant and submit Himself in His incarnation (see Phil. 2:5–8). This great benediction comprehends the entire gospel.

c. **Father of mercies.** Paul borrowed from Jewish liturgical language and a synagogue prayer that called for God to treat the sinful individual with kindness, love, and tenderness (see Rom. 12:1; cf. 2 Sam. 24:14; Ps. 103:13, 14; Mic. 7:18–20).

d. **God of all comfort.** An OT description of God (cf. Is. 40:1; 51:3, 12; 66:13), who is the ultimate source of every true act of comfort. The Gr. word for "comfort" is related to the familiar word paraclete, "one who comes alongside to help," another name for the Holy Spirit (see John 14:26; Phil. 2:1). "Comfort" often connotes softness and ease, but that is not its meaning here. Paul was saying that God came to him in the middle of his sufferings and troubles to strengthen him and give him courage and boldness (cf. 2 Cor. 1:4–10).

e. **tribulation.** This term refers to crushing pressure, because in Paul's life and ministry there was always something attempting to weaken him, restrict or confine his ministry, or even crush out his life. But no matter what confronted him, Paul knew God would sustain and strengthen him (see 2 Cor. 12:9, 10; Rom. 8:31–38; cf. Phil. 1:6).

f. **we may be able to comfort.** Comfort from God is not an end in itself. Its purpose is that believers also might be comforters. Having humiliated and convicted the Corinthians, God used Paul to return to them with a strengthening message after he himself had received divine strengthening (2 Cor. 6:1–13; 12:6–11; cf. Luke 22:31, 32).

g. **sufferings of Christ abound.** God's comfort to believers extends to the boundaries of their suffering for Christ. The more they endure righteous suffering, the greater will be their comfort and reward (cf. 1 Pet. 4:12–14). Paul knew first hand that these many sufferings would seem never-ending (2 Cor. 4:7–11; 6:5–10; 11:23–27; cf. Gal. 6:17; Phil. 3:10; Col. 1:24), and all genuine believers should expect the same (cf. Matt. 10:18–24).

h. **salvation.** This refers to the Corinthians' ongoing perseverance to final, completed salvation when they will be glorified (see Rom. 13:11). Paul's willingness, by God's grace and the Spirit's power, to suffer and be comforted and then comfort and strengthen the Corinthians enabled them to persevere.

enduring the same sufferings which we also suffer. Or if we are comforted, it is for your consolation and salvation. And our hope for you is steadfast, because we know that as you are [a]partakers of the sufferings, so also you will partake of the consolation.

For we do not want you to be ignorant, brethren, of [b]our [c]trouble which came to us in Asia: that we were burdened beyond measure, above strength, so that we [d]despaired even of life. Yes, we had the [e]sentence of death in ourselves, that we should [f]not trust in ourselves but in God [g]who raises the dead, who delivered us from so great a death, and does deliver us; in whom we trust that [h]He will still deliver us, you also [i]helping together in prayer for us, that [j]thanks may be given by many persons on our behalf for [k]the gift granted to us through many.

---

a. **partakers of the sufferings.** Some in the church at Corinth, perhaps the majority, were suffering for righteousness, as Paul was. Although that church had caused him much pain and concern, Paul saw its members as partners to be helped, because of their faithfulness in mutual suffering.

b. **our.** An editorial plural, which Paul used throughout the letter. It usually was a humble reference to Paul himself, but in this instance it could include others as well.

c. **trouble which came to us in Asia.** This was a recent occurrence (following the writing of 1 Corinthians) that happened in or around the city of Ephesus. The details of this situation are not known.

d. **despaired even of life.** Paul faced something that was beyond human survival and was extremely discouraging because he believed it threatened to end his ministry prematurely. The Gr. word for "despaired" lit. means "no passage," the total absence of an exit (cf. 2 Tim. 4:6). The Corinthians were aware of what had happened to Paul, but did not realize the utter severity of it, or what God was doing through those circumstances.

e. **sentence of death.** The word for "sentence" is a technical term that indicated the passing of an official resolution, in this case the death sentence. Paul was so absolutely sure he was going to die for the gospel that he had pronounced the sentence upon himself.

f. **not trust in ourselves but in God.** God's ultimate purpose for Paul's horrible extremity. The Lord took him to the point at which he could not fall back on any intellectual, physical, or emotional human resource (cf. 2 Cor. 12:9, 10).

g. **who raises the dead.** A Jewish descriptive term for God used in synagogue worship language. Paul understood that trust in God's power to raise the dead was the only hope of rescue from his extreme circumstances.

h. **He will still deliver us.** See 2 Tim. 4:16, 17; 2 Pet. 2:9.

i. **helping together in prayer.** Intercessory prayer is crucial to the expression of God's power and sovereign purpose. In this regard, Paul wanted the faithful Corinthians to know he needed their prayers now and in the future (cf. Eph. 6:18; James 5:16).

j. **thanks may be given.** Prayer's duty is not to change God's plans, but to glorify Him and give thanks for them. Paul was confident that God's sovereign purpose would be accomplished, balanced by the prayerful participation of believers.

k. **the gift.** Probably better translated "favor," or "blessing," as in God's undeserved favor or the divine answer to prayer Paul would receive in being delivered from death.

III. PAUL'S MINISTRY PLANS

2 Cor. 1:12–24

[a]For our [b]boasting is this: the testimony of our [c]conscience that we [d]conducted ourselves in the world in simplicity and godly sincerity, not with [e]fleshly wisdom but by the grace of God, and more abundantly toward you. For we are not writing any other things to you than what you read or understand. Now I trust you will understand, even to the end (as also you have understood us in part), that [f]we are your boast as you also are ours, in [g]the day of the Lord Jesus.

And in this confidence I intended to come to you before, that you might have [h]a second benefit—to pass by way of you to Macedonia, to [i]come again

---

a. **For.** Paul faced his critics' many accusations against his character and integrity (they had accused him of being proud, self-serving, untrustworthy and inconsistent, mentally unbalanced, incompetent, unsophisticated, and an incompetent preacher) by appealing to the highest human court, his conscience.

b. **boasting.** Paul often used this word, and it can also be rendered "proud confidence." Used negatively, it refers to unwarranted bragging about one's own merits and achievements; but Paul used it positively to denote legitimate confidence in what God had done in his life (cf. Jer. 9:23, 24; Rom. 15:18; 1 Cor. 1:31; 15:9, 10; 1 Tim. 1:12–17).

c. **conscience.** The soul's warning system, which allows human beings to contemplate their motives and actions and make moral evaluations of what is right and wrong (see Rom. 2:14, 15). In order to work as God designed it, the conscience must be informed to the highest moral and spiritual level and best standard, which means submitting it to the Holy Spirit through God's Word (cf. Rom. 12:1, 2; 1 Tim. 1:19; 2 Tim. 2:15; Heb. 9:14; 10:22). Paul's fully enlightened conscience exonerated him completely (cf. Acts 23:1; 24:16; 1 Tim. 1:5; 3:9; 2 Tim. 1:3). But ultimately, only God can accurately judge a man's motives (1 Cor. 4:1–5).

d. **conducted ourselves.** This broadly answers the accusation that Paul had engaged in deceptive personal relationships (cf. 2 Cor. 7:2; 11:9). His continuing flow of information to the Corinthians was always clear, straightforward and understandable, consistent, and genuine. Paul wanted them to know that he was not holding anything back, nor did he have any secret agenda (2 Cor. 10:11). He simply wanted them to understand all that he had written and spoken to them.

e. **fleshly wisdom.** Wisdom that is based on worldly, human insight (see James 3:15).

f. **we are your boast.** More clearly translated, "we are your reason to be proud."

g. **the day of the Lord Jesus.** When He returns (see Phil. 1:6; 2 Tim. 1:12; 4:8). Paul eagerly longed for the Lord's coming when they would rejoice over each other in glory (cf. 1 Thess. 2:19, 20).

h. **a second benefit.** Or, "twice receive a blessing." Paul's original plan was to visit the Corinthians twice so that they might receive a double blessing. His travel plans were not the result of selfishness, but of the genuine relationship he enjoyed with the Corinthians and their mutual loyalty and godly pride in each other.

i. **come again.** Paul had planned to leave Ephesus, stop at Corinth on the way to Macedonia, and return to Corinth again after his ministry in Macedonia (cf. 1 Cor. 16:5–7). For some reason, Paul's plans changed and he was unable to stop in Corinth the first time. The false apostles who had invaded the church seized upon that honest change of schedule as evidence of his untrustworthiness and tried to use it to discredit him.

from Macedonia to you, and be helped by you on my way to Judea. [a]Therefore, when I was planning this, did I do it lightly? Or the things I plan, do I plan [b]according to the flesh, that with me there should be Yes, Yes, and No, No? But [c]as God is faithful, our word to you was [d]not Yes and No. For the Son of God, [e]Jesus Christ, who was preached among you by us—by me, [f]Silvanus, and Timothy—was not Yes and No, but in Him was Yes. For all the promises of God [g]in Him are Yes, and in Him [h]Amen, to the glory of God through us. Now [i]He who establishes us with you in [j]Christ and has [k]anointed us is God, who also has [l]sealed us and given us the Spirit in our hearts as a [m]guarantee.

---

a. **Therefore . . . did I do it lightly?** The Gr. words that introduce this question call for an indignant, negative answer. Paul declared that he was in no way operating as a vacillating, fickle, unstable person who could not be trusted.

b. **according to the flesh.** Purely from a human viewpoint, apart from the leading of the Holy Spirit, this is someone who is unregenerate (see Gal. 5:19–21). He affirmed that his "yes" and "no" words to them really meant what they said.

c. **as God is faithful.** Paul may have been making an oath and calling God to give testimony (cf. 2 Cor. 11:10, 31; Rom. 1:9; Gal. 1:20; Phil. 1:8; 1 Thess. 2:5, 10). Whatever the case, he refers to God's trustworthiness and the fact that he represented such a God as an honest spokesman.

d. **not Yes and No.** He was not saying "yes" and meaning "no." There was no duplicity with Paul (nor with Timothy and Silas). He said what he meant and did what he said, unless there was compelling reason to change his plans.

e. **Jesus Christ.** The firmness of Paul's statement, and his use of Jesus' full title, indicates that the person and work of Christ were under attack from the false teachers at Corinth. The proof of his truthfulness with them was the truthful gospel which he faithfully preached.

f. **Silvanus.** The Lat. name for Silas, Paul's companion on his second missionary journey (Acts 16–18) and fellow preacher at Corinth (see Acts 15:22).

g. **in Him are Yes.** All God's OT and NT promises of peace, joy, love, goodness, forgiveness, salvation, sanctification, fellowship, hope, glorification, and heaven are made possible and fulfilled in Jesus Christ (cf. Luke 24:44).

h. **Amen.** The Heb. word of affirmation (cf. Matt. 5:18; John 3:3; Rom. 1:25). Paul reminded them that they had said a collective "yes" to the truth of his preaching and teaching.

i. **He who establishes us.** Christ's saving work of grace stabilizes believers and places them on a firm foundation in Him (cf. Rom. 16:25; 1 Cor. 15:58; 1 Pet. 5:10).

j. **Christ . . . God . . . Spirit.** A clear reference to the 3 members of the Trinity. The authenticity of Paul's spiritual life and that of every genuine believer is verified by these 4 divine works ("establishes us," "anointed us," "sealed us," "given us the Spirit") accomplished in their lives. For the critics to attack Paul's authenticity was equal to tearing down God's work as well as the church's unity.

k. **anointed.** This word is borrowed from a commissioning service that would symbolically set apart kings, prophets, priests, and special servants. The Holy Spirit sets apart believers and empowers them for the service of gospel proclamation and ministry (cf. Acts 1:8; 1 John 2:20, 27).

l. **sealed us.** Refers to the ancient practice of placing soft wax on a document and imprinting the wax with a stamp that indicated authorship or ownership, authenticity, and protection. The Holy Spirit attaches all these meanings to His act of spiritually sealing believers (see Eph. 1:13; cf. Hag. 2:23; Eph. 4:30).

m. **guarantee.** A pledge or down payment. The Spirit is the down payment on the believer's eternal inheritance (see Eph. 1:14; cf. 2 Pet. 1:4, 11).

Moreover I call God as witness against my soul, that ᵃto spare you I came no more to Corinth. ᵇNot that we have dominion over your faith, but are fellow workers for your joy; for by faith you stand.

112. THE APOSTLE'S SORROW AND CONFIDENCE
2 *Cor.* 2:1–17

But I determined this within myself, that I would not ᶜcome again to you in sorrow. For if I make you ᵈsorrowful, then who is he who makes me glad but the one who is made sorrowful by me? And ᵉI wrote this very thing to you, lest, when I came, I should have sorrow over those from whom I ought to have joy, having confidence in you all that my joy is the joy of you all. For out of much affliction and anguish of heart I wrote to you, with many tears, not that you should be grieved, but that you might know the love which I have so abundantly for you.

But ᶠif anyone has caused grief, he has not grieved me, but all of you to some extent—not to be too severe. This ᵍpunishment which was inflicted by the

---

a. **to spare you.** Paul finally explained why he said he was coming, but did not. He did not come earlier because he wanted them to have time to repent of and correct their sinful behavior (see 1 Cor. 4:21). He waited instead for a report from Titus before taking further action (see chap. 7), hoping he would not have to come again, as he had earlier, to face their rebellion.

b. **Not that we have dominion over your faith.** Paul did not want to lord it over the Corinthians when he ministered and worked among them (see 1 Pet. 5:2, 3).

c. **come again . . . in sorrow.** Paul, who had already had a painful confrontation at Corinth, was not eager to have another one (see 2 Cor. 1:23).

d. **sorrowful.** Although Paul was sensitive to the Corinthians' pain and sadness from the past confrontation, because of his commitment to purity he would confront them again if necessary. "The one who is made sorrowful" refers to one convicted by his sin. In particular, there was apparently on Paul's last visit, a man in the church who confronted him with the accusations taken from the false teachers. The church had not dealt with that man in Paul's defense, and Paul was deeply grieved over that lack of loyalty. The only thing that would bring Paul joy would be repentance from such a one and any who agreed with him, and Paul had been waiting for it.

e. **I wrote this very thing.** Paul's reason for writing was that those in sin would repent—then there could be mutual joy when the apostle came.

f. **if anyone has caused grief.** The Gr. construction of this clause assumes the condition to be true—Paul is acknowledging the reality of the offense and its ongoing effect, not on him, but on the church. With this deflection of any personal vengeance, he sought to soften the charge against the penitent offender and allow the church to deal with the man and those who were with him objectively, apart from Paul's personal anguish or offense.

g. **punishment . . . inflicted by the majority.** This indicates that the church in Corinth had followed the biblical process in disciplining the sinning man (cf. Matt. 18:15–20; 1 Cor.

majority [a]is sufficient for such a man, so that, on the contrary, you ought rather [b]to forgive and comfort him, lest perhaps such a one be swallowed up with too much sorrow. Therefore I urge you to reaffirm your love to him. For to this end I also wrote, that I might put you to the test, whether you are obedient in all things. Now whom you forgive anything, I also forgive. For if indeed I have forgiven anything, I have forgiven that one for your sakes [c]in the presence of Christ, lest Satan should take advantage of us; for we are not ignorant of his [d]devices.

Furthermore, [e]when I came to Troas to preach Christ's gospel, and [f]a door was opened to me by the Lord, [g]I had no rest in my spirit, because I did not find [h]Titus my brother; but [i]taking my leave of them, I departed for [j]Macedonia.

5:4–13; 2 Thess. 3:6, 14). The Gr. word for "punishment," used frequently in secular writings but only here in the NT, denoted an official legal penalty or commercial sanction that was enacted against an individual or group (city, nation).

a. **is sufficient.** The process of discipline and punishment was enough; now it was time to show mercy because the man had repented (cf. Matt. 18:18, 23–35; Gal. 6:1, 2; Eph. 4:32; Col. 3:13; Heb. 12:11).

b. **to forgive.** It was time to grant forgiveness so the man's joy would be restored (cf. Ps. 51:12, 14; Is. 42:2, 3). Paul knew there was—and is—no place in the church for man-made limits on God's grace, mercy, and forgiveness toward repentant sinners. Such restrictions could only rob the fellowship of the joy of unity (cf. Matt. 18:34, 35; Mark 11:25, 26).

c. **in the presence of Christ.** Paul was constantly aware that his entire life was lived in the sight of God, who knew everything he thought, did, and said (cf. 2 Cor. 2:17; 4:2; 2 Tim. 4:1).

d. **devices.** The devil wants to produce sin and animosity that will destroy church unity. He uses every possible approach to accomplish this—from legalism to libertinism, intolerance to excessive tolerance (cf. 2 Cor. 11:13, 14; Eph. 4:14; 6:11, 12; 1 Pet. 5:8). Paul used a different word (but with similar meaning) for "devices" (wiles) in Eph. 6:11. It, along with the words for "take advantage" and "ignorant," strongly implies that Satan targets the believer's mind, but God has provided protection by unmasking Satan's schemes in Scripture, along with providing the counteracting truth.

e. **when I came to Troas.** "Troas" was a seaport city N of Ephesus in the western Asia Minor province of Mysia (cf. Acts 16:7). The riots in Ephesus probably caused Paul to leave for Troas, but his main reason for going was to meet Titus, returning from Corinth after delivering "the severe letter," and to hear how the Corinthians had responded to that letter.

f. **a door was opened to me.** God sovereignly provided a great evangelistic opportunity for Paul, which may have led to the planting of the church in Troas (cf. Acts 20:5–12). Because of the success of his preaching, Paul was assured that this opportunity was from God (cf. 1 Cor. 16:8, 9).

g. **I had no rest in my spirit.** Paul's concern for the problems in the Corinthian church and how its members were responding to both those problems and his instructions caused Paul debilitating restlessness and anxiety (cf. 2 Cor. 7:5, 6). These concerns became so heavy and distracting that he was unable to give full attention to his ministry.

h. **Titus.** One of Paul's most important Gentile converts and closest associates in ministry (see v. 12; Gal. 2:1).

i. **taking my leave of them.** Because of his troubled heart and mind and his anxiety to see Titus, Paul turned his back on the open door in Troas.

j. **Macedonia.** A province that bordered the NW shore of the Aegean Sea, N of Achaia

ᵃNow thanks be to God who always ᵇleads us in triumph in Christ, and through us ᶜdiffuses the fragrance of His knowledge in every place. For we are ᵈto God the fragrance of Christ among those who are being saved and among those who are perishing. To the one we are the ᵉaroma of death leading to death, and to the other the aroma of life leading to life. And who is ᶠsufficient for these things? For we are ᵍnot, as so many, ʰpeddling the word of God; but as of sincerity, but as from God, we speak in the sight of God in Christ.

(see Acts 16:9). Paul headed there in hopes of intersecting with Titus, whom he knew would have to pass through there on his journey back from Corinth.

a. **Now thanks be to God.** Paul made an abrupt transition from his narrative and looked above and beyond his troubles to praise and thank God. By turning from the difficulties of ministry and focusing on the privileges of his position in Christ, Paul regained his joyful perspective. He picked the narrative back up in 2 Cor. 7:5.

b. **leads us in triumph in Christ.** Paul drew from the imagery of the official and exalted Roman ceremony called the Triumph, in which a victorious general was honored with a festive, ceremonial parade through the streets of Rome. First, Paul gave thanks for being led by a sovereign God at all times (cf. 1 Tim. 1:17); and second, for the promised victory in Jesus Christ (cf. Matt. 16:18; Rom. 8:37; Rev. 6:2).

c. **diffuses the fragrance of His knowledge.** Paul was also grateful for the privilege of being used as an influence for Christ (cf. Rom. 10:14, 15) wherever he went. The imagery comes from the strong, sweet smell of incense from censers in the Triumph parade, which, along with the fragrance of crushed flowers strewn under horses' hooves, produced a powerful aroma that filled the city. By analogy, every believer is transformed and called by the Lord to be an influence for His gospel throughout the world.

d. **to God the fragrance of Christ.** Paul was further thankful for the privilege of pleasing God. Continuing his analogy, Paul pictured God as the emperor at the end of the Triumph who also smells the pervasive fragrance and is pleased with the victorious efforts it represents. Wherever God's servant is faithful and is an influence for the gospel, God is pleased (cf. 2 Cor. 5:9; Matt. 25:21).

e. **the aroma of death . . . life.** Paul used the style of Heb. superlatives to emphasize the twofold effect of gospel preaching. To some, the message brings eternal life and ultimate glorification. To others, it is a stumbling stone of offense that brings eternal death (cf. 1 Pet. 2:6–8).

f. **sufficient for these things.** No one in his own strength is adequate or competent to serve God in the ways and with the power that Paul has been describing (cf. 2 Cor. 3:5; 1 Cor. 15:10; Gal. 2:20; Eph. 1:19; 3:20; Phil. 2:13; Col. 1:29).

g. **not, as so many.** Or, "not as the majority." This specifically refers to the false teachers in Corinth and to the many other teachers and philosophers of that day who operated by human wisdom (cf. 1 Cor. 1:19, 20).

h. **peddling.** From a Gr. verb that means "to corrupt," this word came to refer to corrupt hucksters, or con men who by their cleverness and deception were able to sell as genuine an inferior product that was only a cheap imitation. The false teachers in the church were coming with clever, deceptive rhetoric to offer a degraded, adulterated message that mixed paganism and Jewish tradition. They were dishonest men seeking personal profit and prestige at the expense of gospel truth and people's souls.

113. The Spirit and the Letter

2 Cor. 3:1–6

[a]Do we begin again to commend ourselves? Or do we need, as some others, epistles of commendation to you or [b]letters of commendation from you? You are our epistle [c]written in our hearts, [d]known and read by all men; clearly you are an [e]epistle of Christ, ministered by us, [f]written not with ink but by the [g]Spirit of the living God, not on [h]tablets of stone but on [i]tablets of flesh, that is, of the heart.

And we have [j]such trust through Christ toward God. Not that we are sufficient of ourselves [k]to think of anything as being from ourselves, but our

---

a. **Do we begin again to commend ourselves?** The Gr. word for "commend" means "to introduce." Thus Paul was asking the Corinthians if he needed to reintroduce himself, as if they had never met, and prove himself once more. The form of the question demanded a negative answer. The false teachers in Corinth constantly attacked Paul's competency as a minister of the gospel; these verses form his defense.

b. **letters of commendation.** The false teachers also accused Paul of not possessing the appropriate documents to prove his legitimacy. Such letters were often used to introduce and authenticate someone to the first-century churches (cf. 1 Cor. 16:3, 10, 11). The false teachers undoubtedly arrived in Corinth with such letters, which they may have forged (cf. Acts 15:1, 5) or obtained under false pretenses from prominent members of the Jerusalem church. Paul's point was that he did not need secondhand testimony when the Corinthians had firsthand proof of his sincere and godly character, as well as the truth of his message that regenerated them.

c. **written in our hearts.** An affirmation of Paul's affection for the believers in Corinth—he held them close to his heart (cf. 2 Cor. 12:15).

d. **known and read by all men.** The transformed lives of the Corinthians were Paul's most eloquent testimonial, better than any secondhand letter. Their changed lives were like an open letter that could be seen and read by all men as a testimony to Paul's faithfulness and the truth of his message.

e. **epistle of Christ.** The false teachers did not have a letter of commendation signed by Christ, but Paul had the Corinthian believers' changed lives as proof that Christ had transformed them.

f. **written not with ink.** Paul's letter was no human document written with ink that can fade. It was a living one.

g. **Spirit of the living God.** Paul's letter was alive, written by Christ's divine, supernatural power through the transforming work of the Holy Spirit (cf. 1 Cor. 2:4, 5; 1 Thess. 1:5).

h. **tablets of stone.** A reference to the Ten Commandments (see Ex. 24:12; 25:16).

i. **tablets of flesh . . . of the heart.** More than just writing His law on stone, God was writing His law on the hearts of those people He transformed (cf. Jer. 31:33; 32:38, 39; Ezek. 11:19; 36:26, 27). The false teachers claimed external adherence to the Mosaic law as the basis of salvation, but the transformed lives of the Corinthians proved that salvation was an internal change wrought by God in the heart.

j. **such trust.** The Gr. word for "trust" can mean "to win." Paul was confident in his ministry, and that confidence resulted in his ability to stay the course and continue moving toward the goal (cf. Acts 4:13, 29).

k. **to think of anything.** The Gr. word for "think" can also mean "to consider" or "to reason." Paul disdained his own ability to reason, judge, or assess truth. Left to his own abilities, he was useless. He was dependent on divine revelation and the Holy Spirit's power.

ᵃsufficiency is from God, ᵇwho also made us sufficient as ministers of the new covenant, not of ᶜthe letter but of the Spirit; for ᵈthe letter kills, but the Spirit gives life.

114. UNVEILED GLORY

2 Cor. 3:7–18

But if the ᵉministry of death, written and engraved on stones, ᶠwas glorious, so that the children of Israel ᵍcould not look steadily at the face of Moses because of ʰthe glory of his countenance, which glory was passing away, how will the ⁱministry of the Spirit not be more glorious? For if the ʲministry of

---

a. **our sufficiency is from God.** Only God can make a person adequate to do his work, and Paul realized that truth (see 2 Cor. 2:16; cf. 9:8, 10; 2 Thess. 2:13).

b. **new covenant.** The covenant that provides forgiveness of sins through the death of Christ (see Jer. 31:31–34; Matt. 26:28; Heb. 8:7–12).

c. **the letter.** A shallow, external conformity to the law that missed its most basic requirement of absolutely holy and perfect love for God and man (Matt. 22:34–40) and distorted its true intention, which was to make a person recognize his sinfulness (cf. Rom. 2:27–29).

d. **the letter kills, but the Spirit gives life.** The letter kills in two ways: 1) it results in a living death. Before Paul was converted, he thought he was saved by keeping the law, but all it did was kill his peace, joy, and hope; and 2) it results in spiritual death. His inability to truly keep the law sentenced him to an eternal death (see Rom. 7:9–11; cf. Rom. 5:12; Gal. 3:10). Only Jesus Christ through the agency of the Holy Spirit can produce eternal life in one who believes.

e. **ministry of death.** The law is a killer in the sense that it brings knowledge of sin. It acts as a ministry of death because no one can satisfy the demands of the law on his own and is therefore condemned (cf. Gal. 3:22; see Rom. 7:1–13; 8:4; Gal. 3:10–13; 3:19—4:5).

f. **was glorious.** When God gave Moses the law, His glory appeared on the mountain (Ex. 19:10–25; 20:18–26). Paul was not depreciating the law; he was acknowledging that it was glorious because it reflected God's nature, will, and character (see Ex. 33:18—34:9).

g. **could not look steadily at the face of Moses.** The Israelites could not look intently or stare at Moses' face for too long because the reflective glory of God was too bright for them. It was similar to staring into the sun (see Ex. 34:29–35).

h. **the glory of his countenance.** When God manifested Himself, He did so by reducing His attributes to visible light. That's how God manifested Himself to Moses (Ex. 34:29), whose face in turn reflected the glory of God to the people (cf. the Transfiguration of Jesus in Matt. 17:1–8; 2 Pet. 1:16–18; and His second coming in Matt. 24:29, 30; 25:31).

i. **ministry of the Spirit . . . exceeds much more in glory.** The "ministry of the Spirit" is Paul's descriptive term for the New Covenant (see Jer. 31:31–34; Matt. 26:28; 1 Cor. 11:25; Heb. 8:8, 13; 9:15; 12:24). Paul is arguing that if such glory attended the giving of the law under the ministry that brought death, how much more glorious will be the ministry of the Spirit in the New Covenant which brings righteousness. The law pointed to the superior New Covenant and thus a glory that must also be superior.

j. **ministry of condemnation.** Another name for the ministry of death (see 2 Cor. 3:7).

condemnation had glory, the [a]ministry of righteousness exceeds much more in glory. For even what was made glorious had no glory in this respect, because of the glory that excels. For if [b]what is passing away was glorious, [c]what remains is much more glorious.

[d] Therefore, since we have such hope, we use great [e]boldness of speech— unlike [f]Moses, who put a veil over his face so that the children of Israel could not look steadily at the end of what was passing away. But their minds were blinded. For until this day [g]the same veil remains unlifted in the reading of the Old Testament, because [h]the veil is taken away in Christ. But even to this day, when Moses is read, a veil lies on their heart. Nevertheless when one turns to the Lord, the veil is taken away. Now [i]the Lord is the Spirit; and where the Spirit of the Lord is, [j]there is liberty. But [k]we all, [l]with unveiled

a. **ministry of righteousness.** The New Covenant. The emphasis here is on the righteousness it provides (cf. Rom. 3:21, 22; Phil. 3:9).

b. **what is passing away.** The law had a fading glory (cf. 2 Cor. 3:7). It was not the final solution or the last word on the plight of sinners.

c. **what remains.** The New Covenant is "what" remains because it is the consummation of God's plan of salvation. It has permanent glory.

d. **such hope.** The belief that all the promises of the New Covenant will occur. It is hope in total and complete forgiveness of sins for those who believe the gospel (cf. Rom. 8:24, 25; Gal. 5:5; Eph. 1:18; 1 Pet. 1:3, 13, 21).

e. **boldness of speech.** The Gr. word for "boldness" means "courageously." Because of his confidence, Paul preached the New Covenant fearlessly, without any hesitation or timidity.

f. **Moses, who put a veil over his face.** This physical action pictured the fact that Moses did not have the confidence or boldness of Paul because the Old Covenant was veiled. It was shadowy. It was made up of types, pictures, symbols, and mystery. Moses communicated the glory of the Old Covenant with a certain obscurity (cf. 1 Pet. 1:10, 11).

g. **the same veil remains . . . a veil lies on their heart.** The "veil" here represents unbelief. Those Israelites did not grasp the glory of the Old Covenant because of their unbelief. As a result, the meaning of the Old Covenant was obscure to them (cf. Heb. 3:8, 15; 4:7). Paul's point was that just as the Old Covenant was obscure to the people of Moses' day, it was still obscure to those who trusted in it as a means of salvation in Paul's day. The veil of ignorance obscures the meaning of the Old Covenant to the hardened heart (cf. John 5:38).

h. **the veil is taken away in Christ.** Without Christ the OT is unintelligible. But when a person comes to Christ, the veil is lifted and his spiritual perception is no longer impaired (Is. 25:6–8). With the veil removed, believers are able to see the glory of God revealed in Christ (John 1:14). They understand that the law was never given to save them, but to lead them to the One who would.

i. **the Lord is the Spirit.** Yahweh of the OT is the same Lord who is saving people in the New Covenant through the agency of the Holy Spirit. The same God is the minister of both the Old and New Covenants.

j. **there is liberty.** Freedom from sin and the futile attempt to keep the demands of the law as a means of earning righteousness (cf. John 8:32–36; Rom. 3:19, 20). The believer is no longer in bondage to the law's condemnation and Satan's dominion.

k. **we all.** Not just Moses, or prophets, apostles, and preachers, but all believers.

l. **with unveiled face.** Believers in the New Covenant have nothing obstructing their vision of Christ and His glory as revealed in the Scripture.

face, ᵃbeholding as in a mirror the glory of the Lord, are ᵇbeing transformed ᶜinto the same image ᵈfrom glory to glory, just as by the Spirit of the Lord.

115. THE TRIALS OF THE MINISTRY

2 Cor. 4:1–18

Therefore, since we have ᵉthis ministry, as we have received mercy, we do not ᶠlose heart. But ᵍwe have renounced the hidden things of shame, not walking in craftiness nor ʰhandling the word of God deceitfully, but by manifestation of the truth commending ourselves to every man's conscience in the sight of God. But even ⁱif our gospel is veiled, it is veiled to those who are perishing,

---

a. **beholding as in a mirror.** Paul's emphasis here is not so much on the reflective capabilities of the mirror as it is on the intimacy of it. A person can bring a mirror right up to his face and get an unobstructed view. Mirrors in Paul's day were polished metal (see James 1:23), and thus offered a far from perfect reflection. Though the vision is unobstructed and intimate, believers do not see a perfect representation of God's glory now, but will one day (cf. 1 Cor. 13:12).

b. **being transformed.** A continual, progressive transformation (see Rom. 12:2).

c. **into the same image.** As they gaze at the glory of the Lord, believers are continually being transformed into Christlikeness. The ultimate goal of the believer is to be like Christ (cf. Rom. 8:29; Phil. 3:12–14; 1 John 3:2), and by continually focusing on Him the Spirit transforms the believer more and more into His image.

d. **from glory to glory.** From one level of glory to another level of glory—from one level of manifesting Christ to another. This verse describes progressive sanctification. The more believers grow in their knowledge of Christ, the more He is revealed in their lives (cf. Phil. 3:12–14).

e. **this ministry.** The New Covenant gospel of Jesus Christ.

f. **lose heart.** A strong Gr. term which refers to abandoning oneself to cowardly surrender. That was not how Paul responded to the continual attacks he faced. The task of ministering the New Covenant was too noble to lose heart over (cf. Gal. 6:9; Eph. 3:13). Since God had called him to proclaim it, Paul could not abandon his calling. Instead, he trusted God to strengthen him (cf. Acts 20:24; 1 Cor. 9:16, 17; Col. 1:23, 25).

g. **we have renounced the hidden things of shame.** "Renounced" means "to turn away from" or "to repent," and "shame" means "ugly" or "disgraceful." The phrase "hidden things of shame" refers to secret immoralities, hypocrisies, and the sins hidden deep in the darkness of one's life. At salvation every believer repents and turns away from such sin and devotes his life to the pursuit of godliness. This appears to be a reply by Paul to a direct and slanderous accusation against him, that he was a hypocrite, whose mask of piety hid a corrupt and shameful life.

h. **handling . . . deceitfully.** This Gr. word means "to tamper with," and was used in nonbiblical sources to speak of the dishonest business practice of diluting wine with water. The false teachers accused Paul of being a deceiver ("craftiness") who was twisting and perverting the teaching of Jesus and the OT Scripture.

i. **if our gospel is veiled . . . to those who are perishing.** The false teachers accused Paul of preaching an antiquated message. So Paul showed that the problem was not with the

whose minds [a]the god of this age [b]has blinded, who do not believe, lest the light of the gospel of the glory of Christ, who is the [c]image of God, should shine on them. For [d]we do not preach ourselves, but Christ Jesus the Lord, and ourselves your bondservants for Jesus' sake. For it is the God who [e]commanded light to shine out of darkness, who has shone in our hearts to give [f]the light of the knowledge of the glory of God in the face of Jesus Christ.

But we have this treasure in [g] earthen vessels, that the [h]excellence of the power may be of God and not of us. We are hard-pressed on every side, yet not crushed; we are perplexed, but not in despair; persecuted, but not forsaken; struck down, but not destroyed—[i]always carrying about in the body the dying

message or the messenger, but with the hearers headed for hell (cf. 1 Cor. 2:14). The preacher cannot persuade people to believe; only God can do that.

a. **the god of this age.** Satan (cf. Matt. 4:8; John 12:31; 14:30; 16:11; Eph. 2:2; 2 Tim. 2:26; 1 John 5:19). "This age" refers to the current world mind-set expressed by the ideals, opinions, goals, hopes, and views of the majority of people. It encompasses the world's philosophies, education, and commerce.

b. **has blinded.** Satan blinds men to God's truth through the world system he has created. Without a godly influence, man left to himself will follow that system, which panders to the depravity of unbelievers and deepens their moral darkness (cf. Matt. 13:19). Ultimately, it is God who allows such blindness (John 12:40).

c. **image of God.** Jesus Christ is the exact representation of God Himself (see Col. 1:15; 2:9; Heb. 1:3).

d. **we do not preach ourselves.** The false teachers accused Paul of preaching for his own benefit, yet they were the ones guilty of doing so. In contrast, Paul was always humble (2 Cor. 12:5, 9; cf. 1 Cor. 2:3); he never promoted himself, but always preached Christ Jesus as Lord (1 Cor. 2:2).

e. **commanded light to shine out of darkness.** A direct reference to God as Creator, who commanded physical light into existence (Gen. 1:3).

f. **the light of the knowledge of the glory of God.** The same God who created physical light in the universe is the same God who must create supernatural light in the soul and usher believers from the kingdom of darkness to His kingdom of light (Col. 1:13). The light is expressed as "the knowledge of the glory of God." That means to know that Christ is God incarnate. To be saved, one must understand that the glory of God shone in Jesus Christ. That is the theme of John's gospel (see John 1:4).

g. **earthen vessels.** The Gr. word means "baked clay," and refers to clay pots. They were cheap, breakable, and replaceable, but they served necessary household functions. Sometimes they were used as a vault to store valuables, such as money, jewelry, or important documents. But they were most often used for holding garbage and human waste. The latter is the use Paul had in mind, and it was how Paul viewed himself—as lowly, common, expendable, and replaceable (cf. 1 Cor. 1:20–27; 2 Tim. 2:20, 21).

h. **excellence of the power may be of God and not of us.** By using frail and expendable people, God makes it clear that salvation is the result of His power and not any power His messengers could generate (cf. 2:16). The great power of God overcomes and transcends the clay pot. The messenger's weakness is not fatal to what he does; it is essential (cf. 2 Cor. 12:9, 10).

i. **always carrying about in the body the dying of the Lord Jesus.** "Always" indicates that the suffering Paul experienced was endless. And the suffering a result of attacks against the "Lord Jesus," not Paul and other believers. Those who hated Jesus took out was their vengeance on those who represented Him (cf. John 15:18–21; Gal. 6:17; Col. 1:24).

of the Lord Jesus, [a]that the life of Jesus also may be manifested in our body. For we who live are always [b]delivered to death for Jesus' sake, that the life of Jesus also may be manifested in [c]our mortal flesh. So then death is working in us, but life in you.

And since we have the same [d]spirit of faith, according to what is written, [e]"I believed and therefore I spoke," we also believe and therefore speak, knowing that He who raised up the Lord Jesus will also raise us up with Jesus, and will present us with you. For all things are for your sakes, that grace, having spread through the many, may cause thanksgiving to abound to the glory of God.

Therefore we do not lose heart. Even though [f]our outward man is perishing, yet the [g]inward man is [h]being renewed day by day. For [i]our light affliction, which is but for a moment, is working for us a far more exceeding and [j]eternal

---

a. **that the life of Jesus also may be manifested in our body.** Through Paul's weakness, Christ was put on display (cf. Gal. 2:20). His suffering, the false apostles said, was evidence that God was not with him and he was a fraud. On the contrary, Paul affirmed that his suffering was the badge of his loyalty to Christ and the source of his power (2 Cor. 12:9, 10).

b. **delivered to death.** Refers to the transferring of a prisoner to the executioner. It was used to refer to Christ's being delivered to those who crucified Him (Matt. 27:2). In this case, it refers to the potential physical death constantly faced by those who represented Christ.

c. **our mortal flesh.** Another term for Paul's humanness—his physical body (cf. 2 Cor. 5:3). Paul faced death every day, yet he was willing to pay that price if it meant salvation for those to whom he preached (cf. Phil. 2:17; Col. 1:24; 2 Tim. 2:10). Paul remained true to his convictions, no matter the cost. He was not a pragmatist who would alter his message to suit his listeners. He was convinced of the power of God to act through the message he preached.

d. **spirit of faith.** The attitude of faith, not the Holy Spirit. Paul had the same conviction about the power of the message as did the psalmist.

e. **I believed and therefore I spoke.** A quotation from the LXX (the Gr. translation of the OT) version of Ps. 116:10. In the midst of his troubles, the psalmist confidently asked God to deliver him out of his troubles. He could confidently do so because he believed God would answer his prayer.

f. **our outward man is perishing.** The physical body is in the process of decay and will eventually die. On the surface Paul was referring to the normal aging process, but with the added emphasis that his lifestyle sped up that process. While not an old man, Paul wore himself out in ministry, both in the effort and pace he maintained, plus the number of beatings and attacks he absorbed from his enemies (cf. 2 Cor. 6:4–10; 11:23–27).

g. **inward man.** The soul of every believer i.e., the new creation—the eternal part of the believer (cf. Eph. 4:24; Col. 3:10).

h. **being renewed.** The growth and maturing process of the believer is constantly occurring. While the physical body is decaying, the inner self of the believer continues to grow and mature into Christlikeness (cf. Eph. 3:16–20).

i. **our light affliction . . . for a moment.** The Gr. word for "light" means "a weightless trifle" and "affliction" refers to intense pressure. From a human perspective, Paul's own testimony lists a seemingly unbearable litany of sufferings and persecutions he endured throughout his life (2 Cor. 11:23–33), yet he viewed them as weightless and lasting for only a brief moment.

j. **eternal weight of glory.** The Gr. word for "weight" refers to a heavy mass. For Paul, the future glory he would experience with the Lord far outweighed any suffering he experienced

weight of glory, while we do not look at the things which are seen, but at the things which are not seen. For the ᵃthings which are seen are temporary, but the ᵇthings which are not seen are eternal.

116. The Motivation of the Ministry
2 Cor. 5:1—10

For we know that if our ᶜearthly house, this tent, is destroyed, we have ᵈa building from God, ᵉa house ᶠnot made with hands, eternal in the heavens. For in this ᵍwe groan, earnestly desiring to be ʰclothed with our habitation which is from heaven, if indeed, having been clothed, ⁱwe shall not be found naked. For we who are in this tent groan, being burdened, not because we

in this world (cf. Rom. 8:17, 18; 1 Pet. 1:6, 7). Paul understood that the greater the suffering, the greater would be his eternal glory (cf. 1 Pet. 4:13).

a. **things which are seen . . . not seen.** Endurance is based on one's ability to look beyond the physical to the spiritual; beyond the present to the future, and beyond the visible to the invisible. Believers must look past what is temporary—what is perishing (i.e., the things of the world).

b. **things . . . not seen are eternal.** Pursuing God, Christ, the Holy Spirit, and the souls of men should consume the believer.

c. **earthly house . . . tent.** Paul's metaphor for the physical body (cf. 2 Pet. 1:13, 14). The imagery was quite natural for that time because many people were nomadic tent dwellers, and Paul as a tentmaker (Acts 18:3) knew much about tents' characteristics. Also, the Jewish tabernacle had symbolized God's presence among the people as they left Egypt and became a nation. Paul's point is that like a temporary tent, man's earthly existence is fragile, insecure, and lowly (cf. 1 Pet. 2:11).

d. **a building from God.** Paul's metaphor for the believer's resurrected, glorified body (cf. 1 Cor. 15:35–50). "Building" implies solidity, security, certainty, and permanence, as opposed to the frail, temporary, uncertain nature of a tent. Just as the Israelites replaced the tabernacle with the temple, so believers ought to long to exchange their earthly bodies for glorified ones (see 2 Cor. 4:16; Rom. 8:19–23; 1 Cor. 15:35–50; Phil. 3:20, 21).

e. **a house . . . in the heavens.** A heavenly, eternal body. Paul wanted a new body that would forever perfectly express his transformed nature.

f. **not made with hands.** A glorified body, by definition, is not of this earthly creation (see Mark 14:58; Heb. 9:11; cf. John 2:19; Col. 2:11).

g. **we groan.** Paul had a passionate longing to be free from his earthly body and all the accompanying sins, frustrations, and weaknesses that were so relentless (see Rom. 7:24; 8:23).

h. **clothed with our habitation . . . from heaven.** The perfections of immortality.

i. **we shall not be found naked.** Paul clarified the fact that the believer's hope for the next life is not a disembodied spiritual life, but a real, eternal, resurrection body. Unlike the pagans who viewed matter as evil and spirit as good, Paul knew that Christian death would not mean being released into a nebulous, spiritual infinity. Rather, it would mean the receiving of a glorified, spiritual, immortal, perfect, qualitatively different but nonetheless real body, just as Jesus received (see 1 Cor. 15:35–44; Phil. 3:20, 21; cf. 1 John 3:2).

want to be ªunclothed, but further clothed, that ᵇmortality may be swallowed up by life. Now He who has prepared us ᶜfor this very thing is God, who also has given us the Spirit as a guarantee.

So we are always confident, knowing that while we are ᵈat home in the body we are absent from the Lord. For we ᵉwalk by faith, not by sight. We are confident, yes, well pleased rather to be ᶠabsent from the body and to be present with the Lord.

Therefore ᵍwe make it our aim, ʰwhether present or absent, to be ⁱwell pleasing to Him. For we must all appear before ʲthe judgment seat of Christ,

---

a. **unclothed . . . further clothed.** Paul reiterated that he could hardly wait to get his glorified body (cf. Phil. 1:21–23).

b. **mortality . . . swallowed up by life.** Paul wanted the fullness of all that God had planned for him in eternal life, when all that is earthly and human will cease to be.

c. **for this very thing.** More precisely translated "purpose." Paul emphatically states that the believer's heavenly existence will come to pass according to God's sovereign purpose (see Rom. 8:28–30; cf. John 6:37–40, 44).

d. **at home in the body . . . absent from the Lord.** While a believer is alive on earth he is away from the fullness of God's presence. However, Paul was not saying he had absolutely no contact, because there is prayer, the indwelling Spirit, and fellowship through the Word. Paul was simply expressing a heavenly homesickness, a strong yearning to be at home with his Lord (cf. Ps. 73:25; 1 Thess. 4:17; Rev. 21:3, 23; 22:3).

e. **walk by faith.** The Christian can hope for a heaven he has not seen. He does so by believing what Scripture says about it and living by that belief (see Heb. 11:1; cf. John 20:29).

f. **absent from the body . . . present with the Lord.** Because heaven is a better place than earth, Paul would rather have been there, with God. This sentiment simply states Paul's feelings and longings of v. 6 from a reverse perspective (see Phil. 1:21, 23).

g. **we make it our aim.** Paul was speaking of his ambition in life, but not the kind of proud, selfish desire that "ambition" expresses in English. "Aim" is from the Gr. word that means "to love what is honorable." Paul demonstrated that it is right and noble for the believer to strive for excellence, spiritual goals, and all that is honorable before God (cf. Rom. 15:20; 1 Tim. 3:1).

h. **whether present or absent.** Paul's ambition was not altered by his state of being— whether he should be in heaven or on earth—he cared how he lived for the Lord (see Rom. 14:6; Phil. 1:20; cf. 1 Cor. 9:27).

i. **well pleasing to Him.** This was Paul's highest goal (cf. 1 Cor. 4:1–5), and should be so for every believer (cf. Rom. 12:2; Eph. 5:10; Col. 1:9; 1 Thess. 4:1). The term translated "well pleasing" is the same one used in Titus 2:9 to describe slaves who were passionate to please their masters. This describes the believer's deepest motivation and highest aim in pleasing God—the realization that every Christian is inevitably and ultimately accountable to Him.

j. **the judgment seat of Christ.** "Judgment seat" metaphorically refers to the place where the Lord will sit to evaluate believers' lives for the purpose of giving them eternal rewards. It is translated from the Gr. word *bēma*, which was an elevated platform where victorious athletes (e.g., during the Olympics) went to receive their crowns. The term is also used in the NT to refer to the place of judging, as when Jesus stood before Pontius Pilate (Matt. 27:19; John 19:13), but here the reference is definitely from the athletic analogy. Corinth had such a platform where both athletic rewards and legal justice were dispensed (Acts 18:12–16), so the Corinthians understood Paul's reference.

that each one may receive [a]the things done in the body, according to what he has done, [b]whether good or bad.

117. The Message of the Ministry

2 Cor. 5:11–21

Knowing, therefore, [c]the terror of the Lord, [d]we persuade men; but we are well known to God, and I also trust are [e]well known in your consciences.

For we do not commend ourselves again to you, but give you opportunity to boast on our behalf, that you may have an answer for those who [f]boast in appearance and not in heart. For if we are [g]beside ourselves, it is for God;

---

a. **the things done in the body.** Actions which happened during the believer's time of earthly ministry. This does not include sins, since their judgment took place at the cross (Eph 1:7). Paul was referring to all those activities believers do during their lifetimes, which relate to their eternal reward and praise from God. What Christians do in their temporal bodies will, in His eyes, have an impact for eternity (see 1 Cor. 4:3–5; cf. Rom. 12:1, 2; Rev. 22:12).

b. **whether good or bad.** These Gr. terms do not refer to moral good and moral evil. Matters of sin have been completely dealt with by the death of the Savior. Rather, Paul was comparing worthwhile, eternally valuable activities with useless ones. His point was not that believers should not enjoy certain wholesome, earthly things, but that they should glorify God in them and spend most of their energy and time with what has eternal value (see 1 Cor. 3:8–14).

c. **the terror of the Lord.** This is more clearly rendered, "the fear of the Lord." It is not referring to being afraid, but to Paul's worshipful reverence for God as his essential motivation to live in such a way as to honor his Lord and maximize his reward for his Lord's glory (cf. 2 Cor. 7:1; Prov. 9:10; Acts 9:31).

d. **we persuade men.** The Gr. word for "persuade" means to seek someone's favor, as in getting the other person to see you in a certain favorable or desired way (cf. Gal. 1:10). This term can mean gospel preaching (Acts 18:4; 28:23), but here Paul was persuading others not about salvation, but about his own integrity. The Corinthians' eternal reward would be affected if they defected to the false teachers and left the divine teaching of Paul.

e. **well known.** Paul's true spiritual condition of sincerity and integrity was manifest to God (see 2 Cor. 1:12; cf. Acts 23:1; 24:16), and he also wanted the Corinthians to believe the truth about him.

f. **boast in appearance.** Those who have no integrity, such as Paul's opponents at Corinth, have to take pride in externals, which can be any false doctrine accompanied by showy hypocrisy (cf. Matt. 5:20; 6:1; Mark 7:6, 7).

g. **beside ourselves.** This Gr. phrase usually means to be insane, or out of one's mind, but here Paul used the expression to describe himself as one dogmatically devoted to truth. In this way, he answered those critics who claimed he was nothing more than an insane fanatic (cf. John 8:48; Acts 26:22–24).

or if we are ªof sound mind, it is for you. For the ᵇlove of Christ ᶜcompels us, because we judge thus: that if ᵈOne died for all, ᵉthen all died; and He died for all, that those who live should live no longer for themselves, but for Him who died for them and rose again.

Therefore, from now on, we regard no one ᶠaccording to the flesh. Even though we have known Christ according to the flesh, yet now ᵍwe know Him thus no longer. Therefore, if anyone is ʰin Christ, he is a ⁱnew creation; ʲold things have passed away; behold, ᵏall things have become new. Now

---

a. **of sound mind.** The original word meant to be moderate, sober minded, and in complete control. Paul also behaved this way among the Corinthians as he defended his integrity and communicated truth to them.

b. **the love of Christ.** Christ's love for Paul and all believers at the cross (cf. Rom. 5:6–8). Christ's loving, substitutionary death motivated Paul's service for Him (cf. Gal. 2:20; Eph. 3:19).

c. **compels.** This refers to pressure that causes action. Paul emphasized the strength of his desire to offer his life to the Lord.

d. **One died for all.** This expresses the truth of Christ's substitutionary death. The preposition "for" indicates He died "in behalf of," or "in the place of" all (cf. Is. 53:4–12; Gal. 3:13; Heb. 9:11–14). This truth is at the heart of the doctrine of salvation. God's wrath against sin required death; Jesus took that wrath and died in the sinner's place. Thus He took away God's wrath and satisfied God's justice as a perfect sacrifice (see Rom. 5:6–11, 18, 19; 1 Tim. 2:5, 6; cf. Eph. 5:2; 1 Thess. 5:10; Titus 2:14; 1 Pet. 2:24).

e. **then all died.** Everyone who died in Christ receives the benefits of His substitutionary death (see Rom. 3:24–26; 6:8). With this short phrase, Paul defined the extent of the atonement and limited its application. This statement logically completes the meaning of the preceding phrase, in effect saying, "Christ died for all who died in Him," or "One died for all, therefore all died" (cf. John 10:11–16; Acts 20:28). Paul was overwhelmed with gratitude that Christ loved him and was so gracious as to make him a part of the "all" who died in Him.

f. **according to the flesh.** Paul no longer evaluated people according to external, human, worldly standards (cf. 10:3). Since Paul's conversion, his priority was to meet people's spiritual needs (cf. Acts 17:16; Rom. 1:13–16; 9:1–3; 10:1).

g. **we know Him thus no longer.** Paul, as a Christian, also no longer had merely a fallible, human assessment of Jesus Christ (cf. Acts 9:1–6; 26:9–23).

h. **in Christ.** These two words comprise a brief but most profound statement of the inexhaustible significance of the believer's redemption, which includes the following: 1) the believer's security in Christ, who bore in His body God's judgment against sin; 2) the believer's acceptance in Him with whom God alone is well pleased; 3) the believer's future assurance in Him who is the resurrection to eternal life and the sole guarantor of the believer's inheritance in heaven; and 4) the believer's participation in the divine nature of Christ, the everlasting Word (cf. 2 Pet. 1:4).

i. **new creation.** This describes something that is created at a qualitatively new level of excellence. It refers to regeneration or the new birth (cf. John 3:3; Eph. 2:1–3; Titus 3:5; 1 Pet. 1:23; 1 John 2:29; 3:9; 5:4). This expression encompasses the Christian's forgiveness of sins paid for in Christ's substitutionary death (cf. Gal. 6:15; Eph. 4:24).

j. **old things have passed away.** After a person is regenerate, old value systems, priorities, beliefs, loves, and plans are gone. Evil and sin are still present, but the believer sees them in a new perspective, and they no longer control him.

k. **all things . . . new.** The Gr. grammar indicates that this newness is a continuing condition of fact. The believer's new spiritual perception of everything is a constant reality for him, and he now lives for eternity, not temporal things. James identifies this transformation as the faith that produces works (see Eph. 2:10; James 2:14–26).

ᵃall things are of God, who has reconciled us to Himself through Jesus Christ, and has given us the ᵇministry of reconciliation, that is, that ᶜGod was in Christ ᵈreconciling the world to Himself, not ᵉimputing their trespasses to them, and has committed to us the ᶠword of reconciliation.

Now then, we are ᵍambassadors for Christ, ʰas though God were pleading through us: we implore you on Christ's behalf, be reconciled to God. ⁱFor He

---

a. **all things are of God.** Many modern translations add the article "these" before "things," which connects the word "things" to all that Paul has just asserted in 2 Cor. 5:14–17. All the aspects related to someone's conversion and newly transformed life in Christ are accomplished by sovereign God. Sinners on their own cannot decide to participate in these new realities (see Rom. 5:10; cf. 1 Cor. 8:6; 11:12; Eph. 2:1).

b. **ministry of reconciliation.** This speaks to the reality that God wills to be reconciled with sinners (cf. Rom. 5:10; Eph. 4:17–24). God has called believers to proclaim the gospel of reconciliation to others (cf. 1 Cor. 1:17). The concept of service, such as waiting on tables, derives from the Gr. word for "ministry." Lit. God wants Christians to accept the privilege of serving unbelievers by proclaiming a desire to be reconciled.

c. **God was in Christ.** God by His own will and design used His Son, the only acceptable and perfect sacrifice, as the means to reconcile sinners to Himself (see Acts 2:23; Col. 1:19, 20; cf. John 14:6; Acts 4:12; 1 Tim. 2:5, 6).

d. **reconciling the world.** God initiates the change in the sinner's status in that He brings him from a position of alienation to a state of forgiveness and right relationship with Himself. This again is the essence of the gospel. The word "world" should not be interpreted in any universalistic sense, which would say that everyone will be saved, or even potentially reconciled. "World" refers rather to the entire sphere of mankind or humanity (cf. Titus 2:11; 3:4), the category of beings to whom God offers reconciliation—people from every ethnic group, without distinction. The intrinsic merit of Christ's reconciling death is infinite and the offer is unlimited. However, actual atonement was made only for those who believe; cf. John 10:11, 15; 17:9; Acts 13:48; 20:28; Rom. 8:32, 33; Eph. 5:25). The rest of humanity will pay the price personally for their own sin in eternal hell.

e. **imputing.** This may also be translated "reckoning," or "counting." This is the heart of the doctrine of justification whereby God declares the repentant sinner righteous and does not count his sins against him because He covers him with the righteousness of Christ the moment he places wholehearted faith in Christ and His sacrificial death (see Rom. 3:24—4:5; cf. Ps. 32:2; Rom. 4:8).

f. **word of reconciliation.** Here Paul presents another aspect to the meaning of the gospel. He used the Gr. word for "word" (cf. Acts 13:26), which indicated a true and trustworthy message, as opposed to a false or unsure one. In a world filled with false messages, believers have the solid, truthful message of the gospel.

g. **ambassadors.** A term that is related to the more familiar Gr. word often translated "elder." It described an older, more experienced man who served as a representative of a king from one country to another. Paul thus described his role—and the role of all believers—as a messenger representing the King of heaven with the gospel, who pleads with the people of the world to be reconciled to God, who is their rightful King (cf. Rom. 10:13–18).

h. **as though God were pleading.** As believers present the gospel, God speaks (lit. "calls," or "begs") through them and urges unbelieving sinners to come in an attitude of faith and accept the gospel, which means to repent of their sins and believe on Jesus (cf. Acts 16:31; James 4:8).

i. **For He made Him.** In this verse, Paul summarized the heart of the gospel, resolving the mystery and paradox of 2 Cor. 5:18–20, and explaining how sinners can be reconciled to God through Jesus Christ. These 15 Gr. words express the doctrines of imputation and substitution like no other single verse.

made Him ªwho knew no sin to be ᵇsin for us, that we might become ᶜthe righteousness of God in Him.

118. THE CONDUCT OF THE MINISTRY

2 Cor. 6:1–10

We then, as workers together with Him also plead with you not ᵈto receive the grace of God in vain. ᵉFor He says:

"In an acceptable time I have heard you,

And in the day of salvation I have helped you."

Behold, now is the accepted time; behold, ᶠnow is the day of salvation.

ᵍWe give no offense in anything, that our ministry may not be blamed. But

---

a. **who knew no sin.** Jesus Christ, the sinless Son of God (see Gal. 4:4, 5; cf. Luke 23:4, 14, 22, 47; John 8:46; Heb. 4:15; 7:26; 1 Pet. 1:19; 2:22–24; 3:18; Rev. 5:2–10).

b. **sin for us.** God the Father, using the principle of imputation, treated Christ as if He were a sinner though He was not, and had Him die as a substitute to pay the penalty for the sins of those who believe in Him (cf. Is. 53:4–6; Gal. 3:10–13; 1 Pet. 2:24). On the cross, He did not become a sinner (as some suggest), but remained as holy as ever. He was treated as if He were guilty of all the sins ever committed by all who would ever believe, though He committed none. The wrath of God was exhausted on Him and the just requirement of God's law met for those for whom He died.

c. **the righteousness of God.** Another reference to justification and imputation. The righteousness that is credited to the believer's account is the righteousness of Jesus Christ, God's Son (see Rom. 1:17; 3:21–24; Phil. 3:9). As Christ was not a sinner, but was treated as if He were, so believers who have not yet been made righteous (until glorification) are treated as if they were righteous. He bore their sins so that they could bear His righteousness. God treated Him as if He committed believers' sins, and treats believers as if they did only the righteous deeds of the sinless Son of God.

d. **to receive the grace of God in vain.** Most of the Corinthians were saved but hindered by legalistic teaching regarding sanctification (see 2 Cor. 11:3; Gal. 6:1). Some were not truly saved but deceived by a gospel of works (cf. 13:5; Gal. 5:4), which was being taught by the false teachers. In either case, Paul's proclamation of the gospel of grace would not have been having its desired effect, and he would have had cause for serious concern that his many months of ministry at Corinth were for nothing. Both cases also prevented the people from effectively assuming any "ministry of reconciliation."

e. **For He says.** Paul emphasized his point by quoting Is. 49:8. He was passionately concerned that the Corinthians adhere to the truth because it was God's time to save and they were messengers for helping to spread that message.

f. **now is the day of salvation.** Paul applied Isaiah's words to the present situation. There is a time in God's economy when He listens to sinners and responds to those who are repentant—and it was and is that time (cf. Prov. 1:20–23; Is. 55:6; Heb. 3:7, 8; 4:7). However, there will also be an end to that time (cf. Gen. 6:3; Prov. 1:24–33; John 9:4), which is why Paul's exhortation was so passionate.

g. **We give no offense in anything.** The faithful ambassador of Christ does nothing to discredit his ministry, but everything he can to protect its integrity, the gospel's integrity, and God's integrity (cf. Rom. 2:24; 1 Cor. 9:27; Titus 2:1–10).

in all things ᵃwe commend ourselves as ministers of God: in much patience, ᵇin tribulations, in needs, in distresses, in stripes, in imprisonments, in tumults, in labors, in sleeplessness, in fastings; by purity, by knowledge, by longsuffering, by kindness, ᶜby the Holy Spirit, by sincere love, ᵈby the word of truth, ᵉby the power of God, ᶠby the armor of righteousness on ᵍthe right hand and on the left, by ʰhonor and dishonor, by evil report and good report; ⁱas deceivers, and yet true; as ʲunknown, and yet well known; as dying, and behold we live; as chastened, and yet not killed; as sorrowful, yet always rejoicing; as poor, yet ᵏmaking many rich; as having nothing, and yet possessing all things.

119. SEPARATION FROM UNBELIEVERS
2 Cor. 6:11—7:1

O Corinthians! We have spoken openly to you, ˡour heart is wide open. You are not restricted by us, but you are restricted by your own affections. Now in return for the same (I speak as to children), you also be open.

---

a. **we commend ourselves as ministers of God.** "Commend" means "introduce," with the connotation of proving oneself (see 2 Cor. 3:1). The most convincing proof is the patient endurance of character reflected in Paul's hardships (2 Cor. 6:5) and the nature of his ministry (vv. 6, 7).

b. **In tribulations.** Like Paul, any believer who engages in a faithful ministry of reconciliation should expect to be rejected and accepted, to be hated and loved, to encounter joy and hardship. This is what Jesus had already taught His disciples (cf. Matt. 5:10–16; Luke 12:2–12).

c. **by the Holy Spirit.** Paul lived and walked by the power of the Spirit (see Gal. 5:16). It was the central reason that all the other positive elements of his endurance were a reality.

d. **by the word of truth.** The Scriptures, the revealed Word of God (cf. Col. 1:5; James 1:18). During his entire ministry, Paul never operated beyond the boundaries of the direction and guidance of divine revelation.

e. **by the power of God.** Paul did not rely on his own strength when he ministered (see 1 Cor. 1:18; 2:1–5; cf. Rom. 1:16).

f. **by the armor of righteousness.** Paul did not fight Satan's kingdom with human resources, but with spiritual virtue (see 2 Cor. 10:3–5; Eph. 6:10–18).

g. **the right hand . . . the left.** Paul had both offensive tools, such as the sword of the Spirit, and defensive tools, such as the shield of faith and the helmet of salvation, at his disposal (see Eph. 6:16, 17).

h. **honor and dishonor.** The mark of a ministry that has genuine character is paradoxical, and here Paul gave a series of paradoxes regarding his service for Christ.

i. **as deceivers.** Paul's opponents at Corinth had accused him of being an impostor and a false apostle (cf. John 7:12).

j. **as unknown.** This is a twofold reference to: 1) the fact that Christians did not know him before he began persecuting them (cf. Acts 8:1; 1 Tim. 1:12, 13); and 2) his rejection by the community of leading Jews and Pharisees following his conversion. He had become unknown to his former world, and well-known and well-loved by the Christian community.

k. **making many rich.** The spiritual wealth Paul possessed and imparted did much to make his hearers spiritually wealthy (cf. Acts 3:6).

l. **our heart is wide open.** Lit. "our heart is enlarged" (cf. 1 Kin. 4:29). The evidence of

Do not be ªunequally yoked together ᵇwith unbelievers. For what fellowship has righteousness with lawlessness? And what communion has light with darkness? And what accord has Christ with ᶜBelial? Or what part has a believer with an unbeliever? And what ᵈagreement has the temple of God with idols? For ᵉyou are the temple of the living God. ᶠAs God has said:

> "I will dwell in them
> And walk among them.
> I will be their God,
> And they shall be My people."
> ᵍ Therefore
> "Come out from among them
> And ʰbe separate, says the Lord.
> Do not touch what is unclean,

Paul's genuine love for the Corinthians was that no matter how some of them had mistreated him, he still loved them and had room for them in his heart (cf. Phil. 1:7).

a. **unequally yoked together.** An illustration taken from OT prohibitions to Israel regarding the work-related joining together of two different kinds of livestock (see Deut. 22:10). By this analogy, Paul taught that it is not right to join together in common spiritual enterprise with those who are not of the same nature (unbelievers). It is impossible under such an arrangement for things to be done to God's glory.

b. **with unbelievers.** Christians are not to be bound together with non-Christians in any spiritual enterprise or relationship that would be detrimental to the Christian's testimony within the body of Christ (see 1 Cor. 5:9–13; cf. 1 Cor. 6:15–18; 10:7–21; James 4:4; 1 John 2:15). This was especially important for the Corinthians because of the threats from the false teachers and the surrounding pagan idolatry. But this command does not mean believers should end all associations with unbelievers; that would defy the purpose for which God saved believers and left them on earth (cf. Matt. 28:19, 20; 1 Cor. 9:19–23). The implausibility of such religious alliances is made clear in 2 Cor. 6:14b–17.

c. **Belial.** An ancient name for Satan, the utterly worthless one (see Deut. 13:13). This contrasts sharply with Jesus Christ, the worthy One with whom believers are to be in fellowship.

d. **agreement . . . temple of God with idols.** The temple of God (true Christianity) and idols (idolatrous, demonic false religions) are utterly incompatible (cf. 1 Sam. 4–6; 2 Kin. 21:1–15; Ezek. 8).

e. **you are the temple of the living God.** Believers individually are spiritual houses (cf. 5:1) in which the Spirit of Christ dwells (see 1 Cor. 3:16, 17; 6:19, 20; Eph. 2:22).

f. **As God has said.** Paul supported his statement by referring to a blend of OT texts (Lev. 26:11, 12; Jer. 24:7; 31:33; Ezek. 37:26, 27; Hos. 2:2, 3).

g. Paul drew from Is. 52:11 and elaborated on the command to be spiritually separated. It is not only irrational and sacrilegious but disobedient to be bound together with unbelievers. When believers are saved, they are to disengage themselves from all forms of false religion and make a clean break from all sinful habits and old idolatrous patterns (see Eph. 5:6–12; 2 Tim. 2:20–23; cf. Rev. 18:4).

h. **be separate.** This is a command for believers to be as Christ was (Heb. 7:26). As a result of separating themselves from false doctrine and practice, believers will know the full richness of what it means to be children of God (see Rom. 8:14–17; cf. 2 Sam. 7:14; Ezek. 20:34).

And I will receive you."
"I will be a Father to you,
And you shall be My sons and daughters,
Says the Lord Almighty."

Therefore, having ªthese promises, beloved, ᵇlet us cleanse ourselves from all ᶜfilthiness of the ᵈflesh and spirit, ᵉperfecting holiness in the fear of God.

120. ASSURANCE OF PAUL'S LOVE

2 Cor. 7:2–16

Open your hearts to us. ᶠWe have wronged no one, ᵍwe have corrupted no one, we have cheated no one. I do not say this to condemn; for I have said before that ʰyou are in our hearts, to die together and to live together. ⁱGreat is my

---

a. **these promises.** The OT promises Paul quoted in 6:16–18. Scripture often encourages believers to action based on God's promises (cf. Rom. 12:1; 2 Pet. 1:3).

b. **let us cleanse ourselves.** The form of this Gr. verb indicates that this is something each Christian must do in his own life.

c. **filthiness.** This Gr. word, which appears only here in the NT, was used 3 times in the Greek OT to refer to religious defilement, or unholy alliances with idols, idol feasts, temple prostitutes, sacrifices, and festivals of worship.

d. **flesh and spirit.** False religion panders to the human appetites, represented by both "flesh and spirit." While some believers for a time might avoid succumbing to fleshly sins associated with false religion, the Christian who exposes his mind to false teaching cannot avoid contamination by the devilish ideologies and blasphemies that assault the purity of divine truth and blaspheme God's name.

e. **perfecting holiness.** The Gr. word for "perfecting" means "to finish" or "to complete" (cf. 8:6). "Holiness" refers to separation from all that would defile both the body and the mind. Complete or perfect holiness was embodied only in Christ, thus believers are to pursue Him (cf. 2 Cor. 3:18; Lev. 20:26; Matt. 5:48; Rom. 8:29; Phil. 3:12–14; 1 John 3:2, 3).

f. **We have wronged no one.** The Gr. word for "wronged" means "to treat someone unjustly," "to injure someone," or "to cause someone to fall into sin." Paul could never be accused of injuring or leading any Corinthian into sin (see Matt. 18:5–14).

g. **we have corrupted no one.** "Corrupted" could refer to corruption by doctrine or money, but probably refers to corrupting one's morals (cf. 1 Cor. 15:33). Paul could never be accused of encouraging any immoral conduct.

h. **you are in our hearts.** Paul had a forgiving heart. Rather than only condemning the Corinthians for believing the false teachers and rejecting him, Paul reminded them of his love for them and his readiness to forgive them.

i. **Great is my boldness.** "Boldness" can be translated "confidence." Paul was confident of God's ongoing work in their lives (cf. Phil. 1:6)—another proof of Paul's love for the Corinthian believers.

boldness of speech toward you, great is my boasting on your behalf. I am filled with comfort. I am exceedingly joyful in all our tribulation.

For indeed, when we came to Macedonia, our bodies had no rest, but we were troubled on every side. Outside were ᵃconflicts, inside were fears. Nevertheless God, who comforts ᵇthe downcast, ᶜcomforted us by the coming of Titus, and not only by his coming, but also by the consolation with which he was comforted in you, when he told us of your earnest desire, your mourning, your zeal for me, so that I rejoiced even more.

For even if ᵈI made you sorry with ᵉmy letter, ᶠI do not regret it; though I did regret it. For I perceive that the same epistle made you sorry, though only for a while. Now I rejoice, not that you were made sorry, but that ᵍyour sorrow led to repentance. For you were made sorry in a godly manner, that you might suffer loss from us in nothing. For ʰgodly sorrow produces repentance

---

a. **conflicts.** Here, Paul continued the narrative he left off in 2 Cor. 2:13. When he arrived in Macedonia after leaving Troas, he had no rest from external "conflicts." The Gr. word is used of quarrels and disputes, and probably refers to the ongoing persecution Paul faced. He was also burdened by internal "fears"—the concern he had for the church and the anti-Paul faction prevalent there.

b. **the downcast.** This refers not to the spiritually humble, but to those who are humiliated. Such people are lowly in the economic, social, or emotional sense (cf. Rom. 12:16).

c. **comforted us by the coming of Titus . . . when he told us.** The Gr. word for "coming" refers to the actual presence of Titus with Paul. But comforting Paul beyond just the arrival of Titus, which was a blessing, was the encouraging report he gave regarding the repentance of the Corinthians and their positive response to Paul's letter carried by Titus. Paul was encouraged by the manner in which the Corinthians comforted Titus, since he brought them such a confrontational. Paul was also encouraged by their response to himself, which was manifested in 3 ways: 1) "earnest desire"—they longed to see Paul again and resume their relationship with him; 2) "mourning"—they were sorrowful over their sin and the breach it created between themselves and Paul; and 3) "zeal"—they loved Paul to such a degree that they were willing to defend him against those who sought to harm him, specifically the false teachers.

d. **I made you sorry.** This can also be translated "I caused you sorrow" (see 2 Cor. 2:1).

e. **my letter.** The severe letter that confronted the mutiny in the church at Corinth (see 2 Cor. 2:3).

f. **I do not regret it . . . I did regret it. . . . Now I rejoice.** Paul did not regret sending the letter, even though it caused them sorrow, because he knew that sorrow over their sin would affect in them repentance leading to obedience. Yet Paul did regret having sent it for a brief time while awaiting Titus' return, fearing that his letter was too harsh, and that he might have driven them further away from him. In the end, however, he rejoiced because the letter accomplished what he had hoped.

g. **your sorrow led to repentance.** The letter produced a sorrow in the Corinthian believers that led them to repent of their sins. "Repentance" refers to the desire to turn from sin and restore one's relationship to God (see Matt. 3:2, 8).

h. **godly sorrow produces repentance leading to salvation.** "Godly sorrow" refers to sorrow that is according to the will of God and produced by the Holy Spirit (see 2 Tim. 2:25). True repentance cannot occur apart from such a genuine sorrow over one's sin. The word "leading" is supplied by the translators; Paul was saying that repentance belongs to the realm or sphere of salvation. Repentance is at the very heart of and proves one's salvation:

leading to salvation, not to be regretted; but the ᵃsorrow of the world produces death. For observe this very thing, that you sorrowed in a godly manner: What ᵇdiligence it produced in you, ᶜwhat clearing of yourselves, what ᵈindignation, what ᵉfear, what ᶠvehement desire, what ᵍzeal, what ʰvindication! In all things you proved yourselves ⁱto be clear in this matter. ʲTherefore, although I wrote to you, I did not do it for the sake of him who had done the wrong, nor for the sake of him who suffered wrong, but that our care for you in the sight of God might appear to you.

Therefore we have been comforted in your comfort. And we rejoiced exceedingly more for the joy of Titus, because his spirit has been refreshed by you all. For if in anything I have boasted to him about you, I am not ashamed. But as we spoke all things to you in truth, even so our boasting to Titus was found true. And his affections are greater for you as he remembers the obedience of you all, how with ᵏfear and trembling you received him. Therefore I rejoice that I have confidence in you in everything.

---

unbelievers repent of their sin initially when they are saved, and then as believers, repent of their sins continually to keep the joy and blessing of their relationship to God (see 1 John 1:7–9).

a. **sorrow of the world produces death.** Human sorrow is unsanctified remorse and has no redemptive capability. It is nothing more than the wounded pride of getting caught in a sin and having one's lusts go unfulfilled. That kind of sorrow leads only to guilt, shame, despair, depression, self-pity, and hopelessness. People can die from such sorrow (cf. Ps. 32:3, 4).

b. **diligence.** Better translated, "earnestness" or "eagerness." It is the initial reaction of true repentance to eagerly and aggressively pursue righteousness. This is an attitude that ends indifference to sin and complacency about evil and deception.

c. **what clearing of yourselves.** A desire to clear one's name of the stigma that accompanies sin. The repentant sinner restores the trust and confidence of others by making his genuine repentance known.

d. **indignation.** Often associated with righteous indignation and holy anger. Repentance leads to anger over one's sin and displeasure at the shame it has brought on the Lord's name and His people.

e. **fear.** This is reverence toward God, who is the One most offended by sin. Repentance leads to a healthy fear of the One who chastens and judges sin.

f. **vehement desire.** This could be translated "yearning," or "a longing for," and refers to the desire of the repentant sinner to restore the relationship with the one who was sinned against.

g. **zeal.** This refers to loving someone or something so much that one hates anyone or anything that harms the object of this love.

h. **vindication.** This could be translated "avenging of wrong," and refers to the desire to see justice done. The repentant sinner no longer tries to protect himself; he wants to see the sin avenged no matter what it might cost him.

i. **to be clear in this matter.** The essence of repentance is an aggressive pursuit of holiness, which was characteristic of the Corinthians. The Gr. word for "clear" means "pure" or "holy." They demonstrated the integrity of their repentance by their purity.

j. **him who had done the wrong.** The leader of the mutiny in the Corinthian church (see 2 Cor. 12:7).

k. **fear and trembling.** Reverence toward God and a healthy fear of judgment (see 1 Cor. 2:3).

121. Patterns and Purpose for Giving

2 Cor. 8:1–15

^aMoreover, brethren, we make known to you the ^bgrace of God bestowed on the ^cchurches of Macedonia: that in a great trial of affliction the ^dabundance of their joy and their ^edeep poverty abounded in the ^friches of their liberality. For ^gI bear witness that according to their ability, yes, and beyond their ability, they were freely willing, imploring us with much urgency that we would receive ^hthe gift and the fellowship of the ministering to the saints. And ⁱnot

---

a. **Moreover.** While this section specifically deals with Paul's instruction to the Corinthians about a particular collection for the saints in Jerusalem, it also provides the richest, most detailed model of Christian giving in the NT.

b. **grace of God.** The generosity of the churches of Macedonia was motivated by God's grace. Paul did not merely commend those churches for a noble human work, but instead gave the credit to God for what He did through them.

c. **churches of Macedonia.** Macedonia was the northern Roman province of Greece. Paul's reference was to the churches at Philippi, Thessalonica, and Berea (cf. Acts 17:11). This was basically an impoverished province that had been ravaged by many wars and even then was being plundered by Roman authority and commerce.

d. **abundance of their joy.** "Abundance" means "surplus." In spite of their difficult circumstances, the churches' joy rose above their pain because of their devotion to the Lord and the causes of His kingdom.

e. **deep poverty.** "Deep" means "according to the depth," or "extremely deep." "Poverty" refers to the most severe type of economic deprivation, the kind that caused a person to become a beggar.

f. **riches of their liberality.** The Gr. word for "liberality" can be translated "generosity" or "sincerity." It is the opposite of duplicity or being double-minded. The Macedonian believers were rich in their single-minded, selfless generosity to God and to others.

g. **I bear witness.** Paul highlighted 3 elements of the Macedonians' giving which summed up the concept of freewill giving: 1) "according to their ability." Giving is proportionate—God sets no fixed amount or percentage and expects His people to give based on what they have (Luke 6:38; 1 Cor. 16:2); 2) "beyond their ability." Giving is sacrificial. God's people are to give according to what they have, yet it must be in proportions that are sacrificial (cf. Matt. 6:25–34; Mark 12:41–44; Phil. 4:19); and 3) "freely willing"—lit. "one who chooses his own course of action." Giving is voluntary—God's people are not to give out of compulsion, manipulation, or intimidation. Freewill giving has always been God's plan (cf. 9:6; Gen. 4:2–4; 8:20; Ex. 25:1, 2; 35:4, 5, 21, 22; 36:5–7; Num. 18:12; Deut. 16:10, 17; 1 Chr. 29:9; Prov. 3:9, 10; 11:24; Luke 19:1–8). Freewill giving is not to be confused with tithing, which related to the national taxation system of Israel (see Lev. 27:30) and is paralleled in the NT and the present by paying taxes (see Matt. 22:21; Rom. 13:6, 7).

h. **the gift and the fellowship.** "Gift" means "grace." The Macedonian Christians implored Paul for the special grace of being able to have fellowship and be partners in supporting the poor saints in Jerusalem. They viewed giving as a privilege, not an obligation (cf. 2 Cor. 9:7).

i. **not only as we had hoped.** The response of the Macedonian churches was far more than Paul had expected.

only as we had hoped, but they [a]first gave themselves to the Lord, and then to us by the will of God. So [b]we urged Titus, that as he had begun, so he would also complete this grace in you as well. [c]But as you abound in everything—in faith, in speech, in knowledge, in all diligence, and in your love for us—see that you abound in this grace also.

I speak [d]not by commandment, but I am testing the sincerity of your love by the diligence of others. For you know the grace of our Lord Jesus Christ, that [e]though He was rich, yet for your sakes [f]He became poor, [g]that you through His poverty might become rich.

And in this I give [h]advice: It is to your advantage not only to be doing what you began and were desiring to do a year ago; but now you also must [i]complete the doing of it; that as there was a readiness to desire it, so there also may be a completion out of what you have. For if there is first a [j]willing

---

a. **first.** Refers not to time but priority. Of first priority to the Macedonians was to present themselves as sacrifices to God (cf. Rom. 12:1, 2; 1 Pet. 2:5). Generous giving follows personal dedication.

b. **we urged Titus.** Titus initially encouraged the Corinthians to begin the collection at least one year earlier. When he returned to Corinth with the severe letter, Paul encouraged him to help the believers finish the collection of the money for the support of the poor saints in Jerusalem.

c. **you abound in everything.** The giving of the Corinthians was to be in harmony with other Christian virtues that Paul already recognized in them: "faith"—sanctifying trust in the Lord; "speech"—sound doctrine; "knowledge"—the application of doctrine; "diligence"—eagerness and spiritual passion; and "love"—the love of choice, inspired by their leaders.

d. **not by commandment.** Freewill giving is never according to obligation or command.

e. **though He was rich.** A reference to the eternality and pre-existence of Christ. As the second person of the Trinity, Christ is as rich as God is rich. He owns everything, and possesses all power, authority, sovereignty, glory, honor, and majesty (cf. Is. 9:6; Mic. 5:2; John 1:1; 8:58; 10:30; 17:5; Col. 1:15–18; 2:9; Heb. 1:3).

f. **He became poor.** A reference to Christ's incarnation (cf. John 1:14; Rom. 1:3; 8:3; Gal. 4:4; Col. 1:20; 1 Tim. 3:16; Heb. 2:7). He laid aside the independent exercise of all His divine prerogatives, left His place with God, took on human form, and died on a cross like a common criminal (Phil. 2:5–8).

g. **that you . . . might become rich.** Believers become spiritually rich through the sacrifice and impoverishment of Christ (Phil. 2:5–8). They become rich in salvation, forgiveness, joy, peace, glory, honor, and majesty (cf. 1 Cor. 1:4, 5; 3:22; Eph. 1:3; 1 Pet. 1:3, 4). They become joint heirs with Christ (Rom. 8:17).

h. **advice.** Paul was not commanding the Corinthians to give any specific amount. It was his opinion, however, that it was to their advantage to give generously so they might receive abundantly more from God in either material blessings, spiritual blessings, or eternal reward (cf. 9:6; Luke 6:38).

i. **complete the doing of it.** The Corinthians needed to finish what they had started by completing the collection (cf. Luke 9:62; 1 Cor. 16:2). They needed this reminder since they likely stopped the process due to the influence of the false teachers, who probably accused Paul of being a huckster who would keep the money for himself (cf. 2 Cor. 2:17).

j. **willing mind.** Paul spoke of a readiness and eagerness to give. God is most concerned with the heart attitude of the giver, not the amount he gives (cf. 2 Cor. 9:7; Mark 12:41–44).

mind, it is accepted ᵃaccording to what one has, and ᵇnot according to what he does not have.

For I do not mean that others should be eased and you burdened; ᶜbut by an equality, that now at this time your abundance may supply their lack, that their abundance also may supply your lack—that there may be equality. ᵈAs it is written, "He who gathered much had nothing left over, and he who gathered little had no lack."

122. PROCEDURES OF GIVING

2 Cor. 8:16—9:5

But thanks be to God who puts the same earnest care for you into the heart of Titus. For he not only accepted the exhortation, but being more diligent, he went to you of his own accord. And we have sent with him ᵉ the brother whose praise is in the gospel throughout all the churches, and not only that, but who was also ᶠchosen by the churches to travel with us with this gift, which is administered by us ᵍto the glory of the Lord Himself and to show

---

a. **according to what one has.** Whatever one has is the resource out of which he should give (see v. 3). That is why there are no set amounts or percentages for giving anywhere stated in the NT. The implication is that if one has much, he can give much; if he has little, he can give only little (cf. 2 Cor. 9:6).

b. **not according to what he does not have.** Believers do not need to go into debt to give, nor lower themselves to a poverty level. God never asks believers to impoverish themselves. The Macedonians received a special blessing of grace from God to give the way they did.

c. **equality.** This Gr. word gives us the Eng. word "isostasy," which refers to a condition of equilibrium. Thus the term could also be translated "balance" or "equilibrium." The idea is that in the body of Christ some believers who have more than they need should help those who have far less than they need (cf. 1 Tim. 6:17, 18). This is not, however, a scheme of Paul's to redistribute wealth within the church, but rather to meet basic needs.

d. **As it is written.** Quoted from Ex. 16:18. The collecting of the manna by the Israelites in the wilderness was an appropriate illustration of sharing of resources. Some were able to gather more than others, and apparently shared it so that no one lacked what they needed.

e. **the brother.** This man is unnamed because he was so well known, prominent and unimpeachable. He was a distinguished preacher, and he was able to add credibility to the enterprise of taking the collection to Jerusalem.

f. **chosen by the churches.** To protect Paul and Titus from false accusations regarding the mishandling of the money, the churches picked the unbiased brother as their representative to lend accountability to the enterprise.

g. **to the glory of the Lord Himself.** Paul wanted careful scrutiny as protection against bringing dishonor to Christ for any misappropriation of the money. He wanted to avoid any offenses worthy of justifiable criticisms or accusations.

your ready mind, avoiding this: that anyone should blame us in this lavish gift which is administered by us—[a]providing honorable things, not only in the sight of the Lord, but also in the sight of men.

And we have sent with them [b]our brother whom we have often proved diligent in many things, but now much more diligent, because of the great confidence which we have in you. If anyone inquires about Titus, he is my [c]partner and fellow worker concerning you. Or if our brethren are inquired about, they are [d]messengers of the churches, the [e]glory of Christ. Therefore show to them, and before the churches, the proof of your love and of our boasting on your behalf.

Now concerning the [f]ministering to the saints, it is superfluous for me to write to you; [g]for I know your willingness, about which I boast of you to [h]the Macedonians, that [i]Achaia was ready a year ago; and your zeal has stirred up the majority. Yet I have sent the brethren, lest our boasting of you should be in vain in this respect, that, as I said, you may be ready; lest if some Macedonians come with me and find you unprepared, we (not to mention you!) should be ashamed of this confident boasting. Therefore I thought it necessary to exhort the brethren to go to you ahead of time, and prepare [j]your generous gift beforehand, which you had previously promised, that it may be ready as a matter of generosity and not as a [k]grudging obligation.

---

a. **providing honorable things.** A better rendering is "have regard for what is honorable," or "take into consideration what is honorable." Paul cared greatly about what people thought of his actions, especially considering how large the gift was.

b. **our brother.** A third member of the delegation sent to deliver the gift, also unnamed.

c. **partner and fellow worker.** Titus was Paul's "partner"—his close companion—and fellow laborer among the Corinthians. They already knew of his outstanding character.

d. **messengers of the churches.** The two men who went with Titus were apostles in the sense of being commissioned and sent by the churches. They were not apostles of Christ (2 Cor. 11:13; 1 Thess. 2:6), because they were not eyewitnesses of the resurrected Lord or commissioned directly by Him (see Rom. 1:1).

e. **glory of Christ.** The greatest of all commendations is to be characterized as bringing glory to Christ. Such was the case of the two messengers.

f. **ministering to the saints.** The offering they were collecting for the believers in Jerusalem (see 2 Cor. 8:4).

g. Paul was simply calling the Corinthians back to their original eagerness and readiness to participate in the offering project. The confusion and lies spread by the false teachers (i.e., Paul was a deceiver ministering only for the money) had sidetracked the believers on this issue.

h. **the Macedonians.** Believers in the churches in the province of Macedonia, which was the northern part of Greece (see 2 Cor. 8:1–5; Acts 16:9).

i. **Achaia.** A province in southern Greece, where Corinth was located (see Acts 18:12).

j. **your generous gift.** On first hearing of the need, the Corinthians had undoubtedly promised Paul that they would raise a large amount.

k. **grudging obligation.** More clearly translated "covetousness," or "greed," it denotes a

123. Promise of Giving

2 Cor. 9:6–15

But this I say: He who ᵃsows sparingly will also reap sparingly, and he who sows ᵇbountifully will also reap bountifully. So let each one give ᶜas he purposes in his heart, not ᵈgrudgingly or ᵉof necessity; for ᶠGod loves a cheerful giver. And God is able to make ᵍall grace abound toward you, that you, always having ʰall sufficiency in all things, may have an ⁱabundance for every good work. ʲAs it is written:

---

grasping to get more and keep it at the expense of others. This attitude emphasizes selfishness and pride, which can have a very detrimental effect on giving, and is natural for unbelievers but should not be for professed believers (cf. Ps. 10:3; Eccl. 5:10; Mic. 2:2; Mark 7:22; Rom. 1:29; 1 Cor. 5:11; 6:9, 10; Eph. 5:3–5; 1 Tim. 6:10; 2 Pet. 2:14).

a. **sows.** The simple, self-evident agrarian principle—which Paul applied to Christian giving—that the harvest is directly proportionate to the amount of seed sown (cf. Prov. 11:24, 25; 19:17; Luke 6:38; Gal. 6:7).

b. **bountifully.** This is derived from the Gr. word which gives us the word "eulogy" ("blessing"). When a generous believer gives by faith and trust in God, with a desire to produce the greatest possible blessing, that person will receive that kind of a harvest of blessing (cf. Prov. 3:9, 10; 28:27; Mal. 3:10). God gives a return on the amount one invests with Him. Invest a little, receive a little, and vice versa (cf. Luke 6:38).

c. **as he purposes.** The term translated "purposes" occurs only here in the NT and indicates a premeditated, predetermined plan of action that is done from the heart voluntarily, but not impulsively. This is an age-old biblical principle of giving (see 2 Cor. 8:3; cf. Ex. 25:2).

d. **grudgingly.** Lit. "with grief," "sorrow," or "sadness," which indicates an attitude of depression, regret, and reluctance that accompanies something done strictly out of a sense of duty and obligation, but not joy.

e. **of necessity.** Or "compulsion." This refers to external pressure and coercion, quite possibly accompanied by legalism. Believers are not to give based on the demands of others, or according to any arbitrary standards or set amounts.

f. **God loves a cheerful giver.** God has a unique, special love for those who are happily committed to generous giving. The Gr. word for "cheerful" is the word from which we get "hilarious," which suggests that God loves a heart that is enthusiastically thrilled with the pleasure of giving.

g. **all grace abound toward you.** God possesses an infinite amount of grace, and He gives it lavishly, without holding back (cf. 1 Chr. 29:14). Here "grace" does not refer to spiritual graces, but to money and material needs. When the believer generously—and wisely—gives of his material resources, God graciously replenishes them so he always has plenty and will not be in need (cf. 2 Chr. 31:10).

h. **all sufficiency.** In secular Greek philosophy, this was the proud contentment of self-sufficiency that supposedly led to true happiness. Paul sanctifies the secular term and says that God, not man, will supply everything needed for real happiness and contentment (cf. Phil. 4:19).

i. **abundance for every good work.** God gives back lavishly to generous, cheerful givers, not so they may satisfy selfish, nonessential desires, but so they may meet the variety of needs others have (cf. Deut. 15:10, 11).

j. **As it is written.** Paul marshals OT support (Ps. 112:9) for what he has been saying

"He has dispersed abroad,

He has given to the poor;

His righteousness endures forever."

Now may He who supplies seed to the sower, and bread for food, supply and multiply the seed you have sown and increase the [a]fruits of your righteousness, while you are enriched in everything for all liberality, which causes thanksgiving through us to God. For the [b]administration of this service not only [c]supplies the needs of the saints, but also is abounding through many thanksgivings to God, while, through the [d]proof of this ministry, they glorify God for the [e]obedience of your confession to the gospel of Christ, and for your liberal sharing with them and all men, and by [f]their prayer for you, who long for you because of [g]the exceeding grace of God in you. Thanks be to God for His [h]indescribable gift!

---

about the divine principles of giving. God replenishes and rewards the righteous giver both in time and eternity.

a. **fruits of your righteousness.** God's temporal and eternal blessings to the cheerful giver (cf. Hos. 10:12).

b. **administration of this service.** "Administration," which may also be translated "service," is a priestly word from which we get "liturgy." Paul viewed the entire collection project as a spiritual, worshipful enterprise that was primarily being offered to God to glorify Him.

c. **supplies the needs of the saints.** The Gr. word for "supplies" is a doubly intense term that could be rendered "really, fully supplying." This indicates the Jerusalem church had an extremely great need. Many of its members had gone to Jerusalem as pilgrims to celebrate the feast of Pentecost (see Acts 2:1, 5–11), had been converted through Peter's message, and had then remained in the city without adequate financial support. Many residents of Jerusalem had undoubtedly lost their jobs in the waves of persecution that came after the martyrdom of Stephen (Acts 8:1). However, the Corinthians were wealthy enough (they had not yet suffered persecution and deprivation like the Macedonians; 2 Cor. 8:1–4) to help meet the huge need with a generous monetary gift (see 2 Cor. 9:5).

d. **proof of this ministry.** The collection also provided an important opportunity for the Corinthians to test the genuineness of their faith (cf. James 1:22; 1 John 2:3, 4). The Jewish believers, who already doubted the validity of Gentile salvation, were especially skeptical of the Corinthians since their church had so many problems. The Corinthians' involvement in the collection would help to put those doubts to rest.

e. **obedience of your confession.** Obedient submission to God's Word is always evidence of a true confession of Christ as Lord and Savior (Eph. 2:10; James 2:14–20; cf. Rom. 10:9, 10). If the Corinthians had a proper response to and participation in Paul's collection ministry, the Jewish believers would know the Gentile conversions had been real.

f. **their prayer for you.** This verse illustrates the truth that mutual prayer is at the heart of authentic Christian unity. When the Jerusalem believers recognized God was at work in the Corinthian church as a result of its outreach through the collection, they would have become friends in Christ and prayed for the Corinthians, thanking God for their loving generosity.

g. **the exceeding grace of God.** The Spirit of God was at work in the Corinthians in a special way.

h. **indescribable gift.** Paul summarized his discourse by comparing the believer's act of

124. PAUL'S APOSTOLIC AUTHORITY

2 Cor. 10:1–18

[a]Now I, Paul, myself am pleading with you by the [b]meekness and [c]gentleness of Christ—who in presence am [d]lowly among you, but being absent am bold toward you. But I beg you that when I am present I may not be bold with that confidence by which I intend to be bold against some, who think of us as if we walked according to the flesh. For though we [e]walk in the flesh, we do not

---

giving with what God did in giving Jesus Christ (cf. Rom. 8:32), "His indescribable gift." God buried His Son and reaped a vast harvest of those who put their faith in the resurrected Christ (cf. John 12:24). That makes it possible for believers to joyfully, sacrificially, and abundantly sow and reap. As they give in this manner, they show forth Christ's likeness (cf. John 12:25, 26; Eph. 5:1, 2).

a. **Now.** The abrupt change in tone from 2 Cor. 1–9 has prompted various explanations of the relationship between chaps. 10–13 and 1–9. Some argue that chaps. 10–13 were originally part of the "severe letter" (2:4), and hence belong chronologically before chaps. 1–9. Chapters 10–13 cannot, however, have been written before chaps. 1–9, since they refer to Titus' visit as a past event (12:18; cf. 8:6). Further, the offender whose defiance of Paul prompted the "severe letter" (2:5–8) is nowhere mentioned in chaps. 10–13. Others agree that chaps. 10–13 belong after chaps. 1–9, but believe they form a separate letter. They assume that Paul, after sending chaps. 1–9 to the Corinthians, received reports of new trouble at Corinth and wrote chaps. 10–13 in response. A variation of this view is that Paul paused in his writing of 2 Corinthians after chaps. 1–9, then heard bad news from Corinth before he resumed writing chaps. 10–13. This view preserves the unity of 2 Corinthians; however Paul does not mention anywhere in chaps. 10–13 that he received any fresh news from Corinth. The best interpretation views 2 Corinthians as a unified letter, with chaps. 1–9 addressed to the repentant majority (cf. 2:6) and chaps. 10–13 to the minority still influenced by the false teachers. The support for this view is that: 1) there is no historical evidence (from Gr. manuscripts, the writings of the church Fathers, or early translations) that chaps. 10–13 ever circulated as a separate letter; all Gr. manuscripts have them following chaps. 1–9; 2) the differences in tone between chaps. 10–13 and 1–9 have been exaggerated (cf. 11:11; 12:14 with 6:11; 7:2); and 3) chaps. 10–13 form the logical conclusion to chaps. 1–9, as Paul prepared the Corinthians for his promised visit (1:15, 16; 2:1–3).

b. **meekness.** The humble and gentle attitude that expresses itself in patient endurance of unfair treatment. A meek person is not bitter or angry, and he does not seek revenge when wronged. See Matt. 5:5.

c. **gentleness.** This is similar in meaning to meekness. When applied to someone in a position of authority it refers to leniency. Gentle people refuse to retaliate, even when it is in their power to do so (Phil. 4:5).

d. **lowly . . . bold toward you.** Paul sarcastically repeated another feature of the Corinthians' accusation against him; sadly, they had mistaken his gentleness and meekness toward them for weakness. Further, they accused him of cowardice, of being bold only when writing to them from a safe distance. Paul was quite capable of bold, fearless confrontation (cf. Gal. 2:11). But seeking to spare the Corinthians (2 Cor. 1:23), the apostle begged the rebellious minority not to force him to display his boldness by confronting them—something he would do, he warned, if necessary.

e. **walk in the flesh.** Paul's opponents at Corinth had wrongly accused him of walking in the flesh in a moral sense (cf. Rom. 8:4). Playing off that, Paul affirmed that he did walk in the flesh in a physical sense; though possessing the power and authority of an apostle of Jesus Christ, he was a real human being (cf. 2 Cor. 4:7, 16; 5:1).

^awar according to the flesh. ^bFor the weapons of our warfare are not carnal but mighty in God for pulling down ^cstrongholds, casting down ^darguments and every high thing that exalts itself against the knowledge of God, bringing ^eevery thought into captivity to the obedience of Christ, and being ^fready to punish all disobedience when your obedience is fulfilled.

Do you ^glook at things according to the outward appearance? ^hIf anyone is convinced in himself that he is Christ's, let him again consider this in himself, that just as he is Christ's, even so ⁱwe are Christ's. For even if I should boast

---

a. **war according to the flesh.** Although a man, Paul did not fight the spiritual battle for men's souls using human ingenuity, worldly wisdom, or clever methodologies (cf. 1 Cor. 1:17–25; 2:1–4). Such impotent weapons are powerless to free souls from the forces of darkness and bring them to maturity in Christ. They cannot successfully oppose satanic assaults on the gospel, such as those made by the false apostles at Corinth.

b. **our warfare.** The motif of the Christian life as warfare is a common one in the NT (cf. 2 Cor. 6:7; Eph. 6:10–18; 1 Tim. 1:18; 2 Tim. 2:3, 4; 4:7).

c. **strongholds.** The metaphor would have been readily understandable to the Corinthians since Corinth, like most ancient cities, had a fortress (on top of a hill S of the city) in which its residents could take refuge. The formidable spiritual strongholds manned by the forces of hell can be demolished only by spiritual weapons wielded by godly believers—singularly the "sword of the Spirit" (Eph. 6:17), since only the truth of God's Word can defeat satanic falsehoods. This is the true spiritual warfare. Believers are not instructed in the NT to assault demons or Satan (see Jude 9), but to assault error with the truth. That is our battle (cf. John 17:17; Heb. 4:12).

d. **arguments.** Thoughts, ideas, speculations, reasonings, philosophies, and false religions are the ideological forts in which men barricade themselves against God and the gospel (cf. 1 Cor. 3:20).

e. **every thought into captivity.** Emphasizes the total destruction of the fortresses of human and satanic wisdom and the rescuing of those inside from the damning lies that had enslaved them.

f. **ready to punish.** Paul would not stand idly by while enemies of the faith assaulted a church under his care. He was ready to purge them out (as he did at Ephesus; 1 Tim. 1:19, 20) as soon as the Corinthian church was complete in its obedience. When that happened, the lines would be clearly drawn between the repentant, obedient majority and the recalcitrant, disobedient minority.

g. **look . . . outward appearance.** The Gr. verb "look" is better translated as an imperative, or command: "Look at what is obvious, face the facts, consider the evidence." In light of what they knew about him (cf. 1 Cor. 9:1, 2), how could some of the Corinthians possibly believe that Paul was a false apostle and the false teachers were true apostles? Unlike Paul, the false apostles had founded no churches, and had suffered no persecution for the cause of Christ. Paul could call on his companions and even Ananias as witnesses to the reality of his Damascus Road experience; there were no witnesses to verify the false apostles' alleged encounters with the risen, glorified Christ.

h. **If anyone is convinced . . . that he is Christ's.** The false apostles' claim to belong to Christ can be understood in 4 ways: 1) that they were Christians; 2) that they had known Jesus during His earthly life; 3) that they had an apostolic commission from Him; or 4) that they had an elevated, secret knowledge of Him. Their claim that some or all of those things were true about themselves implies that they denied all of them to be true of Paul.

i. **we are Christ's.** For the sake of argument, Paul did not at this point deny the false apostles' claims (as he did later in 2 Cor. 11:13–15). He merely pointed out that he, too, can and does claim to belong to Christ. To decide between the conflicting personal claims, the

somewhat more ᵃabout our authority, which the Lord gave us for edification and not for your destruction, I shall not be ashamed—lest I seem to ᵇterrify you by letters. "For his letters," they say, "are weighty and powerful, but his ᶜbodily presence is weak, and his speech contemptible." Let such a person consider this, that what we are in word by letters when we are absent, such we will also be in deed ᵈwhen we are present.

For we dare not ᵉclass ourselves or compare ourselves with those who commend themselves. But they, measuring themselves by themselves, and ᶠcomparing themselves among themselves, are not wise. We, however, will ᵍnot boast beyond measure, but within the ʰlimits of the sphere which God

---

Corinthians needed only to consider the objective evidence, as he commanded them to do earlier in this verse.

a. **about our authority.** The debate with the false apostles had forced Paul to emphasize his authority more than he cared to; Paul's claims for his authority normally were restrained by his humility. But no matter how much he said about his authority, Paul would never be ashamed. Since he had the authority of which he spoke, he would never be proved guilty of making an empty boast. The Lord gave Paul his authority to edify and strengthen the church; that he had done so at Corinth proves the genuineness of his claim to apostolic calling. Far from edifying the Corinthian church, the false apostles had brought confusion, divisiveness, and turmoil to it. That showed that their authority did not come from the Lord, who seeks only to build His church (cf. Matt. 16:18), not tear it down.

b. **terrify you by letters.** The false apostles had accused Paul of being an abusive leader, of trying to intimidate the Corinthians in his letters. Paul's goal, however, was not to terrify the Corinthians, but to bring them to repentance (cf. 2 Cor. 7:9, 10), because he loved them (cf. 2 Cor. 7:2, 3; 11:11; 12:15).

c. **bodily presence.** In their continuing attempt to discredit Paul, the false apostles claimed that in contrast to his bold, forceful letters, in person he lacked the presence, charisma, and personality of a truly great leader. They no doubt supported their point by portraying Paul's departure after his "painful" visit (2 Cor. 2:1) as a retreat of abject failure. And in a culture that highly valued skillful rhetoric and eloquent oration, Paul's "contemptible" speech was also taken as evidence that he was a weak, ineffective person.

d. **when we are present.** Paul denied the false charges against him and affirmed his integrity. What he was in his letters he was to be when present with them.

e. **class ourselves or compare ourselves.** It is a mark of Paul's humility that he refused to compare himself with others, or engage in self-promotion. His only personal concern was what the Lord thought of him (cf. 1 Cor. 4:4), though he needed to defend his apostleship so the Corinthians would not, in turning from him, turn from the truth to lies.

f. **comparing themselves among themselves.** Paul pointed out the folly of the false apostles' boasting. They invented false standards that they could meet, then proclaimed themselves superior for meeting them.

g. **not boast beyond measure.** In contrast to the proud, arrogant, boastful false apostles, Paul refused to say anything about himself or his ministry that was not true and God-given.

h. **limits of the sphere which God appointed us.** Paul was content to stay within the bounds of the ministry God had given him—that of being the apostle to the Gentiles (Rom. 1:5; 11:13; 1 Tim. 2:7; 2 Tim. 1:11). Thus, contrary to the claims of the false apostles, Paul's sphere of ministry included Corinth. The apostle again demonstrated his humility by refusing to boast of his own accomplishments, preferring to speak only of what Christ had done through him (Rom. 15:18; Col. 1:29).

appointed us—a sphere which especially includes you. For we are not overextending ourselves (as though our authority did not extend to you), for it was to you that we came with the gospel of Christ; not boasting of things beyond measure, that is, in other men's labors, but having hope, that as your faith is increased, we shall be greatly ªenlarged by you in our sphere, to preach the gospel in the ᵇregions beyond you, and not to boast in another man's sphere of accomplishment.

But "he who glories, let him glory in the LORD." For not he who commends himself is approved, but ᵇwhom the Lord commends.

125. PAUL'S APOSTOLIC CONDUCT

2 Cor. 11:1–15

Oh, that you would bear with me in ᵈa little folly—and indeed you do bear with me. For ᵉI am jealous for you with ᶠgodly jealousy. For ᵍI have betrothed you to one husband, that I may present you as a ʰchaste virgin to Christ.

---

a. **enlarged . . . in our sphere.** When the crisis in Corinth had been resolved and the Corinthians' faith strengthened, Paul would, with their help, expand his ministry into new areas.

b. **regions beyond you.** Areas such as Rome (Acts 19:21) and Spain (Rom. 15:24, 28).

b. **whom the Lord commends.** Self-commendation is both meaningless and foolish; the only true, meaningful commendation comes from God.

d. **a little folly.** Having just pointed out the folly of self-commendation (2 Cor. 10:18), Paul certainly did not want to engage in it. But the Corinthians' acceptance of the false apostles' claims forced Paul to set forth his own apostolic credentials (cf. 2 Cor. 12:11); that was the only way he could get them to see the truth (see 2 Cor. 10:7). Unlike the false apostles, however, Paul's boasting was in the Lord (2 Cor. 10:17) and motivated by concern for the Corinthians' well-being under the threat of false teaching (cf. 2 Cor. 12:19).

e. **I am jealous for you.** The reason for Paul's "folly" was his deep concern for the Corinthians—concern to the point of jealousy, not for his own reputation, but zeal for their spiritual purity.

f. **godly jealousy.** Jealousy inspired by zeal for God's causes, and thus similar to God's own jealousy for His holy name and His people's loyalty (cf. Ex. 20:5; 34:14; Deut. 4:24; 5:9; 6:15; 32:16, 21; Josh. 24:19; Ps. 78:58; Ezek. 39:25; Nah. 1:2).

g. **I have betrothed you to one husband.** As their spiritual father (12:14; 1 Cor. 4:15; cf. 9:1, 2), Paul portrayed the Corinthians like a daughter, whom he betrothed to Jesus Christ (at their conversion). The OT pictures Israel as the wife of the Lord (cf. Is. 54:5; Jer. 3:14; Hos. 2:19, 20), while the NT pictures the church as the bride of Christ (Eph. 5:22–32; Rev. 19:7).

h. **chaste virgin.** Having betrothed or pledged the Corinthians to Christ, Paul wanted them to be pure until the marriage day finally arrived (cf. Rev. 19:7). It was that passionate concern which provoked Paul's jealousy and prompted him to set forth his apostolic credentials.

But I fear, lest somehow, as [a]the serpent deceived Eve by his craftiness, so your minds may be corrupted from the simplicity that is in Christ. For if [b]he who comes preaches [c]another Jesus whom we have not preached, or if you receive a different spirit which you have not received, or a different gospel which you have not accepted—[d]you may well put up with it!

For I consider that I am not at all inferior to [e]the most eminent apostles. Even though I am [f]untrained in speech, yet [g]I am not in knowledge. But we have been thoroughly manifested among you in all things.

---

a. **the serpent deceived Eve.** Paul compared the danger facing the Corinthian church to Eve's deception by Satan. He feared the Corinthians, like Eve, would fall prey to satanic lies and have their minds corrupted. The tragic result would be the abandonment of their simple devotion to Christ in favor of the sophisticated error of the false apostles. Paul's allusion to Gen. 3 implies that the false apostles were Satan's emissaries—a truth that he later made explicit.

b. **he who comes.** The false apostles came into the Corinthian church from the outside— just as Satan did into the Garden. Likely they were Palestinian Jews (cf. Acts 6:1) who allegedly sought to bring the Corinthians under the sway of the Jerusalem church. They were in a sense Judaizers, seeking to impose Jewish customs on the Corinthians. Unlike the Judaizers who plagued the Galatian churches (cf. Gal. 5:2), however, the false apostles at Corinth apparently did not insist that the Corinthians be circumcised. Nor did they practice a rigid legalism; in fact, they apparently encouraged licentiousness (cf. 2 Cor. 12:21). Their fascination with rhetoric and oratory (cf. 10:10) suggests they had been influenced by Greek culture and philosophy. They claimed (falsely, cf. Acts 15:24) to represent the Jerusalem church, even possessing letters of commendation (see 2 Cor. 3:1). Claiming to be the most eminent of apostles, they scorned Paul's apostolic claims. Though their teaching may have differed from the Galatian Judaizers, it was just as deadly.

c. **another Jesus . . . a different spirit . . . a different gospel.** Despite their vicious attacks on him, Paul's quarrel with the false apostles was not personal, but doctrinal. He could tolerate those hostile to him, as long as they preached the gospel of Jesus Christ (cf. Phil. 1:15–18). Those who adulterated the true gospel, however, received Paul's strongest condemnation (cf. Gal. 1:6–9). Though the precise details of what the false apostles taught are unknown and don't matter, they preached "another Jesus" and "a different spirit," which added up to "a different gospel."

d. **you may well put up with it!** Paul's fear that the Corinthians would embrace the damning lies of the false apostles prompted his jealous concern for them.

e. **the most eminent apostles.** Possibly a reference to the 12 apostles, in which case Paul was asserting that, contrary to the claims of the false apostles (who said they were sent from the Jerusalem church; see 2 Cor. 11:4), he was in no way inferior to the 12 (cf. 1 Cor. 15:7–9). More likely, Paul was making a sarcastic reference to the false apostles, based on their exalted view of themselves. It is unlikely that he would refer to the 12 in the context of false teaching (cf. 2 Cor. 11:1–4), nor does the comparison that follows seem to be between Paul and the 12 (Paul certainly would not have had to defend his speaking skills against those of the 12; cf. Acts 4:13).

f. **untrained in speech.** Paul acknowledged his lack of training in the rhetorical skills so prized in Greek culture (see 2 Cor. 10:10; cf. Acts 18:24); he was a preacher of the gospel, not a professional orator.

g. **I am not in knowledge.** Whatever deficiencies Paul may have had as an orator, he had none in terms of knowledge. Paul did not refer here to his rabbinic training under Gamaliel (Acts 22:3), but to his knowledge of the gospel (cf. 1 Cor. 2:6–11; Eph. 3:1–5), which he had received directly from God (Gal. 1:12).

Did I commit sin in humbling myself that you might be exalted, because I preached the gospel of God to you ᵃfree of charge? ᵇI robbed other churches, taking wages from them to minister to you. And when I was present with you, and in need, I was a burden to no one, for what I lacked the ᶜbrethren who came from Macedonia supplied. And in everything I kept myself from being burdensome to you, and so I will keep myself. As the truth of Christ is in me, no one shall stop me from ᵈthis boasting in the ᵉregions of Achaia. Why? Because I do not love you? God knows!

But what I do, I will also ᶠcontinue to do, that I may cut off the opportunity from those who desire an opportunity to be regarded just as we are in the things of which they boast. For such are ᵍfalse apostles, deceitful workers, transforming themselves into apostles of Christ. And no wonder! For Satan himself transforms himself into an ʰangel of light. Therefore it is no great thing if his ministers also transform themselves into ministers of righteousness, whose end will be according to their works.

---

a. **free of charge.** Greek culture measured the importance of a teacher by the fee he could command. The false apostles therefore accused Paul of being a counterfeit, since he refused to charge for his services (cf. 1 Cor. 9:1–15). They convinced the Corinthians to be offended by Paul's refusal to accept support from them, offering that as evidence that he did not love them. Paul's resort to manual labor to support himself (Acts 18:1–3) also embarrassed the Corinthians, who felt such work to be beneath the dignity of an apostle. With biting irony Paul asked his accusers how foregoing his right to support could possibly be a sin. In fact, by refusing support he had humbled himself so they could be exalted; that is, lifted out of their sin and idolatry.

b. **I robbed other churches.** "Robbed" is a very strong word, used in extrabiblical Gr. to refer to pillaging. Paul, of course, did not take money from churches without their consent; his point is that the churches who supported him while he ministered in Corinth received no direct benefit from the support they gave him. Why Paul refused to accept the support he was entitled to from the Corinthians (1 Cor. 9:15) is not clear; perhaps some of them were suspicious of his motives in promoting the offering for the Jerusalem church (cf. 2 Cor. 12:16–18).

c. **brethren who came from Macedonia.** Silas and Timothy (Acts 18:5), bringing money from Philippi (Phil. 4:15) and, possibly, Thessalonica (cf. 1 Thess. 3:6). The Macedonians' generous financial support allowed Paul to devote himself full time to preaching the gospel.

d. **this boasting.** About his ministering free of charge (cf. 1 Cor. 9:15, 18).

e. **the regions of Achaia.** The Roman province of which Corinth was the capital and leading city (see 9:2). The false apostles apparently were affecting more than just the city of Corinth.

f. **continue to do.** That Paul refused to accept financial support from the Corinthians was a source of embarrassment to the false apostles, who eagerly sought money for their services. Paul intended to keep his ministry free of charge and thereby undermine the false apostles' claims that they operated on the same basis as he did.

g. **false apostles.** No longer speaking with veiled irony or defending himself, Paul bluntly and directly exposed the false apostles for what they were—emissaries of Satan. Not only was their claim to apostleship false, so also was their doctrine. As satanic purveyors of false teaching, they were under the curse of Gal. 1:8, 9. Paul's forceful language may seem harsh, but it expressed the godly jealousy he felt for the Corinthians (see v. 2). Paul was unwilling to sacrifice truth for the sake of unity. Cf. 1 Tim. 4:12; 2 Pet. 2:1–17; Jude 8–13.

h. **angel of light.** Since the Prince of Darkness (cf. Luke 22:53; Acts 26:18; Eph. 6:12;

126. PAUL'S APOSTOLIC SUFFERING

2 Cor. 11:16–33

I say again, ^alet no one think me a fool. If otherwise, at least receive me as a fool, that I also may boast a little. What I speak, I speak ^bnot according to the Lord, but as it were, foolishly, in this confidence of boasting. Seeing that many boast according to the flesh, I also will boast. For you ^cput up with fools gladly, since you yourselves are wise! For you put up with it if one ^dbrings you into bondage, if one ^edevours you, if one ^ftakes from you, if one ^gexalts himself, if one ^hstrikes you on the face. To our shame I say that we were

---

Col. 1:13) masquerades as an angel of light—that is, deceptively, disguised as a messenger of truth—it is not surprising that his emissaries do as well. Satan deceived Eve (Gen 3:1–7) and holds unbelievers captive (2 Cor. 4:4; cf. Eph. 2:1–3); his emissaries were attempting to deceive and enslave the Corinthians. The terrifying "end" these self-styled "ministers of righteousness" will face is God's judgment—the fate of all false teachers (Rom. 3:8; 1 Cor. 3:17; Phil. 3:19; 2 Thess. 2:8; 2 Pet. 2:1, 3, 17; Jude 4, 13).

a. **let no one think me a fool.** Since some of the Corinthians (following the false apostles' lead) were comparing Paul unfavorably to the false apostles, he decided to answer fools according to their folly (Prov. 26:5). Paul's concern was not personal preservation; rather, the apostle knew that by rejecting him in favor of the false apostles, the Corinthians would be rejecting the true gospel for a false one. So by establishing himself and his ministry as genuine, Paul was defending the true gospel of Jesus Christ.

b. **not according to the Lord.** Paul acknowledged that boasting is "not according to the Lord" (cf. 2 Cor. 10:1), but the desperate situation in Corinth (where the false apostles made their "boast according to the flesh") forced him to boast, not for self-glorification (Gal. 6:14), but to counter the false doctrine threatening the Corinthian church (see v. 16).

c. **put up with fools.** The Corinthians, wrote Paul sarcastically, should have no trouble bearing with a "fool" like him, since they themselves were so wise (cf. 1 Cor. 4:10)! These verses contain some of the most scathing sarcasm Paul ever penned, demonstrating the seriousness of the situation at Corinth and revealing the jealous concern of a godly pastor. Paul did not view his disagreement with the false apostles as a mere academic debate; the souls of the Corinthians and the purity of the gospel were at stake.

d. **brings you into bondage.** The Gr. verb translated by this phrase appears elsewhere in the NT only in Gal. 2:4, where it speaks of the Galatians' enslavement by the Judaizers. The false apostles had robbed the Corinthians of their freedom in Christ (cf. Gal. 5:1).

e. **devours you.** Or "preys upon you." This probably refers to the false teachers' demands for financial support (the same verb appears in Luke 20:47 where Jesus denounces the Pharisees for devouring widows' houses).

f. **takes from you.** Better translated "takes advantage of you" (it is translated "I caught you by cunning" in 2 Cor. 12:16). The false apostles were attempting to catch the Corinthians like fish in a net (cf. Luke 5:5, 6).

g. **exalts himself.** This refers to one who is presumptuous, puts on airs, acts arrogantly, or lords it over people (cf. 1 Pet. 5:3).

h. **strikes you on the face.** The false apostles may have physically abused the Corinthians, but the phrase is more likely used in a metaphorical sense (cf. 1 Cor. 9:27) to speak of the false teachers' humiliation of the Corinthians. To strike someone on the face was a sign of disrespect and contempt (cf. 1 Kin. 22:24; Luke 22:64; Acts 23:2).

^atoo weak for that! But in whatever anyone is bold—I speak foolishly—I am bold also.

^bAre they Hebrews? So am I. Are they Israelites? So am I. Are they the seed of Abraham? So am I. ^dAre they ministers of Christ?—^eI speak as a fool—I am more: ^fin labors more abundant, in stripes above measure, in prisons more frequently, in deaths often. From the Jews five times I received ^gforty stripes minus one. Three times I was ^hbeaten with rods; ⁱonce I was stoned; ^jthree times I was shipwrecked; ^ka night and a day I have been in the deep; in journeys often, ^lin perils of waters, in perils of robbers, in perils of my own countrymen, in perils of the Gentiles, in perils in the city, in perils in the wilderness, in perils in the sea, in perils among ^mfalse brethren; in weariness and toil, in sleeplessness often, in hunger and thirst, in fastings often, in cold and nakedness—besides the other things, what comes upon me daily:

---

a. **too weak for that.** Paul's sarcasm reached its peak as he noted that he was "too weak" to abuse the Corinthians as the false apostles had done.

b. **Are they Hebrews . . . Israelites . . . the seed of Abraham?** To each of these questions Paul replied simply and powerfully, "so am I" (cf. Phil. 3:5).

d. **Are they ministers of Christ?** Paul had already emphatically denied that they were; however, some of the Corinthians still believed they were. Paul accepted that belief for the sake of argument, then went on to show that his ministry was in every way superior to the false apostles' so-called "ministry."

e. **I speak as a fool.** Once again Paul expressed his extreme distaste for the boasting the Corinthians had forced him into.

f. **in labors . . . in deaths often.** A general summation of Paul's sufferings for the gospel; the next few verses give specific examples, many of which are not found in Acts. Paul was often in danger of death (Acts 9:23, 29; 14:5, 19, 20; 17:5; 21:30–32).

g. **forty stripes minus one.** Deuteronomy 25:1–3 set 40 as the maximum number that could legally be administered; in Paul's day the Jews reduced that number by one to avoid accidentally going over the maximum. Jesus warned that His followers would receive such beatings (Matt. 10:17).

h. **beaten with rods.** Refers to Roman beatings with flexible sticks tied together (cf. Acts 16:22, 23).

i. **once I was stoned.** At Lystra (Acts 14:19, 20).

j. **three times I was shipwrecked.** Not including the shipwreck on his journey as a prisoner to Rome (Acts 27), which had not yet taken place. Paul had been on several sea voyages up to this time (cf. Acts 9:30; 11:25, 26; 13:4, 13; 14:25, 26; 16:11; 17:14, 15; 18:18, 21), giving ample opportunity for the 3 shipwrecks to have occurred.

k. **a night and a day I have been in the deep.** At least one of the shipwrecks was so severe that Paul spent an entire day floating on the wreckage, waiting to be rescued.

l. **in perils.** Those connected with his frequent travels. "Waters" (rivers) and "robbers" posed a serious danger to travelers in the ancient world. Paul's journey from Perga to Pisidian Antioch (Acts 13:14), for example, required him to travel through the robber-infested Taurus Mountains, and to cross two dangerous, flood-prone rivers. Paul was frequently in danger from his "own countrymen" (Acts 9:23, 29; 13:45; 14:2, 19; 17:5; 18:6, 12–16; 20:3, 19; 21:27–32) and, less often, from "Gentiles" (Acts 16:16–40; 19:23—20:1).

m. **false brethren.** Those who appeared to be Christians, but were not, such as the false apostles (2 Cor. 11:13) and the Judaizers (Gal. 2:4).

my ᵃdeep concern for all the churches. Who is weak, and I am not weak? Who is made to stumble, and I do not burn with indignation?

ᵇIf I must boast, I will boast in the things which concern my infirmity. The God and Father of our Lord Jesus Christ, who is blessed forever, knows that ᶜI am not lying. In Damascus the governor, under Aretas the king, was guarding the city of the Damascenes with a garrison, desiring to arrest me; but I was ᵈlet down in a basket through a window in the wall, and escaped from his hands.

127. PAUL'S APOSTOLIC CREDENTIALS
2 Cor. 12:1–18

It is doubtless ᵉnot profitable for me to boast. I will come to ᶠvisions and revelations of the Lord: I know ᵍa man in Christ who ʰfourteen years ago—

---

a. **deep concern.** Far worse than the occasional physical suffering Paul endured was the constant, daily burden of concern for the churches that he felt. Those who were "weak" (cf. Rom. 14; 1 Cor. 8) in faith, or were "made to stumble" into sin caused him intense emotional pain. Cf. 1 Thess. 5:14.

b. **I will boast . . . my infirmity.** To do so magnified God's power at work in him (cf. 2 Cor. 4:7; Col. 1:29; 2 Tim. 2:20, 21).

c. **I am not lying.** Realizing how incredible the list of his sufferings must have seemed, Paul called on God to witness that he was telling the truth (cf. 2 Cor. 1:23; Rom. 1:9; 9:1; Gal. 1:20; 1 Thess. 2:5, 10; 1 Tim. 2:7)—that these things really happened.

d. **let down in a basket.** Paul related his humiliating escape from Damascus (cf. Acts 9:23–25) as the crowning example of the weakness and infirmity in which he boasted (2 Cor. 11:30). The Acts narrative names the hostile Jews as those who sought Paul's life, whereas Paul here mentioned the governor under the Nabatean Arab king Aretas (9 B.C.–A.D. 40) as the one who sought him. Evidently the Jews stirred up the secular authorities against him, as they were later to do repeatedly in Acts (cf. Acts 13:50; 14:2; 17:13).

e. **not profitable.** Paul continued, reluctantly, with his boasting (see 2 Cor. 11:1). Though it was "not profitable," since it could tempt his own flesh to be proud, the Corinthians' fascination with the alleged visions and revelations of the false apostles left him little choice.

f. **visions and revelations.** Six of Paul's visions are recorded in Acts (9:12; 16:9, 10; 18:9; 22:17, 18; 23:11; 27:23, 24), and his letters speak of revelations he had received (cf. Gal. 1:12; 2:2; Eph. 3:3).

g. **a man in Christ.** Though Paul's reluctance to boast caused him to refer to himself in the third person, the context makes it obvious that he was speaking about himself; relating the experience of another man would hardly have enhanced Paul's apostolic credentials. Also, Paul's thorn in the flesh afflicted him, not someone else (v. 7).

h. **fourteen years ago.** Since it took place 14 years before the writing of 2 Corinthians, the specific vision Paul relates cannot be identified with any incident recorded in Acts. It probably took place between his return to Tarsus from Jerusalem (Acts 9:30) and the start of his missionary journeys (Acts 13:1–3).

whether in the body I do not know, or whether out of the body I do not know, God knows—such a one was ᵃcaught up to the third heaven. And I know such a man—ᵇwhether in the body or out of the body I do not know, God knows—how he was caught up into Paradise and heard ᶜinexpressible words, which it is not lawful for a man to utter. Of such a one I will boast; yet of myself I will not boast, except in my infirmities. For though I might desire to boast, I will not be a fool; for I will speak the truth. But I refrain, lest anyone should think of me above what he sees me to be or hears from me.

And lest I should be exalted above measure by the abundance of the revelations, ᵈa thorn in the flesh was given to me, a messenger of Satan to buffet me, ᵉlest I be exalted above measure. Concerning this thing ᶠI pleaded with the Lord three times that it might depart from me. And He said to

---

a. **caught up to the third heaven . . . caught up into Paradise.** Paul was not describing two separate visions; "the third heaven" and "Paradise" are the same place (cf. Rev. 2:7, which says the tree of life is in Paradise, with Rev. 22:14, which says it is in heaven). The first heaven is the earth's atmosphere (Gen. 8:2; Deut. 11:11; 1 Kin. 8:35); the second is interplanetary and interstellar space (Gen. 15:5; Ps. 8:3; Is. 13:10); and the third the abode of God (1 Kin. 8:30; 2 Chr. 30:27; Ps. 123:1).

b. **whether in . . . or . . . out of the body.** Paul was so overwhelmed by his heavenly vision that he did not know the precise details. However, whether he was caught up bodily into heaven (like Enoch, Gen. 5:24 and Elijah, 2 Kin. 2:11), or his spirit was temporarily separated from his body, was not important.

c. **inexpressible words . . . not lawful . . . to utter.** Because the words were for him alone, Paul was forbidden to repeat them, even if he could have expressed them coherently.

d. **a thorn in the flesh . . . a messenger of Satan.** This was sent to him by God, to keep him humble. As with Job, Satan was the immediate cause, but God was the ultimate cause. Paul's use of the word "messenger" (Gr., *angellos*, or angel) from Satan suggests the "thorn in the flesh" (lit. "a stake for the flesh") was a demon person, not a physical illness. Of the 188 uses of the Gr. word, *angellos*, in the NT, at least 180 are in reference to angels. This angel was from Satan, a demon afflicting Paul. Possibly, the best explanation for this demon was that he was indwelling the ring leader of the Corinthian conspiracy, the leader of the false apostles. Through them he was tearing up Paul's beloved church and thus driving a painful stake through Paul. Further support for this view comes from the context of 2 Cor. 10–13, which is one of fighting adversaries (the false prophets). The verb translated "buffet" always refers to ill treatment from other people (Matt. 26:67; Mark 14:65; 1 Cor. 4:11; 1 Pet. 2:20). Finally, the OT describes Israel's personal opponents as thorns (Num. 33:55; Josh. 23:13; Judg. 2:3; Ezek. 28:24).

e. **lest I be exalted above measure.** The assault was painful, but purposeful. God was allowing Satan to bring this severe trouble in the church for the purpose of humbling Paul who, having had so many revelations, including a trip to heaven and back, would have been proud. The demonized false apostle attacking his work in Corinth was the stake being driven through his otherwise proud flesh.

f. **I pleaded . . . three times.** Paul, longing for relief from this painful hindrance to his ministry, went to his Lord, begging Him (the use of the definite article with "Lord" shows Paul's prayer was directed to Jesus) to remove it. The demons are only subject to His authority. The threefold repetition of Paul's request parallels that of Jesus in Gethsemane (Mark 14:32–41). Both Paul and Jesus had their requests denied, but were granted grace to endure their ordeals.

me, ^a"My grace is sufficient for you, for ^bMy strength is made perfect in weakness." Therefore most gladly I will rather boast in my infirmities, that the power of Christ may rest upon me. Therefore I take pleasure in infirmities, in reproaches, in needs, in persecutions, in distresses, for Christ's sake. For when I am weak, then I am strong.

I have become a fool in boasting; you have compelled me. For I ought to have been commended by you; for in nothing was I behind the most eminent apostles, though I am nothing. Truly ^cthe signs of an apostle were accomplished among you with all perseverance, in signs and wonders and mighty deeds. For what is it in which you were inferior to other churches, except that I myself was not burdensome to you? ^dForgive me this wrong!

^eNow for the third time I am ready to come to you. And I will ^fnot be burdensome to you; for ^gI do not seek yours, but you. For the ^hchildren ought not to lay up for the parents, but the parents for the children. And I will very gladly spend and ⁱbe spent for your souls; though the more abundantly I love you, the less I am loved.

But be that as it may, I did not burden you. Nevertheless, being crafty, I caught you by cunning! Did I take advantage of you by any of ^jthose whom

---

a. **My grace is sufficient for you.** The present tense of the verb translated "is sufficient" reveals the constant availability of divine grace. God would not remove the thorn, as Paul had requested, but would continually supply him with grace to endure it (cf. 1 Cor. 15:10; Phil. 4:13; Col. 1:29).

b. **My strength is made perfect in weakness.** Cf. 2 Cor. 4:7–11. The weaker the human instrument, the more clearly God's grace shines forth.

c. **the signs of an apostle.** Including, but not limited to, "signs and wonders and mighty deeds" (the miracle of the Corinthians' salvation was also a mark of Paul's apostleship, 1 Cor. 9:2). The purpose of miraculous signs was to authenticate the apostles as God's messengers (cf. Acts 2:22, 43; 4:30; 5:12; 14:3; Rom. 15:18, 19; Heb. 2:3, 4).

d. **Forgive me.** Paul had not slighted the Corinthians except by refusing to be a burden (see 2 Cor. 11:7). With a touch of irony, he begged their forgiveness for that "wrong."

e. **for the third time.** The first was the visit recorded in Acts 18; the second was the "painful visit" (cf. 2 Cor. 2:1).

f. **not be burdensome.** On his upcoming visit, Paul wished to continue his practice of refusing to accept support from the Corinthians.

g. **I do not seek yours, but you.** Paul sought the Corinthians (cf. 2 Cor. 6:11–13; 7:2, 3), not their money.

h. **children . . . parents . . . parents . . . children.** To reinforce his point, Paul cited the axiomatic truth that parents are financially responsible for their children, not children (when they are young, cf. 1 Tim. 5:4) for their parents.

i. **be spent.** Far from seeking to take from the Corinthians, Paul sought to give. The verb translated "spend" refers to spending money, and probably describes Paul's willingness to work to support himself while in Corinth (Acts 18:3). "Be spent" describes Paul's willingness to give of himself—even to the point of sacrificing his life.

j. **those whom I sent you.** Although it was obvious to all that Paul had not personally

I sent to you? I urged Titus, and sent our brother with him. Did Titus take advantage of you? Did we not walk in the same spirit? Did we not walk in the same steps?

128. FINAL WARNINGS

2 Cor. 12:19—13:10

Again, do you think that we excuse ourselves to you? [a]We speak before God in Christ. But we do all things, beloved, for your [b]edification. For I fear lest, when I come, I shall not find you such as I wish, and that I shall be found by you such as you do not wish; lest there be contentions, jealousies, outbursts of wrath, selfish ambitions, backbitings, whisperings, conceits, tumults; lest, when I come again, my God will humble me among you, and I shall mourn for many who have sinned before and have not repented of the uncleanness, fornication, and lewdness which they have practiced.

This will be the [c]third time I am coming to you. "By the mouth of [d]two or three witnesses every word shall be established." I have told you before, and

---

taken advantage of the Corinthians, his opponents circulated an even more vicious rumor—that he was using craftiness and cunning to deceive the Corinthians (cf. 2 Cor. 4:2). Specifically, the false apostles accused Paul of sending his assistants to collect the Jerusalem offering from the Corinthians while intending to keep some of it for himself. Thus, according to his opponents, Paul was both a deceitful hypocrite (because he really did take money from the Corinthians after all, despite his words in 2 Cor. 12:14, 15) and a thief. This charge was all the more painful to Paul because it impugned the character of his friends. Outraged that the Corinthians could believe such ridiculous lies, Paul pointed out that his associates did not take advantage of the Corinthians during their earlier visits regarding the collection (2 Cor. 8:6, 16–22). The simple truth was that neither Paul nor his representatives had in any way defrauded the Corinthians.

a. **We speak before God.** Lest the Corinthians view themselves as judges before whom Paul was on trial, the apostle quickly set them straight: only God was his judge (cf. 2 Cor. 5:10; 1 Cor. 4:3–5). Paul sought to edify the Corinthians, not exonerate himself.

b. **edification.** When he visited them, Paul did not want to find the Corinthians in the same sorry spiritual condition as on his last visit (the "painful visit," 2 Cor. 2:1). If he found that they were not what he wished (i.e., still practicing the sins he listed), they would find him not as they wished—he would have had to discipline them (cf. 2 Cor. 13:2). To find the Corinthians still living in unrepentant sin would both humiliate and sadden Paul. This warning (and the one in 2 Cor. 13:2) was designed to prevent that from happening.

c. **the third time.** See 2 Cor. 12:14.

d. **two or three witnesses.** Not a reference to Paul's 3 visits to Corinth, since he could be only one witness no matter how many visits he made. Paul informed the Corinthians that he would deal biblically (cf. Deut. 19:15; Matt. 18:16; John 8:17; Heb. 10:28) with any sin he found in Corinth.

foretell as if I were present the second time, and now being absent I write to those who have sinned before, and to all the rest, that if I come again I will not spare—since you seek ᵃa proof of Christ speaking in me, ᵇwho is not weak toward you, but mighty in you. For though He was crucified in weakness, yet He lives by the power of God. For we also are weak in Him, but we shall live with Him by the power of God toward you.

Examine ᶜyourselves as to whether you are in the faith. Test yourselves. Do you not know yourselves, that Jesus Christ is in you?—unless indeed you are ᵈdisqualified. But I trust that you will know that we are not disqualified.

Now I pray to God that you do no evil, not that we should appear approved, but that you should ᵉdo what is honorable, though we may seem disqualified. For we can do ᶠnothing against the truth, but for the truth. For we are glad when we are weak and you are strong. And this also we pray, that you may be made complete. Therefore I write these things being absent, lest being present I should use sharpness, according to the authority which the Lord has given me for edification and not for destruction.

---

a. **a proof of Christ speaking in me.** Those Corinthians still seeking proof that Paul was a genuine apostle would have it when he arrived. They may have gotten more than they bargained for, however, for Paul was going to use his apostolic authority and power to deal with any sin and rebellion he found there (see 2 Cor. 12:21).

b. **who is not weak.** Christ's power was to be revealed through Paul against the sinning Corinthians (cf. 1 Cor. 11:30–32). By rebelling against Christ's chosen apostle (2 Cor. 1:1), they were rebelling against Him.

c. **Examine yourselves.** The Gr. grammar places great emphasis on the pronouns "yourselves" and "you." Paul turned the tables on his accusers; instead of presuming to evaluate his apostleship, they needed to test the genuineness of their faith (cf. James 2:14–26). He pointed out the incongruity of the Corinthians' believing (as they did) that their faith was genuine and his apostleship false. Paul was their spiritual father (1 Cor. 4:15); if his apostleship was counterfeit, so was their faith. The genuineness of their salvation was proof of the genuineness of his apostleship.

d. **disqualified.** Lit. "not approved." Here it referred to the absence of genuine saving faith.

e. **do what is honorable.** Paul's deepest longing was for his spiritual children to lead godly lives (cf. 2 Cor. 7:1)—even if they persisted in doubting him. Paul was even willing to appear "disqualified," as long as the Corinthians turned from their sin (cf. Rom. 9:3).

f. **nothing against the truth.** Lest anyone think his reference to being disqualified was an admission of wrongdoing on his part, Paul hastened to add that he had not violated "the truth" of the gospel. The apostle may also have meant that he needed to take no action against the Corinthians if he found them living according to "the truth." In that case, he would rejoice in his "weakness" (that is, his lack of opportunity to exercise his apostolic power), because that would mean that the Corinthians were spiritually "strong."

129. BENEDICTION AND GREETINGS
2 Cor. 13:11—14

Finally, brethren, farewell. Become complete. Be of good comfort, be of one mind, live in peace; and the God of love and peace will be with you.

Greet one another with a holy kiss.

All the saints greet you.

The grace of the Lord Jesus Christ, and the love of God, and the communion of the Holy Spirit be with you all. Amen.

130. THREE MONTHS IN GREECE
Acts 20:2—3a

[a]Now when he had gone over that region [of Macedonia] and encouraged them with many words, he came to Greece and stayed [b]three months.

131. PAUL WRITES A LETTER TO THE ROMANS
Introduction to Romans

This epistle's name comes from its original recipients: the members of the church in Rome, the capital of the Roman Empire (Rom. 1:7).

Author and Date

No one disputes that the apostle Paul wrote Romans. Like his namesake, Israel's first king (Saul was Paul's Hebrew name; Paul his Greek name), Paul was from the tribe of Benjamin (Phil. 3:5). He was also a Roman citizen (Acts 16:37; 22:25). Paul was born about the time of Christ's birth, in Tarsus (Acts 9:11), an important city (Acts 21:39) in the Roman province of Cilicia,

---

a. **he had gone over that region.** Macedonia and Achaia.

b. **three months.** Most or all of it were likely spent in Corinth.

located in Asia Minor (modern Turkey). He spent much of his early life in Jerusalem as a student of the celebrated rabbi Gamaliel (Acts 22:3). Like his father before him, Paul was a Pharisee (Acts 23:6), a member of the strictest Jewish sect (cf. Phil. 3:5).

Miraculously converted while on his way to Damascus (ca. A.D. 33–34) to arrest Christians in that city, Paul immediately began proclaiming the gospel message (Acts 9:20). After narrowly escaping from Damascus with his life (Acts 9:23–25; 2 Cor. 11:32, 33), Paul spent 3 years in Nabatean Arabia, south and east of the Dead Sea (Gal. 1:17, 18). During that time, he received much of his doctrine as direct revelation from the Lord (Gal. 1:11, 12).

More than any other individual, Paul was responsible for the spread of Christianity throughout the Roman Empire. He made 3 missionary journeys through much of the Mediterranean world, tirelessly preaching the gospel he had once sought to destroy (Acts 26:9). After he returned to Jerusalem bearing an offering for the needy in the church there, he was falsely accused by some Jews (Acts 21:27–29), savagely beaten by an angry mob (Acts 21:30, 31), and arrested by the Romans. Though two Roman governors, Felix and Festus, as well as Herod Agrippa, did not find him guilty of any crime, pressure from the Jewish leaders kept Paul in Roman custody. After two years, the apostle exercised his right as a Roman citizen and appealed his case to Caesar. After a harrowing trip (Acts 27, 28), including a violent, two-week storm at sea that culminated in a shipwreck, Paul reached Rome. Eventually released for a brief period of ministry, he was arrested again and suffered martyrdom at Rome in ca. A.D. 65–67 (cf. 2 Tim. 4:6).

Though physically unimpressive (cf. 2 Cor. 10:10; Gal. 4:14), Paul possessed an inner strength granted him through the Holy Spirit's power (Phil. 4:13). The grace of God proved sufficient to provide for his every need (2 Cor. 12:9, 10), enabling this noble servant of Christ to successfully finish his spiritual race (2 Tim. 4:7).

Paul wrote Romans from Corinth, as the references to Phoebe (Rom. 16:1, Cenchrea was Corinth's port), Gaius (Rom. 16:23), and Erastus (Rom. 16:23)—all of whom were associated with Corinth—indicate. The apostle wrote the letter toward the close of his third missionary journey (most likely in A.D. 56), as he prepared to leave for Palestine with an offering for the poor believers in the Jerusalem church (Rom. 15:25). Phoebe was given the great responsibility of delivering this letter to the Roman believers (16:1, 2).

Background and Setting

Rome was the capital and most important city of the Roman Empire. It was founded in 753 B.C., but is not mentioned in Scripture until NT times. Rome is located along the banks of the Tiber River, about 15 miles from the Mediterranean Sea. Until an artificial harbor was built at nearby Ostia, Rome's main harbor was Puteoli, some 150 miles away (see Acts 28:13). In Paul's day, the city had a population of over one million people, many of whom were slaves. Rome boasted magnificent buildings, such as the Emperor's palace, the Circus Maximus, and the Forum, but its beauty was marred by the slums in which so many lived. According to tradition, Paul was martyred outside Rome on the Ostian Way during Nero's reign (A.D. 54–68).

Some of those converted on the Day of Pentecost probably founded the church at Rome (cf. Acts 2:10). Paul had long sought to visit the Roman church, but had been prevented from doing so (Rom. 1:13). In God's providence, Paul's inability to visit Rome gave the world this inspired masterpiece of gospel doctrine.

Paul's primary purpose in writing Romans was to teach the great truths of the gospel of grace to believers who had never received apostolic instruction. The letter also introduced him to a church where he was personally unknown, but hoped to visit soon for several important reasons: to edify the believers (1:11); to preach the gospel (1:15); and to get to know the Roman Christians, so they could encourage him (1:12; 15:32), better pray for him (15:30), and help him with his planned ministry in Spain (15:28).

Unlike some of Paul's other epistles (e.g., 1, 2 Cor., Gal.), his purpose for writing was not to correct aberrant theology or rebuke ungodly living. The Roman church was doctrinally sound, but, like all churches, it was in need of the rich doctrinal and practical instruction this letter provides.

Historical and Theological Themes

Since Romans is primarily a work of doctrine, it contains little historical material. Paul does use such familiar OT figures as Abraham (chap. 4), David (4:6–8), Adam (5:12–21), Sarah (9:9), Rebekah (9:10), Jacob and Esau

(9:10–13), and Pharaoh (9:17) as illustrations. He also recounts some of Israel's history (chaps. 9–11). Chapter 16 provides insightful glimpses into the nature and character of the first-century church and its members.

The overarching theme of Romans is the righteousness that comes from God: the glorious truth that God justifies guilty, condemned sinners by grace alone through faith in Christ alone. Chapters 1–11 present the theological truths of that doctrine, while chaps. 12–16 detail its practical outworking in the lives of individual believers and the life of the whole church. Some specific theological topics include principles of spiritual leadership (1:8–15); God's wrath against sinful mankind (1:18–32); principles of divine judgment (2:1–16); the universality of sin (3:9–20); an exposition and defense of justification by faith alone (3:21—4:25); the security of salvation (5:1–11); the transference of Adam's sin (5:12–21); sanctification (chaps. 6–8); sovereign election (chap. 9); God's plan for Israel (chap. 11); spiritual gifts and practical godliness (chap. 12); the believer's responsibility to human government (chap. 13); and principles of Christian liberty (14:1—15:12).

Interpretive Challenges

As the preeminent doctrinal work in the NT, Romans naturally contains a number of difficult passages. Paul's discussion of the perpetuation of Adam's sin (5:12–21) is one of the deepest, most profound theological passages in all of Scripture. The nature of mankind's union with Adam, and how his sin was transferred to the human race has always been the subject of intense debate. Bible students also disagree on whether 7:7–25 describes Paul's experience as a believer or unbeliever, or is a literary device not intended to be autobiographical at all. The closely related doctrines of election (8:28–30) and the sovereignty of God (9:6–29) have confused many believers. Others question whether chaps. 9–11 teach that God has a future plan for the nation of Israel. Some have ignored Paul's teaching on the believer's obedience to human government (13:1–7) in the name of Christian activism, while others have used it to defend slavish obedience to totalitarian regimes.

All of these and more interpretive challenges are addressed in the notes to the respective passages.

132. Greetings and Theme

Rom. 1:1–17

Paul, a ^abondservant of Jesus Christ, called to be an apostle, separated to the ^bgospel of God ^cwhich He promised before through His prophets in the Holy Scriptures, concerning His Son Jesus Christ our Lord, who was born of the ^dseed of David according to the flesh, ^eand declared to be the ^fSon of God with power according to the ^gSpirit of holiness, by the ^hresurrection from the

---

a. **bondservant.** *Doulos*, the common NT word for servant. Although in Gr. culture it is most often referred to the involuntary, permanent service of a slave, Paul elevates this word by using it in its Heb. sense to describe a servant who willingly commits himself to serve a master he loves and respects (Ex. 21:5, 6; Gal. 1:10; Titus 1:1; cf. Gen. 26:24; Num. 12:7; 2 Sam. 7:5; Is. 53:11).

b. **gospel of God.** Used in its verb and noun forms some 60 times in this epistle, the Gr. word for this phrase means "good news" (see Mark 1:1). Rome incorporated it into its emperor worship. The town herald used this word to begin important favorable announcements about the emperor—such as the birth of a son. But Paul's good news is not from the emperor but "of God"; it originated with Him. Its message that God will forgive sins, deliver from sin's power, and give eternal hope (Rom. 1:16; cf. 1 Cor. 15:1–4) comes not only as a gracious offer, but also as a command to be obeyed (Rom. 10:16). Paul was consumed with this message (1 Cor. 9:23).

c. **which He promised before.** Paul's Jewish antagonists accused him of preaching a revolutionary new message unrelated to Judaism (Acts 21:28). But the OT is replete with prophecies concerning Christ and the gospel (1 Pet. 1:10–12; cf. Matt. 5:17; Heb. 1:1).

d. **seed of David.** The OT had prophesied that Messiah would be in the lineage of David (2 Sam. 7:12, 13; Ps. 89:3, 4, 19, 24; Is. 11:1–5; Jer. 23:5, 6). Both Mary, Jesus' mother (Luke 3:23, 31), and Joseph, his legal father (Matt. 1:6, 16; Luke 1:27), were descendants of David. John makes believing that Christ has come in the flesh a crucial test of orthodoxy (1 John 4:2, 3). Because He is fully human—as well as fully God—He can serve as man's substitute (John 1:29; 2 Cor. 5:21) and as a sympathetic High-Priest (Heb. 4:15, 16).

e. **declared.** The Gr. word, from which the English word "horizon" comes, means "to distinguish." Just as the horizon serves as a clear demarcation line, dividing earth and sky, the resurrection of Jesus Christ clearly divides Him from the rest of humanity, providing irrefutable evidence that He is the Son of God (see Rom. 10:9).

f. **Son of God.** This title, used nearly 30 times in the gospels, identifies Jesus Christ as the same in essence as God. See John 1:34, 49; 10:36; 11:27; 19:7. (cf. Heb. 1:5; 2 Sam. 7:14). The resurrection clearly declared that Jesus was deity, the expression of God Himself in human form. While He was eternally the Son in anticipation of His incarnation, it was when He entered the world in incarnation that He was declared to all the world as the Son of God and took on the role of submission to the Father (See Ps. 2:7; Heb. 1:5, 6).

g. **Spirit of holiness.** In His incarnation, Christ voluntarily submitted Himself to do the will of the Father only through the direction, agency, and power of the Holy Spirit (Matt. 3:16; Luke 4:1; John 3:34; see Acts 1:2).

h. **resurrection from the dead.** His victory over death was the supreme demonstration and most conclusive evidence that He is God the Son (see Rom. 10:9; cf. Acts 13:29–33; 1 Cor. 15:14–17).

dead. Through Him we have received ^agrace and ^bapostleship for ^cobedience to the faith among all nations for His name, among whom you also are the ^dcalled of Jesus Christ;

To all who are in Rome, ^ebeloved of God, called to be saints:

Grace to you and peace from God our Father and the Lord Jesus Christ.

First, I thank my God through Jesus Christ for you all, that your faith is spoken of throughout the whole world. ^fFor God is my witness, whom I serve with my spirit in the gospel of His Son, that without ceasing I make mention of you always in my prayers, making request if, by some means, now at last I may find a way in the will of God to come to you. For I long to see you, that I may impart to you some ^gspiritual gift, so that you may be established—that is, that I may be encouraged together with you by the mutual faith both of you and me.

Now I do not want you to be unaware, brethren, that I often planned to come to you (but was hindered until now), that I might have some ^hfruit

---

a. **grace.** The unmerited favor which God shows guilty sinners. This is the book's first reference to the most crucial part of the gospel message: salvation is a gift from God wholly separate from any human effort or achievement (Rom. 3:24, 27; 4:1–5; 5:20, 21; see Eph. 2:8, 9).

b. **apostleship.** Although the term "apostle" refers to the 12 in a unique way (see Rom. 1:1), in a broader and less official sense it can describe anyone whom God has sent with the message of salvation (cf. Acts 14:14; Rom. 16:7; Heb. 3:1).

c. **obedience to the faith.** True saving faith always produces obedience and submission to the Lordship of Jesus Christ (Rom. 16:19, 26; cf. 10:9, 10; cf. Matt. 7:13, 14, 22–27; James 2:17–20).

d. **called.** See Rom. 1:7. Always in the NT epistles the "call" of God refers to God's effectual call of elect sinners to salvation (cf. Rom. 8:28–30), rather than the general call to all men to believe (cf. Matt. 20:16).

e. **beloved of God, called . . . saints.** The Gr. text records these as 3 separate privileges: 1) God has set His love on His own (Rom. 5:5; 8:35; Eph. 1:6; 2:4, 5; 1 John 3:1); 2) He has extended to them not only the general, external invitation to believe the gospel (Is. 45:22; 55:6; Ezek. 33:11; Matt. 11:28; John 7:37; Rev. 22:17), but His effectual calling—or His drawing to Himself all those He has chosen for salvation (Rom. 8:30; 2 Thess. 2:13, 14; 2 Tim. 1:9; see John 6:44); and 3) God has set believers apart from sin unto Himself, so that they are holy ones (1 Cor. 3:16, 17; 1 Pet. 2:5, 9).

f. **serve with my spirit.** In the NT, this Gr. word for "serve" always refers to religious service, and is sometimes translated "worship." Paul had seen the shallow, hypocritical religion of the Pharisees and the superstitious hedonism of pagan idolatry. His spiritual service (see Rom. 12:1), however, did not result from abject fear or legal obligation, but was genuine and sincere (cf. Phil. 3:3; 2 Tim. 1:3; 2:22).

g. **spiritual gift.** The Gr. word translated "gift" is charisma, which means a "gift of grace"—a spiritual enablement whose source is the Spirit of God. Romans uses this same term to describe: 1) Christ Himself (5:15, 16); 2) general blessings from God (11:29; cf. 1 Tim. 6:17); and 3) specific spiritual gifts given to members of the body to minister to the whole (Rom. 12:6–8; cf. 1 Cor. 12:1–31; 1 Pet. 4:10, 11). Paul probably intends to encompass all 3.

h. **fruit.** Scripture catalogs 3 kinds of spiritual fruit: 1) spiritual attitudes that characterize a Spirit-led believer (Gal. 5:22, 23); 2) righteous actions (Rom. 6:22; Phil. 4:16, 17; Heb. 13:15); and 3) new converts (Rom. 16:5). In this context, Paul is probably referring to the third one—a desire that was eventually realized during his imprisonment in Rome (Phil. 4:22).

among you also, just as among the other Gentiles. ªI am a debtor both to Greeks and to ᵇbarbarians, both to wise and to unwise. So, as much as is in me, I am ready to preach the gospel to you who are in Rome also.

For ᶜI am not ashamed of the gospel of Christ, for it is the ᵈpower of God to ᵉsalvation for everyone who ᶠbelieves, for the ᵍJew first and also for the Greek. ʰFor

a. **Greeks.** People of many different nationalities who had embraced the Gr. language, culture, and education. They were the sophisticated elite of Paul's day. Because of their deep interest in Greek philosophy, they were considered "wise." Because of this prevalence of Greek culture, Paul sometimes used this word to describe all Gentiles (cf. Rom. 3:9).

b. **barbarians.** A derisive term coined by the Greeks for all who had not been trained in Gr. language and culture. When someone spoke in another language, it sounded to the Greeks like "bar-bar-bar," or unintelligible chatter. Although in the narrowest sense "barbarian" referred to the uncultured, uneducated masses, it was often used to describe all non-Greeks—the unwise of the world. Paul's point is that God is no respecter of persons—the gospel must reach both the world's elite and its outcasts (cf. John 4:4–42; James 2:1–9).

c. **I am not ashamed.** He had been imprisoned in Philippi (Acts 16:23, 24), chased out of Thessalonica (Acts 17:10), smuggled out of Berea (Acts 17:14), laughed at in Athens (Acts 17:32), regarded as a fool in Corinth (1 Cor. 1:18, 23), and stoned in Galatia (Acts 14:19), but Paul remained eager to preach the gospel in Rome—the seat of contemporary political power and pagan religion. Neither ridicule, criticism, nor physical persecution could curb his boldness. See 2 Cor. 4:5–18; 11:23–28; 12:9, 10.

d. **power.** The Eng. word "dynamite" comes from this Gr. word. Although the message may sound foolish to some (1 Cor. 1:18), the gospel is effective because it carries with it the omnipotence of God (cf. Ex. 15:6; Deut. 32:39; Job 9:4; Pss. 33:8, 9; 89:13; 106:8, 9; Is. 26:4; 43:13; Jer. 10:12; 27:5; Matt. 28:18; Rom. 9:21). Only God's power is able to overcome man's sinful nature and give him new life (Rom. 5:6; 8:3; John 1:12; 1 Cor. 1:18, 23–25; 2:1–4; 4:20; 1 Pet. 1:23).

e. **salvation.** Used 5 times in Romans (the verb form occurs 8 times), this key word basically means "deliverance" or "rescue." The power of the gospel delivers people from lostness (Matt. 18:11), from the wrath of God (Rom. 5:9), from willful spiritual ignorance (Hos. 4:6; 2 Thess. 1:8), from evil self-indulgence (Luke 14:26), and from the darkness of false religion (Col. 1:13; 1 Pet. 2:9). It rescues them from the ultimate penalty of their sin, i.e., eternal separation from God and eternal punishment (see Rev. 20:6).

f. **believes.** To trust, rely on, or have faith in. When used of salvation, this word usually occurs in the present tense ("is believing") which stresses that faith is not simply a one-time event, but an ongoing condition. True saving faith is supernatural, a gracious gift of God that He produces in the heart (see Eph. 2:8) and is the only means by which a person can appropriate true righteousness (cf. Rom. 3:22, 25; 4:5, 13, 20; 5:1; see 4:1–25). Saving faith consists of 3 elements: 1) mental: the mind understands the gospel and the truth about Christ (Rom. 10:14–17); 2) emotional: one embraces the truthfulness of those facts with sorrow over sin and joy over God's mercy and grace (Rom. 6:17; 15:13); and 3) volitional: the sinner submits his will to Christ and trusts in Him alone as the only hope of salvation (see Rom. 10:9). Genuine faith will always produce authentic obedience (see Rom. 4:3; cf. John 8:31; 14:23, 24).

g. **Jew first.** God chose Israel to be His witness nation (Ex. 19:6) and gave her distinct privileges (Rom. 3:2; 9:4, 5). Christ's ministry was first to Israel (Matt. 15:24), and it was through Israel that salvation was to come to the world (John 4:22; cf. 8:46).

h. **righteousness of God.** Better translated, "righteousness from God." A major theme of the book, appearing over 30 times in one form or another, righteousness is the state or condition of perfectly conforming to God's perfect law and holy character. Other terms from the same Gr. root also occur some 30 times and are usually translated "justified," "justification" or similarly. Only God is inherently righteous (Deut. 32:4; Job 9:2; Pss. 11:7; 116:5; John 17:25; Rom. 3:10; 1 John 2:1; Rev. 16:5), and man falls woefully short of the divine standard of moral perfection (Rom. 3:23; Matt. 5:48). But the gospel reveals that on the basis of faith—and faith alone—God will impute His righteousness to ungodly sinners (see Rom. 3:21–24; 4:5; 2 Cor. 5:21; Phil. 3:8, 9).

in it the righteousness of God is revealed ªfrom faith to faith; as it is written, ᵇ"The just shall live by faith."

133. THE UNRIGHTEOUSNESS OF THE GENTILES
Rom. 1:18–32

ᶜFor the ᵈwrath of God ᵉis revealed from heaven against all ᶠungodliness and ᵍunrighteousness of men, who ʰsuppress the truth in unrighteousness, because

---

a. from faith to faith. This may be a parallel expression to "everyone who believes" (Rom. 1:16), as if Paul were singling out the faith of each individual believer—from one person's faith to another's faith to another's and so on. Or perhaps Paul's point is that the righteousness from God is completely on the basis of faith from beginning to end.

b. The just shall live by faith. See Hab. 2:4. Paul intends to prove that it has always been God's way to justify sinners by grace on the basis of faith alone. God established Abraham as a pattern of faith (Rom. 4:22–25; Gal. 3:6, 7) and thus calls him the father of all who believe (4:11, 16). Elsewhere, Paul uses this same phrase to argue that no one has ever been declared righteous before God except by faith alone (Gal. 3:11) and that true faith will demonstrate itself in action (Phil. 2:12, 13). This expression emphasizes that true faith is not a single event, but a way of life—it endures. That endurance is called the perseverance of the saints (cf. Col. 1:22, 23; Heb. 3:12–14). One central theme of the story of Job is that no matter what Satan does, saving faith cannot be destroyed.

c. After introducing the righteousness which comes from God (1:17), a theme he develops at length (Rom. 3:21—5:21), Paul presents the overwhelming evidence of man's sinfulness, underscoring how desperately he needs this righteousness that only God can provide. He presents God's case against the irreligious, immoral pagan (Rom. 1:18–32; the Gentiles) the religious, outwardly moral person (Rom. 2:1—3:8; the Jews); and concludes by showing that all men alike deserve God's judgment (3:9–20).

is manifest in them. God has sovereignly planted evidence of His existence in the very nature of man by reason and moral law (Rom. 1:20, 21, 28, 32; 2:15).

d. wrath of God. This is not an impulsive outburst of anger aimed capriciously at people whom God does not like. It is the settled, determined response of a righteous God against sin (cf. Pss. 2:5, 12; 45:7; 75:8; 76:6, 7; 78:49–51; 90:7–9; Is. 51:17; Jer. 25:15, 16; John 3:36; Rom. 9:22; Eph. 5:6; Col. 3:5, 6).

e. is revealed. More accurately, "is constantly revealed." The word essentially means "to uncover, make visible, or make known." God reveals His wrath in two ways: 1) indirectly, through the natural consequences of violating His universal moral law, and 2) directly through His personal intervention (the OT record—from the sentence passed on Adam and Eve to the worldwide flood, from the fire and brimstone that leveled Sodom to the Babylonian captivity—clearly displays this kind of intervention). The most graphic revelation of God's holy wrath and hatred against sin was when He poured out divine judgment on His Son on the cross. God has various kinds of wrath: 1) eternal wrath, which is hell; 2) eschatological wrath, which is the final Day of the Lord; 3) cataclysmic wrath like the flood and the destruction of Sodom and Gomorrah; 4) consequential wrath, which is the principle of sowing and reaping; and 5) the wrath of abandonment, which is removing restraint and letting people go to their sins (for examples of this wrath, see Ps. 81:11, 12; Prov. 1:23–31; Hos. 4:17). Here, it is that fifth form, God's abandoning the wicked continually through history to pursue their sin and its consequences (Rom. 1:24–32).

f. ungodliness. This indicates a lack of reverence for, devotion to, and worship of the true God—a defective relationship with Him (cf. Jude 14, 15).

g. unrighteousness. This refers to the result of ungodliness: a lack of conformity in thought, word, and deed to the character and law of God (see Rom. 1:17).

h. suppress the truth. Although the evidence from conscience (Rom. 1:19; 2:14), creation

what may be known of God is manifest in them, for God has shown it to them. For since the creation of the world His invisible attributes are clearly seen, being understood ªby the things that are made, even ᵇHis eternal power and ᶜGodhead, so that they are without excuse, because, although they knew God, ᵈthey did not glorify Him as God, ᵉnor were thankful, but became futile in their thoughts, and their foolish ᶠhearts were darkened. ᵍProfessing to be wise, they became fools, and ʰchanged the glory of the incorruptible God into an image made like corruptible man—and birds and four-footed animals and creeping things.

Therefore ⁱGod also gave them up to uncleanness, in the lusts of their hearts, to dishonor their bodies among themselves, who exchanged the truth of God for the lie, and worshiped and served the creature rather than the Creator, who is blessed forever. Amen.

(Rom. 1:20), and God's Word is irrefutable, men choose to resist and oppose God's truth by holding fast to their sin (cf. Ps. 14:1; John 3:19, 20).

a. **by the things that are made.** The creation delivers a clear, unmistakable message about God's person (cf. Pss. 19:1–8; 94:9; Acts 14:15–17; 17:23–28).

b. **His eternal power.** The Creator, who made all that we see around us and constantly sustains it, must be a being of awesome power.

c. **Godhead.** That is, His divine nature, particularly His faithfulness (Gen. 8:21, 22), kindness, and graciousness (Acts 14:17).

d. **they did not glorify Him.** Man's chief end is to glorify God (Lev. 10:3; 1 Chr. 16:24–29; Ps. 148; Rom. 15:5, 6), and Scripture constantly demands it (Ps. 29:1, 2; 1 Cor. 10:31; Rev. 4:11). To glorify Him is to honor Him, to acknowledge His attributes, and to praise Him for His perfections (cf. Ex. 34:5–7). It is to recognize His glory and extol Him for it. Failing to give Him glory is man's greatest affront to his Creator (Acts 12:22, 23).

e. **nor were thankful.** They refused to acknowledge that every good thing they enjoyed came from God (Matt. 5:45; Acts 14:15–17; 1 Tim. 6:17; James 1:17).

f. **hearts were darkened.** When man rejects the truth, the darkness of spiritual falsehood replaces it (cf. John 3:19, 20).

g. **Professing to be wise, they became fools.** Man rationalizes his sin and proves his utter foolishness by devising and believing his own philosophies about God, the universe, himself (cf. Pss. 14:1; 53:1).

h. **changed the glory . . . into an image.** They substitute the worship of idols for the worship of the true God. Historians report that many ancient cultures did not originally have idols. For example, Persia (Herodotus; The Histories, 1:31), Rome (Varro in Augustine; The City of God, 4:31), even Greece and Egypt (Lucian; The Syrian Goddess, 34) had no idolatry at their founding. The fourth-century A.D. historian Eusebius reported that the oldest civilizations had no idols. The earliest biblical record of idolatry was among Abram's family in Ur (Josh. 24:2). The first commandment forbids it (Ex. 20:3–5), and the prophets continually ridiculed those who foolishly practiced it (Is. 44:9–17; cf. 2 Kin. 17:13–16). Although the false gods which men worship do not exist, demons often impersonate them (1 Cor. 10:20).

i. **God also gave them up.** This is a judicial term in Gr., used for handing over a prisoner to his sentence. When men consistently abandon God, He will abandon them (cf. Judg. 10:13; 2 Chr. 15:2; 24:20; Ps. 81:11, 12; Hos. 4:17; Matt. 15:14; Acts 7:38–42; 14:16). He accomplishes this 1) indirectly and immediately, by removing His restraint and allowing their sin to run its inevitable course, and 2) directly and eventually, by specific acts of divine judgment and punishment.

For this reason God gave them up to ªvile passions. For even their ᵇwomen exchanged the natural use for what is against nature. Likewise also the men, leaving the natural use of the woman, burned in their lust for one another, men with men committing what is shameful, and ᶜreceiving in themselves the penalty of their error which was due.

And even as they did not like to retain God in their knowledge, God gave them over to a ᵈdebased mind, to do those things which are not fitting; being filled with all unrighteousness, sexual immorality, wickedness, covetousness, maliciousness; full of envy, murder, strife, deceit, evil-mindedness; they are whisperers, backbiters, haters of God, violent, proud, boasters, inventors of evil things, disobedient to parents, undiscerning, untrustworthy, unloving, unforgiving, unmerciful; who, knowing the righteous judgment of God, that those who practice such things are deserving of death, not only do the same but also approve of those who practice them.

134. THE CULPABILITY OF THOSE UNDER THE LAW

Rom. 2:1–16

ᵉTherefore you are ᶠinexcusable, O man, whoever you are who judge, for in whatever you judge another you ᵍcondemn yourself; for you who judge

---

a. **vile passions.** Identified in Rom. 1:26, 27 as homosexuality, a sin roundly condemned in Scripture (Gen. 19; Lev. 18:22; 1 Cor. 6:9–11; cf. Gal. 5:19–21; Eph. 5:3–5; 1 Tim. 1:9, 10; Jude 7).

b. **women.** Rather than the normal Gr. term for women, this is a general word for female. Paul mentions women first to show the extent of debauchery under the wrath of abandonment, because in most cultures women are the last to be affected by moral collapse.

c. **receiving in themselves the penalty.** Here the law of sowing and reaping (Gal. 6:7, 8) takes effect, as Paul refers to the self-destructive nature of this sin, of which certain diseases like AIDS are frightening evidence.

d. **debased.** This translates a Gr. word that means "not passing the test." It was often used to describe useless, worthless metals, discarded because they contained too much impurity. God has tested man's minds and found them worthless and useless (cf. Jer. 6:30).

e. Having demonstrated the sinfulness of the immoral pagan (Rom. 1:18–32), Paul presents his case against the religious moralist—Jew or Gentile—by cataloging 6 principles that govern God's judgment: 1) knowledge (Rom. 2:1); 2) truth (vv. 2, 3); 3) guilt (vv. 4, 5); 4) deeds (vv. 6–10); 5) impartiality (vv. 11–15); and 6) motive (v. 16).

f. **inexcusable . . . you . . . who judge.** Both Jews (Paul's primary audience here; cf. Rom. 2:17) and moral Gentiles who think they are exempt from God's judgment because they have not indulged in the immoral excesses described in chap. 1, are tragically mistaken. They have more knowledge than the immoral pagan (Rom. 3:2; 9:4) and thus a greater accountability (cf. Heb. 10:26–29; James 3:1).

g. **condemn yourself.** If someone has sufficient knowledge to judge others, he condemns

[a]practice the same things. But we know that the judgment of God is [b]according to truth against those who practice such things. And do you think this, O man, you who judge those practicing such things, and doing the same, that you will escape the judgment of God? Or do you [c]despise the riches of His [d]goodness, [e]forbearance, and [f]longsuffering, not knowing that the goodness of God leads you to [g]repentance? But in accordance with your [h]hardness and your [i]impenitent heart you are [j]treasuring up for yourself wrath in the [k]day of wrath and revelation of the righteous judgment of God, [l]who "will render to each one according to his deeds": [m]eternal life to those who by patient

himself, because he shows he has the knowledge to evaluate his own condition.

a. practice the same things. In their condemnation of others they have excused and overlooked their own sins. Self-righteousness exists because of two deadly errors: 1) minimizing God's moral standard usually by emphasizing externals; and 2) underestimating the depth of one's own sinfulness (cf. Matt. 5:20–22, 27, 28; 7:1–3; 15:1–3; Luke 18:21).

b. according to truth. The meaning is "right." Whatever God does is by nature right (cf. Rom. 3:4; 9:14; Pss. 9:4, 8; 96:13; 145:17; Is. 45:19).

c. despise. Lit. "to think down on," thus to underestimate someone's or something's value, and even to treat with contempt.

d. goodness. This refers to "common grace," the benefits God bestows on all men (cf. Matt. 5:45; Acts 14:15–17).

e. forbearance. This word, which means "to hold back," was sometimes used of a truce between warring parties. Rather than destroying every person the moment he or she sins, God graciously holds back His judgment (cf. Rom. 3:25). He saves sinners in a physical and temporal way from what they deserve (see 1 Tim. 4:10), to show them His saving character, that they might come to Him and receive salvation that is spiritual and eternal.

f. longsuffering. This word indicates the duration for which God demonstrates His goodness and forbearance—for long periods of time (cf. 2 Pet. 3:5). Together these 3 words speak of God's common grace—the way He demonstrates His grace to all mankind (cf. Job 12:10; Pss. 119:68; 145:9).

g. repentance. The act of turning from sin to Christ for forgiveness and salvation. See 2 Cor. 7:9–11.

h. hardness. The Eng. word "sclerosis" (as in arteriosclerosis, a hardening of the arteries) comes from this Gr. word. But here the danger is not physical, but spiritual hardness (Ezek. 36:26; Matt. 19:8; Mark 3:5; 6:52; 8:17; John 12:40; Heb. 3:8, 15; 4:7).

i. impenitent heart. A refusal to repent (cf. Rom. 2:4) and accept God's pardon of sin through Jesus Christ.

j. treasuring up . . . wrath. To reject God's offer of forgiveness and cling to one's sin is to accumulate more of God's wrath and earn a severer judgment (see Heb. 10:26–30; Rev. 20:12).

k. day of wrath and . . . judgment. Refers to the final judgment of wicked men that comes at the Great White Throne at the end of the Millennium (see Rev. 20:11–15).

l. Although Scripture everywhere teaches that salvation is not on the basis of works (see Rom. 4:1–4; Eph. 2:8, 9), it consistently teaches that God's judgment is always on the basis of a man's deeds (Is. 3:10, 11; Jer. 17:10; John 5:28, 29; 1 Cor. 3:8; 2 Cor. 5:10; Gal. 6:7–9; cf. Rom. 14:12). Paul describes the deeds of two distinct groups: the redeemed (Rom. 2:7, 10) and the unredeemed (vv. 8, 9). The deeds of the redeemed are not the basis of their salvation but the evidence of it. They are not perfect and are prone to sin, but there is undeniable evidence of righteousness in their lives (see James 2:14–20, 26).

m. eternal life. Not simply in duration, because even unbelievers will live forever (2 Thess. 1:9; Rev. 14:9–11), but also in quality (see John 17:3). Eternal life is a kind of life, the holy life of the eternal God given to believers.

continuance in doing good seek for glory, honor, and immortality; but to those who are ᵃself-seeking and do not obey the truth, but obey unrighteousness—indignation and wrath, tribulation and anguish, on every soul of man who does evil, of ᵇthe Jew first and also of the Greek; but glory, honor, and peace to everyone who works what is good, to the Jew first and also to the Greek. For there is no ᶜpartiality with God.

For as many as have ᵈsinned without law will also perish without law, and as many as have sinned in the law will be ᵉjudged by the law (for not the hearers of the law are just in the sight of God, but the doers of the law will be justified; for when Gentiles, who do not have the law, ᶠby nature do the things in the law, these, although not having the law, are ᵍa law to themselves, ʰwho show the work of the law written in their hearts, their ⁱconscience also bearing witness, and between themselves their thoughts accusing or else excusing them) in the day when God will judge the ʲsecrets of men by Jesus Christ, according to my gospel.

a. **self-seeking.** This word may have originally been used to describe a hireling or mercenary; someone who does what he does for money regardless of how his actions affect others.

b. **the Jew first.** Just as the Jews were given the first opportunity to hear and respond to the gospel (Rom. 1:16), they will be first to receive God's judgment if they refuse (cf. Amos 3:2). Israel will receive severer punishment because she was given greater light and blessing (see Rom. 9:3, 4).

c. **partiality.** Lit. "to receive a face," that is, to give consideration to someone simply because of his position, wealth, influence, popularity, or appearance. Because it is God's nature to be just, it is impossible for Him to be anything but impartial (Acts 10:34; Gal. 2:6; Eph. 6:7, 8; Col. 3:25; 1 Pet. 1:17).

d. **sinned without law.** The Gentiles who never had the opportunity to know God's moral law (Ex. 20:1ff) will be judged on their disobedience in relationship to their limited knowledge (see Rom. 1:19, 20).

e. **judged by the law.** The Jews and many Gentiles who had access to God's moral law will be accountable for their greater knowledge (cf. Matt. 11:20–23; Heb. 6:4–6; 10:26–31).

f. **by nature do . . . the law.** Without knowing the written law of God, people in pagan society generally value and attempt to practice its most basic tenets. This is normal for cultures instinctively (see Rom. 2:15) to value justice, honesty, compassion, and goodness toward others, reflecting the divine law written in the heart.

g. **law to themselves.** Their practice of some good deeds and their aversion to some evil ones demonstrate an innate knowledge of God's law—a knowledge that will actually witness against them on the day of judgment.

h. **work of the law.** Probably best understood as "the same works the Mosaic law prescribes."

i. **conscience.** Lit. "with knowledge." That instinctive sense of right and wrong that produces guilt when violated. In addition to an innate awareness of God's law, men have a warning system that activates when they choose to ignore or disobey that law. Paul urges believers not to violate their own consciences or cause others to (Rom. 13:5; 1 Cor. 8:7, 12; 10:25, 29; 2 Cor. 5:11; cf. 9:1; Acts 23:1; 24:16), because repeatedly ignoring the conscience's warnings desensitizes it and eventually silences it (1 Tim. 4:2). See 2 Cor. 1:12; 4:2.

j. **secrets.** This primarily refers to the motives that lie behind men's actions (1 Chr. 28:9; Ps. 139:1–3; Jer. 17:10; Matt. 6:4, 6, 18; cf. Luke 8:17; Heb. 4:12).

135. THE UNRIGHTEOUSNESS OF THE JEWS
Rom. 2:17—3:8

Indeed you are called a [a]Jew, and rest on the law, and make your boast in God, and know His will, and approve the things that are excellent, being instructed out of the law, and are confident that you yourself are a guide to [b]the blind, a light to those who are in darkness, an instructor of the foolish, a teacher of babes, having the form of knowledge and truth in the law. You, therefore, who teach another, do you not teach yourself? You who preach that a man should not steal, do you steal? You who say, "Do not commit adultery," do you commit adultery? You who abhor idols, [c]do you rob temples? You who make your boast in the law, do you dishonor God through breaking the law? For "the name of God is blasphemed among the Gentiles because of you," as [d]it is written.

For circumcision is indeed [e]profitable if you keep the law; but if you are a breaker of the law, your circumcision has become [f]uncircumcision. Therefore, if an uncircumcised man keeps the righteous requirements of the law, will not

---

a. **Jew.** Having shown that outwardly moral people—Jew and Gentiles alike—will stand condemned by God's judgment, Paul turns his argument exclusively to the Jews, God's covenant people. Neither their heritage (Rom. 2:17a), their knowledge (vv. 17b–24), nor their ceremonies, specifically circumcision (vv. 25–29), will protect them from God's righteous judgment. Previously called Hebrews and Israelites, by the first century "Jew" had become the most common name for the descendants of Abraham through Isaac. "Jew" comes from "Judah," (meaning "praise"), one of the 12 tribes and the designation for the southern half of Solomon's kingdom after his death. From the time of the Babylonian captivity, the whole race bore this title. Their great heritage, however, (cf. Gen. 12:3) became a source of pride and complacency (cf. Jon. 4:2; Mic. 3:11, 12; Matt. 3:7–9; John 8:31–34, 40–59), which led to judgment instead of "praise."

b. **the blind . . . babes.** Because they possessed the law, the Jews were confident that they were spiritually superior teachers: guides to blind pagans (cf. Matt. 23:24–28), light (cf. Is. 42:6), wise in God's ways, and able to teach babes (probably a reference to Gentile proselytes to Judaism).

c. **do you rob temples?** May refer to fraudulently skimming funds from money given to the temple or withholding part of their temple tax or offerings (cf. Mal. 3:8–10). More likely, however, it refers to the common practice—in direct violation of God's command (Deut. 7:25)—of looting pagan temples and selling the idols and vessels for personal profit (cf. Acts 19:37) under the pretext of religion.

d. **it is written.** Quoted from Is. 52:5.

e. **profitable.** As an act of obedience and a reminder of their covenant relationship to God (see Gen. 17:10–14).

f. **uncircumcision.** A Jew who continually transgressed God's law had no more of a saving relationship to God than an uncircumcised Gentile. The outward symbol was nothing without the inner reality.

his uncircumcision be ªcounted as circumcision? And will not the physically uncircumcised, ᵇif he fulfills the law, judge you who, even with your written code and circumcision, are a transgressor of the law? For he is not a Jew who is one ᶜoutwardly, nor is circumcision that which is outward in the flesh; but ᵈhe is a Jew who is one inwardly; and ᵉcircumcision is that of the heart, in the ᶠSpirit, not in the letter; whose praise is not from men but from God.

What advantage then has the Jew, or what is the profit of circumcision? Much in every way! Chiefly because to them were committed the ᵍoracles of God. For what if some did not believe? ʰWill their unbelief make ⁱthe faithfulness of God without effect? Certainly not! Indeed, let God be true but ʲevery man a liar. As ᵏit is written:

"That You may be justified in Your words,

And may overcome when You are judged."

But if our unrighteousness ˡdemonstrates the righteousness of God, what

---

a. **counted as circumcision.** God will regard the believing Gentile as favorably as a circumcised, believing Jew.

b. **if he fulfills the law.** A Gentile's humble obedience to the law should serve as a stern rebuke to a Jew who, in spite of his great advantages, lives in disobedience.

c. **outwardly.** This refers to physical descendants of Abraham who have been properly circumcised (cf. 9:6; Matt. 3:9).

d. **he is a Jew.** A true child of God; the true spiritual seed of Abraham. (See Rom. 4:16; cf. Gal. 3:29).

e. **circumcision is that of the heart.** The outward rite is of value only when it reflects the inner reality of a heart separated from sin unto God. Cf. Deut. 10:16; 30:6.

f. **Spirit . . . letter.** Salvation results from the work of God's Spirit in the heart, not mere external efforts to conform to his law.

g. **oracles.** This Gr. word is *logion*, a diminutive form of the common NT word *logos*, which is normally translated "word." These are important sayings or messages, especially supernatural ones. Here Paul uses the word to encompass the entire OT—the Jews received the very words of the true God (Deut. 4:1, 2; 6:1, 2; cf. Mark 12:24; Luke 16:29; John 5:39). The Jews had a great advantage in having the OT, because it contained the truth about salvation (2 Tim. 3:15) and about the gospel in its basic form (Gal. 3:8). When Paul said "preach the Word" (2 Tim. 4:2), he meant the "oracles of God" (1 Pet. 4:11) recorded in Scripture.

h. **Will their unbelief . . . ?** Paul anticipated that Jewish readers would disagree with his statements that God has not guaranteed to fulfill His promises to every physical descendant of Abraham. They would argue that such teaching nullifies all the promises God made to the Jews in the OT. But his answer reflects both the explicit and implicit teaching of the OT; before any Jew, regardless of the purity of his lineage, can inherit the promises, he must come to repentance and faith (cf. Rom. 9:6, 7; Is. 55:6, 7).

i. **the faithfulness of God.** God will fulfill all the promises He made to the nation, even if individual Jews are not able to receive them because of their unbelief.

j. **every man a liar.** If all mankind were to agree that God had been unfaithful to His promises, it would only prove that all are liars and God is true. Cf. Titus 1:1.

k. **it is written.** This is quoted from Ps. 51:4.

l. **demonstrates the righteousness of God.** See Rom.1:17. By contrast, like a jeweler who displays a diamond on black velvet to make the stone appear even more beautiful.

shall we say? Is God unjust who inflicts wrath? [a](I speak as a man.) Certainly not! For then how will God [b]judge the world?

For if the truth of God has increased through my lie to His glory, why am I also still judged as a sinner? And why not say, "Let us do evil that good may come"?—as we are [c]slanderously reported and as some affirm that we say. Their condemnation is just.

136. THE UNRIGHTEOUSNESS OF MANKIND
Rom. 3:9–20

What then? [d]Are we better than they? Not at all. For we have previously charged both Jews and Greeks that they are all [e]under sin.

As [f]it is written:

> "There is [g]none righteous, no, not one;
> There is [h]none who understands;
> There is [i]none who seeks after God.

---

a. **(I speak as a man).** He is simply paraphrasing the weak, unbiblical logic of his opponents—the product of their natural, unregenerate minds.

b. **judge.** A major theme of Scripture (Gen. 18:25; Pss. 50:6; 58:11; 94:2), here it probably refers to the great future day of judgment (see Rom. 2:5). Paul's point is that if God condoned sin, He would have no equitable, righteous basis for judgment.

c. **slanderously reported.** Tragically, the apostle's gospel message of salvation by grace through faith alone had been perverted by his opponents who argued it provided not only a license to sin, but outright encouragement to do so (Rom. 5:20; 6:1, 2).

d. **Are we better?** "We" probably refers to the Christians in Rome who will receive this letter. Christians do not have an intrinsically superior nature to all those Paul has shown to stand under God's condemnation. **Greeks.** See Rom. 1:14.

e. **under sin.** Completely enslaved and dominated by sin.

f. **it is written.** Paul strings together a series of OT quotations that indict the character (Rom. 3:10–12), conversation (vv. 13, 14), and conduct (vv. 15–17) of all men. Nine times he uses words such as "none" and "all" to show the universality of human sin and rebellion.

g. **none righteous.** Man is universally evil (cf. Ps. 14:1; see Rom. 1:17).

h. **none . . . understands.** Man is unable to comprehend the truth of God or grasp His standard of righteousness (see Pss. 14:2; 53:3; cf. 1 Cor. 2:14). Sadly, his spiritual ignorance does not result from a lack of opportunity (Rom. 1:19, 20; 2:15), but is an expression of his depravity and rebellion (Eph. 4:18).

i. **none . . . seeks.** See Ps. 14:2. This verse clearly implies that the world's false religions are fallen man's attempts to escape the true God—not to seek Him. Man's natural tendency is to seek his own interests (cf. Phil. 2:21), but his only hope is for God to seek him (John 6:37, 44). It is only as a result of God's work in the heart that anyone seeks Him (Ps. 16:8; Matt. 6:33).

They have all ªturned aside;

They have together become unprofitable;

There is none who does good, no, not one."

"Their throat is an ᵇopen tomb;

With their tongues they have practiced deceit";

"The poison of asps is under their lips";

"Whose mouth is full of ᶜcursing and ᵈbitterness."

"Their feet are swift to shed blood;

ᵉDestruction and misery are in their ways;

And the ᶠway of peace they have not known."

"There is no ᵍfear of God before their eyes."

Now we know that whatever the law says, it says to ʰthose who are under the law, that ⁱevery mouth may be stopped, and all the world may become guilty before God. Therefore by the ʲdeeds of the law no flesh will be justified in His sight, for ᵏby the law is the knowledge of sin.

---

a. **turned aside.** See Ps. 14:3. This word basically means "to lean in the wrong direction." It was used to describe a soldier's running the wrong way, or deserting. All men are inclined to leave God's way and pursue their own (cf. Is. 53:6).

b. **open tomb.** See Ps. 5:9. Tombs were sealed not only to show respect for the deceased, but to hide the sight and stench of the body's decay. As an unsealed tomb allows those who pass to see and smell what is inside, the unregenerate man's open throat—that is, the foul words that come from it—reveal the decay of his heart (cf. Prov. 10:31, 32; 15:2, 28; Jer. 17:9; Matt. 12:34, 35; 15:18; James 3:1–12).

c. **cursing.** This is quoted from Ps. 10:7. It refers to wanting the worst for someone and publicly expressing that desire in caustic, derisive language.

d. **bitterness.** The open, public expression of emotional hostility against one's enemy (cf. Ps. 64:3, 4).

e. **Destruction and misery.** Man damages and destroys everything he touches, leaving a trail of pain and suffering in his wake. This is quoted from Is. 59:7, 8.

f. **way of peace.** Not the lack of an inner sense of peace, but man's tendency toward strife and conflict, whether between individuals or nations (cf. Jer. 6:14).

g. **fear of God.** See Ps. 36:1. Man's true spiritual condition is nowhere more clearly seen than in the absence of a proper submission to and reverence for God. Biblical fear for God consists of: 1) awe of His greatness and glory, and 2) dread of the results of violating that holy nature (see Prov. 1:7; cf. Prov. 9:10; 16:6; Acts 5:1–11; 1 Cor. 11:30).

h. **those . . . under the law.** Every unredeemed human being. Jews received the written law through Moses (Rom. 3:2), and Gentiles have the works of the law written on their hearts (Rom. 2:15), so that both groups are accountable to God.

i. **every mouth . . . stopped . . . guilty.** There is no defense against the guilty verdict God pronounces on the entire human race.

j. **deeds of the law.** Doing perfectly what God's moral law requires is impossible, so that every person is cursed by that inability (see Gal. 3:10, 13).

k. **by the law is the knowledge of sin.** The law makes sin known, but can't save.

137. THE SOURCE OF JUSTIFYING RIGHTEOUSNESS

Rom. 3:21–31

ᵃBut now the ᵇrighteousness of God ᶜapart from the law is revealed, being witnessed by the Law and the Prophets, even the righteousness of God, through faith in Jesus Christ, to all and on all who believe. For ᵈthere is no difference; for ᵉall have sinned and fall short of the glory of God, being ᶠjustified ᵍfreely by His grace through the ʰredemption that is in Christ Jesus, ⁱwhom God

---

a. **But now.** Not a reference to time, but a change in the flow of the apostle's argument. Having shown the impossibility of gaining righteousness by human effort, he turns to explain the righteousness that God Himself has provided.

b. **righteousness.** See Rom. 1:17. This righteousness is unique: 1) God is its source (Is. 45:8); 2) it fulfills both the penalty and precept of God's law. Christ's death as a substitute pays the penalty exacted on those who failed to keep God's law, and His perfect obedience to every requirement of God's law fulfills God's demand for comprehensive righteousness (2 Cor. 5:21; 1 Pet. 2:24; cf. Heb. 9:28); and 3) because God's righteousness is eternal (Ps. 119:142; Dan. 9:24), the one who receives it from Him enjoys it forever.

c. **apart from the law.** Entirely apart from obedience to any law (Rom. 4:15; Gal. 2:16; 3:10, 11; 5:1, 2, 6; Eph. 2:8, 9; cf. Phil. 3:9; 2 Tim. 1:9; Titus 3:5).

d. **there is no difference . . . glory of God.** A parenthetical comment explaining that God can bestow His righteousness on all who believe, Jew or Gentile, because all men—without distinction—fail miserably to live up to the divine standard.

e. **all have sinned.** Paul has already made this case (Rom. 1:18—3:20).

f. **justified.** This verb, and related words from the same Gr. root (e.g., justification), occur some 30 times in Romans and are concentrated in Rom. 2:13—5:1. This legal or forensic term comes from the Gr. word for "righteous" and means "to declare righteous." This verdict includes: pardon from the guilt and penalty of sin, and the imputation of Christ's righteousness to the believer's account, which provides for the positive righteousness man needs to be accepted by God. God declares a sinner righteous solely on the basis of the merits of Christ's righteousness. God imputed a believer's sin to Christ's account in His sacrificial death (Is. 53:4, 5; 1 Pet. 2:24), and He imputes Christ's perfect obedience to God's law to Christians (cf. Rom. 5:19; 1 Cor. 1:30; see 2 Cor. 5:21; Phil. 3:9). The sinner receives this gift of God's grace by faith alone (Rom. 3:22, 25; see 4:1–25). Sanctification, the work of God by which He makes righteous those whom He has already justified, is distinct from justification but without exception, always follows it (Rom. 8:30).

g. **freely by His grace.** Justification is a gracious gift God extends to the repentant, believing sinner, wholly apart from human merit or work (see Rom. 1:5).

h. **redemption.** The imagery behind this Gr. word comes from the ancient slave market. It meant paying the necessary ransom to obtain the prisoner or slave's release. The only adequate payment to redeem sinners from sin's slavery and its deserved punishment was "in Christ Jesus" (1 Tim. 2:6; 1 Pet. 1:18, 19), and was paid to God to satisfy His justice.

i. **whom God set forth.** This great sacrifice was not accomplished in secret, but God publicly displayed His Son on Calvary for all to see.

set forth as a ªpropitiation by His blood, through faith, ᵇto demonstrate His righteousness, because in His forbearance God had ᶜpassed over the sins that were previously committed, to demonstrate at the present time His righteousness, that He might be ᵈjust and the justifier of the one who has faith in Jesus.

ᵉWhere is boasting then? It is excluded. By what law? Of works? No, but by the law of faith. Therefore we conclude that a man is ᶠjustified by faith apart from the deeds of the law. Or is He the God of the Jews only? Is He not also the ᵍGod of the Gentiles? Yes, of the Gentiles also, since there is one God who will justify the circumcised by faith and the uncircumcised ʰthrough faith. Do we then ⁱmake void the law through faith? Certainly not! On the contrary, we establish the law.

---

a. **propitiation.** Crucial to the significance of Christ's sacrifice, this word carries the idea of appeasement or satisfaction—in this case Christ's violent death satisfied the offended holiness and wrath of God against those for whom Christ died (Is. 53:11; Col. 2:11–14). The Heb. equivalent of this word was used to describe the mercy seat—the cover to the ark of the covenant—where the High-Priest sprinkled the blood of the slaughtered animal on the Day of Atonement to make atonement for the sins of the people. In pagan religions, it is the worshiper not the god who is responsible to appease the wrath of the offended deity. But in reality, man is incapable of satisfying God's justice apart from Christ, except by spending eternity in hell. Cf. 1 John 2:2

b. **to demonstrate . . . His righteousness.** Through the incarnation, sinless life, and substitutionary death of Christ.

c. **passed over the sins.** This means neither indifference nor remission. God's justice demands that every sin and sinner be punished. God would have been just, when Adam and Eve sinned, to destroy them, and with them, the entire human race. But in His goodness and forbearance (see Rom. 2:4), He withheld His judgment for a certain period of time (cf. Ps. 78:38, 39; Acts 17:30, 31; 2 Pet. 3:9).

d. **just and the justifier.** The wisdom of God's plan allowed Him to punish Jesus in the place of sinners and thereby justify those who are guilty without compromising His justice.

e. **Where is boasting then?** Cf. 4:1, 2; 1 Cor. 1:26–29.

f. **justified by faith.** Although the word "alone" does not appear in the Gr. text, that is Paul's clear meaning (cf. 4:3–5; see James 2:24).

g. **God of the Gentiles.** There is only one true God (cf. 1 Cor. 8:5, 6).

h. **through faith . . . we establish the law.** Salvation by grace through faith does not denigrate the law, but underscores its true importance: 1) by providing a payment for the penalty of death, which the law required for failing to keep it; 2) by fulfilling the law's original purpose, which is to serve as a tutor to show mankind's utter inability to obey God's righteous demands and to drive people to Christ (Gal. 3:24); and 3) by giving believers the capacity to obey it (Rom. 8:3, 4).

i. **make void.** Knowing he would be accused of antinomianism (being against the law) for arguing that a man was justified apart from keeping the law, Paul introduced here the defense he later developed in Rom. 6, 7.

138. THE EXAMPLE OF RIGHTEOUSNESS

Rom. 4:1–12

What then shall we say that ᵃAbraham our father has found according to the flesh? For if Abraham was ᵇjustified by works, he has something to ᶜboast about, but not before God. For what does the Scripture say? ᵈ"Abraham ᵉbelieved God, and it was ᶠaccounted to him for righteousness." ᵍNow to him who works, the wages are not counted as grace but as debt.

But to him who does not work but believes on Him who ʰjustifies the ungodly, his faith is accounted for righteousness, just as David also describes the blessedness of the man to whom God imputes righteousness apart from works:

> ⁱ"Blessed are those whose lawless deeds are forgiven,
>
> And whose sins are covered;
>
> Blessed is the man to whom the LORD shall not impute sin."

---

a. **Abraham our father.** Paul uses the model of Abraham to prove justification by faith alone because the Jews held him up as the supreme example of a righteous man (John 8:39), and because it clearly showed that Judaism with its works-righteousness had deviated from the faith of the Jews' patriarchal ancestors. In a spiritual sense, Abraham was the forerunner of the primarily Gentile church in Rome as well (see Rom. 1:13; 4:11, 16; cf. Gal. 3:6, 7).

b. **justified by works.** Declared righteous on the basis of human effort (see Rom. 3:24).

c. **boast.** If Abraham's own works had been the basis of his justification, he would have had every right to boast in God's presence. That makes the hypothetical premise of v. 2 unthinkable (Eph. 2:8, 9; 1 Cor. 1:29).

d. **Abraham . . .** A quotation of Gen. 15:6, one of the clearest statements in all Scripture about justification (see Rom. 3:24.).

e. **believed.** Abraham was a man of faith (see Rom. 1:16; cf. 4:18–21; Gal. 3:6, 7, 9; Heb. 11:8–10). But faith is not a meritorious work. It is never the ground of justification—it is simply the channel through which it is received and it, too, is a gift. See Eph. 2:8.

f. **accounted.** Also translated "imputed" (Rom. 4:6, 8, 11, 23, 24). Used in both financial and legal settings, this Gr. word, which occurs 9 times in chap. 4 alone, means to take something that belongs to someone and credit to another's account. It is a one-sided transaction—Abraham did nothing to accumulate it; God simply credited it to him. God took His own righteousness and credited it to Abraham as if it were actually his. This God did because Abraham believed in Him (see Gen. 15:6).

g. **Now to him . . .** Broadening his argument from Abraham to all men, the apostle here makes it clear that the forensic act of declaring a man righteous is completely apart from any kind of human work. If salvation were on the basis of one's own effort, God would owe salvation as a debt—but salvation is always a sovereignly given gift of God's grace (Rom. 3:24; Eph. 2:8, 9) to those who believe (cf. Rom. 1:16). Since faith is contrasted with work, faith must mean the end of any attempt to earn God's favor through personal merit.

h. **justifies the ungodly.** Only those who relinquish all claims to goodness and acknowledge they are ungodly are candidates for justification (cf. Luke 5:32).

i. **Blessed are those.** Paul turns for support of his argument to Ps. 32:1, 2, a penitential

Does this blessedness then come upon the [a]circumcised only, or upon the [b]uncircumcised also? For we say that faith was accounted to Abraham for righteousness. How then was it accounted? While he was circumcised, or uncircumcised? [c]Not while circumcised, but while uncircumcised. And he received the [d]sign of circumcision, a [e]seal of the righteousness of the faith which he had while still uncircumcised, that he might be [f]the father of all those who believe, though they are uncircumcised, that righteousness might be imputed to them also, and the father of circumcision to those who not only are of the circumcision, but who also walk in the steps of the faith which our father Abraham had while still uncircumcised.

139. Abraham's Righteousness

Rom. 4:13–25

For the [g]promise that he would be the heir of the world was [h]not to Abraham or to his seed through the law, but through the [i]righteousness of faith. For if

---

psalm written by David after his adultery with Bathsheba and his murder of her husband (2 Sam. 11). In spite of the enormity of his sin and the utter absence of personal merit, David knew the blessing of imputed righteousness.

    a. **circumcised.** This refers to Jews (see Gen. 17:10–14; cf. Acts 15:19–29; Rom. 2:25–29; 4:11; Gal. 5:1–4; 6:12; Phil. 3:2–5).

    b. **uncircumcised.** All Gentiles (see 2:25–29).

    c. **Not while . . . but while uncircumcised.** The chronology of Genesis proves Paul's case. Abraham was 86 when Ishmael was born (Gen. 16:16), and Abraham was 99 when he was circumcised. But God declared him righteous before Ishmael had even been conceived (Gen. 15:6; 16:2–4)—at least 14 years before Abraham's circumcision.

    d. **sign.** This indicates man's need for spiritual cleansing (cf. Rom. 2:28, 29; Jer. 4:3, 4; 9:24–26) and of the covenant relationship between God and His people (see Gen. 17:11).

    e. **seal.** An outward demonstration of the righteousness God had credited to him by faith.

    f. **the father of all those who believe.** Racially, Abraham is the father of all Jews (circumcised); spiritually, he is the father of both believing Jews (Rom. 4:12) and believing Gentiles (uncircumcised; v. 11). Cf. Rom. 4:16; Gal. 3:29.

    g. **promise . . . heir of the world.** This refers to Christ and is the essence of the covenant God made with Abraham and his descendants (see Gen. 12:3; 15:5; 18:18; 22:18). The final provision of that covenant was that through Abraham's seed all the world would be blessed (Gen. 12:3). Paul argues that "the seed" refers specifically to Christ and that this promise really constituted the gospel (Gal. 3:8; cf. John 8:56). All believers, by being in Christ, become heirs of the promise (Gal. 3:29; cf. 1 Cor. 3:21–23).

    h. **not . . . through the law.** That is, not as a result of Abraham's keeping the law.

    i. **righteousness of faith.** Righteousness received from God by faith (see Rom. 1:17).

[a]those who are of the law are heirs, faith is made void and the [b]promise made of no effect, because the [c]law brings about wrath; for where there is no law there is no transgression.

Therefore it is [d]of faith that it might be [e]according to grace, so that the promise might be sure to all the seed, not only to [f]those who are of the law, but also to [g]those who are of the faith of Abraham, who is the father of us all ([h]as it is written, "I have made you a father of many nations") in the presence of Him whom he believed—God, who [i]gives life to the dead and [j]calls those things which do not exist as though they did; who, [k]contrary to hope, in hope believed, so that he became the father of many nations, according to [l]what was spoken, "So shall your descendants be." And not being [m]weak in faith, he did not consider his own body, already dead (since he was about a hundred years old), and [n]the deadness of Sarah's womb. He did not waver at [o]the promise of God through unbelief, but was strengthened in faith, [p]giving glory to God, and being fully convinced that what He had promised He was also able to perform. And [q]therefore "it was accounted to him for righteousness."

---

a. **those who are of the law.** If only those who perfectly keep the law—an impossibility—receive the promise, faith has no value.

b. **promise . . . of no effect.** Making a promise contingent on an impossible condition nullifies the promise (see v. 13).

c. **law brings about wrath.** By exposing man's sinfulness (cf. Rom. 7:7–11; Gal. 3:19, 24).

d. **of faith.** Justification is through faith alone (see Rom. 1:16, 17 and 3:24).

e. **according to grace.** But the power of justification is God's great grace (see Rom. 1:5), not man's faith.

f. **those who are of the law.** Believing Jews.

g. **those who are of the faith of Abraham.** Believing Gentiles.

h. **as it is written.** Quoted from Gen. 17:5.

i. **gives life to the dead.** Abraham had experienced this firsthand (Heb. 11:11, 12; cf. Rom. 4:19).

j. **calls those things which do not exist as though they did.** This is another reference to the forensic nature of justification. God can declare believing sinners to be righteous even though they are not, by imputing His righteousness to them, just as God made or declared Jesus "sin" and punished Him, though He was not a sinner. Those whom He justifies, He will conform to the image of His Son (Rom. 8:29, 30).

k. **contrary to hope.** From the human perspective, it seemed impossible. Cf. Gen. 17:5.

l. **what was spoken.** Quoted from Gen. 15:5.

m. **weak in faith.** When doubt erodes one's confidence in God's Word.

n. **the deadness of Sarah's womb.** She was only 10 years younger than Abraham (Gen. 17:17), 90 years old (well past childbearing age) when they received the promise of Isaac.

o. **the promise.** Of the birth of a son (Gen. 15:4; 17:16; 18:10).

p. **giving glory to God.** Believing God affirms His existence and character and thus gives Him glory (cf. Heb. 11:6; 1 John 5:10).

q. **therefore.** Because of his genuine faith (see Gen. 15:6).

Now ᵃit was ᵇnot written for his sake alone that it was imputed to him, but also for us. It shall be imputed to us who believe in Him who raised up Jesus our Lord from the dead, who was ᶜdelivered up because of our offenses, and was raised ᵈbecause of our justification.

140. The Blessings of Righteousness
Rom. 5:1–11

ᵉTherefore, ᶠhaving been justified by faith, we have ᵍpeace with God through our Lord Jesus Christ, through whom also we have ʰaccess by faith into this grace in which we ⁱstand, and rejoice in ʲhope of the glory of God. And not

---

a. **it was not written.** A paraphrase of the LXX (Gr. translation of the OT) rendering of Is. 53:12. Perhaps these words were adapted to and quoted from an early Christian confession or hymn.

b. **not . . . for his sake alone.** All Scripture has universal application (cf. Rom. 15:4; 2 Tim. 3:16, 17), and Abraham's experience is no exception. If Abraham was justified by faith, then all others are justified on the same basis.

c. **delivered up.** I.e., crucified.

d. **because of our justification.** The resurrection provided proof that God had accepted the sacrifice of His Son and would be able to be just and yet justify the ungodly.

e. **Therefore.** Paul completed his case that God justifies sinners on the basis of faith alone, and he turned his pen to counter the notion that although believers receive salvation by faith, they will preserve it by good works. He argues that they are bound eternally to Jesus Christ, preserved by His power and not by human effort (cf. Is. 11:5; Ps. 36:5; Lam. 3:23; Eph. 1:18–20; 2 Tim. 2:13; Heb. 10:23). For the Christian, the evidences of that eternal tie are: 1) his peace with God (Rom. 5:1); 2) his standing in grace (v. 2a); 3) his hope of glory (vv. 2b–5a); 4) his receiving of divine love (vv. 5b–8); 5) his certain escape of divine wrath (vv. 9, 10); and 6) his joy in the Lord (v. 11).

f. **having been justified.** The Gr. construction—and its Eng. translation—underscores that justification is a one-time legal declaration with continuing results (see Rom. 3:24), not an ongoing process.

g. **peace with God.** Not a subjective, internal sense of calm and serenity, but an external, objective reality. God has declared Himself to be at war with every human being because of man's sinful rebellion against Him and His laws (cf. Rom. 1:18; 8:7; Ex. 22:24; Deut. 32:21, 22; Ps. 7:11; John 3:36; Eph. 5:6). But the first great result of justification is that the sinner's war with God is ended forever (Col. 1:21, 22). Scripture refers to the end of this conflict as a person's being reconciled to God (2 Cor. 5:18–20).

h. **access.** Used only twice elsewhere in the NT (Eph. 2:18; 3:12), this word always refers to the believer's access to God through Jesus Christ. What was unthinkable to the OT Jew (cf. Ex. 19:9, 20, 21; 28:35) is now available to all who come (Jer. 32:38, 40; Heb. 4:16; 10:19–22; cf. Matt. 27:51).

i. **stand.** This refers to the permanent, secure position believers enjoy in God's grace (cf. Rom. 8:1–34; John 6:37; Phil. 1:6; 2 Tim. 1:12; Jude 24).

j. **hope of the glory of God.** Unlike the Eng. word "hope," the NT word contains no uncertainty; it speaks of something that is certain, but not yet realized. The believer's ultimate

only that, but we also glory in ªtribulations, knowing that tribulation produces perseverance; and ᵇperseverance, ᶜcharacter; and character, hope. Now hope does not disappoint, because ᵈthe love of God has been poured out in our hearts by the Holy ᵉSpirit who was given to us.

ᶠFor when we were still without strength, ᵍin due time ʰChrist died for the ungodly. For scarcely for a ⁱrighteous man will one die; yet perhaps for a good man someone would even dare to die. But God demonstrates His own love toward us, in that while we were still sinners, Christ died for us. ʲMuch more then, having now been justified ᵏby His blood, we shall be saved from

destiny is to share in the very glory of God (Rom. 8:29, 30; John 17:22; 2 Cor. 3:18; Phil. 3:20, 21; 1 John 3:1, 2), and that hope will be realized because Christ Himself secures it (1 Tim. 1:1). Without the clear and certain promises of the Word of God, the believer would have no basis for hope (Rom. 15:4; Ps. 119:81, 114; Eph. 2:12; cf. Jer. 14:8).

a. **tribulations.** A word used for pressure, like that of a press squeezing the fluid from olives or grapes. Here they are not the normal pressures of living (cf. Rom. 8:35), but the inevitable troubles that come to followers of Christ because of their relationship with Him (Matt. 5:10–12; John 15:20; 2 Cor. 4:17; 1 Thess. 3:3; 2 Tim. 3:12; 1 Pet. 4:19). Such difficulties produce rich spiritual benefits.

b. **perseverance.** Sometimes translated "patience," this word refers to endurance, the ability to remain under tremendous weight and pressure without succumbing (Rom. 15:5; Col. 1:22, 23; 2 Thess. 1:4; Rev. 14:12).

c. **character.** A better translation is "proven character." The Gr. word simply means "proof." It was used of testing metals to determine their purity. Here the proof is Christian character (cf. James 1:12). Christians can glory in tribulations because of what those troubles produce.

d. **the love of God . . . poured out.** God's love for us has been lavishly poured out to the point of overflowing within our hearts. Paul moves from the objective aspects of our security in Christ to the internal, more subjective. God has implanted within our hearts evidence that we belong to Him in that we love the One who first loved us (1 Cor. 16:22; cf. Gal. 5:22; Eph. 3:14–19; 1 John 4:7–10).

e. **Spirit who was given.** A marvelous testimony to God's love for us (Rom. 8:9, 14, 16, 17; John 7:38, 39; 1 Cor. 6:19, 20; 12:13; Eph. 1:18).

f. **without strength.** Lit. "helpless." Unregenerate sinners are spiritually dead and incapable of doing anything to help themselves (John 6:44; Eph. 2:1).

g. **in due time.** At the moment God had chosen (cf. Gal. 4:4).

h. **Christ died for the ungodly.** God's love for His own is unwavering because it is not based on how lovable we are, but on the constancy of His own character; God's supreme act of love came when we were at our most undesirable (cf. Matt. 5:46).

i. **righteous man . . . good man.** As uncommon as such a sacrifice is, Paul's point is that we were neither of these persons—yet Christ sacrificed Himself for us.

j. **Much more.** What Paul is about to say is even more amazing and wonderful.

k. **by His blood.** Through His violent, substitutionary death. References to the blood of the Savior include the reality that He bled in His death (a necessity to fulfill the OT imagery of sacrifice), but are not limited to the fluid itself. NT writers also use the term "blood" as a graphic way to describe violent death (see Matt. 23:30, 35; 27:4–8, 24, 25; John 6:53–56; Acts 5:28; 20:26). References to the Savior's blood are not simply pointing to the fluid, but at His death and entire atoning work (cf. 3:25; Eph. 1:7; 2:13; Col. 1:14, 20; Heb. 9:12; 10:19; 13:12; 1 Pet. 1:2, 19; 1 John 1:7; Rev. 1:5).

[a]wrath through Him. For if when we were enemies we were reconciled to God through the death of His Son, much more, having been reconciled, we shall be [b]saved by His life. And not only that, but we also rejoice in God through our Lord Jesus Christ, through whom we have now received the [c]reconciliation.

141. THE IMPUTATION OF RIGHTEOUSNESS
Rom. 5:12–21

Therefore, [d]just as [e]through one man sin entered the world, and death through sin, and thus [f]death spread to all men, [g]because all sinned— (For until the law sin was in the world, but [h]sin is not imputed [i]when there is no law. [j]Nevertheless death reigned from Adam to Moses, even over those who had [k]not

a. **wrath.** Christ bore the full fury of God's wrath in the believing sinner's place, and there is none left for him (see Rom. 8:1; 1 Thess. 1:10; 5:9).

b. **saved by His life.** When we were God's enemies, Christ was able by His death to reconcile us to God. Certainly now that we are God's children, the Savior can keep us by His living power.

c. **reconciliation.** This is between God and sinners. See 2 Cor. 5:18–20.

d. **just as . . . sin entered.** Not a particular sin, but the inherent propensity to sin entered the human realm; men became sinners by nature. Adam passed to all his descendants the inherent sinful nature he possessed because of his first disobedience. That nature is present from the moment of conception (Ps. 51:5), making it impossible for man to live in a way that pleases God. Satan, the father of sin (1 John 3:8), first brought temptation to Adam and Eve (Gen. 3:1–7).

e. **through one man.** When Adam sinned, all mankind sinned in his loins (cf. Heb. 7:7–10). Since his sin transformed his inner nature and brought spiritual death and depravity, that sinful nature would be passed on seminally to his posterity as well (Ps. 51:5).

f. **death.** Adam was not originally subject to death, but through his sin it became a grim certainty for him and his posterity. Death has 3 distinct manifestations: 1) spiritual death or separation from God (cf. Eph. 1:1, 2; 4:18); 2) physical death (Heb. 9:27); and 3) eternal death (also called the second death), which includes not only eternal separation from God, but eternal torment in the lake of fire (Rev. 20:11–15).

g. **because all sinned.** Because all humanity existed in the loins of Adam, and have through procreation inherited his fallenness and depravity, it can be said that all sinned in him. Therefore, humans are not sinners because they sin, but rather they sin because they are sinners.

h. **sin is not imputed.** See Acts 17:3; 2 Cor. 5:19. Though all men were regarded as sinners (Rom. 5:12), because there was no explicit list of commands, there was no strict accounting of their specific points of violation.

i. **when there is no law.** The period from Adam to Moses, when God had not yet given the Mosaic law.

j. **Nevertheless death reigned.** But even without the law, death was universal. All men from Adam to Moses were subject to death, not because of their sinful acts against the Mosaic law (which they did not yet have), but because of their own inherited sinful nature.

k. **not sinned . . . likeness . . . of Adam.** Those who had no specific revelation as did Adam (Gen. 2:16, 17) or those who had the Mosaic law (cf. Rom. 5:13), but nevertheless sinned against the holiness of God, i.e., those who "sinned without law" (Rom. 2:12).

sinned according to the likeness of the transgression of Adam, who is [a]a type of Him who was to come. But the free gift is not like the offense. For if by the one man's offense [b]many died, [c]much more the grace of God and [d]the gift by the grace of the one Man, Jesus Christ, abounded to many. And the gift is not like that which came through the one who sinned. For the judgment which came from one offense resulted in [e]condemnation, but the free gift which came from [f]many offenses resulted in justification. For if by the one man's offense [g]death reigned through the one, much more those who receive abundance of grace and of the [h]gift of righteousness [i]will reign in life through the One, Jesus Christ.)

Therefore, as through one man's offense judgment came to all men, resulting in condemnation, even so through [j]one Man's righteous act the [k]free gift came to all men, resulting in justification of life. For as by one man's disobedience many were made sinners, so also by one Man's obedience many will be [l]made righteous.

---

a. **a type of Him . . . to come.** Both Adam and Christ were similar in that their acts affected many others. This phrase serves as transition from the apostle's discussion of the transference of Adam's sin to the crediting of Christ's righteousness.

b. **many died.** Paul uses the word "many" with two distinct meanings in Rom. 5;15, just as he will the word "all" in v. 18. He has already established that all men, without exception, bear the guilt of sin and are therefore subject to death (see v. 12). So the "many" who die must refer to all Adam's descendants.

c. **much more.** Christ's one act of redemption was immeasurably greater than Adam's one act of condemnation.

d. **the gift.** Salvation by grace.

e. **condemnation.** The divine guilty verdict; the opposite of justification.

f. **many offenses.** Adam brought upon all men the condemnation for only one offense—his willful act of disobedience. Christ, however, delivers the elect from the condemnation of many offenses.

g. **death reigned.** Adam's sin brought universal death—exactly opposite the result he expected and Satan had promised: "You will be like God" (Gen. 3:5). Christ's sacrifice brought salvation to those who believe.

h. **gift of righteousness.** See Rom. 1:17 and 3:24; see also 2 Cor. 5:21; Phil. 3:8, 9.

i. **will reign in life.** Unlike Adam's act, Christ's act has—and will—accomplish exactly what He intended (cf. Phil. 1:6), i.e., spiritual life (cf. Eph. 2:5).

j. **one Man's righteous act.** Not a reference to a single event, but generally to Christ's obedience (cf. Luke 2:49; John 4:34; 5:30; 6:38), culminating in the greatest demonstration of that obedience, death on a cross (Phil. 2:8).

k. **free gift . . . to all men.** This cannot mean that all men will be saved; salvation is only for those who exercise faith in Jesus Christ (cf. Rom. 1:16, 17; 3:22, 28; 4:5, 13). Rather, like the word "many" in v. 15, Paul is using "all" with two different meanings for the sake of parallelism, a common practice in the Heb. OT.

l. **made righteous.** This expression probably refers to one's legal status before God and not an actual change in character, since Paul is contrasting justification and condemnation throughout this passage, and he has not yet introduced the doctrine of sanctification (Rom. 6–8) which deals with the actual transformation of the sinner as a result of redemption.

Moreover ᵃthe law entered that the offense might abound. But where sin abounded, grace abounded much more, so that as sin reigned in death, even so grace might reign through righteousness to eternal life through Jesus Christ our Lord.

142. FREEDOM FROM SIN

Rom. 6:1 –14

ᵇWhat shall we say then? ᶜShall we continue in sin that grace may abound? ᵈCertainly not! How shall ᵉwe who died to sin live any longer in it? Or do you not know that as many of us as were ᶠbaptized into Christ Jesus were baptized ᵍinto His death? Therefore we were ʰburied with Him through baptism into

---

a. **the law entered.** Cf. Gal. 3:19. Although the Mosaic law is not flawed (Rom. 7:12), its presence caused man's sin to increase (cf. 7:8–11). Thus it made men more aware of their own sinfulness and inability to keep God's perfect standard (7:7; Gal. 3:21, 22), and it served as a tutor to drive them to Christ (Gal. 3:24).

b. **What shall we say then?** Paul moves from demonstrating the doctrine of justification, which is God's declaring the believing sinner righteous (Rom. 3:20—5:21), to demonstrating the practical ramifications of salvation on those who have been justified. He specifically discusses the doctrine of sanctification, which is God's producing actual righteousness in the believer (Rom. 6:1—8:39). He begins his lesson on sanctification by arguing that in spite of their past, all whom God has justified will experience personal holiness (cf. 1 Cor. 6:9–11a; 1 Tim. 1:12, 13).

c. **Shall we continue in sin.** Because of his past Pharisaic experience, Paul was able to anticipate the major objections of his critics. He had already alluded to this criticism, that by preaching a justification based solely on the free grace of God, he was encouraging people to sin (cf. Rom. 3:5, 6, 8).

d. **Certainly not!** Lit. "may it never be!" Used 14 times in Paul's epistles (10 in Romans: 3:4, 6, 31; 6:2, 15; 7:7, 13; 9:14; 11:1, 11), this expression is the strongest Gr. idiom for repudiating a statement, and it contains a sense of outrage that anyone would ever think the statement was true.

e. **we . . . died to sin.** Not a reference to the believer's ongoing daily struggle with sin, but to a one-time event completed in the past. Because we are "in Christ" (Rom. 6:11; 8:1), and He died in our place (5:6–8), we are counted dead with Him. This is the fundamental premise of chap. 6, and Paul spends the remainder of the chapter explaining and supporting it.

f. **baptized into Christ Jesus.** This does not refer to water baptism. Paul is actually using the word "baptized" in a metaphorical sense, as we might in saying someone was immersed in his work, or underwent his baptism of fire when experiencing some trouble. All Christians have, by placing saving faith in Him, been spiritually immersed into the person Christ, that is, united and identified with Him (cf. 1 Cor. 6:17; 10:2; Gal. 3:27; 1 Pet. 3:21; 1 John 1:3; see Acts 2:38). Certainly water baptism pictures this reality, which is the purpose—to show the transformation of the justified.

g. **into His death.** This means that immersion or identification is specifically with Christ's death and resurrection, as the apostle will explain (see Rom. 6:4–7).

h. **buried with Him.** Since we are united by faith with Him, as baptism symbolizes, His death and burial become ours.

death, that just as Christ was raised from the dead by the glory of the Father, even so we also should walk in ᵃnewness of life.

For if we have been united together in the likeness of His death, certainly we also shall be in the likeness of His resurrection, knowing this, that ᵇour old man was crucified with Him, that the ᶜbody of sin might be ᵈdone away with, that we should no longer be slaves of sin. For he who ᵉhas died has been ᶠfreed from sin. Now if we died with Christ, we believe that ᵍwe shall also live with Him, knowing that Christ, having been raised from the dead, dies no more. Death no longer has ʰdominion over Him. For the death that He died, ⁱHe died to sin once for all; but the life that He lives, ʲHe lives to God. ᵏLikewise you also, ˡreckon

---

a. **newness of life.** This is true if, in Christ, we died and were buried with Him, we have also been united with Him in His resurrection. There is a new quality and character to our lives, a new principle of life. This speaks of the believer's regeneration (cf. Ezek. 36:26; 2 Cor. 5:17; Gal. 6:15; Eph. 4:24). Whereas sin describes the old life, righteousness describes the new.

b. **our old man.** A believer's unregenerate self. The Gr. word for "old" does not refer to something old in years but to something that is worn out and useless. Our old self died with Christ, and the life we now enjoy is a new divinely-given life that is the life of Christ Himself (cf. Gal. 2:20). We have been removed from the unregenerate self's presence and control, so we should not follow the remaining memories of its old sinful ways as if we were still under its evil influence (see Eph. 4:20–24; Gal. 5:24; Col. 3:9, 10).

c. **body of sin.** Essentially synonymous with "our old man." Paul uses the terms "body" and "flesh" to refer to sinful propensities that are intertwined with physical weaknesses and pleasures (e.g., Rom. 8:10, 11, 13, 23). Although the old self is dead, sin retains a foothold in our temporal flesh or our unredeemed humanness, with its corrupted desires (Rom. 7:14–24). The believer does not have two competing natures, the old and the new; but one new nature that is still incarcerated in unredeemed flesh (see Rom. 6:12). But the term "flesh" is not equivalent to the physical body, which can be an instrument of holiness (Rom. 6:19; 12:1; 1 Cor. 6:20).

d. **done away.** Rendered powerless or inoperative.

e. **has died.** Through his union with Christ (see Rom. 6:3).

f. **freed from sin.** No longer under its domination and control.

g. **we shall also live with Him.** The context suggests that Paul means not only that believers will live in the presence of Christ for eternity, but also that all who have died with Christ, which is true of all believers, will live a life here that is fully consistent with His holiness.

h. **dominion.** Mastery, control, or domination. Cf. Rom. 6:11, 12.

i. **He died to sin.** Christ died to sin in two senses: 1) in regard to sin's penalty—He met its legal demands upon the sinner; and 2) in regard to sin's power—forever breaking its power over those who belong to Him. And His death will never need repeating (Heb. 7:26, 27; 9:12, 28; 10:10; cf. 1 Pet. 3:18). Paul's point is that believers have died to sin in the same way.

j. **He lives to God.** For God's glory.

k. **Likewise.** This implies the importance of his readers knowing what he just explained. Without that foundation, what he is about to teach will not make sense. Scripture always identifies knowledge as the foundation for one's practice (cf. Col. 3:10).

l. **reckon.** While it simply means to count or number something, it was often used metaphorically to refer to having an absolute, unreserved confidence in what one's mind knows to be true—the kind of heartfelt confidence that affects his actions and decisions. Paul is not referring to mind games in which we trick ourselves into thinking a certain way. Rather he is urging us to embrace by faith what God has revealed to be true.

yourselves to be dead indeed to sin, but alive to God in [a]Christ Jesus our Lord.

Therefore do not let sin reign in your [b]mortal body, that you should obey it in its lusts. And do not [c]present [d]your members as [e]instruments of unrighteousness to sin, but present yourselves to God as being alive from the dead, and your members as instruments of righteousness to God. For [f]sin shall not have dominion over you, for you are [g]not under law but under grace.

143. SLAVES OF RIGHTEOUSNESS

Rom. 6:15–23

[h]What then? Shall we sin because we are not under law but under grace? Certainly not! Do you not know that to whom you present yourselves slaves to obey, you are that one's slaves whom you obey, whether of sin leading to death, or of obedience leading to righteousness? But God be thanked that though

---

a. **in Christ.** Paul's favorite expression of our union with Christ. This is its first occurrence in Romans (cf. Eph. 1:3–14).

b. **mortal body.** The only remaining repository where sin finds the believer vulnerable. The brain and its thinking processes are part of the body and thus tempt our souls with its sinful lusts (cf. Rom. 8:22, 23; 1 Cor. 15:53; 1 Pet. 2:9–11).

c. **present.** Refers to a decision of the will. Before sin can have power over a believer, it must first pass through his will (cf. Phil. 2:12, 13).

d. **your members.** The parts of the physical body, the headquarters from which sin operates in the believer (7:18, 22–25; cf. 12:1; 1 Cor. 9:27).

e. **instruments of unrighteousness.** Tools for accomplishing that which violates God's holy will and law.

f. **sin shall not have dominion.** Sin must be able to exercise control in our bodies or Paul's admonition becomes unnecessary (Rom. 6:13). But sin does not have to reign there; so the apostle expresses his confidence that those who are Christ's will not allow it to.

g. **not under law but under grace.** This does not mean God has abrogated His moral law (Rom. 3:31; cf. Matt. 5:17–19). The law is good, holy, and righteous (Rom. 7:12; cf. 1 Tim. 1:8), but it cannot be kept, so it curses. Since it cannot assist anyone to keep God's moral standard (cf. Rom. 7:7–11), it can only show the standard and thus rebuke and condemn those who fail to keep it. But the believer is no longer under the law as a condition of acceptance with God—an impossible condition to meet and one designed only to show man his sinfulness (see Rom. 3:19, 20; cf. Gal. 3:10–13)—but under grace, which enables him to truly fulfill the law's righteous requirements (Rom. 7:6; 8:3, 4). Chapter 7 is Paul's complete commentary on this crucial expression.

h. **What then?** This section continues Paul's discussion of sanctification by reminding his readers of their past slavery to sin and their new slavery to righteousness. He wants them to live in submission to their new master, Jesus Christ, and not to be entangled again with the sins that characterized their old life, sins which no longer have any claim over them.

you were slaves of sin, yet you obeyed from the heart that [a]form of doctrine to which you were delivered. And having been set free from sin, you became slaves of righteousness. I speak in [b]human terms because of the weakness of your flesh. For just as you presented your members as slaves of uncleanness, and of lawlessness leading to [c]more lawlessness, so now present your members as slaves of righteousness for holiness.

For when you were slaves of sin, you were free in regard to righteousness. What [d]fruit did you have then in the things of which you are now ashamed? For the end of those things is death. But now having been set free from sin, and having become slaves of God, you have your fruit to [e]holiness, and the end, everlasting life. [f]For the wages of sin is death, but the gift of God is eternal life in Christ Jesus our Lord.

144. SIN AND THE LAW

Rom. 7:1–12

Or do you not know, brethren (for I speak to those who [g]know the law), that the law has [h]dominion over a man as long as he lives? [i]For the woman who has

---

a. **form of doctrine . . . delivered.** In the Gk. "form" is a word for a mold such as a craftsman would use to cast molten metal. Paul's point is that God pours His new children into the mold of divine truth (Rom. 12:2; cf. Titus 2:1). New believers have an innate and compelling desire to know and obey God's Word (1 Pet. 2:2).

b. **human terms . . . weakness of your flesh.** Paul's use of the master/slave analogy was an accommodation to their humanness and their difficulty in grasping divine truth.

c. **more lawlessness.** Like a vicious animal, sin's appetite only grows when it is fed (Gen. 4:7).

d. **fruit.** Or benefit.

e. **holiness.** The benefit of being slaves to God is sanctification, the outcome of which is eternal life.

f. **For the wages . . .** This verse describes two inexorable absolutes: 1) spiritual death is the paycheck for every man's slavery to sin; and 2) eternal life is a free gift God gives undeserving sinners who believe in His Son (cf. Eph. 2:8, 9).

g. **know the law.** Lit. "those who know law." Although Paul intends to include God's written law, he is not referring to any specific law code, but to a principle that is true of all law—Greek, Roman, Jewish, or biblical. Knowing that his readers—especially Jewish ones—would have many questions about how the law relates to their faith in Christ, Paul sets out to explain that relationship (he refers to the law 27 times in this passage). In a detailed explanation of what it means not to be under law, but under grace (Rom. 6:14, 15), Paul teaches that: 1) the law can no longer condemn a believer (Rom. 7:1–6); 2) it convicts unbelievers (and believers) of sin (Rom. 7:7–13); 3) it cannot deliver a believer from sin (Rom. 7:14–25); and 4) believers who walk in the power of the Spirit can fulfill the law (Rom. 8:1–4).

h. **dominion.** I.e., jurisdiction. No matter how serious a criminal's offenses may be, he is no longer subject to prosecution and punishment after he dies.

i. **For the woman . . .** These two verses are not a complex allegory, but a simple analogy,

289

a husband is bound by the law to her husband as long as he lives. But if the husband dies, she is [a]released from the law of her husband. So then if, while her husband lives, she marries another man, she will be called an adulteress; but if her husband dies, she is free from that law, so that she is no adulteress, though she has married another man. Therefore, my brethren, you also have [b]become dead to the law [c]through the body of Christ, that you may [d]be married to another—to Him who was raised from the dead, that we should bear [e]fruit to God. For when we were in the [f]flesh, the [g]sinful passions which were [h]aroused by the law were at work in our members to bear fruit to death. But now we have been [i]delivered from the law, having died to what we were

---

using marriage law to illustrate the point Paul just made about law's jurisdiction (Rom. 7:1). This passage is not teaching that only the death of a spouse frees a Christian to remarry; it is not teaching about divorce and remarriage at all. Both Christ and Paul have fully addressed those issues elsewhere (cf. Matt. 5:31, 32; 19:3–12; 1 Cor. 7:10–15).

a. **released from the law.** The law that governs a married woman's actions no longer has any jurisdiction over her once her husband dies. Widows are free to marry again, and Paul even encourages younger ones to remarry as long as their potential mate is a believer (1 Cor. 7:39; 1 Tim. 5:14). Even the illegitimately divorced can marry again (see 1 Cor. 7:8, 9).

b. **become dead.** The Gr. construction of this verb emphasizes two important points: 1) this death happened at a point in time, with results that are complete and final; and 2) someone else—in this case God Himself—initiated this death (lit. "you were made to die"). In response to faith in His Son, God makes the believing sinner forever dead to the condemnation and penalty of the law (cf. Rom. 8:1).

c. **through the body of Christ.** Because, as the substitute for sinners, He suffered the penalty of death that the law demanded.

d. **be married to another.** Just as the widow in Paul's analogy (Rom. 7:2, 3) was freed to remarry, the believer has been freed from his hostile relationship to a law that condemned him, and can, therefore, be remarried—this time to Christ (cf. 2 Cor. 11:5; Eph. 5:24–27).

e. **fruit.** A transformed life that manifests new attitudes (Gal. 5:22, 23) and actions (John 15:1, 2; Phil. 1:11; cf. 2 Cor. 5:21; Gal. 2:19, 20; Eph. 2:10; see Rom. 1:13). This is in contrast to the "fruit to death," which refers to the sinful passions at work in unbelievers produce a harvest of eternal death (see Rom. 5:12; cf. Gal. 6:7, 8).

f. **flesh.** Scripture uses this term in a non-moral sense to describe man's physical being (John 1:14), and in a morally evil sense to describe man's unredeemed humanness (see Rom. 6:6; Rom. 8; Gal. 5; Eph. 2), i.e., that remnant of the old man which will remain with each believer until each receives his or her glorified body (Rom. 8:23). "In the flesh" here describes a person who is able to operate only in the sphere of fallen mankind—an unredeemed, unregenerate person (Rom. 8:9). Although the believer can manifest some of the deeds of the flesh, he can never again be "in the flesh."

g. **sinful passions.** The overwhelming impulses to think and do evil, which characterize those who are "in the flesh" (Eph. 2:3).

h. **aroused by the law.** The unbeliever's rebellious nature is awakened when restrictions are placed on him and makes him want to do the very things the law forbids (cf. Rom. 1:32).

i. **delivered from the law.** Not freedom to do what God's law forbids (Rom. 6:1, 15; 8:4; cf. 3:31), but freedom from the spiritual liabilities and penalties of God's law (cf. Gal. 3:13). Because we died in Christ when He died (see 6:2), the law with its condemnation and penalties no longer has jurisdiction over us (Rom. 7:1–3).

held by, so that we should ^aserve in the ^bnewness of the Spirit and not in the oldness of the letter.

What shall we say then? ^cIs the law sin? Certainly not! On the contrary, I would not have known sin except through the law. For ^dI would not have known covetousness unless the law had said, "You shall not ^ecovet." But sin, taking ^fopportunity by the commandment, produced in me all manner of evil desire. For apart from the law ^gsin was dead. I was alive once ^hwithout the law, but ⁱwhen the commandment came, ^jsin revived and ^kI died. And the commandment, which ^lwas to bring life, I found to bring death. For ^msin, taking occasion by the commandment, deceived me, and by it killed me. Therefore ⁿthe law is holy, and the commandment holy and just and good.

---

a. **serve.** This is the verb form of the word for "bondservant" (see Rom. 1:1), but here it is parallel to being slaves of righteousness (cf. Rom. 6:22), emphasizing that this service is not voluntary. Not only is the believer able to do what is right, he will do what is right.

b. **the newness of the Spirit.** A new state of mind which the Spirit produces, characterized by a new desire and ability to keep the law of God (see Rom. 8:4). This is in contrast to the "oldness of the letter"—the external, written law code that produced only hostility and condemnation.

c. **Is the law sin?** Paul wanted to make certain his readers did not conclude that the law itself was evil.

d. **I would not have known sin.** The law reveals the divine standard, and as believers compare themselves against that standard, they can accurately identify sin, which is the failure to meet the standard. Paul uses the personal pronoun "I" throughout the rest of the chapter, using his own experience as an example of what is true of unredeemed mankind (Rom. 7:7–12) and true of Christians (vv. 13–25).

e. **covet.** Quoted from Ex. 20:17; Deut. 5:21.

f. **opportunity by the commandment.** The word "opportunity" describes a starting point or base of operations for an expedition. Sin uses the specific requirements of the law as a base of operation from which to launch its evil work. Confronted by God's law, the sinner's rebellious nature finds the forbidden thing more attractive, not because it is inherently attractive, but because it furnishes an opportunity to assert one's self-will.

g. **sin was dead.** Not lifeless or nonexistent (see Rom. 5:12, 13), but dormant. When the law comes, sin becomes fully active and overwhelms the sinner.

h. **without the law.** Not ignorance of or lack of concern for the law (cf. Phil. 3:6), but a purely external, imperfect conception of it.

i. **when the commandment came.** When he began to understand the true requirements of God's moral law at some point prior to his conversion.

j. **sin revived.** He realized his true condition as a desperately wicked sinner (cf. 1 Tim. 1:15).

k. **I died.** He realized his deadness, spiritually; that all his religious credentials and accomplishments were rubbish (Phil. 3:7, 8).

l. **was to bring life.** Theoretically, perfect obedience to the law could bring eternal life, and with it happiness and holiness. But no one except Christ has—or could—ever fully obey it (2 Cor. 5:21; see Rom. 10:5).

m. **sin . . . deceived me.** By leading him to expect life from his keeping of the law, when what he found was death; and by convincing him that he is acceptable to God because of his own merit and good works.

n. **the law is holy.** The fact that the law reveals and condemns sin, bringing death to the

145. The Fight against the Flesh

Rom. 7:13–25

[a]Has then what is good become death to me? Certainly not! But [b]sin, that it might appear sin, was producing death in me through what is good, so that sin through the commandment might become exceedingly sinful. For we know that the [c]law is spiritual, but I am [d]carnal, [e]sold under sin. For [f]what I am doing, I do not [g]understand. For what I will to do, that I do not practice; but what I hate, that I do. If, then, I do what I will not to do, [h]I agree with the law that

sinner, does not mean that the law is evil. Rather the law is a perfect reflection of God's holy character (cf. Rom. 7:14, 16, 22; Ps. 19:7–11) and the standard for believers to please Him.

a. **Has then what is good become death.** Sin is the cause of spiritual death, not the good law.

b. **sin . . . might become . . . sinful.** An awareness of the true nature of sin and its deadly character, which brings the sinner to see his need of salvation—the very purpose God intended the law to serve (Gal. 3:19–22).

c. **the law is spiritual.** I.e., it reflects God's holy character.

d. **carnal.** Lit. "of flesh." This means earthbound, mortal, and still incarcerated in unredeemed humanness. Paul does not say he is still "in the flesh" (see Rom. 7:5), but the flesh is in him.

e. **sold under sin.** Sin no longer controls the whole man (as with an unbeliever; cf. Rom. 6:6), but it does hold captive the believer's members, or his fleshly body. Sin contaminates him and frustrates his inner desire to obey the will of God.

f. **what I am doing.** Some interpret this chronicle of Paul's inner conflict as describing his life before Christ. They point out that Paul describes the person as "sold under sin" (Rom. 7:14); as having "nothing good" in him (v. 18); and as a "wretched man" trapped in a "body of death" (v. 24). Those descriptions seem to contradict the way Paul describes the believer in chap. 6 (cf. vv. 2, 6, 7, 11, 17, 18, 22). However, it is correct to understand Paul here to be speaking about a believer. This person desires to obey God's law and hates his sin (vv. 15, 19, 21); he is humble, recognizing that nothing good dwells in his humanness (v. 18); he sees sin in himself, but not as all that is there (vv. 17, 20–22); and he serves Jesus Christ with his mind (v. 25). Paul has already established that none of those attitudes ever describe the unsaved (cf. 1:18–21, 32; 3:10–20). Paul's use of present tense verbs in vv. 14–25 strongly supports the idea that he is describing his life currently as a Christian. For those reasons, it seems certain that chap. 7 describes a believer. However, of those who agree that this is a believer, there is still disagreement. Some see a carnal, fleshly Christian; others a legalistic Christian, frustrated by his feeble attempts in his own power to please God by keeping the Mosaic law. But the personal pronoun "I" refers to the apostle Paul, a standard of spiritual health and maturity. So, in vv. 14–25 Paul must be describing all Christians—even the most spiritual and mature—who, when they honestly evaluate themselves against the righteous standard of God's law, realize how far short they fall. He does so in a series of 4 laments (vv. 14–17, 18–20, 21–23, 24, 25).

g. **understand.** This refers to knowledge that goes beyond the factual and includes the idea of an intimate relationship (cf. Gal. 4:9). By extension, this word was sometimes used to express approving or accepting (cf. 1 Cor. 8:3). That is its sense here, i.e., Paul found himself doing things he did not approve of.

h. **I agree with the law that it is good.** Paul's new nature defends the divine standard—the perfectly righteous law is not responsible for his sin. His new self longs to honor the law and keep it perfectly (Rom. 7:22).

it is good. But now, it is [a]no longer I who do it, but [b]sin that dwells in me. For I know that [c]in me (that is, in [d]my flesh) nothing good dwells; for to will is present with me, but how to perform what is good I do not find. For the good that I will to do, I do not do; but the evil I will not to do, that I practice. Now if I do what I will not to do, it is no longer I who do it, but sin that dwells in me.

I find then a [e]law, that evil is present with me, the one who wills to do good. For [f]I delight in the law of God according to the inward man. But I see [g]another law in my members, warring against the [h]law of my mind, and bringing me into captivity to the law of sin which is in my members. O [i]wretched man that I am! Who will [j]deliver me from this [k]body of death? I thank God—[l]through Jesus Christ our Lord!

---

a. **no longer I who do it.** The Gr. adverb for "no longer" signifies a complete and permanent change. Paul's new inner self (see Rom. 6:6), the new "I," no longer approved of the sin that was still residing in his flesh, like his old self did (cf. Gal. 2:20), but rather, strongly disapproved. Many have misconstrued Paul's comments as abdicating personal responsibility for his sin by embracing a form of Greek dualism (which would later spawn Gnosticism). Dualism taught that the body is evil and the spirit is good, so its adherents sinned with impunity by claiming they were not responsible; their sin was entirely the product of their physical bodies, while their spirits remained untouched and unsullied. But the apostle has already acknowledged personal guilt for his sin (cf. 1 John 1:10).

b. **sin that dwells in me.** His sin does not flow out of his new redeemed innermost self ("I"), but from his unredeemed humanness, his flesh "in me" (Gal. 5:17).

c. **in me . . . nothing good dwells.** The flesh serves as a base camp from which sin operates in the Christian's life. It is not sinful inherently, but because of its fallenness, it is still subject to sin and is thoroughly contaminated.

d. **my flesh.** The part of the believer's present being that remains unredeemed (see Rom. 6:6, 12; 7:5).

e. **law.** Not a reference to God's law, but to an inviolable spiritual principle.

f. **I delight in the law of God.** The believer's justified, new inner self no longer sides with sin, but joyfully agrees with the law of God against sin (Pss. 1:2; 119:14, 47, 77, 105, 140; cf. 2 Cor. 4:16; Eph. 3:16).

g. **another law.** A corresponding spiritual principle to the one in Rom. 7:21. But this principle, which Paul identifies as "the law of sin," operates in the members of his body—that is, his unredeemed and still sinful humanness (see 6:6)—waging war against his desire to obey God's law.

h. **law of my mind.** Equivalent to the new inner self (2 Cor. 5:17; see 6:6), which longs to obey the law of God (see Rom. 7:21, 22). Paul is not saying his mind is spiritual and his body is inherently evil (see Rom. 7:17).

i. **wretched man.** In frustration and grief, Paul laments his sin (cf. Pss. 38:14; 130:1–5). A believer perceives his own sinfulness in direct proportion to how clearly he sees the holiness of God and perfection of His law.

j. **deliver.** This word means "to rescue from danger" and was used of a soldier pulling his wounded comrade from the battlefield. Paul longed to be rescued from his sinful flesh (cf. Rom. 8:23).

k. **body of death.** The believer's unredeemed humanness, which has its base of operation in the body (see Rom. 6:6, 12; 7:5). Tradition says that an ancient tribe near Tarsus tied the corpse of a murder victim to its murderer, allowing its spreading decay to slowly infect and execute the murderer—perhaps that is the image Paul has in mind.

l. **through Jesus Christ.** The first half of this verse answers the question Paul just raised—

So then, with the mind [a]I myself serve the law of God, but with the flesh the law of sin.

146. No Condemnation in Christ

Rom. 8:1–8

There is [b]therefore now [c]no condemnation to [d]those who are in Christ Jesus, who do not walk according to the flesh, but according to the Spirit. [e]For [f]the law of [g]the Spirit of life in Christ Jesus has made me free from [h]the law of sin and death. For [i]what the law could not do in that it was [j]weak through the flesh, God did by sending [k]His own Son [l]in the likeness of sinful flesh, on

---

he is certain that Christ will eventually rescue him when He returns (cf. Rom. 8:18, 23; 1 Cor. 15:52, 53, 56, 57; 2 Cor. 5:4). The second half summarizes the two sides of the struggle Paul has described (vv. 14–24).

    a. **I myself.** Paul's new redeemed self (see Rom. 6:6).

    b. **therefore.** The result or consequence of the truth just taught. Normally it marks the conclusion of the verses immediately preceding it. But here it introduces the staggering results of Paul's teaching in the first 7 chapters of Romans: that justification is by faith alone on the basis of God's overwhelming grace.

    c. **no condemnation.** Occurring only 3 times in the NT, all in Romans (cf. Rom. 5:16, 18), "condemnation" is used exclusively in judicial settings as the opposite of justification. It refers to a verdict of guilty and the penalty that verdict demands. No sin a believer can commit—past, present, or future—can be held against him, since the penalty was paid by Christ and righteousness was imputed to the believer. And no sin will ever reverse this divine legal decision (see Rom. 8:33).

    d. **those . . . in Christ Jesus.** I.e., every true Christian; to be in Christ means to be united with Him (see Rom. 6:2, 11; cf. 6:1–11; 1 Cor. 12:13, 27; 15:22).

    e. **For.** The word "for" introduces the reason there is no condemnation for the believer, the Spirit has replaced the law that produced only sin and death (Rom. 7:5, 13) with a new, simple law that produces life: the law of faith (Rom. 3:27), or the message of the gospel.

    f. **the law of the Spirit of life.** Synonymous with the gospel, the law of faith.

    g. **the Spirit.** The Spirit, who was mentioned only once in Rom. 1–7 (cf. 1:4), is referred to nearly 20 times in chap. 8. He frees us from sin and death (Rom. 8:2, 3); enables us to fulfill God's law (v. 4); changes our nature and grants us strength for victory over our unredeemed flesh (vv. 5–13); confirms our adoption as God's children (vv. 14–16); and guarantees our ultimate glory (vv. 17–30).

    h. **the law of sin and death.** The law of God. Although it is good, holy, and righteous (Rom. 7:12), because of the weakness of the flesh (see Rom. 7:7–11; 8:3), it can produce only sin and death (Rom. 7:5, 13).

    i. **what the law could not do.** Deliver sinners from its penalty (Acts 13:38, 39; Gal. 3:10) or make them righteous (Gal. 3:21).

    j. **weak . . . the flesh.** Because of the sinful corruption of unregenerate men, the law was powerless to produce righteousness (Gal. 3:21).

    k. **His own Son.** See Ps. 2:7; Gal. 4:4; Phil. 2:6, 7; Heb. 1:1–5.

    l. **in the likeness of sinful flesh.** Although in His incarnation Christ became fully man (see

account of sin: He [a]condemned sin in the flesh, that the [b]righteous requirement of the law might be [c]fulfilled in us who do [d]not walk according to the flesh but according to the Spirit. For those who live according to the flesh [e]set their minds on the things of the flesh, but [f]those who live according to the Spirit, the things of the Spirit. For to be [g]carnally minded is death, but to be [h]spiritually minded is life and peace. Because the carnal mind is [i]enmity against God; for it is not subject to the law of God, nor indeed can be. So then, those who are in the flesh cannot please God.

Rom. 1:3), He took only the outward appearance of sinful flesh, because He was completely without sin (Heb. 4:15).

a. **condemned sin in the flesh.** God's condemnation against sin was fully poured out on the sinless flesh of Christ (Is. 53:4–8; cf. Phil. 2:7).

b. **righteous requirement of the law.** The thoughts, words, and deeds which the moral law of God demands. The ceremonial aspect of the Mosaic law has been set aside (Col. 2:14–17), and the basic responsibility for the civil aspect, which shows the application of the moral law in a community, has been transferred to human government (Rom. 13:1–7). The moral law finds its basis in the character of God and is presented in outline form in the Ten Commandments; its most condensed form is in Jesus' commands to love God and to love one's neighbor as one's self. It has never been abrogated, but finds its authority in the New Covenant. Every unbeliever is still under its requirement of perfection and its condemnation, until he comes to Christ (Gal. 3:23–25) and every believer still finds in it the standard for behavior.

c. **fulfilled.** Although the believer is no longer in bondage to the moral law's condemnation and penalty (Rom. 7:6), the law still reflects the moral character of God and His will for His creatures. But what the external, written code was unable to accomplish, the Spirit is able to do by writing the law on our hearts (Jer. 31:33, 34) and giving us the power to obey it.

d. **not walk according to the flesh but . . . the Spirit.** Not an admonition, but a statement of fact that applies to all believers. "Walk" refers to a lifestyle, the habits of living and thinking that characterize a person's life (cf. Luke 1:6; Eph. 4:17; 1 John 1:7). Since every true Christian is indwelt by the Spirit, every Christian will manifest the fruit He produces in their life (Gal. 5:22, 23).

e. **set their minds.** This Gr. verb refers to a basic orientation of the mind—a mindset that includes one's affections, mental processes, and will (cf. Phil. 2:2, 5; 3:15, 19; Col. 3:2). Paul's point is that unbelievers' basic disposition is to satisfy the cravings of their unredeemed flesh (Phil. 3:19; 2 Pet. 2:10).

f. **those who live . . . the flesh.** All unbelievers.

g. **carnally minded.** In the Gr. "minded" is a noun form of the verb in Rom. 8:5. "Carnally" means "of flesh." This is a simple spiritual equation: The person with the mind set on the flesh is spiritually dead (cf. 1 Cor. 2:14; Eph. 2:1).

h. **spiritually minded.** This describes every Christian. The person with his mind set on the things of the Spirit is very much spiritually alive and at peace with God (see Rom. 5:1; cf. Eph. 2:5).

i. **enmity against God.** The unbeliever's problem is much deeper than acts of disobedience, which are merely outward manifestations of inner fleshly compulsions. His basic inclinations and orientation toward gratifying himself—however outwardly religious or moral he may appear—are directly hostile to God. Even the good deeds unbelievers perform are not truly a fulfillment of God's law, because they are produced by the flesh, for selfish reasons, and from a heart that is in rebellion (see Rom. 5:1).

147. FREEDOM IN THE SPIRIT

Rom. 8:9–17

But you are not in the flesh but in the Spirit, if indeed the Spirit of God ᵃdwells in you. Now if anyone does not have the Spirit of Christ, he is not His. And if Christ is in you, ᵇthe body is dead because of sin, but the ᶜSpirit is life because of righteousness. But if the Spirit of Him who raised Jesus from the dead dwells in you, He who raised Christ from the dead will also give life to your mortal bodies through His Spirit who dwells in you.

Therefore, brethren, we are debtors—not to the flesh, to live according to the flesh. For if you live according to ᵈthe flesh you will die; but if by the Spirit you ᵉput to death the deeds of the body, you will live. For as many as are ᶠled by the Spirit of God, these are ᵍsons of God. For you did not receive the ʰspirit of bondage again to fear, but you received the ⁱSpirit of adoption by whom we cry

a. **dwells.** Refers to being in one's own home. The Spirit of God makes His home in every person who trusts in Jesus Christ. Cf. 1 Cor. 6:19, 20; 12:13. When there is no evidence of His presence by the fruit He produces (Gal. 5:22, 23), a person has no legitimate claim to Christ as Savior and Lord.

b. **the body is dead because of sin.** The body is unredeemed and dead in sin (see Rom. 6:6, 12; 7:5; cf. 8:11, 23).

c. **Spirit is life because of righteousness.** It is best to translate the word "spirit" as the person's spirit, not the Holy Spirit. Paul is saying that if God's Spirit indwells you (Rom. 7:9), the human spirit is alive (cf. Eph. 2:5) and can manifest true righteousness.

d. **the flesh.** Our unredeemed humanness—that complex of sinful passions that sin generates through its one remaining domain, our bodies (see Rom. 6:6, 12; 7:5).

e. **put to death the deeds of the body.** Paul's first instruction concerning what his readers must do in the struggle with sin destroys several false views of how believers are made holy: 1) that in a crisis-moment we are immediately made perfect; 2) that we must "let God" take over while we remain idle; and 3) that some turning-point decision will propel us to a higher level of holiness. Rather, the apostle says the Spirit provides us with the energy and power to continually and gradually be killing our sins, a process never completed in this life. The means the Spirit uses to accomplish this process is our faithful obedience to the simple commands of Scripture (see Eph. 5:18; Col. 3:16; cf. 13:14; Pss. 1:2; 119:11; Luke 22:40; John 17:17; 1 Cor. 6:18; 9:25–27; 1 Pet. 2:11).

f. **led by the Spirit.** Believers are not led through subjective, mental impressions or promptings to provide direction in making life's decisions—something Scripture nowhere teaches. Instead, God's Spirit objectively leads His children sometimes through the orchestration of circumstances (Acts 16:7) but primarily through: 1) illumination, divinely clarifying Scripture to make it understandable to our sinful, finite minds (Luke 24:44, 45; 1 Cor. 2:14–16; Eph. 1:17–19; cf. Eph. 3:16–19; Col. 1:9); and 2) sanctification, divinely enabling us to obey Scripture (Gal. 5:16, 17; 5:25).

g. **sons of God.** When a person experiences the Spirit's leading in those ways, he gains assurance that God has adopted him into His family (see Rom. 8:15–17; 1 John 3:2).

h. **spirit of bondage . . . to fear.** Because of their life of sin, unregenerate people are slaves to their fear of death (Heb. 2:14, 15), and to their fear of final punishment (1 John 4:18).

i. **Spirit of adoption.** Not primarily a reference to the transaction by which God adopts us (see Eph. 1:5; Gal. 4:5–7), but to a Spirit-produced awareness of the rich reality that God has

out, ᵃ"Abba, Father." The Spirit Himself ᵇbears witness with our spirit that we are children of God, and if children, then ᶜheirs—heirs of God and ᵈjoint heirs with Christ, ᵉif indeed we suffer with Him, that we may also be glorified together.

148. THE ASSURANCE OF SALVATION GLORY
Rom. 8:18–30

ᶠFor I consider that the sufferings of this present time are not worthy to be compared with the glory which shall be revealed in us. For the earnest expectation of ᵍthe creation eagerly waits for ʰthe revealing of the sons of God. For the creation was subjected to ⁱfutility, not willingly, but because of Him who subjected it in hope; because the creation itself also will be delivered from the bondage of corruption into the glorious liberty of the children of God. For we

made us His children, and, therefore, that we can come before Him without fear or hesitation as our beloved Father. It includes the confidence that we are truly sons of God.

a. **Abba.** An informal, Aram. term for Father that conveys a sense of intimacy. Like the Eng. terms "Daddy" or "Papa," it connotes tenderness, dependence, and a relationship free of fear or anxiety (cf. Mark 14:36).

b. **bears witness with our spirit.** In Roman culture, for an adoption to be legally binding, 7 reputable witnesses had to be present, attesting to its validity. God's Holy Spirit confirms the validity of our adoption, not by some inner, mystical voice, but by the fruit He produces in us (Gal. 5:22, 23) and the power He provides for spiritual service (Acts 1:8).

c. **heirs.** Every believer has been made an heir of God, our Father (Matt. 25:34; Gal. 3:29; Eph. 1:11; Col. 1:12; 3:24; Heb. 6:12; 9:15; 1 Pet. 1:4). We will inherit eternal salvation (Titus 3:7), God Himself (Lam. 3:24; cf. Ps. 73:25; Rev. 21:3), glory (5:2), and everything in the universe (Heb. 1:2). Unlike the Jewish practice of the primacy of the firstborn son, under Roman law the inheritance was divided equally between the children, where the law more carefully protected possessions that had been inherited.

d. **joint heirs.** God has appointed His Son to be heir of all things (Heb. 1:2). Every adopted child will receive by divine grace the full inheritance Christ receives by divine right (cf. Matt. 25:21; John 17:22; 2 Cor. 8:9).

e. **if . . . we suffer with Him.** Proof of the believer's ultimate glory is that he suffers—whether it comes as mockery, ridicule, or physical persecution—because of His Lord (Matt. 5:10–12; John 15:18–21; 2 Cor. 4:17; 2 Tim. 3:12).

f. **glory . . . revealed in us.** This looks forward to the resurrection of the body (Rom.8:23) and the subsequent complete Christlikeness which is the believer's eternal glory. See Phil. 3:20, 21; Col. 3:4; 1 John 3:2.

g. **the creation.** This includes everything in the physical universe except human beings, whom he contrasts with this term (Rom.8:22, 23). All creation is personified to be, as it were, longing for transformation from the curse and its effects.

h. **the revealing.** Lit. "an uncovering," or "an unveiling." When Christ returns, God's children will share His glory.

i. **futility.** This refers to the inability to achieve a goal or purpose. Because of man's sin, God cursed the physical universe (Gen. 3:17–19), and now, no part of creation entirely fulfills God's original purpose.

know that the whole creation groans and labors with birth pangs together until now. Not only that, but we also who have the [a]firstfruits of the Spirit, even we ourselves [b]groan within ourselves, eagerly waiting for the [c]adoption, the [d]redemption of our body. For we were saved in this hope, but hope that is seen is not hope; for why does one still hope for what he sees? But if we hope for what we do not see, we eagerly wait for it with perseverance.

[e]Likewise the Spirit also helps in our weaknesses. For we do not know what we should pray for as we ought, but the Spirit Himself makes intercession for us with [f]groanings which cannot be uttered. Now He who searches the hearts knows what [g]the mind of the Spirit is, because He makes intercession for the saints according to the will of God.

And we know that [h]all things work together for [i]good to those who love God, to those who are the [j]called according to His purpose. For whom He [k]foreknew, He also [l]predestined to be [m]conformed to the image of His Son,

a. **firstfruits of the Spirit.** Just as the first pieces of produce to appear on a tree provide hope of a future harvest, the fruit which the Spirit produces in us now (Gal. 5:22, 23) provides hope that we will one day be like Christ.

b. **groan.** With grief over our remaining sinfulness (Rom.7:24; cf. Ps. 38:4, 9, 10).

c. **adoption.** The process that began with God's choice (Eph. 1:5) and included our actually becoming His children at salvation (Gal. 4:5–7) will culminate with our glorification—the full realization of our inheritance (see Rom. 8:29, 30).

d. **redemption of our body.** Not the physical body only, but all of man's remaining fallenness (see 6:6, 12; 7:5; cf. 1 Cor. 15:35–44; Phil. 3:20, 21; 2 Pet. 1:3, 4; 1 John 3:2).

e. **Likewise.** As the creation (Rom. 8:22) and believers (v. 23) both groan for ultimate restoration, the Spirit does as well.

f. **groanings which cannot be uttered.** Divine articulations within the Trinity that cannot be expressed in words, but carry profound appeals for the welfare of every believer (cf. 1 Cor. 2:11). This work of the Holy Spirit parallels the high priestly work of intercession by the Lord Jesus on behalf of believers (see Heb. 2:17, 18; 4:14–16; 7:24–26).

g. **the mind of the Spirit.** No words are necessary because the Father understands and agrees with what the Spirit thinks. See Jude 20.

h. **all things.** The best manuscript evidence records this verse as, "we know that God causes all things . . ."

i. **good.** In His providence, God orchestrates every event in life—even suffering, temptation, and sin—to accomplish both our temporal and eternal benefit (cf. Deut. 8:15, 16).

j. **called.** Cf. Rom.8:30; see 1:7. As always, in the NT epistles, this call is God's effectual calling of His elect that brings them to salvation.

k. **foreknew.** Not a reference simply to God's omniscience—that in eternity past He knew who would come to Christ. Rather, it speaks of a predetermined choice to set His love on us and established an intimate relationship—or His election (cf. Acts 2:23—an inviolable rule of Gr. grammar, called the Granville Sharp rule, equates "predestined" and "foreknowledge;" see 1 Pet. 1:1, 2, and cf. with Rom.1:20—the term must be interpreted the same in both verses). See election in Rom.9:10–24.

l. **predestined.** Lit. "to mark out, appoint, or determine beforehand." Those God chooses, He destines for His chosen end—that is, likeness to His Son (see Eph. 1:4, 5, 11).

m. **conformed to the image of His Son.** The goal of God's predestined purpose for His own is that they would be made like Jesus Christ. This is the "prize of the upward call" (Phil. 3:14); cf. Eph. 4:13; Col. 1:28; Phil. 3:20, 21; 1 John 3:2).

that He might be the ᵃfirstborn among many brethren. Moreover whom He predestined, these He also called; whom He called, these He also justified; and whom He justified, these He also ᵇglorified.

149. SECURE IN GOD'S LOVE

Romans 8:31–39

ᶜWhat then shall we say to these things? ᵈIf God is for us, who can be against us? He who did not spare His own Son, but delivered Him up for us all, how shall He not with Him also ᵉfreely give us ᶠall things? Who shall bring a charge against God's elect? ᵍIt is God who justifies. Who is he who ʰcondemns? It is Christ who died, and furthermore is also risen, who is even at the right hand of God, who also makes intercession for us. Who shall separate us from ⁱthe love of Christ? Shall ʲtribulation, or ᵏdistress, or ˡpersecution, or famine, or nakedness, or peril, or sword? As ᵐit is written:

---

a. **firstborn.** The preeminent one, the only one who is the rightful heir (cf. Ps. 89:27; Col. 1:15–18; Rev. 1:5). Jesus Christ is the most notable one among those who have become "brethren" by being made like Him.

b. **glorified.** Paul uses the past tense for a future event to stress its certainty (cf. Rom.8:18, 21; 2 Tim. 2:10).

c. **What shall we say to these things?** Paul closes his teaching about the believer's security in Christ with a crescendo of questions and answers for the concerns his readers might still have. The result is an almost poetic expression of praise for God's grace in bringing salvation to completion for all who are chosen and believe—a hymn of security.

d. **If God is for us.** The Gr. construction is better translated "Since God is for us."

e. **freely give.** This word means "to bestow out of grace." Paul often uses it to denote forgiveness (2 Cor. 2:7, 10; 12:13; Col. 2:13; 3:13) and may intend that here.

f. **all things.** Referring either to every sin the believer commits (if "freely give" is translated "forgiveness") or to whatever is necessary to complete the purpose He had in choosing us (Rom. 8:29, 30; cf. Phil. 1:6)

g. **It is God who justifies.** See Rom. 3:24. Who can successfully accuse someone whom God has declared righteous?

h. **condemns.** To declare guilty and sentence to punishment. There are 4 reasons the believer can never be found guilty: 1) Christ's death; 2) His resurrection; 3) His exalted position; and 4) His continual intercession for them.

i. **the love of Christ.** Not our love for Christ, but His love for us (John 13:1), specifically here as He demonstrated it in salvation (1 John 4:9, 10).

j. **tribulation.** See Rom.5:3. Here the word probably refers to the kind of adversity common to all men.

k. **distress.** This refers to being strictly confined in a narrow, difficult place or being helplessly hemmed in by one's circumstances.

l. **persecution.** Suffering inflicted on us by men because of our relationship with Christ (Matt. 5:10–12).

m. **it is written.** This is a quotation from the LXX (the ancient Gr. translation of the Heb. OT) of Ps. 44:22.

"For Your sake we are killed all day long;
We are accounted as sheep for the slaughter."

Yet in all these things we are ᵃmore than conquerors through Him who loved us. For I am persuaded that neither death nor life, nor angels nor ᵇprincipalities nor ᶜpowers, nor things present nor things to come, ᵈnor height nor depth, ᵉnor any other created thing, shall be able to separate us from the love of God which is in Christ Jesus our Lord.

150. ISRAEL'S REJECTION OF THE GOSPEL
Rom. 9:1–13

I tell the truth in Christ, I am not lying, my conscience also bearing me witness ᶠin the Holy Spirit, that I have great sorrow and continual grief in my heart. For I could wish that I myself were ᵍaccursed from Christ for my brethren, my countrymen according to the flesh, who are ʰIsraelites, to whom pertain the ⁱadoption, the ʲglory, the ᵏcovenants, the giving of the law,

---

a. **more than conquerors.** A compound Gr. word, which means to over-conquer, to conquer completely, without any real threat to personal life or health.

b. **principalities.** Fallen angels or demons (cf. Eph. 6:12; Col. 2:15; Jude 6).

c. **powers.** The plural form of this common word for "power" is used to refer to either miracles or to persons in positions of authority.

d. **nor height nor depth.** Common astronomical terms used to refer to the high and low points of a star's path; nothing in life's path, from beginning to end, can separate us from Christ's love. Possibly, Paul may intend to describe all of space from top to bottom.

e. **nor any other created thing.** In case anything or anyone might be left out, this covers everything but the Creator Himself.

f. **in the Holy Spirit.** Only when the Spirit controls the conscience can it be trusted—but it remains imperfect and its warnings must always be evaluated against the Word of God (cf. 1 Cor. 4:3–5).

g. **accursed.** The Gr. word is *anathema*, which means "to devote to destruction in eternal hell" (cf. 1 Cor. 12:3; 16:22; Gal. 1:8, 9). Although Paul understood the exchange he was suggesting was impossible (8:38, 39; John 10:28), it was still the sincere expression of his deep love for his fellow Jews (cf. Ex. 32:32).

h. **Israelites.** The descendants of Abraham through Jacob, whose name God changed to Israel (Gen. 32:28).

i. **adoption.** Not in the sense of providing salvation to every person born a Jew (see Rom. 8:15–23; cf. 9:6), but sovereignly selecting an entire nation to receive His special calling, covenant, and blessing and to serve as His witness nation (Ex. 4:22; 19:6; Hos. 11:1; cf. Is. 46:3, 4).

j. **glory.** The glory cloud (Shekinah) that pictured God's presence in the OT (Ex. 16:10; 24:16, 17; 29:42, 43; Lev. 9:23). His glory was supremely present in the Holy of Holies in both the tabernacle and the temple, which served as the throne room of Yahweh, Israel's King (Ex. 25:22; 40:34; 1 Kin. 8:11).

k. **covenants.** See Gen. 9:16. A covenant is a legally binding promise, agreement, or contract.

the [a]service of God, and the [b]promises; of whom are the [c]fathers and from whom, according to the flesh, [d]Christ came, who is over all, the eternally blessed God. Amen.

But it is not that the [e]word of God has taken no effect. For they are [f]not all Israel who are of Israel, nor are they all [g]children because they are the seed of Abraham; but, "In Isaac your seed shall be called." That is, those who are the [h]children of the flesh, these are not the [i]children of God; but the children of the promise are counted as the seed. For this is [j]the word of promise: "At this time I will come and Sarah shall have a son."

And not only this, but when Rebecca also had conceived by one man, even by our father Isaac (for [k]the children not yet being born, nor having [l]done any good or evil, that [m]the purpose of God according to election might stand,

---

Three times in the NT the word "covenants" is used in the plural (Gal. 4:24; Eph. 2:12). All but one of God's covenants with man are eternal and unilateral—that is, God promised to accomplish something based on His own character and not on the response or actions of the promised beneficiary. The 6 biblical covenants include: 1) the covenant with Noah (Gen. 9:8–17); 2) the covenant with Abraham (Gen. 12:1–3; see 4:13); 3) the covenant of law given through Moses at Sinai (Ex. 19–31; cf. Deut. 29, 30); 4) the priestly covenant (Num. 25:10–13); 5) the covenant of an eternal kingdom through David's greatest Son (2 Sam. 7:8–16); and 6) the New Covenant (Jer. 31:31–34; Ezek. 37:26; cf. Heb. 8:6–13). All but the Mosaic Covenant are eternal and unilateral. It is neither, since Israel's sin abrogated it and it has been replaced by the New Covenant (cf. Heb. 8:7–13).

a. **service.** Better translated "temple service," this refers to the entire sacrificial and ceremonial system that God revealed through Moses (cf. Ex. 29:43–46).

b. **promises.** Probably this refers to the promised Messiah, who would come out of Israel, bringing eternal life and an eternal kingdom (cf. Acts 2:39; 13:32–34; 26:6; Gal. 3:16, 21).

c. **fathers.** The patriarchs Abraham, Isaac, and Jacob, through whom the promises of the Messiah were fulfilled.

d. **Christ . . . the eternally blessed God.** This is not intended primarily as a benediction, but as an affirmation of the sovereignty and deity of Christ.

e. **word of God.** This refers specifically to the privileges and promises God had revealed to Israel (Rom. 9:4; cf. Is. 55:11; Jer. 32:42).

f. **not all Israel who are of Israel.** Not all the physical descendants of Abraham are true heirs of the promise (see Rom. 2:28, 29).

g. **children.** Only Isaac's descendants could truly be called the children of Abraham, the inheritors of those racial and national promises (Gen. 17:19–21).

h. **children of the flesh.** Abraham's other children by Hagar and Keturah were not chosen to receive the national promises made to him.

i. **children of God.** Paul's point is that just as not all of Abraham's descendants belonged to the physical people of God—or national Israel—not all of those who are true children of Abraham through Isaac are the true spiritual people of God and enjoy the promises made to Abraham's spiritual children (Rom. 4:6, 11; cf. 11:3, 4).

j. **word of promise.** This quote is from Gen. 18:10.

k. **the children.** The twins Jacob and Esau.

l. **done any good or evil.** God's choice of Jacob, instead of Esau, to continue the physical line was not based on his personal merit or demerit.

m. **the purpose of God according to election.** Rather, God's choice of Jacob resides solely in His own sovereign plan, a perfect example of election unto salvation. God has chosen some Jews—and some Gentiles—but not all, for salvation.

ᵃnot of works but of Him who calls), ᵇit was said to her, "The older shall serve the younger." As it is written, ᶜ"Jacob I have loved, but Esau I have hated."

151. GOD'S SOVEREIGNTY AND ISRAEL'S REJECTION

Rom. 9:14–33

What shall we say then? ᵈIs there unrighteousness with God? Certainly not! For ᵉHe says to Moses, "I will have mercy on whomever I will have mercy, and I will have compassion on whomever I will have compassion." So then ᶠit is not of him ᵍwho wills, nor of him ʰwho runs, but of God who shows mercy. For the Scripture says to the Pharaoh, ⁱ"For this very purpose I have ʲraised you up, that I may show My power in you, and that My name may be

---

a. **not of works but of Him who calls.** The fact that God made His choice of Jacob before the boys were born and apart from personal merit demonstrates that election unto spiritual life is unrelated to any human effort, and is based only on the prerogative of God who makes His selection (see Rom. 8:29; cf. 1 Cor. 1:9).

b. **it was said.** This quote is from Gen. 25:23.

c. **Jacob I have loved, but Esau I have hated.** Quoted from Mal. 1:2, 3. Actual emotional hatred for Esau and his offspring is not the point here. Malachi, who wrote this declaration more than 1,500 years after their death, was looking back at these two men—and by extension the nations (Israel and Edom) that came from their loins. God chose one for divine blessing and protection, and the other He left to divine judgment.

d. **Is there unrighteousness with God?** Paul once again anticipates his readers' objection to Paul's theology: If God were to choose some people for salvation and pass over others apart from their merits or actions that would make God arbitrary and unfair (cf. Gen. 18:25; Pss. 7:9; 48:10; 71:19; 119:137, 142; Jer. 9:23, 24).

e. **He says to Moses.** This quote is from Ex. 33:19. In response to the accusation that such a teaching about God's sovereign election is inconsistent with His fairness, Paul cites this text from the OT that clearly indicates that God is absolutely sovereign and does elect who will be saved without violating His other attributes. He determines who receives mercy.

f. **it.** God's gracious choice of certain people unto eternal life (see Rom. 8:29).

g. **who wills.** Salvation is not initiated by human choice—even faith is a gift of God (see Rom. 1:16; cf. John 6:37; Eph. 2:8, 9).

h. **who runs.** Salvation is not merited by human effort (see Rom. 9:11).

i. Quoted from Ex. 9:16. This again (as Rom. 9:15) is an OT quote to prove that God does sovereignly choose who will serve His purposes and how.

j. **raised you up.** Refers to bringing forward or lifting up and was often used to describe the rise of leaders and countries to positions of prominence (cf. Hab. 1:6; Zech. 11:16). Undoubtedly, Pharaoh thought his position and actions were of his own free choice to accomplish his own purposes, but in reality he was there to serve God's purpose. The mighty act of God in freeing Israel from the hand of Pharaoh demonstrated two corollary truths. Both Moses and Pharaoh were wicked sinners, even murderers, and were equally worthy of God's wrath and eternal punishment. But Moses received mercy while Pharaoh received God's

declared in all the earth." Therefore He has mercy on whom He wills, and whom He wills He [a]hardens.

You will say to me then, [b]"Why does He still find fault? For who has resisted His will?" But indeed, [c]O man, who are you to reply against God? Will the thing formed say to him who formed it, "Why have you made me like this?" Does not the potter have power over the clay, from the same lump to make one vessel for honor and another for dishonor?

[d]What if God, wanting to show His wrath and to make His power known, [e]endured with much longsuffering the [f]vessels of wrath [g]prepared for destruction, and that He might make known the riches of His [h]glory on the [i]vessels of mercy, which [j]He had prepared beforehand for glory, even us whom He called, not of the Jews only, but also of the Gentiles?

---

judgment, because that was God's sovereign will (cf. Rom. 11:7; Josh. 11:18–20; 1 Thess. 5:9; 2 Pet. 2:12).

a. **hardens.** The Gr. word literally means to make something hard, but is often used figuratively to refer to making stubborn or obstinate. Ten times Exodus refers to God's hardening Pharaoh's heart (e.g., Rom. 4:21; 7:3, 13), and other times to Pharaoh's hardening his own heart (e.g., Rom. 8:32; 9:34). This does not mean that God actively created unbelief or some other evil in Pharaoh's heart (cf. James 1:13), but rather that He withdrew all the divine influences that ordinarily acted as a restraint to sin and allowed Pharaoh's wicked heart to pursue its sin unabated (cf. Rom. 1:24, 26, 28).

b. **Why does He still find fault?** The objection is: How can God blame anyone for sin and unbelief when He has sovereignly determined that person's destiny?

c. **O man, who are you to reply against God?** The nature of Paul's reply makes it clear that he is not addressing those with honest questions about this difficult doctrine, but those who seek to use it to excuse their own sin and unbelief. Using the familiar OT analogy of the potter (cf. Is. 64:6–8; Jer. 18:3–16), Paul argues that it is as irrational, and far more arrogant, for men to question God's choice of certain sinners for salvation, as for a piece of pottery to question the purposes of the potter.

d. **What if.** This introduces a statement of fact in the form of a rhetorical question. These verses are not intended to identify the origin of evil or explain fully why God has allowed it, but they do provide 3 reasons He has permitted its presence and contamination: 1) to demonstrate His wrath; 2) to make His power known; and 3) to put the riches of His glorious mercy on display. No one is treated unfairly: Some receive the justice they earn and deserve (Rom. 6:23), others graciously receive mercy.

e. **endured.** God could justly destroy sinners the first time they sin. But He patiently endures their rebellion rather than giving them what every sin immediately deserves: eternal punishment. See Rom. 2:4.

f. **vessels of wrath.** Continuing the analogy of a potter, Paul refers to those whom God has not chosen for salvation, but rather allowed to incur the just penalty for their sin—God's wrath (see Rom. 1:18).

g. **prepared for destruction.** By their own rejection of Him. God does not make men sinful, but He leaves them in the sin they have chosen (see Rom. 9:18).

h. **glory.** The greatness of His character, seen especially in the grace, mercy, compassion, and forgiveness He grants sinners in Christ.

i. **vessels of mercy.** Those He has chosen for salvation.

j. **He had prepared beforehand.** Refers to divine election (see Rom. 9:29).

As He says also in ªHosea:

> "I will call them My people, who were not My people,
> And her beloved, who was not beloved."
> "And it shall come to pass in the place where it was said to them,
> 'You are not My people,'
> There they shall be called sons of the living God."

ᵇIsaiah also cries out concerning Israel:

> "Though the number of the children of Israel be as the sand
>   of the sea,
> The remnant will be saved.
> For He will finish the work and cut it short in righteousness,
> Because the LORD will make a short work upon the earth."

And as ᶜIsaiah said before:

> "Unless the ᵈLord of Sabaoth had left us a seed,
> We would have become like Sodom,
> And we would have been made like Gomorrah."

ᵉWhat shall we say then? That Gentiles, who did not pursue righteousness, have attained to righteousness, even the ᶠrighteousness of faith; but Israel,

---

a. Paul quotes Hos. 1:9, 10; 2:23. Hosea spoke of the ultimate restoration of Israel to God, but Paul's emphasis is that restoration necessarily implies her present alienation from God. Therefore, Israel's unbelief is consistent with the OT revelation.

b. See Is. 10:22, 23. Isaiah prophesied that the southern kingdom of Judah would be conquered and scattered—temporarily rejected by God—because of her unbelief. Paul's point is that the scattering Isaiah described was only a preview of Israel's rejection of the Messiah and her subsequent destruction and scattering.

c. See Is. 1:9. Again, only a remnant of Israel will survive God's wrath, solely because of His mercy.

d. **Lord of Sabaoth.** Cf. James 5:4. This OT title for God is translated "Lord of hosts" and refers to His all-encompassing sovereignty.

e. **What shall we say then?** Paul concludes the lesson on God's divine choice by reminding his readers that although God chooses some to receive His mercy, those who receive His judgment do so not because of something God has done to them, but because of their own unwillingness to believe the gospel (cf. 1 Thess. 2:10). Sinners are condemned for their personal sins, the supreme one being rejection of God and Christ (cf. Rom. 2:2–6, 9, 12; John 8:21–24; 16:8–11).

f. **righteousness of faith.** Righteousness which comes from God on the basis of faith (see Rom. 1:17).

pursuing the law of righteousness, has not attained to ^athe law of righteousness. Why? Because they did not seek it by faith, but as it were, by the ^bworks of the law. For they stumbled at that stumbling stone. As ^cit is written:

> "Behold, I lay in Zion a stumbling stone and rock of offense,
> And whoever believes on Him will not be put to shame."

152. ISRAEL'S NEED FOR THE GOSPEL
Rom. 10:1–21

Brethren, my heart's desire and ^dprayer to God for Israel is that they may be saved. For I bear them witness that they have a ^ezeal for God, but not according to knowledge. For they being ^fignorant of God's righteousness, and seeking to establish ^gtheir own righteousness, have not submitted to the righteousness of God. For ^hChrist is the end of the law for righteousness to everyone who believes.

---

a. **the law of righteousness.** Righteousness earned by keeping the law (cf. Rom. 3:20; see 8:3).

b. **works of the law.** By doing everything the law prescribed (cf. Gal. 2:16; 3:2, 5, 10).

c. See Is. 8:14 and 28:16. Long before His coming, the OT prophets had predicted that Israel would reject her Messiah, illustrating again that her unbelief is perfectly consistent with the Scripture.

d. **prayer to God for Israel.** Paul's calling as an apostle to the Gentiles (Rom. 11:13; Acts 9:15) did not diminish his continual entreaties to God (cf. 1 Tim. 2:1–3) for Israel to be saved (cf. Rom. 1:16; John 4:22; Acts 1:8), or his own evangelistic efforts toward Jews.

e. **zeal for God.** Demonstrated by legalistic conformity to the law and fierce opposition to Judaism's opponents (Acts 22:3; 26:4, 5; Gal. 1:13, 14; Phil. 3:5, 6).

f. **ignorant of God's righteousness.** Ignorant both of God's inherent righteousness revealed in the law and the rest of the OT (which should have shown the Jews their own unrighteousness) and of the righteousness which comes from Him on the basis of faith (see Rom.:17).

g. **their own righteousness.** Based on their conformity to God's law and often to the less demanding standards of their own traditions (Mark 7:1–13).

h. **Christ is the end of the law.** Although the Gr. word translated "end" can mean either "fulfillment" or "termination," this is not a reference to Christ's having perfectly fulfilled the law through His teaching (Matt. 5:17, 18) or through His sinless life (2 Cor. 5:21). Instead, as the second half of the verse shows, Paul means that belief in Christ as Lord and Savior ends the sinner's futile quest for righteousness through his imperfect attempts to save himself by efforts to obey the law (cf. Rom. 3:20–22; Is. 64:6; Col. 2:13, 14).

For Moses writes about [a]the righteousness which is of the law, [b]"The man who does those things shall live by them." But the [c]righteousness of faith speaks in this way, "Do not say in your heart, 'Who will ascend into heaven?'" (that is, to bring Christ down from above) or, "'Who will descend into the abyss?'" (that is, to bring Christ up from the dead). But what does it say? [d]"The word is near you, in your mouth and in your heart" (that is, the [e]word of faith which we preach): that if you [f]confess with your mouth the Lord Jesus and believe in your heart that [g]God has raised Him from the dead, you will be saved. For with the heart one believes unto righteousness, and with the mouth [h]confession is made unto salvation. For the Scripture says, [i]"Whoever believes on Him will not be put to shame." For there is no distinction between Jew and Greek, for the same Lord over all is rich to all who call upon Him. For [j]"whoever [k]calls on the name of the LORD shall be saved."

---

a. **the righteousness which is of the law.** A righteous standing before God on the basis of obedience to the law.

b. **The man who does those things shall live by them.** Quoted from Lev. 18:5. To hope for a righteousness based on obedience to the law requires perfect conformity in every detail (Gal. 3:10; James 2:10; cf. Deut. 27:26)—an utter impossibility.

c. **righteousness of faith.** Paul speaks of the righteousness based on faith as if it were a person and puts in its mouth a quotation from Deut. 30:12, 13. His point is that the righteousness of faith does not require some impossible odyssey through the universe to find Christ.

d. **The word is near you.** Quoted from Deut. 30:14. The journey of Rom. 10:6, 7 is unnecessary because God has clearly revealed the way of salvation: It is by faith.

e. **word of faith.** The message of faith is the way to God.

f. **confess . . . the Lord Jesus.** Not a simple acknowledgment that He is God and the Lord of the universe, since even demons acknowledge that to be true (James 2:19). This is the deep personal conviction, without reservation, that Jesus is that person's own master or sovereign. This phrase includes repenting from sin, trusting in Jesus for salvation, and submitting to Him as Lord. This is the volitional element of faith (see Rom. 1:16).

g. **God has raised Him from the dead.** Christ's resurrection was the supreme validation of His ministry (cf. John 2:18–21). Belief in it is necessary for salvation because it proved that Christ is who He claimed to be and that the Father had accepted His sacrifice in the place of sinners (Rom. 4:24; cf. Acts 13:32, 33; 1 Pet. 1:3, 4). Without the resurrection, there is no salvation (1 Cor. 15:14–17).

h. **confession.** This Gr. word basically means to say the same thing, or to be in agreement with someone. The person who confesses Jesus as Lord (Rom. 10:9),with the Father's declaration that Jesus is Savior and Lord.

i. Quoted from Is. 28:16 and 49:23. This quotation not only demonstrates that salvation by grace through faith alone has always been God's salvation plan, but that no one—including Gentiles—was ever to be excluded (Rom. 1:16; 3:21, 22; 2 Pet. 3:9; see also Jon. 3:5).

j. Paul quoted Joel (Rom. 2:32) to further emphasize that salvation is available for people of all nations and races.

k. **calls on the name.** This familiar OT expression (e.g., Pss. 79:5, 6; 105:1; 116:4, 5) does not refer to some desperate cry to just any deity but to the one true God as He has revealed Himself—a revelation which now includes recognition of Jesus as Lord and of the One who raised up Jesus from the dead.

[a]How then shall they call on Him in whom they have not believed? And how shall they believe in Him of whom they have not heard? And how shall they hear without a preacher? And how shall they preach unless they are sent? As it is written:

"How [b]beautiful are the feet of those who preach the gospel of peace,
Who bring glad tidings of good things!"

But they have not all [c]obeyed the gospel. For Isaiah says, "LORD, who has [d]believed our report?" So then faith comes by hearing, and hearing by [e]the word of God. But I say, have they not heard? Yes indeed:

[f]"Their sound has gone out to all the earth,
And their words to the ends of the world."

But I say, did Israel not know? First Moses says:

[g]"I will provoke you to jealousy by [h]those who are not a nation,
I will move you to anger by a foolish nation."

But Isaiah is very bold and says:

[i]"I was found by those who did not seek Me;
I was made manifest to those who did not ask for Me."

---

a. **How then . . . ?** Paul's main point in this series of rhetorical questions is that a clear presentation of the gospel message must precede true saving faith. True faith always has content—the revealed Word of God. Salvation comes to those who hear and believe the facts of the gospel.

b. **beautiful . . . feet of those who preach the gospel.** Quoted from Is. 52:7. It is the message of good news which those feet carry that is so welcome.

c. **obeyed the gospel.** The good news is not only a gracious offer but a command to believe and repent (Rom. 1:4–6; 2:8; 6:17; Acts 6:7; 2 Thess. 1:7, 8; Heb. 5:9).

d. **believed our report.** Quoted from Is. 53:1. The report Isaiah described was of the substitutionary death of Christ (Is. 53:5)—the good news of the gospel.

e. **the word of God.** The preferred rendering is "the word of Christ," which means "the message about Christ"—the gospel (cf. Matt. 28:19, 20; Acts 20:21).

f. Paul cited this quotation from the LXX (the Gr. translation of the Heb. OT) version of Ps. 19:4 to show that even David understood that God's revelation of Himself has reached the entire earth (cf. Rom. 1:18–20; Jer. 29:13; Matt. 24:14; John 1:9; Col. 1:5, 6).

g. Israel was ignorant of the salvation truth contained in her own Scriptures, including that the gospel would reach the Gentiles, as promised in Deut. 32:21; Is. 65:1, 2.

h. **those who are not a nation.** The Gentiles, who are not a part of Israel, God's special, chosen nation.

i. Quoted from Is. 65:1, 2.

But to Israel he says:

> "All day long I have stretched out My hands
> To a [a]disobedient and contrary people."

153. Israelite Rejection and the Remnant

Rom. 11:1–10

[b]I say then, has God [c]cast away His people? [d]Certainly not! For I also am an Israelite, of the seed of Abraham, of the tribe of Benjamin. God has not cast away His people [e]whom He foreknew. Or do you not know what the Scripture says of [f]Elijah, how he pleads with God against Israel, saying, [g]"Lord, they have killed Your prophets and torn down Your altars, and I alone am left, and they seek my life"? But what does the divine response say to him? [h]"I have reserved for Myself seven thousand men who have not bowed the knee to [i]Baal." Even so then, at this present time there is [j]a remnant according to the [k]election of grace. And if by [l]grace, then it is no longer of works; otherwise grace is no longer grace. But if it is of works, it is no longer grace; otherwise work is no longer work.

---

a. **disobedient.** Lit. "to contradict," or "to speak against." As throughout her history, Israel once again had contradicted the Word of God—this time it was the truth of the gospel (cf. Matt. 21:33–41; Luke 14:21–24).

b. **I say then . . .** In this section Paul answers the question that logically arises from 10:19—21: "Is God's setting aside of Israel for rejecting Christ permanent?" At stake is whether God can be trusted to keep His unconditional promises to that nation (cf. Jer. 33:19–26).

c. **cast away.** To thrust away from oneself. The form of the question in the Gr. text expects a negative answer. Despite Israel's disobedience (Rom. 9:1–13; 10:14–21), God has not rejected His people (cf. 1 Sam. 12:22; 1 Kin. 6:13; Pss. 89:31–37; 94:14; Is. 49:15; 54:1–10; Jer. 33:19–26).

d. **Certainly not!** The strongest form of negation in Gr. (see Rom. 6:2).

e. **whom He foreknew.** See Rom. 8:29. Israel's disobedience does not nullify God's predetermined love relationship with her.

f. **Elijah.** See 1 Kin. 17:1.

g. Quoted from 1 Kin. 19:10.

h. Quoted from 1 Kin. 19:18.

i. **Baal.** See 1 Kin. 16:31, 32; cf. Num. 22:41.

j. **a remnant.** Although the nation had rejected Jesus, thousands of individual Jews had come to faith in Him (cf. Acts 2:41; 4:4; 6:1).

k. **election of grace.** God did not choose this remnant because of its foreseen faith, good works, spiritual worthiness, or racial descent, but solely because of His grace (cf. Deut. 7:7, 8; Eph. 2:8, 9; 2 Tim. 1:9).

l. **grace . . . no longer of works.** Human effort and God's grace are mutually exclusive ways to salvation (cf. Rom. 3:21–31; 4:1–11; 9:11; Gal. 2:16, 21; 3:11, 12, 18; Titus 3:5).

What then? ᵃIsrael has not obtained what it seeks; but ᵇthe elect have obtained it, and the rest ᶜwere blinded. Just as ᵈit is written:

> "God has given them a spirit of stupor,
> Eyes that they should not see
> And ears that they should not hear,
> To this very day."

And David says:

> ᵉ"Let their table become a snare and a trap,
> A stumbling block and a recompense to them.
> Let their eyes be darkened, so that they do not see,
> And bow down their back always."

154. GENTILES GRAFTED IN

Rom. 11:11–18

I say then, have they ᶠstumbled that they should fall? Certainly not! But through ᵍtheir fall, to ʰprovoke them to jealousy, ⁱsalvation has come to the

---

a. **Israel . . . what it seeks.** In spite of their intense religious zeal, the Jews of Paul's day had failed to obtain God's righteousness (Rom. 9:31, 32; 10:2, 3).

b. **the elect.** Those whom God graciously had chosen in turn sought and found His righteousness (see Rom. 9:30; 10:4).

c. **were blinded.** By a judicial act of God (cf. Ex. 4:21; 7:3; 9:12; 10:20, 27; 11:10; 14:4, 8, 17; Deut. 2:30; John 12:40), in response to their hardened hearts (cf. Ex. 8:15, 32; 9:34; 10:1; 2 Chr. 36:13; Ps. 95:8; Prov. 28:14; Matt. 19:8; Mark 3:5; Eph. 4:18; Heb. 3:8, 15; 4:7).

d. **it is written.** See Rom. 3:10. The first line was quoted from Is. 29:10 and the last lines are adapted from Deut. 29:4. These OT quotes both illustrate God's judicial hardening of unbelieving Israel, and show that what Paul is teaching is not in violation of or inconsistent with the OT.

e. Adapted from Ps. 69:22, 23. A person's "table" was thought to be a place of safety, but the table of the ungodly is a trap. Many people trust in the very things that damn them.

f. **stumbled . . . fall.** The form of Paul's question and his strong response confirms that Israel's blindness, hardening, and apostasy are not irreversible.

g. **their fall.** Israel's rejection of Jesus Christ.

h. **provoke . . . to jealousy.** God intends to use His offer of salvation to the despised Gentiles (see Acts 22:21–23) to draw the nation back to Him.

i. **salvation . . . to the Gentiles.** Something the OT had long prophesied (cf. Gen. 12:3; Is. 49:6; Matt. 8:11, 12; 21:43; 22:1–14; Acts 13:46, 47; 28:25–28).

Gentiles. Now if their fall is [a]riches for the world, and [b]their failure riches for the Gentiles, how much more [c]their fullness!

For I speak to you Gentiles; inasmuch as I am an [d]apostle to the Gentiles, I magnify my ministry, if by any means I may provoke to jealousy those who are [e]my flesh and save some of them. For if their being cast away is the reconciling of the world, what will their acceptance be but [f]life from the dead?

For if the [g]firstfruit is holy, [h]the lump is also holy; and if the [i]root is holy, so are the [j]branches. And if some of the [k]branches were broken off, and you, being [l]a wild olive tree, were grafted in among them, and with them became a partaker of [m]the root and fatness of [n]the olive tree, [o]do not boast against the [p]branches. But if you do boast, remember that you do not support the root, but [q]the root supports you.

---

a. **riches for the world.** The rich truths of salvation (Gen. 12:3; Is. 49:6; cf. 2 Cor. 8:9).

b. **their failure.** To acknowledge Jesus of Nazareth as their Messiah and be God's witness nation resulted in the Gentile church being given that privilege.

c. **their fullness.** Their future spiritual renewal (Rev. 7:4, 9; cf. Zech. 8:23; 12:10; 13:1; 14:9, 11, 16). Israel's "fall" and "failure" is temporary.

d. **apostle to the Gentiles.** See Acts 18:6; 22:21; 26:17, 18; Eph. 3:8; 1 Tim. 2:7.

e. **my flesh.** His fellow Israelites (see Rom. 9:3).

f. **life from the dead.** Not bodily resurrection, but the passing from spiritual death to spiritual life (John 5:24). This phrase also describes the future spiritual rebirth of Israel (cf. Zech. 12:10; 13:1).

g. **firstfruit.** The first portion of the harvest, which was to be given to the Lord (Ex. 23:19; 34:26; Lev. 2:12; 23:10; Num. 15:19–21; 18:12, 13; Deut. 18:4).

h. **the lump is also holy.** Because the firstfruit offering represented the entire portion, the entire piece of dough could be said to be holy, set apart to God (cf. Ex. 31:15; Lev. 27:14, 30, 32; Josh. 6:19).

i. **root.** The patriarchs Abraham, Isaac, and Jacob. See Rom. 4:13.

j. **branches.** The patriarchs' descendants: the nation of Israel.

k. **branches were broken off.** See Jer. 5:10; 11:16, 17; Matt. 21:43. Some, but not all, of the branches of Israel (see Rom. 11:16) were removed; God always preserved a believing remnant.

l. **a wild olive tree . . . grafted in.** Olives were an important crop in the ancient world. Although trees often lived for hundreds of years, individual branches eventually stopped producing olives. When that happened, branches from younger trees were grafted in to restore productivity. Paul's point is that the old, unproductive branches (Israel) were broken off and branches from a wild olive tree (Gentiles) were grafted in.

m. **the root and fatness.** Once grafted in, Gentiles partake of the richness of God's covenant blessings as the spiritual heirs of Abraham (see Rom. 4:11; Gal. 3:29).

n. **the olive tree.** The place of divine blessing; God's covenant of salvation made with Abraham (Gen. 12:1–3; 15:1–21; 17:1–27).

o. **do not boast.** There is no place in the church for spiritual pride, still less for anti-Semitism—we are the spiritual offspring of Abraham (Rom. 4:11, 16; Gal. 3:29).

p. **branches.** The unbelieving Jews who had been broken off.

q. **the root supports you.** Gentiles are not the source of blessing, but have been grafted into the covenant of salvation that God made with Abraham (cf. Gal. 3:6–9, 13, 14).

155. God's Plan for the Future Salvation of Israel

Rom. 11:19–36

You will say then, "Branches were broken off that I might be grafted in." Well said. Because of [a]unbelief they were broken off, and you stand by faith. Do not be haughty, but [b]fear. For if God did not spare the natural branches, He may not spare you either. Therefore [c]consider the goodness and severity of God: on [d]those who fell, severity; but toward you, goodness, [e]if you continue in His goodness. Otherwise you also will be [f]cut off. And they also, if they do not continue in unbelief, will be grafted in, for God is able to graft them in again. For if you were cut out of the olive tree which is wild by nature, and were grafted contrary to nature into a cultivated olive tree, how much more will these, who are natural branches, be grafted into their own olive tree?

For I do not desire, brethren, that you should be ignorant of this [g]mystery, lest you should be [h]wise in your own opinion, that [i]blindness in part has

---

a. **unbelief . . . faith.** Branches were broken off and others grafted in based solely on the issue of faith, not race, ethnicity, social or intellectual background, or external morality. Salvation is ever and always by faith alone (cf. Rom. 1:16, 17; Eph. 2:8, 9).

b. **fear.** See 1 Cor. 10:12; 2 Cor. 13:5. God will judge the apostate church (cf. Rev. 2:15, 16; 3:16) just as surely as He judged apostate Israel. If Israel (the "natural branches") was not spared despite being God's covenant nation, why should Gentiles, strangers to God's covenants (Eph. 2:11, 12; see 9:4), expect to be spared if they sin against the truth of the gospel?

c. **consider the goodness and severity.** All of God's attributes work in harmony; there is no conflict between His goodness and love, and His justice and wrath. Those who accept His gracious offer of salvation experience His goodness (Rom. 2:4); those who reject it experience His severity (2:5).

d. **those who fell.** The unbelieving Jews described in Rom. 11:12–21. "Fell" translates a Gr. word meaning "to fall so as to be completely ruined." Those who reject God's offer of salvation bring upon themselves utter spiritual ruin.

e. **if you continue.** Genuine saving faith always perseveres (cf. John 8:31; 15:5, 6; Col. 1:22, 23; Heb. 3:12–14; 4:11; 1 John 2:19).

f. **cut off.** From the same Gr. root word translated "severity" earlier in the verse. God will deal swiftly and severely with those who reject Him.

g. **mystery.** This word is used to refer to NT truth previously not revealed (see 1 Cor. 2:7; Eph. 3:3–6). This mystery has two components: 1) Israel has experienced a partial spiritual hardening, and 2) that hardening will last only for a divinely specified period of time.

h. **wise in your own opinion.** Another warning to the Gentiles against spiritual pride and arrogance (see vv. 17–24).

i. **blindness in part.** The nation's blindness does not extend to every individual Jew. Through all of history God has always preserved a believing remnant.

happened to Israel ªuntil the fullness of the Gentiles has come in. And so ᵇall Israel will be saved, as it is written:

> ᶜ"The Deliverer will come out of Zion,
>
> And He will turn away ungodliness from Jacob;
>
> For this is My ᵈcovenant with them,
>
> ᵉWhen I take away their sins."

Concerning the ᶠgospel they are enemies for your sake, but ᵍconcerning the election they are beloved for ʰthe sake of the fathers. For ⁱthe gifts and the calling of God are irrevocable. For as you were once disobedient to God, yet have now obtained mercy through their disobedience, even so these also have now been disobedient, that through the mercy shown you ʲthey also may obtain mercy. For God has ᵏcommitted them all to disobedience, that He might have mercy on all.

---

a. **until the fullness of the Gentiles has come in.** "Until" refers to a specific point in time; "fullness" refers to completion; "has come in" translates a Gr. verb often used to speak of coming to salvation (cf. Matt. 5:20; Mark 9:43, 45, 47; John 3:5; Acts 14:22). Israel's spiritual hardening (which began with rejecting Jesus as Messiah) will last until the complete number of elect Gentiles has come to salvation.

b. **all Israel.** All the elect Jewish people alive at the end of the Tribulation, not the believing remnant of Jews within the church during this church age (see Rom. 11:5, 17). Since the remnant has already embraced the truth of the gospel (see v. 25), it could not be in view here, since it no longer needs the salvation this verse promises. In the future, Israel will repent of unbelief and embrace the Messiah (Zech. 12:10). In the terms of Paul's analogy, God will at that time gladly graft the (believing) Jewish people back into the olive tree of His covenant blessings because it was theirs originally (Rom. 9:4)—unlike the wild branches (the Gentiles, cf. Eph. 2:11, 12).

c. **The Deliverer will come out of Zion.** Quoted from Is. 59:20, 21. See Pss. 14:7; 53:6; Is. 46:13. The Lord Jesus Christ's millennial rule will be associated with Mt. Zion (Ps. 110:2).

d. **covenant.** The Abrahamic Covenant (Gen. 12:1–3; Is. 59:21).

e. **When I take away their sins.** Quoted from Is. 27:9. A necessary prerequisite for Israel's salvation (cf. Ezek. 36:25–29; Heb. 8:12).

f. **gospel . . . enemies.** Israel's temporary situation during her time of spiritual hardening.

g. **concerning the election.** From the perspective of God's eternal choice, Israel will always be His covenant people.

h. **the sake of the fathers.** The patriarchs (Abraham, Isaac, and Jacob), recipients of the Abrahamic Covenant (Ex. 2:24; Lev. 26:4; 2 Kin. 13:23).

i. **the gifts . . . are irrevocable.** God's sovereign election of Israel, like that of individual believers, is unconditional and unchangeable, because it is rooted in His immutable nature and expressed in the unilateral, eternal Abrahamic Covenant (see Rom. 9:4).

j. **they also may obtain mercy.** God will extend His grace to unbelieving Israel, just as He did to unbelieving Gentiles (cf. Rom. 5:8). Salvation, whether of Jews or Gentiles, flows from God's mercy (cf. 1 Tim. 1:12–14).

k. **committed them.** Though not the author of sin (Ps. 5:4; Hab. 1:13; James 1:13), God allowed man to pursue his sinful inclinations so that He could receive glory by demonstrating His grace and mercy to disobedient sinners (cf. Eph. 2:2; 5:6).

ᵃOh, the depth of the riches both of the wisdom and knowledge of God! How unsearchable are His ᵇjudgments and His ᶜways past finding out!

> ᵈ"For who has known the mind of the Lᴏʀᴅ?
> Or who has become His counselor?"
> ᵉ"Or who has first given to Him
> And it shall be repaid to him?"

ᶠFor of Him and through Him and to Him are all things, to whom be glory forever. Amen.

156. Spiritual Giftedness in the Church
Rom. 12:1–8

ᵍI ʰbeseech you therefore, brethren, by the ⁱmercies of God, that you ʲpresent your bodies a living sacrifice, holy, acceptable to God, which is your

---

a. **Oh, the depths . . .** The majesty, grandeur, and wisdom of God's plan revealed in Rom. 11:1–32 caused Paul to burst out in praise. This doxology is a fitting response not only to God's future plans for Israel (Rom. 9–11), but to Paul's entire discussion of justification by faith (Rom. 1–11).

b. **judgments.** God's purposes or decrees, which are beyond human understanding (cf. Ps. 36:6).

c. **ways.** The methods God chooses to accomplish His purposes (cf. Job 5:9; 9:10; 26:14).

d. Quoted from Is. 40:13.

e. Quoted from Job 41:11.

f. See 1 Cor. 8:6; 15:28; Eph. 1:23; 4:6; Heb. 2:10. God is the source, the sustainer, and the rightful end of everything that exists.

g. In these final 5 chapters of Romans, Paul explains in great detail how believers are to practically live out the rich theological truths of chaps. 1–11. God has graciously given believers so much, that Paul exhorts them to respond in grateful obedience.

h. **beseech.** This Gr. word comes from a root which means "to call alongside to help." Jesus used a related word, often translated "comforter," in reference to the Holy Spirit (John 14:16, 26; 15:26; 16:7). This family of words later came to connote exhorting, encouraging, or counseling. Paul was speaking as a counselor to his readers, but his counsel carried the full weight of his apostleship.

i. **mercies of God.** The gracious, extravagant, divine graces Paul expounded in the first 11 chapters of Romans, including God's love (1:7; cf. 5:5; 8:35, 39), grace (1:6, 7; 3:24; 5:2, 20, 21; 6:15), righteousness (1:17; 3:21, 22; 4:5, 6, 22–24; 5:17, 19), and the gift of faith (1:5, 17; 3:22, 26; 4:5, 13; 5:1; 10:17; 12:3).

j. **present your bodies a living sacrifice.** Under the Old Covenant, God accepted the sacrifices of dead animals. But because of Christ's ultimate sacrifice, the OT sacrifices are no longer of any effect (Heb. 9:11, 12). For those in Christ, the only acceptable worship is to offer themselves completely to the Lord. Under God's control, the believer's yet-unredeemed body (see Rom. 6:6, 12; 7:5; cf. 8:11, 23) can and must be yielded to Him as an instrument of righteousness (Rom. 6:12, 13; cf. 8:11–13).

^areasonable service. And ^bdo not be conformed to ^cthis world, but be ^dtransformed by the ^erenewing of your mind, that you may prove what is that ^fgood and acceptable and perfect will of God.

For I say, through the ^ggrace given to me, to everyone who is among you, not to think of himself more highly than he ought to think, but to think ^hsoberly, as God has dealt to each one a ^hmeasure of faith. ⁱFor as we have ^jmany members in one body, but all the members do not have the same function, so we, being many, are one body in Christ, and individually

---

a. **reasonable service.** "Reasonable" is from the Gr. for "logic." In light of all the spiritual riches believers enjoy solely as the fruit of God's mercies (Rom. 11:33, 36), it logically follows that they owe God their highest form of service. Understood here is the idea of priestly, spiritual service, which was such an integral part of OT worship.

b. **do not be conformed.** "Conformed" refers to assuming an outward expression that does not reflect what is really inside, a kind of masquerade or act. The word's form implies that Paul's readers were already allowing this to happen and must stop.

c. **this world.** Better translated, "age," which refers to the system of beliefs, values—or the spirit of the age—at any time current in the world. This sum of contemporary thinking and values forms the moral atmosphere of our world and is always dominated by Satan (cf. 2 Cor. 4:4).

d. **transformed.** The Gr. word, from which the Eng. word "metamorphosis" comes, connotes a change in outward appearance. Matthew uses the same word to describe the Transfiguration (Matt. 17:2). Just as Christ briefly and in a limited way displayed outwardly His inner, divine nature and glory at the Transfiguration, Christians should outwardly manifest their inner, redeemed natures, not once, however, but daily (cf. 2 Cor. 3:18; Eph. 5:18).

e. **renewing of your mind.** That kind of transformation can occur only as the Holy Spirit changes our thinking through consistent study and meditation of Scripture (Ps. 119:11; cf. Col. 1:28; 3:10, 16; Phil. 4:8). The renewed mind is one saturated with and controlled by the Word of God.

f. **good . . . acceptable . . . perfect.** Holy living of which God approves. These words borrow from OT sacrificial language and describe a life that is morally and spiritually spotless, just as the sacrificial animals were to be (cf. Lev. 22:19–25).

g. **grace.** The divine, undeserved favor that called Paul to be an apostle and gave him spiritual authority (Rom. 1:1–5; cf. 1 Cor. 3:10; Gal. 2:9) and also produced sincere humility (1 Tim. 1:12–14).

h. **soberly.** The exercise of sound judgment, which will lead believers to recognize that in themselves they are nothing (cf. 1 Pet. 5:5), and will yield the fruit of humility (cf. 3 John 9).

h. **measure of faith.** The correct proportion of the spiritual gift—or supernatural endowment and ability—the Holy Spirit gives each believer (see 1 Pet. 4:10, 11) so he may fulfill his role in the body of Christ (1 Cor. 12:7, 11). "Faith" is not saving faith, but rather faithful stewardship, the kind and quantity required to use one's own particular gift (cf. 1 Cor. 12:7, 11). Every believer receives the exact gift and resources he needs to fulfill his role in the body of Christ.

i. **For as we . . .** One of two NT passages (cf. 1 Cor. 12:12–14) listing the general categories of spiritual gifts. The emphasis in each list is not on believers' identifying their gift perfectly, but on faithfully using the unique enablement God has given each. The fact that the two lists differ clearly implies the gifts are like a palette of basic colors, from which God selects to blend a unique hue for each disciple's life (see 1 Cor. 12:12–14).

j. **many members . . . one body.** Just as in the natural body, God has sovereignly given the body of Christ a unified diversity (see 1 Cor. 12:14–20).

members of one another. Having then ªgifts differing according to the grace that is given to us, let us use them: if ᵇprophecy, let us prophesy ᶜin proportion to our faith; or ᵈministry, let us use it in our ministering; he who teaches, in ᵉteaching; he who exhorts, in ᶠexhortation; he who ᵍgives, with ʰliberality; he who ⁱleads, with diligence; he who ʲshows mercy, with ᵏcheerfulness.

---

a. **gifts.** See 12:3. **according to the grace . . . given.** Undeserved and unmerited. The gift itself (1 Cor. 12:4), the specific way in which it is used (1 Cor. 12:5), and the spiritual results (1 Cor. 12:6) are all sovereignly chosen by the Spirit completely apart from personal merit (1 Cor. 12:11).

b. **prophecy.** See 1 Cor. 12:10. This Gr. word means "speaking forth" and does not necessarily include prediction of the future or any other mystical or supernatural aspects. Although some prophets in Acts did make predictions of future events (Rom. 11:27, 28; 21:10, 11), others made no predictions but spoke the truth of God to encourage and strengthen their hearers (Rom. 15:32; cf. vv. 22–31). The evidence does suggest, however, that in the first century, before the NT was complete and the sign gifts had ceased (see 1 Cor. 13:8; cf. 2 Cor. 12:12; Heb. 2:3, 4), this word may have had both non-revelatory and revelatory facets. In its non-revelatory sense, the word "prophecy" simply identifies the skill of public proclamation of the Word of God (see 1 Cor. 14:3, 24, 25; 1 Pet. 4:11).

c. **in proportion to our faith.** Lit. "the faith," or the full revealed message or body of Christian faith (Jude 3; cf. 2 Tim. 4:2). The preacher must be careful to preach the same message the apostles delivered. Or, it could also refer to the believer's personal understanding and insight regarding the gospel.

d. **ministry.** From the same Gr. word as "deacon," "deaconess" come from, it refers to those who serve. This gift, similar to the gift of helps (1 Cor. 12:28), has broad application to include every kind of practical help (cf. Acts 20:35; 1 Cor. 12:28).

e. **teaching.** The ability to interpret, clarify, systematize, and explain God's truth clearly (cf. Acts 18:24, 25; 2 Tim. 2:2). Pastors must have the gift of teaching (1 Tim. 3:2; Titus 1:9; cf. 1 Tim. 4:16), but many mature, qualified laymen also have this gift. This differs from preaching (prophecy), not in content, but in the unique skill for public proclamation.

f. **exhortation.** The gift which enables a believer to effectively call others to obey and follow God's truth (see v. 1). It may be used negatively to admonish and correct regarding sin (2 Tim. 4:2), or positively, to encourage, comfort, and strengthen struggling believers (cf. 2 Cor. 1:3–5; Heb. 10:24, 25).

g. **gives.** This denotes the sacrificial sharing and giving of one's resources and self to meet the needs of others (cf. 2 Cor. 8:3–5, 9; 11; Eph. 4:28).

h. **liberality.** Simplicity, single-mindedness, and openhearted generosity. The believer who gives with a proper attitude does not do so for thanks and personal recognition, but to glorify God (cf. Matt. 6:2; Acts 2:44, 45; 4:37—5:11; 2 Cor. 8:2–5).

i. **leads.** Lit. "standing before." Paul calls this gift "administrations" (1 Cor. 12:28), a word that means "to guide" and is used of the person who steers a ship (Acts 27:11; Rev. 18:17). In the NT, this word is used to describe only leadership in the home (1 Tim. 3:4, 5, 12) and the church (1 Cor. 12:28; 1 Tim. 5:17; cf. Acts 27:11; Rev. 18:17). Again, the church's leaders must exercise this gift, but it is certainly not limited to them.

j. **shows mercy.** One who actively shows sympathy and sensitivity to those in suffering and sorrow, and who has both the willingness and the resources to help lessen their afflictions. Frequently, this gift accompanies the gift of exhortation.

k. **cheerfulness.** This attitude is crucial to ensure that the gift of mercy becomes a genuine help, not a discouraging commiseration with those who are suffering (cf. Prov. 14:21, 31; Luke 4:18, 19).

157. THE EXERCISE OF LOVE

Rom. 12:9—21

^aLet ^blove be without ^chypocrisy. Abhor what is evil. Cling to what is good. Be ^dkindly affectionate to one another with brotherly love, ^ein honor giving preference to one another; not lagging in ^fdiligence, ^gfervent in spirit, serving the Lord; ^hrejoicing in hope, ⁱpatient in tribulation, ^jcontinuing steadfastly in prayer; ^kdistributing to the needs of the saints, ^lgiven to hospitality.

---

a. This passage (Rom. 12:9–21) provides a comprehensive and mandatory list of traits that characterize the Spirit-filled life (cf. John 15:8; Eph. 2:10). Paul presents these characteristics under 4 categories: 1) personal duties (v. 9); 2) family duties (vv. 10–13); 3) duties to others (vv. 14–16); and 4) duties to those who consider us enemies (vv. 17–21).

b. **love.** The supreme NT virtue, which centers completely on the needs and welfare of the one loved and does whatever necessary to meet those needs (cf. Matt. 22:37–39; Gal. 5:22; 1 Pet. 4:8; 1 John 4:16; see 1 Cor. 13).

c. **hypocrisy.** See Matt. 6:2. Christian love is to be shown purely and sincerely, without self-centeredness or guile.

d. **kindly affectionate . . . with brotherly love.** To be devoted to other Christians with a family sort of love, not based on personal attraction or desirability (cf. 1 Thess. 4:9). This quality is the primary way the world can recognize us as followers of Christ (John 13:35; cf. 1 John 3:10, 17–19).

e. **in honor giving preference.** To show genuine appreciation and admiration for fellow believers by putting them first (Phil. 2:3).

f. **diligence.** Whatever is worth doing in the Christian life is valuable enough to be done with enthusiasm and care (John 9:4; Gal. 6:10; Heb. 6:10, 11: cf. Eccl. 9:10; 2 Thess. 3:13). Sloth and indifference not only prevent good, but allow evil to prosper (Prov. 18:9; Eph. 5:15, 16).

g. **fervent in spirit.** Lit. "to boil in spirit." This phrase suggests having plenty of heat to produce adequate, productive energy, but not so much heat that one goes out of control (cf. Acts 18:25; 1 Cor. 9:26; Gal. 6:9).

h. **rejoicing in hope.** Of Christ's return and our ultimate redemption (see 5:2; 8:19; cf. Matt. 25:21; 1 Cor. 15:58; 2 Tim. 4:8).

i. **patient.** Perseverance (see Rom. 5:3).

j. **continuing steadfastly in prayer.** Cf. Acts 2:42; 1 Thess. 5:17; 1 Tim. 2:8.

k. **distributing.** From a Gr. word that means commonality, partnership, or mutual sharing, which is often translated "fellowship," and "communion" (Acts 2:42, 44; cf. 4:32; 1 Tim. 6:17, 18).

l. **given to hospitality.** Lit. "pursuing the love of strangers" (Heb. 13:2)—not merely entertaining one's friends. In NT times, travel was dangerous and inns were evil, scarce, and expensive. So the early believers often opened their homes to travelers, especially to fellow believers (2 Tim. 1:16–18; 3 John 5–8; cf. Luke 14:12–14; 1 Pet. 4:9). Church leaders should be role models of this virtue (Titus 1:8).

[a]Bless those who persecute you; bless and do not curse. [b]Rejoice with those who rejoice, and weep with those who weep. Be of the [c]same mind toward one another. Do not [d]set your mind on high things, but associate with the humble. Do not be [e]wise in your own opinion.

[f]Repay no one evil for evil. Have [g]regard for good things in the sight of all men. [h]If it is possible, as much as depends on you, live peaceably with all men. Beloved, do not avenge yourselves, but rather give place to [i]wrath; for it is written, [j]"Vengeance is Mine, I will repay," says the Lord. Therefore

> "If your enemy is hungry, feed him;
> If he is thirsty, give him a drink;
> For in so doing you will [k]heap coals of fire on his head."

Do not be overcome by evil, but overcome evil with good.

---

a. **Bless those who persecute you.** Treat enemies as if they were your friends (Luke 6:27–33; cf. Matt. 5:44; Luke 23:34; Acts 7:60; 1 Pet. 2:21–23).

b. **Rejoice . . . weep.** To be glad in the blessings, honor, and welfare of others—no matter what one's own situation (cf. 1 Cor. 12:26; 2 Cor. 2:3), and to be sensitive or compassionate to the hardships and sorrows of others (Col. 3:12; James 5:11; cf. Luke 19:41–44; John 11:35).

c. **same mind toward one another.** To be impartial (see Rom. 2:11; James 2:1–4, 9; cf. Acts 10:34; 1 Tim. 5:21; 1 Pet. 1:17).

d. **set your mind . . . high things.** To be haughty with self-seeking pride (cf. Phil. 2:3).

e. **wise in your own opinion.** Christians are not to have conceit or feelings of superiority toward fellow believers (cf. Rom. 1:22).

f. **Repay no one evil for evil.** The OT law of "eye for eye, tooth for tooth" was never intended to be applied by individuals in the OT or NT; but it was a standard for the collective society to use to enforce good conduct among people (1 Thess. 5:15; see Ex. 21:23, 24; cf. Lev. 24:20; Deut. 19:21; 1 Pet. 3:8, 9).

g. **regard for good things.** Christians are to respect what is intrinsically proper and honest. "Good" also carries the idea of visibly and obviously having the right behavior when they are around others, especially unbelievers.

h. **If it is possible.** Although we should do everything possible to be at peace with others, it will not always come, because it also depends on others' attitudes and responses.

i. **wrath.** Of God (see Rom. 1:18).

j. **Vengeance.** Divine retribution as quoted from Deut. 32:35.

k. **heap coals of fire on his head.** Refers to an ancient Egyptian custom in which a person who wanted to show public contrition carried a pan of burning coals on his head. The coals represented the burning pain of his shame and guilt. When believers lovingly help their enemies, it should bring shame to such people for their hate and animosity (cf. Prov. 25:21, 22).

158. Subjection to Government

Rom. 13:1–7

Let every soul [a]be subject to the [b]governing authorities. For [c]there is no authority except from God, and the authorities that exist are [d]appointed by God. Therefore whoever resists the authority [e]resists the ordinance of God, and those who resist will bring [f]judgment on themselves. For rulers are [g]not a terror to good works, but to evil. Do you want to be unafraid of the authority? [h]Do what is good, and you will have praise from the same. For he is [i]God's minister to you for good. But if you do evil, be afraid; for he does not [j]bear the sword in vain; for he is God's minister, an avenger [k]to execute wrath on him who practices evil. Therefore you must be subject, not only [l]because of wrath but also for conscience' sake. For [m]because of this

---

a. **be subject.** This Gr. word was used of a soldier's absolute obedience to his superior officer. Scripture makes one exception to this command: when obedience to civil authority would require disobedience to God's Word (Ex. 1:17; Dan. 3:16–18; 6:7, 10; see Acts 4:19, 20; 5:28, 29).

b. **governing authorities.** Every position of civil authority without regard to competency, morality, reasonableness, or any other caveat (1 Thess. 4:11, 12; 1 Tim. 2:1, 2; Titus 3:1, 2).

c. **there is no authority except from God.** Since He alone is the sovereign ruler of the universe (Pss. 62:11; 103:19; 1 Tim. 6:15), He has instituted 4 authorities on earth: 1) the government over all citizens; 2) the church over all believers; 3) the parents over all children; and 4) the masters over all employees.

d. **appointed.** Human government's authority derives from and is defined by God. He instituted human government to reward good and to restrain sin in an evil, fallen world.

e. **resists the ordinance of God.** Since all government is God-ordained, disobedience is rebellion against God.

f. **judgment.** Not God's judgment, but punishment from the government for breaking the law.

g. **not a terror to good works, but to evil.** Even the most wicked, godless governments act as a deterrent to crime.

h. **Do what is good . . . have praise.** Peaceful, law-abiding citizens need not fear the authorities. Few governments will harm those who obey their laws. In fact, governments usually commend such people.

i. **God's minister . . . for good.** By helping restrain evil and protecting life and property. Paul took advantage of his government's role in promoting what is good when he exercised his rights as a Roman citizen to obtain justice (Acts 16:37; 22:25, 29; 25:11).

j. **bear the sword.** This symbolizes the government's right to inflict punishment on wrongdoers—especially capital punishment (Gen. 9:6; cf. Matt. 26:52; Acts 25:11).

k. **to execute wrath.** Not God's wrath, but the punishment inflicted by the civil authorities.

l. **because of . . . conscience' sake.** Out of a sense of obligation to God and to keep a clear conscience before Him (see 2 Cor. 1:12), not merely to avoid punishment from the civil authorities.

m. **because of this.** Because God ordained human government and demands submission to it.

you also pay ᵃtaxes, for they are God's ministers attending continually to this very thing. ᵇRender therefore to all their due: taxes to whom taxes are due, ᶜcustoms to whom customs, fear to whom ᵈfear, honor to whom honor.

159. CHRISTIAN BEHAVIOR IN SECULAR SOCIETY

Rom. 13:1–7

ᵉOwe no one anything except to ᶠlove one another, for he who loves another has fulfilled the law. For ᵍthe commandments, "You shall not commit adultery," "You shall not murder," "You shall not steal," "You shall not bear false witness," "You shall not covet," and if there is any other commandment, are all ʰsummed up in this saying, namely, "You shall love your neighbor as yourself." Love does no harm to a neighbor; therefore ⁱlove is the fulfillment of the law.

---

a. **taxes.** The Gr. word referred specifically to taxes paid by individuals, particularly those living in a conquered nation to their foreign rulers—which makes the tax even more onerous. That tax was usually a combined income and property tax. In this context, however, Paul uses the term in the broadest possible sense to speak of all kinds of taxes. Jesus explicitly taught that taxes are to be paid—even to the pagan Roman government (Matt. 22:17–21). He also set an example by willingly paying the temple tax (Matt. 17:24–27).

b. **Render . . . to all their due.** "Render" translates a Gr. word signifying the payment of something owed—not a voluntary contribution—and is reinforced by the word "due." The apostle reiterates that paying taxes is mandatory.

c. **customs.** Tolls or taxes on goods.

d. **fear . . . honor.** God demands that we show sincere respect and an attitude of genuine high esteem for all public officials.

e. **Owe no one anything.** Not a prohibition against borrowing money, which Scripture permits and regulates (cf. Ex. 22:25; Lev. 25:35–37; Deut. 15:7–9; Neh. 5:7; Pss. 15:5; 37:21, 26; Ezek. 22:12; Matt. 5:42; Luke 6:34). Paul's point is that all our financial obligations must be paid when they are due. See Deut. 23:19, 20; 24:10–13.

f. **love one another.** Believers are commanded to love not only other Christians (John 13:34, 35; 1 Cor. 14:1; Phil. 1:9; Col. 3:14; 1 Thess. 4:9; 1 Tim. 2:15; Heb. 6:10; 1 Pet. 1:22; 4:8; 1 John 2:10; 3:23; 4:7, 21), but also non-Christians (Matt. 5:44; Luke 6:27, 35; cf. Luke 6:28, 34; Rom. 12:14, 20; Gal. 6:10; 1 Thess. 5:15).

g. **the commandments.** To demonstrate that love fulfills the law, Paul cites 4 of the Ten Commandments dealing with human relations and ties them in with an overarching OT command. He quotes Ex. 20:13–15, 17 (cf. Deut. 5:17–19, 21).

h. **summed up . . . love your neighbor as yourself.** This command, quoting Lev. 19:18, encompasses all of God's laws concerning human relationships (Matt. 22:39); if we truly love our neighbor (anyone with whom we have contact, cf. Luke 10:25–37), we will only do what is in his best interest (Rom. 13:10).

i. **love is the fulfillment of the law.** If we treat others with the same care that we have

And do this, knowing the [a]time, that now it is high time to awake out of [b]sleep; for now [c]our salvation [d]is nearer than when we first believed. The [e]night is far spent, the [f]day is at hand. Therefore let us [g]cast off the works of darkness, and let us put on [h]the armor of light. [i]Let us walk properly, as in the day, not in [j]revelry and drunkenness, not in [k]lewdness and lust, not in [l]strife and envy. [m]But put on the Lord Jesus Christ, and make [n]no provision for the flesh, to fulfill its lusts.

---

for ourselves, we will not violate any of God's laws regarding interpersonal relationships (Matt. 7:12; James 2:8).

a. **time.** The Gr. word views time not in terms of chronology, but as a period, era, or age (cf. Rom. 3:26; Matt. 16:3; Mark 1:15; Luke 21:8; Acts 1:7; 3:19; Rev. 1:3).

b. **sleep.** Spiritual apathy and lethargy, i.e. unresponsiveness to the things of God.

c. **our salvation.** Not our justification, but the final feature of our redemption, glorification (see Rom. 8:23).

d. **is nearer.** We will be glorified when Jesus returns (see Rom. 8:23), which draws closer with each passing day. The Bible frequently uses the return of Jesus Christ to motivate believers to holy living (2 Cor. 5:10; Titus 2:11–13; Heb. 10:24, 25; James 5:7, 8; 1 Pet. 4:7–11; 2 Pet. 3:11–14).

e. **night.** Of man's depravity and Satan's dominion (cf. 1 Thess. 5:4, 5).

f. **day.** Of Christ's return and reign (cf. 1 Thess. 5:2–4).

g. **cast off.** In light of Christ's imminent return, Paul exhorts believers to repent of and forsake their sins (2 Pet. 3:14; 1 John 2:28; cf. Eph. 4:22; Col. 3:8–10; Heb. 12:1, 14; James 1:21; 1 Pet. 2:1; 4:1–3).

h. **the armor of light.** The protection that practical righteousness provides (cf. Eph. 6:11–17).

i. **Let us walk properly.** By living a life pleasing to God, manifesting in our outward behavior the inner reality of a redeemed life (cf. Rom. 6:4; 8:4; Luke 1:6; Gal. 5:16; 25; Eph. 2:10; 4:1, 17; 5:2, 8, 15; Phil. 1:27; 3:16, 17; Col. 1:10; 2:6; 1 Thess. 2:12; 4:1, 12; 1 Pet. 2:12; 1 John 2:6; 2 John 4, 6).

j. **revelry.** Wild parties, sexual orgies, brawls, riots (cf. Gal. 5:21; 1 Pet. 4:3).

k. **lewdness and lust.** Sexual immorality (cf. 1 Cor. 6:18; Eph. 5:3; Col. 3:5; 1 Thess. 4:3; 2 Tim. 2:22).

l. **strife and envy.** Closely associated iniquities (cf. 1 Cor. 3:3; 2 Cor. 12:20; Gal. 5:20; Phil. 1:15; 1 Tim. 6:4), since the former is often the result of the latter.

m. **But put on the Lord Jesus Christ.** This phrase summarizes sanctification, the continuing spiritual process in which those who have been saved by faith are transformed into His image and likeness (cf. 2 Cor. 3:18; Gal. 4:19; Phil. 3:13, 14; Col. 2:7; 1 John 3:2, 3). The image Paul uses to describe that process is taking off and putting on clothing, which is symbolic of thoughts and behavior. See Eph. 4:20–24.

n. **no provision.** This word has the basic meaning of planning ahead or forethought. Most sinful behavior results from wrong ideas and lustful desires we allow to linger in our minds (cf. James 1:14, 15).

160. CHRISTIAN LIBERTY

Rom. 14:1–13

ªReceive one who is ᵇweak in the faith, but not to ᶜdisputes over doubtful things. For ᵈone believes he may eat all things, but he who is weak eats ᵉonly vegetables. Let not him who eats ᶠdespise him who does not eat, and let not him who does not eat judge him who eats; for God has received him. Who are you to judge another's servant? ᵍTo his own master he stands or falls. Indeed, he will be made to stand, for God is able to make him stand.

---

a. **Receive.** The Gr. word refers to personal and willing acceptance of another. The diversity of the church displays Christ's power to bring together dissimilar people in genuine unity. Yet Satan often works on man's unredeemed flesh to create division and threaten that unity. The threat to unity Paul addresses in this passage arises when mature (strong) believers—both Jews and Gentiles—conflict with immature (weak) believers. The strong Jewish believers understood their freedom in Christ and realized the ceremonial requirements of the Mosaic law were no longer binding. The mature Gentiles understood that idols are not gods and, therefore, that they could eat meat that had been offered to them. But in both cases the weaker brothers' consciences were troubled, and they were even tempted to violate their consciences (a bad thing to train oneself to do), become more legalistic under the feelings of guilt, or even to sin. Knowing that the mature Jews and Gentiles would be able to understand these struggles, Paul addresses most of his comments to them.

b. **weak in the faith.** This characterizes those believers who are unable to let go of the religious ceremonies and rituals of their past. The weak Jewish believer had difficulty abandoning the rites and prohibitions of the Old Covenant; he felt compelled to adhere to dietary laws, observe the Sabbath, and offer sacrifices in the temple. The weak Gentile believer had been steeped in pagan idolatry and its rituals; he felt that any contact with anything remotely related to his past, including eating meat that had been offered to a pagan deity and then sold in the marketplace, tainted him with sin. Both had very sensitive consciences in these areas, and were not yet mature enough to be free of those convictions. Cf. 1 Cor. 8:1–13

c. **disputes over doubtful things.** Better translated, "for the purpose of passing judgment on his opinions (or scruples)." The mature believer should not sit in judgment on the sincere but underdeveloped thoughts that govern the weak believer's conduct.

d. **one believes.** The strong believer, whose mature faith allows him to exercise his freedom in Christ by eating the inexpensive meat sold at the pagan meat markets—inexpensive because a worshiper had first offered it as a sacrifice to a pagan deity (see 1 Cor. 8:1–13).

e. **only vegetables.** The strict diet weak Jewish and Gentile believers ate to avoid eating meat that was unclean or may have been sacrificed to idols.

f. **despise . . . judge.** "Despise" indicates a contempt for someone as worthless, who deserves only disdain and abhorrence. "Judge" is equally strong and means "to condemn." Paul uses them synonymously: The strong hold the weak in contempt as legalistic and self-righteous; the weak judge the strong to be irresponsible at best and perhaps depraved.

g. **To his own master he stands or falls.** How Christ evaluates each believer is what matters, and His judgment does not take into account religious tradition or personal preference (cf. Rom. 8:33, 34; 1 Cor. 4:3–5).

One person ᵃesteems one day above another; another ᵇesteems every day alike. ᶜLet each be fully convinced in his own mind. ᵈHe who observes the day, observes it ᵉto the Lord; and he who does not observe the day, to the Lord he does not observe it. He who eats, eats to the Lord, for he gives God thanks; and he who does not eat, to the Lord he does not eat, and gives God thanks. For none of us ᶠlives to himself, and no one dies to himself. For if we live, we live to the Lord; and if we die, we die to the Lord. Therefore, whether we live or die, we are the Lord's. For to this end Christ died and rose and lived again, that He might be ᵍLord of both the dead and the living. But why do you judge your brother? Or why do you show contempt for ʰyour brother? For we shall all stand before ⁱthe judgment seat of Christ. For ʲit is written:

> "As I live, says the Lᴏʀᴅ,
> Every knee shall bow to Me,
> And every tongue shall confess to God."

---

a. **esteems one day.** Though it was no longer required by God, the weak Jewish believer felt compelled to observe the Sabbath and other special days associated with Judaism (cf. Gal. 4:9, 10; see Col. 2:16, 17). On the other hand, the weak Gentile wanted to separate himself from the special days of festivities associated with his former paganism because of its immorality and idolatry.

b. **esteems every day alike.** The mature believers were unaffected by those concerns.

c. **Let each be fully convinced.** Each Christian must follow the dictates of his own conscience in matters not specifically commanded or prohibited in Scripture. Since conscience is a God-given mechanism to warn, and responds to the highest standard of moral law in the mind (Rom. 2:14, 15), it is not sensible to train yourself to ignore it. Rather, respond to its compunctions and as you mature, by learning more, your mind will not alert it to those things which are not essential.

d. **He who observes . . .** The strong believer eats whatever he pleases and thanks the Lord. The weak brother eats according to his ceremonial diet and thanks the Lord that he made a sacrifice on His behalf. In either case, the believer thanks the Lord, so the motive is the same.

e. **to the Lord.** Whether weak or strong, the motive behind a believer's decisions about issues of conscience must be to please the Lord.

f. **lives to himself . . . dies to himself.** The focus of Christian living is never oneself—everything we do should be to please our sovereign Lord (cf. 1 Cor. 6:20; 10:31).

g. **Lord of both the dead and the living.** Christ died not only to free us from sin, but to enslave us to Himself (Rom. 6:22); to establish Himself as Sovereign over the saints in His presence and those still on earth (cf. Phil. 2:11; 1 Tim. 6:15; Rev. 17:14; 19:16).

h. **your brother.** A fellow believer in Christ.

i. **the judgment seat of Christ.** The preferred rendering is "the judgment seat of God" (see 1 Cor. 3:13–15). Every believer will give an account of himself, and the Lord will judge the decisions he made—including those concerning issues of conscience. That verdict is the only one that matters (see 1 Cor. 4:1–5; 2 Cor. 5:9, 10).

j. **it is written.** Paul quotes Is. 45:23; 49:18 (cf. Phil. 2:10, 11).

So then each of us shall give account of himself to God. Therefore let us not judge one another anymore, [a]but rather resolve this, not to put a [b]stumbling block or a cause to fall in our brother's way.

161. LIBERTY AND LOVE

Rom. 14:14–23

[c]I know and am convinced by the Lord Jesus that there is [d]nothing [e]unclean of itself; but [f]to him who considers anything to be unclean, to him it is unclean. Yet if your brother is [g]grieved because of your food, you are no longer walking in [h]love. Do not [i]destroy with your food [j]the one for whom Christ died. Therefore do not let [k]your good be [l]spoken of as evil; for the [m]kingdom of God is not [n]eating and drinking, but [o]righteousness and [p]peace and

a. **but rather resolve.** The same Gr. word translated "judge" (Rom. 14:3, 10, 13) is here translated "resolve." In vv. 3, 10, 13a the meaning is negative: to condemn. In v. 13b, the meaning is positive: to determine or make a careful decision. The point of Paul's play on words is that instead of passing judgment on their brothers, they should use their best judgment to help fellow believers.

b. **stumbling block.** Anything a believer does—even though Scripture may permit it—that causes another to fall into sin (1 Cor. 8:9).

c. **I know and am convinced by the Lord Jesus.** This truth was not the product of his own thinking or the teaching of others, but of divine revelation (cf. Gal. 1:12). See 1 Cor. 7:12.

d. **nothing unclean of itself.** See Acts 10:15; cf. Mark 7:15; 1 Tim. 4:3–5; Titus 1:15).

e. **unclean.** The Gr. word originally meant "common" but came to mean "impure" or "evil" (see Acts 10:14).

f. **to him who considers . . . to him it is unclean.** If a believer is convinced a certain behavior is sin—even if his assessment is wrong—he should never do it. If he does, he will violate his conscience, experience guilt (cf. 1 Cor. 8:4–7; see Rom. 2:15), and perhaps be driven back into deeper legalism instead of moving toward freedom (see v. 5).

g. **grieved.** The Gr. word refers to causing pain or distress. A weak believer may be hurt when he sees a brother do something he believes is sinful. But still worse, the strong believer may cause his weaker brother to violate his own conscience (cf. 1 Cor. 8:8–13).

h. **love.** See 1 Cor. 13:1–13. Love will ensure that the strong Christian is sensitive and understanding of his brother's weaknesses (1 Cor. 8:8–13).

i. **destroy.** This refers to complete devastation. In the NT, it is often used to indicate eternal damnation (Matt. 10:28; Luke 13:3; John 3:16; Rom. 2:12). In this context, however, it refers to a serious devastation of one's spiritual growth (cf. Matt. 18:3, 6, 14).

j. **the one for whom Christ died.** Any Christian (cf. 1 Cor. 8:11).

k. **your good.** The rightful exercise of one's Christian liberty (cf. 1 Cor. 10:23–32).

l. **spoken of as evil.** To blaspheme. When unbelievers see a strong Christian abusing his freedom in Christ and harming a weaker brother, they will conclude that Christianity is filled with unloving people, which reflects badly on God's reputation (cf. Rom. 2:24).

m. **kingdom of God.** The sphere of salvation where God rules in the hearts of those He has saved (see Acts 1:3; 1 Cor. 6:9).

n. **eating and drinking.** Non-essentials and external observances.

o. **righteousness.** Holy, obedient living (cf. Eph. 6:14; Phil. 1:11).

p. **peace.** The loving tranquility, produced by the Spirit, that should characterize believers' relationships with God and each other (Gal. 5:22).

[a]joy in the Holy Spirit. For he who serves Christ in these things is acceptable to God and [b]approved by men.

Therefore let us pursue the things which make for peace and the things by which one may edify another. Do not destroy the [c]work of God for the sake of food. [d]All things indeed are pure, but it is evil for the man [e]who eats with offense. It is good neither to eat meat nor drink wine nor do anything by which your brother [f]stumbles or is offended or is made weak. Do you have faith? [g]Have it to yourself before God. Happy is he who does not condemn himself in [h]what he approves. But he [i]who doubts is condemned if he eats, because he does not eat from faith; for [j]whatever is not from faith is sin.

162. LIBERTY AND THE GLORY OF GOD

Rom. 15:1–13

We then who are strong ought [k]to bear with the [l]scruples of the weak, and not to please ourselves. Let each of us please his neighbor for his good, leading

---

a. **joy in the Holy Spirit.** Another part of the Spirit's fruit, this describes an abiding attitude of praise and thanksgiving regardless of circumstances, which flows from one's confidence in God's sovereignty (Gal. 5:22; 1 Thess. 1:6).

b. **approved by men.** This refers to approving something after a careful examination, like a jeweler inspecting a stone to determine its quality and value. Christians are under the microscope of a skeptical world that is assessing how they live with and treat each other (cf. John 13:35; Phil. 2:15).

c. **work of God.** A fellow Christian who has been redeemed by the efforts of the Father, Son, and Holy Spirit, not his own (cf. Eph. 2:10).

d. **All things . . . pure.** The discretionary liberties which God has given to believers and are good in themselves (Rom. 14:14, 16).

e. **who eats with offense.** One who uses those God-given liberties carelessly and selfishly, offending his weaker brother.

f. **stumbles.** The strongest Christian can bring harm to himself in the area of Christian liberty by denouncing or belittling the freedom God has given him (Gal. 5:1), or by carelessly flaunting his liberty without regard for how that might affect others (cf. 1 Cor. 10:23–32).

g. **Have it to yourself before God.** This is better translated, "have as your own conviction before God." Paul urges the strong believer to understand his liberty, enjoy it, and keep it between God and himself.

h. **what he approves.** The strong believer maintains a healthy conscience because he does not give a weak believer a cause to stumble.

i. **who doubts is condemned.** When the weak brother violates his conscience, he sins.

j. **whatever is not from faith.** The thoughts and actions that our conscience condemns.

k. **to bear.** The word means "to pick up and carry a weight." It is used of carrying a pitcher of water (Mark 14:13), of carrying a man (Acts 21:35), and figuratively of bearing an obligation (Acts 15:10). The strong are not to simply tolerate the weaknesses of their weaker brothers; they are to help the weak shoulder their burdens by showing loving and practical consideration for them (Gal. 6:2; cf. 1 Cor. 9:19–22; Phil. 2:2–4).

l. **scruples.** Better translated, "weaknesses."

to ªedification. For even ᵇChrist did not please Himself; but as ᶜit is written, ᵈ"The reproaches of those who reproached You fell on Me." For whatever ᵉthings were written before were ᶠwritten for our learning, that we through the patience and ᵍcomfort of the Scriptures might have ʰhope. Now may the God of patience and comfort grant you ⁱto be like-minded toward one another, according to Christ Jesus, that you may ʲwith one mind and one mouth glorify the ᵏGod and Father of our Lord Jesus Christ.

Therefore receive one another, just ˡas Christ also received us, to the glory of God. Now I say that Jesus Christ has become ᵐa servant to the circumcision for the truth of God, to confirm the ⁿpromises made to the

---

a. **edification.** To build up and strengthen. This is essentially the same appeal Paul made earlier (Rom. 14:19), only with the additional qualification of self-sacrifice (1 Cor. 10:23, 24; cf. Phil. 2:2–5).

b. **Christ did not please Himself.** His ultimate purpose was to please God and accomplish His will (John 4:34; 5:30; 6:38; 8:25, 27–29; Phil. 2:6–8).

c. **it is written.** Quoted from Ps. 69:9.

d. **The reproaches . . . fell on Me.** "Reproaches" refers to slander, false accusations, and insults. Men hate God, and they manifested that same hate toward the One He sent to reveal Himself (cf. John 1:10, 11, 18).

e. **things . . . written before.** The divinely revealed OT.

f. **written for our learning.** Although Christians live under the New Covenant and are not under the authority of the Old Covenant, God's moral law has not changed and all Scripture is of spiritual benefit (1 Cor. 10:6, 10, 11; 2 Pet. 1:20, 21). Paul's description of the benefits of Scripture certainly includes the NT, but speaks primarily about "the sacred writings"—or the OT (2 Tim. 3:15–17).

g. **comfort.** Lit. "encouragement." The Word of God not only informs believers how to endure, but it also encourages them in the process.

h. **hope.** Without the clear and certain promises of the Word of God, the believer has no basis for hope (cf. Ps. 119:81, 114; Eph. 2:12; Jer. 14:8).

i. **to be like-minded toward one another.** Paul urges the strong and the weak (see Rom. 14:1–12), despite their differing views on these non-essential issues, to pursue loving, spiritual harmony in regard to matters on which the Bible is silent.

j. **with one mind and one mouth.** Our unity should be both real (one mind) and apparent (one mouth). But the consummate purpose of unity is not to please other believers but to glorify God.

k. **God and Father.** This expression emphasizes the deity of Christ. Jesus is not an adopted son of God; He is of the same essential being and nature as God. This is such an important connection that it appears frequently in the NT (2 Cor. 1:3; 11:31; Eph. 1:3; Col. 1:3; 1 Pet. 1:3).

l. **as Christ . . . received us.** If the perfect, sinless Son of God was willing to bring sinners into God's family, how much more should forgiven believers be willing to warmly embrace and accept each other in spite of their disagreements over issues of conscience (Matt. 10:24; 11:29; Eph. 4:32—5:2).

m. **a servant to the circumcision.** Jesus was born a Jew (see Matt. 1:1), and as a child, He was circumcised and identified physically with the sign of the covenant (see Rom. 4:11; Gen. 17:10–14).

n. **promises made to the fathers.** The covenant with Abraham that God reiterated to both Isaac and Jacob (see Rom. 4:13).

fathers, and ᵃthat the Gentiles might glorify God for His mercy, as ᵇit is written:

> ᶜ"For this reason I will confess to You among the Gentiles,
> And sing to Your name."

And again he says:

> ᵈ"Rejoice, O Gentiles, with His people!"

And again:

> ᶠ"Praise the Lᴏʀᴅ, all you Gentiles!
> Laud Him, all you peoples!"

And again, Isaiah says:

> ᵍ"There shall be a ʰroot of Jesse;
> And He who shall rise to reign over the Gentiles,
> In Him the Gentiles shall hope."

Now may the ⁱGod of hope fill you with all joy and peace in believing, that you may abound in hope ʲby the power of the Holy Spirit.

---

a. **that the Gentiles might glorify God for His mercy.** Because He extended His grace and mercy to a people outside the covenant (see Rom. 10:11–21; 11:11–18).

b. **it is written.** To show that God's plan has always been to bring Jew and Gentile alike into His kingdom and to soften the prejudice of Christian Jews against their Gentile brothers, Paul quotes from the Law, the Prophets, and twice from the Psalms—all the recognized divisions of the OT—proving God's plan from their own Scriptures.

c. Quoted from 2 Sam. 22:50; Ps. 18:49. The psalmist sings praise to God among the nations, which alludes to Gentile salvation.

d. Quoted from Deut. 32:43.

f. Quoted from Ps. 117:1.

g. Quoted from Is. 11:10.

h. **root of Jesse.** A way of referring to Jesus as the descendant of David, and thus of David's father Jesse (see Rev. 5:5).

i. **God of hope.** God is the source of eternal hope, life, and salvation, and He is the object of hope for every believer (see Rom. 5:2).

j. **by the power of the Holy Spirit.** The believer's hope comes through the Scripture (cf. 15:4; Eph. 1:13, 14), which was written and is applied to every believing heart by the Holy Spirit.

163. PAUL'S MINISTRY TRAVELS

Rom. 15:14–33

^aNow I myself am confident concerning you, my brethren, that you also are full of ^bgoodness, filled with all ^cknowledge, able also to ^dadmonish one another. Nevertheless, brethren, I have written more boldly to you on some points, ^eas reminding you, because of the grace given to me by God, that I might be a ^fminister of Jesus Christ ^gto the Gentiles, ministering the gospel of God, that the ^hoffering of the Gentiles might be acceptable, sanctified by the Holy Spirit. Therefore I have reason to ⁱglory in Christ Jesus in the things which pertain to God. For I will not dare to speak of any of those things which Christ has not accomplished through me, in word and deed, to make the Gentiles obedient—in mighty ^jsigns and wonders, by the power of the Spirit of God, so that from Jerusalem and round about ^kto Illyricum I have fully preached the gospel of Christ. And so I have made it my aim to preach

a. Not wanting to jeopardize his relationship with the believers in Rome by seeming to be insensitive, presumptuous, or unloving, Paul sets out to explain how he could write such a forthright letter to a church he did not found and had never visited.

b. **goodness.** High moral character. The believers in Rome hated evil and loved righteousness, attitudes their lives clearly displayed.

c. **knowledge.** Refers to deep, intimate knowledge indicating that the Roman believers were doctrinally sound (Col. 2:2, 3), illustrating the fact that truth and virtue are inseparable (cf. 1 Tim. 1:19).

d. **admonish.** To encourage, warn, or advise—a comprehensive term for preaching (1 Cor. 14:3) and personal counseling (see 12:1). Every believer is responsible to encourage and strengthen other believers with God's Word and is divinely equipped to do so (2 Tim. 3:16).

e. **as reminding you.** In spite of their spiritual strength, these Christians needed to be reminded of truths they already knew but could easily neglect or even forget (cf. 1 Tim. 4:6; 2 Tim. 2:8–14; Titus 3:1).

f. **minister.** "Minister" was a general Gr. term used of public officials. But in the NT it is used most often of those who serve God in some form of public worship (e.g., Phil. 2:17; Heb. 1:7, 14; 8:1, 2, 6), including that of a priest (Luke 1:23).

g. **to the Gentiles.** Although Paul's practice was always to present the gospel to the Jews first in every city he visited (see Acts 13:5), his primary apostolic calling was to the Gentiles (Rom. 11:13; Acts 9:15).

h. **offering.** Having referred to himself as a minister, a word with priestly overtones, Paul explains that his priestly ministry is to present to God an offering of a multitude of Gentile converts.

i. **glory.** Lit. "to boast. Paul never boasted in his accomplishments as an apostle, but only in what Christ had accomplished through him (1 Cor. 1:27–29, 31; 2 Cor. 10:13–17; 12:5, 9; Gal. 6:14; 1 Tim. 1:12–16).

j. **signs and wonders.** See Acts 2:19; 2 Cor. 12:12. God used them to authenticate true preaching and teaching.

k. **to Illyricum.** The region that roughly corresponds to the former European country of Yugoslavia. From Jerusalem to Illyricum was a span of some 1,400 miles.

the gospel, not where Christ was named, lest I should build on ᵃanother man's foundation, but as ᵇit is written:

"To whom He was not announced, they shall see;
And those who have not heard shall understand."

For this reason I also have been much ᶜhindered from coming to you. But now ᵈno longer having a place in these parts, and having a great desire these many years to come to you, whenever I journey to ᵉSpain, I shall come to you. For I hope to see you on my journey, and to be ᶠhelped on my way there by you, if first I may enjoy your company for a while. But now I am going to Jerusalem to minister to the saints. For it pleased those from ᵍMacedonia and Achaia to make a certain ʰcontribution for the poor among the saints who are in Jerusalem. It pleased them indeed, and they are their debtors. For if the Gentiles have been partakers of ⁱtheir spiritual things, their duty is also to minister to them in material things. Therefore, when I have performed this and have sealed to them ʲthis fruit, I shall go by way of you to Spain. But I know that when I come to you, I shall come in the fullness of the blessing of the gospel of Christ.

---

a. **another man's foundation.** Paul's goal was to reach those who had never heard the gospel—the primary function of a NT evangelist (Eph. 4:11). But for pastor-teachers, building on the foundation laid by such an evangelist is the crucial part of their ministry (cf. 1 Cor. 3:6).

b. **it is written.** Quoted from Is. 52:15; see 3:10. The OT quotation refers primarily to Christ's second coming, but in its broader application it refers to the process of evangelism that began in Paul's day and continues throughout church history until Christ returns.

c. **hindered from coming.** The form of this Gr. verb indicates an ongoing problem, and that something external created the hindrance. Paul was providentially being prevented by God from going to Rome (cf. Acts 16:7).

d. **no longer having a place.** Paul believed he had covered the region with the gospel sufficiently and could move on to other areas.

e. **Spain.** The city and region referred to in the OT as Tarshish (1 Kin. 10:22; Jon. 1:3), located on the far western end of the European continent. It had become a major center of commerce and culture, made accessible by the vast network of Roman roads. Its most famous ancient son was Seneca, the philosopher and statesman who tutored Nero and served as prime minister of the Empire.

f. **helped on my way there by you.** Paul hoped the church at Rome would supply him with an escort and supplies to make the journey to Spain.

g. **Macedonia and Achaia.** See Acts 16:9; 18:12. Paul ministered in these regions during his first and second missionary journeys.

h. **contribution.** The Gr. word carries the basic idea of sharing and is usually translated "fellowship" or "communion." The context indicates that here it is the sharing of a financial gift to help support the poor in Jerusalem (1 Cor. 16:1; 2 Cor. 8:2–4; Gal. 2:9, 10).

i. **their spiritual things.** The "things" were gospel truths first preached to the Gentile believers by the Jewish apostles, prophets, teachers, and evangelists.

j. **this fruit.** The financial gift for the Jerusalem church; the fruit of their genuine love and gratitude.

Now I beg you, brethren, through the Lord Jesus Christ, and through ᵃthe love of the Spirit, that you strive together with me in ᵇprayers to God for me, that I may be delivered from those in Judea who do not believe, and that my service for Jerusalem ᶜmay be acceptable to the saints, that I may come to you with joy by the will of God, and may be ᵈrefreshed together with you. Now ᵉthe God of peace be with you all. Amen.

164. COMMENDATIONS AND GREETINGS
Rom. 16:1–16

ᶠI commend to you ᵍPhoebe our sister, who is a ʰservant of the church in ⁱCenchrea, that you may receive her in the Lord in a manner worthy of the saints, and assist her in whatever business she has need of you; for indeed she has been a helper of many and of myself also.

---

a. **the love of the Spirit.** This phrase occurs only here in Scripture and refers to Paul's love for the Holy Spirit, not the Spirit's love for him (cf. Ps. 143:10).

b. **prayers . . . that I may be delivered.** Many Jews in Judea rejected the gospel and were prepared to attack Paul when he returned. Aware of the trouble that awaited him (Acts 20:22–24), he wanted the Roman Christians to pray for his deliverance only so he could complete the ministry the Lord had given him. Their prayers were answered in that he met with success in Jerusalem (Acts 21:17, 19, 20) and was delivered from death, but not imprisonment (Acts 21:10, 11; 23:11).

c. **may be acceptable.** Paul wanted the Jewish Christians in Jerusalem to receive the financial gift from the Gentiles with loving gratitude, recognizing it as a gesture of brotherly love and kindness.

d. **refreshed together with you.** Paul eventually found the joy and rest he was looking for (Acts 28:15).

e. **the God of peace.** Just as He is the God of hope, God is also the source of true peace (cf. Eph. 2:11–14; Phil. 4:7).

f. This chapter (Rom. 16), which has almost no explicit teaching and contains several lists of mostly unknown people, is the most extensive and intimate expression of Paul's love and affection for other believers and co-workers found anywhere in his NT letters. It also provides insights into the lives of ordinary first-century Christians and gives an inside look at the nature and character of the early church.

g. **Phoebe.** Means "bright and radiant," which aptly fits Paul's brief description of her personality and Christian character.

h. **servant.** The term from which we get "deacon" and "deaconess" (see 1 Tim. 3:10, 11, 13). In the early church, women servants cared for sick believers, the poor, strangers, and those in prison. They instructed the women and children (cf. Titus 2:3–5). Whether Phoebe had an official title or not, she had the great responsibility of delivering this letter to the Roman church. When they had served faithfully and become widowed and destitute, such women were to be cared for by the church (see 1 Tim. 5:3–16).

i. **Cenchrea.** A neighboring port city of Corinth, where Paul wrote Romans. The church in Cenchrea was probably planted by the Corinthian church.

Greet Priscilla and Aquila, my fellow workers in Christ Jesus, who [a]risked their own necks for my life, to whom not only I give thanks, but also all the churches of the Gentiles. Likewise greet the church that is in their house.

Greet my beloved [b]Epaenetus, who is the [c]firstfruits of Achaia to Christ. Greet [d]Mary, who labored much for us. Greet [e]Andronicus and Junia, my countrymen and my [f]fellow prisoners, who are [g]of note among the apostles, who also were in Christ before me.

Greet [h]Amplias, my beloved in the Lord. Greet Urbanus, our fellow worker in Christ, and [i]Stachys, my beloved. Greet Apelles, approved in Christ. Greet those who are of the household of [j]Aristobulus. Greet [k]Herodion, [l]my countryman. Greet those who are of the household of [m]Narcissus who are in the Lord.

Greet [n]Tryphena and Tryphosa, who have labored in the Lord. Greet the beloved [o]Persis, who labored much in the Lord. Greet [p]Rufus,

---

a. **risked their own necks for my life.** Probably at Corinth or Ephesus, but the details are not known.

b. **Epaenetus.** Probably saved through Paul's preaching and lovingly discipled by the apostle.

c. **firstfruits.** See Rom. 1:13. He was the first convert in Asia Minor (modern Turkey), which in the best manuscripts replaces the word "Achaia."

d. **Mary, who labored much for us.** "Labored much" connotes hard work to the point of exhaustion. The context suggests she might have ministered in the church at Rome since its founding and been mentioned to Paul by others (possibly Priscilla and Aquila). But nothing more is known of her.

e. **Andronicus and Junia.** Perhaps a married couple, since "Junia" can be a woman's name.

f. **fellow prisoners.** Probably a reference to their actually sharing the same cell or adjacent cells at some point.

g. **of note among the apostles.** Their ministry with Paul, and perhaps with Peter and some of the other apostles in Jerusalem before Paul was converted, was well known and appreciated by the apostles.

h. **Amplias.** A common name among the emperor's household slaves at that time; he may have been one of those in "Caesar's household" (Phil. 4:22).

i. **Stachys.** An uncommon Gr. name meaning "ear of corn." He was obviously close to Paul, but the details are unknown.

j. **Aristobulus.** Since Paul does not greet him personally, he was probably not a believer, although some relatives and household servants apparently were. One noted biblical scholar believes that he was the brother of Herod Agrippa I and the grandson of Herod the Great.

k. **Herodion.** Related to the Herod family, and so perhaps associated with the household of Aristobulus.

l. **my countryman.** The preferred reading is "my kinsman," indicating that he may have been one of Paul's Jewish relatives.

m. **Narcissus.** See Rom. 16:10. Some scholars believe that this was the Emperor Claudius' secretary. If so, two households within the palace had Christians in them (cf. Phil. 4:22).

n. **Tryphena and Tryphosa.** Possibly twin sisters, whose names mean "delicate" and "dainty."

o. **Persis.** Named after her native Persia; since her work is spoken of in the past tense, she was probably older than the other two women in this verse.

p. **Rufus.** Biblical scholars generally agree that he was one of the sons of Simon of Cyrene, the man enlisted to carry Jesus' cross (cf. Mark 15:21) and was likely saved through that contact with Christ. Mark wrote his gospel in Rome, possibly after the letter to Rome was written, and circulated. Paul would not have mentioned Rufus if that name were not well known to the church in Rome.

[a]chosen in the Lord, and [b]his mother and mine. Greet Asyncritus, Phlegon, Hermas, Patrobas, Hermes, and the [c]brethren who are with them. Greet Philologus and Julia, Nereus and his sister, and Olympas, and all the saints who are with them.

Greet one another with a [d]holy kiss. The churches of Christ greet you.

165. FINAL INSTRUCTIONS AND BENEDICTIONS
Rom. 16:17—27

[e]Now I urge you, brethren, note those who cause [f]divisions and offenses, contrary to the doctrine which you learned, and avoid them. For those who are such do not serve our Lord Jesus Christ, but their own [g]belly, and by smooth words and flattering speech deceive the hearts of the simple. For your obedience has become known to all. Therefore I am glad on your behalf; but I want you to be wise in what is good, and [h]simple concerning evil. And the [i]God of peace [j]will crush Satan under your feet shortly.

The grace of our Lord Jesus Christ be with you. Amen.

---

a. **chosen in the Lord.** Elected to salvation. Some translations render "chosen" as "choice," which indicates he was widely known as an extraordinary believer because of his great love and service.

b. **his mother and mine.** Rufus was not Paul's natural brother. Rather, Rufus' mother, the wife of Simon of Cyrene, at some time had cared for Paul during his ministry travels.

c. **brethren.** "Brethren" in this context, probably refers to both men and women, which indicates that these names represent the outstanding leaders of two of the assemblies in Rome.

d. **holy kiss.** Kissing of friends on the forehead, cheek, or beard was common in the OT. The Jews in the NT church carried on the practice, and it became especially precious to new believers, who were often outcasts from their own families because of their faith, because of the spiritual kinship it signified.

e. **Now . . .** Paul considered it necessary to insert into his greetings of love this caution against harmful teachings and practices that undermine the truth of Christianity and are its greatest threat. Genuine love will be ready to forgive evil, but it will not condone or ignore it. Those such as Paul, who truly love other believers who are dear to them, will warn them about sin and harm (cf. 1 Cor. 13:6).

f. **divisions and offenses.** Doctrinal falsehood and unrighteous practices (cf. Matt. 24:24; Acts 20:27–32; Gal. 1:6–8; Eph. 4:14).

g. **belly.** Driven by self-interest and self-gratification, often seen in their pretentious, extravagant, and immoral lifestyles (cf. Phil. 3:18, 19; 2 Tim. 3:7, 8; 2 Pet. 1:20—2:3, 10–19; Jude 12, 13).

h. **simple.** The unsuspecting or naive person (cf. 2 Cor. 11:13–15).

i. **God of peace.** See Rom. 15:33; Heb. 13:20.

j. **will crush Satan.** See Gen. 3:15.

Timothy, my fellow worker, and ^aLucius, ^bJason, and ^cSosipater, my countrymen, greet you.

I, ^dTertius, who wrote this epistle, greet you in the Lord.

^eGaius, my host and the host of ^fthe whole church, greets you. ^gErastus, the ^htreasurer of the city, greets you, and ⁱQuartus, a brother. The grace of our Lord Jesus Christ be with you all. Amen.

^jNow to Him who is able to establish you according to ^kmy gospel and the ^lpreaching of Jesus Christ, according to the revelation of ^mthe mystery kept secret since the world began but now made manifest, and by the ⁿprophetic Scriptures made known to all nations, according to the commandment of the everlasting God, for obedience to the faith—^oto God, alone wise, be glory through Jesus Christ forever. Amen.

---

a. **Lucius.** Either 1) a native of Cyrene, one of the prophets and teachers in Antioch who participated in Paul and Barnabas' commissioning (Acts 13:1–3) or 2) another form of "Luke," the author of the Gospel of Luke and the book of Acts.

b. **Jason.** One of the first converts in Thessalonica, who evidently let Paul stay in his home for a short time before Paul and Silas were sent to Berea (see Acts 17:5–10).

c. **Sosipater.** A longer form of "Sopater" (Acts 20:4–6), a Berean (cf. Acts 17:10–12) who joined other believers in meeting Paul at Troas after the apostle left Ephesus.

d. **Tertius.** Paul's secretary, who wrote this letter as Paul dictated it, inserts a personal greeting.

e. **Gaius.** One of Paul's converts at Corinth (cf. 1 Cor. 1:14). His full name was most likely "Gaius Titius Justus" (Acts 18:7).

f. **the whole church.** The congregation that met in Gaius' house.

g. **Erastus.** A common name in NT times, but probably not the same man referred to in Acts 19:22 or 2 Tim. 4:20

h. **treasurer.** In Corinth. This was a prominent position with political clout.

i. **Quartus.** May have been a physical brother of Erastus, but more likely just the final brother in Christ listed here.

j. **Now to Him . . .** The letter concludes with a beautiful doxology that praises God for His work through Jesus Christ and thereby summarizes the major themes in Romans (see Rom. 11:33–36; cf. Matt. 6:13; Luke 19:37, 38; Eph. 3:20, 21; Heb. 13:20, 21; Rev. 5:9, 10).

k. **my gospel.** See Rom. 1:1; 2:16; cf. Gal. 1:11; 2:2.

l. **preaching of Jesus Christ.** Synonymous with the gospel, it was Paul's supreme life commitment (see Rom. 10:14, 15, 17; cf. 1 Cor. 1:23, 24; 2 Cor. 4:5, 6).

m. **the mystery.** See Rom. 11:25. In the NT, this word does not have its modern connotation. Instead, it refers to something hidden in former times but now made known (1 Cor. 4:1; Eph. 5:32; 6:19; Col. 1:25, 26; 2 Thess. 2:7, 8; 1 Tim. 3:9, 16). The NT's most common mystery is that God would provide salvation for Gentiles as well as Jews (Eph. 3:3–9).

n. **prophetic Scriptures made known.** God had told Israel that He would not only call her to righteousness, but appoint her as a light (of the gospel) to the nations (see Is. 42:6; 49:6; 1 Pet. 1:10, 11; cf. Gen. 12:3; Ex. 19:6; Is. 49:22; 53:11; 60:3–5; Jer. 31:31, 33).

o. **to God . . . be glory.** It was through the Father that the gospel was ultimately revealed, therefore He deserves all the credit, praise, and worship.

166. MINISTRY IN TROAS

Acts 20:3b–12

And when the [a]Jews plotted against him as he was about to sail to Syria, he decided to return through Macedonia. And [b]Sopater of Berea accompanied him to Asia—also Aristarchus and Secundus of the Thessalonians, and Gaius of Derbe, and Timothy, and Tychicus and Trophimus of Asia. These men, going ahead, waited [c]for us at Troas. But we sailed away [d]from Philippi after the [e]Days of Unleavened Bread, and in five days joined them at Troas, where we stayed seven days.

Now on the [f]first day of the week, when the disciples came together [g]to break bread, Paul, ready to depart the next day, spoke to them and continued

---

a. **Jews plotted against him.** See Acts 9:20, 23; 13:45; 14:2, 19; 17:5–9, 13; 18:6, 12, 13; 19:9; 21:27–36; 23:12–15. Tragically, most of the opposition to Paul's ministry stemmed from his fellow countrymen (cf. 2 Cor. 11:26). The Jewish community of Corinth hated Paul because of its humiliating debacle before Gallio (Acts 18:12–17), and the stunning conversions of two of its most prominent leaders, Crispus (18:8), and Sosthenes (18:17; 1 Cor. 1:1). Luke does not record the details of the Jews' plot, but it undoubtedly involved murdering Paul during the voyage to Palestine. The apostle would have been an easy target on a small ship packed with Jewish pilgrims. Because of that danger, Paul canceled his plans to sail from Greece to Syria. Instead, he decided to go N into Macedonia, cross the Aegean Sea to Asia Minor, and catch another ship from there. That delay cost Paul his opportunity to reach Palestine in time for Passover; but he hurried to be there in time for Pentecost.

b. **Sopater of Berea . . . Trophimus of Asia.** Paul's traveling companions came from the various provinces in which he had ministered. These men were likely the official representatives of their churches, chosen to accompany Paul as he took the offering to Jerusalem (see Acts 19:21; cf. 1 Cor. 16:3, 4).

c. **for us.** The first person plural pronoun reveals that Luke rejoined Paul in Philippi. Being a Gentile, he was able to remain there to minister after Paul and Silas were forced to leave (Acts 16:20, 39, 40). This verse begins the second of the three "we passages" in which Luke accompanied Paul on his travels.

d. **from Philippi.** Paul, along with Luke, and possibly Titus, crossed the Aegean Sea from Philippi to Troas. That crossing, due to unfavorable winds, took 5 days; Paul's earlier crossing from Troas to Neapolis (Philippi's port) had taken only two days (Acts 16:11). In Troas, they were reunited with the rest of their party.

e. **Days of Unleavened Bread.** I.e., Passover (Ex. 12:17).

f. **first day of the week.** Sunday, the day the church gathered for worship, because it was the day of Christ's resurrection. Cf. Matt. 28:1; Mark 16:2, 9; Luke 24:1; John 20:1, 19; 1 Cor. 16:2. The writings of the early church Fathers confirm that the church continued to meet on Sunday after the close of the NT period. Scripture does not require Christians to observe the Saturday Sabbath: 1) the Sabbath was the sign of the Mosaic Covenant (Ex. 31:16, 17; Neh. 9:14; Ezek. 20:12), whereas Christians are under the New Covenant (2 Cor. 3; Heb. 8); 2) there is no NT command to keep the Sabbath; 3) the first command to keep the Sabbath was not until the time of Moses (Ex. 20:8); 4) the Jerusalem Council (chap. 15) did not order Gentile believers to keep the Sabbath; 5) Paul never cautioned Christians about breaking the Sabbath; and 6) the NT explicitly teaches that Sabbath keeping was not a requirement (see Rom. 14:5; Gal. 4:10, 11; Col. 2:16, 17).

g. **to break bread.** The common meal associated with the communion service (1 Cor. 11:20–22).

his message until midnight. There were [a]many lamps in the [b]upper room where they were gathered together. And in a window sat a certain [c]young man named Eutychus, who was sinking into a deep sleep. He was overcome by sleep; and as Paul continued speaking, he fell down from the third story and was taken up dead. But Paul went down, fell on him, and embracing him said, "Do not trouble yourselves, for [d]his life is in him." Now when he had come up, had broken bread and eaten, and talked a long while, even till daybreak, he departed. And they brought the young man in alive, and they were not a little comforted.

167. MEETING AT MILETUS WITH THE EPHESIAN ELDERS

Acts 20:13—38

[e]Then we went ahead to the ship and sailed to Assos, there intending to take Paul on board; for so he had given orders, intending himself to go [f]on foot. And when he met us at Assos, we took him on board and came to [g]Mitylene. We sailed from there, and the next day came opposite Chios. The following day we arrived at Samos and stayed at Trogyllium. The next day we came to [h]Miletus. For Paul had [i]decided to sail past Ephesus, so that he would not

---

a. **lamps.** The fumes given off by these oil-burning lamps help explain why Eutychus fell asleep.

b. **upper room.** See Acts 1:13. The early church met in homes (Rom. 16:5; 1 Cor. 16:19; Col. 4:15; Philem. 2); the first church buildings date from the third century.

c. **young man.** The Gr. word suggests he was between 7 and 14 years old. His youth, the fumes from the lamps, and the lateness of the hour gradually overcame his resistance. He dozed off, fell out of the open window, and was killed.

d. **his life is in him.** This does not mean that he had not died, but that his life had been restored. As a physician, Luke knew whether someone had died, as he plainly states (Acts 20:9) was the case with Eutychus.

e. **Assos.** Located 20 mi. S of Troas, across the neck of a small peninsula.

f. **on foot.** Because the ship had to sail around the peninsula, Paul could have arrived in Assos not long after it did. Paul presumably chose to walk to Assos so he could continue to teach the believers from Troas who accompanied him.

g. **Mitylene . . . Chios . . . Samos . . . Trogyllium.** Mitylene was the chief city of the island of Lesbos, S of Assos. Chios was an island off the coast of Asia Minor, S of Lesbos. Chios was the birthplace of the Greek poet Homer. Samos refers to an island off the coast near Ephesus. The famed mathematician Pythagoras was born on Samos. Trogyllium was the name of a promontory jutting into the Aegean Sea between Samos and Miletus. Whether the ship actually stopped there is unclear, since many Gr. manuscripts do not mention Trogyllium.

h. **Miletus.** A city in Asia Minor, about 30 mi. S of Ephesus.

i. **decided to sail past Ephesus.** Still trying to reach Jerusalem before Pentecost (50

have to spend time in Asia; for he was hurrying to be at Jerusalem, if possible, on the Day of Pentecost.

From Miletus he sent to Ephesus and called for the elders of the church. And when they had come to him, he said to them: "You know, from the first day that I came to Asia, in what manner I always lived among you, serving the Lord with all humility, [a]with many tears and trials which happened to me by the [b]plotting of the Jews; how I kept back nothing that was helpful, but proclaimed it to you, and taught you [c]publicly and from house to house, testifying to Jews, and also to Greeks, repentance toward God and faith toward our Lord Jesus Christ. And see, now I go [d]bound in the spirit to Jerusalem, not knowing the things that will happen to me there, except that the [e]Holy Spirit testifies in every city, saying that chains and tribulations await me. But none of these things move me; nor do I count my life dear to myself, so that I may finish my race with joy, and the ministry which I received from the Lord Jesus, to testify to the [f]gospel of the grace of God.

"And indeed, now I know that [g]you all, among whom I have gone preaching the kingdom of God, will see my face no more. Therefore I testify to you this day that I am innocent of the blood of all men. For I have not shunned to declare to you the [h]whole counsel of God. Therefore [i]take heed to yourselves and to all

---

days after Passover), Paul decided to have the elders (i.e., pastors, overseers) of the Ephesian church meet him in Miletus.

a. **with many tears.** Paul wept because of: 1) those who did not know Christ (cf. Rom. 9:2, 3); 2) struggling, immature believers (2 Cor. 2:4); and 3) the threat of false teachers (Acts 20:29, 30).

b. **plotting of the Jews.** See 2 Cor. 11:24, 26. Ironically, it was the plot of the Jews at Corinth that allowed the Ephesian elders this opportunity to spend time with Paul.

c. **publicly and from house to house.** Paul taught in the synagogue (Acts 19:8; see 6:9) and the school of Tyrannus (Acts 19:10). He reinforced that public teaching with practical instruction of individuals and households.

d. **bound in the spirit.** Paul's deep sense of duty toward the Master who had redeemed him and called him to service drove him onward despite the threat of danger and hardship (Acts 20:23).

e. **Holy Spirit testifies.** Paul knew he faced persecution in Jerusalem (cf. Rom. 15:31), though he would not know the details until he heard Agabus' prophecy (Acts 21:10, 11).

f. **gospel of the grace of God.** An apt description, since salvation is solely by God's grace (Eph. 2:8, 9; Titus 2:11).

g. **you all . . . will see my face no more.** Aware that he faced severe opposition in Jerusalem, Paul did not anticipate ever returning to Asia Minor. Though he may have done so after his release from his first Roman imprisonment, he could not at this time have foreseen that possibility.

h. **whole counsel of God.** The entire plan and purpose of God for man's salvation in all its fullness: divine truths of creation, election, redemption, justification, adoption, conversion, sanctification, holy living, and glorification. Paul strongly condemned those who adulterate the truth of Scripture (2 Cor. 2:17; 2 Tim. 4:3, 4; cf. Rev. 22:18, 19).

i. **take heed to yourselves.** Paul repeated this call to self-examination to Timothy when his young son in the faith served as pastor of the Ephesian congregation (1 Tim. 4:16; 2 Tim.

the flock, among which the Holy Spirit has made you ᵃoverseers, to shepherd the church of God which He purchased ᵇwith His own blood. For I know this, that after my departure ᶜsavage wolves will come in among you, not sparing the flock. Also ᵈfrom among yourselves men will rise up, speaking ᵉperverse things, to draw away the disciples after themselves. Therefore watch, and remember that for ᶠthree years I did not cease to warn everyone night and day with tears.

"So now, brethren, I commend you to God and to the ᵍword of His grace, which is able to ʰbuild you up and give you an inheritance among all those who are sanctified. I have ⁱcoveted no one's silver or gold or apparel. Yes, you yourselves know that ʲthese hands have provided for my necessities, and for those who were with me. I have shown you in every way, by laboring like this, that you must support the weak. And remember ᵏthe words of the Lord Jesus, that He said, 'It is more blessed to give than to receive.'"

And when he had said these things, he knelt down and prayed with

---

2:20, 21). This was a timely warning, proven true by later events at Ephesus (1 Tim. 1:3–7, 19, 20; 6:20, 21; Rev. 2:2). False teachers were already plaguing the churches of Galatia (Gal. 1:6) and the Corinthian church (2 Cor. 11:4).

a. **overseers.** These are the same as elders and pastors (see 1 Tim. 3:1). The word stresses the leaders' responsibility to watch over and protect their congregations—an appropriate usage in the context of a warning against false teachers. Church rule, which minimizes the biblical authority of elders in favor of a cultural, democratic process, is foreign to the NT (cf. 1 Thess. 5:12, 13; Heb. 13:17).

b. **with His own blood.** See 1 Pet. 1:18. Paul believed so strongly in the unity of God the Father and the Lord Jesus Christ that he could speak of Christ's death as shedding the blood of God—who has no body (John 4:24; cf. Luke 24:39) and hence no blood.

c. **savage wolves.** Borrowed from Jesus (Matt. 7:15; 10:16), this metaphor stresses the extreme danger false teachers pose to the church.

d. **from among yourselves.** Even more deadly than attacks from outside the church are the defections of those (especially leaders) within the church (1 Tim. 1:20; 2 Tim. 1:15; 2:17; cf. Jude 3, 4, 10–13).

e. **perverse things.** The Gr. word means "distorted," or "twisted." False teachers twist God's Word for their own evil ends (Acts 13:10; 2 Pet. 3:16).

f. **three years.** The total length of Paul's Ephesian ministry, including the two years he taught in the school of Tyrannus (Acts 19:10).

g. **word of His grace.** The Scriptures, the record of God's gracious dealings with mankind.

h. **build you up.** The Bible is the source of spiritual growth (1 Thess. 2:13; 2 Tim. 3:16, 17; 1 Pet. 2:2) for all Christians. And since the church is "the pillar and ground of the truth" (1 Tim. 3:15), its leaders must be familiar with that truth.

i. **coveted.** Love of money is a hallmark of false teachers (cf. Is. 56:11; Jer. 6:13; 8:10; Mic. 3:11; Titus 1:11; 2 Pet. 2:3), but did not characterize Paul's ministry. See 1 Tim. 6:3, 5.

j. **these hands . . . provided for my necessities.** Paul had the right to earn his living from the gospel (1 Cor. 9:3–14) and sometimes accepted support (2 Cor. 11:8, 9; Phil. 4:10–19). Yet, he often worked to support himself so he could "present the gospel of Christ without charge" (1 Cor. 9:18).

k. **the words of the Lord Jesus.** This is the only direct quote from Jesus' earthly ministry recorded outside the gospels. The Bible does not record all the words or deeds of Jesus (John 21:25).

them all. Then they all wept freely, and ªfell on Paul's neck and kissed him, sorrowing most of all for the words which he spoke, that they would see his face no more. And they accompanied him to the ship.

168. JOURNEY TO JERUSALEM

Acts 21:1–14

Now it came to pass, that when we had ᵇdeparted from them and set sail, running a ᶜstraight course we came to Cos, the following day to ᵈRhodes, and from there to ᵉPatara. And ᶠfinding a ship sailing over to Phoenicia, we went aboard and set sail. When we had sighted Cyprus, we passed it on the left, sailed to Syria, and landed at ᵍTyre; for there the ship was to unload her cargo. And finding ʰdisciples, we stayed there seven days. They ⁱtold Paul through the Spirit not to go up to Jerusalem. When we had come to the end of those days, we departed and went on our way; and they all accompanied us, with wives and children, till we were out of the city. And we knelt down on the

---

a. **fell on Paul's neck.** A common biblical way of expressing extreme emotion and affection (cf. Gen. 33:4; 45:14; 46:29).

b. **departed.** Lit. means "to tear away." It reiterates the difficulty of Paul's parting from the Ephesian elders (20:37, 38).

c. **straight course . . . to Cos.** The chief city of the island of Cos.

d. **Rhodes.** An island SE of Cos; also the name of its capital city. Its harbor was home to the great statue known as the Colossus of Rhodes, one of the 7 Wonders of the Ancient World.

e. **Patara.** A busy port city in the extreme southern portion of Asia Minor. Paul and the others had now rounded the southwestern corner of Asia Minor. Each of the ports they stopped in represented one day's sailing; the ship did not sail at night.

f. **finding a ship . . . Phoenicia.** Realizing he would never reach Jerusalem in time for Pentecost if he continued to hug the coast, Paul decided to risk sailing directly across the Mediterranean Sea to Tyre (Acts 21:3). The ship they embarked on would have been considerably larger than the small coastal vessels on which they had been sailing. The ship that later took Paul on his ill-fated voyage to Rome held 276 people (Acts 27:37); this one was probably of comparable size.

g. **Tyre.** See 12:20; cf. Josh. 19:29; Matt. 11:21. The voyage across the Mediterranean from Patara to Tyre normally took 5 days.

h. **disciples.** The church in Tyre had been founded by some of those who fled Jerusalem after Stephen's martyrdom (Acts 11:19)—a persecution Paul himself had spearheaded.

i. **told Paul . . . not to go.** This was not a command from the Spirit for Paul not to go to Jerusalem. Rather, the Spirit had revealed to the believers at Tyre that Paul would face suffering in Jerusalem. Understandably, they tried (as his friends shortly would) to dissuade him from going there. Paul's mission to Jerusalem had been given him by the Lord Jesus (Acts 20:24); the Spirit would never command him to abandon it.

shore and prayed. When we had taken our leave of one another, we boarded the ship, and they returned home.

And when we had finished our voyage from Tyre, we came to ªPtolemais, greeted the brethren, and stayed with them one day. On the next day we who were ᵇPaul's companions departed and came to Caesarea, and entered the house of ᶜPhilip the evangelist, who was one of the seven, and stayed with him. Now this man had four ᵈvirgin daughters who ᵉprophesied. And as we stayed many days, a certain ᶠprophet named Agabus came ᵍdown from Judea. When he had come to us, he took Paul's ʰbelt, bound his own hands and feet, and said, "Thus says the Holy Spirit, 'So shall the Jews at Jerusalem bind the man who owns this belt, and deliver him into the ⁱhands of the Gentiles.'"

Now when we heard these things, both ʲwe and those from that place pleaded with him not to go up to Jerusalem. Then Paul answered, "What do you mean by weeping and breaking my heart? For I am ready not only to be bound, but also to die at Jerusalem ᵏfor the name of the Lord Jesus."

So when he would not be persuaded, we ceased, saying, "The ˡwill of the Lord be done."

---

a. **Ptolemais.** Old Testament Acco (Judg. 1:31), located 25 mi. S of Tyre.

b. **Paul's companions.** This phrase is omitted by the better Gr. manuscripts. As is clear from Acts 21:11, Paul accompanied his companions to Caesarea.

c. **Philip the evangelist.** See Acts 6:5. No one else in Scripture is called an evangelist, though Paul commanded Timothy to do the work of an evangelist (2 Tim. 4:5). Once enemies, Philip and Paul were now fellow preachers of God's gospel of grace.

d. **virgin daughters.** That they were virgins may indicate that they had been called by God for special ministry (cf. 1 Cor. 7:34). The early church regarded these women as important sources of information on the early years of the church.

e. **prophesied.** Luke does not reveal the nature of their prophesy. They may have had an ongoing prophetic ministry, or prophesied only once. Since women are not to be preachers or teachers in the church (1 Cor. 14:34–36; 1 Tim. 2:11, 12), they probably ministered to individuals. For an explanation of NT prophets see 11:27; 1 Cor. 12:28; Eph 4:11.

f. **prophet named Agabus.** See Acts 11:28.

g. **down from Judea.** Although it was located in Judea, the Jews considered Caesarea, seat of the Roman government, to be a foreign city (see Acts 18:22).

h. **belt.** Old Testament prophets sometimes acted out their prophecies (cf. 1 Kin. 11:29–39; Is. 20:2–6; Jer. 13:1–11; Ezek. 4, 5). Agabus' action foreshadowed Paul's arrest and imprisonment by the Romans.

i. **hands of the Gentiles.** Though falsely accused by the Jews (Acts 21:27, 28), Paul was arrested and imprisoned by the Romans (vv. 31–33).

j. **we and those from that place.** Both Paul's friends (Luke and the others traveling with him) and the Caesarean Christians.

k. **for the name.** Baptism (see Acts 2:38; cf. 8:16; 10:48; 19:5), healing (Acts 3:6, 16; 4:10), signs and wonders (Acts 4:30), and preaching (Acts 4:18; 5:40; 8:12), were all done in the name of the Lord Jesus. His name represents all that He is.

l. **will of the Lord be done.** A confident expression of trust that God's will is best (cf. 1 Sam. 3:18; Matt. 6:10; Luke 22:42; James 4:13–15).

PART V

ARREST AND IMPRISONMENT

ca. A.D. 57–62

169. ARRIVAL IN JERUSALEM

Acts 21:15–26

^aAnd after those days we packed and went up to Jerusalem. Also some of the disciples from Caesarea went with us and brought with them a certain ^bMnason of Cyprus, an ^cearly disciple, with whom we were to lodge.

And when we had ^dcome to Jerusalem, ^ethe brethren received us gladly. On the following day Paul went in with us to ^fJames, and ^gall the elders were present. When he had greeted them, he ^htold in detail those things which God had done among the Gentiles through his ministry. And when they heard it, they glorified the Lord. And they said to him, "You see, brother, how many myriads of Jews there are who have believed, and they are all ⁱzealous for the law; but they have been informed about you that you teach all the Jews who are among the Gentiles ^jto forsake Moses, saying that they ought not to

a. **up to Jerusalem.** Jerusalem was SE of Caesarea, located on a plateau so travelers were always said to go up to it (cf. Acts 11:2; 15:2; 18:22; Mark 10:32; Luke 2:22; John 2:13; Gal. 1:17, 18).

b. **Mnason.** His Gr. name may mean he was a Hellenistic Jew. If so, Paul and his Gentile companions may have chosen to stay with him because of his acquaintance with Gr. culture. That would have made him more comfortable in housing a party of Gentiles than the Palestinian Jews would have been.

c. **early disciple.** Possibly one of those saved on the Day of Pentecost. If so, Mnason could have been another source of historical information for Luke.

d. **come to Jerusalem.** Presumably in time to celebrate Pentecost, as Paul had planned (Acts 20:16).

e. **the brethren received us gladly.** This was because of the much-needed offering they brought. Also, and more importantly, the Jerusalem believers rejoiced because the Gentile converts with Paul provided visible evidence of God's work of salvation in the Roman world. This initial, unofficial reception may have taken place at Mnason's house.

f. **James.** The brother of Jesus and head of the Jerusalem church (see Acts 12:17), not James, the brother of John, who had been executed by Herod (Acts 12:2).

g. **all the elders.** The mention of elders indicates that the apostles, often away on evangelistic work, had turned over rule of the Jerusalem church to them. Some have speculated that there were 70 elders, paralleling the Sanhedrin. Given the large size of the Jerusalem church, there probably were at least that many. God had decreed that after the apostles were gone, the church was to be ruled by elders (cf. Acts 11:30; 20:17; 1 Tim. 5:17; Titus 1:5; James 5:14; 1 Pet. 5:1, 5).

h. **told in detail.** Paul's official report of his missionary work did not involve meaningless generalities; he related specific incidents from his journeys (cf. Acts 11:4). As always (cf. Acts 14:27; 15:4, 12), Paul gave all credit and glory for his accomplishments to God.

i. **zealous for the law.** Some Jewish believers continued to observe the ceremonial aspects of the Mosaic law. Unlike the Judaizers (see Acts 15:1), they did not view the law as a means of salvation.

j. **to forsake Moses.** The Judaizers were spreading false reports that Paul was teaching Jewish believers to forsake their heritage. That Paul had not abandoned Jewish customs is evident from his circumcision of Timothy (Acts 16:1–3) and his own taking of a Nazirite vow (Acts 18:18).

circumcise their children nor to walk according to the customs. What then? The assembly must certainly meet, for they will hear that you have come. Therefore do what we tell you: We have four men who have ^ataken a vow. Take them and ^bbe purified with them, and ^cpay their expenses so that they may ^dshave their heads, and that all may know that those things of which they were informed concerning you are nothing, but that you yourself also walk orderly and keep the law. But concerning the Gentiles who believe, we have written and decided that they should observe ^eno such thing, except that they should keep themselves from things offered to idols, from blood, from things strangled, and from sexual immorality."

Then Paul took the men, and the next day, having been purified with them, entered the temple to announce the expiration of the days of purification, at which time an offering should be made for each one of them.

170. Arrest at the Temple

Acts 21:27–39

^fNow when the seven days were almost ended, the ^gJews from Asia, seeing him in the temple, stirred up the whole crowd and laid hands on him, crying out, "Men of Israel, help! This is the man who teaches all men everywhere against ^hthe

---

a. **taken a vow.** A Nazirite vow, symbolizing total devotion to God (see Acts 18:18; Num. 6:1–21).

b. **be purified.** Having just returned from an extended stay in Gentile lands, Paul was considered ceremonially unclean. He therefore needed to undergo ritual purification before participating (as their sponsor) in the ceremony marking the end of the 4 men's vows.

c. **pay their expenses.** For the temple ceremony in which the 4 would shave their heads, and the sacrifices associated with the Nazirite vow. Paying those expenses for another was considered an act of piety, and by so doing, Paul would give further proof that he had not forsaken his Jewish heritage.

d. **shave their heads.** A practice commonly associated with a Nazirite vow (Num. 6:18).

e. **no such thing.** James made it clear that what he was asking Paul to do by no means changed the decision of the Jerusalem Council regarding Gentiles. Since Paul was Jewish, that decision did not apply to him.

f. **seven days.** The length of the purification process (see Acts 21:24). Paul had to appear at the temple on the third and seventh days. The incident that follows took place on the seventh day, when the process was almost completed.

g. **Jews from Asia.** Probably from Ephesus, since they recognized Trophimus as a Gentile (Acts 21;29). They were in Jerusalem celebrating the Feast of Pentecost.

h. **the people, the law, and this place.** Paul's enemies leveled 3 false charges against him. They claimed that he taught Jews to forsake their heritage—the same lie told by the people, the law, and this place; and furthermore he also ᵃbrought Greeks into the temple and has defiled this holy place." (For they had previously seen Trophimus the Ephesian with him in the city, whom they supposed that Paul had brought into the temple.)

And all the city was disturbed; and the people ran together, seized Paul, and dragged him out of the temple; and immediately the ᵇdoors were shut. Now as they were seeking to kill him, news came to the ᶜcommander of the ᵈgarrison that all Jerusalem was in an uproar. He immediately took ᵉsoldiers and centurions, and ran down to them. And when they saw the commander and the soldiers, they stopped beating Paul. Then the commander came near and took him, and commanded him to be bound with ᶠtwo chains; and he asked who he was and what he had done. And some among the multitude cried one thing and some another.

So when he could not ascertain the truth because of the tumult, he commanded him to be taken into the ᵍbarracks. When he reached the stairs, he had to be carried by the soldiers because of the violence of the mob. For the multitude of the people followed after, crying out, ʰ"Away with him!"

Then as Paul was about to be led into the barracks, he said to the commander, "May I speak to you?"

Judaizers (see Acts 21:21). The second charge, that Paul opposed the law, was a very dangerous one, albeit false, in this setting. Originally, Pentecost was a celebration of the firstfruits of the harvest. But by this time, it had become a celebration of Moses' receiving the law on Mt. Sinai. Thus, the Jewish people were especially zealous for the law during this feast. The third charge, of blaspheming or defiling the temple, had helped bring about the deaths of Jesus (Mark 14:57, 58) and Stephen (Acts 6:13). All 3 charges were, of course, totally false.

a. **brought Greeks into the temple.** The Asian Jews accused Paul of having brought Trophimus past the Court of the Gentiles into the part of the temple which Gentiles were forbidden. Such a charge was absurd, for it would have entailed Paul's risking his friend's life (the Romans had granted the Jews permission to execute any Gentile who so defiled the temple).

b. **doors were shut.** This was done by the temple guards, since Paul's death on the temple grounds would defile the temple (cf. 2 Kin. 11:15). They made no effort, however, to rescue the apostle from the crowd, which was intent on beating him to death.

c. **commander.** The tribune (Claudias Lysias, Acts 23:26) commanding the Roman cohort based in Jerusalem. He was the highest ranking Roman official stationed in Jerusalem (the governor's official residence was in Caesarea, see Acts 8:40).

d. **the garrison.** The 1,000 man Roman occupation force. Their headquarters was Fort Antonia, located on a precipice overlooking the temple complex. From that vantage point, Roman sentries spotted the riot and informed their commander.

e. **soldiers and centurions.** The use of the plural "centurions" suggests Lysias took at least 200 soldiers with him, since each centurion commanded 100 men.

f. **two chains.** Assuming Paul to be guilty of something (since the Jews were so enraged at him), Lysias arrested him. The tribune thought he knew who Paul was (Acts 21:38).

g. **barracks.** In Fort Antonia, overlooking the temple grounds.

h. **"Away with him!"** Or, "Kill him" (cf. Acts 22:22; Luke 23:18; John 19:15).

He replied, ᵃ"Can you speak Greek? Are you not ᵇthe Egyptian who some time ago stirred up a rebellion and led the four thousand ᶜassassins out into the wilderness?"

But Paul said, "I am a Jew from ᵈTarsus, in Cilicia, a citizen of no mean city; and I implore you, permit me to speak to the people."

171. PAUL ADDRESSES HIS ATTACKERS
Acts 21:40 — 22:11

So when he had given him permission, ᵉPaul stood on the stairs and motioned with his hand to the people. And when there was a great silence, he spoke to them in the Hebrew language, saying,

"Brethren and fathers, hear my defense before you now." And when they heard that he spoke to them in the ᶠHebrew language, they kept all the more silent.

Then he said: ᵍ"I am indeed a Jew, born in Tarsus of ʰCilicia, but ⁱbrought up in this city at the feet of ʲGamaliel, taught according to the strictness of our ᵏfathers' law, and was zealous toward God as you all are today.

---

a. **"Can you speak Greek?"** Paul's use of the language of educated people startled Lysias, who assumed his prisoner was an uncultured criminal.

b. **the Egyptian . . . stirred up a rebellion.** Lysias' question revealed who he (wrongly) assumed Paul was. The Egyptian was a false prophet who, several years earlier, had promised to drive out the Romans. Before he could do so, however, his forces were attacked and routed by Roman troops led by governor Felix. Though several hundred of his followers were killed or captured, he managed to escape. Lysias assumed he had returned and been captured by the crowd.

c. **assassins.** Called "sicarii," they were a terrorist group whose Jewish nationalism led them to murder Romans and Jews perceived as sympathetic to Rome. Since they often used the cover of a crowd to stab their victims, Lysias assumed the mob had caught one of their leaders in the act.

d. **Tarsus.** See Acts 9:11. Tarsus was an important cultural city, with a university rivaling those at Athens and Alexandria.

e. **Paul stood.** Paul's first of 6 defenses (cf. Acts 22:30—23:10; 24:10–21; 25:1–12; 26:1–29; 28:17–29).

f. **Hebrew language.** Aramaic, the language commonly spoken in Palestine (cf. 2 Kin. 18:26; Is. 36:11). See Acts 21:37.

g. **I am indeed a Jew.** A response to the false charges raised by the Asian Jews (see Acts 21:21).

h. **Cilicia.** See Acts 6:9. Tarsus was the chief city of Cilicia.

i. **brought up in this city.** Paul was born among the Hellenistic Jews of the Diaspora, but had been brought up in Jerusalem.

j. **Gamaliel.** See Acts 5:34. That Paul had studied under the most celebrated rabbi of that day was further evidence that the charges against him were absurd.

k. **fathers' law.** As a student of Gamaliel, Paul received extensive training both in the OT law, and in the rabbinic traditions. Also, though he did not mention it to the crowd, he

^aI persecuted this Way to the death, binding and delivering into prisons both men and women, as also the high priest bears me witness, and all the ^bcouncil of the elders, from whom I also received letters to the brethren, and went to Damascus to bring in chains even those who were there to Jerusalem to be punished.

^c"Now it happened, as I journeyed and came near Damascus at ^dabout noon, suddenly a great light from heaven shone around me. And I fell to the ground and heard a voice saying to me, 'Saul, Saul, why are you persecuting Me?' So I answered, 'Who are You, Lord?' And He said to me, 'I am Jesus of Nazareth, whom you are persecuting.'

"And those who were with me indeed saw the light and were afraid, but they ^edid not hear the voice of Him who spoke to me. So I said, 'What shall I do, Lord?' And the Lord said to me, 'Arise and go into Damascus, and there you will be told all things which are appointed for you to do.' And since I could not see for the ^fglory of that light, being led by the hand of those who were with me, I came into Damascus.

172. PAUL'S ADDRESS CONTINUES

Acts 22:12—30

"Then a certain ^gAnanias, a devout man according to the law, having a good testimony with all the Jews who dwelt there, came to me; and he stood and

---

also had been a Pharisee. In light of all that, the charge that Paul opposed the law (see Acts 21:21) was ridiculous.

    a. **I persecuted this Way.** See Acts 9:2. As the leading persecutor of the Christian church after Stephen's martyrdom (cf. Gal. 1:13), Paul's zeal for his Jewish heritage far outstripped that of his hearers.

    b. **council of the elders.** The Sanhedrin (see Acts 4:15; Matt. 26:59).

    c. **Now it happened . . .** The second of 3 NT accounts of Paul's conversion (cf. Acts 9:1–19; 26:12–18).

    d. **about noon.** Paul's reference to the time of day emphasizes how bright the light from heaven really was. It outshone the sun at its peak.

    e. **did not hear the voice.** This is no contradiction with 9:7. Since Jesus spoke only to Paul, only he understood the Lord's words. His companions heard the sound, but could not make out the words (cf. John 12:29).

    f. **glory of that light.** Paul's companions saw the light, but only he saw the Lord Jesus Christ (Acts 9:7, 17, 27; 26:16; 1 Cor. 9:1; 15:8).

    g. **Ananias.** See Acts 9:10. His testimony as a respected member of Damascus' Jewish community would carry weight with Paul's hostile audience.

said to me, 'Brother Saul, receive your sight.' And at that same hour I looked up at him. Then he said, 'The God of our fathers has chosen you that you should know His will, and see ªthe Just One, and hear the voice of His mouth. For you will be ᵇHis witness to all men of what you have seen and heard. And now why are you waiting? Arise and be baptized, and ᶜwash away your sins, calling on the name of the Lord.'

"Now it happened, ᵈwhen I returned to Jerusalem and was praying in the temple, that I was in ᵉa trance and saw Him saying to me, 'Make haste and get out of Jerusalem quickly, for they will not receive your testimony concerning Me.' So I said, 'Lord, they know that in every synagogue I imprisoned and beat those who believe on You. And when the blood of Your martyr Stephen was shed, I also was standing by consenting to his death, and guarding the clothes of those who were killing him.' Then He said to me, 'Depart, for I will send you far from here ᶠto the Gentiles.'"

And they listened to him until this word, and then they raised their voices and said, "Away with such a fellow from the earth, for he is not fit to live!" Then, as they cried out and ᵍtore off their clothes and ʰthrew dust into the air, ⁱthe commander ordered him to be brought into the barracks, and said ʲthat he should be examined under scourging, so that he might know why

---

a. **the Just One.** A title given to the Messiah (cf. Acts 3:14; 7:52; Is. 53:11).

b. **His witness.** Paul never wavered in his claim to have seen the risen, glorified Christ on the Damascus road (see Acts 22:11).

c. **wash away your sins.** Grammatically this phrase, "calling on the name of the Lord," precedes "arise and be baptized." Salvation comes from calling on the name of the Lord (Rom. 10:9, 10, 13), not from being baptized (see Acts 2:38).

d. **when I returned to Jerusalem.** After a brief ministry in Damascus (Acts 9:20–25) and 3 years in Nabatean Arabia (Gal. 1:17, 18).

e. **a trance.** Paul was carried beyond his senses into the supernatural realm to receive revelation from Jesus Christ. The experience was unique to the apostles, since only Peter (Acts 10:10; 11:5) and John (Rev. 1:10) had similar revelations. This was the fourth of 6 visions received by Paul in Acts (cf. Acts 9:3–6; 16:9, 10; 18:9, 10; 23:11; 27:23, 24).

f. **to the Gentiles.** Paul's insistence that the Lord had sent him to minister to the despised Gentiles was too much for the crowd. They viewed the teaching that Gentiles could be saved without first becoming Jewish proselytes (thus granting them equal status with the Jewish people before God) as intolerable blasphemy.

g. **tore off their clothes.** They did this in preparation to stone Paul, in horror at his "blasphemy" (see Acts 14:14) or in uncontrollable rage—or, most likely, for all 3 reasons. Their passions inflamed by racial pride, the members of the crowd lost any semblance of self control.

h. **threw dust.** A sign of intense emotion (cf. 2 Sam. 16:13; Job 2:12; Rev. 18:19).

i. **the commander ordered him to be brought into the barracks.** Lysias realized he would have to interrogate Paul privately. He ordered his soldiers to bring the prisoner into Fort Antonia, away from the angry mob.

j. **that he should be examined under scourging.** A brutal Roman interrogation method. Prisoners frequently died after being flogged with the Roman flagellum (metal-tipped leather thongs attached to a wooden handle).

they shouted so against him. And as they ᵃbound him with thongs, Paul said to the ᵇcenturion who stood by, "Is it lawful for you to scourge a man ᶜwho is a Roman, and uncondemned?"

When the centurion heard that, he went and told the commander, saying, ᵈ"Take care what you do, for this man is a Roman."

Then the commander came and said to him, "Tell me, are you a Roman?" He said, "Yes."

The commander answered, ᵉ"With a large sum I obtained this citizenship." And Paul said, "But I was born a citizen."

Then immediately those who were about to examine him withdrew from him; and the commander was also afraid after he found out that he was a Roman, and because he had bound him.

The next day, because he wanted to know for certain why he was accused by the Jews, he released him from his bonds, and commanded the ᶠchief priests and all their council to appear, and brought Paul down and set him before them.

173. Paul Speaks before the Sanhedrin
Acts 23:1–10

ᵍThen Paul, looking earnestly at the council, said, "Men and brethren, I have lived in all ʰgood conscience before God until this day." And the ⁱhigh priest

---

a. **bound him.** This was done in preparation for his examination by scourging. Stretching Paul taut would magnify the effects of the flagellum on his body.

b. **centurion.** See Acts 10:1; Matt. 8:5. There would have been 10 centurions in the 1,000 man Roman garrison in Jerusalem.

c. **who is a Roman.** Roman citizens were exempted (by the Valerian and Porcian laws) from such brutal methods of interrogation. Paul now exerted his rights as a Roman citizen. His claim would not have been questioned, because the penalty for falsely claiming Roman citizenship was death.

d. **"Take care . . . this man is a Roman."** The centurion informed his commander of Paul's citizenship, cautioning him against an act that could have ended Lysias' military career—or even cost him his life.

e. **With a large sum.** Roman citizenship was officially not for sale, but could sometimes be obtained by bribing corrupt officials.

f. **chief priests and all their council.** He convened an unofficial meeting of the Sanhedrin (see Acts 4:15, 23).

g. **the council.** The Sanhedrin (see Acts 4:15; Matt. 26:59).

h. **good conscience.** See 2 Cor. 1:12; cf. 24:16; 2 Tim. 1:3.

i. **high priest Ananias.** Not the Annas of the gospels (see Luke 3:2), this man was one of

Ananias [a]commanded those who stood by him to strike him on the mouth. Then Paul said to him, "God will strike you, you [b]whitewashed wall! For you sit to judge me according to the law, and do you command me to be struck [c]contrary to the law?"

And those who stood by said, "Do you [d]revile God's high priest?"

Then Paul said, [e]"I did not know, brethren, that he was the high priest; for [f]it is written, 'You shall not speak evil of a ruler of your people.'"

But when [g]Paul perceived that one part were Sadducees and the other Pharisees, he cried out in the council, "Men and brethren, I am a Pharisee, the son of a Pharisee; concerning the hope and resurrection of the dead I am being judged!"

And when he had said this, [h]a dissension arose between the Pharisees and

---

Israel's cruelest and most corrupt High-Priests (see Acts 4:6). His pro-Roman policies alienated him from the Jewish people, who murdered him at the outset of the revolt against Rome (A.D. 66).

a. **commanded . . . to strike him.** An illegal act in keeping with Ananias' brutal character. The verb translated "strike" is used of the mob's beating of Paul (Acts 21:32) and the Roman soldiers' beating of Jesus (Matt. 27:30). It was no mere slap on the face, but a vicious blow.

b. **whitewashed wall.** Cf. Ezek. 13:10–16; Matt. 23:27.

c. **contrary to the law.** Outraged by the High-Priest's flagrant violation of Jewish law, Paul flared up in anger. When Jesus was similarly struck in violation of the law, He reacted by calmly asking the reason for the blow (John 18:23). Paul's reaction was wrong, as he would shortly admit (Acts 23:5). Although an evil man, Ananias still held a God-ordained office, and was to be granted the respect that position demanded.

d. **revile.** Those standing near Paul were appalled by his harsh rebuke of the High-Priest. "Revile" is the same word used in John 9:28 to describe the Jewish leaders' insulting remarks to the blind man whom Jesus had healed. Peter used it to speak of the abuse Jesus endured (1 Pet. 2:23).

e. **I did not know.** Some believe this to be another manifestation of Paul's eye problems (cf. Gal. 4:15); or that Paul was so angry that he forgot to whom he was speaking; or that he was being sarcastic, since Ananias was not acting like a High-Priest should. The simplest explanation is to take Paul's words at face value. He had been gone from Jerusalem for many years and would not likely have recognized Ananias by sight. That this was an informal gathering of the Sanhedrin (see Acts 22:30) would have meant the High-Priest would not have been wearing his official garments.

f. **it is written.** Quoted from Ex. 22:28.

g. **Paul perceived.** Ananias' haughty attitude and illegal act convinced Paul he would not receive a fair hearing before the Sanhedrin. Accordingly, he decided on a bold step. As a Pharisee, and possibly a former member of the Sanhedrin (see Acts 26:10), Paul was well aware of the tensions between the Sanhedrin's two factions. He appealed to the Pharisees for support, reminding them that he himself was a Pharisee, and appealing to the major theological difference between them and the Sadducees (see Acts 23:7). Paul thus created a split between the Sanhedrin's factions.

h. **a dissension arose.** There were major social, political, and theological differences between the Sadducees and Pharisees. By raising the issue of the resurrection, Paul appealed to the Pharisees for support on perhaps the most important theological difference (see Acts 23:8). Since the resurrection of Jesus Christ is also the central theme of Christianity, this was no cynical ploy on Paul's part to divide the Sanhedrin over a trivial point of theology.

the Sadducees; and the assembly was divided. For ᵃSadducees say that there is no resurrection—and no angel or spirit; but the Pharisees confess both. Then there arose a loud outcry. And the ᵇscribes of the Pharisees' party arose and protested, saying, "We find no evil in this man; but if a spirit or an angel has spoken to him, let us not fight against God."

Now when there arose a great dissension, the commander, fearing lest Paul might be pulled to pieces by them, commanded the soldiers to go down and take him by force from among them, and bring him into the barracks.

174. Transport to Caesarea

Acts 23:11–35

ᶜBut the following night the Lord stood by him and said, "Be of good cheer, Paul; for as you have testified for Me in Jerusalem, so you must also ᵈbear witness at Rome."

And when it was day, some of the Jews banded together and ᵉbound themselves under an oath, saying that they would neither eat nor drink till they had killed Paul. Now there were more than forty who had formed this conspiracy. They came to the ᶠchief priests and elders, and said, "We have bound ourselves under a great oath that we will eat nothing until we have

---

a. **Sadducees . . . Pharisees.** The Sadducees accepted only the Pentateuch as divinely inspired Scripture. Since they claimed (wrongly, cf. Matt. 22:23–33) that the Pentateuch did not teach that there would be a resurrection, they rejected it. The Pharisees, however, believed in the resurrection and afterlife. Their beliefs were thus closer to Christianity than those of the Sadducees. Significantly, the Scripture records the conversion of Pharisees (Acts 15:5; John 3:1), but not of Sadducees.

b. **scribes of the Pharisees' party.** So intense was their theological disagreement with the Sadducees that they were willing to defend Paul—even though he was a leader of the hated sect of the Christians (cf. Acts 24:5).

c. **the Lord stood by him.** The fifth of 6 visions Paul received in Acts (cf. Acts 9:3–6; 16:9, 10; 18:9, 10; 22:17, 18; 27:23, 24), all coming at crucial points in his ministry.

d. **bear witness at Rome.** Jesus encouraged Paul by telling him that his desire (Rom. 1:9–11; 15:23) to visit Rome would be granted.

e. **bound themselves under an oath.** Lit. they "anathematized" themselves (cf. Gal. 1:8, 9), thus invoking divine judgment if they failed (cf. 1 Sam. 14:44; 2 Sam. 3:35; 19:13; 1 Kin. 2:23; 2 Kin. 6:31).

f. **chief priests and elders.** See Acts 4:23; Matt. 16:21. Being Sadducees, they would be more inclined to help the conspirators. Significantly excluded are the scribes who, being mostly Pharisees, had already shown their willingness to defend Paul (Acts 23:9).

killed Paul. Now you, therefore, together with the council, suggest to the commander that he be brought down to you tomorrow, as though you were going to make further inquiries concerning him; but we are ready to kill him before he comes near."

So when [a]Paul's sister's son heard of their ambush, he went and [b]entered the barracks and told Paul. Then Paul called one of the centurions to him and said, "Take this young man to the commander, for he has something to tell him." So he took him and brought him to the commander and said, "Paul the prisoner called me to him and asked me to bring this young man to you. He has something to say to you."

Then the commander took him by the hand, went aside, and asked privately, "What is it that you have to tell me?"

And he said, "The Jews have agreed to ask that you bring Paul down to the council tomorrow, as though they were going to inquire more fully about him. But do not yield to them, for more than forty of them lie in wait for him, men who have bound themselves by an oath that they will neither eat nor drink till they have killed him; and now they are ready, waiting for the promise from you."

So the commander let the young man depart, and commanded him, "Tell no one that you have revealed these things to me."

And he called for two centurions, saying, "Prepare two hundred [c]soldiers, seventy horsemen, and two hundred spearmen to go to Caesarea at the [d]third hour of the night; and provide mounts to set Paul on, and bring him safely to Felix the governor." He wrote a letter in the following manner:

---

a. **Paul's sister's son.** The only clear reference in Scripture to Paul's family (for other possible references see Rom. 16:7, 11, 21). Why he was in Jerusalem, away from the family home in Tarsus is not known. Nor is it evident why he would want to warn his uncle, since Paul's family possibly disinherited him when he became a Christian (Phil. 3:8).

b. **entered the barracks and told Paul.** Since Paul was not under arrest, but merely in protective custody, he was able to receive visitors.

c. **soldiers . . . horsemen . . . spearmen.** The "soldiers" were legionnaires, the elite soldiers of the Roman army; the "horsemen" were from the garrison's cavalry detachment; and the "spearmen," or javelin throwers, were soldiers less heavily armed than the legionnaires. Lysias sent almost half of his 1,000 man garrison, showing how seriously he viewed the plot against Paul. To foil the conspirators' plot, avoid a potentially explosive confrontation with the Jews, and save Paul's life, Lysias realized he had to get the apostle out of Jerusalem and to his superior, Governor Felix in Caesarea.

d. **third hour of the night.** 9:00 p.m.

Claudius Lysias,

To the most excellent governor Felix:

Greetings.

This man was seized by the Jews and was about to be killed by them. Coming with the troops I rescued him, [a]having learned that he was a Roman. And when I wanted to know the reason they accused him, I brought him before their council. I found out that he was accused concerning [b]questions of their law, but had nothing charged against him deserving of death or chains. And when it was told me that the Jews lay in wait for the man, I sent him immediately to you, and also commanded his accusers [c]to state before you the charges against him.

Farewell.

Then the soldiers, as they were commanded, took Paul and brought him by night to [d]Antipatris. The next day they left the [e]horsemen to go on with him, and returned to the barracks. When they came to [f]Caesarea and had delivered the letter to the governor, they also presented Paul to him. And when the governor had read it, he asked [g]what province he was from. And when he understood that he was [h]from Cilicia, he said, "I will hear you when your accusers also have come." And he commanded him to be kept in [i]Herod's Praetorium.

---

a. **having learned that he was a Roman.** Actually, Lysias did not find this out until after he arrested Paul (Acts 22:25, 26). Lysias sought to portray himself in the best possible light before the governor. For that reason, he also neglected to mention his order to have Paul scourged (Acts 22:24), and his mistaken assumption that he was the notorious Egyptian assassin (Acts 21:38).

b. **questions of their law.** Lysias' failure to mention any crimes against Roman law was tantamount to declaring Paul innocent.

c. **to state before you the charges.** The plot against Paul's life rendered any further hearings at Jerusalem unsafe, thus requiring Lysias to burden Felix with the case.

d. **Antipatris.** A Roman military post about 40 mi. from Jerusalem. Travelers from Jerusalem to Caesarea often rested there. To get there from Jerusalem in one night (Acts 23:32) would have been an exhausting forced march for the foot soldiers.

e. **horsemen.** Since there was much less danger of ambush in the largely Gentile region of Samaria, the foot soldiers were no longer needed.

f. **Caesarea.** See Acts 8:40.

g. **what province he was from.** Felix needed to determine whether he had jurisdiction to hear Paul's case.

h. **from Cilicia.** Judea and Cilicia were at that time both under the legate of Syria, so Felix had the authority to hear his case.

i. **Herod's Praetorium.** Felix's official residence in Caesarea.

351

175. Accusations before Felix

Acts 24:1–9

ᵃNow after five days Ananias the high priest came down with the ᵇelders and a certain orator named ᶜTertullus. These gave evidence to the governor against Paul.

And when he was called upon, Tertullus began his accusation, saying: "Seeing that through you we enjoy great peace, and prosperity is being brought to this nation by your foresight, we accept it always and in all places, most noble ᵈFelix, with all thankfulness. ᵉNevertheless, not to be tedious to you any further, I beg you to hear, by your courtesy, a few words from us. For we have found this man ᶠa plague, a ᵍcreator of dissension among all the Jews throughout the world, and a ʰringleader of the sect of the Nazarenes. ⁱHe

---

a. **after five days.** A very short period of time for the Jewish leaders to put their case together, hire an attorney ("orator"), and make the trip to Caesarea. Perhaps they feared Felix would dismiss the case against Paul if they did not pursue it rapidly.

b. **elders.** Important leaders of the Sanhedrin (see Acts 4:5).

c. **Tertullus.** Possibly a Roman, but more likely a Hellenistic Jew (cf. Acts 24:6).

d. **Felix.** Governor of Judea from A.D. 52 to 59. Felix was a former slave whose brother (a favorite of Emperor Claudius) had obtained for him the position as governor. He was not highly regarded by the influential Romans of his day and accomplished little during his term as governor. He defeated the Egyptian and his followers (see Acts 21:38), but his brutality angered the Jews and led to his ouster as governor by Emperor Nero two years after Paul's hearing.

e. **Nevertheless.** Having dispensed with the obligatory flattery of Felix, Tertullus set forth the specific charges against Paul. They included sedition (a violation of Roman law), sectarianism (a violation of Jewish law), and sacrilege (a violation of God's law).

f. **a plague.** This statement, while reflecting the Sanhedrin's hatred of the apostle and Christianity, was not a specific charge of wrongdoing.

g. **creator of dissension.** The first and (in a Roman court) most serious charge leveled against Paul: sedition (rebellion). The Romans did not tolerate those who incited rebellion (as the Jews present would learn a few years later in A.D. 66). Had the Jewish leaders been able to substantiate this charge, Paul would have faced severe punishment, possibly even execution. Tertullus carefully avoided naming any specific incidents, since Felix could then have transferred Paul's case to the governor in whose jurisdiction the incident took place. The Jews wanted Paul tried before a governor over whom they had some influence.

h. **ringleader . . . sect of the Nazarenes.** The second charge brought against Paul was sectarianism (heresy). Tertullus' contemptuous reference to Christianity as "the sect of the Nazarenes" (cf. Acts 6:14; John 1:46; 7:41, 52) was intended to portray Paul as the leader of a messianic sect posing a danger to Rome.

i. **He even . . . to you.** Many ancient manuscripts omit this passage, raising the question of who Tertullus was urging Felix to examine. If the passage is omitted, Tertullus would be asking Felix to examine Paul; but the apostle would merely have denied Tertullus' false accusations. If the passage is genuine, Tertullus would be falsely accusing Lysias of overstepping his authority by meddling in a proper Jewish legal proceeding. He would then be claiming that an examination of Lysias would confirm the Jewish leaders' false interpretation of the events. That would help explain Felix's decision to adjourn the hearing until he sent for Lysias (Acts 24:22).

even ᵃtried to profane the temple, and we seized him, and wanted to judge him according to our law. But the commander Lysias came by and with great violence took him out of our hands, commanding his accusers to come to you. By examining him yourself you may ascertain all these things of which we accuse him." And the Jews also assented, maintaining that these things were so.

176. Defense before Felix

Acts 24:10—27

ᵇThen Paul, after the governor had nodded to him to speak, answered: "Inasmuch as I know that you have been for ᶜmany years a judge of this nation, I do the more cheerfully answer for myself, because you may ascertain that it is no more than ᵈtwelve days since I went up to Jerusalem to worship. And they neither found me in the temple disputing with anyone nor inciting the crowd, either in the synagogues or in the city. Nor can they prove the things of which they now accuse me. But this I confess to you, that according to the Way which they call a sect, so I worship the God of my fathers, believing all things which are written in ᵉthe Law and in the Prophets. I have ᶠhope in God, which they themselves also accept, that there will be a resurrection of the dead, both of the just and the unjust. This being so, I myself always strive to have a conscience without offense toward God and men.

---

a. **tried to profane the temple.** The third accusation leveled against Paul was sacrilege, blasphemy against God. The Jewish leaders, through their spokesman, repeated the false charges of the Asian Jews (Acts 21:28). Trying to whitewash the angry crowd's savage beating of Paul, they claimed (falsely) to have arrested him.

b. Paul's third of 6 defenses (cf. Acts 22:1–21; 22:30—23:10; 25:1–12; 26:1–29; 28:17–19).

c. **many years a judge.** Both as governor, and before that during his service under the governor of Samaria. Unlike Tertullus, Paul was not flattering Felix, but reminding him of his acquaintance with Jewish laws, customs, and beliefs. Felix was thus bound to give a just verdict.

d. **twelve days.** Five of which had been spent at Caesarea waiting for his accusers to arrive. Several of the remaining 7 had been taken up with his purification rites (see Acts 21:24, 27). Paul's point was that, even if he had wanted to, he had not had the time to incite a revolt.

e. **the Law and in the Prophets.** The "Law and the Prophets" refers to the OT (see Matt. 7:12). The Sadducees rejected much of the OT (see Acts 23:8), while both they and the Pharisees rejected the OT's witness to Jesus Christ (cf. Luke 24:27, 44; John 1:45; 5:39, 46). In contrast, Paul viewed the entire OT as the inspired Word of God, and believed everything it taught.

f. **hope in God.** The great hope of the Jewish people was the resurrection (Job 19:25–27; Is. 26:19; Dan. 12:2). It was Paul, not the skeptical Sadducees, who stood in the mainstream of traditional Jewish theology.

"Now after many years I came to bring ªalms and offerings to my nation, in the midst of which some Jews from Asia found me purified in the temple, neither with a mob nor with tumult. They ought to have been here before you to object if they had anything against me. Or else let those who are here themselves say if they found any wrongdoing in me while I stood before the council, unless it is for this one statement which I cried out, standing among them, ᵇ'Concerning the resurrection of the dead I am being judged by you this day.'"

But when Felix heard these things, ᶜhaving more accurate knowledge of the Way, he ᵈadjourned the proceedings and said, "When Lysias the ᵉcommander comes down, I will make a decision on your case." So he commanded the centurion to keep Paul and to let him have liberty, and told him not to forbid any of his friends to provide for or visit him.

And after some days, when Felix came with his wife ᶠDrusilla, who was Jewish, he sent for Paul and heard him concerning the faith in Christ. Now as he reasoned about ᵍrighteousness, self-control, and the judgment to come, ʰFelix was afraid and answered, "Go away for now; ⁱwhen I have a convenient

a. **alms and offerings.** The only reference in Acts to the delivery of the offering Paul had been collecting for the poor saints in Jerusalem (see Acts 19:21). Far from seeking to stir up strife, Paul had gone to Jerusalem on a humanitarian mission.

b. **Concerning the resurrection of the dead.** Belief in the resurrection was not a crime under either Jewish or Roman law. Nor was Paul responsible for the longstanding feud between the Sadducees and Pharisees that erupted into open dissension when he made his statement.

c. **having more accurate knowledge of the Way.** Probably from his wife Drusilla, who was Jewish (Acts 25:24).

d. **adjourned the proceedings.** The witnesses to Paul's alleged crime (the Jews from Asia) had failed to show up for the hearing. Nor could the Jewish leaders prove him guilty of a crime. The only verdict Felix could render consistent with Roman law was not guilty, which would infuriate the Jews, and possibly lead to further trouble. Since as governor, Felix's primary responsibility was to maintain order, he decided the best decision was no decision, and adjourned the proceedings on the pretext of needing further information from Lysias.

e. **commander comes down.** Lysias' written report had already stated that the dispute involved questions of Jewish law (Acts 23:29), and that Paul was not guilty of any crime (Acts 23:29). It is difficult to see what more he could have added, and there is no evidence that Felix ever summoned him.

f. **Drusilla.** The youngest daughter of Agrippa I (see Acts 12:1), and Felix's third wife. Felix, struck by her beauty, had lured her away from her husband. At the time of Paul's hearing, she was not yet 20 years old.

g. **righteousness, self-control, and the judgment.** God demands "righteousness" of all men, because of His holy nature (Matt. 5:48; 1 Pet. 1:15, 16). For men and women to conform to that absolute standard requires "self-control." The result of failing to exhibit self-control and to conform oneself to God's righteous standard is (apart from salvation) "judgment."

h. **Felix was afraid.** Living with a woman he had lured away from her husband, Felix obviously lacked "righteousness" and "self-control." The realization that he faced "judgment" alarmed him, and he hastily dismissed Paul.

i. **when I have a convenient time.** The moment of conviction passed, and Felix foolishly passed up his opportunity to repent (cf. 2 Cor. 6:2).

time I will call for you." Meanwhile he also hoped that ᵃmoney would be given him by Paul, that he might release him. Therefore he sent for him more often and conversed with him.

But after two years ᵇPorcius Festus succeeded Felix; and Felix, wanting to ᶜdo the Jews a favor, left Paul bound.

177. Appeal to Caesar

Acts 25:1–12

Now when Festus had come to the province, ᵈafter three days he went up from Caesarea to Jerusalem. Then the high priest and the chief men of the Jews informed him against Paul; and they petitioned him, asking a favor against him, that he would summon him to Jerusalem—while they lay in ᵉambush along the road to kill him. But Festus answered that Paul should be kept at Caesarea, and that he himself was going there shortly. "Therefore," he said, "let those who have authority among you go down with me and accuse this man, to see if there is any fault in him."

And when he had remained among them more than ten days, he went down to ᶠCaesarea. And the next day, sitting on ᵍthe judgment seat, he commanded Paul to be brought. When he had come, the Jews who had come

---

a. **money would be given him by Paul.** Roman law prohibited the taking of bribes, which was nonetheless commonplace.

b. **Porcius Festus succeeded Felix.** Festus was a member of the Roman nobility, unlike the former slave, Felix. Little is known of his brief tenure as governor (he died two years after assuming office), but the Jewish historian Josephus described him as better than either his predecessor or his successor.

c. **do the Jews a favor.** He did this since Jewish complaints to Rome about his brutality eventually led to his ouster from office. He had brutally suppressed a riot in Caesarea and infuriated the Jews who managed to complain to Rome and have him replaced. Emperor Nero recalled him to Rome where he would have faced severe punishment if his influential brother, Pallas, had not interceded for him.

d. **after three days . . . Caesarea to Jerusalem.** To acquaint himself with the situation in his new province.

e. **ambush.** A second ambush plot. This time, however, the members of the Sanhedrin were not accomplices (cf. Acts 23:14, 15), but the plotters.

f. **Caesarea.** See Acts 8:40. As the headquarters of Roman government in Judea, Caesarea was the proper place for Paul, a Roman citizen, to be tried.

g. **the judgment seat.** This signified that this hearing was an official Roman trial (see Acts 25:10, 17; 18:12; Matt. 27:19; John 19:13).

down from Jerusalem stood about and laid many serious complaints against Paul, which they could not prove, while ªhe answered for himself, "Neither against the law of the Jews, nor against the temple, nor against Caesar have I offended in anything at all."

But Festus, ᵇwanting to do the Jews a favor, answered Paul and said, "Are you willing to go up to Jerusalem and there be judged before me concerning these things?"

So Paul said, "I stand at ᶜCaesar's judgment seat, where I ought to be judged. To the Jews I have done no wrong, as you very well know. For if I am an offender, or have committed anything deserving of death, I do not object to dying; but if there is nothing in these things of which these men accuse me, no one can deliver me to them. ᵈI appeal to Caesar."

Then Festus, when he had conferred with ᵉthe council, answered, "You have appealed to Caesar? ᶠTo Caesar you shall go!"

178. ARRIVAL OF KING AGRIPPA

Acts 25:13–27

And after some days ᵍ King Agrippa and ʰBernice came to Caesarea to greet Festus. When they had been there many days, Festus laid Paul's case before the

---

a. **he answered.** Paul's fourth of 6 defenses (cf. Acts 22:1–21; 22:30—23:10; 24:10–21; 26:1–29; 28:17–29).

b. **wanting to do the Jews a favor.** Cf. Acts 24:27.

c. **Caesar's judgment seat.** Festus' compromise gave the Jewish leaders all that they hoped for; they intended to murder Paul before he got to Jerusalem. The apostle therefore rejected Festus' attempt at compromise and reminded the governor that he was standing at Caesar's judgment seat where, as a Roman citizen, he had every right to be judged.

d. **I appeal to Caesar.** He declared his right as a Roman citizen to have a trial in Rome.

e. **the council.** Festus' advisers.

f. **To Caesar you shall go!** By granting the appeal, the governor removed himself from the case and transferred it to the emperor.

g. **King Agrippa.** Herod Agrippa II, son of the Herod who killed James and imprisoned Peter (see Acts 12:1). He was the last of the Herods, who play a prominent role in NT history. His great-uncle, Herod Antipas, was the Herod of the gospels (Mark 6:14–29; Luke 3:1; 13:31–33; 23:7–12), while his great-grandfather, Herod the Great, ruled at the time Jesus was born (Matt. 2:1–19; Luke 1:5). Though not the ruler of Judea, Agrippa was well versed in Jewish affairs (cf. Acts 26:3).

h. **Bernice.** Not Agrippa's wife, but his consort and sister. (Their sister, Drusilla, was married to the former governor, Felix). Their incestuous relationship was the talk of Rome, where Agrippa grew up. Bernice for a while became the mistress of Emperor Vespasian, then of his son, Titus, but always returned to her brother.

king, saying: "There is a certain man left a prisoner by Felix, about whom the chief priests and the elders of the Jews informed me, when I was in Jerusalem, asking for a judgment against him. To them I answered, 'It is not the custom of the Romans to deliver any man to destruction before the accused meets the accusers face to face, and has opportunity to answer for himself concerning the charge against him.' Therefore when they had come together, without any delay, the next day I sat on the judgment seat and commanded the man to be brought in. When the accusers stood up, they brought no accusation against him of such things as I supposed, but had some questions against him about their own ªreligion and about a certain Jesus, who had died, whom Paul affirmed to be alive. And because ᵇI was uncertain of such questions, I asked whether he was willing to go to Jerusalem and there be judged concerning these matters. But when Paul appealed to be reserved for the decision of ᶜAugustus, I commanded him to be kept till I could send him to Caesar."

Then Agrippa said to Festus, ᵈ"I also would like to hear the man myself."

"Tomorrow," he said, "you shall hear him."

So the next day, when ᵉAgrippa and Bernice had come with great pomp, and had entered the auditorium with the ᶠcommanders and the ᵍprominent men of the city, at Festus' command Paul was brought in. And Festus said: "King Agrippa and all the men who are here present with us, you see this man about whom the whole assembly of the Jews petitioned me, both at Jerusalem and here, crying out that he was not fit to live any longer. But when I found that he had committed nothing deserving of death, and that he himself had appealed to Augustus, I decided to send him. ʰI have nothing certain to write

a. **religion.** Such charges did not belong in a Roman court (cf. Acts 18:12–16).

b. **I was uncertain of such questions.** Festus, a pagan Roman and new in Judea, could not be expected to understand the theological differences between Christians and Jews.

c. **Augustus . . . Caesar.** "Augustus," meaning "revered" or "worshiped one," was a title commonly applied to the emperor. The "Caesar" ruling at this time was the infamous Nero.

d. **I also would like to hear.** The Gr. verb tense implies Herod had been wanting to hear Paul for a long time. As an expert on Jewish affairs (cf. Acts 26:3), he relished hearing Christianity's leading spokesman in person.

e. **Agrippa and Bernice.** The two are inseparable in Luke's account (cf. Acts 26:30); she is a constant reminder of Agrippa's scandalous private life (see Acts 25:13).

f. **commanders.** The 5 tribunes commanding the 5 cohorts stationed in Caesarea (see Acts 10:1).

g. **prominent men.** The civic leaders of the city.

h. **I have nothing certain.** Since Festus did not understand the nature of the charges against Paul, he did not know what to write in his official report to Nero. For a provincial governor to send a prisoner to the emperor with no clear charges against him was foolish, if not dangerous.

to my lord concerning him. Therefore I have brought him out before you, and ᵃespecially before you, King Agrippa, so that after the examination has taken place I may have something to write. For it seems to me unreasonable to send a prisoner and not to specify the charges against him."

179. Defense before Agrippa

Acts 26:1–18

Then Agrippa said to Paul, "You are ᵇpermitted to speak for yourself."

So Paul ᶜstretched out his hand and ᵈanswered for himself: "I think myself happy, King Agrippa, because today I shall answer for myself before you concerning all the things of which I am accused by the Jews, especially because you are ᵉexpert in all customs and questions which have to do with the Jews. Therefore I beg you to hear me patiently.

"My manner of life from my youth, which was spent from the beginning among my own nation at Jerusalem, all the Jews know. They knew me from the first, if they were willing to testify, that according to the strictest sect of our religion I ᶠlived a Pharisee. And now I stand and am judged for ᵍthe hope of the promise made by God to our fathers. To this promise our ʰtwelve tribes, earnestly serving God night and day, hope to attain. ⁱFor this hope's sake, King

---

a. **especially before you, King Agrippa.** Festus hoped Herod's expertise in Jewish affairs (Acts 26:3) would enable him to make sense of the charges against Paul.

b. **permitted to speak.** Since no one was there to accuse Paul, Herod permitted him to speak in his defense.

c. **stretched out his hand.** A common gesture at the beginning of a speech (cf. Acts 12:17; 13:16; 19:33).

d. **answered for himself.** Paul's fifth of 6 defenses (cf. Acts 22:1–21; 22:30—23:10; 24:10–21; 25:1–12; 28:17–19).

e. **expert in all customs and questions . . . with the Jews.** See Acts 25:26. Paul's main purpose was not to defend himself but to convert Agrippa and the others (Acts 26:28, 29).

f. **lived a Pharisee.** See Matt. 3:7; cf. Phil. 3:5.

g. **the hope of the promise.** The coming of the Messiah and His kingdom (cf. Acts 1:6; 3:22–24; 13:23–33; Gen. 3:15; Is. 7:14; 9:6; Dan. 7:14; Mic. 5:2; Titus 2:13; 1 Pet. 1:11, 12).

h. **twelve tribes.** A common NT designation for Israel (cf. Matt. 19:28; James 1:1; Rev. 21:12). The 10 northern tribes were not lost. Representatives from each intermingled with the two southern tribes before and after the Exile—a process that had begun during the reigns of Hezekiah (2 Chr. 30:1–11) and Josiah (2 Chr. 34:1–9).

i. **For this . . .** Paul found it inconceivable that he should be condemned for believing in the resurrection—the great hope of the Jewish people (see Acts 24:15).

Agrippa, I am accused by the Jews. Why should it be thought incredible by you that God raises the dead?

"Indeed, I myself thought I must do many things contrary to the name of Jesus of Nazareth. This I also did in Jerusalem, and many of the ᵃsaints I shut up in prison, having received authority from the chief priests; and when they were put to death, ᵇI cast my vote against them. And I punished them often in every synagogue and ᶜcompelled them to blaspheme; and being exceedingly enraged against them, I persecuted them even to foreign cities.

"While thus occupied, ᵈas I journeyed to Damascus with authority and commission from the chief priests, at midday, O king, along the road I saw a light from heaven, brighter than the sun, shining around me and those who journeyed with me. And when we all had fallen to the ground, I heard a voice speaking to me and saying in the Hebrew language, 'Saul, Saul, why are you persecuting Me? It is hard for you to kick against the goads.' So I said, 'Who are You, Lord?' And He said, 'I am Jesus, whom you are persecuting. But rise and stand on your feet; for I have appeared to you for this purpose, to make you a minister and a witness both of the things which you have seen and of the ᵉthings which I will yet reveal to you. I will deliver you from the Jewish people, as well as from the ᶠGentiles, to whom I now send you, ᵍto open their eyes, in order to turn them ʰfrom darkness to light, and from the power of Satan to God, that they may receive ⁱforgiveness of sins and ʲan inheritance among those who are ᵏsanctified by faith in Me.'"

---

a. **saints.** Christian believers (1 Cor. 1:2).

b. **I cast my vote.** Lit. "I threw my pebble"—a reference to the ancient custom of recording votes by means of colored pebbles. This verse may also indicate that Paul had once been a member of the Sanhedrin.

c. **compelled them to blaspheme.** To renounce their faith in Jesus Christ.

d. The third NT account of Paul's conversion (see Acts 9:1–19; 22:6–21).

e. **things which I will yet reveal to you.** See Acts 18:9, 10; 22:17–21; 23:11; 2 Cor. 12:1–7; Gal. 1:11, 12.

f. **Gentiles to whom I now send you.** Paul's commissioning as the apostle to the Gentiles (Rom. 11:13; 1 Tim. 2:7).

g. **to open their eyes.** Unbelievers are blinded to spiritual truth by Satan (2 Cor. 4:4; 6:14; cf. Matt. 15:14).

h. **from darkness to light.** Since unbelievers are in the darkness of their spiritual blindness, the Bible often uses light to picture salvation (see Acts 13:47; Matt. 4:16; John 1:4, 5, 7–9; 3:19–21; 8:12; 9:5; 12:36; 2 Cor. 4:4; 6:14; Eph. 5:8, 14; Col. 1:12, 13; 1 Thess. 5:5; 1 Pet. 2:9; 1 John 1:7; 2:8–10).

i. **forgiveness of sins.** This is the most significant result of salvation (see Acts 2:38; cf. 3:19; 5:31; 10:43; 13:38; Matt. 1:21; 26:28; Luke 1:77; 24:47; 1 Cor. 15:3; Gal. 1:4; Col. 1:14; Heb. 8:12; 9:28; 10:12; 1 Pet. 2:24; 3:18; 1 John 2:1, 2; 3:5; 4:10; Rev. 1:5).

j. **an inheritance.** The blessings believers will enjoy throughout eternity in heaven (cf. Acts 20:32; Eph. 1:11, 14, 18; Col. 1:12; 3:24; Heb. 9:15).

k. **sanctified by faith.** The Bible plainly and repeatedly teaches that salvation comes

180. PAUL CONTINUES HIS DEFENSE

Acts 26:19–32

ᵃ"Therefore, King Agrippa, I was not disobedient to the heavenly vision, but declared first to those in Damascus and in Jerusalem, and throughout all the region of Judea, and then to the Gentiles, that they should repent, turn to God, and do works befitting repentance. For these reasons ᵇthe Jews seized me in the temple and tried to kill me. Therefore, having obtained help from God, to this day I stand, witnessing both to small and great, saying no other things than those which ᶜthe prophets and Moses said would come—that the ᵈChrist would suffer, that He would be the first to rise from the dead, and would proclaim light to the Jewish people and to the Gentiles."

Now as he thus made his defense, Festus said with a loud voice, "Paul, ᵉyou are beside yourself! Much learning is driving you mad!"

But he said, "I am not mad, most noble Festus, but speak the words of truth and reason. For the king, before whom I also speak freely, knows these things; for I am convinced that none of these things escapes his attention, since this thing was ᶠnot done in a corner. King Agrippa, ᵍdo you believe the prophets? I know that you do believe."

Then Agrippa said to Paul, ʰ"You almost persuade me to become a Christian."

---

solely through faith apart from human works (Acts 13:39; 15:9; 16:31; John 3:14–17; 6:69; Rom. 3:21–28; 4:5; 5:1; 9:30; 10:9–11; Gal. 2:16; 3:11, 24; Eph. 2:8, 9; Phil. 3:9).

a. **works befitting repentance.** Genuine repentance is inseparably linked to a changed lifestyle (see Acts 2:38; Matt. 3:8; James 2:18).

b. **the Jews . . . tried to kill me.** See Acts 21:27–32. The true reason in contrast to the lies of the Jewish leaders (24:6).

c. **the prophets and Moses.** See Acts 24:14. The term "Moses" is used interchangeably with "law," since he was the author of the Pentateuch, the 5 books of law.

d. **Christ would suffer . . . rise from the dead.** Messiah's suffering (Ps. 22; Is. 53) and resurrection (Ps. 16:10; cf. 13:30–37), the central themes of Paul's preaching, are clearly taught in the OT.

e. **you are beside yourself!** Festus was astonished that a learned scholar like Paul could actually believe that the dead would live again—something no intelligent Roman would accept. Unable to contain himself, he interrupted the proceedings, shouting that Paul's tremendous learning had driven him insane (cf. Mark 3:21; John 8:48, 52; 10:20).

f. **not done in a corner.** The death of Jesus and the Christians' claim that He rose from the dead were common knowledge in Palestine.

g. **do you believe the prophets?** Paul's shrewd question put Herod in a dilemma. If he affirmed his belief in the prophets, he would also have to admit that what they taught about Jesus' death and resurrection was true—an admission that would make him appear foolish before his Roman friends. Yet to deny the prophets would outrage his Jewish subjects.

h. **You almost persuade me.** A better translation is "Do you think you can convince me

And Paul said, "I would to God that not only you, but also all who hear me today, might become both almost and altogether such as I am, except for these chains."

When he had said these things, the king stood up, as well as the governor and Bernice and those who sat with them; and when they had gone aside, they talked among themselves, saying, "This man is doing nothing deserving of death or chains."

Then [a]Agrippa said to Festus, "This man might have been set free if he had not appealed to Caesar."

181. JOURNEY TO ROME

Acts 27:1–20

[b]And when it was decided that we should sail to Italy, they delivered Paul and some other prisoners to one named Julius, a [c]centurion of the Augustan Regiment. So, entering a ship of [d]Adramyttium, [e]we put to sea, meaning to sail along the coasts of Asia. [f]Aristarchus, a Macedonian of Thessalonica, was with us. And the next day we [g]landed at Sidon. And Julius treated Paul kindly and gave him liberty to go to his friends and receive care. When we had put to sea from there, we [h]sailed under the shelter of Cyprus, because the winds

---

to become a Christian in such a short time?" Recognizing his dilemma, Agrippa parried Paul's question with one of his own.

a. **Agrippa said.** The hearing over, Agrippa and Festus met privately to discuss Paul's case. Both agreed that he was innocent of any crime and could be set free, had he not appealed to Caesar.

b. **we.** The use of the pronoun "we" marks the return of Paul's close friend Luke, who has been absent since Acts 21:18. He had likely been living near Caesarea so he could care for Paul during his imprisonment. Now he rejoined the apostle for the journey to Rome.

c. **centurion of the Augustan Regiment.** A cohort (regiment) of that name was stationed in Palestine during the reign of Agrippa II (see Acts 25:13). Julius may have been on detached duty, performing such tasks as escorting important prisoners.

d. **Adramyttium.** A city on the NW coast of Asia Minor (modern Turkey) near Troas, where the centurion planned to find a ship sailing to Italy.

e. **we put to sea.** From Caesarea the ship sailed 70 mi. N to Sidon.

f. **Aristarchus . . . with us.** He had been seized by the crowd during the riot at Ephesus (Acts 19:29), while accompanying Paul to Jerusalem with the offering (Acts 20:4). Aristarchus would be with Paul during the apostle's first Roman imprisonment (Col. 4:10).

g. **landed at Sidon.** See Acts 12:20. The Christians there ministered to Paul—possibly by providing him with provisions for his trip.

h. **sailed under the shelter of Cyprus.** They kept to the lee side of the island (passing between it and the mainland), seeking shelter from the strong winds.

were contrary. And when we had sailed over the sea which is off Cilicia and Pamphylia, we came to ᵃMyra, a city of Lycia. There the centurion found an ᵇAlexandrian ship sailing to Italy, and he put us on board.

When we had sailed slowly many days, and arrived with difficulty off ᶜCnidus, the wind not permitting us to proceed, we sailed under ᵈthe shelter of Crete off ᵉSalmone. Passing it with difficulty, we came to a place called ᶠFair Havens, near the city of Lasea.

Now when much time had been spent, and sailing was now dangerous because ᵍthe Fast was already over, Paul advised them, saying, "Men, I perceive that this voyage will ʰend with disaster and much loss, not only of the cargo and ship, but also our lives." Nevertheless the ⁱcenturion was more persuaded by the ʲhelmsman and the owner of the ship than by the things spoken by Paul. And because the harbor was ᵏnot suitable to winter in, the majority advised to set sail from there also, if by any means they could reach ˡPhoenix, a harbor of Crete opening toward the southwest and northwest, and winter there.

When the south wind blew softly, supposing that they had obtained their desire, putting out to sea, they sailed close by Crete. But not long after, a tempestuous head wind arose, called ᵐEuroclydon. So when the ship was caught, and

---

a. **Myra . . . Lycia.** One of the main ports of the imperial grain fleet, whose ships brought Egyptian grain to Italy.

b. **Alexandrian ship.** Part of the imperial grain fleet.

c. **Cnidus.** Located on a peninsula in extreme SW Asia Minor, this port also served ships of the imperial grain fleet. Having reached Cnidus, the ship could not sail farther W due to the strong headwinds. It was forced to turn S and head for the island of Crete.

d. **the shelter of Crete.** This large island off the SW coast of Asia Minor provided some relief from the strong NW winds buffeting the ship.

e. **Salmone.** A promontory on Crete's NE coast.

f. **Fair Havens . . . Lasea.** The ship fought its way around the SE corner of Crete, finally reaching the shelter of the bay known as Fair Havens.

g. **the Fast was already over.** See Zech. 7:3; cf. Lev. 23:26–32. Travel in the open sea was dangerous from mid-Sept. to mid-Nov., after which it ceased altogether until Feb. Since the Fast (the Day of Atonement) of late Sept. or early Oct. was past, further travel was already extremely hazardous.

h. **end with disaster.** Because of the lateness of the season, and the difficulties they had already experienced, Paul wisely counseled them to spend the winter at Fair Havens.

i. **centurion.** See Acts 10:1. Because the ship was part of the Imperial grain fleet (see Acts 27:5) Julius, not the helmsman nor the ship's owner, was the ranking official on board.

j. **helmsman.** The ship's pilot, or captain.

k. **not suitable to winter in.** The professional sailors deemed Fair Havens an unsuitable location to wait out the winter (Acts 27:9).

l. **Phoenix.** Located 40 mi. from Fair Havens with a harbor that provided better shelter from the winter storms.

m. **Euroclydon.** Euraquilon is the preferred reading (see marginal note), from the Gr.

could not head into the wind, we let her drive. And running under the shelter of an island called ^aClauda, we ^bsecured the skiff with difficulty. When they had taken it on board, they ^cused cables to undergird the ship; and fearing lest they should run aground on the ^dSyrtis Sands, they ^estruck sail and so were driven. And because we were exceedingly tempest-tossed, the next day they ^flightened the ship. On the third day we threw the ship's tackle overboard with our own hands. Now when neither sun nor stars appeared for many days, and no small tempest beat on us, all hope that we would be saved was finally given up.

182. SHIPWRECK AT SEA

Acts 27:21–44

But after long abstinence from food, then Paul stood in the midst of them and said, "Men, you should have listened to me, and not have sailed from Crete and incurred this disaster and loss. And now I urge you to take heart, for there will be no loss of life among you, but only of the ship. For there stood by me this night ^gan angel of the God to whom I belong and whom I serve, saying, 'Do not be afraid, Paul; you must be ^hbrought before Caesar; and indeed God has granted you all those who sail with you.' Therefore take heart, men, for I believe God that it will be just as it was told me. However, we must run aground on a certain island."

---

word euros ("east wind") and the Lat. word aquilo ("north wind"). It is a strong, dangerous windstorm greatly feared by those who sailed the Mediterranean.

a. **Clauda.** An island 23 mi. SW of Crete.

b. **secured the skiff.** Taking advantage of Clauda's shelter, the sailors began to rig the ship for the storm by hauling the ship's dinghy on board.

c. **used cables to undergird the ship.** A procedure known as frapping. The cables, wrapped around the hull and winched tight, helped the ship endure the battering of the wind and waves.

d. **Syrtis.** A region of sandbars and shoals off the coast of Africa, much feared as a graveyard of ships.

e. **struck sail.** This phrase could best be translated "let down the sea anchor." The sailors undoubtedly did both, since putting out an anchor with the sails up would be self-defeating.

f. **lightened the ship.** Throwing all unnecessary gear and cargo overboard would lighten the ship, enabling it to ride more easily over the waves.

g. **an angel.** The last of 6 visions Paul received as recorded by Luke (cf. Acts 9:3–6; 16:9, 10; 18:9, 10; 22:17, 18; 23:11).

h. **brought before Caesar.** The angel reaffirmed the promise Jesus Himself had earlier made to Paul (Acts 23:11).

Now when the [a]fourteenth night had come, as we were driven up and down in the [b]Adriatic Sea, about midnight the sailors [c]sensed that they were drawing near some land. And they [d]took soundings and found it to be [e]twenty fathoms; and when they had gone a little farther, they took soundings again and found it to be fifteen fathoms. Then, fearing lest we should run aground on the rocks, they [f]dropped four anchors from the stern, and prayed for day to come. And as the sailors were seeking to escape from the ship, when they had let down the [g]skiff into the sea, under pretense of [h]putting out anchors from the prow, Paul said to the centurion and the soldiers, "Unless these men stay in the ship, you cannot be saved." Then the soldiers cut away the ropes of the skiff and let it fall off.

And as day was about to dawn, Paul implored them all to take food, saying, "Today is the fourteenth day you have waited and continued [i]without food, and eaten nothing. Therefore I urge you to take nourishment, for this is for your survival, since [j]not a hair will fall from the head of any of you." And when he had said these things, he took bread and gave thanks to God in the presence of them all; and when he had broken it he began to eat. Then they were all encouraged, and also took food themselves. And in all we were [k]two hundred and seventy-six persons on the ship. So when they had eaten enough, they lightened the ship and threw out the wheat into the sea.

When it was day, they did not recognize the land; but they observed a bay with a beach, onto which they planned to run the ship if possible. And they let go

---

a. **fourteenth night.** Since they sailed from Fair Havens (Acts 27:13).

b. **Adriatic Sea.** The central Mediterranean Sea, not the present Adriatic Sea located between Italy and Croatia. The modern Adriatic was known in Paul's day as the Gulf of Adria.

c. **sensed.** The sailors probably heard the sound of waves breaking on a shore.

d. **took soundings.** With a weight attached to a length of rope they measured the depth of the sea.

e. **twenty fathoms . . . fifteen fathoms.** 120 feet . . . 90 feet. The decreasing depth of the water confirmed the ship was approaching land.

f. **dropped four anchors from the stern.** An attempt to hold the ship in place and keep the bow pointed toward the shore.

g. **skiff.** The same dinghy hauled aboard earlier (Acts 27:16).

h. **putting out anchors from the prow.** This would have been for additional stability (cf. Acts 27:29).

i. **without food.** Because of seasickness and the difficulty of preparing and preserving food, the passengers and crew had eaten little or nothing in the two weeks since they left Fair Havens.

j. **not a hair will fall.** A common Jewish saying (1 Sam. 14:45; 2 Sam. 14:11; 1 Kin. 1:52; Luke 21:18) denoting absolute protection.

k. **two hundred and seventy-six persons on the ship.** As an ocean-going vessel, this ship was considerably larger than the smaller vessel Paul sailed in from Caesarea to Lycia.

the anchors and left them in the sea, meanwhile loosing the rudder ropes; and they hoisted the mainsail to the wind and made for shore. But striking ᵃa place where two seas met, they ran the ship aground; and the prow stuck fast and remained immovable, but the stern was being broken up by the violence of the waves.

And ᵇthe soldiers' plan was to kill the prisoners, lest any of them should swim away and escape. But the centurion, wanting to save Paul, kept them from their purpose, and commanded that those who could swim should jump overboard first and get to land, and the rest, some on boards and some on parts of the ship. And so it was that they all escaped safely to land.

183. FROM MALTA TO ROME

Acts 28:1–15

Now when they had escaped, they then found out that the island was called ᶜMalta. And the natives showed us unusual kindness; for they kindled a fire and made us all welcome, because of the rain that was falling and because of the cold. But when Paul had gathered a bundle of sticks and laid them on the fire, ᵈa viper came out because of the heat, and fastened on his hand. So when the natives saw the creature hanging from his hand, they said to one another, "No doubt this man is a murderer, whom, though he has escaped the sea, yet justice does not allow to live." But he shook off the creature into the fire and suffered no harm. However, they were expecting that he would swell up or suddenly fall down dead. But after they had looked for a long time and saw no harm come to him, they changed their minds and said that ᵉhe was a god.

In that region there was an estate of the ᶠleading citizen of the island, whose name was Publius, who received us and entertained us courteously for three days. And it happened that the father of Publius lay ᵍsick of a fever

---

a. **a place where two seas met.** A sandbar or reef short of the shore.

b. **the soldiers' plan was to kill the prisoners.** Knowing they could face punishment or death if their prisoners escaped (cf. Acts 12:19; 16:27).

c. **Malta.** An island, 17 mi. long and 9 mi. wide, about 60 mi. S of Sicily. None of the sailors had previously been to the bay (known today as St. Paul's Bay) where they were shipwrecked.

d. **a viper.** A venomous snake. Cf. Mark 16:18.

e. **said that he was a god.** See Acts 14:11, 12.

f. **leading citizen.** The Gr. phrase indicates Publius was the Roman governor of Malta.

g. **sick of a fever and dysentery.** The gastric fever (caused by a microbe found in goat's

and dysentery. Paul went in to him and prayed, and he laid his hands on him and healed him. So when this was done, the rest of those on the island who had diseases also came and were healed. They also honored us in many ways; and when we departed, they provided such things as were necessary.

^aAfter three months we sailed in an ^bAlexandrian ship whose figurehead was the ^cTwin Brothers, which had wintered at the island. And landing at ^dSyracuse, we stayed three days. From there we circled round and reached R^ehegium. And after one day the south wind blew; and the next day we came to ^fPuteoli, where we found brethren, and were invited to stay with them seven days. And so we went toward ^gRome. And from there, when the brethren heard about us, they came to meet us as far as ^hAppii Forum and ⁱThree Inns. When Paul saw them, he thanked God and took courage.

184. House Arrest in Rome

Acts 28:16–31

Now when we came to Rome, the ^jcenturion delivered the prisoners to the captain of the guard; but Paul was permitted to ^kdwell by himself with the soldier who guarded him.

---

milk) that was common on Malta. Dysentery, often the result of poor sanitation, was widespread in the ancient world.

a. **After three months.** Since sea travel was dangerous during this period (see Acts 27:9).

b. **Alexandrian ship.** Probably another in the imperial grain fleet (see Acts 27:5, 6).

c. **Twin Brothers.** Castor and Pollux, Zeus' sons according to Gr. mythology, were believed to protect sailors.

d. **Syracuse.** An important city on the island of Sicily. Tradition holds that Paul established a church during the ship's 3-day stopover there.

e. **Rhegium.** A harbor on the southern tip of the Italian mainland. There the ship waited one day for a favorable wind to permit it to sail through the Straits of Messina (separating Sicily from the Italian mainland).

f. **Puteoli.** Modern Pozzuoli, located on the Bay of Naples near Pompeii. Rome's main port and the most important one in Italy, Puteoli was also the main port for the Egyptian grain fleet (see Acts 27:5).

g. **Rome.** Almost as a footnote, Luke mentions the party's arrival in the Imperial capital —Paul's longtime goal (see Acts 19:21).

h. **Appii Forum.** A market town 43 mi. S of Rome on the Appian Way.

i. **Three Inns.** A rest stop on the Appian Way, about 30 mi. S of Rome.

j. **centurion delivered the prisoners to the captain of the guard.** Many Gr. manuscripts omit this phrase. If part of the original text, it indicates either that Julius delivered the prisoners to his commanding officer, or to the commander of the Praetorian Guard.

k. **dwell by himself . . . guarded.** Possibly through Julius' intervention, Paul was allowed to live under guard in his own rented quarters (cf. Acts 28:30).

And it came to pass after three days that Paul called the ªleaders of the Jews together. So when they had come together, ᵇhe said to them: "Men and brethren, though I have done nothing against our people or ᶜthe customs of our fathers, yet I was delivered as a prisoner from Jerusalem into the hands of the Romans, who, when they had examined me, wanted to let me go, because there was no cause for putting me to death. But when the Jews spoke against it, I was compelled to ᵈappeal to Caesar, not that I had anything of which to accuse my nation. For this reason therefore I have called for you, to see you and speak with you, because for ᵉthe hope of Israel I am bound with this chain."

Then they said to him, "We neither received letters from Judea concerning you, nor have any of the brethren who came reported or spoken any evil of you. But we desire to hear from you what you think; for concerning this sect, we know that it is spoken against everywhere."

So when they had appointed him a day, many came to him at his lodging, to whom he explained and solemnly testified of the kingdom of God, ᶠpersuading them concerning Jesus from both the Law of Moses and the Prophets, from morning till evening. And some were persuaded by the things which were spoken, and some disbelieved.

So when they did not agree among themselves, they departed after Paul had said one word: "The Holy Spirit spoke rightly through Isaiah the prophet to our fathers, saying,

> ᵍ"Go to this people and say:
> "Hearing you will hear, and shall not understand;
> And seeing you will see, and not perceive;
> For the hearts of this people have grown dull.
> Their ears are hard of hearing,
> And their eyes they have closed,

---

a. **leaders of the Jews.** The most prominent men from Rome's synagogues (see Acts 6:9).

b. Paul's sixth and final defense recorded in Acts (cf. Acts 22:1–21; 22:30—23:10; 24:10–21; 25:1–12; 26:1–29).

c. **the customs of our fathers.** Paul began by denying that he was guilty of any infraction against the Jewish people or their traditions (cf. Acts 22:3; 24:14; 26:4, 5).

d. **appeal to Caesar.** See Acts 25:11.

e. **the hope of Israel.** See Acts 24:15; 26:6.

f. **persuading them . . . Law of Moses . . . Prophets.** Paul's method of Jewish evangelism throughout Acts was to prove from the OT that Jesus was the Messiah (cf. Acts 13:16–41).

g. Quoted from Is. 6:9, 10.

> Lest they should see with their eyes and hear with their ears,
> Lest they should understand with their hearts and turn,
> So that I should heal them."ᶜ

"Therefore let it be known to you that the ᵃsalvation of God has been sent to the Gentiles, and they will hear it!" And when he had said these words, the Jews departed and had a great dispute among themselves.

ᵇThen Paul dwelt two whole years in his own rented house, and received all who came to him, preaching the kingdom of God and teaching the things which concern the Lord Jesus Christ ᶜwith all confidence, no one forbidding him.

185. PAUL WRITES THE EPISTLE OF EPHESIANS
Introduction to Ephesians

The letter is addressed to the church in the city of Ephesus, capital of the Roman province of Asia (Asia Minor, modern Turkey). Because the name Ephesus is not mentioned in every early manuscript, some scholars believe the letter was an encyclical, intended to be circulated and read among all the churches in Asia Minor and was simply sent first to believers in Ephesus.

Author and Date

There is no indication that the authorship of Paul should be in question. He is indicated as author in the opening salutation (Eph. 1:1; 3:1). The letter was written from prison in Rome (Acts 28:16–31) sometime between A.D. 60–62 and is, therefore, often referred to as a prison epistle (along with Philippians, Colossians, and Philemon). It may have been composed almost contemporaneously with Colossians and initially sent with that epistle and Philemon by

---

a. **salvation of God has been sent to the Gentiles.** See Acts 11:18; 13:46, 47; 14:27; 15:14–17; 18:6.

b. The best explanation for this rather abrupt ending to the book is that Luke wrote Acts before Paul's release from his first Roman imprisonment.

c. **with all confidence, no one forbidding him.** Helped by his loyal fellow workers (cf. Col. 4:10; Philem. 24), Paul evangelized Rome (cf. Phil. 1:13; 4:22).

Tychicus (Eph. 6:21, 22; Col. 4:7, 8). See Introduction to Philippians: Author and Date for a discussion of the city from which Paul wrote.

Background and Setting

It is likely that the gospel was first brought to Ephesus by Priscilla and Aquila, an exceptionally gifted couple (see Acts 18:26) who were left there by Paul on his second missionary journey (Acts 18:18, 19). Located at the mouth of the Cayster River, on the east side of the Aegean Sea, the city of Ephesus was perhaps best known for its magnificent temple of Artemis, or Diana, one of the 7 wonders of the ancient world. It was also an important political, educational, and commercial center, ranking with Alexandria in Egypt and Antioch of Pisidia in southern Asia Minor.

The fledgling church begun by Priscilla and Aquila was later firmly established by Paul on his third missionary journey (Acts 19) and was pastored by him for some 3 years. After Paul left, Timothy pastored the congregation for perhaps a year and a half, primarily to counter the false teaching of a few influential men (such as Hymenaeus and Alexander), who were probably elders in the congregation there (1 Tim. 1:3, 20). Because of those men, the church at Ephesus was plagued by "fables and endless genealogies" (Eph. 1:4) and by such ascetic and unscriptural ideas as the forbidding of marriage and abstaining from certain foods (4:3). Although those false teachers did not rightly understand Scripture, they propounded their ungodly interpretations with confidence (1:7), which produced in the church harmful "disputes rather than godly edification which is in faith" (1:4). Thirty years or so later, Christ gave to the Apostle John a letter for this church indicating its people had left their first love for Him (Rev. 2:1–7).

Historical and Theological Themes

The first 3 chapters are theological, emphasizing NT doctrine, whereas the last 3 chapters are practical and focus on Christian behavior. Perhaps, above all, this is a letter of encouragement and admonition, written to remind believers of their immeasurable blessings in Jesus Christ; and not only to be thankful for those blessings, but also to live in a manner worthy of them. Despite, and partly even because of, a Christian's great blessings in Jesus Christ, he is sure to be tempted by Satan to self-satisfaction and complacency. It was for that reason that, in the last chapter, Paul reminds believers of the full and sufficient spiritual armor supplied to them through God's Word and by His Spirit (Eph. 6:10–17) and of their need for vigilant and persistent prayer (6:18).

A key theme of the letter is the mystery (meaning a heretofore unrevealed truth) of the church, which is "that the Gentiles should be fellow heirs, of the same body, and partakers of His promise in Christ through the gospel" (3:6), a truth completely hidden from the OT saints (cf. 3:5, 9). All believers in Jesus Christ, the Messiah, are equal before the Lord as His children and as citizens of His eternal kingdom, a marvelous truth that only believers of this present age possess. Paul also speaks of the mystery of the church as the bride of Christ (5:32; cf. Rev. 21:9).

A major truth emphasized is that of the church as Christ's present spiritual, earthly body, also a distinct and formerly unrevealed truth about God's people. This metaphor depicts the church, not as an organization, but as a living organism composed of mutually related and interdependent parts. Christ is Head of the body and the Holy Spirit is its lifeblood, as it were. The body functions through the faithful use of its members' various spiritual gifts, sovereignly and uniquely bestowed by the Holy Spirit on each believer.

Other major themes include the riches and fullness of blessing to believers. Paul writes of "the riches of His [God's] grace (1:7), "the unsearchable riches of Christ" (3:8), and "the riches of His glory" (3:16). Paul admonishes believers to "be filled with all the fullness of God" (3:19), to "come to the unity of the faith and of the knowledge of the Son of God, to a perfect man, to the measure of the stature of the fullness of Christ" (4:13), and to "be filled with the Spirit" (5:18). Their riches in Christ are based on His grace (1:2, 6, 7; 2:7), His peace (1:2), His will (1:5), His pleasure and purpose (1:9), His glory (1:12, 14), His calling and inheritance (1:18), His power and strength (1:19; 6:10), His love (2:4), His workmanship (2:10), His Holy Spirit (3:16), His offering and sacrifice (5:2), and His armor (6:11, 13). The word "riches" is used 5 times in this letter; "grace" is used 12 times; "glory" 8 times; "fullness" or "filled" 6 times; and the key phrase "in Christ" (or "in Him") some 12 times.

Interpretive Challenges

The general theology of Ephesians is direct, unambiguous, and presents no ideas or interpretations whose meanings are seriously contended. There are, however, some texts that require careful thought to rightly interpret, namely: 1)

2:8, in which one must decide if the salvation or the faith is the gift; 2) 4:5, in which the type of baptism must be discerned; and 3) 4:8, in its relationship to Ps. 68:18. These issues are addressed in the notes on the appropriate passages.

186. PREDESTINATION AND REDEMPTION IN CHRIST

Eph. 1:1–10

Paul, an ᵃapostle of Jesus Christ by the will of God,

> To the saints ᵇwho are in Ephesus, and faithful in Christ Jesus:
>
> ᶜGrace to you and peace from ᵈGod our Father and the Lord Jesus Christ.
>
> ᵉBlessed be the ᶠGod and Father of our Lord Jesus Christ, who has blessed us with every spiritual blessing ᵍin the heavenly places ʰin Christ, just as ⁱHe

---

a. **apostle.** The word means "messenger" and served as an official title for Paul and the 12 disciples (including Matthias, Acts 1:26), who were eyewitnesses of the resurrected Jesus and were chosen by God to lay the foundation for the church by preaching, teaching, and writing Scripture, accompanied by miracles (cf. 2 Cor. 12:12). See Eph. 4:11.

b. **saints . . . faithful.** Designates those whom God has set apart from sin to Himself, made holy through their faith in Jesus Christ.

c. **Grace to you and peace.** A common greeting in the early church which Paul used in all his letters.

d. **God our Father and the Lord Jesus Christ.** From them came the authority with which Paul spoke as well as the blessings of grace and peace to all believers. The conjunction "and" indicates equivalence; that is, the Lord Jesus Christ is equally divine with the Father.

e. **Blessed.** Derived from the same Gr. word as "eulogy," which means to praise or commend. This is the supreme duty of all creatures (see Rom. 1:18–21; cf. Rev. 5:13). This passage (Eph. 1:3–14) describes God's master plan for salvation in terms of the past (election, vv. 3–6a), the present (redemption, vv. 6b–11), and the future (inheritance, vv. 12–14). It can also be viewed as emphasizing the Father (vv. 3–6), the Son (vv. 7–12), and the Spirit (vv. 13–16).

f. **God . . . who has blessed us with every spiritual blessing.** In His providential grace, God has already given believers total blessing (Rom 8:28; Col. 2:10; James 1:17; 2 Pet. 1:3). "Spiritual" does not refer to immaterial blessings as opposed to material ones, but rather to the work of God, who is the divine and spiritual source of all blessings.

g. **in the heavenly places.** Lit. "in the heavenlies." This refers to the realm of God's complete, heavenly domain, from which all his blessings come (cf. Eph.1;20; 2:6; 3:10; 6:12).

h. **in Christ.** God's superabundant blessings belong only to believers who are His children, by faith in Christ, so that what He has is theirs—including His righteousness, resources, privilege, position, and power (cf. Rom 8:16, 17).

i. **He chose us.** The doctrine of election is emphasized throughout Scripture (cf. Deut. 7:6; Is. 45:4; John 6:44; Acts 13:48; Rom 8:29; 9:11; 1 Thess. 1:3, 4; 2 Thess. 2:13; 2 Tim 2:10; see 1 Pet. 1:2). The form of the Gr. verb behind "chose" indicates that God not only chose by Himself but for Himself to the praise of His own glory (Eph.1;6, 12, 14). God's election or predestination does not operate apart from or nullify man's responsibility to believe in Jesus as Lord and Savior (cf. Matt. 3:1, 2; 4:17; John 5:40).

chose us in Him ᵃbefore the foundation of the world, that we should be ᵇholy and without blame before Him ᶜin love, ᵈhaving predestined us to adoption as sons by Jesus Christ to Himself, according to the good pleasure of His will, ᵉto the praise of the glory of His grace, ᶠby which He made us accepted in the Beloved.

In Him we have ᵍredemption through His blood, ʰthe forgiveness of sins, according to the riches of His grace which He made to abound toward us in all wisdom and prudence, having made known to us the mystery of His will, according to His good pleasure which He purposed in Himself, that in the dispensation of the fullness of the times ⁱHe might gather together in one all things in Christ, both which are in heaven and which are on earth—in Him.

a. **before the foundation of the world.** Through God's sovereign will before the creation of the world and, therefore, obviously independent of human influence and apart from any human merit, those who are saved have become eternally united with Christ Jesus. Cf. 1 Pet. 1:20; Rev. 13:8; 17:8.

b. **holy and without blame before Him.** This describes both a purpose and a result of God's choosing those who are to be saved. Unrighteous persons are declared righteous, unworthy sinners are declared worthy of salvation, all because they are chosen "in Him" (Christ). This refers to Christ's imputed righteousness granted to us (see 2 Cor. 5:21; Phil 3:9), a perfect righteousness which places believers in a holy and blameless position before God (Eph. 5:27; Col. 2:10), though daily living inevitably falls far short of His holy standard.

c. **in love.** This phrase belongs at the start of v. 5, since it introduces the divine motive for God's elective purpose. Cf. Eph. 2:4–5; Deut. 7:8.

d. **having predestined us to adoption as sons.** Human parents can bestow their love, resources, and inheritance on an adopted child, but not their own distinct characteristics. But God miraculously gives His own nature to those whom He has elected and who have trusted in Christ. He makes them his children in the image of His divine Son, giving them not just Christ's riches and blessings but also His very nature (cf. John 15:15; Rom. 8:15).

e. **to the praise of the glory of His grace.** The ultimate purpose of election to salvation is the glory of God (cf. Eph. 1;12, 14; Phil. 2:13; 2 Thess. 1:11, 12).

f. **by which . . . accepted in the Beloved.** "Which" refers to the divine grace (undeserved love and favor) that has made it possible for sinners to be accepted by God through the substitutionary death and imputed righteousness provided by Jesus Christ ("the Beloved," cf. Matt. 3:17; Col. 1:13). Because believers are accepted in Him, then they, like Him, are beloved of God.

g. **redemption through His blood.** The term used here relates to paying the required ransom to God for the release of a person from bondage. Christ's sacrifice on the cross paid that price for every elect person enslaved by sin, buying them out of the slave market of iniquity (see 2 Cor. 5:18, 19). The price of redemption was death (cf. Lev. 17:11; Rom. 3:24, 25; Heb. 9:22; 1 Pet. 1:18, 19; Rev. 5:8–10).

h. **the forgiveness of sins . . . in all wisdom and prudence.** Redemption brings in the limitless grace of God (Rom. 5:20) and forgiveness of sin (cf. Matt. 26:28; Acts 13:38, 39; Eph 4:32; Col. 2:13; 1 John 1:9). It brings divinely-bestowed spiritual understanding. Cf. 1 Cor. 2:6, 7, 12, 16.

i. **He might gather.** At the end of this world's history, God will gather believers together in the millennial kingdom, called here the "dispensation of the fullness of the times," meaning the completion of history (Rev. 20:1–6). After that, God will gather everything to Himself in eternity future, and the new heaven and new earth will be created (Rev. 21:1ff.). The new universe will be totally unified under Christ (cf. 1 Cor. 15:27, 28; Phil. 2:10, 11).

187. INHERITANCE AND RESOURCES IN CHRIST
Eph. 1:11–23

[a]In Him also we have obtained an inheritance, [b]being predestined according to the purpose of Him [c]who works all things according to the counsel of His will, that we who first trusted in Christ should be [d]to the praise of His glory.

In Him you also [e]trusted, after you heard the word of truth, the gospel of your salvation; in whom also, having believed, you were [f]sealed with the Holy Spirit of promise, who is the guarantee of our inheritance until the redemption of the purchased possession, to the praise of His glory.

Therefore I also, after I heard of your faith in the Lord Jesus and [g]your love for all the saints, do not cease to give thanks for you, making mention of you in my prayers: that [h]the God of our Lord Jesus Christ, the Father of glory, may give to you [i]the spirit of wisdom and revelation in the knowledge of Him,

---

a. **In Him also we have obtained an inheritance.** Christ is the source of the believer's divine inheritance, which is so certain that it is spoken of as if it has already been received. Cf. 1 Cor. 3:22, 23; 2 Pet. 1:3, 4.

b. **being predestined.** Before the earth was formed, God sovereignly determined that every elect sinner—however vile, useless, and deserving of death—by trusting in Christ would be made righteous.

c. **who works all things.** The word translated "works" is the same one from which "energy," "energetic," and "energize" are derived. When God created the world, He gave it sufficient energy to begin immediately to operate as He had planned. It was not simply ready to function, but was created functioning. As God works out His plan according "to the counsel of His will," He energizes every believer with the power necessary for his spiritual completion (cf. Phil 1:6; 2:13).

d. **to the praise of His glory.** God's glory is the supreme purpose of redemption (cf. Eph.1;6, 14).

e. **trusted, after you heard the word.** The God-revealed gospel of Jesus Christ must be heard (Rom. 10:17) and believed (John 1:12) to bring salvation.

f. **sealed with the Holy Spirit.** God's own Spirit comes to indwell the believer and secures and preserves his eternal salvation. The sealing of which Paul speaks refers to an official mark of identification placed on a letter, contract, or other document. That document was thereby officially under the authority of the person whose stamp was on the seal. Four primary truths are signified by the seal: 1) security (cf. Dan. 6:17; Matt. 27:62–66); 2) authenticity (cf. 1 Kin. 21:6–16); 3) ownership (cf. Jer. 32:10); and 4) authority (cf. Esth. 8:8–12). The Holy Spirit is given by God as His pledge of the believer's future inheritance in glory (cf. 2 Cor. 1:21).

g. **your love for all the saints.** Love for other believers evidences saving faith (cf. John 13:34, 35; 1 John 4:16–18; 4:20; 5:1) and is a cause of thanksgiving (Eph. 1:16).

h. **the God of our Lord Jesus Christ.** This is a designation of God that links Father and Son in essential nature as deity (cf. Rom. 1:5, 6; 1 Cor. 1:3; Phil 2:9–11; 1 Pet. 1:3; 2 John 3).

i. **the spirit of wisdom . . . understanding.** Paul was praying that believers will have the disposition of godly knowledge and insight of which the sanctified mind is capable (Eph. 1:8), so as to grasp the greatness of the hope (Rom. 8:29; 1 John 3:2) and the inheritance that is theirs in Christ (Eph. 1:3–14).

ᵃthe eyes of your understanding being enlightened; that you may know what is the hope of His calling, what are the riches of the glory of His inheritance in the saints, and what is the ᵇexceeding greatness of His power toward us who believe, according to the working of His mighty power which He worked in Christ when He raised Him from the dead and seated Him at His right hand in the heavenly places, ᶜfar above all principality and power and might and dominion, and every name that is named, not only in this age but also in that which is to come.

And He put all things under His ᵈfeet, and gave Him to be head over all things to the church, which is ᵉHis body, the fullness of Him who fills all in all.

188. New Life in Christ

Eph. 2:1–10

And you He made alive, who were dead in trespasses and sins, in which you once walked according to the ᶠcourse of this world, according to ᵍthe prince of the power of the air, the spirit who now works in the sons of disobedience, among whom also we all once conducted ourselves in the lusts of our flesh, fulfilling the desires of the flesh and of the mind, and were by nature children of wrath, just as the others.

---

a. **the eyes of your understanding being enlightened.** A spiritually enlightened mind is the only means of truly understanding and appreciating the hope and inheritance in Christ and of living obediently for Him.

b. **exceeding greatness of His power.** God's great power, that very power which raised Jesus from the dead and lifted Him by ascension back to glory to take His seat at God's right hand, is given to every believer at the time of salvation and is always available (cf. Acts 1:8; Col. 1:29). Paul therefore did not pray that God's power be given to believers but that they be aware of the power they already possessed in Christ and use it (cf. Eph. 3:20).

c. **far above.** Paul wanted believers to comprehend the greatness of God compared to other heavenly beings. "Principality, power, might, and dominion" were traditional Jewish terms to designate angelic beings having a high rank among God's hosts. God is above them all (cf. Rev. 20:10–15).

d. **feet . . . head.** This is a quote from Ps. 8:6 indicating that God has exalted Christ over everything (cf. Heb. 2:8), including His church (cf. Col. 1:18). Christ is clearly the authoritative Head (not "source") because all things have been placed under His feet. See Eph. 4:15; 5:23.

e. **His body.** A metaphor for God's redeemed people, used exclusively in the NT of the church (cf. Eph. 4:12–16; 1 Cor. 12:12–27).

f. **course of this world.** See John 1:9. This refers to the world order, i.e., humanity's values and standards apart from God and Christ. In 2 Cor. 10:4, 5, Paul refers to these ideologies that are like fortresses in which people are imprisoned, need to be set free, and brought captive to Christ and obedience to the truth.

g. **the prince of the power of the air.** Satan. Cf. John 12:31; 14:30; 16:11; 2 Cor. 4:4.

But God, who is rich in ªmercy, because of His great love with which He loved us, even ᵇwhen we were dead in trespasses, made us alive together with Christ (by grace you have been saved), and ᶜraised us up together, and made us sit together ᵈin the heavenly places in Christ Jesus, that in the ages to come He might show the exceeding ᵉriches of His grace in His kindness toward us in Christ Jesus. For by grace you have been saved through ᶠfaith, and that not of yourselves; it is the gift of God, not of works, lest anyone should boast. For we are His workmanship, ᵍcreated in Christ Jesus for good works, ʰwhich God prepared beforehand that we should walk in them.

189. Unity in Christ

Eph. 2:11–22

Therefore remember that you, once ⁱGentiles in the flesh—who are called Uncircumcision by what is called the Circumcision made in the flesh by

a. **mercy . . . love.** Salvation is for God's glory by putting on display His boundless mercy and love for those who are spiritually dead because of their sinfulness.

b. **when we were dead . . . made us alive.** Far more than anything else, a spiritually dead person needs to be made alive by God. Salvation brings spiritual life to the dead. The power that raises believers out of death and makes them alive (cf. Rom. 6:1–7) is the same power that energizes every aspect of Christian living (cf. Rom. 6:11–13).

c. **raised us up together, and made us sit together.** The tense of "raised" and "made" indicates that these are immediate and direct results of salvation. Not only is the believer dead to sin and alive to righteousness through Christ's resurrection, but he also enjoys his Lord's exaltation and shares in His pre-eminent glory.

d. **in the heavenly places.** The supernatural realm where God reigns. In Eph. 3:10 and 6:12, however, it also refers to the supernatural sphere where Satan temporarily rules. This spiritual realm is where believers' blessings are (cf. Eph. 1:3), their inheritance is (1 Pet. 1:4), their affections should be (Col. 3:3), and where they enjoy fellowship with the Lord. It is the realm from which all divine revelation has come and where all praise and petitions go.

e. **riches of His grace.** Salvation, of course, is very much for the believer's blessing, but it is even more for the purpose of eternally glorifying God for bestowing on believers His endless and limitless grace and kindness. The whole of heaven glorifies Him for what He has done in saving sinners (cf. Eph. 3:10; Rev. 7:10–12).

f. **faith, and that not of yourselves.** "That" refers to the entire previous statement of salvation, not only the grace but the faith. Although men are required to believe for salvation, even that faith is part of the gift of God which saves and cannot be exercised by one's own power. God's grace is preeminent in every aspect of salvation (cf. Rom. 3:20; Gal. 2:16).

g. **created in . . . for good works.** Good works cannot produce salvation but are subsequent and resultant God-empowered fruits and evidences of it (cf. John 15:8; Phil. 2:12, 13; 2 Tim. 3:17; Titus 2:14; James 2:16–26).

h. **which God prepared beforehand.** Like his salvation, a believer's sanctification and good works were ordained before time began (see Rom. 8:29, 30).

i. Gentiles (the "uncircumcision") experienced two types of alienation. The first was social, resulting from the animosity that had existed between Jews and Gentiles for thousands of years.

hands—that at that time you were without Christ, being aliens from the commonwealth of Israel and strangers from the covenants of promise, having no hope and without God in the world. But now in Christ Jesus you who once were [a]far off have been [b]brought near by the blood of Christ.

For [c]He Himself is our peace, who has made both one, and has broken down [d]the middle wall of separation, having [e]abolished in His flesh the enmity, that is, the law of commandments contained in ordinances, so as to create in Himself one [f]new man from the two, thus making peace, and that He might [g]reconcile them both to God in one body through the cross, thereby putting to death the enmity. And He came and [h]preached peace to you who were [i]afar

---

Jews considered Gentiles to be outcasts, objects of derision, and reproach. The second and more significant type of alienation was spiritual, because Gentiles as a people were cut off from God in 5 different ways: 1) they were "without Christ," the Messiah, having no Savior and Deliverer and without divine purpose or destiny. 2) They were "aliens from the commonwealth of Israel." God's chosen people, the Jews, were a nation whose supreme King and Lord was God Himself, and from whose unique blessing and protection they benefitted. 3) Gentiles were "strangers from the covenants of promise," not able to partake of God's divine covenants in which He promised to give His people a land, a priesthood, a people, a nation, a kingdom, and a King—and to those who believe in Him, eternal life and heaven. 4) They had "no hope" because they had been given no divine promise. 5) They were "without God in the world." While Gentiles had many gods, they did not recognize the true God because they did not want Him (see Rom. 1:18–26).

a. **far off.** A common term in rabbinical writings used to describe Gentiles, those who were apart from the true God (cf. Is. 57:19; Acts 2:39).

b. **brought near.** Every person who trusts in Christ alone for salvation, Jew or Gentile, is brought into spiritual union and intimacy with God. This is the reconciliation of 2 Cor. 5:18–21. The atoning work accomplished by Christ's death on the cross washes away the penalty of sin and ultimately even its presence.

c. **He Himself.** This emphatically indicates that Jesus alone is the believer's source of peace (cf. Is. 9:6).

d. **the middle wall of separation.** This alludes to a wall in the temple that partitioned off the Court of the Gentiles from the areas accessible only to Jews. Paul referred to that wall as symbolic of the social, religious, and spiritual separation that kept Jews and Gentiles apart.

e. **abolished in His flesh the enmity.** Through His death, Christ abolished OT ceremonial laws, feasts, and sacrifices which uniquely separated Jews from Gentiles. God's moral law (as summarized in the Ten Commandments and written on the hearts of all men, Rom. 2:15) was not abolished but subsumed in the New Covenant, however, because it reflects His own holy nature (Matt. 5:17–19.) See Matt. 22:37–40; Rom. 13:8–10.

f. **one new man.** Christ does not exclude anyone who comes to Him, and those who are His are not spiritually distinct from one another. "New" translates a Gr. word that refers to something completely unlike what it was before. It refers to being different in kind and quality. Spiritually, a new person in Christ is no longer Jew or Gentile, only Christian (cf. Rom. 10:12, 13; Gal. 3:28).

g. **reconcile them both to God.** As Jews and Gentiles are brought to God through Christ Jesus, they are brought together with each other. This was accomplished by the cross where Jesus became a curse (Gal. 3:10–13), taking God's wrath so that divine justice was satisfied and reconciliation with God became a reality (see 2 Cor. 5:19–21). For more on reconciliation, see Rom. 5:8–10; Col. 1:19–23.

h. **preached peace.** The Gr. word for "preached" lit. means "to bring or announce good news," and in the NT is almost always used of proclaiming the good news that sinners can be reconciled to God by the salvation which is through Jesus Christ. In this context, Christ, the One who "Himself is our peace" (Eph. 2:14), also announced the good news of peace.

i. **afar off and . . . near.** That is to Gentiles and Jews alike.

off and to those who were near. For through Him we both have [a]access by one Spirit to the Father.

Now, therefore, you are no longer strangers and foreigners, but [b]fellow citizens with the saints and [c]members of the household of God, having been built on [d]the foundation of the apostles and prophets, Jesus Christ Himself being the chief [e]cornerstone, in whom the whole building, being fitted together, grows into [f]a holy temple in the Lord, in whom you also are being built together for [g]a dwelling place of God in the Spirit.

190. THE GOSPEL REVEALED

Eph. 3:1–13

[h]For this reason I, Paul, [i]the prisoner of Christ Jesus for you Gentiles—if indeed you have heard of the [j]dispensation of the grace of God which was

---

a. **access by one Spirit to the Father.** No sinner has any right or worthiness in himself for access to God, but believers have been granted that right through faith in Christ's sacrificial death (cf. Eph. 3:12; Rom. 5:2). The resources of the Trinity belong to believers the moment they receive Christ, and the Holy Spirit presents them before the heavenly throne of God the Father, where they are welcome to come with boldness at any time. See Rom. 8:15–17; Gal. 4:6, 7; Heb. 4:16.

b. **fellow citizens with the saints.** God's kingdom is made up of the people from all time who have trusted in Him. There are no strangers, foreigners, or second-class citizens there (cf. Phil. 3:20).

c. **members of the household of God.** Redeemed sinners not only become heavenly citizens but also members of God's own family. The Father bestows on believers the same infinite love He gives His Son. See Eph. 1:5; Heb. 3:6.

d. **the foundation of the apostles and prophets.** For discussion of these gifted men, see Eph. 4:11. As important as they were, it was not them personally, but the divine revelation they taught, as they authoritatively spoke the word of God to the church before the completion of the NT, that provided the foundation (cf. Rom. 15:20).

e. **cornerstone.** Cf. Ps. 118:22; Is. 28:16; Matt. 21:42; Acts 4:11; 1 Pet. 2:6, 7. This stone set the foundation and squared the building.

f. **a holy temple in the Lord.** Every new believer is a new stone in Christ's temple, the church, Christ's body of believers (see 1 Pet. 2:5). Christ's building of His church will not be complete until every person who will believe in Him has done so (2 Pet. 3:9).

g. **a dwelling place of God in the Spirit.** The term for "dwelling" connotes a permanent home. God the Holy Spirit takes up permanent residence in His earthly sanctuary, the church, the vast spiritual body of all the redeemed (cf. 1 Cor. 6:19, 20; 2 Cor. 6:16).

h. **For this reason.** This refers back to the truths about the unity of believers that Paul has just discussed and introduces the motive for his prayer which begins in Eph. 3:14.

i. **the prisoner of Christ Jesus.** Although Paul had been a prisoner for about two years in Caesarea and two years in Rome, he did not consider himself to be a prisoner of any government or person. Rather, he knew he was under Christ's control, and every aspect of his life was in the Lord's hands. He suffered imprisonment for preaching to Gentiles. See 2 Cor. 4:8–15.

j. **dispensation . . . given to me.** "Dispensation" means a stewardship, an administration, or management. Paul did not choose the stewardship of his apostleship or ministry. God had

given to me for you, how that by revelation He made known to me the mystery (ᵃas I have briefly written already, by which, when you read, you may understand my knowledge in ᵇthe mystery of Christ), which ᶜin other ages was not made known to the sons of men, as it has now been revealed by the Spirit to His holy apostles and prophets: that the ᵈGentiles should be fellow heirs, of the same body, and partakers of His promise in Christ through the gospel, of which I ᵉbecame a minister according to the gift of the grace of God given to me by the effective working of His power.

To me, who am less than ᶠthe least of all the saints, this grace was given, that I should preach among the Gentiles ᵍthe unsearchable riches of Christ, and to make all see what is the fellowship of the mystery, which from the beginning of the ages has been hidden in God who created all things through Jesus Christ; to the intent that now the manifold wisdom of God might be made known by the church to the ʰprincipalities and powers ⁱin the heavenly places, according to ʲthe

---

sovereignly commissioned him with the calling, spiritual gifts, opportunities, knowledge, and authority to minister as the apostle to the Gentiles (see Acts 9:1–19; 1 Tim 1:12, 13; cf. Rom 15:15, 16; 1 Cor. 4:1; 9:16, 17; Gal. 2:9).

a. **as I have briefly written.** In this parenthetical passage, Paul interrupted the thought begun in Eph. 3:1 to re-emphasize and to expand upon the truths he had just written. He was compelled to affirm his authority for teaching the oneness of Jew and Gentile in Christ (Eph. 3;2–7), a new and far-reaching truth that most of the Ephesians doubtless found difficult to comprehend or accept.

b. **the mystery of Christ.** See 1:9–12; 2:11, 12; Matt. 13:11; 1 Cor. 2:7; Col. 4:3. There were many truths hidden and later revealed in the NT that are called mysteries. Here is one: Jew and Gentile brought together in one body in the Messiah. For others, see 1 Cor. 15:51; Col. 1:27; 1 Tim. 3:16. Paul not only wrote of the mystery that, in Christ, Jew and Gentile become one in God's sight and in His kingdom and family, but also explained and clarified that truth. He realized that spiritual knowledge must precede practical application. What is not properly understood cannot properly be applied.

c. **in other ages was not made known.** Though God had promised universal blessing through Abraham (Gen. 12:3), the full meaning of that promise became clear when Paul wrote Gal. 3:28. Isaiah 49:6 predicted salvation to all races, but it was Paul who wrote of the fulfillment of that pledge (Acts 13:46, 47). Paul disclosed a truth that not even the greatest prophets understood—that within the church, composed of all the saved since Pentecost in one united body, there would be no racial, social, or spiritual distinctions.

d. **Gentiles should be fellow heirs.** A summary of 2:11–22. See 1 Cor. 12:12, 13; Gal. 3:29.

e. **became a minister.** No man can make himself a minister (lit. servant) of God,

f. **the least of all the saints.** In light of God's perfect righteousness, Paul's assessment of himself was not false humility but simple honesty. He knew his unworthiness. See 1 Tim. 1:12, 13 (cf. Judg. 6:15, 16; Is. 6:1–9).

g. **the unsearchable riches of Christ.** All God's truths, all His blessings, all that He is and has (cf. Eph. 1:3; Col. 2:3; 2 Pet. 1:3).

h. **principalities and powers.** Angels, both holy and unholy (Eph. 1:21; 6:12; see Col. 1:16). God, through the church manifests His glory to all the angels. The holy angels rejoice (see Luke 15:10; cf. 1 Pet. 1:12) because they are involved with the church (see 1 Cor. 11:10; Heb. 1:14). Although they have no desire or capacity to praise God, even fallen angels see the glory of God in the salvation and preservation of the church.

i. **in the heavenly places.** As in Eph. 1:3; 6:12, this refers to the entire realm of spiritual beings.

j. **the eternal purpose.** The supreme purpose of the church is to glorify God, which

eternal purpose which He accomplished in Christ Jesus our Lord, in whom we have boldness and ᵃaccess with confidence through faith in Him. Therefore I ask that you do not lose heart at my ᵇtribulations for you, which is your glory.

191. God's Fullness for the Church
Eph. 3:14–21

ᶜFor this reason I bow my knees to the Father of our Lord Jesus Christ, from whom the ᵈwhole family in heaven and earth is named, ᵉthat He would grant you, ᶠaccording to the riches of His glory, to be ᵍstrengthened with might through His Spirit in the inner man, ʰthat Christ may dwell in your hearts ⁱthrough faith; that you, being ʲrooted and grounded in love, may be ᵏable to comprehend ˡwith all the

---

includes the displaying of His wisdom (Eph. 3:10) before the angels, who then honor Him with even greater praise.

a. **access with confidence.** Every person who comes to Christ in faith can come before God at any time, not in self-confidence but in Christ-confidence. See Heb. 4:15, 16.

b. **tribulations . . . your glory.** Through trouble and suffering, God produces glory.

c. **For this reason.** Paul repeated what he wrote in Eph. 3:1 as he began his prayer. Because of their new identity in Christ, stated in chap. 2, believers are spiritually alive (v. 5), they are unified into God's household (v. 19), and, as the church, they are the dwelling place of God, built on the words and work of the apostles and prophets (vv. 20–22). **I bow my knees.** Not an instruction for physical posture during prayer, but suggesting an attitude of submission, reverence, and intense passion (cf. Ezra 9:5, 6; Ps. 95:1–6; Dan. 6:10; Acts 20:36).

d. **whole family in heaven and earth is named.** Paul was not teaching the universal fatherhood of God and the universal brotherhood of man (cf. John 8:39–42; 1 John 3:10), but was simply referring to believers from every era of history, those who are dead (in heaven) and those who are alive (on earth).

e. **that He would grant you.** Paul's prayers are almost always for the spiritual welfare of others (cf. Phil. 1:4; Col. 1:9–11; 1 Thess. 1:2).

f. **according to the riches of His glory.** They are limitless and available to every believer.

g. **strengthened . . . His Spirit in the inner man.** Spiritual power is a mark of every Christian who submits to God's Word and Spirit. It is not reserved for some special class of Christian, but for all those who discipline their minds and spirits to study the Word, understand it, and live by it. Although the outer, physical person becomes weaker with age (cf. 2 Cor. 4:16), the inner, spiritual person should grow stronger through the Holy Spirit, who will energize, revitalize, and empower the obedient, committed Christian (cf. Acts 1:8; Rom. 8:5–9, 13; Gal. 5:16).

h. **that Christ may dwell in your hearts.** Every believer is indwelt by Christ at the moment of salvation (Rom. 8:9; 1 Cor. 12:13), but He is "at home," finding comfort and satisfaction, only where hearts are cleansed of sin and filled with His Spirit (cf. John 14:23).

i. **through faith.** This speaks of Christians' continuing trust in Christ to exercise His lordship over them.

j. **rooted and grounded in love.** I.e., established on the strong foundation of self-giving, serving love for God and for His people (cf. Matt. 22:37–39; 1 John 4:9–12, 19–21).

k. **able to comprehend.** A believer cannot understand the fullness of God's love apart from genuine, Spirit-empowered love in his own life.

l. **with all the saints.** Love is both granted to (Rom. 5:5; 1 Thess. 4:9) and commanded

saints what is the ᵃwidth and length and depth and height—ᵇto know the love of Christ ᶜwhich passes knowledge; that you may be ᵈfilled with all the fullness of God.

Now to Him who is able to do exceedingly abundantly ᵉabove all that we ask or think, according to the power that works in us, ᶠto Him be glory in the church by Christ Jesus to all generations, forever and ever. Amen.

192. THE UNITY OF THE CHURCH

Eph. 4:1–10

I, ᵍtherefore, ʰthe prisoner of the Lord, beseech you to ⁱwalk worthy of the ʲcalling with which you were called, with all ᵏlowliness and

---

of (John 13:34, 35) every Christian, not just those who have a naturally pleasant temperament or have great spiritual maturity.

a. **width . . . length . . . depth . . . height.** Not 4 different features of love, but an effort to suggest its vastness and completeness.

b. **to know the love of Christ.** Not the love believers have for Christ, but the love of and from Christ that He places in their hearts before they can truly and fully love Him or anyone else (Rom. 5:5).

c. **which passes knowledge.** Knowledge of Christ's love is far beyond the capability of human reason and experience. It is only known by those who are God's children (cf. Phil. 4:7).

d. **filled with all the fullness of God.** To be so strong spiritually, so compelled by divine love, that one is totally dominated by the Lord with nothing left of self. Human comprehension of the fullness of God is impossible, because even the most spiritual and wise believer cannot completely grasp the full extent of God's attributes and characteristics—His power, majesty, wisdom, love, mercy, patience, kindness, and everything He is and does. But believers can experience the greatness of God in their lives as a result of total devotion to Him. Note the fullness of God, here; the fullness of Christ in Eph. 4:13; and the fullness of the Spirit in Eph. 5:18. Paul prayed for believers to become as Godlike as possible (Matt. 5:48; 1 Pet. 1:15, 16).

e. **above all.** When the conditions of Eph. 3:16–19 are met, God's power working in and through believers is unlimited and far beyond their comprehension.

f. **to Him be glory.** Only when His children meet this level of faithfulness will Christ be fully glorified with the honor He deserves from His church.

g. **therefore.** This word marks the transition from doctrine to duty, principle to practice, position to behavior. This is typical of Paul (see Rom. 12:1; Gal. 5:1; Phil. 2:1; Col. 3:5; 1 Thess. 4:1).

h. **the prisoner of the Lord.** By mentioning his imprisonment again (see Eph. 4:1), Paul gently reminded Ephesian believers that the faithful Christian walk can be costly and that he had paid a considerable personal price because of his obedience to the Lord.

i. **walk worthy.** "Walk" is frequently used in the N.T. to refer to daily conduct. It sets the theme for the final 3 chapters of Ephesians. "Worthy" has the idea of living to match one's position in Christ. The apostle urged his readers to be everything the Lord desires and empowers them to be.

j. **calling.** This refers to God's sovereign call to salvation, as always in the epistles. See Rom. 8:30. The effectual call that saves is mentioned in Eph. 1:18; Rom. 11:29; 1 Cor. 1:26; Phil. 3:14; 2 Thess. 1:11; 2 Tim. 1:9; Heb. 3:1.

k. **lowliness.** "Humility" is a term not found in the Rom. or Gr. vocabularies of Paul's day.

ᵃgentleness, with ᵇlongsuffering, ᶜbearing with one another in love, endeavoring to keep the ᵈunity of the Spirit in the bond of peace. ᵉThere is ᶠone body and one Spirit, just as you were called in ᵍone hope of your calling; ʰone Lord, ⁱone faith, ʲone baptism; ᵏone God and Father of all, who is above all, and through all, and in you all.

ˡBut to each one of us ᵐgrace was given according to ⁿthe measure of Christ's gift. Therefore He says:

The Gr. word apparently was coined by Christians, perhaps even by Paul himself, to describe a quality for which no other word was available. Humility, the most foundational Christian virtue (James 4:6), is the quality of character commanded in the first beatitude (Matt. 5:3), and describes the noble grace of Christ (Phil. 2:7, 8).

a. **gentleness.** "Meekness," an inevitable product of humility, refers to that which is mild-spirited and self-controlled (cf. Matt. 5:5; 11:29; Gal. 5:23; Col. 3:12).

b. **longsuffering.** The Gr. word lit. means long-tempered, and refers to a resolved patience that is an outgrowth of humility and gentleness (cf. 1 Thess. 5:14; James 5:10).

c. **bearing with one another in love.** Humility, gentleness, and patience are reflected in a forbearing love for others that is continuous and unconditional (cf. 1 Pet. 4:8).

d. **unity of the Spirit.** The Spirit-bestowed oneness of all true believers (see 1 Cor. 6:17; 12:11–13; Phil. 1:27; 2:2) has created the bond of peace, the spiritual cord that surrounds and binds God's holy people together. This bond is love (Col. 3:14).

e. **There is . . .** In this passage, Paul lists the particular areas of oneness, or unity: body, Spirit, hope, Lord, faith, baptism, and God and Father. He focuses on the Trinity—the Spirit in Eph. 4:4, the Son in v. 5, and the Father in v. 6. His point is not to distinguish between the Persons of the Godhead but to emphasize that, although they have unique roles, they are completely unified in every aspect of the divine nature and plan.

f. **one body.** The church, the body of Christ, is composed of every believer since Pentecost without distinction, by the work of the "one Spirit" (see 1 Cor. 12:11–13).

g. **one hope.** This is the pledge and promise of eternal inheritance given each believer (Eph. 1:11–14) and sealed to each believer by the one Spirit (Eph. 4:13).

h. **one Lord.** See Acts 4:12; Rom. 10:12; Gal. 1:8.

i. **one faith.** The body of doctrine revealed in the NT (cf. Jude 3).

j. **one baptism.** This probably refers to the water baptism following salvation, a believer's public confession of faith in Jesus Christ. Spiritual baptism, by which all believers are placed into the body of Christ (1 Cor. 12:11–13) is implied in Eph. 4:4.

k. **one God.** This is the basic doctrine of God taught in Scripture (see Deut. 4:35; 6:4; 32:39; Is. 45:14; 46:9; 1 Cor. 8:4–6).

l. **But to each one.** This could be translated "in spite of that," or "on the other hand," contrasting what has just been said with what is about to be said, moving from the subject of the unity of believers ("all," Eph. 4:6) to that of the uniqueness of believers ("each one").

m. **grace.** Grace is a single-word definition of the gospel, the good news of God's offering salvation to sinful and unworthy mankind. God is the God of grace because He is a God who freely gives; His giving has nothing to do with anything we have done, but is unmerited, unearned, and undeserved. See Eph. 2:7–9.

n. **the measure of Christ's gift.** Each believer has a unique spiritual gift that God

[a]"When He ascended on high,
He [b]led captivity captive,
And [c]gave gifts to men."

(Now this, "He [d]ascended"—what does it mean but that He also [e]first descended into the [f]lower parts of the earth? He who descended is also the One who ascended far above all the heavens, [g]that He might fill all things.)

---

individually portions out according to His sovereign will and design. The Gr. term for "gift" focuses not on the Spirit as the source like the term used in 1 Cor. 12:1, nor on the grace that prompted it in Rom. 12:6, but on the freeness of the gift. For discussions of the gifts, see Rom. 12:6–8; 1 Cor. 12:4–10; 1 Pet. 4:10.

a. **When He ascended on high.** Paul used an interpretive rendering of Ps. 68:18 as a parenthetical analogy to show how Christ received the right to bestow the spiritual gifts (Eph. 4:7). Psalm 68 is a victory hymn composed by David to celebrate God's conquest of the Jebusite city of Jerusalem and the triumphant assent of God up to Mt. Zion (cf. 2 Sam. 6, 7; 1 Chr. 13). After such a triumph, the king would bring home the spoils and the prisoners. Here Paul depicts Christ returning from His battle on earth back into the glory of the heavenly city with the trophies of His great victory at Calvary (see 2 Cor. 2:14–16).

b. **led captivity captive.** Through His crucifixion and resurrection, Christ conquered Satan and death, and in triumph returned to God those who were once sinners and prisoners of Satan (cf. Col. 2:15).

c. **gave gifts to men.** He distributes the spoils throughout His kingdom. After His ascension came all the spiritual gifts empowered by the Spirit, who was then sent (see John 7:39; 14:12; Acts 2:33).

d. **ascended.** Jesus' ascension from earth to heaven (Acts 1:9–11), where He forever reigns with His Father.

e. **first descended.** This refers to Christ's incarnation, when He came down from heaven as a man into the earth of suffering and death.

f. **the lower parts of the earth.** These are in contrast to the highest heavens to which He afterward ascended (cf. Ps. 139:8, 15; Is. 44:23). The phrase here does not point to a specific place, but to the great depth, as it were, of the incarnation, including Christ's descent, between His crucifixion and resurrection beyond the earth, the grave, and death, into the very pit of the demons, "the spirits in prison" (see Col. 2:14, 15; 1 Pet. 3:18, 19).

g. **that He might fill all things.** After the Lord ascended, having fulfilled all prophecies and all His divinely-ordained redemptive tasks, He gained the right to rule the church and to give gifts, as He was then filling the entire universe with His divine presence, power, sovereignty, and blessing (cf. Phil. 2:9–11).

193. THE BUILDING UP OF THE CHURCH
Eph. 4:11–16

And [a]He Himself gave some to be [b]apostles, some [c]prophets, some [d]evangelists, and some [e]pastors and teachers, for the [f]equipping of the [g]saints for [h]the work of ministry, for [i]the edifying of the body of Christ, till we all come to

---

a. **He Himself gave some to be.** As evidenced by His perfect fulfillment of His Father's will, Christ possessed the authority and sovereignty to assign the spiritual gifts (Eph. 4:7, 8) to those He has called into service in His church. He gave not only gifts, but gifted men.

b. **apostles.** See Eph. 2:20. A term used particularly of the 12 disciples who had seen the risen Christ (Acts 1:22), including Matthias, who replaced Judas. Later, Paul was uniquely set apart as the apostle to the Gentiles (Gal. 1:15–17) and was numbered with the other apostles. He, too, miraculously encountered Jesus at his conversion on the Damascus Road (Acts 9:1–9; Gal. 1:15–17). Those apostles were chosen directly by Christ, so as to be called "apostles of Christ" (Gal. 1:1; 1 Pet. 1:1). They were given 3 basic responsibilities: 1) to lay the foundation of the church (2:20); 2) to receive, declare and write God's Word (3:5; Acts 11:28; 21:10, 11); and 3) to give confirmation of that Word through signs, wonders, and miracles (2 Cor. 12:12; cf. Acts 8:6, 7; Heb. 2:3, 4). The term "apostle" is used in more general ways of other men in the early church, such as Barnabas (Acts 14:4), Silas, Timothy, (1 Thess. 2:6) and others (Rom. 16:7; Phil. 2:25). They are called "apostles of the churches" (2 Cor. 8:23), rather than "apostles of Jesus Christ" like the 13. They were not self-perpetuating, nor was any apostle who died replaced.

c. **prophets.** See Eph. 2:20. Not ordinary believers who had the gift of prophecy but specially commissioned men in the early church. The office of prophet seems to have been exclusively for work within a local congregation. They were not "sent ones" as were the apostles (see Acts 13:1), but, as with the apostles, their office ceased with the completion of the NT. They sometimes spoke practical direct revelation for the church from God (Acts 11:21–28) or expounded revelation already given (implied in Acts 13:1). They were not used for the reception of Scripture. Their messages were to be judged by other prophets for validity (1 Cor. 14:32) and had to conform to the teaching of the apostles (v. 37). Those two offices were replaced by the evangelists and teaching pastors.

d. **evangelists.** Men who proclaim the good news of salvation in Jesus Christ to unbelievers. Cf. the use of this term in Acts 21:8; 2 Tim. 4:5. The related verb translated "to preach the gospel" is used 54 times and the related noun translated "gospel" is used 76 times in the NT.

e. **pastors and teachers.** This phrase is best understood in context as a single office of leadership in the church. The Gr. word translated "and" can mean "in particular" (see 1 Tim. 5:17). The normal meaning of pastor is "shepherd," so the two functions together define the teaching shepherd. He is identified as one who is under the "great Pastor" Jesus (Heb. 13:20, 21; 1 Pet. 2:25). One who holds this office is also called an "elder" (see Titus 1:5–9) and "bishop" (see 1 Tim. 3:1–7). Acts 20:28 and 1 Pet. 5:1, 2 bring all 3 terms together.

f. **equipping.** This refers to restoring something to its original condition, or its being made fit or complete. In this context, it refers to leading Christians from sin to obedience. Scripture is the key to this process (see 2 Tim. 3:16, 17; cf. John 15:3).

g. **saints.** All who believe in Jesus Christ. See Eph. 1:1.

h. **the work of ministry.** The spiritual service required of every Christian, not just of church leaders (cf. 1 Cor. 15:58).

i. **the edifying of the body of Christ.** The spiritual edification, nurturing, and development of the church (cf. Acts 20:32).

the ᵃunity of the faith and of ᵇthe knowledge of the Son of God, to a perfect man, to the measure of the stature of ᶜthe fullness of Christ; that we should no longer be children, tossed to and fro and ᵈcarried about with every wind of doctrine, by the trickery of men, in the cunning craftiness of deceitful plotting, but, ᵉspeaking the truth in love, may ᶠgrow up in all things into Him who is ᵍthe head—Christ—ʰfrom whom the whole body, joined and knit together by what every joint supplies, according to the effective working by which ⁱevery part does its share, causes growth of the body for the edifying of itself in love.

a. **unity of the faith.** Faith here refers to the body of revealed truth that constitutes Christian teaching, particularly featuring the complete content of the gospel. Oneness and harmony among believers is possible only when it is built on the foundation of sound doctrine.

b. **the knowledge of the Son of God.** This does not refer to salvation knowledge but to the deep knowledge of Christ that a believer comes to have through prayer, faithful study of His Word, and obedience to His commands (cf. Phil. 3:8–10, 12; Col. 1:9, 10; 2:2; see 1 John 2:12–14).

c. **the fullness of Christ.** God wants every believer to manifest the qualities of His Son, who is Himself the standard for their spiritual maturity and perfection. See Rom. 8:29; 2 Cor. 3:18; Col. 1:28, 29.

d. **carried about with every wind of doctrine.** Spiritually immature believers who are not grounded in the knowledge of Christ through God's Word are inclined to uncritically accept every sort of beguiling doctrinal error and fallacious interpretation of Scripture promulgated by deceitful, false teachers in the church. They must learn discernment (1 Thess. 5:21, 22). See Eph. 3:1; 4:20. The NT is replete with warnings of such danger (Acts 20:30, 31; Rom. 16:17, 18; Gal. 1:6, 7; 1 Tim. 4:1–7; 2 Tim. 2:15–18; 2 Pet. 2:1–3).

e. **speaking the truth in love.** Evangelism is most effective when the truth is proclaimed in love. This can be accomplished only by the spiritually mature believer who is thoroughly equipped in sound doctrine. Without maturity, the truth can be cold and love little more than sentimentality.

f. **grow up . . . into Him.** Christians are to be completely yielded and obedient to the Lord's will, subject to His controlling power and Christlike in all areas of their lives (cf. Gal. 2:20; Phil. 1:21).

g. **the head.** Given the picture of the church as a body whose head is Christ, "head" is used in the sense of authoritative leader, not "source," which would have required a different anatomical picture. See Eph. 1:22; 5:23.

h. **from whom.** This refers to the Lord. Power for producing mature, equipped believers comes not from the effort of those believers alone but from their Head, the Lord Jesus Christ (cf. Col. 2:19).

i. **every part does its share.** Godly, biblical church growth results from every member of the body fully using his spiritual gift, in submission to the Holy Spirit and in cooperation with other believers (cf. Col. 2:19).

194. PATTERN AND PRINCIPLES FOR CHURCH MEMBERS

Eph. 4:17–32

This I say, therefore, and testify in the Lord, that you should ᵃno longer walk as the rest of the ᵇGentiles walk, in ᶜthe futility of their mind, having their understanding darkened, being ᵈalienated from the life of God, because of the ignorance that is in them, because of the blindness of their heart; who, ᵉbeing past feeling, have given themselves over to ᶠlewdness, to work all uncleanness with greediness.

But you have not so ᵍlearned Christ, if indeed you have heard Him and have been taught by Him, ʰas the truth is in Jesus: that you ⁱput off, concerning your former conduct, ʲthe old man which grows corrupt according to the

---

a. **no longer walk.** "Walk" expresses daily conduct and refers back to what Paul has said about the believer's high calling in Christ Jesus (Eph. 4:1). Because Christians are part of the body of Christ, have been spiritually gifted by the Holy Spirit, and are edified through other believers, they should not continue to live like the rest of the ungodly (1 John 2:6).

b. **Gentiles.** All ungodly, unregenerate pagans (cf. 1 Thess. 4:5 which defines them).

c. **the futility of their mind.** First, unbelievers are intellectually unproductive. As far as spiritual and moral issues are concerned, their rational processes are distorted and inadequate, inevitably failing to produce godly understanding or moral living. Their life is empty, vain, and without meaning (cf. Rom. 1:21–28; 1 Cor. 2:14; Col. 2:18).

d. **alienated from the life of God.** Second, unbelievers are spiritually separated from God, thus ignorant of God's truth (1 Cor. 2:14), and their willing spiritual darkness and moral blindness is the result (cf. Rom. 1:21–24; 2 Tim. 3:7). They are blind, or "hard" like a rock.

e. **being past feeling.** Third, unbelievers are morally insensitive. As they continue to sin and turn away from God, they become still more apathetic about moral and spiritual things (cf. Rom. 1:32).

f. **lewdness . . . uncleanness.** Fourth, unbelievers are behaviorally depraved (cf. Rom. 1:28). As they willingly keep succumbing to sensuality and licentiousness, they increasingly lose moral restraint, especially in the area of sexual sins. Impurity is inseparable from greediness, which is a form of idolatry (5:5; Col. 3:5). That some souls may not reach the extremes of Eph. 4:17–19 is due only to God's common grace and the restraining influence of the Holy Spirit.

g. **learned . . . heard . . . taught.** Three figurative descriptions of salvation, the new birth.

h. **as the truth is in Jesus.** The truth about salvation leads to the fullness of truth about God, man, creation, history, life, purpose, relationships, heaven, hell, judgment, and everything else that is truly important. John summed this up in 1 John 5:20.

i. **put off.** To strip away, as in taking off old, filthy clothes. This describes repentance from sin and submission to God at the point of salvation. See Col. 3:3–9 (cf. Is. 55:6, 7; Matt. 19:16–22; Acts 2:38–40; 20:21; 1 Thess. 1:9).

j. **the old man.** The worn out, useless, and unconverted sinful nature corrupted by deceit. Salvation is a spiritual union with Jesus Christ that is described as the death plus burial of the old self and the resurrection of the new self walking in newness of life. This transformation is Paul's theme in Rom. 6:2–8.

deceitful lusts, and ªbe renewed in the spirit of your mind, and that you ᵇput on the new man which was created according to God, ᶜin true righteousness and holiness.

Therefore, ᵈputting away lying, "Let each one of you ᵉspeak truth with his neighbor," for we are members of one another. ᶠ"Be angry, and do not sin": do not let the ᵍsun go down on your wrath, nor give place to the devil. Let him who stole ʰsteal no longer, but rather let him labor, working with his hands what is good, that he may have something to ⁱgive him who has need. Let no ʲcorrupt word proceed out of your mouth, but what is ᵏgood for necessary

---

a. **be renewed in the spirit of your mind.** Salvation involves the mind (see Rom. 12:2; 2 Cor. 10:5), which is the center of thought, understanding, and belief, as well as of motive and action (cf. Col. 3:1, 2, 10). When a person becomes a Christian, God gives him a completely new spiritual and moral capability that a mind apart from Christ could never achieve (cf. 1 Cor. 2:9–16).

b. **put on the new man.** The renewal of the mind in salvation brings not simply a renovation of character, but transformation of the old to the new self (cf. 2 Cor. 5:17). In Christ, the old self no longer exists as it had in the past; the new self is created in the very likeness of God (cf. Gal. 2:20).

c. **in true righteousness and holiness.** Righteousness relates to the Christian's moral responsibility to his fellow men reflecting the second table of the law (Ex. 20:12–17), while holiness refers to his responsibilities to God, reflecting the first table (Ex. 20:3–11). There is still sin in the believer's unredeemed human flesh (see Rom. 7:17, 18, 20, 23, 25; 8:23).

d. **putting away lying.** More than simply telling direct falsehoods, lying also includes exaggeration and adding fabrications to something that is true. Cheating, making foolish promises, betraying a confidence, and making false excuses are all forms of lying, with which Christians should have no part (cf. John 8:44; 1 Cor. 6:9; Rev. 21:8).

e. **speak truth with his neighbor.** Quoted from Zech. 8:16. God's work in the world is based on truth, and neither the church nor individual believers can be fit instruments for the Lord to use if they are not truthful.

f. **Be angry, and do not sin.** Quoted from Ps. 4:4. By NT standards, anger can be either good or bad, depending on motive and purpose. Paul may have been sanctioning righteous indignation, anger at evil. This type of anger hates injustice, immorality, ungodliness, and every other sin. When such anger is unselfish and based on love for God and others, it not only is permissible but commanded. Jesus expressed this righteous anger (see Matt. 21:12; Mark 3:5; John 2:15).

g. **sun go down.** Even righteous anger can turn to bitterness, so should be set aside by the end of each day. If anger is prolonged, it may become hostile and violate the instruction of Rom. 12:17–21.

h. **steal no longer.** Stealing in any form is a sin and has no part in the life of a Christian. Rather, let him work, producing what is beneficial (cf. Ex. 20:15). The alternative to stealing is to provide for oneself, one's family, and others what is God-honoring through honest, honorable means (cf. 2 Thess. 3:10, 11; 1 Tim. 5:8).

i. **give him who has need.** A Christian not only should harm no one but should continually endeavor to help those who are in need. See Luke 14:13, 14; Acts 20:33–35.

j. **corrupt word.** The word for "corrupt" refers to that which is foul or rotten, such as spoiled fruit or putrid meat. Foul language of any sort should never pass a Christian's lips, because it is totally out of character with his new life in Christ (see Col. 3:8; James 3:6–8; cf. Ps. 141:3).

k. **good for necessary edification.** The Christian's speech should be instructive, encouraging, uplifting, (even when it must be corrective), and suited for the moment (cf. Prov. 15:23; 25:11; 24:26).

edification, that it may impart ^agrace to the hearers. And ^bdo not grieve the Holy Spirit of God, by whom you were ^csealed for the day of redemption. ^dLet all bitterness, wrath, anger, clamor, and evil speaking be put away from you, with all malice. And be kind to one another, tenderhearted, forgiving one another, ^eeven as God in Christ forgave you.

195. Walking in Love and Light
Eph. 5:1–14

^fTherefore be imitators of God as dear children. And walk in love, as ^gChrist also has loved us and given Himself for us, an offering and a sacrifice to God for ^ha sweet-smelling aroma.

---

a. **grace to the hearers.** Cf. Col. 4:6. Because believers have been saved by grace and kept by grace, they should live and speak with grace. Our Lord set the standard (Luke 4:22).

b. **do not grieve the Holy Spirit of God.** God is grieved when His children refuse to change the old ways of sin for those righteous ways of the new life. It should be noted that such responses by the Holy Spirit indicate He is a person. His personhood is also indicated by personal pronouns (John 14:17; 16:13), His personal care of believers (John 14:16, 26; 15:26), His intellect (1 Cor. 2:11), feelings (Rom. 8:27; 15:30), will (1 Cor. 12:11), speaking (Acts 13:2), convicting (John 16:8–11), interceding (Rom. 8:26), guiding (John 16:13), glorifying Christ (John 16:14), and serving God (Acts 16:6, 7).

c. **sealed for the day of redemption.** The Holy Spirit is the guarantor of eternal redemption in Christ for those who believe in Him (see Eph. 1:13, 14).

d. **Let all . . .** There verses summarize the changes in the life of a believer mentioned in Eph. 4:17–30. "Bitterness" reflects a smoldering resentment. "Wrath" has to do with rage, the passion of a moment. "Anger" is a more internal, deep hostility. "Clamor" is the outcry of strife out of control. "Evil speaking" is slander. "Malice" is the general Gr. term for evil, the root of all vices.

e. **even as God in Christ forgave you.** Those who have been forgiven so much by God should, of all people, forgive the relatively small offenses against them by others. The most graphic illustration of this truth is the parable of Matt. 18:21–35.

f. **be imitators of God.** The Christian has no greater calling or purpose than that of imitating his Lord (see Eph. 3:16, 19). That is the very purpose of sanctification, growing in likeness to the Lord while serving Him on earth (cf. Matt. 5:48). The Christian life is designed to reproduce godliness as modeled by the Savior and Lord, Jesus Christ, in whose image believers have been recreated through the new birth (cf. Rom. 8:29; 2 Cor. 3:18; 1 Pet. 1:14–16). As God's dear children, believers are to become more and more like their heavenly Father (Matt. 5:48; 1 Pet. 1:15, 16).

g. **Christ also has loved us and given Himself for us.** The Lord is the supreme example in His self-sacrificing love for lost sinners (Eph. 4:32; Rom. 5:8–10). He took human sin upon Himself and gave up His very life that men might be redeemed from their sin, receive a new and holy nature, and inherit eternal life (see 2 Cor. 5:21). They are henceforth to be imitators of His great love in the newness and power of the Holy Spirit, who enables them to demonstrate divine love.

h. **a sweet-smelling aroma.** Christ's offering of Himself for fallen man pleased and

But ª fornication and all uncleanness or covetousness, let it not even be named among you, as is fitting for saints; neither filthiness, nor foolish talking, nor coarse jesting, which are ᵇnot fitting, but rather giving of thanks. ᶜFor this you know, that no fornicator, unclean person, nor covetous man, who is an idolater, has any inheritance in ᵈthe kingdom of Christ and God. Let no one ᵉdeceive you with empty words, for because of these things the wrath of God comes upon the sons of disobedience. Therefore do not be partakers with them.

For you were once ᶠdarkness, but now you are light in the Lord. Walk as children of light (for the ᵍfruit of the Spirit is in all goodness, righteousness,

---

glorified His heavenly Father, because it demonstrated in the most complete and perfect way God's sovereign, perfect, unconditional, and divine kind of love. Leviticus describes 5 offerings commanded by God for Israel. The first 3 were: 1) the burnt offering (Lev. 1:1–17), depicting Christ's perfection; 2) the grain offering (Lev. 2:1–16), depicting Christ's total devotion to God in giving His life to please the Father; and 3) the peace offering (Lev. 3:1–17; 4:27–31), depicting His peacemaking between God and man. All 3 of these were a "soothing aroma to the Lord" (Lev. 1:9, 13, 17; 2:2, 9, 12; 3:5, 16). The other two offerings, the sin offering (Lev. 4:1–26, 32–35) and the trespass offering (Lev. 5:1–19), were repulsive to God because, though they depicted Christ, they depicted Him as bearing sin (cf. Matt. 27:46). In the end, when redemption was accomplished, the whole work pleased God completely.

a. **fornication . . . covetousness.** In absolute contrast to God's holiness and love, such sins as these exist (also in Eph. 5:5), by which Satan seeks to destroy God's divine work in His children and turn them as far away as possible from His image and will. As do many other Scriptures, this verse shows the close connection between sexual sin and other forms of impurity and greed. An immoral person is inevitably greedy. Such sins are so godless that the world should never have reason even to suspect their presence in Christians.

b. **not fitting.** These 3 inappropriate sins of the tongue include any speech that is obscene and degrading or foolish and dirty, as well as suggestive and immoral wit. All such are destructive of holy living and godly testimony and should be confessed, forsaken, and replaced by open expressions of thankfulness to God (cf. Col. 3:8).

c. **For this you know.** Paul had taught this truth many times when he pastored the church at Ephesus and it should have been clear in their minds. God never tolerates sin, which has no place at all in His kingdom, nor will any person whose life pattern is one of habitual immorality, impurity, and greed (see Eph. 5:3) be in His kingdom, because no such person is saved (see 1 Cor. 6:9, 10; Gal. 5:17–21; 1 John 3:9, 10).

d. **the kingdom of Christ and God.** A reference to the sphere of salvation where Christ rules the redeemed. See Acts 1:3.

e. **deceive you.** No Christian will be sinless in this present life, but it is dangerously deceptive for Christians to offer assurance of salvation to a professing believer whose life is characterized by persistent sin and who shows no shame for that sin or hunger for the holy and pure things of God. They are headed for wrath (Eph. 2:2) and believers must not partner in any of their wickedness (Eph. 5:7).

f. **darkness . . . light.** "Darkness" describes the character of the life of the unconverted as void of truth and virtue in intellectual and moral matters (cf. 1 John 1:5–7). The realm of darkness is presided over by the "power of darkness," (Luke 22:53; Col. 1:13) who rules those headed for "eternal darkness" (Matt. 8:12; 2 Pet. 2:17). Tragically, sinners love the darkness (John 3:19–21). It is that very darkness from which salvation in Christ delivers sinners (see John 8:12; Col. 1:13; 1 Pet. 2:9; cf. Ps. 27:1).

g. **fruit of the spirit.** Better, as in marginal reading, "fruit of the light." This speaks of that which is produced by walking in the light (cf. 1 John 1:5–7), namely moral excellence of heart, righteous behavior, and truthfulness (honesty or integrity). See Gal. 5:22, 23.

and truth), [a]finding out what is acceptable to the Lord. And have [b]no fellowship with the unfruitful works of darkness, [c]but rather expose them. For it is [d]shameful even to speak of those things which are done by them in secret. But all things that are exposed are made manifest by the light, [e]for whatever makes manifest is light. Therefore He says:

> [f]"Awake, you who sleep,
> Arise from the dead,
> And Christ will give you light."

196. WALKING IN WISDOM

Eph. 5:15–21

See then that you walk [g]circumspectly, not as fools but as wise, [h]redeeming the time, because the days are evil.

---

a. **finding out what is acceptable to the Lord.** "Finding out" carries the idea of testing or proving to learn by clear and convincing evidence what is truly honoring to God. The point is that, as believers walk in the light of the truth, the knowledge of the Lord's will becomes clear. See Rom. 12:1, 2 where Paul says the same thing, stating that it is only after presenting ourselves as living sacrifices to God that we can know His acceptable will. This relates to assurance of salvation also (see 1 Pet. 1:5–11).

b. **no fellowship with . . . darkness.** Paul's instruction is plain and direct: Christians are to faithfully live in righteousness and purity and have nothing at all to do with the evil ways and works of Satan and the world. The two ways of living are unalterably opposed to each other and mutually exclusive. Cf. 1 Cor. 5:9–11; 2 Cor. 6:14–18; 2 Thess. 3:6, 14.

c. **but rather expose them.** The Christian's responsibility does not stop with his own rejection of evil. He is also responsible for exposing and opposing darkness wherever it is found, especially when it is found in the church. See Matt. 18:15–17; Gal. 6:1–3.

d. **shameful even to speak.** Some sins are so despicable that they should be sealed off from direct contact and not even mentioned, much less discussed, except in order to contradict and oppose them. Merely talking about them can be morally and spiritually corruptive. Positive proclamation of the pure truth in the light of the Word exposes all evil (cf. Prov. 6:23; 2 Tim. 3:16).

e. **for whatever makes manifest is light.** This phrase should probably be part of Eph. 5:14, and is better translated, "for it is light that makes everything visible." The pure and illuminating light of God's Word exposes all the secrets of sin.

f. **Awake . . .** Using this quotation from Is. 60:1, Paul extended an invitation for salvation to the unsaved, in order that they may be transformed from children of darkness into children of God's holy light (cf. Prov. 4:18). These words may have been part of an early church Easter hymn used as an invitation to unbelievers. They express a capsule view of the gospel. Cf. the invitations in Is. 55:1–3, 6, 7 and in James 4:6–10.

g. **circumspectly, not as fools but as wise.** This term means "accurately or precisely with great care" (cf. Ps. 1:1; Matt. 7:14). To live morally is to live wisely. Biblically, a "fool" is not so named because of intellectual limits, but because of unbelief and the consequent abominable deeds (Ps. 14:1; Rom. 1:22). He lives apart from God and against God's law (Prov. 1:7, 22; 14:9), and can't comprehend the truth (1 Cor. 2:14) or his true condition (Rom. 1:21, 22). Certainly believers are to avoid behaving like fools (see Luke 24:25; Gal. 3:1–3).

h. **redeeming the time.** The Gr. word for "time" denotes a fixed, measured, allocated

ᵃTherefore do not be unwise, but understand what the will of the Lord is. ᵇAnd do not be drunk with wine, in which is dissipation; ᶜbut be filled with the Spirit, ᵈspeaking to one another in ᵉpsalms and ᶠhymns and ᵍspiritual songs, singing and ʰmaking melody ⁱin your heart to the Lord, ʲgiving thanks always for all things to God the Father in the name of our Lord Jesus Christ, ᵏsubmitting to one another ˡin the fear of God.

---

season; with the definite article "the," it likely refers to one's lifetime as a believer. We are to make the most of our time on this evil earth in fulfilling God's purposes, lining up every opportunity for useful worship and service. See 1 Pet. 1:17. Be aware of the brevity of life (Pss. 39:4, 5; 89:46, 47; James 4:14, 17).

a. **Therefore do not be unwise, but understand what the will of the Lord is.** Knowing and understanding God's will through His Word is spiritual wisdom. For example, God's will revealed to us is that people should be saved (1 Tim. 2:3, 4), Spirit-filled (Eph. 5:18), sanctified (1 Thess. 4:3), submissive (1 Pet. 2:13–15), suffering (1 Pet. 2:20) and thankful (1 Thess. 5:18). Jesus is the supreme example for all (see John 4:4; 5:19, 30; 1 Pet. 4:1, 2).

b. **And do not be drunk with wine.** Although Scripture consistently condemns all drunkenness (see Prov. 23:20, 21, 29–35; 31:4, 5; Is. 5:11, 12; 28:7, 8; cf. 1 Cor. 5:11; 1 Pet. 4:3), the context suggests that Paul is here speaking especially about the drunken orgies commonly associated with many pagan worship ceremonies of that day. They were supposed to induce some ecstatic communion with the deities. Paul refers to such as the "cup of demons" (see 1 Cor. 10:20, 21).

c. **but be filled with the Spirit.** See Acts 2:4; 4:8, 31; 6:3. True communion with God is not induced by drunkenness, but by the Holy Spirit. Paul is not speaking of the Holy Spirit's indwelling (Rom. 8:9) or the baptism by Christ with the Holy Spirit (1 Cor. 12:13), because every Christian is indwelt and baptized by the Spirit at the time of salvation. He is rather giving a command for believers to live continually under the influence of the Spirit by letting the Word control them (see Col. 3:16), pursuing pure lives, confessing all known sin, dying to self, surrendering to God's will, and depending on His power in all things. Being filled with the Spirit is living in the conscious presence of the Lord Jesus Christ, letting His mind, through the Word, dominate everything that is thought and done. Being filled with the Spirit is the same as walking in the Spirit (see Gal. 5:16–23). Christ exemplified this way of life (Luke 4:1).

d. **speaking to one another.** This is to be public (Heb. 2:12). Cf. Pss. 33:1; 40:3; 96:1, 2; 149:1; Acts 16:25; Rev. 14:3.

e. **psalms.** Old Testament psalms put to music, primarily, but the term was used also of vocal music in general. The early church sang the Psalms.

f. **hymns.** Perhaps songs of praise distinguished from the Psalms which exalted God, in that they focused on the Lord Jesus Christ.

g. **spiritual songs.** Probably songs of personal testimony expressing truths of the grace of salvation in Christ.

h. **making melody.** Lit. means to pluck a stringed instrument, so it could refer primarily to instrumental music, while including vocal also.

i. **in your heart to the Lord.** Not just public, but private. The Lord Himself is both the source and the object of the believer's song-filled heart. That such music pleases God can be seen in the account of the temple dedication, when the singing so honored the Lord that His glory came down (2 Chr. 5:12, 14).

j. **giving thanks always for all things.** See 1 Thess. 5:18; cf. 2 Cor. 4:15; 9:12, 15; Phil. 4:6; Col. 2:7; Heb. 13:15. Believers' thankfulness is for who God is and for what He has done through His Son, their Savior and Lord.

k. **submitting to one another.** Paul here made a transition and introduced his teaching about specific relationships of authority and submission among Christians (Eph. 5:22—6:9) by declaring unequivocally that every spirit-filled Christian is to be a humble, submissive Christian. This is foundational to all the relationships in this section. No believer is inherently superior to any other believer. In their standing before God, they are equal in every way (Gal 3:28).

l. **in the fear of God.** The believer's continual reverence for God is the basis for his submission to other believers. Cf. Prov. 9:10.

197. HUSBANDS AND WIVES

Eph. 5:22–33

^aWives, submit to your own husbands, ^bas to the Lord. For the ^chusband is head of the wife, as also Christ is head of the church; and He is the ^dSavior of the body. Therefore, just as the church is subject to Christ, so let the wives be to their own husbands in everything.

Husbands, ^elove your wives, just as Christ also loved the church and gave Himself for her, that He might ^fsanctify and cleanse her with the washing of water by the word, that He might present her to Himself a glorious church, not having spot or wrinkle or any such thing, but that she should be holy and without blemish. So husbands ought to love their own wives ^gas their own

a. **Wives, submit to your own husbands.** Having established the foundational principle of submission (v. 21), Paul applied it first to the wife. The command is unqualified, applying to every Christian wife, no matter what her own abilities, education, knowledge of Scripture, spiritual maturity, or any other qualifications might be in relation to those of her husband. The submission is not the husband's to command but for the wife to willingly and lovingly offer. "Your own husbands" limits her submission to the one man God has placed over her, and also gives a balancing emphasis that he is hers as a personal intimate possession (Song 2:16; 6:3; 7:10). She submits to the man she possesses as her own.

b. **as to the Lord.** Because the obedient, spiritual wife's supreme submission is to the Lord, her attitude is that she lovingly submits as an act of obedience to the Lord who has given this command as His will for her, regardless of her husband's personal worthiness or spiritual condition. Cf. Eph. 5:5–9.

c. **husband is head . . . Christ is head.** The Spirit-filled wife recognizes that her husband's role in giving leadership is not only God-ordained, but is a reflection of Christ's own loving, authoritative headship of the church. See 1 Cor. 11:3; cf. 1:22, 23; 4:15; Col. 1:18; Titus 2:4, 5.

d. **Savior.** As the Lord delivered His church from the dangers of sin, death, and hell, so the husband provides for, protects, preserves, and loves his wife, leading her to blessing as she submits. Cf. Titus 1:4; 2:13; 3:6.

e. **love your wives.** Though the husband's authority has been established (Eph. 5:22–24), the emphasis moves to the supreme responsibility of husbands in regard to their wives, which is to love them with the same unreserved, selfless, and sacrificial love that Christ has for His church. Christ gave everything He had, including His own life, for the sake of His church, and that is the standard of sacrifice for a husband's love of his wife. Cf. Col. 3:19.

f. **sanctify . . . cleanse . . . holy . . . without blemish.** This speaks of the love of Christ for His church. Saving grace makes believers holy by the agency of the Word of God (Titus 2:1–9; 3:5) so that they may be a pure bride. For husbands to love their wives as Christ does His church, demands a purifying love. Since divine love seeks to completely cleanse those who are loved from every form of sin and evil, a Christian husband should not be able to bear the thought of anything sinful in the life of his wife that displeases God. His greatest desire for her should be that she become perfectly conformed to Christ, so he leads her to purity. See 2 Cor. 11:23.

g. **as their own bodies.** Here is one of the most poignant and compelling descriptions of the oneness that should characterize Christian marriage. A Christian husband is to care for his wife with the same devotion that he naturally manifests as he cares for himself (Eph. 5:29)—even more so, since his self-sacrificing love causes him to put her first (cf. Phil. 2:1–4).

bodies; he who ªloves his wife loves himself. For no one ever hated his own flesh, but ᵇnourishes and cherishes it, just as the Lord does the church. For we are ᶜmembers of His body, of His flesh and of His bones. ᵈ"For this reason a man shall leave his father and mother and be joined to his wife, and the two shall become one flesh." This is ᵉa great mystery, but I speak concerning Christ and the church. Nevertheless ᶠlet each one of you in particular so love his own wife as himself, and let the wife see that she respects her husband.

198. PARENTS AND CHILDREN; MASTERS AND BONDSERVANTS

Eph. 6:1–9

Children, ᵍobey your parents in the Lord, for this is right. ʰ"Honor your father and mother," which is the ⁱfirst commandment with promise: "that it may be well with you and you may live long on the earth."

---

a. **loves his wife loves himself.** In the end, a husband who loves his wife in these ways brings great blessing to himself from her and from the Lord.

b. **nourishes and cherishes.** These express the twin responsibilities of providing for her needs so as to help her grow mature in Christ and to provide warm and tender affection to give her comfort and security.

c. **members of His body.** The Lord provides for His church because it is so intimately and inseparably connected to Him. If He did not care for His church, He would be diminishing His own glory which the church brings to Him by praise and obedience. So, in marriage, the husband's life is so intimately joined to the wife's that they are one. When he cares for her, he cares for himself (Eph. 5:29).

d. **For this reason . . .** Quoted from Gen. 2:24. Paul reinforces the divine plan for marriage which God instituted at creation, emphasizing its permanence and unity. The union of marriage is intimate and unbreakable. "Joined" is a word used to express having been glued or cemented together, emphasizing the permanence of the union (see Mal. 2:16; Matt. 19:6–9).

e. **a great mystery.** In the NT, "mystery" identifies some reality hidden in the past and revealed in the NT age to be written in Scripture. Marriage is a sacred reflection of the magnificent and beautiful mystery of union between the Messiah and His church, completely unknown until the NT. See Eph. 3:4, 5; Matt. 13:11; 1 Cor. 2:7.

f. **let each one of you.** The intimacy and sacredness of the love relationship between believing marriage partners is to be a visual expression of the love between Christ and His church.

g. **obey . . . in the Lord.** See Col. 3:20. The child in the home is to be willingly under the authority of parents with obedient submission to them as the agents of the Lord placed over him, obeying parents as if obeying the Lord Himself. The reasoning here is simply that such is the way God has designed and required it ("right"). Cf. Hos. 14:9.

h. **Honor.** While v. 1 speaks of action, this term speaks of attitude, as Paul deals with the motive behind the action. When God gave His law in the Ten Commandments, the first law governing human relationships was this one (Ex. 20:12; Deut. 5:16). It is the only command of the 10 that relates to the family because that principle alone secures the family's fulfillment. Cf. Ex. 21:15, 17; Lev. 20:9; Matt. 15:3–6. Proverbs affirms this principle (see Eph. 1:8; 3:1; 4:1–3; 7:1–3; 10:1; 17:21; 19:13, 26; 28:24).

i. **the first commandment with promise.** Although submission to parents should first

And you, ᵃfathers, ᵇdo not provoke your children to wrath, but bring them up in the ᶜtraining and admonition of the Lord.

ᵈBondservants, be obedient to those who are your masters ᵉaccording to the flesh, ᶠwith fear and trembling, in sincerity of heart, as to Christ; not with ᵍeyeservice, as ʰmen-pleasers, but as bondservants of Christ, doing the will of God from the heart, with goodwill doing service, as to the Lord, and not to men, knowing that whatever good anyone does, he will receive the same ⁱfrom the Lord, whether he is a slave or free.

ʲAnd you, masters, do the same things to them, ᵏgiving up threatening, knowing that your own Master also is in heaven, and there is no partiality with Him.

---

of all be for the Lord's sake, He has graciously added the promise of special blessing for those who obey this command. See Ex. 20:12, the verse from which Paul quotes (cf. Deut. 5:16).

a. **fathers.** The word technically refers to male parents, but was also used of parents in general. Since Paul had been speaking of both parents (vv. Eph. 6;1–3) he probably had both in mind here. The same word is used in Heb. 11:23 for Moses' parents.

b. **do not provoke.** In the pagan world of Paul's day, and even in many Jewish households, most fathers ruled their families with rigid and domineering authority. The desires and welfare of wives and children were seldom considered. The apostle makes clear that a Christian father's authority over his children does not allow for unreasonable demands and strictures that might drive his children to anger, despair, and resentment.

c. **training and admonition of the Lord.** This calls for systematic discipline and instruction, which brings children to respect the commands of the Lord as the foundation of all of life, godliness, and blessing. Cf. Prov. 13:24; Heb. 12:5–11.

d. **Bondservants, be obedient.** See Col. 3:22–24. Slaves in both Greek and Roman culture had no rights legally and were treated as commodities. There was much abuse and seldom good treatment of slaves. The Bible does not speak against slavery itself, but against its abuses (cf. Ex. 21:16, 26, 27; Lev. 25:10; Deut. 23:15, 16). Paul's admonition applies equally well to all employees. The term "obedient" refers to continuous, uninterrupted submission to one's earthly master or employer, the only exception being in regard to a command that involves clear disobedience of God's Word as illustrated in Acts 4:19, 20. See 1 Tim. 6:1, 2; Titus 2:9, 10; 1 Pet. 2:18–20.

e. **according to the flesh.** Human masters, that is.

f. **with fear and trembling.** This is not fright, but respect for their authority. Even if an employer does not deserve respect in his own right (see 1 Pet. 2:18), it should nevertheless be given to him with genuine sincerity as if one was serving Christ Himself. To serve one's employer well is to serve Christ well. Cf. Col. 3:23, 24.

g. **eyeservice.** Working well only when being watched by the boss.

h. **men-pleasers.** Working only to promote one's welfare, rather than to honor the employer and the Lord, whose servants we really are.

i. **from the Lord.** Cf. Col. 3:23. God's credits and rewards will be appropriate to the attitude and action of our work. No good thing done for His glory will go unrewarded.

j. **And you, masters, do the same things to them.** There should be mutual honor and respect from Christian employers to their employees, based on their common allegiance to the Lord.

k. **giving up threatening.** The Spirit-filled boss uses his authority and power with justice and grace—never putting people under threats, never abusive or inconsiderate. He realizes that he has a heavenly Master who is impartial (cf. Acts 10:34; Rom. 2:11; James 2:9).

199. THE BELIEVER'S SPIRITUAL ARMOR
Eph. 6:10–20

ªFinally, my brethren, ᵇbe strong in the Lord and in the power of His might.
ᶜPut on the whole armor of God, that you may be able to stand against the
ᵈwiles of ᵉthe devil. For we do not ᶠwrestle against flesh and blood, but against
principalities, against powers, against the rulers of the darkness of this age,
against ᵍspiritual hosts of wickedness ʰin the heavenly places. ⁱTherefore take

---

a. **Finally . . .** The true believer described in Eph. 1–3, who lives the Spirit-controlled life
of Eph. 4:1—6:9, can be sure to be in a spiritual war, as described here. Paul closes this letter
with both warning about that war and instructions on how to win it. The Lord provides His
saints with sufficient armor to combat and thwart the adversary. In Eph. 6:10–13, the apostle
briefly sets forth the basic truths regarding the believer's necessary spiritual preparation as
well as truths regarding his enemy, his battle, and his victory. In vv. 14–17, he specifies the
6 most necessary pieces of spiritual armor with which God equips His children to resist and
overcome Satan's assaults.

b. **be strong in the Lord and in the power of His might.** Cf. Phil. 4:13; 2 Tim. 2:1.
Ultimately, Satan's power over Christians is already broken and the great war is won through
Christ's crucifixion and resurrection, which forever conquered the power of sin and death
(Rom. 5:18–21; 1 Cor. 15:56, 57; Heb. 2:14). However, in life on earth, battles of temptation go
on regularly. The Lord's power, the strength of His Spirit, and the force of biblical truth are
required for victory (see 2 Cor. 10:3–5).

c. **Put on the whole armor of God.** "Put on" conveys the idea of permanence, indicating
that armor should be the Christian's sustained, life-long attire. Paul uses the common armor
worn by Roman soldiers as the analogy for the believer's spiritual defense and affirms its
necessity if one is to hold his position while under attack.

d. **wiles.** This is the Gr. word for "schemes," carrying the idea of cleverness, crafty
methods, cunning, and deception. Satan's schemes are propagated through the evil world
system over which he rules, and are carried out by his demon hosts. "Wiles" is all-inclusive,
encompassing every sin, immoral practice, false theology, false religion, and worldly entice-
ment. See 2 Cor. 2:11.

e. **the devil.** Scripture refers to him as "the anointed cherub" (Ezek. 28:14), "the ruler of
the demons" (Luke 11:15), "the god of this world" (2 Cor. 4:4), and "the prince of the power of
the air" (2:2). Scripture depicts him opposing God's work (Zech. 3:1), perverting God's Word
(Matt. 4:6), hindering God's servant (1 Thess. 2:18), hindering the gospel (2 Cor. 4:4), snaring
the righteous (1 Tim. 3:7), and holding the world in his power (1 John 5:19).

f. **wrestle.** A term used of hand-to-hand combat. Wrestling features trickery and deception, like Satan and his hosts when they attack. Coping with deceptive temptation requires
truth and righteousness. The 4 designations describe the different strata and rankings of those
demons and the evil supernatural empire in which they operate. Satan's forces of darkness
are highly structured for the most destructive purposes. Cf. Col. 2:15; 1 Pet. 3:22.

g. **spiritual hosts of wickedness.** This possibly refers to the most depraved abomina-
tions, including such things as extreme sexual perversions, occultism, and Satan worship. See
Col. 1:16.

h. **in the heavenly places.** As in 1:3; 3:10, this refers to the entire realm of spiritual beings.

i. **Therefore take up the whole armor of God.** Paul again emphasized the necessity of
the Christian's appropriating God's full spiritual armor by obedience in taking it up, or putting
it on (Eph. 6:11). The first 3 pieces of armor (girdle, breastplate, and shoes/boots, vv. 14, 15)

up the whole armor of God, that you may be able to withstand in the [a]evil day, and [b]having done all, to stand.

[c]Stand therefore, having [d]girded your waist with truth, having put on [e]the breastplate of righteousness, and having [f]shod your feet with the preparation of the gospel of peace; above all, taking [g]the shield of faith with which you will be able to quench all the [h]fiery darts of the wicked one. And take [i]the

---

were worn continually on the battlefield; the last 3 (shield, helmet, and sword, vv. 16, 17) were kept ready for use when actual fighting began.

a. **evil day.** Since the fall of man, every day has been evil, a condition that will persist until the Lord returns and establishes His own righteous kingdom on earth.

b. **having done all, to stand.** Standing firm against the enemy without wavering or falling is the goal. See James 4:17; 1 Pet. 5:8, 9.

c. **Stand therefore.** For the third time (see Eph. 6:11, 13), the apostle calls Christians to take a firm position in the spiritual battle against Satan and his minions. Whether confronting Satan's efforts to distrust God, forsaking obedience, producing doctrinal confusion and falsehood, hindering service to God, bring division, serving God in the flesh, living hypocritically, being worldly, or in any other way reject biblical obedience, this armor is our defense.

d. **girded . . . with truth.** The soldier wore a tunic of loose-fitting cloth. Since ancient combat was largely hand-to-hand, a loose tunic was a potential hindrance and danger. A belt was necessary to cinch up the loosely hanging material. Cf. Ex. 12:11; Luke 12:35; 1 Pet. 1:13. Girding up was a matter of pulling in the loose ends as preparation for battle. The belt that pulls all the spiritual loose ends in is "truth" or better, "truthfulness." The idea is of sincere commitment to fight and win without hypocrisy—self-discipline in devotion to victory. Everything that hinders is tucked away. Cf. 2 Tim. 2:4; Heb. 12:1.

e. **the breastplate of righteousness.** The breastplate was usually a tough, sleeveless piece of leather or heavy material with animal horn or hoof pieces sewn on, covering the soldier's full torso, protecting his heart and other vital organs. Because righteousness, or holiness, is such a distinctive characteristic of God Himself, it is not hard to understand why that is the Christian's chief protection against Satan and his schemes. As believers faithfully live in obedience to and communion with Jesus Christ, His own righteousness produces in them the practical, daily righteousness that becomes their spiritual breastplate. Lack of holiness, on the other hand, leaves them vulnerable to the great enemy of their souls (cf. Is. 59:17; 2 Cor. 7:1; 1 Thess. 5:8).

f. **shod . . . with . . . the gospel of peace.** Roman soldiers wore boots with nails in them to grip the ground in combat. The gospel of peace pertains to the good news that, through Christ, believers are at peace with God and He is on their side (Rom. 5:6–10). It is that confidence of divine support which allows the believer to stand firm, knowing that since he is at peace with God, and God is his strength (see Rom. 8:31, 37–39).

g. **the shield of faith.** This Gr. word usually refers to the large shield (2.5 × 4.5 ft.) that protected the entire body. The faith to which Paul refers is not the body of Christian doctrine (as the term is used in 4:13) but basic trust in God. The believer's continual trust in God's word and promise is "above all" absolutely necessary to protect him from temptations to every sort of sin. All sin comes when the victim falls to Satan's lies and promises of pleasure, rejecting the better choice of obedience and blessing.

h. **fiery darts.** Temptations are likened to the flaming arrows shot by the enemy and quenched by the oil-treated leather shield (cf. Ps. 18:30; Prov. 30:5, 6; 1 John 5:4).

i. **the helmet of salvation.** The helmet protected the head, always a major target in battle. Paul is speaking to those who are already saved, and is therefore not speaking here about attaining salvation. Rather, Satan seeks to destroy a believer's assurance of salvation with his weapons of doubt and discouragement. This is clear from Paul's reference to "the helmet of the hope of salvation" (Is. 59:17; see 1 Thess. 5:8). But although a Christian's feelings

helmet of salvation, and ªthe sword of the Spirit, which is the word of God; ᵇpraying always with all prayer and supplication in the Spirit, being watchful to this end with all perseverance and supplication for all the saints—and for me, that utterance may be given to me, that I may open my mouth boldly to make known the mystery of the gospel, for which I am an ambassador in chains; that in it I may speak boldly, as I ought to speak.

200. FINAL BENEDICTION

Eph. 6:21–24

But that you also may know my affairs and how I am doing, ᶜTychicus, a beloved brother and faithful minister in the Lord, will make all things known to you; whom I have sent to you for this very purpose, that you may know our affairs, and that he may comfort your hearts.

ᵈPeace to the brethren, and love with faith, from God the Father and the Lord Jesus Christ. Grace be with all those who love our Lord Jesus Christ in sincerity. Amen.

---

about his salvation may be seriously damaged by Satan-inspired doubt, his salvation itself is eternally protected and he need not fear its loss. Satan wants to curse the believer with doubts, but the Christian can be strong in God's promises of eternal salvation in Scripture (see John 6:37–39; 10:28, 29; Rom. 5:10; 8:31–39; Phil. 1:6; 1 Pet. 1:3–5). Security is a fact; assurance is a feeling that comes to the obedient Christian (1 Pet. 1:3–10).

a. **the sword of the Spirit.** As the sword was the soldier's only weapon, so God's Word is the only needed weapon, infinitely more powerful than any of Satan's. The Gr. term refers to a small weapon (6–18 in. long). It was used both defensively to fend off Satan's attacks, and offensively to help destroy the enemy's strategies. It is the truth of Scripture. See 2 Cor. 10:3–5; Heb. 4:12.

b. **praying always.** This verse introduces the general character of a believer's prayer life: 1) "all prayer and supplication" focuses on the variety; 2) "always" focuses on the frequency (cf. Rom. 12:12; Phil. 4:6; 1 Thess. 5:17); 3) "in the Spirit" focuses on submission, as we line up with the will of God (cf. Rom. 8:26, 27); 4) "being watchful" focuses on the manner (cf. Matt. 26:41; Mark 13:33); 5) "all perseverance" focuses on the persistence (cf. Luke 11:9; 18:7, 8); and 6) "all saints" focuses on the objects (cf. 1 Sam. 12:23). Paul does not ask for prayer for his personal well-being or physical comfort in the imprisonment from which he wrote, but for boldness and faithfulness to continue proclaiming the gospel to the unsaved no matter what the cost.

c. **Tychicus.** A convert from Asia Minor (modern Turkey) who was with the apostle during his first imprisonment in Rome, from where this epistle was written (see Eph. 3:1). He accompanied Paul in taking an offering to the church in Jerusalem (Acts 20:4–6) and was sent by him on several missions (2 Tim. 4:12; Titus 3:12).

d. **Peace.** This beautiful benediction sums up the major themes of this very personal letter, reminding readers of the peace (Eph. 6:15; 1:2; 2:14, 15, 17; 4:3), love (Eph. 1:15; 4:2, 15, 16; 5:25, 28, 33), and faith (Eph. 6:16; 1:15; 2:8; 3:12, 17; 4:5, 13) from God and Jesus Christ.

201. PAUL WRITES A LETTER TO THE COLOSSIAN CHURCH
Introduction to Colossians

Colossians is named for the city of Colosse, where the church it was addressed to was located. It was also to be read in the neighboring church at Laodicea (Col. 4:16).

Author and Date

Paul is identified as author at the beginning (Col. 1:1; cf. v. 23; 4:18), as customarily in his epistles. The testimony of the early church, including such key figures as Irenaeus, Clement of Alexandria, Tertullian, Origen, and Eusebius, confirms that the opening claim is genuine. Additional evidence for Paul's authorship comes from the book's close parallels with Philemon, which is universally accepted as having been written by Paul. Both were written (ca. A.D. 60–62) while Paul was a prisoner in Rome (Col. 4:3, 10, 18; Philem. 9, 10, 13, 23); plus the names of the same people (e.g., Timothy, Aristarchus, Archippus, Mark, Epaphras, Luke, Onesimus, and Demas) appear in both epistles, showing that both were written by the same author at about the same time.

Background and Setting

Colosse was a city in Phrygia, in the Roman province of Asia (part of modern Turkey), about 100 mi. E of Ephesus in the region of the 7 churches of Rev. 1–3. The city lay alongside the Lycus River, not far from where it flowed into the Maender River. The Lycus Valley narrowed at Colosse to a width of about two mi., and Mt. Cadmus rose 8,000 feet above the city.

Colosse was a thriving city in the fifth century B.C. when the Persian king Xerxes (Ahasuerus, cf. Esth. 1:1) marched through the region. Black wool and dyes (made from the nearby chalk deposits) were important products. In addition, the city was situated at the junction of the main north-south and east-west trade routes. By Paul's day, however, the main road had been rerouted through nearby Laodicea, thus bypassing Colosse and leading to its decline and the rise of the neighboring cities of Laodicea and Hierapolis.

Although Colosse's population was mainly Gentile, there was a large

Jewish settlement dating from the days of Antiochus the Great (223–187 B.C.). Colosse's mixed population of Jews and Gentiles manifested itself both in the composition of the church and in the heresy that plagued it, which contained elements of both Jewish legalism and pagan mysticism.

The church at Colosse began during Paul's three-year ministry at Ephesus (Acts 19). Its founder was not Paul, who had never been there (Col. 2:1); but Epaphras (1:5–7), who apparently was saved during a visit to Ephesus, then likely started the church in Colosse when he returned home. Several years after the Colossian church was founded, a dangerous heresy arose to threaten it— one not identified with any particular historical system. It contained elements of what later became known as Gnosticism: that God is good, but matter is evil, that Jesus Christ was merely one of a series of emanations descending from God and being less than God (a belief that led them to deny His true humanity), and that a secret, higher knowledge above Scripture was necessary for enlightenment and salvation. The Colossian heresy also embraced aspects of Jewish legalism, e.g., the necessity of circumcision for salvation, observance of the ceremonial rituals of the OT law (dietary laws, festivals, Sabbaths), and rigid asceticism. It also called for the worship of angels and mystical experience. Epaphras was so concerned about this heresy that he made the long journey from Colosse to Rome (4:12, 13), where Paul was a prisoner.

This letter was written from prison in Rome (Acts 28:16–31) sometime between A.D. 60–62 and is, therefore, referred to as a Prison Epistle (along with Ephesians, Philippians, and Philemon). It may have been composed almost contemporaneously with Ephesians and initially sent with that epistle and Philemon by Tychicus (Eph. 6:21, 22; Col. 4:7, 8). See Introduction to Philippians: Author and Date for a discussion of the city from which Paul wrote. He wrote this letter to warn the Colossians against the heresy they faced, and sent the letter to them with Tychicus, who was accompanying the runaway slave Onesimus back to his master, Philemon, a member of the Colossian church (Col. 4:7–9; see Introduction to Philemon: Background and Setting). Epaphras remained behind in Rome (cf. Philem. 23), perhaps to receive further instruction from Paul.

Historical and Theological Themes

Colossians contains teaching on several key areas of theology, including the deity of Christ (1:15–20; 2:2–10), reconciliation (1:20–23), redemption

(1:13, 14; 2:13, 14; 3:9–11), election (3:12), forgiveness (3:13), and the nature of the church (1:18, 24, 25; 2:19; 3:11, 15). Also, as noted above, it refutes the heretical teaching that threatened the Colossian church (chap. 2).

Interpretive Challenges

Those cults that deny Christ's deity have seized upon the description of Him as "the firstborn over all creation" (1:15) as proof that He was a created being. Paul's statement that believers will be "holy, and blameless, and above reproach" if they "continue in the faith" (1:22, 23) has led some to teach that believers can lose their salvation. Some have argued for the existence of purgatory based on Paul's statement, "I . . . fill up in my flesh what is lacking in the afflictions of Christ" (1:24), while others see support for baptismal regeneration (2:12). The identity of the "epistle from Laodicea" (4:16) has also prompted much discussion. These issues will be treated in the notes.

202. PRAYERFUL GRATITUDE

Col. 1:1–14

Paul, an apostle of Jesus Christ by the will of God, and ªTimothy our brother,

To the saints and faithful brethren in Christ who are in ᵇColosse:

ᶜGrace to you and peace from God our Father and the Lord Jesus Christ.

We give thanks to the ᵈGod and Father of our Lord Jesus Christ, praying always for you, since we heard of your ᵉfaith in Christ Jesus and of your ᶠlove for all the saints; because of ᵍthe hope which is laid up for you in heaven, of

---

a. **Timothy.** Paul's co-laborer and true child in the faith (see Acts 16:1) was able to be with him because, although Paul was a prisoner, he had personal living quarters (Acts 28:16–31).

b. **Colosse.** One of 3 cities in the Lycus River valley in the region of Phyrgia, in the Roman province of Asia (part of modern Turkey), about 100 mi. E of Ephesus.

c. **Grace . . . and peace.** Paul's greeting in all 13 of his epistles (see Rom. 1:7).

d. **God and Father of our Lord Jesus Christ.** This designation was often used to show that Jesus was one in nature with God, as any true son is with his father. It was an affirmation of Christ's deity (cf. Rom. 15:6; 2 Cor. 1:3; 11:13; Eph. 1:3; 3:14; 1 Pet. 1:3).

e. **faith in Christ Jesus.** For discussion of saving faith see Rom. 1:16; 10:4–17; James 2:14–26.

f. **love for all the saints.** Cf. Col. 1:8. One of the visible fruits of true saving faith is love for fellow believers (John 13:34, 35; Gal. 5:22; 1 John 2:10; 3:14–16).

g. **the hope which is laid up.** The believer's hope is inseparable from his faith. See Rom. 5:2; 1 Pet. 1:3–5.

which you heard before in the word of the truth of [a]the gospel, which has come to you, as it has also [b]in all the world, and is bringing forth [c]fruit, as it is also among you since the day you heard and knew the grace of God in truth; as you also learned from [d]Epaphras, our dear fellow servant, who is a faithful minister of Christ on your behalf, who also declared to us your love in the Spirit.

For this reason we also, since the day we heard it, do not cease to pray for you, and to ask that you may be filled with [e]the knowledge of His will in all [f]wisdom and spiritual understanding; that you may [g]walk worthy of the Lord, fully pleasing Him, [h]being fruitful in every good work and [i]increasing in the knowledge of God; strengthened with all might, according to His glorious power, for all [j]patience and longsuffering with joy; giving thanks to the Father who has [k]qualified us to be partakers of the [l]inheritance of the saints

---

a. **the gospel.** See Rom. 1:1. The Gr. word lit. means "good news," and was used in classical Greek to express the good news of victory in a battle. The gospel is the good news of Christ's victory over Satan, sin, and death.

b. **in all the world.** Cf. Col. 1;23, "every creature under heaven." The gospel was never intended for an exclusive group of people; it is good news for the whole world (Matt. 24:14; 28:19, 20; Mark 16:15; Rom. 1:8, 14, 16; 1 Thess. 1:8). It transcends all ethnic, geographic, cultural, and political boundaries.

c. **fruit.** Refers to the saving effect of gospel preaching and to the growth of the church. See Rom. 1:13; Phil. 1:22; cf. Matt. 13:3–8, 31, 32.

d. **Epaphras.** The likely founder of the church at Colosse.

e. **the knowledge of His will.** The Gr. word for "knowledge" is the usual one, with an added preposition that intensifies its meaning. This is not an inner impression or feeling, but a deep and thorough knowledge of the will of God that is finally and completely revealed in the Word of God (Col. 3:16; Eph. 5:17; 1 Thess. 4:3; 5:18; 1 Tim. 2:4; 1 Pet. 2:13, 15; 4:19).

f. **wisdom and spiritual understanding.** "Spiritual" modifies both "wisdom" (the ability to accumulate and organize principles from Scripture) and "understanding" (the application of those principles to daily living).

g. **walk worthy.** This is a key NT concept which calls the believer to live in a way that is consistent with his identification with the Lord who saved Him. See Eph. 4:1; Phil. 1:27.

h. **being fruitful in every good work.** See Rom. 1:13; Phil. 4:17. Spiritual fruit is the by-product of a righteous life. The Bible identifies spiritual fruit as leading people to Christ (1 Cor. 16:15), praising God (Heb. 13:15), giving money (Rom. 15:26–28), living a godly life (Heb. 12:11), and displaying holy attitudes (Gal. 5:22, 23).

i. **increasing in the knowledge of God.** Spiritual growth cannot occur apart from this knowledge (1 Pet. 2:2; 2 Pet. 3:18). The evidences of spiritual growth include a deeper love for God's Word (Ps. 119:97), a more perfect obedience (1 John 2:3–5), a strong doctrinal foundation (1 John 2:12–14), an expanding faith (2 Thess. 1:3; cf. 2 Cor. 10:5), and a greater love for others (Phil. 1:9).

j. **patience and longsuffering.** These terms are closely related and refer to the attitude one has during trials. "Patience" looks more at enduring difficult circumstances while "longsuffering" looks at enduring difficult people.

k. **qualified us.** The Gr. word means "to make sufficient," "to empower," or "to authorize." God qualifies us only through the finished work of the Savior. Apart from God's grace through Jesus Christ, all people would be qualified only to receive His wrath.

l. **inheritance.** Lit. "for the portion of the lot." Each believer will receive his own individual portion of the total divine inheritance (see Rom. 8:17), an allusion to the partitioning of Israel's inheritance in Canaan (cf. Num. 26:52–56; 33:51–54; Josh. 14:1, 2). See 1 Pet. 1:3–5.

[a]in the light. He has [b]delivered us from the power of darkness and conveyed us into the [c]kingdom of [d]the Son of His love, in whom we have [e]redemption [f]through His blood, [g]the forgiveness of sins.

203. The Deity of Christ

Col. 1:15–23

[h]He is the [i]image of the invisible God, [j]the firstborn over all creation. For by Him all things were created that are in heaven and that are on earth, visible

---

a. **in the light.** Scripture represents "light" intellectually as divine truth (Ps. 119:130) and morally as divine purity (Eph. 5:8–14; 1 John 1:5). The saints' inheritance exists in the spiritual realm of truth and purity where God Himself dwells (1 Tim. 6:16). Light, then, is a synonym for God's kingdom. Cf. John 8:12; 2 Cor. 4:6; Rev. 21:23; 22:5.

b. **delivered us.** The Gr. term means "to draw to oneself" or "to rescue," and refers to the believer's spiritual liberation by God from Satan's kingdom, which, in contrast to the realm of light with truth and purity, is the realm of darkness (cf. Luke 22:53) with only deception and wickedness (1 John 2:9, 11). See Acts 26:18.

c. **kingdom.** In its basic sense, a group of people ruled by a king. More than just the future, earthly millennial kingdom, this everlasting kingdom (2 Pet. 1:11) speaks of the realm of salvation in which all believers live in current and eternal spiritual relationship with God under the care and authority of Jesus Christ (see Matt. 3:2).

d. **the Son of His love.** Cf. Matt. 3:17; 12:18; 17:5; Mark 1:11; 9:7; Luke 3:22; 9:35; Eph. 1:6; 2 Pet. 1:17; see John 17:23–26. The Father gave this kingdom to the Son He loves, as an expression of eternal love. That means that every person the Father calls and justifies is a love gift from Him to the Son. See John 6:37, 44.

e. **redemption.** The Gr. word means "to deliver by payment of a ransom," and was used of freeing slaves from bondage. Here it refers to Christ freeing believing sinners from slavery to sin (cf. Eph. 1:7; 1 Cor. 1:30; see Rom. 3:24).

f. **through His blood.** Cf. Col. 1:20. A reference, not limited to the fluid as if the blood had saving properties in its chemistry, but an expression pointing to the totality of Christ's atoning work as a sacrifice for sin. This is a frequently used metonym in the NT (see Eph. 1:7; 2:13; Heb. 9:14; 1 Pet. 1:19). The word "cross" is used similarly to refer to the whole atoning work (see 1 Cor. 1:18; Gal. 6:12, 14; Eph. 2:16). See Rom. 5:9.

g. **the forgiveness of sins.** The Gr. word is a composite of two words that mean "to pardon" or "grant remission of a penalty." Cf. Ps. 103:12; Mic. 7:19; Eph. 1:7; see 2 Cor. 5:19–21.

h. One component in the heresy threatening the Colossian church was the denial of the deity of Christ. Paul combats that damning element of heresy with an emphatic defense of Christ's deity.

i. **image of the invisible God.** See Heb. 1:3. The Gr. word for "image" is eikōn, from which the Eng. word "icon" derives. It means, "copy" or "likeness." Jesus Christ is the perfect image—the exact likeness—of God and is in the very form of God (Phil. 2:6; cf. John 1:14; 14:9), and has been so from all eternity. By describing Jesus in this manner, Paul emphasizes that He is both the representation and manifestation of God. Thus, He is fully God in every way (cf. Col. 2:9; John 8:58; 10:30–33; Heb. 1:8).

j. **the firstborn over all creation.** Cf. Col. 1:18. The Gr. word for "firstborn" can refer to one who was born first chronologically, but most often refers to pre-eminence in position, or rank (see Heb. 1:6; cf. Rom. 8:29). In both Greek and Jewish culture, the firstborn was the ranking son who had received the right of inheritance from his father, whether he was born first

and invisible, whether ªthrones or dominions or principalities or powers. ᵇAll things were created through Him and for Him. And ᶜHe is before all things, and in Him all things ᵈconsist. And He is the ᵉhead of the body, the church, who is ᶠthe beginning, ᵍthe firstborn from the dead, that in all things He may have the preeminence.

For it pleased the Father that in Him ʰall the fullness should dwell, and by Him to ⁱreconcile all things to Himself, by Him, whether things on earth

or not. It is used of Israel who, not being the first nation, was however the preeminent nation (cf. Ex. 4:22; Jer. 31:9). Firstborn in this context clearly means highest in rank, not first created (cf. Ps. 89:27; Rev. 1:5) for several reasons: 1) Christ cannot be both "first begotten" and "only begotten" (cf. John 1:14, 18; 3:16, 18; 1 John 4:9); 2) when the "firstborn" is one of a class, the class is in the plural form (cf. Col. 1:18; Rom. 8:29), but "creation," the class here, is in a singular form; 3) if Paul was teaching that Christ was a created being, he was agreeing with the heresy he was writing to refute; and 4) it is impossible for Christ to be both created, and the Creator of everything (Col. 1:16). Thus Jesus is the firstborn in the sense that He has the preeminence (v. 18) and possesses the right of inheritance "over all creation" (cf. Heb. 1:2; Rev. 5:1–7, 13). He existed before the creation and is exalted in rank above it. See Ps. 2:7; Rom. 8:29.

a. **thrones or dominions or principalities or powers.** Cf. Col. 2:15; Rom. 8:38; Eph. 1:21; 3:10; 6:12; 1 Pet. 3:22; Jude 6. These are various categories of angels whom Christ created and rules over. There is no comment regarding whether they are holy or fallen, since He is Lord of both groups. The false teachers had incorporated into their heresy the worship of angels (see Col. 2:18), including the lie that Jesus was one of them, merely a spirit created by God and inferior to Him. Paul rejected that and made it clear that angels, whatever their rank, whether holy or fallen, are mere creatures, and their Creator is none other than the preeminent One, the Lord Savior, Jesus Christ. The purpose of His catalog of angelic ranks is to show the immeasurable superiority of Christ over any being the false teachers might suggest.

b. **All things were created through Him and for Him.** Cf. Rom. 11:33–36. See John 1:3; Heb. 1:2. As God, Jesus created the material and spiritual universe for His pleasure and glory.

c. **He is before all things.** When the universe had its beginning, Christ already existed, thus by definition He must be eternal (Mic. 5:2; John 1:1, 2; 8:58; 1 John 1:1; Rev. 22:13).

d. **consist.** Lit. "to hold together." Christ sustains the universe, maintaining the power and balance necessary to life's existence and continuity (cf. Heb. 1:3).

e. **head of the body.** Cf. Col. 2:19. Paul uses the human body as a metaphor for the church, of which Christ serves as the "head." Just as a body is controlled from the brain, so Christ controls every part of the church and gives it life and direction. Cf. Eph. 4:15; 5:23. For a detailed discussion of the church as a body, see 1 Cor. 12:4–27.

f. **the beginning.** This refers to both source and preeminence. The church had its origins in the Lord Jesus (Eph. 1:4), and He gave life to the church through His sacrificial death and resurrection to become its Sovereign.

g. **the firstborn from the dead.** Jesus was the first chronologically to be resurrected, never to die again. Of all who have been or ever will be raised from the dead, and that includes all men (John 5:28, 29), Christ is supreme (see Col. 1:15; Phil. 2:8–11).

h. **all the fullness.** A term likely used by those in the Colossian heresy to refer to divine powers and attributes they believed were divided among various emanations. Paul countered that by asserting that the fullness of deity—all the divine powers and attributes—was not spread out among created beings, but completely dwelt in Christ alone (cf. Col. 2:9).

i. **reconcile all things to Himself.** The Gr. word for "reconcile" means "to change" or "exchange." Its NT usage refers to a change in the sinner's relationship to God. See Rom. 5:10; 2 Cor. 5:18–21. Man is reconciled to God when God restores man to a right relationship with Him through Jesus Christ. An intensified form for "reconcile" is used in this verse to refer to the total and complete reconciliation of believers and ultimately "all things" in the created universe (cf. Rom. 8:21; 2 Pet. 3:10–13; Rev. 21:1). This text does not teach that, as a result, all will believe; rather it teaches that all will ultimately submit (cf. Phil. 2:9–11).

or things in heaven, ᵃhaving made peace through the blood of His cross.

And you, who once were ᵇalienated and enemies in your mind by wicked works, yet now He has ᶜreconciled in the body of His flesh through death, to present you ᵈholy, and blameless, and above reproach in His sight—if indeed you ᵉcontinue in the faith, grounded and steadfast, and are not moved away from the hope of the gospel which you heard, which was ᶠpreached to every creature under heaven, of which I, Paul, became a minister.

204. THE MINISTRY OF THE GOSPEL
Col. 1:24—2:7

ᵍI now rejoice in my sufferings for you, and ʰfill up in my flesh what is lacking in the afflictions of Christ, for ⁱthe sake of His body, which is the church, of

---

a. **having made peace.** See Rom. 5:1. God and those He saved are no longer at enmity with each other.

b. **alienated . . . enemies.** The Gr. term for "alienated" means "estranged," "cut off," or "separated." Before they were reconciled, all people were completely estranged from God (cf. Eph. 2:12, 13). The Gr. word for "enemies" can also be translated "hateful." Unbelievers hate God and resent His holy standard because they love "wicked works" (cf. John 3:19, 20; 15:18, 24, 25). Actually, there is alienation from both sides, since God "hates all workers of iniquity" (Ps. 5:5).

c. **reconciled . . . through death.** Christ's substitutionary death on the cross that paid the full penalty for the sin of all who believe made reconciliation possible and actual. See 2 Cor. 5:18–21; cf. Rom. 3:25; 5:9, 10; 8:3.

d. **holy . . . in His sight.** "Holy" refers to the believer's positional relationship to God—he is separated from sin and set apart to God by imputed righteousness. This is justification (see Rom. 3:24–26; Phil. 3:8, 9). As a result of the believer's union with Christ in His death and resurrection, God considers Christians as holy as His Son (Eph. 1:4; 2 Cor. 5:21). Christians are also "blameless" (without blemish) and "above reproach" (no one can bring a charge against them; Rom. 8:33; cf. Phil. 2:15). We are to be presented to Christ, when we meet Him, as a chaste bride (Eph. 5:25–27; 2 Cor. 11:2).

e. **continue in the faith.** Cf. Acts 11:23; 14:22. Those who have been reconciled will persevere in faith and obedience because, in addition to being declared righteous, they are actually made new creatures (2 Cor. 5:17) with a new disposition that loves God, hates sin, desires obedience, and is energized by the indwelling Holy Spirit (cf. John 8:30–32; 1 John 2:19). Rather than defect from the gospel they heard, true believers will remain solid on Christ who is the only foundation (1 Cor. 3:11), and faithful by the enabling grace of God (Phil. 1:6; 2:11–13). For discussion on perseverance of the saints, see Matt. 24:13.

f. **preached to every creature.** Cf. Mark 16:15. The gospel has no racial boundaries. Having reached Rome, where Paul was when he wrote Colossians, it had reached the center of the known world.

g. **my sufferings.** Paul's present imprisonment (Acts 28:16, 30).

h. **fill up . . . what is lacking.** Paul was experiencing the persecution intended for Christ. In spite of His death on the cross, Christ's enemies had not gotten their fill of inflicting injury on Him. So they turned their hatred on those who preached the gospel (cf. John 15:18, 24; 16:1–3). It was in that sense that Paul filled up what was lacking in Christ's afflictions (see 2 Cor. 1:5; Gal. 6:17).

i. **the sake of His body.** Paul's motivation for enduring suffering was to benefit and

which I became a minister according to the ᵃstewardship from God which was given to me for you, ᵇto fulfill the word of God, the mystery which has been hidden from ages and from generations, but now has been revealed to His saints. To them God willed to make known what are the riches of the glory of this ᶜmystery among the ᵈGentiles: which is Christ in you, ᵉthe hope of glory. Him we preach, warning every man and teaching every man in all wisdom, that we may present every man ᶠperfect in Christ Jesus. To this end ᵍI also labor, striving according to His working which works in me mightily.

For I want you to know what a ʰgreat conflict I have for you and those

---

build Christ's church. Cf. Phil. 1:13, 29, 30; see 2 Cor. 4:8–15; 6:4–10; 11:23–28; 12:9, 10.

a. **stewardship.** Cf. 1 Cor. 4:1, 2; 9:17. A steward was a slave who managed his master's household, supervising the other servants, dispensing resources, and handling business and financial affairs. Paul viewed his ministry as a stewardship from the Lord. The church is God's household (1 Tim. 3:15), and Paul was given the task of caring for, feeding, and leading the churches, for which he was accountable to God (cf. Heb. 13:17). All believers are responsible for managing the abilities and resources God gives them (see 1 Pet. 4:10).

b. **to fulfill the word of God.** This refers to Paul's single-minded devotion to completely fulfill the ministry God gave him to preach the whole counsel of God to those to whom God sent him (Acts 20:27; 2 Tim. 4:7).

c. **mystery.** Cf. Col. 2:2; 4:3. See Matt. 13:11; 1 Cor. 2:7; Eph. 3:4, 5. This refers to truth, hidden until now, but revealed for the first time to the saints in the NT. Such truth includes the mystery of the incarnate God (2:2, 3, 9), Israel's unbelief (Rom. 11:25), lawlessness (2 Thess. 2:7), the unity of Jew and Gentile made one in the church (Eph. 3:3–6), and the rapture of the church (1 Cor. 15:51). In this passage, the mystery is specifically identified in v. 27.

d. **Gentiles . . . Christ in you.** The OT predicted the coming of the Messiah and that the Gentiles would partake of salvation (cf. Is. 42:6; 45:21, 22; 49:6; 52:10; 60:1–3; Pss. 22:27; 65:5; 98:2, 3), but it did not reveal that the Messiah would actually live in each member of His redeemed church, made up mostly of Gentiles. That believers, both Jew and Gentile, now possess the surpassing riches of the indwelling Christ is the glorious revealed mystery (John 14:23; Rom. 8:9, 10; Gal. 2:20; Eph. 1:7, 17, 18; 3:8–10, 16–19).

e. **the hope of glory.** The indwelling Spirit of Christ is the guarantee to each believer of future glory (Rom. 8:11; Eph. 1:13, 14; 1 Pet. 1:3, 4).

f. **perfect.** To be complete or mature—to be like Christ. See Rom. 8:29; 1 Cor. 11:1; Phil. 3:12–14, 19, 20; 1 John 2:6; 3:2. This spiritual maturity is defined in Col. 2:2.

g. **I . . . labor, striving according to His working.** Here is the balance of Christian living. Paul gave the effort to serve and honor God with all his might. "Labor" refers to working to the point of exhaustion. The Gr. word for "striving" gives us the Eng. word "agonize" and refers to the effort required to compete in an athletic event. At the same time, he knew the effective "striving" or work, with spiritual and eternal results was being done by God through him (see Phil. 2:11–13; cf. 1 Cor. 15:10, 58).

h. **great conflict.** The word means "striving" and comes from the same root as in Col. 1:29. Both the Colossians and Laodiceans were among those for whom Paul struggled so hard in order to bring them to maturity.

in ᵃLaodicea, and for as many as have not seen my face in the flesh, that their hearts may be encouraged, being knit together in love, and attaining to all riches of the ᵇfull assurance of understanding, to the knowledge of the mystery ᶜof God, both of the Father and of Christ, in whom are hidden ᵈall the treasures of wisdom and knowledge.

Now this I say ᵉlest anyone should deceive you with persuasive words. For though I am ᶠabsent in the flesh, yet I am with you in spirit, rejoicing to see your good order and the steadfastness of your faith in Christ.

As you therefore have received Christ Jesus the Lord, so ᵍwalk in Him, rooted and built up in Him and established in ʰthe faith, as you have been taught, abounding in it with thanksgiving.

---

a. **Laodicea.** The chief city of Phrygia in the Roman province of Asia, located just S of Hierapolis in the Lycus River valley (see Rev. 3:14; cf. 4:13).

b. **full assurance of understanding.** "Understanding" of the fullness of the gospel, along with inner encouragement and shared love, mark mature believers who, thereby, enjoy the "assurance" of salvation (see 2 Pet. 1:5–8). **mystery.** See Col. 1:26.

c. **of God . . . Christ.** Cf. 4:3. Leaving out the phrase between "God" and "Christ." which was probably not in the original text, changes nothing. The point is that the mystery Paul referred to here is that the Messiah Christ is God incarnate Himself (cf. 1 Tim. 3:16).

d. **all the treasures.** Cf. Col. 2:9, 10; 1:19. The false teachers threatening the Colossians claimed to possess a secret wisdom and transcendent knowledge available only to the spiritual elite. In sharp contrast, Paul declared that all the richness of truth necessary for either salvation, sanctification, or glorification is found in Jesus Christ, who Himself is God revealed. Cf. John 1:14; Rom. 11:33–36; 1 Cor. 1:24, 30; 2:6–8; Eph. 1:8, 9; 3:8, 9.

e. **lest anyone should deceive you.** Paul did not want the Colossians to be deceived by the persuasive rhetoric of the false teachers which assaulted the person of Christ. That is why throughout Col. 1, 2 he stressed Christ's deity, and His sufficiency both to save believers and bring them to spiritual maturity.

f. **absent in the flesh . . . with you in spirit.** Because he was a prisoner, Paul was unable to be present with the Colossians. That did not mean, however, that his love and concern for them was any less (cf. 1 Cor. 5:3, 4; 1 Thess. 2:17). Their "good order" and "steadfast faith" (both military terms depicting a solid rank of soldiers drawn up for battle) brought great joy to the apostle's heart.

g. **walk in Him.** "Walk" is the familiar NT term denoting the believer's daily conduct (Col. 1:10; 4:5; Rom. 6:4; 8:1, 4; 13:13; 1 Cor. 7:17; 2 Cor. 5:7; 10:3; 12:18; Gal. 5:16, 25; 6:16; Eph. 2:10; 4:1, 17; 5:2, 8, 15; Phil. 3:16–18; 1 Thess. 2:12; 4:1, 12; 2 Thess. 3:11; 1 John 1:6, 7; 2:6; 2 John 6; 3 John 3, 4). To walk in Christ is to live a life patterned after His.

h. **the faith.** The sense here is objective, referring to the truth of Christian doctrine. Spiritual maturity develops upward from the foundation of biblical truth as taught and recorded by the apostles. Cf. Col. 3:16. This rooting, building, and establishing is in sound doctrine (cf. 1 Tim. 4:6; 2 Tim. 3:16, 17; Titus 2:1).

205. WARNINGS AGAINST WORLDLY PHILOSOPHY

Col. 2:8–15

[a]Beware lest anyone cheat you through [b]philosophy and empty deceit, according to the tradition of men, according to [c]the basic principles of the world, and not according to Christ. For in Him dwells all the [d]fullness of the Godhead [e]bodily; and you are [f]complete in Him, who is [g]the head of all principality and power.

In Him you were also circumcised with the [h]circumcision made without hands, by putting off the body of the sins of the flesh, by the circumcision of Christ, buried with Him in baptism, in which you also were raised with

---

a. **cheat you.** Here is the term for robbery. False teachers who are successful in getting people to believe lies, rob them of truth, salvation, and blessing.

b. **philosophy and empty deceit.** "Philosophy" (lit. "love of wisdom") appears only here in the NT. The word referred to more than merely the academic discipline, but described any theory about God, the world, or the meaning of life. Those embracing the Colossian heresy used it to describe the supposed higher knowledge they claimed to have attained. Paul, however, equates the false teachers' philosophy with "empty deceit"; that is, with worthless deception. Cf. 1 Tim. 6:20; see 2 Cor. 10:5.

c. **the basic principles of the world.** See Col. 2:20; Gal. 4:3. Far from being advanced, profound knowledge, the false teachers' beliefs were simplistic and immature like all the rest of the speculations, ideologies, philosophies, and psychologies the fallen satanic and human system invents.

d. **fullness of the Godhead.** Christ possesses the fullness of the divine nature and attributes (see Col. 1:19; John 1:14–16).

e. **bodily.** In Greek philosophical thought, matter was evil; spirit was good. Thus, it was unthinkable that God would ever take on a human body. Paul refutes that false teaching by stressing the reality of Christ's incarnation. Jesus was not only fully God, but fully human as well. See Phil. 2:5–11.

f. **complete in Him.** See Col. 2:3, 4; cf. John 1:16; Eph. 1:3. Believers are complete in Christ, both positionally by the imputed perfect righteousness of Christ (see Col. 1:22), and the complete sufficiency of all heavenly resources for spiritual maturity (see 2 Pet. 1:3, 4).

g. **the head of all principality and power.** Jesus Christ is the creator and ruler of the universe and all its spiritual beings (see 1:16), not a lesser being emanating from God as the Colossian errorists maintained.

h. **circumcision made without hands.** See circumcision in Gen. 17:11. Circumcision symbolized man's need for cleansing of the heart (cf. Deut. 10:16; 30:6; Jer. 4:4; 9:26; Acts 7:51; Rom. 2:29) and was the outward sign of that cleansing of sin that comes by faith in God (Rom. 4:11; Phil. 3:3). At salvation, believers undergo a spiritual "circumcision" "by putting off the body of the sins of the flesh" (cf. Rom. 6:6; 2 Cor. 5:17; Phil 3:3; Titus 3:5). This is the new birth, the new creation in conversion. The outward affirmation of the already accomplished inner transformation is now the believer's baptism by water (Acts 2:38).

Him through faith in the working of God, who raised Him from the dead. And you, being ᵃdead in your trespasses and the uncircumcision of your flesh, ᵇHe has made alive together with Him, having ᶜforgiven you all trespasses, having ᵈwiped out the handwriting of requirements that was against us, which was contrary to us. And He has taken it out of the way, having ᵉnailed it to the cross. ᶠHaving disarmed ᵍprincipalities and powers, He ʰmade a public spectacle of them, triumphing over them in it.

---

a. **dead in your trespasses.** See Eph. 2:1, 5. So bound in the sphere of sin, the world (Eph. 2:12), the flesh (Rom. 8:8), and the devil (1 John 5:19) as to be unable to respond to spiritual stimuli; totally devoid of spiritual life. Paul further defines this condition of the unsaved in 1 Cor. 2:14; Eph. 4:17–19; Titus 3:3.

b. **He has made alive together with Him.** See Eph. 2:1, 5. Only through union with Jesus Christ (Col. 2:10–12) can those hopelessly dead in their sins receive eternal life (cf. Eph. 2:5). Note that God takes the initiative and exerts the life-giving power to awaken and unite sinners with His Son; the spiritually dead have no ability to make themselves alive (cf. Rom. 4:17; 2 Cor. 1:9).

c. **forgiven you all trespasses.** Cf. Col. 1:14. God's free (Rom. 3:24) and complete (Rom. 5:20; Eph. 1:7) forgiveness of guilty sinners who put their faith in Jesus Christ is the most important reality in Scripture (cf. Pss. 32:1; 130:3, 4; Is. 1:18; 55:7; Mic. 7:18; Matt. 26:28; Acts 10:43; 13:38, 39; Titus 3:4–7; Heb. 8:12).

d. **wiped out the handwriting.** The Gr. work translated "handwriting" referred to the handwritten certificate of debt by which a debtor acknowledged his indebtedness. All people (Rom. 3:23) owe God an unpayable debt for violating His law (Gal. 3:10; James 2:10; cf. Matt. 18:23–27), and are thus under sentence of death (Rom. 6:23). Paul graphically compares God's forgiveness of believers' sins to wiping ink off a parchment. Through Christ's sacrificial death on the cross, God has totally erased our certificate of indebtedness and made our forgiveness complete.

e. **nailed it to the cross.** This is another metaphor for forgiveness. The list of the crimes of a crucified criminal were nailed to the cross with that criminal to declare the violations he was being punished for (as in the case of Jesus, as noted in Matt. 27:37). Believers' sins were all put to Christ's account, nailed to His cross as He paid the penalty in their place for them all, thus satisfying the just wrath of God against crimes requiring punishment in full.

f. **Having disarmed.** In yet another element of the cross work, Paul tells that the cross spelled the ultimate doom of Satan and his evil host of fallen angels (cf. Gen. 3:15; John 12:31; 16:11; Heb. 2:14).

g. **principalities and powers.** See 1:16. While His body was dead, His living, divine spirit actually went to the abode of demons and announced His triumph over sin, Satan, death, and hell. See 1 Pet. 3:18, 19.

h. **made a public spectacle . . . triumphing over them.** The picture is that of a victorious Roman general parading his defeated enemies through the streets of Rome (see 2 Cor. 2:14–16). Christ won the victory over the demon forces on the cross, where their efforts to halt God's redemptive plan were ultimately defeated. For more on that triumphant imagery, see 2 Cor. 2:14–16.

206. AVOID LEGALISM

Col. 2:16–23

So ^alet no one judge you in ^bfood or in drink, or regarding a ^cfestival or a ^dnew moon or ^esabbaths, which are a ^fshadow of things to come, but the substance is of Christ. Let no one ^gcheat you of your reward, taking delight in ^hfalse humility and ⁱworship of angels, intruding into those things ^jwhich he has not seen, vainly puffed up by his ^kfleshly mind, and not holding fast to the Head, from whom all the body, nourished and knit together by joints and ligaments, grows with the increase that is from God.

Therefore, if you ^ldied with Christ from the ^mbasic principles of the world,

---

a. **let no one . . .** Paul warns the Colossians against trading their freedom in Christ for a set of useless, man-made, legalistic rules (cf. Gal. 5:1). Legalism is powerless to save or to restrain sin.

b. **food . . . drink.** The false teachers sought to impose some sort of dietary regulations, probably based on those of the Mosaic law (cf. Lev. 11). Since they were under the New Covenant, the Colossians (like all Christians) were not obligated to observe the OT dietary restrictions (cf. Mark 7:14–19; Acts 10:9–15; Rom. 14:17; 1 Cor. 8:8; 1 Tim. 4:1–5; Heb. 9:9, 10).

c. **festival.** The annual religious celebrations of the Jewish calendar (e.g., Passover, Pentecost, or Tabernacles; cf. Lev. 23).

d. **new moon.** The monthly sacrifice offered on the first day of each month (Num. 10:10; 28:11–14; Ps. 81:3).

e. **sabbaths.** The weekly celebration of the seventh day, which pictured God's rest from creation. The NT clearly teaches that Christians are not required to keep it (see Acts 20:7; Rom. 14:5, 6).

f. **shadow . . . substance.** The ceremonial aspects of the OT law (dietary regulations, festivals, sacrifices) were mere shadows pointing to Christ. Since Christ, the reality has come, the shadows have no value. Cf. Heb. 8:5; 10:1.

g. **cheat you.** Paul warns the Colossians not to allow the false teachers to cheat them of their temporal blessings or eternal reward (cf. 2 John 8) by luring them into irrational mysticism.

h. **false humility.** Since the false teachers took great delight in it, their "humility" was actually pride, which God hates (Prov. 6:16, 17).

i. **worship of angels.** The beginning of a heresy that was to plague the region around Colosse for several centuries and far beyond—a practice the Bible clearly prohibits (Matt. 4:10; Rev. 19:10; 22:8, 9).

j. **which he has not seen.** Like virtually all cults and false religions, the Colossian false teachers based their teaching on visions and revelations they had supposedly received. Their claims were false, since Jesus Christ is God's final and complete (see Col. 2:3, 4) revelation to mankind (Heb. 1:1, 2).

k. **fleshly mind.** See Rom. 8:6. This describes the unregenerate and is further defined in Eph. 4:17–19.

l. **died with Christ.** Refers to the believer's union with Christ in His death and resurrection (see Rom. 6:1–11) by which he has been transformed to new life from all worldly folly. Cf. Col. 1:18; see Eph. 4:15, 16. There is no spiritual growth for the body (the church) apart from union with the Head, Christ (cf. John 15:4, 5; 2 Pet. 1:3).

m. **basic principles.** See Col. 2:8. These are the same as "the commandments and doctrines of men."

why, as though living in the world, do you subject yourselves to ᵃregulations—"Do not touch, do not taste, do not handle," which all concern things which perish with the using—according to the commandments and doctrines of men? These things indeed have an appearance of wisdom in self-imposed religion, false humility, and neglect of the body, but are of no value against the indulgence of the flesh.

207. PUT OFF WICKEDNESS

Col. 3:1–11

ᵇIf then ᶜyou were raised with Christ, seek those things which are above, where Christ is, ᵈsitting at the right hand of God. ᵉSet your mind on things above, not on things on the earth. For ᶠyou died, and your life is ᵍhidden with Christ

---

a. **regulations . . .** These verses point out the futility of asceticism, which is the attempt to achieve holiness by rigorous self-neglect (Col. 2:23), self-denial (v. 21), and even self-infliction. Since it focuses on temporal "things which perish with the using," asceticism is powerless to restrain sin or bring one to God. While reasonable care and discipline of one's body is of temporal value (1 Tim. 4:8), it has no eternal value, and the extremes of asceticism serve only to gratify the flesh. All too often, ascetics seek only to put on a public show of their supposed holiness (Matt. 6:16–18).

b. **If.** Better translated, "since."

c. **you were raised.** This verb actually means "to be co-resurrected." Because of their union with Christ, believers spiritually entered His death and resurrection at the moment of their conversion (see Rom. 6:3, 4; Gal. 2:20) and have been and are now alive in Him so as to understand spiritual truths, realities, blessings, and the will of God. Those glorious benedictions (cf. Eph. 1:3) are the privileges and riches of the heavenly kingdom, all of which are at our disposal. Paul called them "things above." To understand what these are, see Col. 2:3.

d. **sitting at the right hand of God.** The position of honor and majesty (cf. Ps. 110:1; Luke 22:69; Acts 2:33; 5:31; 7:56; Eph. 1:20; Heb. 1:3; 8:1; 1 Pet. 3:22) that Christ enjoys as the exalted Son of God (see Phil. 2:9). That exaltation makes Him the fountain of blessing for His people (John 14:13, 14; cf. 2 Cor. 1:20).

e. **Set your mind.** This can also be translated "think," or "have this inner disposition." As a compass points N, the believer's entire disposition should point itself toward the things of heaven. Heavenly thoughts can only come by understanding heavenly realities from Scripture (cf. Rom. 8:5; 12:2; Phil. 1:23; 4:8; 1 John 2:15–17; see Matt. 6:33).

f. **you died.** See Rom. 6:1–11; 2 Cor. 5:17; Gal. 6:14. The verb's tense indicates that a death occurred in the past, in this case at the death of Jesus Christ, where believers were united with Him, their penalty of sin was paid, and they arose with Him in new life.

g. **hidden with Christ in God.** This rich expression has a threefold meaning: 1) believers have a common spiritual life with the Father and Son (1 Cor. 6:17; 2 Pet. 1:4); 2) the world cannot understand the full import of the believer's new life (Rom. 8:19; 1 Cor. 2:14; 1 John 3:2); and 3) believers are eternally secure, protected from all spiritual enemies, and with access to all God's blessings (John 10:28; Rom. 8:31–39; Heb. 7:25; 1 Pet. 1:4).

in God. When Christ who is our life appears, then you also will appear with Him in glory.

Therefore [a]put to death your members which are on the earth: [b]fornication, [c]uncleanness, [d]passion, evil desire, and [e]covetousness, [f]which is idolatry. Because of these things the [g]wrath of God is coming upon the [h]sons of disobedience, [i]in which you yourselves once walked when you lived in them.

But now you yourselves are to [j]put off all these: [k]anger, wrath, malice, [l]blasphemy, filthy language out of your mouth. Do not lie to one another, since you have [m]put off the [n]old man with his deeds, and have put on the new man

---

a. **put to death.** See Rom. 8:13; cf. Zech. 4:6; Eph. 5:18; 6:17; 1 John 2:14. This refers to a conscious effort to slay the remaining sin in our flesh.

b. **fornication.** Also translated "immorality," it refers to any form of sexual sin (see Gal. 5:19; cf. 1 Thess. 4:3).

c. **uncleanness.** Also translated "impurity," this term goes beyond sexual acts of sin to encompass evil thoughts and intentions as well (see Gal. 5:19; cf. Matt. 5:28; Mark 7:21, 22; 1 Thess. 4:7).

d. **passion, evil desire.** Similar terms that refer to sexual lust. "Passion" is the physical side of that vice, and "evil desire" is the mental side (see Rom. 1:26; 1 Thess. 4:5; cf. James 1:15).

e. **covetousness.** Also rendered "greed," lit. it means "to have more." It is the insatiable desire to gain more, especially of things that are forbidden (cf. Ex. 20:17; Deut. 5:21; James 4:2).

f. **which is idolatry.** When people engage in either greed or the sexual sins Paul has cataloged, they follow their desires rather than God's, in essence worshiping themselves—which is idolatry (Num. 25:1–3; Eph. 5:3–5).

g. **wrath of God.** His constant, invariable reaction against sin (see John 3:36; Rom. 1:18; Rev. 11:18).

h. **sons of disobedience.** See Eph. 2:2. This expression designates unbelievers as bearing the very nature and character of the disobedient, rebellious sinfulness they love.

i. **in which you . . . once walked.** Before their conversion (cf. Eph. 2:1–5; Titus 3:3, 4).

j. **put off.** A Gr. word used for taking off clothes (cf. Acts 7:58; Rom. 13:12–14; 1 Pet. 2:1). Like one who removes his dirty clothes at day's end, believers must discard the filthy garments of their old, sinful lives.

k. **anger . . . wrath . . . malice.** "Anger" speaks of a deep, smoldering bitterness; the settled heart attitude of an angry person (cf. Eph. 4:31; James 1:19, 20). "Wrath" is a sudden outburst of sinful anger, usually the eruption that flows out of "anger" (see Gal. 5:20; cf. Luke 4:28; Acts 19:28; Eph. 4:31). "Malice" comes from the Gr. term that denotes general moral evil. Here it probably refers to the damage caused by evil speech (cf. 1 Pet. 2:1).

l. **blasphemy.** The normal translation when this word refers to God. But here, since it refers to people, it is better translated "slander." To slander people, however, is to blaspheme God (James 3:9; cf. Matt. 5:22; James 3:10).

m. **put off . . . put on.** See Eph. 4:24, 25. These words are the basis for the command of Col. 3:8. Because the old man died in Christ, and the new man lives in Christ—because that is the fact of new creation or regeneration (2 Cor. 5:17)—believers must put off remaining sinful deeds and be being continually renewed into the Christlikeness to which they are called.

n. **old man . . . new man.** The old man is the old, unregenerate self, originating in Adam (see Rom. 5:12–14; 6:6; cf. Eph. 4:22). The new man refers to the new, regenerate self, which replaces the old man; this is the essence of what believers are in Christ (cf. Eph. 4:17; 5:1, 8, 15). The reason believers still sin is their unredeemed flesh (see Rom. 6:6, 12; 7:5).

who is [a]renewed in knowledge according to the [b]image of Him who created him, where there is [c]neither Greek nor Jew, circumcised nor uncircumcised, barbarian, [d]Scythian, [e]slave nor free, but [f]Christ is all and in all.

208. Put on Righteousness

Col. 3:12–17

[g]Therefore, as the [h]elect of God, holy and [i]beloved, put on [j]tender mercies, [k]kindness, [l]humility, [m]meekness, [n]longsuffering; bearing with one another, and forgiving one another, if anyone has a complaint against another; even

---

a. **renewed in knowledge.** See 2 Cor. 4:16; cf. Rom. 12:2; 2 Cor. 3:18. This Gr. verb ("renewed") contains a sense of contrast with the former reality. It describes a new quality of life that never before existed (cf. Rom. 12:2; Eph. 4:22). Just like a baby is born complete but immature, the new man is complete, but has the capacity to grow. "Knowledge" refers to a deep, thorough knowledge, without which there can be no spiritual growth or renewal (2 Tim. 3:16, 17; 1 Pet. 2:2).

b. **image of Him who created him.** It is God's plan that believers become progressively more like Jesus Christ, the one who made them (cf. Rom. 8:29; 1 Cor. 15:49; 1 John 3:2). See Phil. 3:12–14, 19, 20.

c. **neither Greek nor Jew.** Even as individual believers must discard old, sinful habits, the body of Christ must realize its unity and destroy the old barriers that separated people (cf. Gal. 3:28; Eph. 2:15).

d. **Scythian.** An ancient nomadic and warlike people that invaded the Fertile Crescent in the seventh century B.C. Noted for their savagery, they were the most hated and feared of all the so-called barbarians.

e. **slave nor free.** A social barrier had always existed between slaves and freemen; Aristotle had referred to slaves as "a living tool." But faith in Christ removed the separation (1 Cor. 12:13; Gal. 3:28; cf. Philem. 6).

f. **Christ is all and in all.** Because Jesus Christ is the Savior of all believers, He is equally the all-sufficient Lord of them all.

g. **Therefore.** In view of what God has done through Jesus Christ for the believer, Paul described the behavior and attitude God expects in response (Col. 3:12–17).

h. **elect of God.** This designates true Christians as those who have been chosen by God. No one is converted solely by his own choice, but only in response to God's effectual, free, uninfluenced, and sovereign grace (see John 15:16; Rom. 8:29; 9:10–24; Eph. 1:4; 2 Thess. 2:13; 2 Tim. 1:8, 9; 1 Pet. 1:1, 2; cf. Acts 13:46–48; Rom. 11:4, 5).

i. **beloved.** Election means believers are the objects of God's incomprehensible special love (cf. John 13:1; Eph. 1:4, 5).

j. **tender mercies.** This may also be rendered "heart of compassion." It is a Hebraism that connotes the internal organs of the human body as used figuratively to describe the seat of the emotions (cf. Matt. 9:36; Luke 6:36; James 5:11).

k. **kindness.** Refers to a goodness toward others that pervades the entire person, mellowing all harsh aspects (cf. Matt. 11:29, 30; Luke 10:25–37).

l. **humility.** See Rom. 12:3, 10; Phil. 2:3; cf. Matt. 18:4; John 13:14–16; James 4:6, 10. This is the perfect antidote to the self-love that poisons human relationships.

m. **meekness.** See Matt. 5:5, Gal. 5:23. Sometimes translated "gentleness," it is the willingness to suffer injury or insult rather than to inflict such hurts.

n. **longsuffering.** See Col. 1:11; cf. Rom. 2:4. It is also translated "patience," the opposite

ªas Christ forgave you, so you also must do. But above all these things put on love, which is the ᵇbond of perfection. And let ᶜthe peace of God rule in your hearts, to which also you were called in one body; and be thankful. Let the ᵈword of Christ ᵉdwell in you richly in all wisdom, teaching and admonishing one another in psalms and hymns and spiritual songs, singing with grace in your hearts to the Lord. And whatever you do in word or deed, ᶠdo all in the name of the Lord Jesus, giving thanks to God the Father through Him.

209. CHRISTIAN RELATIONSHIPS

Col. 3:18—4:6

ᵍWives, ʰsubmit to your own husbands, as is fitting in the Lord.

Husbands, ⁱlove your wives and do not ʲbe bitter toward them.

---

of quick anger, resentment, or revenge and thus epitomizes Jesus Christ (1 Tim. 1:16; cf. 2 Pet. 3:15). It endures injustice and troublesome circumstances with hope for coming relief.

a. **as Christ forgave you.** See Matt. 18:23–35; Eph. 4:32. Because Christ as the model of forgiveness has forgiven all our sins totally (Col. 1:14; 2:13, 14), believers must be willing to forgive others.

b. **bond of perfection.** A better rendering is "perfect bond of unity" (see Eph. 4:3; Phil. 1:27; 2:2). Supernatural love poured into the hearts of believers is the adhesive of the church. Cf. Rom. 5:5; 1 Thess. 4:9.

c. **the peace of God.** The Gr. word "peace" here refers to both the call of God to salvation and consequent peace with Him (see Rom. 5:1), and the attitude of rest or security (Phil. 4:7) believers have because of that eternal peace.

d. **word of Christ.** This is Scripture, the Holy Spirit inspired Scripture, the word of revelation He brought into the world.

e. **dwell in you richly.** See Eph. 5:18. "Dwell" means "to live in" or "to be at home," and "richly" may be more fully rendered "abundantly or extravagantly rich." Scripture should permeate every aspect of the believer's life and control every thought, word, and deed (cf. Ps. 119:11; Matt. 13:9; Phil. 2:16; 2 Tim. 2:15). This concept is parallel to being filled with the Spirit in Eph. 5:18 since the results of each are the same. In Eph. 5:18, the power and motivation for all the effects is the filling of the Holy Spirit; here it is the word richly dwelling. Those two realities are really one. The Holy Spirit fills the life controlled by His Word. This emphasizes that the filling of the Spirit is not some ecstatic or emotional experience, but a steady controlling of the life by obedience to the truth of God's Word.

f. **do all in the name of the Lord Jesus.** This simply means to act consistently with who He is and what He wants (see 1 Cor. 10:31).

g. In this section of Colossians, Paul discusses the new man's relationships to others. This passage is also a brief parallel to Eph. 5:19—6:9.

h. **submit.** See Eph. 5:22–24. The Gr. verb means "to subject oneself," which denotes willingly putting oneself under someone or something (cf. Luke 2:51; 10:17, 20; Rom. 8:7; 13:1, 5; 1 Cor. 15:27, 28; Eph. 1:22).

i. **love.** See Eph. 5:25–29. This is a call for the highest form of love which is rendered selflessly (cf. Gen. 24:67; Eph. 5:22–28; 1 Pet. 3:7).

j. **be bitter.** The form of this Gr. verb is better translated "stop being bitter," or "do not have

Children, obey your parents ᵃin all things, for this is well pleasing to the Lord.

Fathers, do not ᵇprovoke your children, lest they become discouraged.

ᶜBondservants, obey in all things your masters ᵈaccording to the flesh, not with ᵉeyeservice, as men-pleasers, but in sincerity of heart, fearing God. And whatever you do, do it heartily, as to the Lord and not to men, knowing that from the Lord you will receive the ᶠreward of the inheritance; for you serve the Lord Christ. But he who does wrong will be repaid for what he has done, and there is no partiality.

Masters, give your bondservants what is just and fair, knowing that you also have a Master in heaven.

ᵍContinue earnestly in prayer, ʰbeing vigilant in it with thanksgiving; meanwhile praying also for us, that God would open to us ⁱa door for the word, to speak ʲthe mystery of Christ, for which I am also in chains, that I may make it manifest, as I ought to speak.

---

the habit of being bitter." Husbands must not be harsh or angrily resentful toward their wives.

a. **in all things.** See Eph. 6:1–3. The only limit on a child's obedience is when parents demand something contrary to God's Word. For example, some children will act contrary to their parents' wishes even in coming to Christ (cf. Luke 12:51–53; 14:26).

b. **provoke.** See Eph. 6:4. Also translated "do not exasperate," this word has the connotation of not stirring up or irritating.

c. **Bondservants.** I.e., slaves (see Rom. 1:1). See Eph. 6:5. Paul upholds the duties of slave and master, of which the modern parallel is the duties of employee and employer. Scripture never advocates slavery, but recognizes it as an element of ancient society that could have been more beneficial if slaves and masters had treated each other properly. Here, Paul followed Christ's example and used slavery as a motif for spiritual instruction, likening the believer to one who is a slave and servant to Jesus Christ and seeing service to an earthly master as a way to serve the Lord.

d. **according to the flesh.** I.e., human inclination (cf. 2 Cor. 10:2, 3).

e. **eyeservice.** See Eph. 6:6. Better translated, "external service." It refers to working only when the master is watching, rather than recognizing the Lord is always watching, and how our work concerns Him. Cf. 1 Tim. 6:1, 2; Titus 2:9, 10; 1 Pet. 2:18–21.

f. **reward of the inheritance.** See Eph. 6:8. The Lord ensures the believer that he will receive a just, eternal compensation for his efforts (cf. Rev. 20:12, 13), even if his earthly boss or master does not compensate fairly (v. 25). God deals with obedience and disobedience impartially (cf. Acts 10:34; Gal. 6:7). Christians are not to presume on their faith in order to justify disobedience to an authority or employer (cf. Philem. 18).

g. **Continue earnestly.** The Gr. word means "to be courageously persistent" or "to hold fast and not let go" and refers here to persistent prayer (Acts 1:14; Rom. 12:12; Eph. 6:18; 1 Thess. 5:17; cf. Luke 11:5–10; 18:1–8).

h. **being vigilant.** In its most general sense this means to stay awake while praying. But Paul has in mind the broader implication of staying alert for specific needs about which to pray, rather than being vague and unfocused. Cf. Matt. 26:41; Mark 14:38; Luke 21:36.

i. **a door.** An opportunity (1 Cor. 16:8, 9; 2 Cor. 2:12).

j. **the mystery of Christ.** See Col. 1:26, 27; 2:2, 3.

Walk in wisdom toward ^athose who are outside, redeeming the time. Let your speech always be ^bwith grace, ^cseasoned with salt, that you may know how you ought to answer each one.

210. COWORKERS IN MINISTRY

Col. 4:7–18

^dTychicus, a beloved brother, faithful minister, and fellow servant in the Lord, will tell you all the news about me. I am sending him to you for this very purpose, that he may know your circumstances and comfort your hearts, with ^eOnesimus, a faithful and beloved brother, who is one of you. They will make known to you all things which are happening here.

^fAristarchus my fellow prisoner greets you, with ^gMark the cousin of Barnabas (about whom you received instructions: if he comes to you, welcome him), and ^hJesus who is called Justus. These are my only fellow workers for the kingdom of God who are of the circumcision; they have proved to be a comfort to me.

---

a. **those . . . outside.** This refers to unbelievers. See Eph. 5:15, 16. Believers are called to so live that they establish the credibility of the Christian faith and that they make the most of every evangelistic opportunity.

b. **with grace.** To speak what is spiritual, wholesome, fitting, kind, sensitive, purposeful, complimentary, gentle, truthful, loving, and thoughtful (see Eph. 4:29–31).

c. **seasoned with salt.** Just as salt not only flavors, but prevents corruption, the Christian's speech should act not only as a blessing to others, but as a purifying influence within the decaying society of the world.

d. **Tychicus.** The name means, "fortuitous" or "fortunate." He was one of the Gentile converts Paul took to Jerusalem as a representative of the Gentile churches (Acts 20:4). He was a reliable companion of Paul and a capable leader, since he was considered as a replacement for Titus and Timothy on separate occasions (2 Tim. 4:12; Titus 3:12). He had the responsibility to deliver Paul's letters to the Colossians, the Ephesians (Eph. 6:21), and Philemon (Col. 4:9).

e. **Onesimus.** The runaway slave whose return to his master was the basis for Paul's letter to Philemon.

f. **Aristarchus.** The Gr. name of a Jewish (cf. Col. 4:11) native of Thessalonica (Acts 20:4; 27:2). He was one of Paul's companions who was seized by a rioting mob in Ephesus (Acts 19:29) and also accompanied Paul on his trip to Jerusalem and his voyage to Rome (Acts 27:4).

g. **Mark.** See Acts 13:5, 13. After having fallen out of favor with Paul for some time, Mark is seen here as one of Paul's key helpers (cf. 2 Tim. 4:11).

h. **Jesus who is called Justus.** Possibly one of the Roman Jews who believed Paul's message (Acts 28:24).

Epaphras, who is one of you, a bondservant of Christ, greets you, always laboring fervently for you in prayers, that you may stand perfect and complete in all the will of God. For I bear him witness that he has a great zeal for you, and those who are in Laodicea, and those in ᵃHierapolis. ᵇLuke the beloved physician and ᶜDemas greet you. Greet the brethren who are in Laodicea, and ᵈNymphas and the church that is in his house.

Now ᵉwhen this epistle is read among you, see that it is read also in the church of the Laodiceans, and that you likewise read the ᶠepistle from Laodicea. And say to ᵍArchippus, "Take heed to the ministry which you have received in the Lord, that you may fulfill it."

This salutation ʰby my own hand—Paul. Remember my chains. Grace be with you. Amen.

211. PAUL WRITES A LETTER TO PHILEMON
Introduction to Philemon

Philemon, the recipient of this letter, was a prominent member of the church at Colosse (vv. 1, 2; cf. Col. 4:9), which met in his house (v. 2). The letter was for him, his family, and the church.

---

a. **Hierapolis.** A city in Phrygia 20 mi. W of Colosse and 6 mi. N of Laodicea.

b. **Luke.** Paul's personal physician and close friend who traveled frequently with him on his missionary journeys and wrote the Gospel of Luke and Acts.

c. **Demas.** A man who demonstrated substantial commitment to the Lord's work before the attraction of the world led him to abandon Paul and the ministry (2 Tim. 4:9, 10; Philem. 24).

d. **Nymphas and the church . . . in his house.** Other manuscripts make the name feminine (Nympha) and indicate the church met in her house, probably in Laodicea.

e. **when this epistle is read among you.** This letter was to be publicly read in the churches in Colosse and in Laodicea.

f. **epistle from Laodicea.** A separate letter from Paul, usually identified as the epistle to the Ephesians. The oldest manuscripts of Ephesians do not contain the words "in Ephesus," indicating that in all likelihood it was a circular letter intended for several churches in the region. Tychicus may have delivered Ephesians to the church at Laodicea first.

g. **Archippus.** Most likely the son of Philemon (Philem. 2). Paul's message to him to fulfill his ministry is similar to the exhortation to Timothy (2 Tim. 4:5).

h. **by my own hand.** Paul usually dictated his letters to an amanuensis (recording secretary), but would often add his own greeting in his own writing at the end of his letters (cf. 1 Cor. 16:21; Gal. 6:11; 2 Thess. 3:17; Philem. 19).

Author and Date

The book claims that the Apostle Paul was its writer (vv. 1, 9, 19), a claim that few in the history of the church have disputed, especially since there is nothing in Philemon that a forger would have been motivated to write. It is one of the Prison Epistles, along with Ephesians, Philippians, and Colossians. Its close connection with Colossians, which Paul wrote at the same time (ca. A.D. 60–62; cf. vv. 1, 16), brought early and unquestioned vindication of Paul's authorship by the early church fathers (e.g., Jerome, Chrysostom, and Theodore of Mopsuestia). The earliest of NT canons, the Muratorian (ca. A.D. 170), includes Philemon.

Background and Setting

Philemon had been saved under Paul's ministry, probably at Ephesus (v. 19), several years earlier. Wealthy enough to have a large house (cf. v. 2), Philemon also owned at least one slave, a man named Onesimus (lit."useful"; a common name for slaves). Onesimus was not a believer at the time he stole some money (v. 18) from Philemon and ran away. Like countless thousands of other runaway slaves, Onesimus fled to Rome, seeking to lose himself in the Imperial capital's teeming and nondescript slave population. Through circumstances not recorded in Scripture, Onesimus met Paul in Rome and became a Christian.

The apostle quickly grew to love the runaway slave (vv. 12, 16) and longed to keep Onesimus in Rome (v. 13), where he was providing valuable service to Paul in his imprisonment (v. 11). But by stealing and running away from Philemon, Onesimus had both broken Roman law and defrauded his master. Paul knew those issues had to be dealt with, and decided to send Onesimus back to Colosse. It was too hazardous for him to make the trip alone (because of the danger of slave-catchers), so Paul sent him back with Tychicus, who was returning to Colosse with the epistle to the Colossians (Col. 4:7–9). Along with Onesimus, Paul sent Philemon this beautiful personal letter, urging him to forgive Onesimus and welcome him back to service as a brother in Christ (vv. 15–17).

Historical and Theological Themes

Philemon provides valuable historical insights into the early church's relationship to the institution of slavery. Slavery was widespread in the Roman

Empire (according to some estimates, slaves constituted one third, perhaps more, of the population) and an accepted part of life. In Paul's day, slavery had virtually eclipsed free labor. Slaves could be doctors, musicians, teachers, artists, librarians, or accountants; in short, almost all jobs could be and were filled by slaves.

Slaves were not legally considered persons, but were the tools of their masters. As such, they could be bought, sold, inherited, exchanged, or seized to pay their master's debt. Their masters had virtually unlimited power to punish them, and sometimes did so severely for the slightest infractions. By the time of the NT, however, slavery was beginning to change. Realizing that contented slaves were more productive, masters tended to treat them more leniently. It was not uncommon for a master to teach a slave his own trade, and some masters and slaves became close friends. While still not recognizing them as persons under the law, the Roman Senate in A.D. 20 granted slaves accused of crimes the right to a trial. It also became more common for slaves to be granted (or to purchase) their freedom. Some slaves enjoyed very favorable and profitable service under their masters and were better off than many freemen because they were assured of care and provision. Many freemen struggled in poverty.

The NT nowhere directly attacks slavery; had it done so, the resulting slave insurrections would have been brutally suppressed and the message of the gospel hopelessly confused with that of social reform. Instead, Christianity undermined the evils of slavery by changing the hearts of slaves and masters. By stressing the spiritual equality of master and slave (v. 16; Gal. 3:28; Eph. 6:9; Col. 4:1; 1 Tim. 6:1, 2), the Bible did away with slavery's abuses. The rich theological theme that alone dominates the letter is forgiveness, a featured theme throughout NT Scripture (cf. Matt. 6:12–15; 18:21–35; Eph. 4:32; Col. 3:13). Paul's instruction here provides the biblical definition of forgiveness, without ever using the word.

Interpretive Challenges

There are no significant interpretive challenges in this personal letter from Paul to his friend Philemon.

212. Personal Greetings

Philem. 1–7

[a]Paul, a [b]prisoner of Christ Jesus, and [c]Timothy our brother,

To [d]Philemon our beloved friend and fellow laborer, to the beloved [e]Apphia, Archippus our fellow soldier, and to the church [f]in your house:

[g]Grace to you and peace from God our Father and the Lord Jesus Christ.

I thank my God, making mention of you always in my prayers, hearing of your love and faith which you have toward the Lord Jesus and toward all the saints, that the [h]sharing of your faith may become [i]effective by the [j]acknowledgment of every good thing which is in you in Christ Jesus. For we have great joy and consolation in your love, because the [k]hearts of the saints have been [l]refreshed by you, brother.

---

a. Following first century custom, the salutation contains the names of the letter's author and its recipient. This is a very personal letter and Philemon was one of only 3 individuals (Timothy and Titus are the others) to receive a divinely inspired letter from Paul.

b. **prisoner of Christ Jesus.** At the time of writing, Paul was a prisoner in Rome. Paul was imprisoned for the sake of and by the sovereign will of Christ (cf. Eph. 3:1; 4:1; 6:19, 20; Phil. 1:13; Col. 4:3). By beginning with his imprisonment and not his apostolic authority, Paul made this letter a gentle and singular appeal to a friend. A reminder of Paul's severe hardships was bound to influence Philemon's willingness to do the comparatively easy task Paul was about to request.

c. **Timothy.** See Acts 16:1–3; 1 Tim. 1:2; Phil. 1:1. He was not the co-author of this letter, but probably had met Philemon at Ephesus and was with Paul when the apostle wrote the letter. Paul mentions Timothy here and in the other epistles (e.g., Philem. 2 Cor. 1:1; Phil. 1:1; Col. 1:1; 1 Thess. 1:1; 2 Thess. 1:1) because he wanted him recognized as a leader and the non-apostolic heir apparent to Paul.

d. **Philemon.** A wealthy member of the Colossian church which met in his house. Church buildings were unknown until the third century.

e. **Apphia, Archippus.** Philemon's wife and son, respectively.

f. **in your house.** First century churches met in homes, and Paul wanted this personal letter read in the church that met at Philemon's. This reading would hold Philemon accountable, as well as instruct the church on the matter of forgiveness.

g. **Grace to you.** The standard greeting that appears in all 13 of Paul's NT letters. It highlighted salvation's means (grace) and its results (peace) and linked the Father and Son, thus affirming the deity of Christ.

h. **sharing.** Usually rendered "fellowship," the Gr. word means much more than simply enjoying one another's company. It refers to a mutual sharing of all life, which believers do because of their common life in Christ and mutual partnership or "belonging to each other" in the "faith."

i. **effective.** Lit. "powerful." Paul wanted Philemon's actions to send a powerful message to the church about the importance of forgiveness.

j. **acknowledgment.** The deep, rich, full, experiential knowledge of the truth (see Col. 1:9; 3:10).

k. **hearts.** This Gr. word denotes the seat of human feelings (see Col. 3:12 where the same Gr. word is translated "tender mercies").

l. **refreshed.** This comes from the Gr. military term that describes an army at rest from a march.

213. APPEAL FOR FORGIVENESS AND RESTORATION

Philem. 8–25

Therefore, though I might be very ªbold in Christ to command you what is fitting, yet for love's sake ᵇI rather appeal to you—being such a one as Paul, ᶜthe aged, and now also a prisoner of Jesus Christ— I appeal to you for ᵈmy son Onesimus, whom I have ᵉbegotten while in my chains, who once was ᶠunprofitable to you, but now is profitable to you and to me.

I am sending him back. You therefore receive him, that is, my own heart, whom I wished to keep with me, that on your behalf he might minister to me in my chains for the gospel. But without your consent I wanted to do nothing, that your good deed might not be by compulsion, as it were, but ᵍvoluntary.

For ʰperhaps he departed for a while for this purpose, that you might receive him forever, no longer as a slave but ⁱmore than a slave—a beloved brother, especially to me but how much more to you, both ʲin the flesh and ᵏin the Lord.

---

a. **bold . . . to command.** Because of his apostolic authority (see Rom. 1:1; 1 Thess. 2:6), Paul could have ordered Philemon to accept Onesimus.

b. **I rather appeal.** In this situation, however, Paul did not rely on his authority but called for a response based on the bond of love between himself and Philemon (Philem. 7; cf. 1 Cor. 10:1).

c. **the aged.** More than a reference to his chronological age (which at the time of this letter was about 60), this description includes the toll that all the years of persecution, illnesses, imprisonments, difficult journeys, and constant concern for the churches had taken on Paul (see 2 Cor. 11:23–30), making him feel and appear even older than he actually was.

d. **my son Onesimus.** To Paul, he was a son in the faith (see 1 Tim. 1:2).

e. **begotten . . . in my chains.** While in prison at Rome, Paul had led him to faith in Christ.

f. **unprofitable . . . profitable.** Better translated "useless . . . useful," this is the same Gr. root word from which "Onesimus" comes. Paul was making a play on words that basically said, "Useful formerly was useless, but now is useful"—Paul's point is that Onesimus had been radically transformed by God's grace.

g. **voluntary.** Or "of your own personal will." Paul wanted Onesimus to minister alongside him, but only if Philemon openly and gladly agreed to release him.

h. **perhaps.** Paul was suggesting that God providentially ordered the overturning of the evil of Onesimus' running away to produce eventual good (cf. Gen. 50:20; Rom. 8:28).

i. **more than a slave . . . beloved brother.** Paul did not call for Onesimus' freedom (cf. 1 Cor. 7:20–22), but that Philemon would receive his slave now as a fellow-believer in Christ (cf. Eph. 6:9; Col. 4:1; 1 Tim. 6:2). Christianity never sought to abolish slavery, but rather to make the relationships within it just and kind.

j. **in the flesh.** In this physical life (see Phil. 1:22), as they worked together.

k. **in the Lord.** The master and slave were to enjoy spiritual oneness and fellowship as they worshiped and ministered together.

If then you count me as a partner, receive him as you would me. But if he has wronged you or owes anything, put that [a]on my account. I, Paul, am writing [b]with my own hand. I will repay—not to mention to you that you owe me [c]even your own self besides. Yes, brother, [d]let me have joy from you in the Lord; refresh my heart in the Lord.

Having confidence in your obedience, I write to you, knowing that you will do [e]even more than I say. But, meanwhile, also prepare [f]a guest room for me, for I trust that through your prayers [g]I shall be granted to you.

[h]Epaphras, my fellow prisoner in Christ Jesus, greets you, as do [i]Mark, Aristarchus, [j]Demas, Luke, my fellow laborers.

The grace of our Lord Jesus Christ be with your spirit. Amen.

214. PAUL WRITES A LETTER TO THE PHILIPPIAN CHURCH

Introduction to Philippians

Philippians derives its name from the Greek city where the church to which it was addressed was located. Philippi was the first town in Macedonia where Paul established a church.

---

a. **on my account.** Paul offered to pay whatever restitution was necessary for Onesimus to be reconciled to Philemon, following the example of Jesus in reconciling sinners to God.

b. **with my own hand.** See Gal. 6:11; Col. 4:18; cf. 2 Thess. 3:17.

c. **even your own self.** Philemon owed Paul something far greater than the material debt Paul was offering to repay, since Paul had led him to saving faith, a debt Philemon could never repay.

d. **let me have joy.** See Phil. 2:2. By forgiving Onesimus, Philemon would keep the unity in the church at Colosse and bring joy to the chained apostle (cf. Philem. 7).

e. **even more than I say.** The more than forgiveness that Paul was urging upon Philemon was either: 1) to welcome Onesimus back enthusiastically, not grudgingly (cf. Luke 15:22–24); 2) to permit Onesimus, in addition to his menial tasks, to minister spiritually with Philemon; or 3) to forgive any others who might have wronged Philemon. Whichever Paul intended, he was not subtly urging Philemon to grant Onesimus freedom (see Philem. 16).

f. **a guest room.** Lit. "a lodging," a place where Paul could stay when he visited Colosse.

g. **I shall be granted to you.** Paul expected to be released from prison in the near future (cf. Phil. 2:23, 24), after which he could be with Philemon and the other Colossians again.

h. **Epaphras.** See Col. 4:12.

i. **Mark, Aristarchus.** See Col. 4:10. The story of the once severed but now mended relationship between Paul and Mark (Acts 15:38–40; 2 Tim. 4:11) would have been well known to the believers in Colosse (Col. 4:10). Listing Mark's name here would serve to remind Philemon that Paul himself had worked through the issues of forgiveness, and that the instructions he was passing on to his friend were ones the apostle himself had already implemented in his relationship with John Mark.

j. **Demas, Luke.** See Col. 4:14.

Author and Date

The unanimous testimony of the early church was that the Apostle Paul wrote Philippians. Nothing in the letter would have motivated a forger to write it.

The question of when Philippians was written cannot be separated from that of where it was written. The traditional view is that Philippians, along with the other Prison Epistles (Ephesians, Colossians, Philemon), was written during Paul's first imprisonment at Rome (ca. A.D. 60–62). The most natural understanding of the references to the "palace guard" (1:13) and the "saints . . . of Caesar's household" (4:22) is that Paul wrote from Rome, where the emperor lived. The similarities between the details of Paul's imprisonment given in Acts and in the Prison Epistles also argue that those epistles were written from Rome (e.g., Paul was guarded by soldiers, Acts 28:16; cf. 1:13, 14; was permitted to receive visitors, Acts 28:30; cf. 4:18; and had the opportunity to preach the gospel, Acts 28:31; cf. 1:12–14; Eph. 6:18–20; Col. 4:2–4).

Some have held that Paul wrote the Prison Epistles during his two-year imprisonment at Caesarea (Acts 24:27). But Paul's opportunities to receive visitors and proclaim the gospel were severely limited during that imprisonment (cf. Acts 23:35). The Prison Epistles express Paul's hope for a favorable verdict (1:25; 2:24; cf. Philem. 22). In Caesarea, however, Paul's only hope for release was either to bribe Felix (Acts 24:26), or agree to stand trial at Jerusalem under Festus (Acts 25:9). In the Prison Epistles, Paul expected the decision in his case to be final (1:20–23; 2:17, 23). That could not have been true at Caesarea, since Paul could and did appeal his case to the emperor.

Another alternative has been that Paul wrote the Prison Epistles from Ephesus. But at Ephesus, like Caesarea, no final decision could be made in his case because of his right to appeal to the emperor. Also, Luke was with Paul when he wrote Colossians (Col. 4:14), but he apparently was not with the apostle at Ephesus. Acts 19, which records Paul's stay in Ephesus, is not in one of the "we sections" of Acts. The most telling argument against Ephesus as the point of origin for the Prison Epistles, however, is that there is no evidence that Paul was ever imprisoned at Ephesus.

In light of the serious difficulties faced by both the Caesarean and Ephesian views, there is no reason to reject the traditional view that Paul wrote the Prison Epistles—including Philippians—from Rome.

Paul's belief that his case would soon be decided (2:23, 24) points to Philippians being written toward the close of the apostle's two-year Roman imprisonment (ca. A.D. 61).

Background and Setting

Originally known as Krenides ("The Little Fountains") because of the numerous nearby springs, Philippi ("city of Philip") received its name from Philip II of Macedon (the father of Alexander the Great). Attracted by the nearby gold mines, Philip conquered the region in the fourth century B.C. In the second century B.C., Philippi became part of the Roman province of Macedonia.

The city existed in relative obscurity for the next two centuries until one of the most famous events in Roman history brought it recognition and expansion. In 42 B.C., the forces of Antony and Octavian defeated those of Brutus and Cassius at the Battle of Philippi, thus ending the Roman Republic and ushering in the Empire. After the battle, Philippi became a Roman colony (cf. Acts 16:12), and many veterans of the Roman army settled there. As a colony, Philippi had autonomy from the provincial government and the same rights granted to cities in Italy, including the use of Roman law, exemption from some taxes, and Roman citizenship for its residents (Acts 16:21). Being a colony was also the source of much civic pride for the Philippians, who used Latin as their official language, adopted Roman customs, and modeled their city government after that of Italian cities. Acts and Philippians both reflect Philippi's status as a Roman colony.

Paul's description of Christians as citizens of heaven (3:20) was appropriate, since the Philippians prided themselves on being citizens of Rome (cf. Acts 16:21). The Philippians may well have known some of the members of the palace guard (1:13) and Caesar's household (4:22).

The church at Philippi, the first one founded by Paul in Europe, dates from the apostle's second missionary journey (Acts 16:12–40). Philippi evidently had a very small Jewish population. Because there were not enough men to form a synagogue (the requirement was for 10 Jewish men who were heads of a household), some devout women met outside the city at a place of prayer (Acts 16:13) alongside the Gangites River. Paul preached the gospel to them and Lydia, a wealthy merchant dealing in expensive purple dyed goods

(Acts 16:14), became a believer (16:14, 15). It is likely that the Philippian church initially met in her spacious home.

Satanic opposition to the new church immediately arose in the person of a demon-possessed, fortune-telling slave girl (Acts 16:16, 17). Not wanting even agreeable testimony from such an evil source, Paul cast the demon out of her (Acts 16:18). The apostle's act enraged the girl's masters, who could no longer sell her services as a fortune-teller (Acts 16:19). They hauled Paul and Silas before the city's magistrates (Acts 16:20) and inflamed the civic pride of the Philippians by claiming the two preachers were a threat to Roman customs (Acts 16:20, 21). As a result, Paul and Silas were beaten and imprisoned (Acts 16:22–24).

The two preachers were miraculously released from prison that night by an earthquake, which unnerved the jailer and opened his heart and that of his household to the gospel (Acts 16:25–34). The next day the magistrates, panicking when they learned they had illegally beaten and imprisoned two Roman citizens, begged Paul and Silas to leave Philippi.

Paul apparently visited Philippi twice during his third missionary journey, once at the beginning (cf. 2 Cor. 8:1–5), and again near the end (Acts 20:6). About 4 or 5 years after his last visit to Philippi, while a prisoner at Rome, Paul received a delegation from the Philippian church. The Philippians had generously supported Paul in the past (4:15, 16), and had also contributed abundantly for the needy at Jerusalem (2 Cor. 8:1–4). Now, hearing of Paul's imprisonment, they sent another contribution to him (4:10), and along with it Epaphroditus to minister to Paul's needs. Unfortunately Epaphroditus suffered a near-fatal illness (2:26, 27), either while en route to Rome, or after he arrived. Accordingly, Paul decided to send Epaphroditus back to Philippi (2:25, 26) and wrote the letter to the Philippians to send back with him.

Paul had several purposes in composing this epistle. First, he wanted to express in writing his thanks for the Philippians' gift (4:10–18). Second, he wanted the Philippians to know why he decided to return Epaphroditus to them, so they would not think his service to Paul had been unsatisfactory (2:25, 26). Third, he wanted to inform them about his circumstances at Rome (1:12–26). Fourth, he wrote to exhort them to unity (2:1, 2; 4:2). Finally, he wrote to warn them against false teachers (3:1—4:1).

Historical and Theological Themes

Since it is primarily a practical letter, Philippians contains little historical material (there are no OT quotes), apart from the momentous treatment of Paul's spiritual autobiography (3:4–7). There is, likewise, little direct theological instruction, also with one momentous exception. The magnificent passage describing Christ's humiliation and exaltation (2:5–11) contains some of the most profound and crucial teaching on the Lord Jesus Christ in all the Bible. The major theme of pursuing Christlikeness, as the most defining element of spiritual growth and the one passion of Paul in his own life, is presented in 3:12–14. In spite of Paul's imprisonment, the dominant tone of the letter is joyful (1:4, 18, 25, 26; 2:2, 16–18, 28; 3:1, 3; 4:1, 4, 10).

Interpretive Challenges

The major difficulty connected with Philippians is determining where it was written (see Author and Date above). The text itself presents only one significant interpretive challenge: the identity of the "enemies of the cross."

215. GREETING THE BELIEVERS IN PHILIPPI
Phil. 1:1–11

^aPaul and ^bTimothy, ^cbondservants of Jesus Christ,

To all the ^dsaints ^ein Christ Jesus who are in Philippi, with the ^fbishops and ^gdeacons:

---

a. **Paul.** Paul wrote this letter from a Roman prison. First century letters normally began by identifying the sender and the recipient with a basic greeting. One notable variation here is that Paul includes Timothy's name because Timothy was an important gospel co-worker in and around Philippi and a trusted, corroborating witness to the truths Paul expounded.

b. **Timothy.** Timothy, Paul's beloved son in the faith (see Acts 16:1–3), was not the co-author of the letter, but possibly the one to whom Paul dictated it. Regardless, Paul had good reason for including Timothy's name (see Phil. 1:1, 2).

c. **bondservants.** This denotes a willing slave who was happily and loyally linked to his master (see Rom. 1:1; cf. James 1:1; 2 Pet. 1:1; Jude 1).

d. **saints.** See 1 Cor. 1:2. These were believers in the church at Philippi, including those who led the assembly.

e. **in Christ Jesus.** This describes the Philippian believers' union with Christ in His death and resurrection (see Rom. 6:2–9; Gal. 2:20), which was the reason they could be called "saints."

f. **bishops.** Lit. "overseers"; see 1 Tim. 3:1. This is a term used to emphasize the leadership responsibilities of those who are elders, who are also called pastors. All 3 terms are used to describe the same men in Acts 20:28.

g. **deacons.** Lit. "those who serve"; see 1 Tim. 3:8.

ªGrace to you and peace from God our Father and the Lord Jesus Christ.

ᵇI thank my God upon every remembrance of you, always ᶜin every prayer of mine making request for you all with joy, for your ᵈfellowship in the gospel ᵉfrom the first day until now, being confident of this very thing, that ᶠHe who has begun a good work in you will complete it until the ᵍday of Jesus Christ; just as it is right for me to think this of you all, because I have you in my ʰheart, inasmuch as both in my chains and in the ⁱdefense and confirmation of the gospel, you all are ʲpartakers with me of grace. For God is my witness, how greatly I long for you all with the ᵏaffection of Jesus Christ.

And this I pray, that your love may abound still more and more ˡin knowledge and all ᵐdiscernment, that you may ⁿapprove the things that are

---

a. **Grace . . . peace.** Paul's standard greeting (see Rom. 1:7) reminded the believers of their relationship to God.

b. **I thank my God.** Paul's letters usually included such commendation (see Gal. 1:3–5).

c. **in every prayer . . . with joy.** The Gr. word for "prayer" denotes a petition for, or a request made on behalf of, someone else. It was a delight for him to intercede for fellow believers.

d. **fellowship.** This can also be translated "participation" or "partnership." Cf. 2 Cor. 8:4.

e. **from the first day.** These believers eagerly assisted Paul in evangelizing Philippi from the beginning of the church there (Acts 16:12–40).

f. **He . . . will complete it.** The Gr. verb translated "has begun" is used only here and in Gal. 3:3—both times in reference to salvation itself. When God begins a work of salvation in a person, He finishes and perfects that work. Thus the verb "will complete" points to the eternal security of the Christian (see John 6:39, 40, 44; Rom. 5:10; 8:29–39; Eph. 1:13, 14; Heb. 7:25; 12:2).

g. **day of Jesus Christ.** This phrase is not to be confused with the "Day of the Lord," which describes final divine judgment and wrath (cf. Is. 13:9; Joel 1:15; 2:11; 1 Thess. 5:2; 2 Pet. 3:10). "Day of Jesus Christ" is also called the "Day of Christ" (v. 10; 2:16) and the "Day of our Lord Jesus Christ" (1 Cor. 1:8), which looks to the final salvation, reward, and glorification of believers. Cf. 1 Cor. 3:10–15; 4:5; 2 Cor. 5:9, 10.

h. **heart.** A common biblical word used to describe the center of thought and feeling (cf. Prov. 4:23).

i. **defense and confirmation.** Two judicial terms referring either to the first phase of Paul's trial in Rome in which he defended his gospel ministry or in a general sense to his continual defense of the faith, which was the heart of his ministry.

j. **partakers with me of grace.** See Phil. 1:5. During his imprisonment, the Philippians sent Paul money and Epaphroditus' services to support the apostle, thus sharing in God's gracious blessing on his ministry (cf. Phil. 2:30).

k. **affection.** The word lit. refers to the internal organs, which are the part of the body that reacts to intense emotion. It became the strongest Gr. word to express compassionate love—a love that involves one's entire being.

l. **in knowledge.** This is from the Gr. word that describes genuine, full, or advanced knowledge. Biblical love is not an empty sentimentalism but is anchored deeply in the truth of Scripture and regulated by it (cf. Eph. 5:2, 3; 1 Pet. 1:22).

m. **discernment.** The Eng. word "aesthetic" comes from this Gr. word, which speaks of moral perception, insight, and the practical application of knowledge. Love is not blind, but perceptive, and it carefully scrutinizes to distinguish between right and wrong. See 1 Thess. 5:21, 22.

n. **approve the . . . excellent.** "Approve" in classical Gr. described the assaying of metals or the testing of money for authenticity (cf. Luke 12:56; 14:19). "Excellent" means "to differ." Believers need the ability to distinguish those things that are truly important so they can establish the right priorities.

excellent, that you may be ᵃsincere and without offense till the day of Christ, being filled with the ᵇfruits of righteousness ᶜwhich are by Jesus Christ, ᵈto the glory and praise of God.

216. STANDING FIRM IN CHALLENGING CIRCUMSTANCES

Phil. 1:12–18

But I want you to know, brethren, that the ᵉthings which happened to me have actually turned out ᶠfor the furtherance of the gospel, so that it has become ᵍevident to the ʰwhole palace guard, and to ⁱall the rest, that my chains are in Christ; and ʲmost of the brethren in the Lord, having become confident by my chains, are ᵏmuch more bold to speak the word without fear.

---

a. **sincere and without offense.** "Sincere" means "genuine," and may have originally meant "tested by sunlight." In the ancient world, dishonest pottery dealers filled cracks in their inferior products with wax before glazing and painting them, making worthless pots difficult to distinguish from expensive ones. The only way to avoid being defrauded was to hold the pot to the sun, making the wax-filled cracks obvious. Dealers marked their fine pottery that could withstand "sun testing" as sine cera—"Without wax." "Without offense" can be translated "blameless," referring to relational integrity. Christians are to live lives of true integrity that do not cause others to sin (see Rom. 12:9; 1 Cor. 10:31, 32; 2 Cor. 1:12; cf. Rom. 14; 1 Cor. 8).

b. **fruits of righteousness.** This is better translated, "the fruit righteousness produces" (see Rom. 1:13; cf. Prov. 11:30; Amos 6:12; James 3:17, 18).

c. **which are by Jesus Christ.** See John 15:1–5; Eph. 2:10. This speaks of the salvation transformation provided by our Lord and His ongoing work of power through His Spirit in us.

d. **to the glory and praise of God.** See John 15:8; Eph. 1:12–14; 3:20, 21. The ultimate end of all Paul's prayers was that God be glorified.

e. **things which happened to me.** Paul's difficult circumstances, namely, his journey to Rome and imprisonment there (see Acts 21–28).

f. **for the furtherance.** Better translated, "for the progress," which refers to the forward movement of something—often of armies—in spite of obstacles, dangers, and distractions. Paul's imprisonment proved to be no hindrance to spreading the message of salvation (cf. Acts 28:30, 31). Actually, it created new opportunities (see Phil. 4:22).

g. **evident . . . chains are in Christ.** People around him recognized that Paul was no criminal, but had become a prisoner because of preaching Jesus Christ and the gospel (cf. Eph. 6:20).

h. **whole palace guard.** The Gr. word for "palace," often simply used in its transliterated form "praetorion," can denote either a special building (e.g., a commander's headquarters, the emperor's palace) or the group of men in the Imperial guard. Because Paul was in a private house in Rome, "palace guard" probably refers to the members of the Imperial guard who guarded Paul day and night. Cf. Acts 28:16.

i. **all the rest.** Everyone else in the city of Rome who met and heard him (cf. Acts 28:23, 24, 30, 31).

j. **most of the brethren.** With the exception of those detractors identified in Phil. 1:15, 16, who were attacking Paul.

k. **much more bold to speak.** Paul's example of powerful witness to the gospel as a

Some indeed preach Christ even ᵃfrom envy and strife, and some also ᵇfrom goodwill: The former preach Christ from ᶜselfish ambition, ᵈnot sincerely, supposing to add affliction to my chains; but ᵉthe latter out of love, knowing that I am ᶠappointed for the defense of the gospel. What then? Only that in every way, whether in pretense or in truth, Christ is preached; and in this ᵍI rejoice, yes, and will rejoice.

217. TO LIVE IS CHRIST

Phil. 1:19–30

For I know that this will turn out for ʰmy deliverance through your prayer and the supply of the ⁱSpirit of Jesus Christ, according to my ʲearnest expectation

---

prisoner demonstrated God's faithfulness to His persecuted children and that their imprisonment would not halt the progress of the gospel. This encouraged others to be bold and not fear imprisonment.

a. **from envy and strife.** The attitude of Paul's detractors, who really did preach the gospel but were jealous of his apostolic power and authority, his success and immense giftedness. "Strife" connotes contention, rivalry, and conflict, which resulted when Paul's critics began discrediting him.

b. **from goodwill.** "Goodwill" speaks of satisfaction and contentment, the attitude that Paul's supporters had for him personally and for his ministry.

c. **selfish ambition.** This describes those who were interested only in self-advancement, or who ruthlessly sought to get ahead at any cost. Paul's detractors used his incarceration as an opportunity to promote their own prestige by accusing Paul of being so sinful the Lord had chastened him by imprisonment.

d. **not sincerely.** See Phil. 1:10. Paul's preacher critics did not have pure motives.

e. **the latter out of love.** Paul's supporters were motivated by genuine affection for him and confidence in his virtue (cf. 1 Cor. 13:1, 2).

f. **appointed.** The Gr. word describes a soldier's being placed on duty. Paul was in prison because he was destined to be there by God's will, so as to be in a strategic position to proclaim the gospel.

g. **I rejoice . . . will rejoice.** Paul's joy was not tied to his circumstances or his critics (cf. Ps. 4:7, 8; Rom. 12:12; 2 Cor. 6:10). He was glad when the gospel was proclaimed with authority, no matter who received credit. He endured the unjust accusations without bitterness at his accusers. Rather, he rejoiced that they preached Christ, even in a pretense of godliness.

h. **my deliverance.** "Deliverance" is from the basic Gr. term for salvation. But it can also be rendered "well-being" or "escape," which presents 4 possible interpretations: 1) it refers to Paul's ultimate salvation; 2) it alludes to his deliverance from threatened execution; 3) he would finally be vindicated by the emperor's ruling; or 4) Paul is talking about his eventual release from prison. Whatever Paul's precise meaning, he was certain he would be freed from his temporary distress (Job 13:16; cf. Job 19:26; Pss. 22:4, 5, 8; 31:1; 33:18, 19; 34:7; 41:1).

i. **Spirit of Jesus Christ.** The Holy Spirit (Rom. 8:9; Gal. 4:6). Paul had supreme confidence in the Spirit (cf. Zech. 4:6; John 14:16; Rom. 8:26; Eph. 3:20).

j. **earnest expectation.** This Gr. word indicates keen anticipation of the future, as when someone stretches his neck to see what lies ahead. Paul was very confident and excited about Christ's promise (see Matt. 10:32).

and hope that in ᵃnothing I shall be ashamed, but with all boldness, as always, so now also Christ will be magnified in my body, whether by life or by death. For ᵇto me, to live is Christ, and ᶜto die is gain. But if I live on in ᵈthe flesh, this will mean ᵉfruit from my labor; yet what I shall choose I cannot tell. For I am ᶠhard-pressed between the two, having a desire to ᵍdepart and be with Christ, which is ʰfar better. Nevertheless to remain in the flesh is ⁱmore needful for you. And being ʲconfident of this, I know that I shall remain and continue with you all for your ᵏprogress and joy of faith, that your ˡrejoicing for me may be more abundant in Jesus Christ by my coming to you again.

Only let your conduct be ᵐworthy of the gospel of Christ, so that whether I come and see you or am absent, I may hear of your affairs, that you stand fast in ⁿone spirit, with one mind ᵒstriving together for ᵖthe faith of the gospel,

---

a. **nothing . . . ashamed.** See Is. 49:23; Rom. 9:33; cf. Pss. 25:2, 3; 40:15, 16; 119:80; Is. 1:27–29; 45:14–17; Jer. 12:13; Zeph. 3:11.

b. **to me, to live is Christ.** For Paul, life is summed up in Jesus Christ; Christ was his reason for being. See Phil. 3:12–14.

c. **to die is gain.** Death would relieve him of earthly burdens and let him focus totally on glorifying God (see Phil. 1:23, 24; cf. Acts 21:13).

d. **the flesh.** Cf. Phil. 1:24. Here this word refers not to one's fallen humanness (as in Rom. 7:5, 18; 8:1), but simply to physical life (as in 2 Cor. 10:3; Gal. 2:20).

e. **fruit.** See Rom. 1:13. Paul knew that the only reason to remain in this world was to bring souls to Christ and build up believers to do the same. See 2 Cor. 4:15.

f. **hard-pressed.** The Gr. word pictures a traveler on a narrow path, a rock wall on either side allowing him to go only straight ahead.

g. **depart and be with Christ.** Paul knew if he died he would have complete, conscious, intimate, unhindered fellowship with his Lord (see 2 Cor. 5:1, 8; 2 Tim. 4:6–8).

h. **far better.** Lit. "very much better," the highest superlative.

i. **more needful for you.** Paul yielded his personal desire to be with his Lord for the necessity of the building of the church (see Phil. 2:3, 4).

j. **confident . . . I shall remain.** Paul's conviction—not a supernatural revelation—that their need would determine that he stay on earth longer.

k. **progress . . . of faith.** "Progress" pictures trail blazing so that an army can advance (see Phil. 1:12). Paul wanted to cut a new path for the Philippians to follow to victory; the increasing of their faith would result in the increasing of their joy.

l. **rejoicing for me . . . in Jesus Christ.** The Gr. word order is "that your rejoicing may be more abundant in Jesus Christ for me." The point is, as Paul lived on fruitfully, their joy and confidence would overflow because of Christ's working in him, not because of anything he himself did by his own ability.

m. **worthy of the gospel.** Believers are to have integrity, i.e., to live consistent with what they believe, teach, and preach. Cf. Eph. 4:1; Col. 1:10; 1 Thess. 2:11, 12; 4:1; Titus 2:10; 2 Pet. 3:11, 14.

n. **one spirit . . . one mind.** This introduces Paul's theme of unity that continues through Phil. 2:4. His call for genuine unity of heart and mind is based on 1) the necessity of oneness to win the spiritual battle for the faith (Phil. 1:28–30); 2) the love of others in the fellowship (2:1, 2); 3) genuine humility and self-sacrifice (2:3, 4); and 4) the example of Jesus Christ who proved that sacrifice produces eternal glory (2:5–11).

o. **striving together.** Lit. "to struggle along with someone." Paul changed the metaphor from that of a soldier standing at his post ("stand fast") to one of a team struggling for victory against a common foe.

p. **the faith of the gospel.** The Christian faith as revealed by God and recorded in the Scripture (Jude 3; cf. Rom. 1:1; Gal. 1:7).

and not in any way terrified by your adversaries, which is to them a ªproof of perdition, but to you of salvation, and that from God. For to you it has been ᵇgranted on behalf of Christ, not only to believe in Him, but also to suffer for His sake, having the ᶜsame conflict which ᵈyou saw in me and now hear is in me.

218. CHRIST'S PERFECT EXAMPLE OF HUMILITY

Phil. 2:1–11

Therefore if there is any ᵉconsolation in Christ, if any ᶠcomfort of love, if any ᵍfellowship of the Spirit, if any ʰaffection and mercy, fulfill my joy by being ⁱlike-minded, having the ʲsame love, being of ᵏone accord, of one mind. et

---

a. **proof of perdition.** When believers willingly suffer without being "terrified," it is a sign that God's enemies will be destroyed and eternally lost (see 2 Thess. 1:4–8).

b. **granted . . . to suffer.** See Phil. 3:10; 1 Pet. 2:20, 21; cf. Matt. 5:10–12; Acts 5:41. The Gr. verb translated "granted" is from the noun for grace. Believers' suffering is a gift of grace which brings power (2 Cor. 12:9, 10; 1 Pet. 5:10) and eternal reward (1 Pet. 4:13).

c. **same conflict.** The same kind of suffering Paul had experienced (Phil. 1:12–14; Acts 16:22–24).

d. **you saw.** This refers to what the Philippians witnessed when Paul and Silas were imprisoned at Philippi (Acts 16:19–40).

e. **consolation in Christ.** "Consolation" can also be translated "encouragement," and is from the Gr. word that means "to come alongside and help, counsel, exhort" (see John 14:26; Rom. 12:1), which our beloved Lord does for His own.

f. **comfort of love.** The Gr. word translated "comfort" portrays the Lord coming close and whispering words of gentle cheer or tender counsel in a believer's ear.

g. **fellowship of the Spirit.** "Fellowship" refers to the partnership, of common eternal life, provided by the indwelling Holy Spirit (1 Cor. 3:16; 12:13; 2 Cor. 13:14; 1 John 1:4–6).

h. **affection and mercy.** God has extended His deep affection (see Phil. 1:8) and compassion to every believer (cf. Rom. 12:1; 2 Cor. 1:3; Col. 3:12) and that reality should result in unity.

i. **like-minded.** Cf. Phil. 3:15, 16; 4:2; 1 Pet. 3:8. The Gr. word means "think the same way." This exhortation is not optional or obscure, but is repeated throughout the NT (cf. Rom. 15:5; 1 Cor. 1:10; 2 Cor. 13:11–13).

j. **same love.** Believers are to love others in the body of Christ equally—not because they are all equally attractive, but by showing the same kind of sacrificial, loving service to all that was shown to them by Christ (John 15:13; Rom. 12:10; 1 John 3:17; cf. John 3:16).

k. **one accord.** This may also be translated "united in spirit" and perhaps is a term specially coined by Paul. It lit. means "one-souled" and describes people who are knit together in harmony, having the same desires, passions, and ambitions. The next phrase, "of one mind," similarly means "intent on one purpose."

nothing be done through [a]selfish ambition or conceit, but in [b]lowliness of mind let each [c]esteem others better than himself. Let each of you look out not only for his own interests, but also for the interests of others.

[d]Let this mind be in you which was also in Christ Jesus, who, [e]being in the form of God, did [f]not consider it robbery to be [g]equal with God, but [h]made Himself of no reputation, taking the [i]form of a bondservant, and coming in

---

a. **selfish ambition.** This Gr. word, which is sometimes rendered "strife" because it refers to factionalism, rivalry, and partisanship (see Gal. 5:20), speaks of the pride that prompts people to push for their own way. **conceit.** Lit. "empty glory," and often translated "empty conceit." This word refers to the pursuit of personal glory, which is the motivation for selfish ambition.

b. **lowliness of mind.** This translates a Gr. word that Paul and other NT writers apparently coined. It was a term of derision, with the idea of being low, shabby, and humble (cf. 1 Cor. 15:9; 1 Tim. 1:15).

c. **esteem others better than himself.** The basic definition of true humility (cf. Rom. 12:10; Gal. 5:13; Eph. 5:21; 1 Pet. 5:5).

d. Christ is the ultimate example of selfless humility (cf. Matt. 11:29; John 13:12–17). This is the classic Christological passage in the NT, dealing with the Incarnation. It was probably sung as a hymn in the early church (see Col. 3:16).

e. **being in the form of God.** Paul affirms that Jesus eternally has been God. The usual Gr. word for "being" is not used here. Instead, Paul chose another term that stresses the essence of a person's nature—his continuous state or condition. Paul also could have chosen one of two Gr. words for "form," but he chose the one that specifically denotes the essential, unchanging character of something—what it is in and of itself. The fundamental doctrine of Christ's deity has always encompassed these crucial characteristics (cf. John 1:1, 3, 4, 14; 8:58; Col. 1:15–17; Heb. 1:3).

f. **not . . . robbery.** The Gr. word is translated "robbery" here because it originally meant "a thing seized by robbery." It eventually came to mean anything clutched, embraced, or prized, and thus is sometimes translated "grasped" or "held onto." Though Christ had all the rights, privileges, and honors of deity—which He was worthy of and could never be disqualified from—His attitude was not to cling to those things or His position but to be willing to give them up for a season. See John 17:1–5.

g. **equal with God.** The Gr. word for "equal" defines things that are exactly the same in size, quantity, quality, character, and number. In every sense, Jesus is equal to God and constantly claimed to be so during His earthly ministry (cf. John 5:18; 10:33, 38; 14:9; 20:28; Heb. 1:1–3).

h. **made Himself of no reputation.** This is more clearly translated "emptied Himself." From this Gr. word comes the theological word "kenosis"; i.e., the doctrine of Christ's self-emptying in His incarnation. This was a self-renunciation, not an emptying Himself of deity nor an exchange of deity for humanity (see Phil. 2:6). Jesus did, however, renounce or set aside His privileges in several areas: 1) heavenly glory—while on earth He gave up the glory of a face-to-face relationship with God and the continuous outward display and personal enjoyment of that glory (cf. John 17:5); 2) independent authority—during His incarnation Christ completely submitted Himself to the will of His Father (see v. 8; cf. Matt. 26:39; John 5:30; Heb. 5:8); 3) divine prerogatives—He set aside the voluntary display of His divine attributes and submitted Himself to the Spirit's direction (cf. Matt. 24:36; John 1:45–49); 4) eternal riches—while on earth Christ was poor and owned very little (cf. 2 Cor. 8:9); and 5) a favorable relationship with God—He felt the Father's wrath for human sin while on the cross (cf. Matt. 27:46; see 2 Cor. 5:21).

i. **form of a bondservant.** Again, Paul uses the Gr. word "form," which indicates exact essence (see Phil. 2:6). As a true servant (see 1:1), Jesus submissively did the will of His Father (cf. Is. 52:13, 14).

^athe likeness of men. And being found ^bin appearance as a man, ^cHe humbled Himself and became ^dobedient to the point of death, even the death of ^ethe cross. Therefore God also has ^fhighly exalted Him and given Him the ^gname which is above every name, that ^hat the name of Jesus every knee should ⁱbow, of those in heaven, and of those on earth, and of those under the earth, and

---

a. **the likeness of men.** Christ became more than God in a human body, but He took on all the essential attributes of humanity (Luke 2:52; Gal. 4:4; Col. 1:22), even to the extent that He identified with basic human needs and weaknesses (cf. Heb. 2:14, 17; 4:15). He became the God-Man: fully God and fully man.

b. **in appearance as a man.** This is not simply a repetition of the last phrase in Phil.2:7, but a shift from the heavenly focus to an earthly one. Christ's humanity is described from the viewpoint of those who saw Him. Paul is implying that although He outwardly looked like a man, there was much more to Him (His deity) than many people recognized naturally (cf. John 6:42; 8:48).

c. **He humbled Himself.** After the humbling of incarnation, Jesus further humbled Himself in that He did not demand normal human rights, but subjected Himself to persecution and suffering at the hands of unbelievers (cf. Is. 53:7; Matt. 26:62–64; Mark 14:60, 61; 1 Pet. 2:23).

d. **obedient . . . death.** Beyond even persecution, Jesus went to the lowest point or furthest extent in His humiliation in dying as a criminal, following God's plan for Him (cf. Matt. 26:39; Acts 2:23).

e. **the cross.** See on Matt. 27:29–50. Even further humiliation was His because Jesus' death was not by ordinary means, but was accomplished by crucifixion—the cruelest, most excruciating, most degrading form of death ever devised. The Jews hated this manner of execution (Deut. 21:23; see Gal. 3:13).

f. **highly exalted Him.** Christ's exaltation was fourfold. The early sermons of the apostles affirm His resurrection and coronation (His position at the right hand of God), and allude to His intercession for believers (Acts 2:32, 33; 5:30, 31; cf. Eph. 1:20, 21; Heb. 4:15; 7:25, 26). Hebrews 4:14 refers to the final element, His ascension. The exaltation did not concern Christ's nature or eternal place within the Trinity, but His new identity as the God-Man (cf. John 5:22; Rom. 1:4; 14:9; 1 Cor. 15:24, 25). In addition to receiving back His glory (John 17:5), Christ's new status as the God-Man meant God gave Him privileges He did not have prior to the Incarnation. If He had not lived among men, He could not have identified with them as the interceding High-Priest. Had He not died on the cross, He could not have been elevated from that lowest degree back to heaven as the substitute for sin.

g. **name . . . above every name.** Christ's new name which further describes His essential nature and places Him above and beyond all comparison is "Lord." This name is the NT synonym for OT descriptions of God as sovereign ruler. Both before (Is. 45:21–23; Mark 15:2; Luke 2:11; John 13:13; 18:37; 20:28) and after (Acts 2:36; 10:36; Rom. 14:9–11; 1 Cor. 8:6; 15:57; Rev. 17:14; 19:16) the exaltation, Scripture affirms that this was Jesus' rightful title as the God-Man.

h. **at the name of Jesus.** "Jesus" was the name bestowed at His birth (Matt. 1:21), not His new name. The name for Jesus given in the fullest sense after His exaltation, was "Lord" (see Phil. 2:11).

i. **bow . . . confess.** The entire intelligent universe is called to worship Jesus Christ as Lord (cf. Ps. 2). This mandate includes the angels in heaven (Rev. 4:2–9), the spirits of the redeemed (Rev. 4:10, 11), obedient believers on earth (Rom. 10:9), the disobedient rebels on earth (2 Thess. 1:7–9), demons and lost humanity in hell (1 Pet. 3:18–22). The Gr. word for "confess" means "to acknowledge," "affirm," or "agree" which is what everyone will eventually do in response to Christ's lordship, willingly and blessedly or unwillingly and painfully.

that every tongue should confess that Jesus Christ is ªLord, to the glory of God the Father.

219. LIGHTS IN A DARK WORLD

Phil. 2:12–18

Therefore, my beloved, as you have always ᵇobeyed, not as in my presence only, but now much more in my absence, ᶜwork out your own salvation with ᵈfear and trembling; for it is ᵉGod who works in you both ᶠto will and to do for His ᵍgood pleasure.

Do all things ʰwithout complaining and disputing, ⁱthat you may become

---

a. **Lord.** See Phil. 2:9. "Lord" primarily refers to the right to rule, and in the NT it denotes mastery over or ownership of people and property. When applied to Jesus, it certainly implies His deity, but it mainly refers to sovereign authority.

b. **obeyed.** Their faithful response to the divine commands Paul had taught them (cf. Rom. 1:5; 15:18; 2 Cor. 10:5, 6).

c. **work out your own salvation.** The Gr. verb rendered "work out" means "to continually work to bring something to fulfillment or completion." It cannot refer to salvation by works (cf. Rom. 3:21–24; Eph. 2:8, 9), but it does refer to the believer's responsibility for active pursuit of obedience in the process of sanctification (see 3:13, 14; Rom. 6:19; cf. 1 Cor. 9:24–27; 15:58; 2 Cor. 7:1; Gal. 6:7–9; Eph. 4:1; Col. 3:1–17; Heb. 6:10, 11; 12:1, 2; 2 Pet. 1:5–11).

d. **fear and trembling.** The attitude with which Christians are to pursue their sanctification. It involves a healthy fear of offending God and a righteous awe and respect for Him (cf. Prov. 1:7; 9:10; Is. 66:1, 2).

e. **God who works in you.** Although the believer is responsible to work (Phil. 2:12), the Lord actually produces the good works and spiritual fruit in the lives of believers (John 15:5; 1 Cor. 12:6). This is accomplished because He works through us by His indwelling Spirit (Acts 1:8; 1 Cor. 3:16, 17; 6:19, 20; cf. Gal. 3:3).

f. **to will and to do.** God energizes both the believer's desires and his actions. The Gr. word for "will" indicates that He is not focusing on mere desires or whimsical emotions but on the studied intent to fulfill a planned purpose. God's power makes His church willing to live godly lives (cf. Ps. 110:3).

g. **good pleasure.** God wants Christians to do what satisfies Him. Cf. Eph. 1:5, 9; 2 Thess. 1:11.

h. **without complaining and disputing.** The Gr. word for "complaining" is a term that actually sounds like what it means. Its pronunciation is much like muttering or grumbling in a low tone of voice. It is an emotional rejection of God's providence, will, and circumstances for one's life. The word for "disputing" is more intellectual and here means "questionings," or "criticisms" directed negatively toward God.

i. **that you may become.** This introduces the reasons believers should have the right attitude in pursuing godliness. "Become" indicates a process—they are to be growing toward something they do not yet fully possess as children of God (cf. Eph. 5:1; Titus 2:1).

^ablameless and harmless, children of God ^bwithout fault in the midst of a ^ccrooked and perverse generation, among whom you ^dshine as lights in the world, ^eholding fast ^fthe word of life, so that ^gI may rejoice in the day of Christ that I have not ^hrun in vain or labored in vain.

Yes, and if I am ⁱbeing poured out as a ^jdrink offering on the sacrifice and ^kservice of your faith, ^lI am glad and rejoice with you all. For the same reason you also be glad and rejoice with me.

---

a. **blameless and harmless.** "Blameless" describes a life that cannot be criticized because of sin or evil. "Harmless," which can also be translated "innocent," describes a life that is pure, unmixed, and unadulterated with sin, much like high quality metal without any alloy (cf. Matt. 10:16; Rom. 16:19; 2 Cor. 11:3; Eph. 5:27).

b. **without fault.** Can also be translated "above reproach." In the Gr. OT, it is used several times of the kind of sacrifice to be brought to God, i.e., spotless and without blemish (cf. Num. 6:14; 19:2; 2 Pet. 3:14).

c. **crooked and perverse generation.** See Deut. 32:5. "Crooked" is the word from which the Eng. "scoliosis" (curvature of the spinal column) comes. It describes something that is deviated from the standard, which is true of all who stray from God's path (cf. Prov. 2:15; Is. 53:6). "Perverse" intensifies this meaning by referring to one who has strayed so far off the path that his deviation is severely twisted and distorted (cf. Luke 9:41). Paul applies this condition to the sinful world system.

d. **shine as lights.** A metaphorical reference to spiritual character. "Shine" can be more precisely rendered "you have to shine," which means believers must show their character in the midst of a dark culture, as the sun, moon, and stars shine in an otherwise dark sky (see Matt. 5:14; 2 Cor. 4:6; Eph. 5:8).

e. **holding fast.** A slightly different translation—"Holding forth"—more accurately reflects the verb in the original text. Here it refers to believers' holding out or offering something for others to take.

f. **the word of life.** The gospel which, when believed, produces spiritual and eternal life (cf. Eph. 2:1).

g. **I may rejoice.** See Phil. 2:2; 4:1; 1 Thess. 2:19, 20.

h. **run . . . or labored in vain.** See Gal. 2:2. Paul wanted to look back on his ministry and see that all his efforts were worthwhile (cf. 1 Cor. 9:27; 1 Thess. 5:12; 2 Tim. 4:7; Heb. 13:17; 3 John 4).

i. **being poured out.** From the Gr. that means "to be offered as a libation or drink offering." Some connect this with Paul's future martyrdom, but the verb is in the present tense, which means he is referring to his sacrificial ministry among the Philippians.

j. **drink offering.** This refers to the topping off of an ancient animal sacrifice. The offerer poured wine either in front of or on top of the burning animal and the wine would be vaporized. That steam symbolized the rising of the offering to the deity for whom the sacrifice was made (cf. Ex. 29:38–41; 2 Kin. 16:13; Jer. 7:18; Hos. 9:4). Paul viewed his entire life as a drink offering, and here it was poured on the Philippians' sacrificial service.

k. **service of your faith.** "Service" comes from a word that refers to sacred, priestly service (cf. Rom. 12:1; 1 Cor. 9:12) and was so used in the Gr. OT. Paul sees the Philippians as priests who were offering their lives sacrificially and faithfully in service to God (cf. 1 Pet. 2:9).

l. **I . . . rejoice . . . you also . . . rejoice.** An attitude of mutual joy ought to accompany any sacrificial Christian service (see Phil. 1:4, 18, 26; cf. 2 Cor. 7:4; Col. 1:24; 1 Thess. 3:9).

220. PAUL'S COMPANIONS

Phil. 2:19–30

But I trust in the Lord Jesus to send Timothy to you shortly, that I also may be encouraged when I know your state. For [a]I have no one like-minded, who will sincerely care for your state. For all seek their own, not the things which are of Christ Jesus. But you know his proven character, that as a son with his father he served with me in the gospel. Therefore I hope to send him at once, as soon as I see [b]how it goes with me. But I trust [c]in the Lord that I myself shall also come shortly.

Yet I considered it necessary to send to you [d]Epaphroditus, my brother, fellow worker, and fellow soldier, but your [e]messenger and the one who ministered to my need; since he was longing for you all, and was [f]distressed because you had heard that he was sick. For indeed he was [g]sick almost unto death; but God had mercy on him, and not only on him but on me also, lest I should have sorrow upon sorrow. Therefore I sent him the more eagerly, that when you see him again you may rejoice, and I may be less [h]sorrowful. Receive him

---

a. **I have no one like-minded.** See Phil. 2:2. Lit. "one souled," and often translated "kindred spirit." Timothy was one in thought, feeling, and spirit with Paul in love for the church. He was unique in being Paul's protege (see 1 Cor. 4:17; cf. 1 Tim. 1:2; 2 Tim. 1:2). Paul had no other like Timothy because, sadly, "all" the others were devoted to their own purposes rather than Christ's. See 2 Tim. 1:15.

b. **how it goes with me.** Paul was eventually released from prison (cf. Acts 28:30), after which he may have visited the church at Philippi.

c. **in the Lord.** Paul knew his plans were subject to God's sovereignty (cf. James 4:13–17).

d. **Epaphroditus.** Paul wanted to send Timothy (Phil. 2:23) and come himself (v. 24), but found it necessary to send this man, a native Philippian of whom, outside this passage, little is known. His name was a common Gr. one, taken from a familiar word that originally meant "favorite of Aphrodite" (Gr. goddess of love). Later, the name came to mean "lovely" or "loving." He was sent to Paul with gifts (4:18) and was to remain and serve Paul as he could (v. 30).

e. **messenger.** This comes from the same word that yields the Eng. "apostle." He was not an apostle of Christ (see Rom. 1:1), but an apostle ("sent one") in the broader sense (see Rom. 1:5) that he was an apostle of the church in Philippi, sent to Paul with their monetary love gift (see Phil. 1:7; cf. 2 Cor. 8:23). Paul's sending him back to the church with this letter needed an explanation, lest they think Epaphroditus had not served Paul well.

f. **distressed.** The Gr. term describes the confused, chaotic, heavy state of restlessness that results from a time of turmoil or great trauma. Epaphroditus was more concerned about the Philippians' worry for him than he was about his own difficult situation.

g. **sick almost unto death.** Perhaps by the time he arrived in Rome, he had become seriously ill, but now was recovered enough to go back home to labor with the church, who needed him more than Paul did.

h. **sorrowful.** More accurately translated "concern" or "anxiety." Paul had a great burden

therefore in the Lord with all gladness, and hold such men in [a]esteem; because for the work of Christ he came [b]close to death, not regarding his life, to supply what was lacking in your service toward me.

221. LEGALISM VERSUS TRUE RIGHTEOUSNESS
Phil. 3:1–11

Finally, my brethren, [c]rejoice in the Lord. For me to write the same things to you is not tedious, but for you it [d]is safe.

Beware of [e]dogs, beware of [f]evil workers, beware of the [g]mutilation! For [h]we are the circumcision, who [i]worship God in the Spirit, [j]rejoice in Christ

---

for all the people in the churches (cf. 2 Cor. 11:2), and he was concerned here because the Philippians were so distressed about Epaphroditus (see Phil. 1:8).

a. **esteem.** Men like him are worthy of honor. See 1 Thess. 5:12, 13.

b. **close to death.** This refers to the same thing mentioned as sickness in Phil. 2:26, 27.

c. **rejoice in the Lord.** Cf. Phil. 4:1. Paul's familiar theme throughout the epistle, which has already been heard in chaps. 1, 2. This, however, is the first time he adds "in the Lord," which signifies the sphere in which the believers' joy exists—a sphere unrelated to the circumstances of life, but related to an unassailable, unchanging relationship to the sovereign Lord.

d. **is safe.** A safeguard to protect the Philippians from succumbing to the false teachers. Paul had previously given them similar instruction regarding their opponents (cf. Phil. 1:27–30).

e. **dogs.** During the first century, dogs roamed the streets and were essentially wild scavengers. Because dogs were such filthy animals, the Jews loved to refer to Gentiles as dogs. Yet here Paul refers to Jews, specifically the Judaizers, as dogs to describe their sinful, vicious, and uncontrolled character. For more on those who taught that circumcision was necessary for salvation, see Acts 15:1–5; Gal. 2:3.

f. **evil workers.** The Judaizers prided themselves on being workers of righteousness. Yet Paul described their works as evil, since any attempt to please God by one's own efforts and draw attention away from Christ's accomplished redemption is the worst kind of wickedness.

g. **mutilation.** In contrast to the Gr. word for "circumcision," which means "to cut around," this term means "to cut down (off)." Like the prophets of Baal (1 Kin. 18:28) and pagans who mutilated their bodies in their frenzied rituals, which were forbidden in the OT (Lev. 19:28; 21:5; Deut. 14:1; Is. 15:2; Hos. 7:14), the Judaizers' circumcision was, ironically, no spiritual symbol; it was merely physical mutilation (see Gal. 5:12).

h. **we are the circumcision.** The true people of God do not possess merely a symbol of the need for a clean heart (see Gen. 17:10), they actually have been cleansed of sin by God (see Rom. 2:25–29).

i. **worship God in the Spirit.** The first characteristic Paul uses to define a true believer. The Gr. word for "worship" means to render respectful spiritual service, while "Spirit" should have a small "s," to indicate the inner person. See John 4:23, 24.

j. **rejoice in Christ Jesus.** The Gr. word for "rejoice" means "to boast with exultant joy." The true Christian gives all the credit for all that he is to Christ (cf. Rom. 15:17; 1 Cor. 1:31; 2 Cor. 10:17).

Jesus, and have ªno confidence in the flesh, though I also might have confidence in the flesh. If anyone else thinks he may have confidence in the flesh, I more so: circumcised ᵇthe eighth day, of the stock of Israel, ᶜof the tribe of Benjamin, a Hebrew of the Hebrews; concerning the law, ᵈa Pharisee; concerning ᵉzeal, persecuting the church; concerning the ᶠrighteousness which is in the law, blameless.

But ᵍwhat things were gain to me, these I have counted loss for Christ. Yet indeed I also count all things loss for the excellence of the ʰknowledge of Christ Jesus my Lord, for whom I have suffered the loss of all things, and count them as ⁱrubbish, that I may gain Christ and ʲbe found in Him,

---

a. **no confidence in the flesh.** By "flesh" Paul is referring to man's unredeemed humanness, his own ability and achievements apart from God (see Rom. 7:5). The Jews placed their confidence in being circumcised, being descendants of Abraham, and performing the external ceremonies and duties of the Mosaic law—things that could not save them (see Rom. 3:20; Gal. 5:1–12). The true believer views his flesh as sinful, without any capacity to merit salvation or please God.

b. **the eighth day . . . Israel . . . Hebrew of Hebrews.** To counteract the Judaizers' claim that certain ceremonies and rituals of Judaism were necessary for salvation, Paul described his own lofty attainments as a Jew, which were greater than those his opponents could claim, but were of no benefit for salvation. For example, Paul was circumcised on the prescribed day (Gen. 17:12; 21:4; Lev. 12:3). Also, Paul was born to Hebrew parents and maintained the Hebrew tradition and language, even while living in a pagan city (cf. Acts 21:40; 26:4, 5). His Jewish heritage was pure.

c. **of the tribe of Benjamin.** Benjamin was the second son of Rachel (Gen. 35:18), and one of the elite tribes of Israel, who along with Judah, remained loyal to the Davidic dynasty and formed the southern kingdom (1 Kin. 12:21).

d. **a Pharisee.** The legalistic fundamentalists of Judaism, whose zeal to apply the OT Scriptures directly to life led to a complex system of tradition and works righteousness (see Matt. 3:7). Paul may have come from a line of Pharisees (cf. Acts 22:3; 23:6; 26:5).

e. **zeal, persecuting the church.** To the Jew, "zeal" was the highest single virtue of religion. It combines love and hate; because Paul loved Judaism, he hated whatever might threaten it (see Acts 8:3 and 9:1).

f. **the righteousness which is in the law.** The standard of righteous living advocated by God's law. Paul outwardly kept this, so that no one could accuse him of violation. Obviously his heart was sinful and self-righteous. He was not an OT believer, but a proud and lost legalist.

g. **what things were gain . . . I have counted loss.** The Gr. word for "gain" is an accounting term that means "profit." The Gr. word for "loss" also is an accounting term, used to describe a business loss. Paul used the language of business to describe the spiritual transaction that occurred when Christ redeemed him. All his Jewish religious credentials that he thought were in his profit column, were actually worthless and damning (cf. Luke 18:9–14). Thus, he put them in his loss column when he saw the glories of Christ (cf. Matt. 13:44, 45; 16:25, 26).

h. **knowledge of Christ Jesus.** To "know" Christ is not simply to have intellectual knowledge about Him; Paul used the Gr. verb that means to know "experientially" or "personally" (cf. John 10:27; 17:3; 2 Cor. 4:6; 1 John 5:20). It is equivalent to shared life with Christ (see Gal. 2:20). It also corresponds to a Heb. word used of God's knowledge of His people (Amos 3:2) and their knowledge of Him in love and obedience (Jer. 31:34; Hos. 6:3; 8:2).

i. **rubbish.** The Gr. word refers to garbage or waste, and can even be translated "dung" or "manure."

j. **be found in Him.** Paul was "in Christ" (see Phil. 1:1). His union with Christ was possible only because God imputed Christ's righteousness to him so that it was reckoned by God as his own (see Rom. 1:17; 3:24).

[a]not having my own righteousness, which is from the law, but that which is through [b]faith in Christ, the righteousness which is from God by faith; that [c]I may know Him and [d]the power of His resurrection, and the [e]fellowship of His sufferings, being [f]conformed to His death, if, [g]by any means, I may attain to [h]the resurrection from the dead.

222. PRESSING TOWARDS THE GOAL
Phil. 3:12—16

[i]Not that I have already attained, or am already perfected; but I [j]press on, that I may [k]lay hold of that for which Christ Jesus has also laid hold of me. Brethren, I

---

a. **not having my own righteousness . . . from the law.** This is the proud self-righteousness of external morality, religious ritual and ceremony, and good works. It is the righteousness produced by the flesh, which cannot save from sin (Rom. 3:19, 20; Gal. 3:6–25).

b. **faith in Christ.** Faith is the confident, continuous confession of total dependence on and trust in Jesus Christ for the necessary requirement to enter God's kingdom (see Rom. 1:16). And that requirement is the righteousness of Christ, which God imputes to every believer (see Rom. 3:24).

c. **I may know Him.** Paul's emphasis here is on gaining a deeper knowledge and intimacy with Christ.

d. **the power of His resurrection.** Christ's resurrection most graphically demonstrated the extent of His power. By raising Himself from the dead, Christ displayed His power over both the physical and spiritual worlds.

e. **fellowship of His sufferings.** This refers to a partnership—a deep communion of suffering that every believer shares with Christ, who is able to comfort suffering Christians because He has already experienced the same suffering, and infinitely more (Heb. 2:18; 4:15; 12:2–4; cf. 2 Cor. 5:21; 1 Pet. 2:21–24).

f. **conformed to His death.** As Christ died for the purpose of redeeming sinners, so Paul had that same purpose in a lesser sense; he lived and would willingly die to reach sinners with the gospel. His life and death, though not redemptive, were for the same purpose as his Lord's.

g. **by any means.** Reflecting his humility, he didn't care how God brought it to pass, but longed for death and for the fulfillment of his salvation in his resurrection body (cf. Rom. 8:23).

h. **the resurrection from the dead.** Lit. "the resurrection out from the corpses." This is a reference to the resurrection which accompanies the rapture of the church (1 Thess. 4:13–17; cf. 1 Cor. 15:42–44).

i. **Not that I have already attained.** The race toward Christlikeness begins with a sense of honesty and dissatisfaction. Paul uses the analogy of a runner to describe the Christian's spiritual growth. The believer has not reached his goal of Christlikeness (cf. vv. 20, 21), but like the runner in a race, he must continue to pursue it. That this is the goal for every believer is also clear from Rom. 8:29; 2 Thess. 2:14; 1 John 3:2.

j. **press on.** The Gr. word was used of a sprinter, and refers to aggressive, energetic action. Paul pursued sanctification with all his might, straining every spiritual muscle to win the prize (1 Cor. 9:24–27; 1 Tim. 6:12; Heb. 12:1).

k. **lay hold . . . laid hold of me.** "Lay hold" means "to make one's own possession." Christ chose Paul for the ultimate purpose of conforming Paul to His glorious image (Rom. 8:29), and that is the very goal Paul pursued to attain.

do not count myself to have ᵃapprehended; but ᵇone thing I do, ᶜforgetting those things which are behind and reaching forward to those things which are ahead, I press toward ᵈthe goal for ᵉthe prize of the ᶠupward call of God in Christ Jesus.

Therefore let us, ᵍas many as are mature, ʰhave this mind; and ⁱif in anything you think otherwise, ʲGod will reveal even this to you. Nevertheless, ᵏto the degree that we have already attained, let us walk by the same rule, let us be of the same mind.

223. WARNINGS AGAINST LAWLESSNESS
Phil. 3:17—4:1

ˡBrethren, join in following my example, and ᵐnote those who so walk, as you have us for a pattern. For many walk, of whom I have ⁿtold you often, and

---

a. **apprehended.** The same Gr. word translated "laid hold" in Phil. 3:12.

b. **one thing I do.** Paul had reduced the whole of sanctification to the simple and clear goal of doing "one thing"—pursuing Christlikeness (see 2 Cor. 11:1–3).

c. **forgetting . . . which are behind.** The believer must refuse to rely on past virtuous deeds and achievements in ministry or to dwell on sins and failures. To be distracted by the past debilitates one's efforts in the present.

d. **the goal.** Christlikeness here and now (see Phil. 3:12).

e. **the prize.** Christlikeness in heaven (cf. Phil. 3:20, 21; 1 John 3:1, 2).

f. **upward call of God.** The time when God calls each believer up to heaven and into His presence will be the moment of receiving the prize which has been an unattainable goal in earthly life.

g. **as many as are mature.** Since the spiritual perfection of Christlikeness is possible only when the believer receives the upward call, Paul is referring here to mature spirituality. He could be referring to the mature believers who were like-minded with him in this pursuit or he may also have used "mature" here to refer sarcastically to the Judaizers, who thought they had reached perfection.

h. **have this mind.** A better translation is "attitude." Believers are to have the attitude of pursuing the prize of Christlikeness.

i. **if . . . you think otherwise.** Those who continue to dwell on the past and make no progress toward the goal.

j. **God will reveal.** The Gr. word for "reveal" means "to uncover" or "unveil." Paul left in God's hands those who were not pursuing spiritual perfection. He knew God would reveal the truth to them eventually, even if it meant chastening (Heb. 12:5–11).

k. **to the degree . . . already attained, let us walk.** The Gr. word for "walk" refers to walking in line. Paul's directive for the Philippian believers was to stay in line spiritually and keep progressing in sanctification by the same principles that had brought them to this point in their spiritual growth (cf. 1 Thess. 3:10; 1 Pet. 2:2).

l. **my example.** Lit. "be imitators of me." Since all believers are imperfect, they need examples of less imperfect people who know how to deal with imperfection and who can model the process of pursuing the goal of Christlikeness. Paul was that model (1 Cor. 11:1; 1 Thess. 1:6).

m. **note those who so walk.** The Philippian believers were to focus on other godly examples, such as Timothy and Epaphroditus (Phil. 2:19, 20), and see how they conducted themselves in service to Christ.

n. **told you often.** Apparently Paul had warned the Philippians on numerous occasions about the dangers of false teachers, just as he did the Ephesians (Acts 20:28–30).

now tell you even [a]weeping, that they are the [b]enemies of the cross of Christ: whose [c]end is destruction, whose [d]god is their belly, and whose [e]glory is in their shame—who set their mind on [f]earthly things. For [g]our citizenship is [h]in heaven, from which we also [i]eagerly wait for the Savior, the Lord Jesus Christ, who will [j]transform our lowly body that it may be [k]conformed to His glorious body, according to the working by which He is able even to [l]subdue all things to Himself.

---

a. **weeping.** Paul had a similar response as he warned the Ephesian elders about the dangers of false teachers (Acts 20:31).

b. **enemies of the cross.** Implied in Paul's language is that these men did not claim to oppose Christ, His work on the cross, or salvation by grace alone through faith alone, but they did not pursue Christlikeness in manifest godliness. Apparently, they were posing as friends of Christ, and possibly had even reached positions of leadership in the church.

c. **end is destruction.** The Gr. word for "end" refers to one's ultimate destiny. The Judaizers were headed for eternal damnation because they depended on their works to save them. The Gentile libertines were headed for the same destiny because they trusted in their human wisdom and denied the transforming power of the gospel.

d. **god . . . belly.** This may refer to the Judaizers' fleshly accomplishments, which were mainly religious works. It could also refer to their observance of the dietary laws they believed were necessary for salvation. If the Gentile libertines are in view, it could easily refer to their sensual desires and fleshly appetites. As always, false teachers are evident by their wickedness. See 2 Pet. 2:10–19; Jude 8–13.

e. **glory . . . shame.** The Judaizers boasted of their self-effort; but even the best of their accomplishments were no better than filthy rags or dung (Phil. 3:7, 8; Is. 64:6). The Gentile libertines boasted about their sin and abused Christian liberty to defend their behavior (1 Cor. 6:12).

f. **earthly things.** The Judaizers were preoccupied with ceremonies, feasts, sacrifices, and other kinds of physical observances. The Gentile libertines simply loved the world itself and all the things in it (cf. James 4:4; 1 John 2:15).

g. **our citizenship.** The Gr. term refers to a colony of foreigners. In one secular source, it was used to describe a capital city that kept the names of its citizens on a register.

h. **in heaven.** The place where God dwells and where Christ is present. It is the believers' home (John 14:2, 3), where their names are registered (Luke 10:20) and their inheritance awaits (1 Pet. 1:4). Other believers are there (Heb. 12:23). We belong to the kingdom under the rule of our heavenly King, and obey heaven's laws. Cf. 1 Pet. 2:11.

i. **eagerly wait.** The Gr. verb is found in most passages dealing with the second coming and expresses the idea of waiting patiently, but with great expectation (Rom. 8:23; 2 Pet. 3:11, 12).

j. **transform our lowly body.** The Gr. word for "transform" gives us the word "schematic," which is an internal design of something. Those who are already dead in Christ, but alive with Him in spirit in heaven (Phil. 1:23; 2 Cor. 5:8; Heb. 12:23), will receive new bodies at the resurrection and rapture of the church, when those alive on earth will have their bodies transformed (see Rom. 8:18–23; 1 Cor. 15:51–54; 1 Thess. 4:16).

k. **conformed to His glorious body.** The believer's new body will be like Christ's after His resurrection, and will be redesigned and adapted for heaven (1 Cor. 15:42, 43; 1 John 3:2).

l. **subdue.** The Gr. word means "to subject" and refers to arranging things in order of rank or managing something. Christ has the power both to providentially create natural laws and miraculously overrule them (1 Cor. 15:23–27).

Therefore, my ªbeloved and longed-for brethren, ᵇmy joy and crown, so ᶜstand fast in the Lord, beloved.

224. APOSTOLIC ADMONITIONS

Phil. 4:2–9

I ᵈimplore ᵉEuodia and I implore Syntyche to be of ᶠthe same mind in the Lord. And I urge you also, true ᵍcompanion, help these women who labored with me in the gospel, ʰwith Clement also, and the rest of my fellow workers, whose names are in the ⁱBook of Life.

Rejoice in the Lord always. Again I will say, rejoice!

Let your ʲgentleness be known to all men. The Lord is ᵏat hand.

---

a. **beloved and longed-for.** Paul reveals his deep affection for the Philippian believers. The Gr. term for "longed-for" refers to the deep pain of separation from loved ones.

b. **my joy and crown.** Paul did not derive his joy from circumstances, but from his fellow believers in Philippi (cf. 1 Thess. 2:19, 20; 3:9). The Gr. term for "crown" refers to the laurel wreath received by an athlete for winning a contest (1 Cor. 9:25) or by a person honored by his peers at a banquet as a symbol of success or a fruitful life. The Philippian believers were proof that Paul's efforts were successful (cf. 1 Cor. 9:2).

c. **stand fast.** This Gr. word was often used to describe a soldier standing at his post; here it is a military command (cf. Phil. 1:27) which is the dominant expression of Phil. 4:1–9.

d. **implore.** The Gr. term means "to urge," or "to appeal."

e. **Euodia . . . Syntyche.** These two women were prominent church members (Phil. 4:3), who may have been among the women meeting for prayer when Paul first preached the gospel in Philippi (Acts 16:13). Apparently, they were leading two opposing factions in the church, most likely over a personal conflict.

f. **the same mind.** Another possible translation is "harmony" (see Phil. 2:2). Spiritual stability depends on the mutual love, harmony, and peace between believers. Apparently the disunity in the Philippian church was about to destroy the integrity of its testimony.

g. **companion.** The Gr. word pictures two oxen in a yoke, pulling the same load. A companion is a partner or an equal in a specific endeavor—in this case a spiritual one. It is possible that this individual is unnamed, but it is best to take the Gr. word translated "companion" as a proper name ("Syzygos"). He was likely one of the church elders (Phil. 1:1).

h. **with Clement.** Nothing is known of him.

i. **Book of Life.** In eternity past, God registered all the names of His elect in that book which identifies those inheritors of eternal life (see Rev. 3:5; cf. Dan. 12:1; Mal. 3:16, 17; Luke 10:20; Rev. 17:8; 20:12).

j. **gentleness.** This refers to contentment with and generosity toward others. It can also refer to mercy or leniency toward the faults and failures of others. It can even refer to patience in someone who submits to injustice or mistreatment without retaliating. Graciousness with humility encompasses all the above.

k. **at hand.** Can refer to nearness in space or time. The context suggests nearness in space: the Lord encompasses all believers with His presence (Ps. 119:151).

[a]Be anxious for nothing, but [b]in everything by [c]prayer and supplication, with thanksgiving, let your requests be made known to God; and the [d]peace of God, which [e]surpasses all understanding, will [f]guard your [g]hearts and minds through Christ Jesus.

Finally, brethren, whatever things are [h]true, whatever things are [i]noble, whatever things are [j]just, whatever things are [k]pure, whatever things are [l]lovely, whatever things are [m]of good report, if there is any virtue and if there is anything praiseworthy—meditate on these things. The things which you learned and received and heard and saw [n]in me, these do, and [o]the God of peace will be with you.

---

a. **Be anxious for nothing.** See Matt. 6:25–34. Fret and worry indicate a lack of trust in God's wisdom, sovereignty, or power. Delighting in the Lord and meditating on His Word are a great antidote to anxiety (Ps. 1:2).

b. **in everything.** All difficulties are within God's purposes.

c. **prayer and supplication, with thanksgiving . . . requests.** Gratitude to God accompanies all true prayer.

d. **peace of God.** See Phil. 4:9. Inner calm or tranquility is promised to the believer who has a thankful attitude based on unwavering confidence that God is able and willing to do what is best for His children (cf. Rom. 8:28).

e. **surpasses all understanding.** This refers to the divine origin of peace. It transcends human intellect, analysis, and insight (Is. 26:3; John 16:33).

f. **guard.** A military term meaning "to keep watch over." God's peace guards believers from anxiety, doubt, fear, and distress.

g. **hearts . . . minds.** Paul was not making a distinction between the two—he was giving a comprehensive statement referring to the whole inner person. Because of the believer's union with Christ, He guards his inner being with His peace.

h. **true.** What is true is found in God (2 Tim. 2:25), in Christ (Eph. 4:20, 21), in the Holy Spirit (John 16:13), and in God's Word (John 17:17).

i. **noble.** The Gr. term means "worthy of respect." Believers are to meditate on whatever is worthy of awe and adoration, i.e., the sacred as opposed to the profane.

j. **just.** This refers to what is right. The believer is to think in harmony with God's divine standard of holiness.

k. **pure.** That which is morally clean and undefiled.

l. **lovely.** The Gr. term means "pleasing" or "amiable." By implication, believers are to focus on whatever is kind or gracious.

m. **of good report.** That which is highly regarded or thought well of. It refers to what is generally considered reputable in the world, such as kindness, courtesy, and respect for others.

n. **in me.** The Philippians were to follow the truth of God proclaimed, along with the example of that truth lived by Paul before them (see Heb. 13:7).

o. **the God of peace.** See Rom. 15:33; cf. 1 Cor. 14:33. God is peace (Rom. 16:20; Eph. 2:14), makes peace with sinners through Christ (2 Cor. 5:18–20), and gives perfect peace in trouble.

225. Contentment and Concluding Remarks

Phil. 4:10–23

But I rejoiced in the Lord greatly that now ªat last your care for me has flourished again; though you surely did care, but you lacked opportunity. Not that I speak in regard to need, for I have learned in ᵇwhatever state I am, to be ᶜcontent: I know how to be ᵈabased, and I know how to abound. Everywhere and in all things I have learned both ᵉto be full and to be hungry, both to abound and to suffer need. ᶠI can do all things ᵍthrough Christ who strengthens me.

Nevertheless you have done well that you ʰshared in my distress. Now you Philippians know also that ⁱin the beginning of the gospel, ʲwhen I departed

---

a. **at last . . . you lacked opportunity.** About ten years had passed since the Philippians first gave a gift to Paul to help meet his needs when he was first in Thessalonica (Phil. 4:15, 16). Paul was aware of their desire to continue to help, but he realized, within God's providence, that they had not had the "opportunity" (season) to help. In these verses, Paul expressed his gratitude to the Philippians for their kind expressions of love and the generous gift they sent him and thus provides a powerful example of how a Christian can be content regardless of his circumstances.

b. **whatever state I am.** Paul defined the circumstances in the following verse.

c. **content.** The Gr. term means "to be self-sufficient" or "to be satisfied." It is the same word translated "sufficiency" in 2 Cor. 9:8. It indicates independence from any need for help (cf. Luke 3:14; 1 Thess. 4:12; 1 Tim. 6:6, 8; Heb. 13:5).

d. **abased . . . abound.** Paul knew how to get along with humble means (food, clothing, daily necessities) and how to live in prosperity ("to overflow").

e. **to be full and to be hungry.** The Gr. word translated "to be full" was used of feeding and fattening animals. Paul knew how to be content when he had plenty to eat and when he was deprived of enough to eat.

f. **I can do all things.** Paul uses a Gr. verb that means "to be strong" or "to have strength" (cf. Acts 19:16, 20; James 5:16). He had strength to withstand "all things" (Phil. 4:11, 12), including both difficulty and prosperity in the material world.

g. **through Christ who strengthens me.** The Gr. word for strengthen means "to put power in." Because believers are in Christ (Gal. 2:20), He infuses them with His strength to sustain them until they receive some provision (Eph. 3:16–20; 2 Cor. 12:10).

h. **shared.** To join in a partnership with someone. By noting they had done well, Paul adds a word of clarification here so the Philippians would not think he was being ungrateful for their most recent gift, because of what he just wrote (Phil. 4:11–13).

i. **in the beginning of the gospel.** When Paul first preached the gospel in Philippi (Acts 16:13).

j. **when I departed.** When Paul first left Philippi approximately 10 years before (Acts 16:40).

from ᵃMacedonia, no church shared with me ᵇconcerning giving and receiving ᶜbut you only. For ᵈeven in Thessalonica you sent aid once and again for my necessities. Not that I seek the gift, but I seek ᵉthe fruit that ᶠabounds to your account. Indeed I have all and abound. I am full, having received from Epaphroditus the things sent from you, ᵍa sweet-smelling aroma, an acceptable sacrifice, well pleasing to God. And my God shall supply ʰall your need ⁱaccording to His riches in glory by Christ Jesus. Now to our God and Father be glory forever and ever. Amen.

Greet ʲevery saint in Christ Jesus. The ᵏbrethren who are with me greet you. All the saints greet you, but especially those who are of ˡCaesar's household.

The grace of our Lord Jesus Christ be with you all. ᵐAmen.

---

a. **Macedonia.** In addition to Philippi, Paul also ministered in two other towns in Macedonia: Thessalonica and Berea (Acts 17:1–14).

b. **concerning giving and receiving.** Paul used 3 business terms. "Concerning" could be translated "account." "Giving and receiving" refer to expenditures and receipts. Paul was a faithful steward of God's resources and kept careful records of what he received and spent.

c. **but you only.** Only the Philippians sent Paul provisions to meet his needs.

d. **even in Thessalonica.** See Acts 17:1. Paul preached there for a few months, during his second missionary journey.

e. **the fruit.** The Gr. word can be translated "profit."

f. **abounds to your account.** The Philippians were in effect storing up for themselves treasure in heaven (Matt. 6:20). The gifts they gave to Paul were accruing eternal dividends to their spiritual account (Prov. 11:24, 25; 19:17; Luke 6:38; 2 Cor. 9:6).

g. **a sweet-smelling aroma, an acceptable sacrifice, well-pleasing to God.** In the OT sacrificial system, every sacrifice was to provide a fragrant aroma and be acceptable to God. Only if it was offered with the correct attitude would it be pleasing to Him (Gen. 8:20, 21; Ex. 29:18; Lev. 1:9, 13, 17). The Philippians' gift was a spiritual sacrifice (cf. Rom. 12:1; 1 Pet. 2:5) that pleased God.

h. **all your need.** Paul addressed all the Philippians' material needs, which had probably been depleted to some extent because of their gracious gift (Prov. 3:9).

i. **according to His riches.** God would give increase to the Philippians in proportion to His infinite resources, not just a small amount out of His riches.

j. **every saint.** See Phil. 1:1. Instead of using the collective "all," Paul used the individualistic "every" to declare that each saint was worthy of his concern.

k. **brethren who are with me.** They certainly included Timothy and Epaphroditus (Phil. 2:19, 25). Others who were preaching the gospel in Rome were present (Phil. 1:14). It is possible that Tychicus, Aristarchus, Onesimus, and Jesus Justus were also there (Col. 4:7, 9–11).

l. **Caesar's household.** A significant number of people, not limited to Caesar's family, which would include courtiers, princes, judges, cooks, food-tasters, musicians, custodians, builders, stablemen, soldiers, accountants. Within that large group, Paul had in mind those who, through the proclamation of the gospel by members of the church at Rome, had been saved prior to his coming. Newly added to their number were those led to Christ by Paul himself, including those soldiers who were chained to him while he was a prisoner (Phil. 1:13).

m. **Amen.** A confessional affirmation that underscores the preceding truth.

PART VI

FROM MISSIONARY TO MARTYR: FAITHFUL TO THE END

ca. A.D. 62–67

226. PAUL WRITES A LETTER TO TIMOTHY
Introduction to 1 Timothy

This is the first of two inspired letters Paul wrote to his beloved son in the faith. Timothy received his name, which means "one who honors God," from his mother (Eunice) and grandmother (Lois), devout Jews who became believers in the Lord Jesus Christ (2 Tim. 1:5) and taught Timothy the OT Scriptures from his childhood (2 Tim. 3:15). His father was a Greek (Acts 16:1) who may have died before Timothy met Paul.

Timothy was from Lystra (Acts 16:1–3), a city in the Roman province of Galatia (part of modern Turkey). Paul led Timothy to Christ (1:2, 18; 1 Cor. 4:17; 2 Tim. 1:2), undoubtedly during his ministry in Lystra on his first missionary journey (Acts 14:6–23). When he revisited Lystra on his second missionary journey, Paul chose Timothy to accompany him (Acts 16:1–3). Although Timothy was very young (probably in his late teens or early twenties, since about 15 years later Paul referred to him as a young man, 4:12), he had a reputation for godliness (Acts 16:2). Timothy was to be Paul's disciple, friend, and co-laborer for the rest of the apostle's life, ministering with him in Berea (Acts 17:14), Athens (Acts 17:15), Corinth (Acts 18:5; 2 Cor. 1:19), and accompanying him on his trip to Jerusalem (Acts 20:4). He was with Paul in his first Roman imprisonment and went to Philippi (2:19–23) after Paul's release. In addition, Paul frequently mentions Timothy in his epistles (Rom. 16:21; 2 Cor. 1:1; Phil. 1:1; Col. 1:1; 1 Thess. 1:1; 2 Thess. 1:1; Philem. 1). Paul often sent Timothy to churches as his representative (1 Cor. 4:17; 16:10; Phil. 2:19; 1 Thess. 3:2), and 1 Timothy finds him on another assignment, serving as pastor of the church at Ephesus (1:3). According to Heb. 13:23, Timothy was imprisoned somewhere and released.

Author and Date

Many modernist critics delight in attacking the plain statements of Scripture and, for no good reason, deny that Paul wrote the Pastoral Epistles (1, 2 Tim., Titus). Ignoring the testimony of the letters themselves (1:1; 2 Tim. 1:1; Titus 1:1) and that of the early church (which is as strong for the Pastoral Epistles as for any of Paul's epistles, except Rom. and 1 Cor.), these critics maintain that a devout follower of Paul wrote the Pastoral Epistles in the second century. As proof, they offer 5 lines of supposed evidence: 1) The historical references in the Pastoral Epistles cannot be harmonized with the chronology of Paul's life given in Acts; 2) The false teaching described in the Pastoral Epistles is the fully-developed Gnosticism of the second century; 3) The church organizational structure in the Pastoral Epistles is that of the second century, and is too well developed for Paul's day; 4) The Pastoral Epistles do not contain the great themes of Paul's theology; 5) The Greek vocabulary of the Pastoral Epistles contains many words not found in Paul's other letters, nor in the rest of the NT.

While it is unnecessary to dignify such unwarranted attacks by unbelievers with an answer, occasionally such an answer does enlighten. Thus, in reply to the critics' arguments, it can be pointed out that: 1) This contention of historical incompatibility is valid only if Paul was never released from his Roman imprisonment mentioned in Acts. But he was released, since Acts does not record Paul's execution, and Paul himself expected to be released (Phil. 1:19, 25, 26; 2:24; Philem. 22). The historical events in the Pastoral Epistles do not fit into the chronology of Acts because they happened after the close of the Acts narrative which ends with Paul's first imprisonment in Rome. 2) While there are similarities between the heresy of the Pastoral Epistles and second-century Gnosticism (see Introduction to Colossians: Background and Setting), there are also important differences. Unlike second-century Gnosticism, the false teachers of the Pastoral Epistles were still within the church (cf. 1:3–7) and their teaching was based on Judaistic legalism (1:7; Titus 1:10, 14; 3:9). 3) The church organizational structure mentioned in the Pastoral Epistles is, in fact, consistent with that established by Paul (Acts 14:23; Phil. 1:1). 4) The Pastoral Epistles do mention the central themes of Paul's theology, including the inspiration of Scripture (2 Tim. 3:15–17); election (2 Tim. 1:9; Titus 1:1, 2); salvation (Titus 3:5–7); the deity of Christ (Titus 2:13); His mediatorial work (2:5), and substitutionary atonement (2:6). 5) The different subject matter in the Pastoral Epistles required a different vocabulary from that in Paul's other epistles. Certainly a pastor today would use a different vocabulary in a personal letter to a fellow pastor than he would in a work of systematic theology.

The idea that a "pious forger" wrote the Pastoral Epistles faces several further difficulties: 1) The early church did not approve of such practices and surely would have exposed this as a ruse, if there had actually been one (cf. 2 Thess. 2:1, 2; 3:17). 2) Why forge 3 letters that include similar material and no deviant doctrine? 3) If a counterfeit, why not invent an itinerary for Paul that would have harmonized with Acts? 4) Would a later, devoted follower of Paul have put the words of 1:13, 15 into his master's mouth? 5) Why would he include warnings against deceivers (2 Tim. 3:13; Titus 1:10), if he himself were one?

The evidence seems clear that Paul wrote 1 Timothy and Titus shortly after his release from his first Roman imprisonment (ca. A.D. 62–64), and 2 Timothy from prison during his second Roman imprisonment (ca. A.D. 66–67), shortly before his death.

Background and Setting

After being released from his first Roman imprisonment (cf. Acts 28:30), Paul revisited several of the cities in which he had ministered, including Ephesus. Leaving Timothy behind there to deal with problems that had arisen in the Ephesian church, such as false doctrine (1 Tim. 1:3–7; 4:1–3; 6:3–5), disorder in worship (2:1–15), the need for qualified leaders (3:1–14), and materialism (6:6–19), Paul went on to Macedonia, from where he wrote Timothy this letter to help him carry out his task in the church (cf. 3:14, 15).

Historical and Theological Themes:

First Timothy is a practical letter containing pastoral instruction from Paul to Timothy (cf. 1 Tim. 3:14, 15). Since Timothy was well versed in Paul's theology, the apostle had no need to give him extensive doctrinal instruction. This epistle does, however, express many important theological truths, such as the proper function of the law (1:5–11), salvation (1:14–16; 2:4–6); the attributes of God (1:17); the Fall (2:13, 14); the person of Christ (3:16; 6:15, 16); election (6:12); and the second coming of Christ (6:14, 15).

Interpretive Challenges

There is disagreement over the identity of the false teachers (1:3) and the genealogies (1 Tim. 1:4) involved in their teaching. What it means to be "delivered to Satan" (1:20) has also been a source of debate. The letter contains key passages in the debate over the extent of the atonement (2:4–6; 4:10). Paul's teaching on the role of women (2:9–15) has generated much discussion, particularly his declaration that they are not to assume leadership roles in the church (2:11, 12). How women can be saved by bearing children (2:15) has also confused many. Whether the fact that an elder must be "the husband of one wife" excludes divorced or unmarried men has been disputed, as well as whether Paul refers to deacons' wives or deaconesses (3:11). Those who believe Christians can lose their salvation cite 4:1 as support for their view. There is a question about the identity of the widows in 5:3–16—are they needy women ministered to by the church, or an order of older women ministering to the church? Does "double honor" accorded to elders who rule well (5:17, 18) refer to respect or money? These will all be dealt with in their respective notes.

227. FALSE DOCTRINE AT EPHESUS
1 Timothy 1:1–11

Paul, an ᵃapostle of Jesus Christ, by the commandment of ᵇGod our Savior and the Lord ᶜJesus Christ, our hope,

> To Timothy, a ᵈtrue son in the faith:
> ᵉGrace, mercy, and peace from God our Father and Jesus Christ our Lord.
> As I urged you ᶠwhen I went into Macedonia—remain in Ephesus that

---

a. **apostle of Jesus Christ.** See 2 Cor. 12:11, 12; cf. Acts 1:2; 2:42; Rom. 1:1; Eph. 2:20.

b. **God our Savior.** A title unique to the Pastoral Epistles (1, 2 Tim., Titus) that has its roots in the OT (Pss. 18:46; 25:5; 27:9; Mic. 7:7; Hab. 3:18). God is by nature a saving God and the source of our salvation, which He planned from eternity past (see 1 Tim. 4:10; cf. 2 Thess. 2:13).

c. **Jesus Christ, our hope.** Christians have hope for the future because Christ purchased salvation for them on the cross in the past (Rom. 5:1, 2), sanctifies them through His Spirit in the present (Gal. 5:16–25), and will lead them to glory in the future (Col. 1:27; 1 John 3:2, 3).

d. **true son in the faith.** Only Timothy (2 Tim. 1:2; 2:1) and Titus (1:4) received this special expression of Paul's favor. The Gr. word for "son" is better translated "child," which emphasizes Paul's role as spiritual father to Timothy. "True" speaks of the genuineness of Timothy's faith (cf. 2 Tim. 1:5). Timothy was Paul's most cherished pupil, and protégé (1 Cor. 4:17; Phil. 2:19–22).

e. **Grace, mercy, and peace.** Paul's familiar greeting that appears in all his epistles (see Rom. 1:7), but with the addition here of "mercy" (cf. 2 Tim. 1:2). Mercy frees believers from the misery that accompanies the consequences of sin.

f. **when I went into Macedonia—remain in Ephesus.** Before Paul left Ephesus, he likely began the confrontation with the expulsion of Hymenaeus and Alexander (1 Tim. 1:20), then assigned Timothy to stay on and complete what he had begun.

you may ªcharge ᵇsome that they ᶜteach no other doctrine, nor give heed to ᵈfables and endless genealogies, which cause disputes rather than godly edification which is in faith. Now the purpose of ᵉthe commandment is ᶠlove from a pure heart, from a ᵍgood conscience, and from sincere faith, from which some, having strayed, have turned aside to ʰidle talk, ⁱdesiring to be teachers of ʲthe law, understanding neither what they say nor the things which they affirm.

a. **charge.** This refers to a military command—it demands that a subordinate obey an order from a superior (cf. 2 Tim. 4:1).

b. **some.** The false teachers were few in number, yet had a wide influence. Several reasons point toward these men being elders in the church at Ephesus and in the churches in the surrounding region: 1) they presumed to be teachers (1 Tim. 1:7), a role reserved for elders (3:2; 5:17). 2) Paul himself had to excommunicate Hymenaeus and Alexander, which implies they occupied the highest pastoral positions. 3) Paul detailed the qualifications of an elder (3:1–7), implying that unqualified men, who needed to be replaced by qualified ones, were occupying those roles. 4) Paul stressed that sinning elders were to be publicly disciplined (5:19–22).

c. **teach no other doctrine.** A compound word made up of two Gr. words that mean "of a different kind" and "to teach." The false teachers were teaching doctrine different than apostolic doctrine (cf. 1 Tim. 6:3, 4; Acts 2:42; Gal. 1:6, 7). This had to do with the gospel of salvation. Apparently they were teaching another gospel (see Gal. 1:6–9) and not the "glorious gospel of the blessed God" (1 Tim. 1:11).

d. **fables and endless genealogies.** Legends and fanciful stories manufactured from elements of Judaism (1 Tim. 1:7; cf. Titus 1:14), which probably dealt with allegorical or fictitious interpretations of OT genealogical lists. In reality, they were "doctrines of demons" (1 Tim. 4:1), posing as God's truth (cf. 4:7).

e. **the commandment.** See 1 Tim. 1:3, where the verb form "charge" is used (also in v. 8). The purpose of the charge in vv. 3, 4 is the spiritual virtue defined in v. 5. Timothy was to deliver this charge to the church. The goal of preaching the truth and warning of error is to call men to true salvation in Christ, which produces a love for God from a purified heart (2 Tim. 2:22; 1 Pet. 1:22), a cleansed conscience (Heb. 9:22; 10:14), and genuine faith (Heb. 10:22).

f. **love.** This is the love of choice and the will, characterized by self-denial and self-sacrifice for the benefit of others, and it is the mark of a true Christian (John 13:35; Rom. 13:10; 1 John 4:7, 8; see 1 Cor. 13:1–7). In contrast, false doctrine produces only conflict and resultant "disputes" (1 Tim. 1:4; 6:3–5).

g. **good conscience.** Cf. 1 Tim. 1:19; 3:9; 4:2; see 2 Cor. 1:12. The Gr. word for "good" refers to that which is perfect and produces pleasure and satisfaction. God created man with a "conscience" as his self-judging faculty. Because God has written His law on man's heart (see Rom. 2:15), man knows the basic standard of right and wrong. When he violates that standard, his conscience produces guilt, which acts as the mind's security system that produces fear, guilt, shame, and doubt as warnings of threats to the soul's well-being (cf. John 8:9; 1 Cor. 8:7, 10, 12; Titus 1:15; Heb. 10:22). On the other hand, when a believer does God's will, he enjoys the affirmation, assurance, peace, and joy of a good conscience (cf. Acts 23:1; 24:16; 2 Tim. 1:3; Heb. 13:18; 1 Pet. 3:16, 21).

h. **idle talk.** Cf. Titus 1:10. Refers to speech that is aimless and has no logical end. It is essentially irrelevant and will not accomplish anything spiritual or edifying to believers. It can also be translated "fruitless discussion." False doctrine leads nowhere, but to the deadening end of human speculation and demonic deception (cf. 1 Tim. 6:3–5).

i. **desiring to be teachers.** The false teachers wanted the kind of prestige enjoyed by Jewish rabbis; but they were not concerned at all about truly learning the law and teaching it to others (cf. 6:4; Matt. 23:5–7). Instead, they imposed on believers in Ephesus a legalistic heresy that offered salvation by works.

j. **the law.** The Mosaic law is in view here, not just law in general. These were Jewish

But we know that the ªlaw is good if one uses it lawfully, knowing this: that the law is ᵇnot made for a righteous person, but for the ᶜlawless and insubordinate, for the ungodly and for sinners, for the unholy and profane, for ᵈmurderers of fathers and murderers of mothers, for manslayers, for fornicators, for sodomites, for kidnappers, for liars, for perjurers, and if there is any other thing that is contrary to ᵉsound doctrine, according to ᶠthe glorious gospel of the blessed God which was ᵍcommitted to my trust.

---

would-be teachers who wanted to impose circumcision and the keeping of Mosaic ceremonies on the church as necessary for salvation. They plagued the early church (see Gal. 3–5; Phil. 3:1–8).

a. **law is good.** The Gr. word for "good" can be translated "useful." The law is good or useful because it reflects God's holy will and righteous standard (Ps. 19:7; Rom. 7:12) which accomplishes its purpose in showing sinners their sin (Rom. 3:19) and their need for a savior (Gal. 3:24). The law forces people to recognize that they are guilty of disobeying God's commands, and it thereby condemns every person and sentences them to hell (see Rom. 3:19, 20).

b. **not made for a righteous person.** Those who think they are righteous will never be saved (Luke 5:32) because they do not understand the true purpose of the law. The false teachers, with their works system of personally achieved self-righteousness (in their own minds), had shown clearly that they misunderstood the law completely. It was not a means to self-righteousness, but a means to self-condemnation, sin, conviction, repentance, and pleading to God for mercy (1 Tim. 1:15). See Luke 18:9–14; Rom. 5:20; Gal. 3:10–13, 19.

c. **lawless . . . profane.** These first 6 characteristics, expressed in 3 couplets, delineate sins from the first half of the Ten Commandments, which deal with a person's relationship to God. "Lawless" describes those who have no commitment to any law or standard, which makes such people "insubordinate," or rebellious. Those who are "ungodly" have no regard for anything sacred, which means they are "sinners" because they disregard God's law. "Unholy" people are indifferent to what is right, which leads them to be the "profane," who step on or trample what is sacred (cf. Heb. 10:29).

d. **murderers of fathers . . . perjurers.** These sins are violations of the second half of the Ten Commandments—those dealing with relationships among people. These specific sins undoubtedly characterized the false teachers, since they are characteristic behaviors related to false doctrine (v. 10). "Murderers of fathers" and "mothers" is a violation of the fifth commandment (Ex. 20:12; cf. 21:15–17), which forbids everything from dishonor to murder. "Manslayers" (or "murderers") is in violation of the sixth commandment (Ex. 20:13). "Fornicators" and "sodomites" (or "homosexuals") violate the seventh commandment (Ex. 20:14), which prohibits sexual activity outside the marriage bed. Because the theft of children was commonplace in Paul's day, he mentions "kidnappers" in connection with the eighth commandment (Ex. 20:15), which prohibits stealing. Finally, "liars" and "perjurers" are violators of the ninth commandment (Ex. 20:16).

e. **sound doctrine.** A familiar emphasis in the Pastoral Epistles (cf. 2 Tim. 4:3; Titus 1:9; 2:1). "Sound" refers to that which is healthy and wholesome. It is the kind of teaching that produces spiritual life and growth, which implies that false doctrine produces spiritual disease and debilitation.

f. **the glorious gospel.** The gospel reveals God's glory; that is, the perfections of His person or His attributes, including His holiness (hatred of sin) and justice (demand of punishment for violations of His law) and grace (forgiveness of sin). Those particular attributes are key to any effective gospel presentation.

g. **committed.** This Gr. word refers to committing something of value to another, and can be translated "entrusted." God entrusted Paul with the communication and guardianship of His revealed truth. Cf. 2:7; 6:20, 21; Rom. 15:15, 16; 1 Cor. 4:1, 2; 9:17; 2 Cor. 5:18–20; Gal. 2:7; Col. 1:25; 1 Thess. 2:4.

228. THE TRUE DOCTRINE OF PAUL
1 Timothy 1:12–20

And I thank Christ Jesus our Lord who has enabled me, because He ᵃcounted me faithful, putting me into the ministry, although I was formerly ᵇa blasphemer, a persecutor, and an insolent man; but I obtained mercy ᶜbecause I did it ignorantly in unbelief. And the ᵈgrace of our Lord was exceedingly abundant, with ᵉfaith and love which are in Christ Jesus. ᶠThis is a faithful saying and worthy of all acceptance, that Christ Jesus came into the world ᵍto save sinners, of whom ʰI am chief. However, ⁱfor this reason I obtained mercy,

---

a. **counted me faithful.** God's sovereign purpose for Paul and for all believers works through personal faith. Until Paul was turned by the Holy Spirit from self-righteous works (see Phil. 3:4–7) to faith alone in Christ, he could not be used by God. He was in the same condition as the useless false teachers (1 Tim. 1:6, 7).

b. **a blasphemer, a persecutor, and an insolent man.** This verse indicates that experience of Paul when he saw himself, in the light of God's law, for who he really was (see Rom. 7:7–12). A "blasphemer" speaks evil of and slanders God. Paul violated the first half of the Ten Commandments through his overt attacks against Christ (cf. Acts 9:4, 5; 22:7, 8; 26:9, 14, 15). As a "persecutor" and an "insolent man," Paul violated the second half through his attacks on believers. The Gr. word for "insolent man" can be translated "violent aggressor," indicating the violence Paul heaped on Christians.

c. **because I did it ignorantly in unbelief.** Paul was neither a Jewish apostate nor a Pharisee who clearly understood Jesus' teaching and still rejected Him. He was a zealous, fastidious Jew trying to earn his salvation, thus lost and damned (see Phil. 3:4–7). His plea of ignorance was not a claim to innocence nor an excuse denying his guilt. It was simply a statement indicating that he did not understand the truth of Christ's gospel and was honestly trying to protect his religion. His willing repentance when confronted by Christ (cf. Rom. 7:9; Phil. 3:8, 9) is evidence that he had not understood the ramifications of his actions—he truly thought he was doing God a service (Acts 26:9).

d. **grace.** God's loving forgiveness, by which He grants salvation apart from any merit on the part of those He saves (see Rom. 3:24; Gal. 1:6).

e. **faith and love.** Attitudes frequently linked with salvation in the NT (cf. Eph. 1:15; 3:17; Col. 1:4, 23). They are gifts of God's grace in Christ.

f. **This is a faithful saying.** A phrase unique to the Pastoral Epistles (cf. 1 Tim. 3:1; 4:9; 2 Tim. 2:11; Titus 3:8), which announces a statement summarizing key doctrines. The phrase "worthy of all acceptance" gives the statement added emphasis. Apparently, these sayings were well known in the churches, as concise expressions of cardinal gospel truth.

g. **to save sinners.** This faithful saying was based on the statements of Jesus recorded in Matt. 9:13; Luke 19:10.

h. **I am chief.** Lit. "first," in rank. Few could be considered a worse sinner than someone who blasphemed God and persecuted His church (see 1 Cor. 15:9; Eph. 3:8). Paul's attitude toward himself dramatically changed (cf. Phil. 3:7–9; see Rom 7:7–12).

i. **for this reason.** Paul was saved so that God could display to all His gracious and merciful patience with the most wretched sinners.

that in me first Jesus Christ might show all ªlongsuffering, as a ᵇpattern to those who are going to believe on Him for everlasting life. Now to the King eternal, immortal, invisible, to God who alone is wise, be honor and glory forever and ever. Amen.

This charge I commit to you, son Timothy, according to the ᶜprophecies previously made concerning you, that by them you may ᵈwage the good warfare, having ᵉfaith and a good conscience, which some having rejected, concerning the faith have suffered ᶠshipwreck, of whom are ᵍHymenaeus and Alexander, whom ʰI delivered to Satan that they ⁱmay learn not to blaspheme.

---

a. **longsuffering.** Refers to patience with people (cf. Rom. 2:4).

b. **pattern.** A model or example. Paul was living proof that God could save any sinner, no matter how great a one he might be. The account of Paul's conversion has been instrumental in the salvation of many. Paul's testimony is repeated 6 other times in the NT (Acts 9, 22, 26; Gal. 1, 2; Phil. 3:1–14).

c. **prophecies previously made concerning you.** The Gr. word for "previously made" lit. means "leading the way to," implying that a series of prophecies had been given about Timothy in connection with his receiving his spiritual gift (see 1 Tim. 4:14). These prophecies specifically and supernaturally called Timothy into God's service.

d. **wage the good warfare.** Paul urged Timothy to fight the battle against the enemies of Christ and the gospel. Cf. 2 Cor. 10:3–5; 2 Tim. 2:3, 4; 4:7.

e. **faith . . . faith.** The first is subjective and means continuing to believe the truth. The second is objective, referring to the content of the Christian gospel.

f. **shipwreck.** A good conscience serves as the rudder that steers the believer through the rocks and reefs of sin and error. The false teachers ignored their consciences and the truth, and as a result, suffered shipwreck of the Christian faith (the true doctrine of the gospel), which implies severe spiritual catastrophe. This does not imply loss of salvation of a true believer (see Rom. 8:31–39), but likely indicates the tragic loss that comes to the apostate. They had been in the church, heard the gospel and rejected it in favor of the false doctrine defined in 1 Tim. 1:3–7. Apostasy is a turning away from the gospel, having once known it. See Heb. 2:3, 4; 3:12–15; 6:1–8; 10:26–31.

g. **Hymenaeus and Alexander.** Hymenaeus is mentioned in 2 Tim. 2:17 in connection with Philetus, another false teacher. Alexander may be the opponent of the faith referred to in 2 Tim. 4:14, 15. Nothing else is known about these two men (see 1 Tim. 1:3).

h. **I delivered to Satan.** Paul put both men out of the church, thus ending their influence and removing them from the protection and insulation of God's people. They were no longer in the environment of God's blessing but under Satan's control. In some instances God has turned believers over to Satan for positive purposes, such as revealing the genuineness of saving faith, keeping them humble and dependent on Him, enabling them to strengthen others, or offering God praise (cf. Job. 1:1–22; Matt. 4:1–11; Luke 22:31–33; 2 Cor. 12:1–10; Rev. 7:9–15). God hands some people over to Satan for judgment, such as King Saul (1 Sam. 16:12–16; 28:4–20), Judas (John 13:27), and the sinning member in the Corinthian church (see 1 Cor. 5:1–5).

i. **may learn not to blaspheme.** See 1 Tim. 1:13. Paul learned not to blaspheme when confronted by the true understanding of the law and the gospel. That was what those men needed. God, the inspired text seems to indicate, would teach them and show them grace as he had Paul. But that evangelistic work could not go on at the expense of the purity of the church.

229. A CALL TO PRAYER

1 Timothy 2:1–8

Therefore I exhort ᵃfirst of all that ᵇsupplications, prayers, ᶜintercessions, and giving of thanks be made for ᵈall men, for ᵉkings and all who are in authority, that we may lead ᶠa quiet and peaceable life in all ᵍgodliness and reverence. For this is good and acceptable in the sight of God our Savior, who ʰdesires

a. **first of all.** The Ephesian church had evidently stopped praying for the lost, since Paul urged Timothy to make it a priority again. The Judaistic false teachers in Ephesus, by a perverted gospel and the teaching that salvation was only for Jews and Gentile proselytes to Judaism, would have certainly restricted evangelistic praying. Religious exclusivism (salvation only for the elite) would preclude the need for prayer for the lost.

b. **supplications.** The Gr. word is from a root that means "to lack," "to be deprived," or "to be without." Thus this kind of prayer occurs because of a need. The lost have a great need for salvation, and believers should always be asking God to meet that need.

c. **intercessions.** This word comes from a root meaning "to fall in with someone," or "to draw near so as to speak intimately." The verb from which this word derives is used of Christ's and the Spirit's intercession for believers (Rom. 8:26; Heb. 7:25). Paul's desire is for the Ephesian Christians to have compassion for the lost, to understand the depths of their pain and misery, and to come intimately to God pleading for their salvation. See Titus 3:3, 4.

d. **all men.** The lost in general, not the elect only. God's decree of election is secret—believers have no way of knowing who is elect until they respond. The scope of God's evangelistic efforts is broader than election (Matt. 22:14; John 17:21, 23).

e. **kings and all who are in authority.** Because so many powerful and influential political rulers are hostile to God, they are often the targets of bitterness and animosity. But Paul urges believers to pray that these leaders might repent of their sins and embrace the gospel, which meant that the Ephesians were even to pray for the salvation of the Roman emperor, Nero, a cruel and vicious blasphemer and persecutor of the faith.

f. **a quiet and peaceable life.** "Quiet" refers to the absence of external disturbances; "peaceable" refers to the absence of internal ones. While it remains uncompromising in its commitment to the truth, the church is not to agitate or disrupt the national life. When it manifests love and goodness to all and prays passionately for the lost, including rulers, the church may experience a certain amount of religious freedom. Persecution should only be the result of righteous living, not civil disobedience (see Titus 3:1–4; 1 Pet. 2:13–23).

g. **godliness and reverence.** "Godliness" is a key word in this letter (1 Tim. 3:16; 4:7, 8; 6:3, 5, 6, 11; cf. 2 Tim. 3:5; Titus 1:1), indicating that there needed to be a call back to holy living, which had been negatively affected by the false doctrine. Godliness refers to having the proper attitude and conduct before God in everything; "reverence" can be translated "moral earnestness," and refers to moral dignity and holy behavior before men.

h. **desires all men to be saved.** The Gr. word for "desires" is not that which normally expresses God's will of decree (His eternal purpose), but God's will of desire. There is a distinction between God's desire and His eternal saving purpose, which must transcend His desires. God does not want men to sin. He hates sin with all His being (Pss. 5:4; 45:7); thus, He hates its consequences—eternal wickedness in hell. God does not want people to remain wicked forever in eternal remorse and hatred of Himself. Yet, God, for His own

all men to be saved and to come to the knowledge of the truth. For ªthere is one God and one ᵇMediator between God and men, ᶜthe Man Christ Jesus, who gave Himself ᵈa ransom ᵉfor all, to be testified ᶠin due time, ᵍfor which I was appointed a ʰpreacher and an apostle—ⁱI am speaking the truth in Christ and not lying—a ʲteacher of the Gentiles in faith and truth.

---

glory, and to manifest that glory in wrath, chose to endure "vessels . . . prepared for destruction" for the supreme fulfillment of His will (Rom. 9:22). In His eternal purpose, He chose only the elect out of the world (John 17:6) and passed over the rest, leaving them to the consequences of their sin, unbelief, and rejection of Christ (cf. Rom. 1:18–32). Ultimately, God's choices are determined by His sovereign, eternal purpose, not His desires. See 2 Pet. 3:9.

a. **there is one God.** There is no other way of salvation (Acts 4:12); hence there is the need to pray for the lost to come to know the one true God (cf. Deut. 4:35, 39; 6:4; Is. 43:10; 44:6; 45:5, 6, 21, 22; 46:9; 1 Cor. 8:4, 6).

b. **Mediator.** This refers to someone who intervenes between two parties to resolve a conflict or ratify a covenant. Jesus Christ is the only "Mediator" who can restore peace between God and sinners (Heb. 8:6; 9:15; 12:24).

c. **the Man Christ Jesus.** The absence of the article before "Man" in the Gr. suggests the translation, "Christ Jesus, Himself a man." Only the perfect God-Man could bring God and man together. Cf. Job 9:32, 33.

d. **a ransom.** This describes the result of Christ's substitutionary death for believers, which He did voluntarily (John 10:17, 18) and reminds one of Christ's own statement in Matt. 20:28, "a ransom for many." The "all" is qualified by the "many." Not all will be ransomed (though His death would be sufficient), but only the many who believe by the work of the Holy Spirit and for whom the actual atonement was made. See 2 Pet. 3:9. Christ did not pay a ransom only; He became the object of God's just wrath in the believer's place—He died his death and bore his sin (cf. 2 Cor. 5:21; 1 Pet. 2:24).

e. **for all.** This should be taken in two senses: 1) there are temporal benefits of the atonement that accrue to all men universally (see 1 Tim. 4:10), and 2) Christ's death was sufficient to cover the sins of all people. Yet the substitutionary aspect of His death is applied to the elect alone (see 2 Cor. 5:14–21). Christ's death is therefore unlimited in its sufficiency, but limited in its application. Because Christ's expiation of sin is indivisible, inexhaustible, and sufficient to cover the guilt of all the sins that will ever be committed, God can clearly offer it to all. Yet only the elect will respond and be saved, according to His eternal purpose (cf. John 17:12).

f. **in due time.** At the proper time in God's redemptive plan (see Gal. 4:4).

g. **for which.** Paul's divine commission was based on the truths delineated in 1 Tim. 2:3–6.

h. **preacher.** The Gr. word derives from the verb that means, "to herald," "to proclaim," or "to speak publicly." Paul was a public herald proclaiming the gospel of Christ.

i. **I am speaking the truth . . . not lying.** Paul's emphatic outburst of his apostolic authority and integrity is to emphasize that he was a teacher of the Gentiles.

j. **teacher of the Gentiles.** The distinctive feature of Paul's apostolic appointment, which demonstrates the universal scope of the gospel. Paul's need to make this distinction suggests he was dealing with some form of Jewish exclusivism that had crippled the Ephesians' interest in praying for Gentiles to be saved.

I desire therefore that the ᵃmen pray ᵇeverywhere, ᶜlifting up holy hands, ᵈwithout wrath and doubting.

230. GOD'S HIGH CALLING FOR WOMEN
1 Timothy 2:9–15

In like manner also, that the women ᵉadorn themselves in modest apparel, with ᶠpropriety and moderation, not with ᵍbraided hair or gold or pearls or costly clothing, but, which is proper for women professing godliness, with good works. ʰLet a

---

a. **men.** The Gr. word for "men" as opposed to women. God intends for men to be the leaders when the church meets for corporate worship. When prayer for the lost is offered during those times, the men are to lead it.

b. **everywhere.** Paul's reference to the official assembly of the church (cf. 1 Cor. 1:2; 2 Cor. 2:14; 1 Thess. 1:8).

c. **lifting up holy hands.** Paul is not emphasizing a specific posture necessary for prayer, but a prerequisite for effective prayer (cf. Ps. 66:18). Though this posture is described in the OT (1 Kin. 8:22; Pss. 28:2; 63:4; 134:2), so are many others. The Gr. word for "holy" means "unpolluted" or "unstained by evil." "Hands" symbolize the activities of life; thus "holy hands" represent a holy life. This basis of effective prayer is a righteous life (James 5:16).

d. **without wrath and doubting.** "Wrath" and righteousness are mutually exclusive (James 1:20; cf. Luke 9:52–56). A better translation for "doubting" is "dissension," and refers to a hesitant reluctance to be committed to prayer. "Effectual, fervent" prayer is effective (James 5:16). The two refer to one's inner attitude.

e. **adorn . . . modest apparel.** The Gr. word for "adorn" means "to arrange," "to put in order," or "to make ready." A woman is to arrange herself appropriately for the worship service, which includes wearing decent clothing which reflects a properly adorned chaste heart.

f. **propriety and moderation.** The Gr. word for "propriety" refers to modesty mixed with humility, which carries the underlying idea of shame. It can also refer to a rejection of anything dishonorable to God, or refer to grief over sin. "Moderation" basically refers to self-control over sexual passions. Godly women hate sin and control their passions so as not to lead another into sin. See 1 Pet. 3:3, 4.

g. **braided hair or gold or pearls or costly clothing.** Specific practices that were causing distraction and discord in the church. Women in the first century often wove "gold, pearls," or other jewelry into their hair styles ("braided hair") to call attention to themselves and their wealth or beauty. The same was true of those women who wore "costly clothing." By doing so they would draw attention to themselves and away from the Lord, likely causing the poorer women to be envious. Paul's point was to forbid the preoccupation of certain women with flaunting their wealth and distracting people from worshiping the Lord.

h. **Let a woman learn.** Women are not to be the public teachers when the church assembles, but neither are they to be shut out of the learning process. The form of the Gr. verb translated "let . . . learn" is an imperative: Paul is commanding that women be taught in the church. That was a novel concept, since neither first century Judaism nor Greek culture held women in high esteem. Some of the women in Ephesus probably overreacted to the cultural denigration they had typically suffered and took advantage of their opportunity in the church by seeking a dominant role in leadership.

woman learn ᵃin silence with all submission. And ᵇI do not permit a woman ᶜto teach or ᵈto have authority over a man, but to be in silence. ᵉFor Adam was formed first, then Eve. And Adam was not deceived, but the woman being deceived, fell into transgression. Nevertheless ᶠshe ᵍwill be saved ʰin childbearing ⁱif they continue in faith, love, and holiness, with self-control.

a. **in silence with all submission.** "Silence" ("quiet") and "submission" ("to line up under") were to characterize the role of a woman as a learner in the context of the church assembly. Paul explains his meaning in 1 Tim. 2:12: Women are to be silent by not teaching, and they are to demonstrate submission by not usurping the authority of the pastors or elders.

b. **I do not permit.** The Gr. word for "permit" is used in the NT to refer to allowing someone to do what he desires. Paul may have been addressing a real situation in which several women in Ephesus desired to be public preachers.

c. **to teach.** Paul used a verbal form of this Gr. word that indicates a condition or process and is better translated: "to be a teacher." This was an important, official function in the church (see Acts 13:1; 1 Cor. 12:28; Eph. 4:11). Thus Paul is forbidding women from filling the office and role of the pastor or teacher. He is not prohibiting them from teaching in other appropriate conditions and circumstances (cf. Acts 18:26; Titus 2:3, 4).

d. **to have authority over.** Paul forbids women from exercising any type of authority over men in the church assembly, since the elders are those who rule (1 Tim. 5:17). They are all to be men (as is clear from the requirements in 3:2, 5).

e. **For Adam was formed first . . .** A woman's subordinate role did not result after the Fall as a cultural, chauvinistic corruption of God's perfect design; rather, God established her role as part of His original creation (1 Tim. 2:13). God made woman after man to be his suitable helper (see Gen. 2:18; cf. 1 Cor. 11:8, 9). The Fall actually corroborates God's divine plan of creation (see Gen. 3:1–7). By nature Eve was not suited to assume the position of ultimate responsibility. By leaving Adam's protection and usurping his headship, she was vulnerable and fell, thus confirming how important it was for her to stay under the protection and leadership of her husband (see 1 Tim. 5:11, 12; 2 Tim. 3:6, 7). Adam then violated his leadership role, followed Eve in her sin, and plunged the human race into sinfulness—all connected with violating God's planned roles for the sexes. Ultimately, the responsibility for the Fall still rests with Adam, since he chose to disobey God apart from being deceived (Rom. 5:12–21; 1 Cor. 15:21, 22).

f. **she.** That Paul does not have Eve in mind here is clear because the verb translated "will be saved" is future, and he also uses the plural pronoun "they." He is talking about women after Eve.

g. **will be saved.** Better translated in this context, "will be preserved." The Gr. word can also mean "to rescue," "to preserve safe and unharmed," "to heal," or "to deliver from." It appears several times in the NT without reference to spiritual salvation (cf. Matt. 8:25; 9:21, 22; 24:22; 27:40, 42, 49; 2 Tim. 4:18). Paul is not advocating that women are eternally saved from sin through childbearing or that they maintain their salvation by having babies, both of which would be clear contradictions of the NT teaching of salvation by grace alone through faith alone (Rom. 3:19, 20) sustained forever (Rom. 8:31–39). Paul is teaching that even though a woman bears the stigma of being the initial instrument who led the race into sin, it is women through childbearing who may be preserved or freed from that stigma by raising a generation of godly children (cf. 1 Tim. 5:10).

h. **in childbearing.** Because mothers have a unique bond and intimacy with their children, and spend far more time with them than do fathers, they have far greater influence in their lives and thus a unique responsibility and opportunity for rearing godly children. While a woman may have led the human race into sin, women have the privilege of leading many out of sin to godliness. Paul is speaking in general terms; God does not want all women to be married (1 Cor. 7:25–40), let alone bear children.

i. **if they continue in faith, love, and holiness, with self-control.** The godly appearance,

231. QUALIFICATIONS FOR ELDERS

1 Timothy 3:1–7

ªThis is a faithful saying: If a man ᵇdesires the position of a ᶜbishop, he desires a good work. A bishop then ᵈmust be ᵉblameless, ᶠthe husband of one wife,

---

demeanor, and behavior commanded of believing women in the church (1 Tim. 2:9–12) is motivated by the promise of deliverance from any inferior status and the joy of raising godly children.

a. Paul's purpose in writing this letter was to instruct Timothy regarding the church (1 Tim. 3:14, 15). Of primary importance to any church is that its leaders be qualified to teach and set the example for the rest. These verses delineate those qualifications for pastors and deacons (see Titus 1:5–9).

b. **desires . . . desires.** Two different Gr. words are used. The first means "to reach out after." It describes external action, not internal motive. The second means "a strong passion," and refers to an inward desire. Taken together, these two words aptly describe the type of man who belongs in the ministry—one who outwardly pursues it because he is driven by a strong internal desire.

c. **bishop.** The word means "overseer" and identifies the men who are responsible to lead the church (cf. 1 Tim. 5:17; 1 Thess. 5:12; Heb. 13:7). In the NT the words "bishop," "elder," "overseer," and "pastor" are used interchangeably to describe the same men (Acts 20:17, 28; Titus 1:5–9; 1 Pet. 5:1, 2). Bishops (pastors, overseers, elders) are responsible to lead (1 Tim. 5:17), preach and teach (5:17), help the spiritually weak (1 Thess. 5:12–14), care for the church (1 Pet. 5:1, 2), and ordain other leaders (1 Tim. 4:14).

d. **must.** The use of this Gr. particle stresses emphatically that living a blameless life is absolutely necessary for church leaders.

e. **blameless.** Lit. "not able to be held" in a criminal sense; there is no valid accusation of wrongdoing that can be made against him. No overt, flagrant sin can mar the life of one who must be an example for his people to follow (cf. 1 Tim. 3:10; 4:7; 5:7; Ps. 101:6; Phil. 3:17; 2 Thess. 3:9; Heb. 13:7; 1 Pet. 5:3). This is the overarching requirement for elders; the rest of the qualifications elaborate on what it means to be blameless. Titus 1:6, 7 uses another Gr. word to mean the same thing.

f. **the husband of one wife.** Lit. in Gr. a "one-woman man." This says nothing about marriage or divorce (for comments on that, see 1 Tim. 3:4). The issue is not the elder's marital status, but his moral and sexual purity. This qualification heads the list, because it is in this area that leaders are most prone to fail. Various interpretations of this qualification have been offered. Some see it as a prohibition against polygamy—an unnecessary injunction since polygamy was not common in Roman society and clearly forbidden by Scripture (Gen 2:24), the teaching of Jesus (Matt. 19:5, 6; Mark 10:6–9), and Paul (Eph. 5:31). A polygamist could not even have been a church member, let alone a church leader. Others see this requirement as barring those who remarried after the death of their wives. But, as already noted, the issue is sexual purity, not marital status. Further, the Bible encourages remarriage after widowhood (5:14; 1 Cor. 7:39). Some believe that Paul here excludes divorced men from church leadership. That again ignores the fact that this qualification does not deal with marital status. Nor does the Bible prohibit all remarriage after divorce (see Matt. 5:31, 32; 19:9; 1 Cor. 7:15). Finally, some think that this requirement excludes single men from church leadership. But if that were Paul's intent, he would have disqualified himself (1 Cor. 7:8). A "one-woman man" is one totally devoted to his wife, maintaining singular devotion, affection and sexual purity in both thought and deed. To violate this is to forfeit blamelessness and no longer be "above reproach" (Titus 1:6, 7). Cf. Prov. 6:32, 33.

ᵃtemperate, ᵇsober-minded, of ᶜgood behavior, ᵈhospitable, ᵉable to teach; ᶠnot given to wine, ᵍnot violent, ʰnot greedy for money, but ⁱgentle, ʲnot quarrelsome, ᵏnot covetous; one ˡwho rules his own house well, having his children in ᵐsubmission with all reverence (for if a man does not know how to rule his own house, how will he ⁿtake care of the church of God?); ᵒnot a novice, lest

---

a. **temperate.** The Gr. word lit. means "wineless," but is here used metaphorically to mean "alert," "watchful," "vigilant," or "clear-headed." Elders must be able to think clearly.

b. **sober-minded.** A "sober-minded" man is disciplined, knows how to properly order his priorities, and is serious about spiritual matters.

c. **good behavior.** The Gr. word means "orderly." Elders must not lead chaotic lives; if they cannot order their own lives, how can they bring order to the church?

d. **hospitable.** From a compound Gr. word meaning "love of strangers" (see Rom. 12:13; Heb. 13:2; cf. 1 Pet. 4:9). As with all spiritual virtues, elders must set the example; their lives and homes are to be open so all can see their spiritual character.

e. **able to teach.** Used only here and in 2 Tim. 2:24. The only qualification relating to an elder's giftedness and spiritual ability, and the only one that distinguishes elders from deacons. The preaching and teaching of God's Word is the overseer/pastor/elder's primary duty (1 Tim. 4:6, 11, 13; 5:17; 2 Tim. 2:15, 24; Titus 2:1).

f. **not given to wine.** More than a mere prohibition against drunkenness (see Eph. 5:18). An elder must not have a reputation as a drinker; his judgment must never be clouded by alcohol (cf. Prov. 31:4, 5; 1 Cor. 6:12), his lifestyle must be radically different from the world and lead others to holiness, not sin (Rom. 14:21). See 5:23.

g. **not violent.** Lit. "not a giver of blows." Elders must react to difficult situations calmly and gently (2 Tim. 2:24, 25), and under no circumstances with physical violence.

h. **not greedy for money.** The better Gr. manuscripts omit this phrase. The principle is included, however, in Titus 1:7; 1 Pet. 5:2.

i. **gentle.** Considerate, genial, gracious, quick to pardon failure, and one who does not hold a grudge.

j. **not quarrelsome.** "Peaceful," "reluctant to fight"; one who does not promote disunity or disharmony.

k. **not covetous.** Elders must be motivated by love for God and His people, not money (cf. 1 Pet. 5:2). A leader who is in the ministry for money reveals a heart set on the world, not the things of God (Matt. 6:24; 1 John 2:15). Covetousness characterizes false teachers (Titus 1:11; 2 Pet. 2:1–3, 14; Jude 11), but not Paul's ministry (Acts 20:33; 1 Cor. 9:1–16; 2 Cor. 11:9; 1 Thess. 2:5).

l. **who rules his own house well.** The elder's home life, like his personal life, must be exemplary. He must be one who "rules" (presides over, has authority over) "his own house" (everything connected with his home, not merely his wife and children) "well" (intrinsically good; excellently). Issues of divorce should be related to this matter. A divorced man gives no evidence of a well-managed home, but rather that divorce shows weakness in his spiritual leadership. If there has been a biblically permitted divorce, it must have been so far in the past as to have been overcome by a long pattern of solid family leadership and the rearing of godly children (1 Tim. 3:4; Titus 1:6).

m. **submission.** A military term referring to soldiers ranked under one in authority. An elder's children must be believers (see "faithful" in Titus 1:6), well-behaved, and respectful.

n. **take care of the church of God.** An elder must first prove in the intimacy and exposure of his own home his ability to lead others to salvation and sanctification. There he proves God has gifted him uniquely to spiritually set the example of virtue, to serve others, resolve conflicts, build unity, and maintain love. If he cannot do those essential things there, why would anyone assume he would be able to do them in the church?

o. **not a novice, lest . . . puffed up with pride.** Putting a new convert into a leadership role would tempt him to pride. Elders, therefore, are to be drawn from the spiritually mature men of the congregation (see 1 Tim. 5:22).

being puffed up with pride he ᵃfall into the same condemnation as the devil. Moreover he must have a ᵇgood testimony among those who are outside, lest he fall into reproach and the snare of the devil.

232. QUALIFICATIONS FOR DEACONS
1 Timothy 3:8–16

Likewise ᶜdeacons must be ᵈreverent, ᵉnot double-tongued, ᶠnot given to much wine, ᵍnot greedy for money, holding ʰthe mystery of the faith with a pure conscience. But let these also ⁱfirst be tested; then let them serve as deacons, being found blameless. Likewise, ʲtheir wives must be reverent, ᵏnot slanderers,

---

a. **fall into the same condemnation as the devil.** Satan's condemnation was due to pride over his position. It resulted in his fall from honor and authority (Is. 14:12–14; Ezek. 28:11–19; cf. Prov. 16:18). The same kind of fall and judgment could easily happen to a new and weak believer put in a position of spiritual leadership.

b. **good testimony . . . outside.** A leader in the church must have an unimpeachable reputation in the unbelieving community, even though people there may disagree with his moral and theological stands. How can he make a spiritual impact on those who do not respect him? Cf. Matt. 5:48; Phil. 2:15.

c. **deacons.** From a word group meaning "to serve." Originally referring to menial tasks such as waiting on tables (see Acts 6:1–4), "deacon" came to denote any service in the church. Deacons serve under the leadership of elders, helping them exercise oversight in the practical matters of church life. Scripture defines no official or specific responsibilities for deacons; they are to do whatever the elders assign them or whatever spiritual ministry is necessary.

d. **reverent.** Serious in mind and character; not silly or flippant about important matters.

e. **not double-tongued.** Deacons must not say one thing to some people and something else to others; their speech must not be hypocritical, but honest and consistent.

f. **not given to much wine.** Not preoccupied with drink (see 1 Tim. 3:3).

g. **not greedy.** Like elders (see 1 Tim. 3:3), deacons must not abuse their office to make money. Such a qualification was especially important in the early church, where deacons routinely handled money, distributing it to those in need.

h. **the mystery.** See Matt. 13:11; 1 Cor. 2:7; Eph. 3:4, 5. Appearing frequently in Paul's writings (cf. Rom. 11:25; 16:25; Eph. 1:9; 3:9; 6:19; Col. 2:2), the word "mystery" describes truth previously hidden, but now revealed, including Christ's incarnation (v. 16), Christ's indwelling of believers (Col. 1:26, 27), the unity of Jews and Gentiles in the church (Eph. 3:4–6), the gospel (Col. 4:3), lawlessness (2 Thess. 2:7), and the rapture of the church (1 Cor. 15:51, 52).

i. **first be tested.** The present tense of this verb indicates an ongoing evaluation of deacons' character and service by the church.

j. **their wives.** The Gr. word rendered "wives" can also be translated "women." Paul likely here refers not to deacons' wives, but to the women who serve as deacons. The use of the word "likewise" as an introduction (cf. 1 Tim. 3:8) suggests a third group in addition to elders and deacons. Also, since Paul gave no requirements for elders' wives, there is no reason to assume these would be qualifications for deacons' wives.

k. **not slanderers.** "Slanderers" is the plural form of diabolos—a title frequently given

temperate, ᵃfaithful in all things. Let deacons be the husbands of one wife, ruling their children and their own houses well. For those who have served well as deacons obtain for themselves a good standing and great boldness in the faith which is in Christ Jesus.

These things I write to you, though ᵇI hope to come to you shortly; but if I am delayed, I write so that you may know ᶜhow you ought to conduct yourself in the ᵈhouse of God, which is the ᵉchurch of the living God, the ᶠpillar and ground of ᵍthe truth. And without controversy great is the ʰmystery of godliness:

> ⁱGod was manifested ʲin the flesh,
>
> ᵏJustified in the Spirit,

---

to Satan (Matt. 4:5, 8, 11; 13:39; Luke 4:3, 5, 6, 13; 8:12; 1 Pet. 5:8; 1 John 3:8; Rev. 2:10; 12:9, 12; 20:2, 10). The women who serve must not be gossips.

a. **faithful in all things.** Women servants in the church, like their male counterparts (see 1 Tim. 3:2), must be absolutely trustworthy in all aspects of their lives and ministries.

b. **I hope to come to you shortly.** The Gr. grammar suggests Paul's meaning is "These things I write, although I had hoped to come to you sooner." Delayed in Macedonia, Paul sent Timothy this letter.

c. **how you ought to conduct yourself.** The second half of this verse expresses the theme of this epistle—setting things right in the church.

d. **house of God.** This is better translated "household." Believers are members of God's household (Gal. 6:10; Eph. 2:19; Heb. 3:6; 1 Pet. 4:17) and must act accordingly. This is not a reference to any building, but to the people who make up the true church.

e. **church of the living God.** The church is God's possession (Acts 20:28; Eph. 1:14; Titus 2:14; 1 Pet. 2:9). The title "the living God" has a rich OT heritage (Deut. 5:26; Josh. 3:10; 1 Sam. 17:26, 36; 2 Kin. 19:4, 16; Pss. 42:2; 84:2; Is. 37:4, 17; Jer. 10:10; 23:26; Dan. 6:20, 26; Hos. 1:10).

f. **pillar and ground.** Paul's imagery may have referred to the magnificent temple of Diana (Artemis) in Ephesus, which was supported by 127 gold-plated marble pillars. The word translated "ground" appears only here in the NT and denotes the foundation on which a building rests. The church upholds the truth of God's revealed Word.

g. **the truth.** The content of the Christian faith recorded in Scripture and summed up in 1 Tim. 3:16.

h. **mystery of godliness.** "Mystery" is that term used by Paul to indicate truth hidden in the OT age and revealed in the NT (see 1 Tim. 3:9). Godliness refers to the truths of salvation and righteousness in Christ, which produce holiness in believers; namely, the manifestation of true and perfect righteousness in Jesus Christ.

i. **God was manifested.** The better manuscripts read "He who" instead of "God." In either case, the reference is clearly to Christ, who manifested the invisible God to mankind (John 1:1–4; 14:9; Col. 1:15; Heb. 1:3; 2 Pet. 1:16–18). This verse contains part of an early church hymn, as its uniformity, rhythm, and parallelism indicate. Its 6 lines form a concise summary of the truth of the gospel.

j. **in the flesh.** Not sinful, fallen human nature here (cf. Rom. 7:18, 25; 8:8; Gal. 5:16, 17), but merely humanness (cf. John 1:14; Rom. 1:3; 8:3; 9:5; 1 Pet. 3:18; 1 John 4:2, 3; 2 John 7).

k. **Justified in the Spirit.** "Justified" means "righteous," so that "spirit" may be written with lower case "s" indicating a declaration of Christ's sinless spiritual righteousness (John 8:46;

^aSeen by angels,
^bPreached among the Gentiles,
Believed on in the world,
^cReceived up in glory.

233. INSTRUCTIONS REGARDING FALSE TEACHERS

1 Timothy 4:1–16

Now ^dthe Spirit expressly says that ^ein latter times some will ^fdepart from the faith, giving heed to ^gdeceiving spirits and ^hdoctrines of demons, ⁱspeaking lies

---

2 Cor. 5:21; Heb. 4:15; 5:9; 7:26; 1 Pet. 2:21, 22; 1 John 2:1), or it could refer to His vindication by the Holy Spirit (Rom. 1:4).

a. **Seen by angels.** Both by fallen (see Col. 2:15; 1 Pet. 3:18–20) and elect (Matt. 28:2; Luke 24:4–7; Acts 1:10, 11; Heb. 1:6–9) angels.

b. **Preached among the Gentiles.** Or, nations. See Matt. 24:14; 26:13; 28:19, 20; Mark 13:10; Acts 1:8.

c. **Received up in glory.** See Acts 1:9, 10; Phil. 2:8–11; Heb. 1:3. Christ's ascension and exaltation showed that the Father was pleased with Him and accepted His work fully.

d. **the Spirit expressly says.** Paul repeats to Timothy the warning he had given many years earlier to the Ephesian elders (Acts 20:29, 30). The Holy Spirit through the Scriptures has repeatedly warned of the danger of apostasy (cf. Matt. 24:4–12; Acts 20:29, 30; 2 Thess. 2:3–12; Heb. 3:12; 5:11—6:8; 10:26–31; 2 Pet. 3:3; 1 John 2:18; Jude 18).

e. **in latter times.** The period from the first coming of Christ until His return (Acts 2:16, 17; Heb. 1:1, 2; 9:26; 1 Pet. 1:20; 1 John 2:18). Apostasy will exist throughout that period, reaching a climax shortly before Christ returns (cf. Matt. 24:12).

f. **depart from the faith.** Those who fall prey to the false teachers will abandon the Christian faith. The Gr. word for "depart" is the source of the Eng. word "apostatize," and refers to someone moving away from an original position. These are professing or nominal Christians who associate with those who truly believe the gospel, but defect after believing lies and deception, thus revealing their true nature as unconverted. See 1 John 2:19; Jude 24.

g. **deceiving spirits.** Those demonic spirits, either directly or through false teachers, who have wandered away from the truth and lead others to do the same. The most defining word to describe the entire operation of Satan and his demons is "deception" (cf. John 8:44; 1 John 4:1–6).

h. **doctrines of demons.** Not teaching about demons, but false teaching that originates from them. To sit under such teaching is to hear lies from the demonic realm (Eph. 6:12; James 3:15; 2 John 7–11). The influence of demons will reach its peak during the Tribulation (2 Thess. 2:9; Rev. 9:2–11; 16:14; 20:2, 3, 8, 10). Satan and demons constantly work the deceptions that corrupt and pervert God's Word.

i. **speaking lies in hypocrisy.** Lit. "hypocritical lie-speakers." These are the human false teachers who propagate demon doctrine (cf. 1 John 4:1).

in hypocrisy, having their own conscience ªseared with a hot iron, ᵇforbidding to marry, and commanding to abstain from foods which God created to be received with thanksgiving by those who believe and know the truth. For ᶜevery creature of God is good, and nothing is to be refused if it is received with thanksgiving; for it is ᵈsanctified by the word of God and prayer.

If you instruct the brethren in these things, you will be a good minister of Jesus Christ, ᵉnourished in the words of faith and of the good doctrine which you have carefully followed. But ᶠreject profane and old wives' fables, and ᵍexercise yourself toward godliness. For bodily exercise ʰprofits a little, but godliness is profitable for all things, having promise of the life that now

---

a. **seared.** A medical term referring to cauterization. False teachers can teach their hypocritical lies because their consciences have been desensitized (cf. Eph. 4:19), as if all the nerves that make them feel had been destroyed and turned into scar tissue by the burning of demonic deception.

b. **forbidding to marry, and commanding to abstain from foods.** A sample of the false teaching at Ephesus. Typically, it contained elements of truth, since Scripture commends both singleness (1 Cor. 7:25–35) and fasting (Matt. 6:16, 17; 9:14, 15). The deception came in making such human works a prerequisite for salvation—a distinguishing mark of all false religion. This ascetic teaching was probably influenced both by the Jewish sect known as the Essenes, and contemporary Greek thought (which viewed matter as evil and spirit as good). Paul addressed this asceticism in Col. 2:21–23. Neither celibacy nor any form of diet saves or sanctifies.

c. **every creature of God is good.** The false teachers' asceticism contradicted Scripture, which teaches that since God created both marriage and food (Gen. 1:28–31; 2:18–24; 9:3), they are intrinsically good (Gen. 1:31) and to be enjoyed with gratitude by believers. Obviously food and marriage are essential for life and procreation.

d. **sanctified.** Set apart or dedicated to God for holy use. The means for so doing are thankful prayer and an understanding that the Word of God has set aside the temporary Mosaic dietary restrictions (Mark 7:19; Acts 10:9–15; Rom. 14:1–12; Col. 2:16, 17). Contrast the unbeliever whose inner corruption and evil motives corrupt every good thing (Titus 1:15).

e. **nourished . . . words of faith . . . good doctrine.** Continual feeding on the truths of Scripture is essential to the spiritual health of all Christians (2 Tim. 3:16, 17), but especially of spiritual leaders like Timothy. Only by reading the Word, studying it, meditating on it, and mastering its contents can a pastor fulfill his mandate (2 Tim. 2:15). Timothy had been doing so since childhood (2 Tim. 3:15), and Paul urged him to continue (cf. v. 16; 2 Tim. 3:14). "Words of faith" is a general reference to Scripture, God's revealed truth. "Good doctrine" indicates the theology Scripture teaches.

f. **reject profane and old wives' fables.** In addition to being committed to God's Word (see 1 Tim. 4:6), believers must avoid all false teaching. Paul denounced such error as "profane" (worldly; the opposite of what is holy) "fables" (muthos, from which the Eng. word "myths" derives), fit only for "old wives" (a common epithet denoting something fit only for the uneducated and philosophically unsophisticated). See 2 Tim. 2:14–18.

g. **exercise . . . toward godliness.** "Godliness" (a proper attitude and response toward God; see 2:2) is the prerequisite from which all effective ministry flows. "Exercise" is an athletic term denoting the rigorous, self-sacrificing training an athlete undergoes. Spiritual self-discipline is the path to godly living (cf. 1 Cor. 9:24–27).

h. **profits a little.** Bodily exercise is limited both in extent and duration; it affects only the physical body during this earthly life. By contrast, godliness is profitable in both time and eternity.

is and of that which is to come. This is a faithful saying and worthy of all acceptance. For to this end we both labor and suffer reproach, because we [a]trust in the living God, who is [b]the Savior of all men, especially of those who believe. These things command and teach.

[c]Let no one despise your youth, but [d]be an example to the believers in word, in conduct, in love, in spirit, in faith, in purity. Till I come, [e]give attention to reading, to exhortation, to doctrine. Do not neglect [f]the gift

---

a. **trust.** Or "hope." Believers are saved in hope (see Rom. 8:24), and live and serve in light of that hope of eternal life (Titus 1:2; 3:7; see Rom. 5:2). Working to the point of exhaustion and suffering rejection and persecution are acceptable because believers understand they are doing God's work—which is the work of salvation. That makes it worth all of the sacrifices (Phil. 1:12–18, 27–30; 2:17; Col. 1:24, 25; 2 Tim. 1:6–12; 2:3, 4, 9, 10; 4:5–8).

b. **the Savior of all men, especially of those who believe.** Paul is obviously not teaching universalism, that all men will be saved in the spiritual and eternal sense, since the rest of Scripture clearly teaches that God will not save everyone. Most will reject Him and spend eternity in hell (Matt. 25:41, 46; Rev. 20:11–15). Yet, the Gr. word translated "especially" must mean that all men enjoy God's salvation in some way like those who believe enjoy His salvation. The simple explanation is that God is the Savior of all men, only in a temporal sense, while of believers in an eternal sense. Paul's point is that while God graciously delivers believers from sin's condemnation and penalty because He was their substitute (2 Cor. 5:21), all men experience some earthly benefits from the goodness of God. Those benefits are: 1) common grace—a term that describes God's goodness shown to all mankind universally (Ps. 145:9) in restraining sin (Rom. 2:15) and judgment (Rom. 2:3–6), maintaining order in society through government (Rom. 13:1–5), enabling man to appreciate beauty and goodness (Ps. 50:2), and showering him with temporal blessings (Matt. 5:45; Acts 14:15–17; 17:25); 2) compassion—the broken-hearted love of pity God shows to undeserving, unregenerate sinners (Ex. 34:6, 7; Ps. 86:5; Dan. 9:9; Matt. 23:37; Luke 19:41–44; cf. Is. 16:11–13; Jer. 48:35–37); 3) admonition to repent—God constantly warns sinners of their fate, demonstrating the heart of a compassionate Creator who has no pleasure in the death of the wicked (Ezek. 18:30–32; 33:11); 4) the gospel invitation—salvation in Christ is indiscriminately offered to all (Matt. 11:28, 29; 22:2–14; John 6:35–40; Rev. 22:17; cf. John 5:39, 40). God is, by nature, a saving God. That is, He finds no pleasure in the death of sinners. His saving character is revealed even in how He deals with those who will never believe, but only in those 4 temporal ways. See 1 Tim. 2:6.

c. **Let no one despise your youth.** Greek culture placed great value on age and experience. Since Timothy was in his thirties, still young by the standards of that culture, he would have to earn respect by being a godly example. Because he had been with Paul since a young teenager, Timothy had much experience to mature him, so that looking down on him because he was under 40 was inexcusable.

d. **be an example . . . in purity.** Paul lists 5 areas (the better Gr. manuscripts omit "in spirit") in which Timothy was to be an example to the church: "word" (speech; cf. Matt. 12:34–37; Eph. 4:25, 29, 31); "conduct" (righteous living; cf. Titus 2:10; 1 Pet. 1:15; 2:12; 3:16); "love" (self-sacrificial service for others; cf. John 15:13); "faith" (not belief, but faithfulness or commitment; cf. 1 Cor. 4:2); "purity" (especially sexual purity; cf. 1 Tim. 3:2). Timothy's exemplary life in those areas would offset the disadvantage of his youth.

e. **give attention . . . to doctrine.** These things were to be Timothy's constant practice; his way of life. "Reading" refers to the custom of public reading of Scripture in the church's worship service, followed by the exposition of the passage that had been read (cf. Neh. 8:1–8; Luke 4:16–27). "Exhortation" challenges those who hear the Word to apply it in their daily lives. It may involve rebuke, warning, encouragement, or comfort. "Doctrine" (teaching) refers to systematic instruction from the Word of God (cf. 1 Tim. 3:2; Titus 1:9).

f. **the gift.** That grace given to Timothy and to all believers at salvation which consisted of a God-designed, Spirit-empowered spiritual ability for the use of ministry (see Rom. 12:4–8;

that is in you, which was given to you ᵃby prophecy with the ᵇlaying on of the hands of the eldership. Meditate on these things; give yourself entirely to them, that your ᶜprogress may be evident to all. Take heed ᵈto yourself and to the doctrine. Continue in them, for in doing this ᵉyou will save both yourself and ᶠthose who hear you.

234. PASTORAL CARE FOR WIDOWS

1 Timothy 5:1–16

Do not ᵍrebuke ʰan older man, but ⁱexhort him as a father, younger men as brothers, older women as mothers, younger women as sisters, with all purity.

---

1 Cor. 12:4–12; 1 Pet. 4:10, 11). Timothy's gift (cf. 2 Tim. 1:6) was leadership with special emphasis on preaching (2 Tim. 4:2), and teaching (1 Tim. 4:6, 11, 13; 6:2).

a. **by prophecy.** Timothy's gift was identified by a revelation from God (see 1 Tim. 1:18) and apostolic confirmation (2 Tim. 1:6), probably when he joined Paul on the apostle's second missionary journey (Acts 16:1–3).

b. **laying on of the hands of the eldership.** See 1 Tim. 5:22. This public affirmation of Timothy's call to the ministry likely took place at the same time as the prophecy (cf. 2 Tim. 1:6). His call to the ministry was thus confirmed subjectively (by means of his spiritual gift), objectively (through the prophecy made about him), and collectively (by the affirmation of apostles and the church, represented by the elders).

c. **progress.** The word was used in military terms of an advancing force and in general terms of advancement in learning, understanding, or knowledge. Paul exhorted Timothy to let his progress toward Christlikeness be evident to all.

d. **to yourself and to the doctrine.** The priorities of a godly leader are summed up in his personal holiness and public teaching. All of Paul's exhortations in 1 Tim. 4:6–16 fit into one or the other of those two categories.

e. **you will save . . . yourself.** Perseverance in believing the truth always accompanies genuine conversion (see Matt. 24:13; cf. John 8:31; Rom. 2:7; Phil. 2:12, 13; Col. 1:23).

f. **those who hear you.** By careful attention to his own godly life and faithful preaching of the Word, Timothy would continue to be the human instrument God used to bring the gospel and to save some who heard him. Though salvation is God's work, it is His pleasure to do it through human instruments.

g. **rebuke.** Some translations add "sharply" to the word "rebuke," which fills out the intensity of the Gr. term. An older sinning believer is to be shown respect by not being addressed with harsh words (cf. 2 Tim. 2:24, 25).

h. **an older man.** In this context, the Gr. is indicating older men generally, not the office of elder. The younger Timothy was to confront sinning older men with deference and honor, which is clearly inferred from OT principles (cf. Lev. 19:32; Job 32:4, 6; Prov. 4:1–4; 16:31; 20:29).

i. **exhort.** This Gr. word, which is related to a title for the Holy Spirit (paraclētos; cf. John 14:16, 26; 15:26; 16:7), refers to coming alongside someone to help. It may best be translated "strengthen." We are to strengthen our fellow believers (cf. Gal. 6:1, 2) in the same way the Scripture (Rom. 15:4) and the Holy Spirit do.

[a]Honor widows who are [b]really widows. But if any [c]widow has children or grandchildren, let them first learn to show piety at home and to [d]repay their parents; for this is good and acceptable before God. Now she who is really a widow, and [e]left alone, [f]trusts in God and continues in supplications and prayers night and day. But she who lives in pleasure is [g]dead while she lives. And these things command, that they may be [h]blameless. But [i]if anyone does not provide for his own, and especially for those of his household, he has denied the faith and is worse than an unbeliever.

Do not let a widow [j]under sixty years old [k]be taken into the number, and not unless she has been [l]the wife of one man, well reported for good works:

---

a. **Honor.** "To show respect or care," "to support," or "to treat graciously." Although it includes meeting all kinds of needs, Paul had in mind here not only this broad definition, but primarily financial support (cf. Ex. 20:12; Matt. 15:1–6; 27:9).

b. **really widows.** Not all widows are truly alone and without resources. Financial support from the church is mandatory only for widows who have no means to provide for their daily needs.

c. **widow has children or grandchildren.** Families, not the church, have the first responsibility for their own widows.

d. **repay their parents.** Children and grandchildren are indebted to those who brought them into the world, reared them, and loved them. Fulfilling this responsibility is a mark of godly obedience (cf. Ex. 20:12).

e. **left alone.** The form of this Gr. word denotes a permanent condition of being forsaken and left without resources. She is "really" a widow, since there is no family to support her.

f. **trusts in God.** A continual state or settled attitude of hope in God (cf. 1 Kin. 17:8–16; Jer. 49:11). Since she has no one else, she pleads with God as her only hope.

g. **dead while she lives.** A widow who lives a worldly, immoral, ungodly life may be alive physically, but her lifestyle proves she is unregenerate and spiritually dead (cf. Eph. 2:1).

h. **blameless.** See 3:2; Phil. 2:15. "Blameless" means "above reproach," so that no one can fault their conduct.

i. **if.** Better translated, "since." Paul negatively restated the positive principle of 1 Tim. 5:4, using the Gr. construction that implies the condition is true, suggesting that there were numerous violations of that principle at Ephesus. Any believer who fails to obey this command is guilty of: 1) denying the principle of compassionate Christian love (cf. John 13:35; Rom. 5:5; 1 Thess. 4:9); and 2) being "worse than an unbeliever." Most pagans naturally fulfill this duty, so believers who have God's command and power to carry it out and do not, behave worse than pagans. Cf. 1 Cor. 5:1, 2.

j. **under sixty.** In NT culture, 60 was considered retirement age. By that age, older women would have completed their child rearing and would have the time, maturity, and character to devote their lives in service to God and the church. They also would not be likely to remarry and become preoccupied with that commitment.

k. **be taken into the number.** More clearly rendered, "be put on the list." This was not a list of those widows eligible for specially recognized church support (all widows in the church who had no other means of support were), but rather those eligible for specially recognized church ministry (cf. Titus 2:3–5).

l. **the wife of one man.** Lit. "one-man woman" (cf. 1 Tim. 3:2, 12). It does not exclude women who have been married more than once (cf. 1 Tim. 5:14; 1 Cor. 7:39), but it refers to a woman totally devoted and faithful to her husband, a wife who had displayed purity of thought and action in her marriage.

if she [a]has brought up children, if she has lodged strangers, if she has [b]washed the saints' feet, if she has relieved the afflicted, if she has diligently followed [c]every good work.

But refuse the younger widows; for when they have begun [d]to grow wanton against Christ, they desire to marry, having condemnation because they have [e]cast off their first faith. And besides they learn to be idle, wandering about from house to house, and not only idle but also [f]gossips and busybodies, saying things which they ought not. Therefore I desire that the younger widows marry, [g]bear children, [h]manage the house, give no opportunity to the adversary to speak reproachfully. For some have [i]already turned aside after [j]Satan. If any believing man or [k]woman has widows, let them relieve them, and do not let the church be burdened, that it may relieve those who are really widows.

---

a. **has brought up children.** This views the godly widow as a Christian mother who has nourished or reared children that have followed the Lord (see 1 Tim. 2:15).

b. **washed the saints' feet.** The menial duty of slaves. It is used literally and metaphorically of widows who have humble servants' hearts (see John 13:5–17).

c. **every good work.** Cf. Dorcas in Acts 9:36–39.

d. **to grow wanton.** Better translated "to feel the impulses of sensual desires"—an expression that includes all that is involved in the marriage relationship, including sexual passion. Paul saw the danger that younger widows might want to escape from their vows to remain single (see 1 Tim. 5:12) and be devoted only to God's service (cf. Num. 30:9); he knew the negative impact such feelings could have on young widows' personal lives and ministry within the church. Such women were also marked out by false teachers as easy prey (2 Tim. 3:6, 7), causing them to leave the truth (1 Tim. 5:15).

e. **cast off their first faith.** In classical Gr., "faith" could also mean "pledge." Taken that way here, it refers to a specific covenant young widows made when asking to be included on the widows' list. Likely, they promised to devote the rest of their lives in service to the church and the Lord. Though well-meaning at the time of their need and bereavement, they were surely to desire marriage again (see 1 Tim. 5:11), and thus renege on their original pledge.

f. **gossips and busybodies.** "Gossips" are people who speak nonsense, talk idly, make empty charges, or even accuse others with malicious words. This idleness and talk also made them suitable targets for the false teachers (1 Tim. 1:6). The term "busybodies" (lit. "one who moves around") refers to those who pry into things that do not concern them; they do not mind their own business.

g. **bear children.** The younger widows were still of childbearing age. Although they had lost their first husbands, there was still the potential privilege and blessing of remarrying and having children (see 1 Tim. 2:15; cf. Ps. 127:3, 5).

h. **manage the house.** The Gr. term denotes all the aspects of household administration, not merely the rearing of children. The home is the domain where a married woman fulfills herself in God's design. See Titus 2:4, 5.

i. **already turned aside.** Some of the young widows had given up their commitment to serve Christ (see 1 Tim. 5:11, 12), perhaps either by following false teachers and spreading their false doctrine or by marrying unbelievers and bringing disgrace upon the church.

j. **Satan.** The devil, the believer's adversary (see Job 1:6–12; 2:1–7; Is. 14:12–15; Ezek. 28:12–15; Rev. 12:9).

k. **woman.** Paul restates the message of 1 Tim. 5:4–8 with the addition that as the situation warrants, Christian women are included in this responsibility for support of widows.

235. THE PROPER RESPONSE TO ELDERS
1 Timothy 5:17–25

Let the ᵃelders who ᵇrule well be counted worthy of ᶜdouble honor, ᵈespecially those who ᵉlabor in the ᶠword and doctrine. ᵍFor the Scripture says, "You shall not muzzle an ox while it treads out the grain," and, "The laborer is worthy of his wages." Do not receive an accusation against an elder except from ʰtwo or three witnesses. ⁱThose who are sinning rebuke ʲin the presence of all, that the rest also may fear.

---

a. **elders.** This identifies the "bishop" (1 Tim. 3:1) or overseer, who is also called pastor (Eph. 4:11). See 1 Tim. 3:1–7; Titus 1:6–9. The source of much of the Ephesian church's difficulties was the inadequacy of the pastors. So Paul explains to Timothy how to restore proper pastoral oversight. He sets forth the church's obligations in regard to honoring, protecting, rebuking, and selecting elders.

b. **rule well.** Elders are spiritual rulers in the church. Cf. 1 Thess. 5:12, 13; Heb. 13:7, 17.

c. **double honor.** Elders who serve with greater commitment, excellence, and effort should have greater acknowledgment from their congregations. This expression does not mean such men should receive exactly twice as much remuneration as others, but because they have earned such respect they should be paid more generously.

d. **especially.** Means "chiefly" or "particularly." Implicit is the idea that some elders will work harder than others and be more prominent in ministry.

e. **labor.** Lit. "work to the point of fatigue or exhaustion." The Gr. word stresses the effort behind the work more than the amount of work.

f. **word and doctrine.** Or better, "preaching and teaching" (see 1 Tim. 4:13). The first emphasizes proclamation, along with exhortation and admonition, and calls for a heart response to the Lord. The second is an essential fortification against heresy and puts more stress on instruction.

g. **For the Scripture says.** A typical formula for introducing biblical references, in this instance both an OT (Deut. 25:4) and NT (Luke 10:7) one. It is also very significant that this is a case of one NT writer (Paul) affirming the inspiration of another by referring to Luke's writing as "Scripture" (cf. 2 Pet. 3:15, 16), which shows the high view that the early church took of NT Scripture.

h. **two or three witnesses.** Serious accusations against elders must be investigated and confirmed by the same process as established in Matt. 18:15–20. This process for the whole church also applies to elders. This demand does not place elders beyond successful accusation, but protects them from frivolous, evil accusers, by demanding the same process of confirmation of sin as for all in the church.

i. **Those who are sinning.** Elders who continue in any kind of sin after the confrontation of 2 or 3 witnesses, especially any that violates the qualifications to serve (1 Tim. 3:2–7).

j. **in the presence of all.** The other elders and the congregation. The third step of confrontation, established in Matt. 18:17, is to tell the church, so that they can all confront the person and call him to repentance.

I charge you before God and the Lord Jesus Christ and ªthe elect angels that you observe these things ᵇwithout prejudice, doing nothing with partiality. ᶜDo not lay hands on anyone hastily, ᵈnor share in other people's sins; ᵉkeep yourself pure.

ᶠNo longer drink only water, but ᵍuse a little wine for your stomach's sake and your frequent infirmities.

Some men's ʰsins are clearly evident, ⁱpreceding them to judgment, but those of some men ʲfollow later. Likewise, the ᵏgood works of some are clearly evident, and those that are otherwise cannot be hidden.

---

a. **the elect angels.** "Chosen angels," or the unfallen angels, as opposed to Satan and his demons. This indicates that God's sovereign purpose to choose those beings who would be part of His eternal kingdom included angels whom He chose to eternal glory. Christians are also called "elect" (Rom. 8:33; 11:7; Col. 3:12; 2 Tim. 2:10; Titus 1:1; 1 Pet. 1:2; 2 John 1, 13).

b. **without prejudice . . . partiality.** All discipline of elders is to be done fairly, without prejudgment or personal preference, according to the standards of Scripture.

c. **Do not lay hands on . . . hastily.** The ceremony that affirmed a man's suitability for and acceptance into public ministry as an elder/pastor/overseer. This came from the OT practice of laying hands on a sacrificial animal to identify with it (Ex. 29:10, 15, 19; Lev. 4:15; cf. Num. 8:10; 27:18–23; Deut. 34:9; Matt. 19:15; Acts 8:17, 18; 9:17; Heb. 6:2). "Hastily" refers to proceeding with this ceremony without a thorough investigation and preparation period to be certain of the man's qualifications (as in 1 Tim. 3:1–7).

d. **nor share in other people's sins.** This refers to the sin of hasty ordination, which makes those responsible culpable for the man's sin of serving as an unqualified elder and, thus, misleading people.

e. **keep yourself pure.** Some versions translate "pure" as "free from sin." Paul wanted Timothy, by not participating in the recognition of unqualified elders, to remain untainted by others' sins. The church desperately needed qualified spiritual leaders, but the selection had to be carefully executed.

f. **No longer drink only water.** "Water" in the ancient world was often polluted and carried many diseases. Therefore Paul urged Timothy not to risk illness, not even for the sake of a commitment to abstinence from wine. Apparently Timothy avoided wine, so as not to place himself in harm's way (see 1 Tim. 3:3).

g. **use a little wine . . . infirmities.** Paul wanted Timothy to use wine which, because of fermentation, acted as a disinfectant to protect his health problems due to the harmful effects of impure water. With this advice, however, Paul was not advocating that Timothy lower the high standard of behavior for leaders (cf. Num. 6:1–4; Prov. 31:4, 5).

h. **sins are clearly evident.** The sins of some men are manifest for all to see, thus disqualifying them out of hand for service as elders.

i. **preceding them to judgment.** The known sins of the unqualified announce those men's guilt and unfitness before all. "Judgment" refers to the church's process for determining men's suitability to serve as elders.

j. **follow later.** The sins of other candidates for elder will come to light in time, perhaps even during the scrutiny of the evaluation process.

k. **good works.** Time and truth go hand in hand. The whole emphasis in this instruction regarding choosing elders, according to the qualifications of 1 Tim. 3:1–7, is to be patient, fair, impartial, and pure (1 Tim. 5:21–25). Such an approach will yield the right choices.

236. FALSE TEACHERS AND THE LOVE OF MONEY
1 Timothy 6:1–10

Let as many ᵃbondservants as are ᵇunder the yoke count their own ᶜmasters worthy of ᵈall honor, so that the name of God and ᵉHis doctrine may not be blasphemed. And those who have ᶠbelieving masters, let them not despise them because they are brethren, but rather serve them because those who are benefited are believers and beloved. Teach and ᵍexhort these things.

ʰIf anyone teaches otherwise and does not consent to wholesome words, even the words of our Lord Jesus Christ, and to the doctrine which accords with godliness, he is proud, knowing nothing, but is obsessed with ⁱdisputes and arguments over words, from which come envy, strife, reviling, evil

---

a. **bondservants.** This can be translated "slaves." They are people who are in submission to another. It carries no negative connotation and is often positive when used in connection with the Lord serving the Father (Phil. 2:7), and believers serving God (1 Pet. 2:16), the Lord (Rom. 1:1; Gal. 1:10; 2 Tim. 2:24; James 1:1), non-Christians (1 Cor. 9:19), and other believers (Gal. 5:13).

b. **under the yoke.** A colloquial expression describing submissive service under another's authority, not necessarily describing an abusive relationship (cf. Matt. 11:28–30).

c. **masters.** The Gr. word for "master," while giving us the Eng. word "despot," does not carry a negative connotation. Instead, it refers to one with absolute and unrestricted authority.

d. **all honor.** This translates into diligent and faithful labor for one's employer. See Eph. 6:5–9; Col. 3:22–25.

e. **His doctrine.** The revelation of God summed up in the gospel. How believers act while under the authority of another affects how people view the message of salvation Christians proclaim (see Titus 2:5–14). Displaying a proper attitude of submission and respect, and performing quality work, help make the gospel message believable (Matt. 5:48).

f. **believing masters.** The tendency might be to assume one's equality in Christ with a Christian master, and disdain the authority related to work roles. On the contrary, working for a Christian should produce more loyal and diligent service out of love for the brethren.

g. **exhort.** Lit. "to call to one's side." The particular emphasis here is on a strong urging, directing, and insisting on following the principles for correct behavior in the workplace.

h. **If anyone . . .** Paul identifies 3 characteristics of false teachers: 1) they "teach otherwise"—a different doctrine, or any teaching that contradicts God's revelation in Scripture (see Gal. 1:6–9); 2) they do "not consent to wholesome words"—they do not agree with sound, healthy teaching, specifically the teaching contained in Scripture (2 Pet. 3:16); and 3) they reject "doctrine which accords with godliness"—teaching not based on Scripture will always result in an unholy life. Instead of godliness, false teachers will be marked by sin (see 2 Pet. 2:10–22; cf. Jude 4, 8–16).

i. **disputes and arguments over words.** "Disputes" refers to idle speculation; "arguments over words" lit. means "word battles." Because proud, ignorant false teachers do not understand divine truth (2 Cor. 2:14), they obsess over terminology and attack the reliability and authority of Scripture. Every kind of strife is mentioned to indicate that false teachers produce nothing of benefit out of their fleshly, corrupt, and empty minds (1 Tim. 6:5).

suspicions, useless wranglings of men of corrupt minds and ᵃdestitute of the truth, who suppose that godliness is ᵇa means of gain. ᶜFrom such withdraw yourself.

Now godliness with ᵈcontentment is great gain. For we brought nothing into this world, and it is certain we can carry nothing out. And ᵉhaving food and clothing, with these we shall be content. But those who ᶠdesire to be rich fall into temptation and a snare, and into many foolish and harmful lusts which drown men in ᵍdestruction and perdition. For the ʰlove of money is a root of all kinds of evil, for which some have ⁱstrayed from the faith in their greediness, and pierced themselves through with many sorrows.

---

a. **destitute of the truth.** False teachers are in a state of apostasy; that is, although they once knew and seemed to embrace the truth, they turned to openly reject it. The Gr. word for "destitute" means "to steal," "to rob," or "to deprive" and its form here indicates that someone or something was pulled away from contact with the truth (it does not mean they were ever saved; see 1 Tim. 1:19; cf. 2 Tim. 2:18; 3:7, 8; Heb. 6:4–6; 2 Pet. 2:1, 4–9).

b. **a means of gain.** Almost always behind all the efforts of the hypocritical, lying (1 Tim. 4:2) false teachers is the driving motivation of monetary gain (cf. Acts 8:18–23; 2 Pet. 2:15).

c. **From such withdraw yourself.** This phrase does not appear in the better manuscripts, although the idea expressed is self-evident.

d. **contentment.** This Gr. word means "self-sufficiency," and was used by Stoic philosophers to describe a person who was unflappable and unmoved by external circumstances. Christians are to be satisfied and sufficient, and not to seek for more than what God has already given them. He is the source of true contentment (2 Cor. 3:5; 9:8; Phil. 4:11–13, 19).

e. **having food and clothing . . . be content.** The basic necessities of life are what ought to make Christians content. Paul does not condemn having possessions, as long as God graciously provides them (1 Tim. 6:17). He does, however, condemn a self-indulgent desire for money, which results from discontentment. See Matt. 6:33.

f. **desire to be rich fall into temptation.** "Desire" refers to a settled wish born of reason, and clearly describes those guilty of greed. The form of the Gr. verb for "fall" indicates that those who have such a desire are continually falling into temptation. Greedy people are compulsive—they are continually trapped in sins by their consuming desire to acquire more.

g. **destruction and perdition.** Such greed may lead these people to suffer the tragic end of destruction and hell. These terms refer to the eternal punishment of the wicked.

h. **love of money.** Lit. "affection for silver." In the context, this sin applies to false teachers specifically, but the principle is true universally. Money itself is not evil since it is a gift from God (Deut. 8:18); Paul condemns only the love of it (cf. Matt. 6:24) which is so characteristic of false teachers (see 1 Pet. 5:2; 2 Pet. 2:1–3, 15).

i. **strayed from the faith.** From the body of Christian truth. Gold has replaced God for these apostates, who have turned away from pursuing the things of God in favor of money.

237. PROPER MOTIVATION FOR THE MAN OF GOD

1 Timothy 6:11–21

But you, ªO man of God, flee ᵇthese things and pursue ᶜrighteousness, godliness, faith, love, patience, gentleness. ᵈFight the good fight of faith, ᵉlay hold on eternal life, ᶠto which you were also called and have confessed the ᵍgood confession in the presence of many witnesses. I urge you in the sight of God who gives life to all things, and before Christ Jesus who witnessed ʰthe good confession before Pontius Pilate, that you keep ⁱthis commandment without spot, blameless until our Lord Jesus Christ's ʲappearing, which He

---

a. **O man of God.** Cf. 2 Tim. 3:17. This is a term used in the NT only for Timothy; as a technical term it is used about 70 times in the OT, always to refer to a man who officially spoke for God (see Deut. 33:1). This, along with 1:2; 2:1, indicates that the letter is primarily directed to Timothy, exhorting him to be faithful and strong in light of persecution and difficulty—and particularly with Paul's death near. The man of God is known by what he: 1) flees from (1 Tim. 6:11); 2) follows after (v. 11); 3) fights for (v. 12); and 4) is faithful to (vv. 13, 14). The key to his success in all these endeavors is the perfection produced in him by the Scripture (2 Tim. 3:16, 17).

b. **these things.** Love of money and all that goes with it (1 Tim. 6:6–10), along with the other proud obsessions of false teachers (1 Tim. 6:3–5).

c. **righteousness, godliness.** "Righteousness" means to do what is right, in relation to both God and man, and it emphasizes outward behavior. "Godliness" (see 1 Tim. 2:2) refers to one's reverence for God, and could be translated "God-likeness."

d. **Fight the good fight of faith.** The Gr. word for "fight" gives us the Eng. word "agonize," and was used in both military and athletic endeavors to describe the concentration, discipline, and extreme effort needed to win. The "good fight of faith" is the spiritual conflict with Satan's kingdom of darkness in which all men of God are necessarily involved. See 2 Cor. 10:3–5; 2 Tim. 4:2.

e. **lay hold on eternal life.** Paul is here admonishing Timothy to "get a grip" on the reality of the matters associated with eternal life, so that he would live and minister with a heavenly and eternal perspective (cf. Phil. 3:20; Col. 3:2).

f. **to which you were also called.** Refers to God's effectual, sovereign call of Timothy to salvation (see Rom. 1:7).

g. **good confession.** Timothy's public confession of faith in the Lord Jesus Christ, which likely occurred at his baptism and again when he was ordained to the ministry (1 Tim. 4:14; 2 Tim. 1:6).

h. **the good confession before Pontius Pilate.** Knowing that such a confession would cost Him His life, Jesus nevertheless confessed that He was truly the King and Messiah (John 18:33–37). He never evaded danger; He boldly and trustfully committed Himself to God who raises the dead (cf. Col. 2:12).

i. **this commandment.** The entire revealed Word of God, which Paul charged Timothy to preach (2 Tim. 4:2). Paul also repeatedly encouraged Timothy to guard it (1 Tim. 1:18, 19; 4:6, 16; 6:20; 2 Tim. 1:13, 14; 2:15–18).

j. **appearing.** When the Lord returns to earth in glory (cf. 2 Tim. 4:1, 8; Titus 2:13) to judge and to establish His kingdom (Matt. 24:27, 29, 30; 25:31). Because Christ's return is imminent, that ought to be motivation enough for the man of God to remain faithful to his calling until he dies or the Lord returns (cf. Acts 1:8–11; 1 Cor. 4:5; Rev. 22:12).

will manifest ªin His own time, He who is the blessed and only ᵇPotentate, the ᶜKing of kings and Lord of lords, who alone has immortality, dwelling in unapproachable light, ᵈwhom no man has seen or can see, to whom be honor and everlasting power. Amen.

Command those who are rich in this present age not to be ᵉhaughty, nor to trust in ᶠuncertain riches but in the living God, who gives us richly all things to enjoy. Let them do good, that they be rich in good works, ᵍready to give, willing to share, ʰstoring up for themselves a good foundation for the time to come, that they may lay hold on eternal life.

O Timothy! Guard ⁱwhat was committed to your trust, avoiding the profane and idle babblings and contradictions of ʲwhat is falsely called knowledge—by professing it some have strayed concerning the faith.

ᵏGrace be with you. Amen.

---

a. **in His own time.** The time, known only to Him, that God established in eternity past for Christ to return (Mark 13:32; Acts 1:7).

b. **Potentate.** This word comes from a Gr. word group that basically means "power," but here it is best translated "Sovereign." God is absolutely sovereign and omnipotently rules everything everywhere.

c. **King of kings and Lord of lords.** A title used of Christ (Rev. 17:14; 19:16) is here used of God the Father. Paul probably used this title for God to confront the cult of emperor worship, intending to communicate that only God is sovereign and worthy of worship.

d. **whom no man has seen or can see.** God in spirit is invisible (cf. 1 Tim. 1:17; Job 23:8, 9; John 1:18; 5:37; Col. 1:15) and, therefore, unapproachable in the sense that sinful man has never seen nor can he ever see His full glory (cf. Ex. 33:20; Is. 6:1–5).

e. **haughty.** "To have an exalted opinion of oneself." Those who have an abundance are constantly tempted to look down on others and act superior. Riches and pride often go together, and the wealthier a person is, the more he is tempted to be proud (Prov. 18:23; 28:11; James 2:1–4).

f. **uncertain riches . . . gives us richly.** Those who have much tend to trust in their wealth (cf. Prov. 23:4, 5). But God provides far more security than any earthly investment can ever give (Eccl. 5:18–20; Matt. 6:19–21).

g. **ready to give.** The Gr. word means "liberal," or "bountiful." Those believers who have money must use it in meeting the needs of others, unselfishly and generously (see Acts 4:32–37; 2 Cor. 8:1–4).

h. **storing up . . . a good foundation.** "Storing up" can be translated "amassing a treasure," while "foundation" can refer to a fund. The idea is that the rich in this world should not be concerned with receiving a return on their earthly investment. Those who make eternal investments will be content to receive their dividends in heaven. See Luke 16:1–13.

i. **what was committed to your trust.** This translates one Gr. word, which means "deposit." The deposit Timothy was to guard is the truth—the divine revelation that God committed to his care. Every Christian, especially if he is in ministry, has that sacred trust to guard the revelation of God (cf. 1 Cor. 4:1; 1 Thess. 2:3, 4).

j. **what is falsely called knowledge.** False doctrine—anything claiming to be the truth that is in fact a lie. False teachers typically claim to have the superior knowledge (as in gnosticism). They claim to know the transcendent secrets, but actually are ignorant and infantile in their understanding (see Col. 2:8).

k. **Grace be with you.** Paul's closing salutation is plural, i.e., "you all"—it goes beyond Timothy to the entire congregation at Ephesus. All believers require the grace of God to preserve the truth and pass it on to the next generation.

238. PAUL WRITES A LETTER TO TITUS
Introduction to Titus

This epistle is named for its recipient, Titus, who is mentioned by name 13 times in the NT (1:4; Gal. 2:1, 3; 2 Tim 4:10; for the 9 times in 2 Cor., see Background and Setting). The title in the Greek NT literally reads "To Titus." Along with 1, 2 Timothy, these letters to Paul's sons in the faith are traditionally called "The Pastoral Epistles."

Author and Date

Authorship by the Apostle Paul (1:1) is essentially uncontested (see Introduction to 1 Timothy). Titus was written between A.D. 62–64, while Paul ministered to Macedonian churches between his first and second Roman imprisonments, from either Corinth or Nicopolis (cf. 3:12). Most likely, Titus served with Paul on both the second and third missionary journeys. Titus, like Timothy (2 Tim. 1:2), had become a beloved disciple (1:4) and fellow worker in the gospel (2 Cor. 8:23). Paul's last mention of Titus (2 Tim. 4:10) reports that he had gone for ministry in Dalmatia—modern Yugoslavia. The letter probably was delivered by Zenas and Apollos (3:13).

Background and Setting

Although Luke did not mention Titus by name in the book of Acts, it seems probable that Titus, a Gentile (Gal. 2:3), met and may have been led to faith in Christ by Paul (1:4) before or during the apostle's first missionary journey. Later, Titus ministered for a period of time with Paul on the Island of Crete and was left behind to continue and strengthen the work (1:5). After Artemas or Tychicus (3:12) arrived to direct the ministry there, Paul wanted Titus to join him in the city of Nicopolis, in the province of Achaia in Greece, and stay through the winter (3:12).

Because of his involvement with the church at Corinth during Paul's third missionary journey, Titus is mentioned 9 times in 2 Corinthians (2:13; 7:6, 13, 14; 8:6, 16, 23; 12:18), where Paul refers to him as "my brother" (2:13) and "my partner and fellow worker" (8:23). The young elder was already familiar with Judaizers, false teachers in the church, who among other things insisted that all Christians, Gentile as well as Jew, were bound by the Mosaic law. Titus had accompanied Paul and Barnabas years earlier to the Council of Jerusalem where that heresy was the subject (Acts 15; Gal. 2:1–5).

Crete, one of the largest islands in the Mediterranean Sea, measuring 160 mi. long by 35 mi. at its widest, lying S of the Aegean Sea, had been briefly visited by Paul on his voyage to Rome (Acts 27:7–9, 12, 13, 21). He returned there for ministry and later left Titus to continue the work, much as he left Timothy at Ephesus (1 Tim. 1:3), while he went on to Macedonia. He most likely wrote to Titus in response to a letter from Titus or a report from Crete.

Historical and Theological Themes

Like Paul's two letters to Timothy, the apostle gives personal encouragement and counsel to a young pastor who, though well-trained and faithful, faced continuing opposition from ungodly men within the churches where he ministered. Titus was to pass on that encouragement and counsel to the leaders he was to appoint in the Cretan churches (1:5).

In contrast to several of Paul's other letters, such as those to the churches in Rome and Galatia, the book of Titus does not focus on explaining or defending doctrine. Paul had full confidence in Titus' theological understanding and convictions, evidenced by the fact that he entrusted him with such a demanding ministry. Except for the warning about false teachers and Judaizers, the letter gives no theological correction, strongly suggesting that Paul also had confidence in the doctrinal grounding of most church members there, despite the fact that the majority of them were new believers. Doctrines that this epistle affirms include: 1) God's sovereign election of believers (1:1, 2); 2) His saving grace (2:11; 3:5); 3) Christ's deity and second coming (2:13); 4) Christ's substitutionary atonement (2:14); and 5) the regeneration and renewing of believers by the Holy Spirit (3:5).

God and Christ are regularly referred to as Savior (1:3, 4; 2:10, 13; 3:4, 6) and the saving plan is so emphasized in 2:11–14 that it indicates the major thrust of the epistle is that of equipping the churches of Crete for effective evangelism. This preparation required godly leaders who not only would shepherd believers under their care (1:5–9), but also would equip those Christians for evangelizing their pagan neighbors, who had been characterized by one of their own famous natives as liars, evil beasts, and lazy gluttons (1:12).

In order to gain a hearing for the gospel among such people, the believers' primary preparation for evangelization was to live among themselves with the unarguable testimony of righteous, loving, selfless, and godly lives (2:2–14) in marked contrast to the debauched lives of the false teachers (1:10–16). How they behaved with reference to governmental authorities and unbelievers was also crucial to their testimony (3:1–8).

Several major themes repeat themselves throughout Titus. They include: work(s) (1:16; 2:7, 14; 3:1, 5, 8, 14); soundness in faith and doctrine (1:4, 9, 13; 2:1, 2, 7, 8, 10; 3:15); and salvation (1:3, 4; 2:10, 13; 3:4, 6).

Interpretive Challenges

The letter to Titus presents itself in a straightforward manner which should be taken at face value. The few interpretive challenges include: 1) Are the children of 1:6 merely "faithful" or are they "believing"? and 2) What is the "blessed hope" of 2:13? These issues are address in the notes.

239. THE ETERNAL PLAN OF SALVATION
Titus 1:1–4

ªPaul, a ᵇbondservant of God and an ᶜapostle of Jesus Christ, according to the faith of ᵈGod's elect and the acknowledgment of ᵉthe truth which accords

---

a. Paul. This salutation emphasizes the nature of Paul's service as an apostle of Jesus Christ. He proclaimed: 1) salvation: God's purpose to save the elect by the gospel; 2) sanctification: God's purpose to build up the saved by the Word of God; and 3) glorification: God's purpose to bring believers to eternal glory.

b. **bondservant.** Paul pictures himself as the most menial slave of NT times (see Titus 2:9; 1 Cor. 4:1, 2), indicating his complete and willing servitude to the Lord, by whom all believers have been "bought at a price" (1 Cor. 6:20; cf. 1 Pet. 1:18, 19). This the only time Paul referred to himself as a "bondservant of God" (cf. Rom. 1:1; Gal. 1:10; Phil. 1:1). He was placing himself alongside OT men of God (cf. Rev. 15:3).

c. **apostle.** Cf. Rom. 1:1; 1 Cor. 1:1; 2 Cor. 1:1; Eph. 1:1. The word has the basic meaning of messenger or lit. "sent one" and, though often used of royal emissaries who ministered with the extended authority of their sovereign, Paul's exalted position as "an apostle" also was an extension of his bondservice to "God," which came with great authority, responsibility, and sacrifice. See Acts 20:24.

d. **God's elect.** See Eph. 1:4, 5. Those who have been graciously chosen for salvation "before the foundation of the world" (Eph. 1:4), but who must exercise personal faith prompted and empowered by the Holy Spirit. God's choice of believers always precedes and enables their choice of Him (cf. John 15:16; Acts 13:46–48; Rom. 9:15–21; 2 Thess. 2:13; 2 Tim. 1:8, 9; 2:10; 1 Pet. 1:1, 2).

e. **the truth.** Paul had in mind gospel truth, the saving message of the death and

with godliness, in ªhope of eternal life which God, who ᵇcannot lie, promised ᶜbefore time began, but has in due time manifested ᵈHis word through preaching, which was committed to me according to the commandment of ᵉGod our Savior;

To Titus, a ᶠtrue son in our ᵍcommon faith:

Grace, mercy, and peace from God the Father and the Lord Jesus Christ ʰour Savior.

240. Establishing Godly Leaders
Titus 1:5–9

ⁱFor this reason I left you in Crete, that you should ʲset in order the things that are lacking, and appoint ᵏelders in every city as I ˡcommanded you—if

resurrection of Jesus Christ (1 Tim. 2:3, 4; 2 Tim. 2:25). It is that saving truth that leads to "godliness" or sanctification (see Titus 2:11, 12).

a. **hope.** This is divinely promised and divinely guaranteed to all believers, providing endurance and patience (cf. John 6:37–40; Rom. 8:18–23; 1 Cor. 15:51–58; Eph. 1:13, 14; Phil. 3:8–11, 20, 21; 1 Thess. 4:13–18; 1 John 3:2, 3). See 1 Pet. 1:3–9.

b. **cannot lie.** Cf. 1 Sam. 15:29; Heb. 6:18. Because God Himself is truth and the source of truth, it is impossible for Him to say anything untruthful (John 14:6, 17; 15:26; cf. Num. 23:19; Ps. 146:6).

c. **before time began.** God's plan of salvation for sinful mankind was determined and decreed before man was even created. The promise was made to God the Son (see John 6:37–44; Eph. 1:4, 5; 2 Tim. 1:9).

d. **His word . . . preaching.** God's Word is the sole source of content for all faithful preaching and teaching. Cf. 1 Cor. 1:18–21; 9:16, 17; 2:1–4; Gal. 1:15, 16; Col 1:25.

e. **God our Savior.** Cf. Titus 2:10; 3:4. The plan of salvation originated in eternity past with God.

f. **true son.** A spiritual son, a genuine believer in Christ, like Timothy (1 Tim. 1:2).

g. **common faith.** This may refer to saving faith or to the content of the Christian faith, e.g., "The faith which was once for all delivered to the saints" (Jude 3).

h. **our Savior.** Christ is called Savior each time He is mentioned after Titus 1:1 (cf. Titus 2:13; 3:6).

i. God's standards for all believers are high; His requirement for church leaders is to set that standard and model it. Such leaders are not qualified on the basis of natural ability, intelligence, or education but on the basis of moral and spiritual character and the ability to teach with skill as the Spirit sovereignly has equipped them.

j. **set in order.** Titus was to correct wrong doctrine and practices in the Cretan churches, a task that Paul had been unable to complete. This ministry is mentioned nowhere else.

k. **elders.** Cf. similar qualifications in 1 Tim. 3:1–7. Mature spiritual leaders of the church, also called bishops (Titus 1:7; cf. 1 Tim. 3:2) or overseers (see 1 Pet. 2:25 where the same Gr. word is used of Christ), and pastors (lit. shepherds; see Eph. 4:11) were to care for each city's congregation. See also Acts 20:17, 28; 1 Pet. 5:1, 2. This ministry of appointing leaders is consistently Pauline (cf. Acts 14:23).

l. **commanded you.** A reminder of past apostolic instructions.

a man is ᵃblameless, the ᵇhusband of one wife, having ᶜfaithful children not accused of ᵈdissipation or insubordination. For a ᵉbishop must be blameless, as a ᶠsteward of God, not self-willed, not quick-tempered, not given to ᵍwine, not violent, not ʰgreedy for money, but ⁱhospitable, a lover of what is good, ʲsober-minded, just, holy, self-controlled, holding fast the ᵏfaithful word as he has been taught, that he may be able, by sound doctrine, both to ˡexhort and convict those who contradict.

---

a. **blameless.** This word does not refer to sinless perfection but to a personal life that is beyond legitimate accusation and public scandal. It is a general and primary requirement of spiritual leaders that is repeated (v. 7) and explained in the next verses (cf. 1 Tim. 3:2, 10).

b. **husband of one wife.** Lit. "a one-woman man," i.e., a husband who is consistently, both inwardly and outwardly, devoted and faithful to his wife (cf. 1 Tim. 3:2). An otherwise qualified single man is not necessarily disqualified. This is not speaking of divorce, but of internal and external purity in the sexual area. See Prov. 6:32, 33. This necessity was motivation for Paul's commitment to control his body (1 Cor. 9:27).

c. **faithful children.** "Faithful" is always used in the NT of believers and never for unbelievers, so this refers to children who have saving faith in Christ and reflect it in their conduct. Since 1 Tim. 3:4 requires children to be in submission, it may be directed at young children in the home, while this text looks at those who are older.

d. **dissipation or insubordination.** "Dissipation" connotes debauchery, suggesting, again, that the reference is to grown children. "Insubordination" carries the idea of rebelliousness to the gospel. Here the elder shows his ability to lead his family to salvation and sanctification (see 1 Tim. 3:4, 5), an essential prerequisite for leading the church.

e. **bishop.** This is not a hierarchial title, but a word meaning "overseer." Cf. Acts 20:28; Heb. 13:17; 1 Pet. 5:2.

f. **steward.** The term refers to one who manages someone else's properties for the well-being of those his master cares for. In this context, one who manages spiritual truths, lives on God's behalf, and is wholly accountable to Him. The church is God's (Acts 20:28; 1 Tim. 3:15; 1 Pet. 5:2–4) and elders or bishops are accountable to him for the way they lead it (Heb. 13:17).

g. **wine.** Applies to drinking any alcoholic beverage in any way that dulls the mind or subdues inhibitions (cf. Prov. 23:29–35; 31:4–7). By application, it also indicts any other substance, e.g., drugs, which would cloud the mind.

h. **greedy.** Even in the early church, some men became pastors in order to gain wealth (see Titus 1:11; 1 Pet. 5:3; cf. 2 Pet. 2:1–3).

i. **hospitable.** The word actually means "a lover of strangers."

j. **sober-minded.** Serious, with the right priorities, sensible.

k. **faithful word.** Sound biblical doctrine not only should be taught but also adhered to with deep conviction. Cf. 1 Tim. 4:6; 5:17; 2 Tim. 2:15; 3:16, 17; 4:2–4.

l. **exhort and convict.** The faithful teaching and defending of Scripture which encourages godliness and confronts sin and error (those who contradict). See Titus 1:10–16; 3:10, 11; Acts 20:29, 30.

241. CONFRONTING FALSE TEACHERS

Titus 1:10–16

ª For there are many ᵇinsubordinate, both idle talkers and deceivers, especially those of ᶜthe circumcision, whose mouths must be stopped, who subvert whole households, teaching things which they ought not, for the sake of ᵈdishonest gain. One of them, ᵉa prophet of their own, said, "Cretans are always liars, evil beasts, lazy gluttons." This testimony is true. Therefore rebuke them sharply, that they may be ᶠsound in the faith, not giving heed to Jewish ᵍfables and commandments of men who turn from the truth. To the pure all things are pure, but to those who are ʰdefiled and unbelieving nothing is pure; but even their ⁱmind and conscience are defiled. They ʲprofess to know God, but in works they deny Him, being abominable, disobedient, and ᵏdisqualified for every good work.

---

a. The false teachers in the Cretan churches were much like those with whom Timothy had to deal in Ephesus (see 1 Tim. 1:3–7; cf. Rom. 16:17, 18; 2 Pet. 2:1–3).

b. **insubordinate.** Because those men were so numerous, Titus' job was especially difficult, which made the appointment of additional godly elders (Titus 1:5) all the more crucial. Some of the false teachers may have opposed even Paul's apostolic authority during his brief ministry on Crete.

c. **the circumcision.** Cf. Acts 10:45; 11:2. These were Jews who taught that salvation required the physical cutting of circumcision (see Gen. 17:9–14) and adherence to Mosaic ceremonies. See Acts 15:1–12; Gal. 3:1–12; Eph. 2:11; Col. 2:12.

d. **dishonest gain.** False teachers are always in it for the money (1 Tim. 6:4; 1 Pet. 5:2).

e. **a prophet.** Epimenides, the highly esteemed sixth-century B.C. Greek poet and native of Crete, had characterized his own people as the dregs of Greek culture. Elsewhere, Paul also quoted pagan sayings (cf. Acts 17:28; 1 Cor. 15:33). This quote is directed at the false teachers' character.

f. **sound in the faith.** True and pure doctrine was to be required of all who spoke to the church. Any who fell short of that were to be rebuked.

g. **fables and commandments of men.** Paul reemphasized (see Titus 1:10, "hose of the circumcision") that most of the false teachers were Jewish. They taught the same kind of externalism and unscriptural laws and traditions that both Isaiah and Jesus railed against (Is. 29:13; Matt. 15:1–9; Mark 7:5–13).

h. **defiled.** The outwardly despicable things that those men practiced (Titus 1:10–12) were simply reflections of their inner corruption. See Matt. 15:15–20.

i. **mind and conscience.** If the mind is defiled, it cannot accurately inform the conscience, so conscience cannot warn the person. When conscience is accurately and fully infused with God's truth, it functions as the warning system God designed. See 2 Cor. 1:12; 4:2; 1 Tim. 1:19, 20. False teachers are corrupt on the inside ("mind and conscience") and the outside ("works" and "disobedient"). Cf. Matt. 7:15, 16.

j. **profess . . . deny.** Some of the false teachers in the church were not believers at all. Eventually, even the seemingly noble "works" of unbelievers will betray them.

k. **disqualified.** They can do nothing that pleases God. See 1 Cor. 9:27; cf. 2 Tim. 3:8.

242. SOUND CHRISTIAN LIVING

Titus 2:1–10

But as for you, speak the things which are proper for [a]sound doctrine: that the [b]older men be sober, [c]reverent, temperate, sound in faith, in love, in patience; the [d]older women likewise, that they be reverent in behavior, [e]not slanderers, not given to much wine, teachers of [f]good things—that they [g]admonish the young women to [h]love their husbands, to love their children, to be [i]discreet, chaste, [j]homemakers, good, [k]obedient to their own husbands, that the word of God may [l]not be blasphemed.

Likewise, exhort the [m]young men to be sober-minded, [n]in all things showing yourself to be a [o]pattern of good works; [p]in doctrine showing integrity,

a. **sound.** Meaning healthy—Paul uses this word 9 times in the pastoral epistles (5 times in Titus), always in the sense that the truth produces spiritual well-being. The "things" Paul mentions in Titus 2:2–10 pertain to truths, attitudes, and actions that correspond to and are based on biblical truth. In order not only to please God, but also to have an effective witness to unbelievers, God's people must know the truth that leads to spiritual health.

b. **older men.** Paul used this term for himself (Philem. 9) when he was over 60. It refers to those of advanced age, using a different term from the one translated "elder" in 1:5.

c. **reverent.** This requirement is not limited to reverence for God, which is assumed, but also refers to being honorable and dignified. They are to be sensible and spiritually healthy.

d. **older women.** Those who no longer had child-rearing responsibilities, typically around age 60 (cf. 1 Tim. 5:3–10).

e. **not slanderers.** A term used 34 times in the NT to describe Satan, the arch-slanderer.

f. **good things.** Those that please God (Titus 1:16), particularly the lessons in Titus 2:4, 5.

g. **admonish the young women.** Their own examples of godliness (Titus 2:3) give older women the right and the credibility to instruct younger women in the church. The obvious implication is that older women must exemplify the virtues (vv. 4, 5) that they "admonish."

h. **love their husbands.** Like the other virtues mentioned here, this one is unconditional. It is based on God's will, not on a husband's worthiness. The Gr. word phileō emphasizes affection. See Eph. 5:22–24.

i. **discreet.** I.e., pure. Cf. 1 Tim. 2:9–11, 15; 1 Pet. 3:3–6.

j. **homemakers.** Cf. 1 Tim. 5:14. Keeping a godly home with excellence for one's husband and children is the Christian woman's non-negotiable responsibility.

k. **obedient.** The ideas of radical feminism were an integral part of ancient Babylonian and Assyrian mythology as well as of Greek gnosticism, which flourished throughout the Roman Empire during NT times and posed a constant danger to the early church. Modern feminism is neither new nor progressive; it is age-old and regressive. See Eph. 5:22.

l. **not be blasphemed.** This is the purpose of godly conduct—to eliminate any reproach on Scripture. For a person to be convinced God can save from sin, one needs to see someone who lives a holy life. When Christians claim to believe God's Word but do not obey it, the Word is dishonored. Many have mocked God and His truth because of the sinful behavior of those who claim to be Christians. Cf. Matt. 5:16; 1 Pet. 2:9.

m. **young men.** Males, 12 and older.

n. **in all things.** This rightly goes at the end of Titus 2:6, qualifying young men and emphasizing the comprehensiveness of this admonition.

o. **pattern.** Titus had a special obligation to exemplify the moral and spiritual qualities about which he was to admonish others. Cf. 1 Cor. 4:16; 11:1; Phil. 3:17; 2 Thess. 3:8, 9; 1 Tim. 4:12; Heb. 13:7.

p. **in doctrine.** All 3 terms—"Integrity," "reverence," and "incorruptibility"—qualify the appropriate commitment to doctrine.

reverence, incorruptibility, ^asound speech that ^bcannot be condemned, that one who is an opponent may be ashamed, having ^cnothing evil to say of you.

Exhort ^dbondservants to be ^eobedient to their own masters, to be well pleasing in all things, not answering back, ^fnot pilfering, but showing ^gall good fidelity, that they may ^hadorn the doctrine of God our Savior in all things.

243. OUR BLESSED HOPE

Titus 2:11–15

ⁱFor the ^jgrace of God that brings salvation has appeared to ^kall men, teaching us that, ^ldenying ungodliness and worldly lusts, we should live soberly,

---

a. **sound speech.** Daily conversation. Cf. Eph. 4:31; Col. 3:16, 17; 4:6.

b. **cannot be condemned.** Beyond reproach.

c. **nothing evil to say.** Again, as in v. 5, the purpose of godly living is to silence the opponents of Christianity and the gospel (see 1 Pet. 2:11, 12), and make the power of Christ believable.

d. **bondservants.** The term applies generally to all employees, but direct reference is to slaves—men, women, and children who, in the Roman Empire and in much of the ancient world, were owned by their masters. They had few, if any, civil rights and often were accorded little more dignity or care than domestic animals. The NT nowhere condones or condemns the practice of slavery, but it everywhere teaches that freedom from the bondage of sin is infinitely more important than freedom from any human bondage a person may have to endure (see Rom. 6:22).

e. **obedient . . . well pleasing.** Paul clearly teaches that, even in the most servile of circumstances, believers are "to be obedient" and seek to please those for whom they work, whether their "masters" are believers or unbelievers, fair or unfair, kind or cruel. How much more obligated are believers to respect and obey employers for whom they work voluntarily! As with wives' obedience to their husbands (Titus 2:5), the only exception would involve a believer's being required to disobey God's Word. Cf. Eph. 6:5–9; Col. 3:22—4:1; 1 Tim. 6:1, 2.

f. **not pilfering.** A term used to refer to embezzlement.

g. **all good fidelity.** Loyalty.

h. **adorn the doctrine.** Again (cf. Titus 2:5), Paul stresses that the supreme purpose of a virtuous life is to make attractive the teaching that God saves sinners.

i. This is the heart of the letter, emphasizing that God's sovereign purpose in calling out elders (Titus 1:5) and in commanding His people to live righteously (2:1–10) is to provide the witness that brings God's plan and purpose of salvation to fulfillment. Paul condensed the saving plan of God into 3 realities: 1) salvation from the penalty (v. 11); 2) the power (v. 12); and 3) the presence (v. 13) of sin.

j. **grace of God.** Not simply the divine attribute of grace, but Jesus Christ Himself, grace incarnate, God's supremely gracious gift to fallen mankind. Cf. John 1:14.

k. **all men.** This does not teach universal salvation. "All men" is used as "man" in Titus 3:4, to refer to humanity in general, as a category, not to every individual. See 2 Cor. 5:19; 2 Pet. 3:9. Jesus Christ made a sufficient sacrifice to cover every sin of every one who believes (John 3:16–18; 1 Tim. 2:5, 6; 4:10; 1 John 2:2). Paul makes clear in the opening words of this letter to Titus that salvation becomes effective only through "the faith of God's elect" (1:1). See 3:2. Out of all humanity, only those who believe will be saved (John 1:12; 3:16; 5:24, 38, 40; 6:40; 10:9; Rom. 10:9–17).

l. **denying . . . live.** Salvation is transforming (2 Cor. 5:17; Eph. 2:8–10), and transformation

righteously, and godly in the present age, looking for the [a]blessed hope and [b]glorious appearing of our great [c]God and Savior Jesus Christ, who gave Himself for us, that He might [d]redeem us from every lawless deed and purify for Himself His own [e]special people, [f]zealous for good works.

[g]Speak these things, exhort, and rebuke with all [h]authority. [i]Let no one despise you.

244. WALKING IN LIGHT OF THE GOSPEL
Titus 3:1–8

[j]Remind them to be [k]subject to rulers and authorities, to obey, to be ready for every good work, to speak evil of no one, to be peaceable, gentle, showing all

---

(new birth) produces a new life in which the power of sin has been broken (see Rom 6:4–14; Phil. 3:8, 9; Col. 3:9, 10).

    a. **blessed hope.** A general reference to the second coming of Jesus Christ, including the resurrection (cf. Rom. 8:22, 23; 1 Cor. 15:51–58; Phil. 3:20, 21; 1 Thess. 4:13–18; 1 John 3:2, 3) and the reign of the saints with Christ in glory (2 Tim. 2:10).

    b. **glorious appearing.** Cf. 2 Tim. 1:10. Lit. "the appearing of the glory." This will be our salvation from the presence of sin.

    c. **God and Savior.** A clear reference to the deity of Jesus. Cf. 2 Pet. 1:1.

    d. **redeem . . . purify.** Another expression (cf. Titus 2:12) summarizes the dual effect of salvation (regeneration and sanctification). To "redeem" is to release someone held captive, on the payment of a ransom. The price was Christ's blood paid to satisfy God's justice. See Acts 20:28; Gal. 1:4; 2:20; 1 Pet. 1:18, 19; cf. Mark 10:45.

    e. **special people.** People who are special by virtue of God's decree and confirmed by the grace of salvation which they have embraced (see Titus 1:1–4). Cf. 1 Cor. 6:19, 20; 1 Pet. 2:9.

    f. **zealous.** Cf. 3:8. Good works are the product, not the means, of salvation. Cf. Eph. 2:10.

    g. **Speak . . . exhort . . . rebuke.** These 3 verbs identify the need for proclamation, application, and correction by the Word.

    h. **authority.** "Authority" to command people in the spiritual realm comes only from God's Word. Cf. Matt. 7:28, 29.

    i. **Let no one despise you.** See 3:9–11. Rebellion against the truth has to be dealt with. Cf. Matt. 18:15–20; 1 Cor. 5:9–13; 2 Thess. 3:14, 15.

    j. **Remind them . . .** In his closing remarks, Paul admonished Titus to remind believers under his care of their attitudes toward: 1) the unsaved rulers (Titus 3:1) and people in general (v. 2); 2) their previous state as unbelievers lost in sin (v. 3); 3) of their gracious salvation through Jesus Christ (vv. 4–7); 4) of their righteous testimony to the unsaved world (v. 8); 5) and of their responsibility to oppose false teachers and factious members within the church (vv. 9–11). All of these matters are essential to effective evangelism.

    k. **subject.** Submission to the authority of Scripture demands submission to human authorities as part of a Christian's testimony (see Rom. 13:1–7; 1 Pet. 2:12–17).

humility to ªall men. For we ᵇourselves were also once foolish, disobedient, deceived, serving various lusts and pleasures, living in malice and envy, hateful and hating one another. But when the ᶜkindness and the love of God our Savior toward man appeared, ᵈnot by works of righteousness which we have done, but ᵉaccording to His mercy He saved us, through the ᶠwashing of regeneration and ᵍrenewing of the Holy Spirit, whom He poured out on us ʰabundantly through Jesus Christ our Savior, that having been ⁱjustified by His grace we should become ʲheirs according to the hope of eternal life.

This is a ᵏfaithful saying, and these things I want you to affirm constantly, that those who have believed in God should be careful to maintain good works. These things are good and ˡprofitable to men.

---

a. **all men.** Christians are to exemplify these godly virtues in their dealings with everyone. The admonition applies especially to dealings with unbelievers. The use of this phrase here to refer to mankind in general (particularly those who cross our paths), rather than every person who lives, supports the fact that it has the same meaning in Titus 2:11.

b. **ourselves.** It is not that every believer has committed every sin listed here, but rather that before salvation every life is characterized by such sins. That sobering truth should make believers humble in dealing with the unsaved, even those who are grossly immoral and ungodly. If it weren't for God's grace to His own, they would all be wicked. See 1 Pet. 3:15; cf. 2 Tim. 2:25. For other lists of sins, see Rom. 1:18–32; 1 Cor. 6:9, 10; Gal. 5:19–21; Eph. 4:17–19.

c. **kindness . . . appeared.** As in 2:11, Paul is speaking of Jesus Christ, who was kindness and love incarnate, appearing in human form. Cf. Eph. 2:4–6.

d. **not by works.** Salvation has never been by works (see Eph. 2:8, 9; cf. Rom. 3:19–28.)

e. **according to His mercy.** Cf. Eph. 2:4; 1 Tim. 1:13; 1 Pet. 1:3; 2:10.

f. **washing of regeneration.** See Ezek. 36:25–29; Eph. 5:26; James 1:18; 1 Pet. 1:23. Salvation brings divine cleansing from sin and the gift of a new, Spirit-generated, Spirit-empowered, and Spirit-protected life as God's own children and heirs (Titus 3:7). This is the new birth (cf. John 3:5; 1 John 2:29; 3:9; 4:7; 5:1).

g. **renewing of the Holy Spirit.** Cf. Rom. 8:2. He is the agent of the "working of regeneration."

h. **abundantly.** When believers are saved, Christ's Spirit blesses them beyond measure (cf. Acts 2:38, 39; 1 Cor. 12:7, 11, 13; Eph. 3:20; 5:18).

i. **justified.** The central truth of salvation is justification by faith alone. When a sinner repents and places his faith in Jesus Christ, God declares him just, imputes the righteousness of Christ to him, and gives him eternal life by virtue of the substitutionary death of Christ as the penalty for that sinner's iniquity. See Rom. 3:21—5:21; Gal. 3:6–22; Phil. 3:8, 9.

j. **heirs.** As adopted children of God through faith in Jesus Christ, believers become "heirs of God and joint heirs with Christ" (Rom. 8:17; cf. 1 Pet. 1:3, 4).

k. **faithful saying.** A common expression in the early church, used 5 times in the pastoral epistles (cf. 1 Tim. 1:15; 3:1; 4:9; 2 Tim. 2:11).

l. **profitable to men.** That is, for the sake of evangelism. Again "men" (cf. Titus 2:11; 3:2) is general, referring to those who respond by the holy witness to the gospel.

245. FINAL WORDS TO TITUS

Titus 3:9–15

But avoid ªfoolish disputes, genealogies, contentions, and strivings about the law; for they are unprofitable and useless. ᵇReject a divisive man after the first and second admonition, knowing that such a person is warped and sinning, being ᶜself-condemned.

When I send ᵈArtemas to you, or ᵉTychicus, be diligent to come to me at ᶠNicopolis, for I have decided to spend the winter there. Send ᵍZenas the lawyer and ʰApollos on their journey with haste, that they may lack nothing. And let our people also learn to maintain ⁱgood works, to meet urgent needs, that they may not be unfruitful.

ʲAll who are with me greet you. Greet those who love us in the faith. Grace be with you all. Amen.

---

a. **foolish disputes.** Paul again warns against becoming embroiled in senseless discussions with the many false teachers on Crete (see Titus 1:10, 14–15), especially the Judaizers who contended that a Christian must be obedient to "the (Mosaic) law," a view that assaulted the doctrine of justification by grace through faith alone and, contrary to holy living, which was good and profitable, was "unprofitable and useless." Proclaiming the truth, not arguing error, is the biblical way to evangelize.

b. **Reject.** Anyone in the church who is unsubmissive, self-willed, and divisive should be expelled. Two warnings are to be given, following the basic pattern for church discipline set forth by Christ (see Matt. 18:15–17; cf. Rom. 16:17, 18; 2 Thess. 3:14, 15).

c. **self-condemned.** By his own ungodly behavior, a factious believer brings judgment on himself.

d. **Artemis.** Nothing is known of this man beyond Paul's obvious confidence in him.

e. **Tychicus.** This "beloved brother [and] faithful minister" (Col. 4:7) accompanied Paul from Corinth to Asia Minor (Acts 20:4), carried the apostle's letter to the Colossian church (Col. 4:7), and possibly his letter to Ephesus (see Eph. 6:21).

f. **Nicopolis.** The name means "city of victory," and this was but one of perhaps 9 different cities so named because of decisive military battles that were won in or near them. This particular Nicopolis was probably in southern Greece, on the W coast of Achaia, which was a good place "to spend the winter."

g. **Zenas.** Nothing is known of this believer whose expertise was either in biblical law or Roman law.

h. **Apollos.** Originally from Alexandria, he was an outstanding teacher of Scripture who was converted to Christ after being acquainted only with the teaching of John the Baptist (Acts 18:24–28). Some of his followers apparently formed a faction in the church at Corinth (1 Cor. 1:11, 12; 3:4).

i. **good works.** Again the emphasis is on good works as the platform for witnessing effectively (cf. Titus 1:13–16; 2:5, 8, 10, 12, 14).

j. **All who are with me.** Cf. 1 Cor. 16:20; 2 Cor. 13:12; Phil. 4:22; cf. also Rom. 16:21–23; Col. 4:10–14, where those with Paul are mentioned by name.

246. PAUL WRITES HIS FINAL LETTER TO TIMOTHY

Introduction to 2 Timothy

This epistle is the second of two inspired letters Paul the apostle wrote to his son in the faith, Timothy (2 Tim. 1:2; 2:1). For biographical information on Timothy, see Introduction to 1 Timothy. It is titled, as are the other personal letters of Paul to individuals (1 Timothy, Titus, and Philemon), with the name of the addressee (1:2).

Author and Date

The issue of Paul's authorship of the Pastoral Epistles is discussed in the Introduction to 1 Timothy: Author and Date. Paul wrote 2 Timothy, the last of his inspired letters, shortly before his martyrdom (ca. A.D. 67).

Background and Setting

Paul was released from his first Roman imprisonment for a short period of ministry during which he wrote 1 Timothy and Titus. Second Timothy, however, finds Paul once again in a Roman prison (2 Tim. 1:16; 2:9), apparently rearrested as part of Nero's persecution of Christians. Unlike Paul's confident hope of release during his first imprisonment (Phil. 1:19, 25, 26; 2:24; Philem. 22), this time he had no such hopes (4:6–8). In his first imprisonment in Rome (A.D. 60–62), before Nero had begun the persecution of Christians (A.D. 64), he was only under house arrest and had opportunity for much interaction with people and ministry (Acts 28:16–31). At this time, 5 or 6 years later (ca. A.D. 66–67), however, he was in a cold cell (4:13), in chains (2:9), and with no hope of deliverance (4:6). Abandoned by virtually all of those close to him for fear of persecution (cf. 1:15; 4:9–12, 16) and facing imminent execution, Paul wrote to Timothy, urging him to hasten to Rome for one last visit with the apostle (4:9, 21). Whether Timothy made it to Rome before Paul's execution is not known. According to tradition, Paul was not released from this second Roman imprisonment, but suffered the martyrdom he had foreseen (4:6).

In this letter, Paul, aware the end was near, passed the non-apostolic mantle of ministry to Timothy (cf. 2:2) and exhorted him to continue faithful in his duties (1:6), hold on to sound doctrine (1:13, 14), avoid error (2:15–18), accept persecution for the gospel (2:3, 4; 3:10–12), put his confidence in the Scripture, and preach it relentlessly (3:15—4:5).

Historical and Theological Themes

It seems that Paul may have had reason to fear that Timothy was in danger of weakening spiritually. This would have been a grave concern for Paul since Timothy needed to carry on Paul's work (cf. 2 Tim. 2:2). While there are no historical indications elsewhere in the NT as to why Paul was so concerned, there is evidence in the epistle itself from what he wrote. This concern is evident, for example, in Paul's exhortation to "stir up" his gift (1:6), to replace fear with power, love, and a sound mind (1:7), to not be ashamed of Paul and the Lord, but willingly suffer for the gospel (1:8), and to hold on to the truth (1:13, 14). Summing up the potential problem of Timothy, who might be weakening under the pressure of the church and the persecution of the world, Paul calls him to 1) generally "be strong" (2:11), the key exhortation of the first part of the letter, and to 2) continue to "preach the word" (4:2), the main admonition of the last part. These final words to Timothy include few commendations but many admonitions, including about 25 imperatives.

Since Timothy was well versed in Paul's theology, the apostle did not instruct him further doctrinally. He did, however, allude to several important doctrines, including salvation by God's sovereign grace (1:9, 10; 2:10), the person of Christ (2:8; 4:1, 8), and perseverance (2:11–13); plus Paul wrote the crucial text of the NT on the inspiration of Scripture (3:16, 17).

Interpretive Challenges

There are no major challenges in this letter involving theological issues. There is limited data regarding several individuals named in the epistle; e.g., Phygellus and Hermogenes (2 Tim. 1:15), Onesiphorus (1:17; cf. 4:19), Hymenaeus and Philetus (2:17, 18), Jannes and Jambres (3:8), and Alexander (4:14).

247. EXHORTATIONS TO FAITHFULNESS
2 Timothy 1:1–11

[a]Paul, an [b]apostle of Jesus Christ by the will of God, according to the [c]promise of life which is in Christ Jesus,

To Timothy, a beloved son:

[d]Grace, mercy, and peace from God the Father and Christ Jesus our Lord.

I thank God, whom I serve with a pure conscience, as my forefathers did, as without ceasing I remember you in my prayers night and day, [e]greatly desiring to see you, being [f]mindful of your tears, that I may be filled with joy, when I call to remembrance the genuine faith that is in you, which dwelt first in your grandmother [g]Lois and your mother Eunice, and I am persuaded is in you also. Therefore I remind you to [h]stir up the gift of God which is in

---

a. **Paul . . .** Paul reminded Timothy that, despite their intimate spiritual relationship, the apostle wrote to him with spiritual authority given him by God. This established the necessity that not only Timothy, but also all others comply with the inspired mandates of the epistle.

b. **apostle of Jesus Christ by the will of God.** See 1 Tim. 1:1. His call was according to God's sovereign plan and purpose (cf. 1 Cor. 1:1; 2 Cor. 1:1; Eph. 1:1; Col. 1:1).

c. **promise of life . . . in Christ Jesus.** The gospel, which promises that those who are spiritually dead, but by faith embrace the gospel's message, will be united to Christ and find eternal life in Him (John 3:16; 10:10; 14:6; Col. 3:4).

d. **Grace . . . our Lord.** See 1 Tim. 1:2. More than a standard greeting by Paul, this expressed his genuine desire for God's best in Timothy's life.

e. **greatly desiring to see you.** Because of Paul's affection for Timothy and the urgency of the hour in Paul's life, as he faced death, Paul had an intense yearning to see Timothy again (cf. 2 Tim. 4:9, 13, 21).

f. **mindful of your tears.** Paul perhaps remembered this occurring at their latest parting, which occurred after a short visit to Ephesus, following the writing of 1 Timothy, and prior to Paul's arrest at Troas (see 2 Tim. 4:13) and his second imprisonment in Rome. Years before, Paul had a similar parting with the elders at Ephesus (Acts 20:36–38).

g. **Lois . . . Eunice.** Mention of their names suggests that Paul knew them personally, perhaps because he (with Barnabas) led them to faith in Christ during his first missionary journey (cf. Acts 13:13—14:21). The women were true OT Jewish believers, who understood the Scripture well enough to prepare themselves and Timothy (2 Tim. 3:15) to immediately accept Jesus as Messiah when they first heard the gospel from Paul.

h. **stir up the gift of God.** This seems to indicate Paul was unsatisfied with Timothy's level of current faithfulness. "Stir up" means lit. "to keep the fire alive," and "gift" refers to the believer's spiritual gift (see Rom. 12:4–8; 1 Cor. 12:7–11; regarding Timothy's spiritual gift, see 2 Tim. 4:2–6; 1 Tim. 4:14). Paul reminds Timothy that as a steward of his God-given gift for preaching, teaching, and evangelizing, he could not let it fall into disuse (cf. 2 Tim. 4:2–5).

you through the ªlaying on of my hands. For God has not given us ᵇa spirit of fear, but of ᶜpower and of love and of a ᵈsound mind.

Therefore do not be ashamed of the ᵉtestimony of our Lord, nor of ᶠme His prisoner, but share with me in the sufferings for the gospel according to the power of God, who has saved us and called us ᵍwith a holy calling, ʰnot according to our works, but ⁱaccording to His own purpose and grace which was given to us ʲin Christ Jesus ᵏbefore time began, but has now been revealed

---

a. **laying on of my hands.** See 1 Tim. 4:14; 5:22; cf. 6:12. Paul might have done this at the time of Timothy's conversion, in which case it would have corresponded to when Timothy received his spiritual gift. The expression may also refer to an extraordinary spiritual endowment, which was received or enhanced at some point after his conversion.

b. **a spirit of fear.** The Gr. word, which can also be translated "timidity," denotes a cowardly, shameful fear caused by a weak, selfish character. The threat of Roman persecution, which was escalating under Nero, the hostility of those in the Ephesian church who resented Timothy's leadership, and the assaults of false teachers with their sophisticated systems of deceptions may have been overwhelming Timothy. But if he was fearful, it didn't come from God.

c. **power.** Positively, God has already given believers all the spiritual resources they need for every trial and threat (cf. Matt. 10:19, 20). Divine power—effective, productive spiritual energy belongs to believers (Eph. 1:18–20; 3:20; cf. Zech. 4:6). **love.** See 1 Tim. 1:5. This kind of love centers on pleasing God and seeking others' welfare before one's own (cf. Rom. 14:8; Gal. 5:22, 25; Eph. 3:19; 1 Pet. 1:22; 1 John 4:18).

d. **sound mind.** Refers to a disciplined, self-controlled, and properly prioritized mind. This is the opposite of fear and cowardice that causes disorder and confusion. Focusing on the sovereign nature and perfect purposes of our eternal God allows believers to control their lives with godly wisdom and confidence in every situation (cf. Rom. 12:3; 1 Tim. 3:2; Titus 1:8; 2:2).

e. **testimony of our Lord.** The gospel message concerning Jesus Christ. Paul did not want Timothy to be "ashamed" to name the name of Christ because he was afraid of the potential persecution (cf. 2 Tim. 1:12, 16).

f. **me His prisoner.** See Eph. 3:1; Phil. 1:12–14. Being linked to Paul, who was a prisoner because of his preaching of the gospel, could have put Timothy's life and freedom in jeopardy (cf. Heb. 13:23).

g. **with a holy calling.** As always in the NT epistles, this calling is not a general invitation to sinners to believe the gospel and be saved (as in Matt. 20:16), but refers to God's effectual call of the elect to salvation (see Rom. 1:7). This calling results in holiness, imputed (justification) and imparted (sanctification), and finally completed (glorification).

h. **not . . . works, but . . . grace.** This truth is the foundation of the gospel. Salvation is by grace through faith, apart from works (see Rom. 3:20–25; Gal. 3:10, 11; Eph. 2:8, 9; Phil. 3:8, 9). Grace is also the basis for God's sustaining work in believers (cf. Phil. 1:6; Jude 24, 25).

i. **according to His own purpose.** God's sovereign plan of election (see 2 Tim. 2:10; John 6:37–40, 44; Acts 13:48; Rom. 8:29; 9:10–24; Eph. 1:4; 3:11; 2 Thess. 2:13; Titus 1:1, 2; 1 Pet. 1:2).

j. **in Christ Jesus.** His sacrifice made God's salvation plan possible, because He became the substitute sacrifice for the sins of God's people (see 2 Cor. 5:21).

k. **before time began.** The same Gr. phrase appears in Titus 1:2. The destiny of God's chosen was determined and sealed from eternity past (John 17:24; cf. Eph. 1:4, 5; Phil. 1:29; 1 Pet. 1:2).

by the ªappearing of our Savior Jesus Christ, who has ᵇabolished death and brought life and immortality to light through the gospel, to which I was appointed a preacher, an apostle, and a teacher of the Gentiles.

248. Examples of Faithfulness
2 Timothy 1:12–18

For this reason ᶜI also suffer these things; nevertheless I am not ashamed, for I ᵈknow whom I have believed and am persuaded that He is able to keep ᵉwhat I have committed to Him until ᶠthat Day. Hold fast the pattern of ᵍsound words which you have heard ʰfrom me, in ⁱfaith and love which are in Christ Jesus. ʲThat good thing which was committed to you, keep by the Holy Spirit who dwells in us.

---

a. **appearing.** "Epiphany" is the Eng. equivalent of this Gr. word, most often used of Christ's second coming (2 Tim. 4:18; 1 Tim. 6:14; Titus 2:13), but here of His first coming.

b. **abolished death . . . immortality to light.** "Abolished" means "rendered inoperative." Physical death still exists, but it is no longer a threat or an enemy for Christians (1 Cor. 15:54, 55; Heb. 2:14). It was not until the incarnation and the gospel that God chose to fully make known the truth of immortality and eternal life, a reality only partially understood by OT believers (cf. Job 19:26).

c. **I also suffer.** Cf. 2 Tim. 1:8; see 2 Cor. 4:8–18; 6:4–10; 11:23–28; Gal. 6:17; Phil. 3:10. I am not ashamed. See v. 8; Rom. 1:16; 1 Pet. 4:16. Paul had no fear of persecution and death from preaching the gospel in a hostile setting, because he was so confident God had sealed his future glory and blessing.

d. **know whom I have believed.** "Know" describes the certainty of Paul's intimate, saving knowledge—the object of which was God Himself. The form of the Gr. verb translated "I have believed" refers to something that began in the past and has continuing results (see Rom. 1:16). This knowing is equal to "the knowledge of the truth" (1 Tim. 2:4; 2 Tim.3:7).

e. **what I have committed.** Paul's life in time and eternity had been given to his Lord. He lived with unwavering confidence and boldness because of the revealed truth about God's power and faithfulness, and his own experience of an unbreakable relationship to the Lord (Rom. 8:31–39).

f. **that Day.** Cf. 2 Tim. 1:18; 4:8; see Phil. 1:6. Also called "Day of Christ" (see Phil. 1:10), when believers will stand before the judgment seat and be rewarded (see 1 Cor. 3:13; 2 Cor. 5:10; 1 Pet. 1:5).

g. **sound words.** Cf. 1 Tim. 4:6; 6:3. The Scripture and the doctrine it teaches (see 2 Tim. 3:15–17).

h. **from me.** Paul had been the source of this divine revelation (cf. 2 Tim. 2:2; 3:10, 14; Phil. 4:9; see Eph. 3:1–5).

i. **faith and love . . . in Christ Jesus.** "Faith" is confidence that God's Word is true, and "love" is kindness and compassion in teaching that truth (cf. Eph. 4:15).

j. **That good thing . . . committed to you.** The treasure of the good news of salvation revealed in the Scripture (see 1 Tim. 6:20).

This you know, that all those in ᵃAsia have turned away from me, among whom are ᵇPhygellus and Hermogenes. The Lord grant mercy to the household of ᶜOnesiphorus, for he often refreshed me, and was not ashamed of my chain; but ᵈwhen he arrived in Rome, he sought me out very zealously and found me. The Lord grant to him that he may find mercy from the Lord in that Day— and you know very well how many ways he ministered to me at ᵉEphesus.

249. PICTURES OF A MAN OF GOD
2 Timothy 2:1–13

You therefore, ᶠmy son, ᵍbe strong in the grace that is in Christ Jesus. And the things that you have ʰheard from me ⁱamong many witnesses, commit these to ʲfaithful men who will be able to teach others also. You therefore must

---

a. **Asia.** A Roman province that is part of modern Turkey; this is not a reference to the entire region of Asia Minor.

b. **Phygellus and Hermogenes.** Nothing else is known about these two men, who apparently had shown promise as leaders, had been close to Paul, and were well known among the Asian churches, but deserted Paul under the pressure of persecution.

c. **Onesiphorus.** One of Paul's loyal co-workers who had not deserted Paul, but befriended him in prison and was not ashamed or afraid to visit the apostle there regularly and minister to his needs. Since Paul asks Timothy to greet those in his house (2 Tim. 4:19), the family obviously lived in or near Ephesus.

d. **when he arrived in Rome.** Onesiphorus was perhaps on a business trip and the text implies that his search involved time, effort, and possibly even danger.

e. **Ephesus.** Onesiphorus' faithfulness began here many years earlier, when Paul ministered on his third or fourth missionary journey.

f. **my son.** Paul had led Timothy to Christ during his first missionary journey (cf. 1 Cor. 4:17; 1 Tim. 1:2, 18).

g. **be strong.** Here is the main admonition in the first part of the letter. Paul is calling for Timothy to overcome his apparent drift toward weakness and renew his commitment to his ministry.

h. **heard from me.** See 2 Tim. 1:13; cf. 3:14. During Timothy's many years of close association with Paul, he had heard divine truth which God had revealed through the apostle.

i. **among many witnesses.** Such as Silas, Barnabas, and Luke, and many others in the churches who could attest to the divine authenticity of Paul's teaching—a needed reminder to Timothy in light of the many defections at Ephesus (cf. 2 Tim. 1:15).

j. **faithful men who will be able to teach others.** Timothy was to take the divine revelation he had learned from Paul and teach it to other faithful men—men with proven spiritual character and giftedness, who would in turn pass on those truths to another generation. From Paul to Timothy to faithful men to others encompasses 4 generations of godly leaders. That process of spiritual reproduction, which began in the early church, is to continue until the Lord returns.

endure hardship as ᵃa good soldier of Jesus Christ. No one engaged in warfare ᵇentangles himself with the affairs of this life, that he may please him who enlisted him as a soldier. And also if anyone ᶜcompetes in athletics, he is not ᵈcrowned unless he competes according to the rules. ᵉThe hardworking farmer must be first to partake of the crops. ᶠConsider what I say, and may the Lord give you understanding in all things.

ᵍRemember that Jesus Christ, ʰof the seed of David, was ⁱraised from the dead according to my gospel, for which ʲI suffer trouble as an evildoer, even to the point of chains; but the word of God is not chained. Therefore I endure all things ᵏfor the sake of the elect, that they also may obtain ˡthe salvation which is in Christ Jesus with ᵐeternal glory.

---

a. **a good soldier.** The metaphor of the Christian life as warfare (against the evil world system, the believer's sinful human nature, and Satan) is a familiar one in the NT (cf. 2 Cor. 10:3–5; Eph. 6:10–20; 1 Thess. 4:8; 1 Tim. 1:18; 4:7; 6:12). Here Paul is dealing with the conflict against the hostile world and the persecution (cf. v. 9; 1:8; 3:11, 12; 4:7).

b. **entangles himself.** Just as a soldier called to duty is completely severed from the normal affairs of civilian life, so also must the good soldier of Jesus Christ refuse to allow the things of the world to distract him (cf. James 4:4; 1 John 2:15–17).

c. **competes in athletics.** The Gr. verb (athleⓍ) expresses the effort and determination needed to compete successfully in an athletic event (cf. 1 Cor. 9:24). This is a useful picture of spiritual effort and untiring pursuit of the victory to those familiar with events such as the Olympic Games and the Isthmian Games (held in Corinth).

d. **crowned . . . rules.** All an athlete's hard work and discipline will be wasted if he or she fails to compete according to the rules. This is a call to obey the Word of God in the pursuit of spiritual victory.

e. **The hardworking farmer.** "Hardworking" is from a Gr. verb meaning "to labor to the point of exhaustion." Ancient farmers worked long hours of backbreaking labor under all kinds of conditions, with the hope that their physical effort would be rewarded by a good harvest. Paul is urging Timothy not to be lazy or indolent, but to labor intensely (cf. Col. 1:28, 29) with a view to the harvest. See 1 Cor. 3:6, 7.

f. **Consider.** The Gr. word denotes clear perception, full understanding, and careful consideration. The form of the verb suggests a strong admonition by Paul, not mere advice, to give deep thought to what he was writing.

g. **Remember . . . Jesus Christ.** The supreme model of a faithful teacher (2 Tim. 2:2), soldier (vv. 3, 4), athlete (v. 5), and farmer (v. 6). Timothy was to follow His example in teaching, suffering, pursuing the prize, and planting the seeds of truth for a spiritual harvest.

h. **of the seed of David.** See Rom. 1:3; Rev. 22:16. As David's descendant, Jesus is the rightful heir to his throne (Luke 1:32, 33). The Lord's humanity is stressed.

i. **raised from the dead.** The resurrection of Christ is the central truth of the Christian faith (1 Cor. 15:3, 4, 17, 19). By it, God affirmed the perfect redemptive work of Jesus Christ (see Rom. 1:4).

j. **I suffer . . . but the word . . . is not chained.** Paul contrasts his imprisonment for the sake of the gospel to the unfettered power of the Word of God.

k. **for the sake of the elect.** Those of the elect, having been chosen for salvation from before the world began (see 2 Tim. 1:9), who had not yet come to faith in Jesus Christ (see Acts 18:10; Titus 1:1).

l. **the salvation which is in Christ Jesus.** There is salvation in no one else (Acts 4:12; cf. Rom. 8:29; Eph. 1:4, 5). The gospel must be proclaimed (Matt. 28:19; Acts 1:8) because the elect are not saved apart from faith in Christ (Rom. 10:14).

m. **eternal glory.** The ultimate outcome of salvation (see Rom. 5:2; 8:17).

This is a ^afaithful saying:

> For if we ^bdied with Him,
> We shall also live with Him.
> If we ^cendure,
> We shall also ^dreign with Him.
> ^eIf we deny Him,
> He also will deny us.
> If we are ^ffaithless,
> ^gHe remains faithful;
> He cannot deny Himself.

250. USEFUL FOR SERVICE

2 Timothy 2:14–26

Remind them of these things, charging them before the Lord not to ^hstrive about words to no profit, to the ⁱruin of the hearers. ^jBe diligent to present

a. **faithful saying.** The saying is in 2 Tim. 2:11–13. See 1 Tim. 1:15.

b. **died with Him . . . live with Him.** This refers to believers' spiritual participation in Christ's death and resurrection (Rom. 6:4–8), including also the possibility of suffering martyrdom for the sake of Christ, as the context would indicate.

c. **endure.** Believers who persevere give evidence of the genuineness of their faith (see Matt. 10:22; cf. 24:13; John 8:31; Rom. 2:7; Col. 1:23).

d. **reign with Him.** In His future eternal kingdom (Rev. 1:6; 5:10; 20:4, 6).

e. **If we deny Him, He also will deny us.** Speaks of a final, permanent denial, such as that of an apostate (see 1 Tim. 1:19), not the temporary failure of a true believer like Peter (Matt. 26:69–75). Those who so deny Christ give evidence that they never truly belonged to Him (1 John 2:19) and face the fearful reality of one day being denied by Him (Matt. 10:33).

f. **faithless.** This refers to a lack of saving faith, not to weak or struggling faith. Unbelievers will ultimately deny Christ because their faith was not genuine (cf. James 2:14–26).

g. **He remains faithful; He cannot deny Himself.** As faithful as Jesus is to save those who believe in Him (John 3:16), He is equally faithful to judge those who do not (John 3:18). To act any other way would be inconsistent with His holy, unchangeable nature. Cf. Heb. 10:23.

h. **strive about words.** Arguing with false teachers, i.e., deceivers who use human reason to subvert God's Word, is not only foolish (Prov. 14:7) and futile (Matt. 7:6), but dangerous (2 Tim. 2:16, 17; cf. v. 23). This is the first of 3 warnings to avoid useless arguments (see vv. 16, 23). See 1 Tim. 4:6, 7; 6:3–5; 2 Pet. 1–3.

i. **ruin.** The Gr. word means "overturned," or "overthrown." It appears only one other time in the NT (2 Pet. 2:6), where it describes the destruction of Sodom and Gomorrah. Because it replaces the truth with lies, false teaching brings spiritual catastrophe to those who heed it. The ruin can be eternal.

j. **Be diligent.** This word denotes zealous persistence in accomplishing a goal. Timothy,

yourself approved to God, a worker who does not need to be ashamed, [a]rightly dividing [b]the word of truth. But [c]shun profane and idle babblings, for they will increase to more ungodliness. And their message will spread like [d]cancer. [e]Hymenaeus and [f]Philetus are of this sort, who have strayed concerning the truth, saying that [g]the resurrection is already past; and they [h]overthrow the faith of some. Nevertheless [i]the solid foundation of God stands, having this seal: [j]"The Lord knows those who are His," and, [k]"Let everyone who names the name of Christ depart from iniquity."

But in a great house there are not only [l]vessels of gold and silver, but also

---

like all who preach or teach the Word, was to give his maximum effort to impart God's Word completely, accurately, and clearly to his hearers. This is crucial to counter the disastrous effects of false teaching (2 Tim. 2:14, 16, 17).

a. **rightly dividing.** Lit. "cutting it straight"—a reference to the exactness demanded by such trades as carpentry, masonry, and Paul's trade of leather working and tentmaking. Precision and accuracy are required in biblical interpretation, beyond all other enterprises because the interpreter is handling God's Word. Anything less is shameful.

b. **the word of truth.** All of Scripture in general (John 17:17), and the gospel message in particular (Eph. 1:13; Col. 1:5).

c. **shun profane and idle babblings.** See 2 Tim. 2:14; 1 Tim. 6:20; cf. Titus 3:9. Such destructive heresy leads only to "more ungodliness." Heresy can't save or sanctify. This is Paul's second such warning.

d. **cancer.** The word refers to a disease which spreads rapidly in a deadly manner. The metaphor emphasizes the insidious danger of false teaching. It attacks and consumes one's life.

e. **Hymenaeus.** See 1 Tim. 1:20.

f. **Philetus.** Alexander's replacement (1 Tim. 1:20) as Hymenaeus' accomplice.

g. **the resurrection is already past.** Like the false teachers who troubled the Corinthians (1 Cor. 15:12), Hymenaeus and Philetus denied the reality of believers' bodily resurrection. They probably taught that believers' spiritual identification with Christ's death and resurrection (Rom. 6:4, 5, 8) was the only resurrection they would experience and that had already happened. Such heretical teaching reflects the contemporary Greek philosophical view that matter was evil and spirit was good.

h. **overthrow the faith.** This speaks of those whose faith was not genuine (cf. Matt. 24:24). Genuine saving faith cannot be finally and completely overthrown (see 2 Tim. 2:12). False, non-saving faith is common (cf. 2 Tim. 4:10). See Matt. 7:21–27; 13:18–22; John 2:23–25; 6:64–66; 8:31; 1 John 2:19.

i. **the solid foundation of God.** This is likely a reference to the church (cf. 1 Tim. 3:15), which cannot be overcome by the forces of hell (Matt. 16:18) and is made up of those who belong to Him. **seal.** A symbol of ownership and authenticity. Paul gives two characteristics of those with the divine seal of authenticity.

j. **"The Lord knows those who are His."** This is likely a reference to Num. 16:5. He "knows," not the sense of awareness, but as a husband knows his wife in the sense of intimate relationship (see John 10:27, 28; Gal. 4:9). God has known His own ever since He chose them before time began. See 2 Tim. 1:9.

k. **"Let everyone . . . depart from iniquity."** This statement is likely adapted from Num. 16:26, and reflects a second mark of God's ownership of believers, which is their pursuit of holiness (cf. 1 Cor. 6:19, 20; 1 Pet. 1:15, 16).

l. **vessels.** The Gr. word is very general and was used to describe various tools, utensils, and furniture found in the home. In this "great house" analogy, Paul contrasts two kinds of utensils or serving dishes.

of wood and clay, ᵃsome for honor and ᵇsome for dishonor. Therefore if ᶜanyone ᵈcleanses himself from ᵉthe latter, he will be a vessel for honor, sanctified and useful for the Master, prepared for every good work. Flee also ᶠyouthful lusts; but pursue righteousness, faith, love, peace with those who call on the Lord out of a pure heart. But avoid foolish and ignorant ᵍdisputes, knowing that they generate strife. And a servant of the Lord must not quarrel but be gentle to all, ʰable to teach, patient, in humility correcting ⁱthose who are in opposition, if ʲGod perhaps will grant them repentance, so that they may know the truth, and that they may come to their senses and escape ᵏthe snare of the devil, having been taken captive by him to do his will.

251. PERILS OF A MAN OF GOD
2 Timothy 3:1–9

ˡBut know this, that in the last days ᵐperilous times will come: For men will be lovers of themselves, lovers of money, boasters, proud, blasphemers, disobedient

---

a. **some for honor.** In a wealthy home, the ones made of precious "gold and silver" were used for honorable purposes such as serving food to the family and guests.

b. **some for dishonor.** Those made of "wood and clay" were not for any honorable use, but rather those uses which were repulsive—disposing of garbage and the filthy waste of the household. See 2 Cor. 4:7.

c. **anyone.** Whoever wants to be useful to the Lord for noble purposes. Even a common wood bucket or clay pot becomes useful when purged and made holy.

d. **cleanses himself.** See 2 Tim. 2:19. The Gr. word means "to thoroughly clean out," or "to completely purge." For any waste bucket in the house to be used for a noble purpose, it would have had to be vigorously scoured, cleansed, and purged of all vestiges of its former filth.

e. **the latter.** The vessels of dishonor (2 Tim. 2:20). Associating with anyone who teaches error and lives in sin is corrupting (Prov. 1:10–19; 13:20; 1 Cor. 5:6, 11; 15:33; Titus 1:16)—all the more so when they are leaders in the church. This is clearly a call to separate from all who claim to serve God, but do so as filthy implements useful only for the most dishonorable duties.

f. **youthful lusts.** Not merely illicit sexual desires, but also such lusts as pride, desire for wealth and power, jealousy, self-assertiveness, and an argumentative spirit.

g. **disputes . . . strife.** Paul's third warning to avoid useless arguments with false teachers (see 2 Tim. 2:14, 16).

h. **able to teach.** This is one word in Gr. meaning "skilled in teaching." See 1 Tim. 3:2.

i. **those who are in opposition.** Primarily unbelievers (captive to Satan, v. 26), but also could include believers deceived by the "foolish and ignorant" (2 Tim. 2:23) speculations of the false teachers; and, possibly, the false teachers themselves.

j. **God . . . will grant them repentance.** Cf. Acts 11:18; see 2 Cor. 7:9, 10. All true repentance is produced by God's sovereign grace (Eph. 2:7), and without such grace human effort to change is futile (cf. Jer. 13:23).

k. **the snare of the devil.** Deception is Satan's trap. He is an inveterate, scheming, clever, and subtle purveyor of lies. See Gen. 3:4–6; John 8:44; 2 Cor. 11:13–15; Rev. 12:9.

l. **the last days.** This phrase refers to this age, the time since the first coming of the Lord Jesus. See 1 Tim. 4:1.

m. **perilous times.** "Perilous" is used to describe the savage nature of two demon-possessed

to parents, unthankful, unholy, unloving, unforgiving, slanderers, without self-control, brutal, despisers of good, traitors, headstrong, haughty, lovers of pleasure rather than lovers of God, [a]having a form of godliness but denying its power. And from such people turn away! For of this sort are those who creep into households and make captives of [b]gullible women loaded down with sins, led away by various lusts, always learning and never able to come to [c]the knowledge of the truth. Now as [d]Jannes and Jambres resisted Moses, so do these also resist the truth: men of corrupt minds, [e]disapproved concerning the faith; but they will progress no further, for their [f]folly will be manifest to all, as theirs also was.

252. THE SUFFICIENCY OF SCRIPTURE

2 Timothy 3:14–17

But you have carefully followed my doctrine, manner of life, purpose, faith, longsuffering, love, perseverance, [g]persecutions, afflictions, which happened

---

men (Matt. 8:28). The word for "times" had to do with epochs, rather than clock or calendar time. Such savage, dangerous eras or epochs will increase in frequency and severity as the return of Christ approaches (2 Tim. 3:13). The church age is fraught with these dangerous movements accumulating strength as the end nears. Cf. Matt. 7:15; 24:11, 12, 24; 2 Pet. 2:1, 2.

a. **having a form of godliness but denying its power** . "Form" refers to outward shape or appearance. Like the unbelieving scribes and Pharisees, false teachers and their followers are concerned with mere external appearances (cf. Matt. 23:25; Titus 1:16). Their outward form of Christianity and virtue makes them all the more dangerous.

b. **gullible women.** Weak in virtue and the knowledge of the truth, and weighed down with emotional and spiritual guilt over their sins, these women were easy prey for the deceitful false teachers. See 1 Tim. 2:13, 14; 5:11, 12.

c. **the knowledge of the truth.** First Timothy 2:4 uses this same phrase, equating it with being saved. Here Paul identified those women (v. 6) and men who were often jumping from one false teacher or cult to another without ever coming to an understanding of God's saving truth in Jesus Christ. The present age, since the coming of Jesus Christ, has been loaded with perilous false teaching that can't save, but does damn (cf. 2 Tim. 3:14, 16, 17; 1 Tim. 4:1).

d. **Jannes and Jambres.** Although their names are not mentioned in the OT, they were likely two of the Egyptian magicians that opposed Moses (Ex. 7:11, 22; 8:7, 18, 19; 9:11). According to Jewish tradition, they pretended to become Jewish proselytes, instigated the worship of the golden calf, and were killed with the rest of the idolaters (Ex. 32). Paul's choice of them as examples may indicate the false teachers at Ephesus were practicing deceiving signs and wonders.

e. **disapproved.** The same word is translated "debased" in Rom. 1:28 and comes from a Gr. word meaning "useless" in the sense of being tested (like metal) and shown to be worthless.

f. **folly . . . manifest.** Sooner or later, it will be clear that these false teachers are lost fools, as it became clear in the case of Jannes and Jambres.

g. **persecutions.** From a Gr. verb that lit. means "to put to flight." Paul had been forced

to me at [a]Antioch, at Iconium, at Lystra—what persecutions I endured. And out of them all [b]the Lord delivered me. Yes, and all [c]who desire to live godly in Christ Jesus will suffer persecution. But evil men and impostors will grow worse and worse, deceiving and being deceived.

But you must continue in the things which you have learned and been assured of, knowing [d]from whom you have learned them, and that [e]from childhood [f]you have known the Holy Scriptures, which are able to make you [g]wise for salvation through [h]faith which is in Christ Jesus.

[i]All Scripture is [j]given by inspiration of God, and is profitable for [k]doctrine,

---

to flee from Damascus (Acts 9:23–25), Pisidian Antioch (Acts 13:50), Iconium (Acts 14:6), Thessalonica (Acts 17:10), and Berea (Acts 17:14).

a. **Antioch . . . Iconium . . . Lystra.** As a native of Lystra (Acts 16:1), Timothy vividly recalled the persecution Paul faced in those 3 cities.

b. **the Lord delivered me.** Cf. 4:17, 18; Pss. 34:4, 6, 19; 37:40; 91:2–6, 14; Is. 41:10; 43:2; Dan. 3:17; Acts 26:16, 17; 2 Cor. 1:10. The Lord's repeated deliverance of Paul should have encouraged Timothy in the face of persecution by those at Ephesus who opposed the gospel.

c. **who desire to live godly in Christ Jesus will suffer persecution.** Faithful believers must expect persecution and suffering at the hands of the Christ-rejecting world (cf. John 15:18–21; Acts 14:22).

d. **from whom you have learned.** See 2 Tim. 1:13. To further encourage Timothy to stand firm, Paul reminds him of his godly heritage. The plural form of the pronoun "whom" suggests Timothy was indebted not just to Paul, but to others as well (1:5).

e. **from childhood.** Lit. "from infancy." Two people whom Timothy was especially indebted to were his mother and grandmother (see 1:5), who faithfully taught him the truths of OT Scripture from his earliest childhood, so that he was ready to receive the gospel when Paul preached it.

f. **you have known the Holy Scriptures.** Lit. "the sacred writings," a common designation of the OT by Greek-speaking Jews.

g. **wise for salvation.** The OT Scriptures pointed to Christ (John 5:37–39) and revealed the need for faith in God's promises (Gen. 15:6; cf. Rom. 4:1–3). Thus, they were able to lead people to acknowledge their sin and need for justification in Christ (Gal. 3:24). Salvation is brought by the Holy Spirit using the Word. See Rom. 10:14–17; Eph. 5:26; 1 Pet. 1:23–25.

h. **faith which is in Christ Jesus.** Though not understanding all the details involved (cf. 1 Pet. 1:10–12), OT believers including Abraham (John 8:56) and Moses (Heb. 11:26) looked forward to the coming of the Messiah (Is. 7:14; 9:6) and His atonement for sin (Is. 53:5, 6). So did Timothy, who responded when he heard the gospel.

i. **All Scripture.** Grammatically similar Gr. constructions (Rom. 7:12; 2 Cor. 10:10; 1 Tim. 1:15; 2:3; 4:4) argue persuasively that the translation "all Scripture is given by inspiration . . ." is accurate. Both OT and NT Scripture are included (see 2 Pet. 3:15, 16, which identify NT writings as Scripture).

j. **given by inspiration of God.** Lit. "breathed out by God," or "God-breathed." Sometimes God told the Bible writers the exact words to say (e.g., Jer. 1:9), but more often He used their minds, vocabularies, and experiences to produce His own perfect infallible, inerrant Word (see 1 Thess. 2:13; Heb. 1:1; 2 Pet. 1:20, 21). It is important to note that inspiration applies only to the original autographs of Scripture, not the Bible writers; there are no inspired Scripture writers, only inspired Scripture. So identified is God with His Word that when Scripture speaks, God speaks (cf. Rom. 9:17; Gal. 3:8). Scripture is called "the oracles of God" (Rom. 3:2; 1 Pet. 4:11), and cannot be altered (John 10:35; Matt. 5:17, 18; Luke 16:17; Rev. 22:18, 19).

k. **doctrine.** The divine instruction or doctrinal content of both the OT and the NT (cf.

for ᵃreproof, for ᵇcorrection, for ᶜinstruction in righteousness, that the ᵈman of God may be ᵉcomplete, ᶠthoroughly equipped for every good work.

253. THE CHARGE FOR FAITHFUL MINISTRY
2 Timothy 4:1–5

ᵍI charge you therefore ʰbefore God and the Lord Jesus ⁱChrist, who will judge ʲthe living and the dead at ᵏHis appearing and His kingdom: Preach ˡthe word!

---

2 Tim. 2:15; Acts 20:18, 20, 21, 27; 1 Cor. 2:14–16; Col. 3:16; 1 John 2:20, 24, 27). The Scripture provides the comprehensive and complete body of divine truth necessary for life and godliness. Cf. Ps. 119:97–105.

    a. **reproof.** Rebuke for wrong behavior or wrong belief. The Scripture exposes sin (Heb. 4:12, 13) that can then be dealt with through confession and repentance.

    b. **correction.** The restoration of something to its proper condition. The word appears only here in the NT, but was used in extrabiblical Gr. of righting a fallen object, or helping back to their feet those who had stumbled. Scripture not only rebukes wrong behavior, but also points the way back to godly living. Cf. Ps. 119:9–11; John 15:1, 2.

    c. **instruction in righteousness.** Scripture provides positive training ("instruction" originally referred to training a child) in godly behavior, not merely rebuke and correction of wrong behavior (Acts 20:32; 1 Tim. 4:6; 1 Pet. 2:1, 2).

    d. **man of God.** A technical term for an official preacher of divine truth. See 1 Tim. 6:11.

    e. **complete.** Capable of doing everything one is called to do (cf. Col. 2:10).

    f. **thoroughly equipped.** Enabled to meet all the demands of godly ministry and righteous living. The Word not only accomplishes this in the life of the man of God but in all who follow him (Eph. 4:11–13).

    g. **I charge you.** Or better "command." The Gr. has the idea of issuing a forceful order or directive (cf. 2 Tim. 2:14; 1 Tim. 1:18; 5:21).

    h. **before God and the Lord Jesus Christ.** The Gr. construction also allows the translation "in the presence of God, even Christ Jesus," which is probably the best rendering since He is about to be introduced as the judge (cf. John 5:22). Everyone who ministers the Word of God is under the omniscient scrutiny of Christ (see 2 Cor. 2:17; Heb. 13:17).

    i. **Christ, who will judge.** The grammatical construction suggests imminency—that Christ is about to judge. Paul is emphasizing the unique accountability that all believers, and especially ministers of the Word of God, have to Christ as Judge. Service to Christ is rendered both under His watchful eye and with the knowledge that as Judge He will one day appraise the works of every believer (see 1 Cor. 3:12–15; 4:1–5; 2 Cor. 5:10). That is not a judgment of condemnation, but one of evaluation. With regard to salvation, believers have been judged already and declared righteous—they are no longer subject to the condemnation of sin (Rom. 8:1–4).

    j. **the living and the dead.** Christ will ultimately judge all men in 3 distinct settings: 1) the judgment of believers after the Rapture (1 Cor. 3:12–15; 2 Cor. 5:10); 2) the sheep and goats judgment of the nations, in which believers will be separated from unbelievers (Matt. 25:31–33, for entrance into the millennial kingdom); and 3) the Great White Throne judgment of unbelievers only (Rev. 20:11–15). Here, the apostle is referring to judgment in a general sense, encompassing all those elements.

    k. **His appearing.** The Gr. word translated "appearing" lit. means "a shining forth" and was used by the ancient Greeks of the supposed appearance to men of a pagan god. Here, Paul is referring generally to Christ's second coming, when He will judge "the living and the dead" (see previous note) and establish His millennial and eternal kingdom (see 1 Tim. 6:14).

    l. **the word.** The entire written Word of God, His complete revealed truth as contained

[a]Be ready [b]in season and out of season. [c]Convince, rebuke, [d]exhort, with all longsuffering and teaching. For the time will come when they will [e]not endure [f]sound doctrine, but according to [g]their own desires, because they have itching ears, they will heap up for themselves teachers; and they will turn their ears away from the truth, and be turned aside to [h]fables. But you be watchful in all things, endure afflictions, do the work of [i]an evangelist, fulfill your ministry.

---

in the Bible (cf. 2 Tim. 3:15, 16; Acts 20:27).

a. **Be ready.** The Gr. word has a broad range of meanings, including suddenness (Luke 2:9; Acts 12:7) or forcefulness (Luke 20:1; Acts 4:1; 6:12; 23:27). Here the form of the verb suggests the complementary ideas of urgency, preparedness, and readiness. It was used of a soldier prepared to go into battle or a guard who was continually alert for any surprise attack—attitudes which are imperative for a faithful preacher (Jer. 20:9; Acts 21:11–13; Eph. 5:15, 16; 1 Pet. 3:15).

b. **in season and out of season.** The faithful preacher must proclaim the Word when it is popular and/or convenient, and when it is not; when it seems suitable to do so, and when it seems not. The dictates of popular culture, tradition, reputation, acceptance, or esteem in the community (or in the church) must never alter the true preacher's commitment to proclaim God's Word.

c. **Convince, rebuke.** The negative side of preaching the Word (the "reproof" and "correction"; cf. 2 Tim. 3:16). The Gr. word for "convince" refers to correcting behavior or false doctrine by using careful biblical argument to help a person understand the error of his actions. The Gr. word for "rebuke" deals more with correcting the person's motives by convicting him of his sin and leading him to repentance.

d. **exhort . . . teaching.** The positive side of preaching (the "doctrine" and "instruction"; cf. 2 Tim. 3:16).

e. **not endure.** This refers to holding up under adversity, and can be translated "tolerate." Paul here warns Timothy that, in the dangerous seasons of this age, many people would become intolerant of the confrontive, demanding preaching of God's Word (2 Tim. 1:13, 14; 1 Tim. 1:9, 10; 6:3–5).

f. **sound doctrine.** See 2 Tim. 1:13; 1 Tim. 4:6; Titus 2:1.

g. **their own desires . . . itching ears.** Professing Christians, nominal believers in the church follow their own desires and flock to preachers who offer them God's blessings apart from His forgiveness, and His salvation apart from their repentance. They have an itch to be entertained by teachings that will produce pleasant sensations and leave them with good feelings about themselves. Their goal is that men preach "according to their own desires." Under those conditions, people will dictate what men preach, rather than God dictating it by His Word.

h. **fables.** This refers to false ideologies, viewpoints, and philosophies in various forms that oppose sound doctrine (see 2 Cor. 10:3–5; 1 Tim. 1:4; 4:7; cf. Titus 1:14; 2 Pet. 1:16).

i. **an evangelist.** Used only two other times in the NT (see Acts 21:8; Eph. 4:11), this word always refers to a specific office of ministry for the purpose of preaching the gospel to non-Christians. Based on Eph. 4:11, it is very basic to assume that all churches would have both pastor-teachers and evangelists. But the related verb "to preach the gospel" and the related noun "gospel" are used throughout the NT not only in relation to evangelists, but also to the call for every Christian, especially preachers and teachers, to proclaim the gospel. Paul did not call Timothy to the office of an evangelist, but to "do the work" of one.

254. Final Hardships

2 Timothy 4:6–16

For I am [a]already being poured out as [b]a drink offering, and the time of [c]my departure is at hand. I have [d]fought the good fight, I have finished the race, I have kept [e]the faith. Finally, there is laid up for me the [f]crown of righteousness, which the Lord, the righteous Judge, will give to me on that Day, and not to me only but also to all who have loved His appearing.

[g]Be diligent to come to me quickly; for [h]Demas has [i]forsaken me, having [j]loved this present world, and has departed for [k]Thessalonica—

---

a. **already.** Meaning his death was imminent. As Paul neared the end of his life, he was able to look back without regret or remorse. In these verses, he examines his life from 3 perspectives: the present reality of the end of his life, for which he was ready (2 Tim. 4:6); the past, when he had been faithful (v. 7); and the future, as he anticipated his heavenly reward (v. 8).

b. **a drink offering.** In the OT sacrificial system, this was the final offering that followed the burnt and grain offerings prescribed for the people of Israel (Num. 15:1–16). Paul saw his coming death as his final offering to God in a life that had already been full of sacrifices to Him (see Phil. 2:17).

c. **my departure.** Paul's death. The Gr. word essentially refers to the loosening of something, such as the mooring ropes of a ship or the ropes of a tent; thus it eventually acquired the secondary meaning of "departure."

d. **fought . . . finished . . . kept.** The form of the 3 Gr. verbs "have fought, have finished, have kept," indicate completed action with continuing results. Paul saw his life as complete—he had been able to accomplish through the Lord's power all that God called him to do. He was a soldier (2 Tim. 2:3, 4; 2 Cor. 10:3; 1 Tim. 6:12; Philem. 2), an athlete (1 Cor. 9:24–27; Eph. 6:12), and a guardian (2 Tim. 1:13, 14; 1 Tim. 6:20, 21).

e. **the faith.** The truths and standards of the revealed Word of God.

f. **the crown of righteousness.** The Gr. word for "crown" lit. means "surrounding," and it was used of the plaited wreaths or garlands placed on the heads of dignitaries and victorious military officers or athletes. Linguistically, "of righteousness" can mean either that righteousness is the source of the crown, or that righteousness is the nature of the crown. Like the "crown of life" (James 1:12), the "crown of rejoicing" (1 Thess. 2:19), the "imperishable crown" (1 Cor. 9:25), and the "crown of glory" (1 Pet. 5:4), in which life, rejoicing, imperishability, and glory describe the nature of the crown, the context here seems to indicate that, the crown represents eternal righteousness. Believers receive the imputed righteousness of Christ (justification) at salvation (Rom. 4:6, 11). The Holy Spirit works practical righteousness (sanctification) in the believer throughout his lifetime of struggle with sin (Rom. 6:13, 19; 8:4; Eph. 5:9; 1 Pet. 2:24). But only when the struggle is complete will the Christian receive Christ's righteousness perfected in him (glorification) when he enters heaven (see Gal. 5:5).

g. **Be diligent to come to me quickly.** Paul longed to see his beloved co-worker, but it was imperative that Timothy make haste because Paul knew his days were numbered (2 Tim. 4:6).

h. **Demas.** He had been one of Paul's closest associates along with Luke and Epaphras (see Col. 4:14; Philem. 24).

i. **forsaken.** This Gr. word means "to utterly abandon," with the idea of leaving someone in a dire situation. Demas was a fair-weather disciple who had never counted the cost of genuine commitment to Christ. His kind are described by our Lord in Matt. 13:20, 21; cf. John 8:31; 1 John 2:1.

j. **loved this present world.** See James 4:4; 1 John 2:15–17.

k. **Thessalonica.** Demas may have considered this city a safe haven.

[a]Crescens for Galatia, [b]Titus for [c]Dalmatia. Only [d]Luke is with me. [e]Get Mark and bring him with you, for he is useful to me for ministry. And [f]Tychicus I have sent to Ephesus. Bring the [g]cloak that I left with [h]Carpus at [i]Troas when you come—and [j]the books, especially the parchments.

[k]Alexander the coppersmith [l]did me much harm. [m]May the Lord repay him according to his works. You also must beware of him, for he has greatly resisted our words.

At my [n]first defense no one stood with me, but all forsook me. [o]May it not be charged against them.

---

a. **Crescens.** In contrast to Demas, Crescens must have been faithful and dependable, since Paul sent him to Galatia, a Roman province in central Asia Minor, where Paul ministered on each of his 3 missionary journeys.

b. **Titus.** Paul's closest friend and co-worker next to Timothy.

c. **Dalmatia.** Also known as Illyricum (Rom. 15:19), a Roman province on the E coast of the Adriatic Sea, just N of Macedonia.

d. **Luke.** The author of the Gospel of Luke and Acts, and Paul's devoted friend and personal physician, who could not carry the burden of ministry in Rome by himself.

e. **Get Mark and bring him with you.** Evidently Mark lived somewhere along the route Timothy would take from Ephesus to Rome. The one who was the author of the Gospel of Mark (sometimes called John), cousin of Barnabas (Col. 4:10), and devoted fellow worker (Philem. 24), had once left Paul and Barnabas in shame (see Acts 13:13; 15:36–39), but had become by this time a valued servant.

f. **Tychicus.** Paul had either sent him to Ephesus earlier, or he was sending him there to deliver this second letter to Timothy, just as Tychicus had previously delivered Paul's letters to the churches at Ephesus (Eph. 6:12), Colosse (Col. 4:7), and possibly to Titus (Titus 3:12; see Col. 4:7).

g. **cloak.** A large, heavy wool garment that doubled as a coat and blanket in cold weather, which Paul would soon face (v. 21).

h. **Carpus.** An otherwise unknown acquaintance of Paul whose name means "fruit."

i. **Troas.** A seaport of Phyrgia, in Asia Minor.

j. **the books, especially the parchments.** "Books" refers to papyrus scrolls, possibly OT books. "Parchments" were vellum sheets made of treated animal hides, thus they were extremely expensive. They may have been copies of letters he had written or blank sheets for writing other letters. That Paul did not have these already in his possession leads to the possible conclusion that he was arrested in Troas and had no opportunity to retrieve them.

k. **Alexander the coppersmith.** Probably not the same man whom Paul delivered to Satan along with Hymenaeus (1 Tim. 1:20), since Paul singles him out as the one who was a "coppersmith." This Alexander, however, may have been an idol maker (cf. Acts 19:24).

l. **did me much harm.** Alexander opposed Paul's teaching and likely spread his own false doctrine. He may have been instrumental in Paul's arrest and may even have borne false witness against him. Cf. Acts 19:23ff.

m. **May the Lord repay him.** Paul left vengeance in God's hands (Deut. 32:35; Rom. 12:19).

n. **first defense.** The Gr. word for "defense" gives us the Eng. words "apology" and "apologetics." It referred to a verbal defense used in a court of law. In the Roman legal system, an accused person received two hearings: the *prima actio*, much like a contemporary arraignment, established the charge and determined if there was a need for a trial. The *secunda actio* then established the accused's guilt or innocence. The defense Paul referred to was the *prima actio*.

o. **May it not be charged against them.** Like Stephen (Acts 7:60) and the Lord Himself (Luke 23:24).

255. TRIUMPHANT TO THE END

2 Timothy 4:17–22

[a]But the Lord stood with me and strengthened me, so that [b]the message might be preached fully through me, and that [c]all the Gentiles might hear. Also I was delivered out of [d]the mouth of the lion. And the Lord [e]will deliver me from every evil work and [f]preserve me for His heavenly kingdom. To Him be glory forever and ever. Amen!

Greet [g]Prisca and Aquila, and the household of Onesiphorus. [h]Erastus stayed in [i]Corinth, but [j]Trophimus I have left in [k]Miletus sick.

Do your utmost to come [l]before winter.

[m]Eubulus greets you, as well as Pudens, Linus, Claudia, and all the brethren. The Lord Jesus Christ be with your spirit. [n]Grace be with you. Amen.

---

a. **But the Lord stood with me.** The Lord fulfills His promise never to "leave or forsake" His children (Deut. 31:6, 8; Josh. 1:5; Heb. 13:5).

b. **the message might be preached fully through me.** As he had done in the past (Acts 26:2–29), Paul was able to proclaim the gospel before a Roman tribunal.

c. **all the Gentiles might hear.** By proclaiming the gospel to such a cosmopolitan, pagan audience, Paul could say that he had reached all the Gentiles with the gospel. This was a fulfillment of his commission (Acts 9:15, 16; 26:15–18).

d. **the mouth of the lion.** Cf. Dan. 6:26, 27. A common figure for mortal danger (Pss. 22:21; 35:17) and a common occurrence for Paul (cf. Acts 14:19; 2 Cor. 4:8–12; 6:4–10; 11:23–27). Peter pictured Satan as a lion in 1 Pet. 5:8.

e. **will deliver me from every evil work.** On the basis of the Lord's present work—strengthening Paul and standing with him (2 Tim. 4:17)—Paul had hope for the Lord's future work. He knew God would deliver him from all temptations and plots against him (2 Cor. 1:8–10).

f. **preserve me for His heavenly kingdom.** Paul knew the completion of his own salvation was nearer than when he first believed (cf. Rom. 13:11; 2 Cor. 5:8; Phil. 1:21).

g. **Prisca and Aquila.** Paul first met these two faithful friends in Corinth after they fled Italy (see Acts 18:2). They ministered for some time in Ephesus (Acts 18:18, 19), later returned to Rome for a period of time (Rom. 16:3), and had returned to Ephesus.

h. **Erastus.** Probably the city treasurer of Corinth, who sent greetings through Paul to the church at Rome (see Rom. 16:23).

i. **Corinth.** The leading city in Greece (see Acts 18).

j. **Trophimus.** A native of Asia, specifically Ephesus, who had accompanied Paul from Greece to Troas (see Acts 20:4).

k. **Miletus.** A city and seaport in the province of Lycia, located 40 mi. S of Ephesus (see Acts 20:15).

l. **before winter.** In view of the coming season and the cold Roman jail cell, Paul needed the cloak for warmth. He would also have less opportunity to use the books and parchments as the duration of light grew shorter in winter.

m. **Eubulus . . . Pudens, Linus, Claudia.** The first 3 names are Latin, which could indicate they were from Italy and had been members in the church at Rome. "Claudia" was a believer and close friend of whom nothing else is known.

n. **Grace be with you.** This is the same benediction as in Paul's previous letter to Timothy (see 1 Tim. 6:21). The "you" is plural, which means it extended to the entire Ephesian congregation.

ONE-YEAR READING PLAN

The following chart provides a plan for reading through *One Faithful Life* over the course of 50 weeks, with five sections being read each week.

The Book of Hebrews is also added for the final three weeks. Throughout church history, many Christians believed that Paul was the author of Hebrews. Though the authorship of Hebrews is unknown, it was clearly written by someone closely associated with Paul's ministry.

Week	Sections	Week	Sections	Week	Sections
☐ 1	1–5	☐ 18	86–90	☐ 35	171–175
☐ 2	6–10	☐ 19	91–95	☐ 36	176–180
☐ 3	11–15	☐ 20	96–100	☐ 37	181–185
☐ 4	16–20	☐ 21	101–105	☐ 38	186–190
☐ 5	21–25	☐ 22	106–110	☐ 39	191–195
☐ 6	26–30	☐ 23	111–115	☐ 40	196–200
☐ 7	31–35	☐ 24	116–120	☐ 41	201–205
☐ 8	36–40	☐ 25	121–125	☐ 42	206–210
☐ 9	41–45	☐ 26	126–130	☐ 43	211–215
☐ 10	46–50	☐ 27	131–135	☐ 44	216–220
☐ 11	51–55	☐ 28	136–140	☐ 45	221–225
☐ 12	56–60	☐ 29	141–145	☐ 46	226–230
☐ 13	61–65	☐ 30	146–150	☐ 47	231–233
☐ 14	66–70	☐ 31	151–155	☐ 48	Hebrews 1–4
☐ 15	71–75	☐ 32	156–160	☐ 49	Hebrews 5–9
☐ 16	76–80	☐ 33	161–165	☐ 50	Hebrews 10–13
☐ 17	81–85	☐ 34	166–170		

Life *and* Letters
of the Apostle Paul

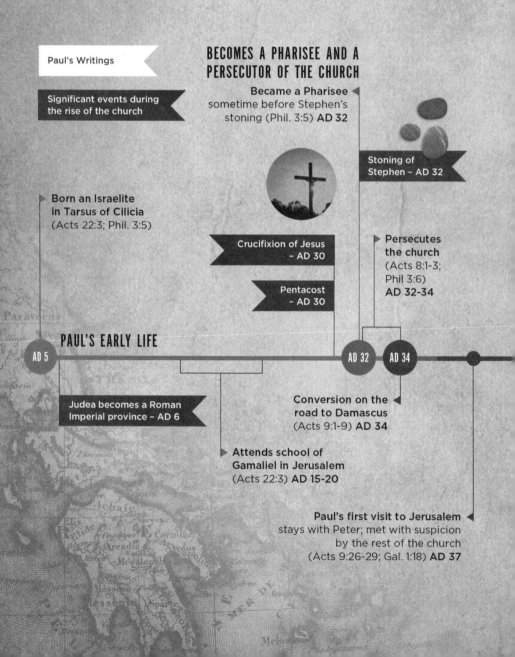

Paul's Writings

Significant events during the rise of the church

BECOMES A PHARISEE AND A PERSECUTOR OF THE CHURCH

Became a Pharisee sometime before Stephen's stoning (Phil. 3:5) **AD 32**

Stoning of Stephen – **AD 32**

Born an Israelite in Tarsus of Cilicia (Acts 22:3; Phil. 3:5)

Crucifixion of Jesus – AD 30

Persecutes the church (Acts 8:1-3; Phil 3:6) **AD 32-34**

Pentacost – AD 30

PAUL'S EARLY LIFE

AD 5

AD 32   AD 34

Judea becomes a Roman Imperial province – AD 6

Conversion on the road to Damascus (Acts 9:1-9) **AD 34**

Attends school of Gamaliel in Jerusalem (Acts 22:3) **AD 15-20**

Paul's first visit to Jerusalem stays with Peter; met with suspicion by the rest of the church (Acts 9:26-29; Gal. 1:18) **AD 37**

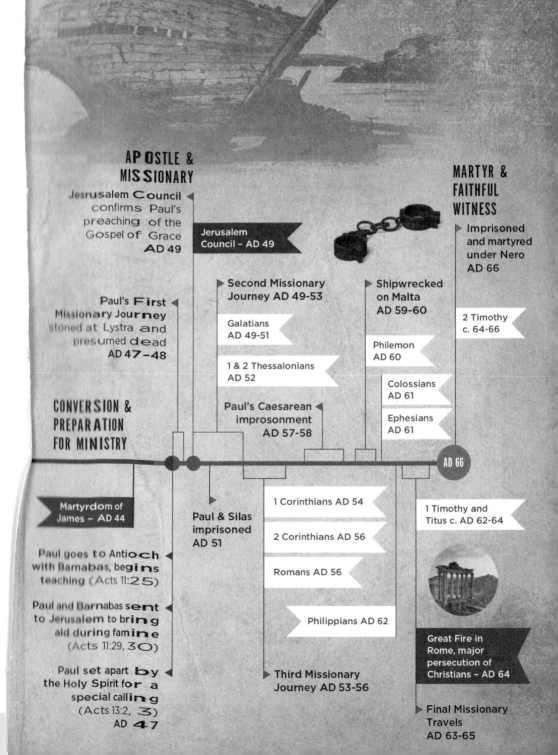

APOSTLE & MISSIONARY

Jesrusalem Council confirms Paul's preaching of the Gospel of Grace AD 49

Jerusalem Council – AD 49

Paul's First Missionary Journey stoned at Lystra and presumed dead AD 47–48

MARTYR & FAITHFUL WITNESS

Imprisoned and martyred under Nero AD 66

Second Missionary Journey AD 49-53

Galatians AD 49-51

1 & 2 Thessalonians AD 52

Shipwrecked on Malta AD 59-60

2 Timothy c. 64-66

Philemon AD 60

Colossians AD 61

Ephesians AD 61

Paul's Caesarean improsonment AD 57-58

CONVERSION & PREPARATION FOR MINISTRY

AD 66

Martyrdom of James – AD 44

Paul goes to Antioch with Barnabas, begins teaching (Acts 11:25)

Paul and Barnabas sent to Jerusalem to bring aid during famine (Acts 11:29, 30)

Paul set apart by the Holy Spirit for a special calling (Acts 13:2, 3) AD 47

Paul & Silas imprisoned AD 51

1 Corinthians AD 54

2 Corinthians AD 56

Romans AD 56

Philippians AD 62

Third Missionary Journey AD 53-56

1 Timothy and Titus c. AD 62-64

Great Fire in Rome, major persecution of Christians – AD 64

Final Missionary Travels AD 63-65